THE BEST PLAYS OF 1994–1995

THE OTIS GUERNSEY
BURNS MANTLE
THEATER YEARBOOK

THE BEST PLAYS OF
1994–1995

EDITED BY OTIS L. GUERNSEY JR.
AND JEFFREY SWEET

Illustrated with photographs and
with drawings by HIRSCHFELD

LIMELIGHT EDITIONS

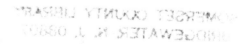

Night School" was developed with David Ford and in association with The Marsh, Stephanie A. Weisman, artistic director, and directed by Martin Higgins. The play was produced in New York by Second Stage Theatre, Carole Rothman artistic director, Suzanne Schwartz Davidson producing director. All inquiries regarding rights should be addressed to: Charlie Varon, 31 Chattanooga Street, San Francisco, CA 94114.

Al Hirschfeld is represented exclusively by The Margo Feiden Galleries, New York City.

EDITOR'S NOTE

THE increasing gravitational pull of the tributary theater on work of substance that can't find a niche in the large venues was dramatically evident during the past two seasons when the Pulitzer Prize was awarded to plays having their first New York runs off off Broadway (*Three Tall Women* last year, *The Young Man From Atlanta* this year). Our *Best Plays* policy of including the occasional, exceptional, presumably "frozen" (unlikely to be extensively rewritten) OOB script on our list of the ten New York bests was activated in both cases. And if the theater's tectonic drift continues in the same direction, we're likely to be doing more of this in the future.

And in this volume, the 76th in continuous publication of our *Best Plays* series, we've also expanded our attention to the cross-country theater by increasing the length of our excerpts from the three outstanding scripts selected by the American Theater Critics Association. And we're introducing each of these excerpts with a descriptive essay by one of the ATCA critics (Misha Berson, Michael Sommers and Michael Grossberg, chairman of the ATCA committee which makes the selections).

But now and forever (as the *Cats* slogan has it) the Broadway and off-Broadway stages hold the central focus of our attention in *The Best Plays of 1994–95,* as in previous volumes. Among their more than 100 productions in 1994–95 there were more than ten outstanding plays to cite here, plus a long list of other major acting, directing and design accomplishments as reported in Jeffrey Sweet's incomparably broad-based review of the theater year. Our coverage of all the casts, credits and other vital statistics of 1994–95 on and off Broadway includes the major cast replacements and touring-company casting recorded by Jeffrey A. Finn. And as the theater's important achievements spread beyond their traditional boundaries into the reaches of off off Broadway, these details are comprehensively collected for the record in Camille Croce Dee's listing of the productions and Mel Gussow's evaluation of them in his survey of the off-off-Broadway season.

In May we received an honorary Drama Desk Award on the occasion of our series's 75th volume, particularly gratifying—as we said in accepting it at their ceremonies—because *Best Plays is* a drama desk: a group of men and women expressing their love for the theater in the diverse work they do for each of these volumes. From our publisher, Melvyn B. Zerman of Limelight Editions, to the newest apprentice press agent who answered one of our hard questions on the telephone, it takes the effort of a great number of devoted people to produce a *Best Plays* yearbook. Not the least of these, perennially, are Jonathan Dodd, who supervises our editorial activities; and the editor's faithful wife, who pores over the copy with a practised eye; Sheridan Sellers, who compiles our listing of new plays produced in regional theater; and Rue E. Canvin, who keeps our record of publications and necrology. Among others on our drama desk are Sally Dixon Wiener (two Best Plays synopses), William Schelble (Tony Awards), Michael Kuchwara (New York Drama Critics Circle voting), Thomas T. Foose (historical advisories), Henry Hewes (former *Best Plays* editor, supervising the Hall of Fame listing), Ralph Newman of the Drama Book Shop and the dozens of cooperative people in the theater's press offices without whom we couldn't get this job done properly.

Al Hirschfeld's drawings distill our memories of the season to their sparkling quintessence, and we are proud to include them in these pages; likewise the examples of the year's outstanding stage designs graciously provided to us by Tony Walton and William Ivey Long. And the "look" of the theater year is dramatically represented in the photographs of onstage action in New York and across the country, made available to us by the production offices, and including the work of Gilles Abegg , T.L. Boston, Bruce Cook, Michael Cooper, Peter Cunningham, T. Charles Erickson, Eric Y. Exit, Ken Friedman, Gerry Goodstein, Randall Hagadorn, Ken Howard, Sherman M. Howe Jr., Susan Johann, Ivan Kyncl, Andrew Leynse, James Leynse, Joan Marcus, Paul Mullins, Timothy Raab, Robert C. Ragsdale, Carol Rosegg, Guy Salvador, Jonathan Slaff, Craig Schwartz, Martha Swope, Jay Thompson, Richard Trigg and Migual Tuason.

The shift of the stage's center of gravity in the 1994–95 season resulted in a majority of the year's Best Plays—six—having made their initial New York appearance off Broadway, with only three from Broadway and the one from OOB. And of course the great majority of them had their world premieres far from the bright lights of Manhattan. Whatever their production origin or scale, our season's new plays and musicals in New York have the one most important thing in common: they are the original products of persevering dramatists with a blank sheet of paper and a play in imagination. It's the playwrights we have to thank most of all for the wonders of our season.

Wherever they choose to go, *Best Plays* will follow in admiration.

OTIS L. GUERNSEY Jr.
Editor

September 1, 1995

CONTENTS

Drawings by HIRSCHFELD

THE SEASON
ON AND OFF
BROADWAY

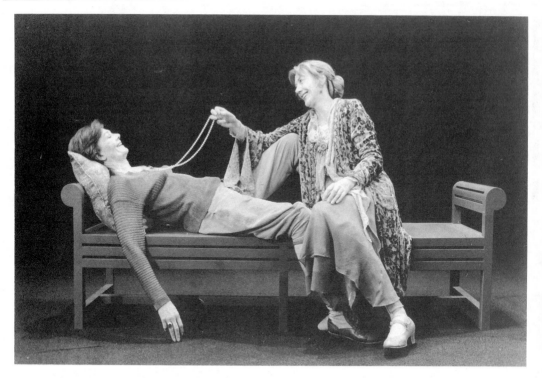

1994–95 PERIOD PIECES—*Above,* Vanessa Redgrave as Vita Sackville-West and Eileen Atkins as Virginia Woolf in *Vita & Virginia; below,* Tammy Amerson with members of the ensemble in the revival of *Show Boat*

BROADWAY AND OFF BROADWAY

By Jeffrey Sweet

GEORGE ABBOTT, the director-writer-producer and sometimes actor who epitomized the vitality of the commercial theater and was particularly known for his contributions to the Broadway musical, died on January 31, 1995 at the age of 107.

This year, though celebrating its much-ballyhooed 100th birthday and its record grosses, Broadway wasn't feeling all that well either.

It was a season in which no American-written musical with a new book and a new score opened on Broadway. (In fact, Broadway hosted only one musical with a new book and score at all, the adaptation by British hands of *Sunset Boulevard.*)

It was a season in which no new American straight play of consequence premiered on the boards that once regularly introduced new works by Tennessee Williams, Eugene O'Neill, Arthur Miller, George S. Kaufman, William Inge, Abe Burrows, Lillian Hellman, Maxwell Anderson and Sidney Kingsley (another major dramatist who died this year).

It was a season in which Neil Simon, the most commercially-successful writer in Broadway history, decided to open his newest effort off Broadway. He had plenty of company—other off-Broadway stages featured such Broadway regulars as Woody Allen, Vanessa Redgrave, Jim Dale, Linda Lavin and David Mamet.

Just because Broadway was ailing doesn't mean that the New York theater didn't offer substantial rewards, however. Broadway is only one of the theater's arenas. Though it may be the most publicized and the one where the biggest financial gambles are taken, these days it is not where much new work is developed or given its first staging.

Those interested in this season's new plays spent comparatively little time in the traditional Times Square theater district and more climbing stairs or squeezing into venues often holding fewer than a hundred seats. Most of the premieres of consequence were presented by non-profit institutional companies working under off-Broadway and Letter of Agreement contracts—Manhattan Theater Club, Playwrights Horizons, the Joseph Papp Public Theater, Circle Rep, Primary Stages, the New York Theater Workshop, the Vineyard Theater, the York Theater, the WPA, etc. In fact, one of these, the Signature Theater, an off-off-Broadway company which each year devotes an entire season to a single writer, premiered this year's Pulitzer

3

The 1994–95 Season on Broadway

PLAYS (6)

What's Wrong With This Picture?
A TUNA CHRISTMAS
LOVE! VALOUR!
COMPASSION!
(transfer)
Having Our Say
On the Waterfront
My Thing of Love

MUSICALS (2)

SUNSET BOULEVARD
A Christmas Carol

REVUE (1)

Smokey Joe's Cafe

SOLO SHOWS (3)

Ian McKellen: A Knight
Out
A Christmas Carol
(return engagement)
Defending the Caveman

SPECIALTIES (4)

Radio City Music Hall:
Christmas Spectacular
Easter Show
The Flying Karamazov
Brothers Do the
Impossible!
Comedy Tonight

REVIVALS (18)

Roundabout:
Hedda Gabler
Philadelphia,
Here I Come!
The Glass Menagerie
The Molière Comedies
A Month in the Country
Show Boat
NYC Opera:
Wonderful Town
The Merry Widow
Circle in the Square:
The Shadow Box
Uncle Vanya
The Rose Tattoo
Jesus Christ Superstar
The Heiress
Translations

How to Succeed in
Business Without
Really Trying
Gentlemen Prefer Blondes
Indiscretions
Hamlet

FOREIGN PLAY
IN ENGLISH (1)

ARCADIA

Categorized above are all the shows listed in the Plays Produced on Broadway section of this volume.
Plays listed in CAPITAL LETTERS have been designated Best Plays of 1994–95.
Plays listed in *italics* were still running on June 1, 1995.

Prize winner, Horton Foote's Best Play, *The Young Man From Atlanta.* (Comment on this play will be found in Mel Gussow's review of the off-off-Broadway season.)

Of the other Best Plays, three (*Love! Valour! Compassion!, After-Play* and *Night and Her Stars*) made their New York debuts at Manhattan Theater Club (*Night and Her Stars* having previously played at California's South Coast Rep). The others were either imports from London—Tom Stoppard's *Arcadia* (Royal National Theater) and *Hapgood* (Royal Shakespeare Company) and *Sunset Boulevard*—or made their way here from regional stagings. *A Tuna Christmas,* the sequel to the long-running off-Broadway hit *Greater Tuna,* was new to New York but had a history of several engagements around the country. The production of *The Cryptogram* that opened off Broadway came from Cambridge's American Repertory Theater (though the play was first produced in London). And *Camping With Henry & Tom* was given its premiere at the Berkshire Theater Festival.

Most of the other works new to New York audiences on and off Broadway also originated elsewhere. Among them, *Having Our Say* (from New Jersey's McCarter Theater), *My Thing of Love* (Chicago's Steppenwolf), *What's Wrong With This Picture?* (Manhattan Theater Club and the Jewish Rep), *London Suite* (Seattle Rep), *Holiday Heart* (Syracuse Stage), *The Old Lady's Guide to Survival* (Actors Theater of Louisville and Chicago's Wisdom Bridge), the stage version of *On the Waterfront* (in an earlier incarnation at the Cleveland Play House), *Das Barbecü* (Seattle Opera via Goodspeed Opera and Baltimore's Center Stage), *Police Boys* (the Pittsburgh Public Theater), *Swingtime Canteen* (New Jersey's American Stage Company and Long Island's Bay Street Theater), *The Cover of Life* (the American Stage Company again), *Inside Out* (the Group Repertory Theater), *The Professional* (Belgrade, Yugoslavia and a stand in London's fringe), *Vita & Virginia* (the Chichester Festival Theater via London), *Travels With My Aunt* (the Citizens' Theater of Glasgow via Long Wharf), *Party* (Chicago's Bailiwick), and Elaine May's contribution to *Death Defying Acts* (Chicago's Goodman Theater).

Many of the revivals, too, began their production histories outside of New York. The Harold Prince edition of *Show Boat* originated in a suburb of Toronto. *How to Succeed in Business Without Really Trying* began at California's La Jolla Playhouse, *Gentlemen Prefer Blondes* at the Goodspeed Opera House (which won a Tony this year for its record of accomplishment in regional theater), Jonathan Kent's production of *Hamlet* in London's Almeida Theater Company, Declan Donnellan's production of *As You Like It* in London's Cheek by Jowl company, and Sean Mathias first staged *Indiscretions* at the Royal National Theater. In addition, Michael Langham's first crack at *The Molière Comedies* with Brian Bedford was given at Ontario's Stratford Festival.

The Roundabout, the reactivated Circle in the Square and Lincoln Center, all non-profit operations, were responsible for the bulk of the revivals of the non-musicals, including *A Month in the Country, The Shadow Box* and the Tony-winning production of *The Heiress.* Among the other Broadway revivals were two works by Tennessee Williams (*The Rose Tattoo* and *The Glass Menagerie*), two by Brian Friel (*Philadelphia, Here I Come!* and *Translations*) and *Hamlet.*

Tom Stoppard was one of several writers to be represented by more than one production this season. The Brian Friel and Tennessee Williams productions were mentioned above, and, of course, *Hamlet* was only one of several productions of Shakespeare (the New York Shakespeare Festival produced *The Two Gentlemen of Verona, The Merry Wives of Windsor* and *The Merchant of Venice,* and the Brooklyn Academy of Music sponsored the visit of *As You Like It*). Within a couple of weeks, Mark St. Germain saw the New York premieres of two projects, both on historical themes—his play *Camping With Henry & Tom* and his musical, co-written with Randy Courts, *Jack's Holiday.* (Courts was also represented by incidental music for *The Cover of Life.*) David Mamet was represented by one short one-act (*An Interview*) and a full-length one-act (*The Cryptogram*). Charles Busch had the solo writing credit for *You Should Be So Lucky* and collaborated on the book of the cabaret musical *Swingtime Canteen,* both of which were directed by Kenneth Elliott.

A number of other directors had multiple credits, too. In addition to *Show Boat,* Harold Prince directed the premiere of *The Petrified Prince.* (At one point, he had four shows running in town, the other two being *The Phantom of the Opera* and *Kiss of the Spider Woman.*) Joe Mantello did a superb job with Terrence McNally's *Love! Valour! Compassion!* and fumbled Donald Margulies's *What's Wrong With This Picture?.* Trevor Nunn guided two blockbusters—*Sunset Boulevard* and *Arcadia.* Daniel Sullivan directed *The Merry Wives of Windsor* and *London Suite.* Adrian Hall's credits included both *The Two Gentlemen of Verona* and *On the Waterfront.* Gerald Gutierrez staged *The Heiress,* a story of 19th century Manhattan, and later in the season guided the premiere of Constance Congdon's 20th century tale on the perils of New York coupling, *Dog Opera.*

Some writers directed their own work, with mixed results. Sam Shepard did not fare well with his staging of *Simpatico.* David Mamet was praised by many for his production of *The Cryptogram.* Giles Havergal did the honors with his adaptation of *Travels With My Aunt,* as did Emily Mann with her staging of her adaptation of *Having Our Say.*

Mann and Congdon were among the comparatively few women who had new works produced this season. Manhattan Theater Club presented two of the others— Cheryl West's *Holiday Heart* and Anne Meara's *After-Play.* Broadway's *My Thing of Love* was by Alexandra Gersten, and *The Truth Teller,* which was offered by Circle Rep, was by Joyce Carol Oates. Eileen Atkins adapted the correspondence between Vita Sackville-West and Virginia Woolf into a vehicle for herself and Vanessa Redgrave called *Vita & Virginia.*

Though it wasn't a stellar season for women writers, one would have to look long and hard to find a season that offered more brilliant female performances—Cherry Jones in *The Heiress,* Mary Alice and Gloria Foster in *Having Our Say,* Laurie Metcalf in *My Thing of Love,* Helen Mirren in *A Month in the Country,* Kathleen Turner and Eileen Atkins in *Indiscretions,* Stockard Channing in *Hapgood,* Linda Lavin and Debra Monk in *Death Defying Acts,* June Havoc in *The Old Lady's Guide to Survival,* Rue McClanahan and Barbara Barrie in *After-Play,* Mercedes Ruehl in *The Rose Tattoo* and *The Shadow Box,* Elizabeth Marvel in *Silence, Cunning, Exile,*

OUTSTANDING 1994–95 MUSICAL PERFORMANCES—Matthew Broderick as J. Pierrepont Finch in the revival of *How To Succeed in Business Without Really Trying;* Glenn Close as Norma Desmond in *Sunset Boulevard*

Francesca Annis in *Hamlet,* Lonette McKee and Elaine Stritch in *Show Boat,* Blair Brown in *Arcadia* and Aideen O'Kelly in *Philadelphia, Here I Come!*—and, of course, Glenn Close in *Sunset Boulevard.*

Among the most notable male performances: Philip Bosco in *The Heiress,* Matthew Broderick's Tony-winner in *How to Succeed,* Ralph Fiennes's Tony-winner in *Hamlet,* Peter Frechette in *Night and Her Stars,* Anthony LaPaglia in *The Rose Tattoo* and the male ensembles of *Travels With My Aunt, A Tuna Christmas, The Compleat Works of Wllm Shkspr (Abridged)* and *Love! Valour! Compassion!*

Not only the actors' talents were on display in *Love! Valour! Compassion!.* At one point or another most of its cast played in the nude. Male nudity was an element in several works this season. Among the other plays displaying members of the cast (I apologize) were *Party, Indiscretions, My Thing of Love, The Two Gentlemen of Verona* and *Dancing on Moonlight.* Men either playing women or dressing in women's clothes were also elements in an unusual number of shows: *Travels With My Aunt, Dog Opera, The Truth Teller, What's Wrong With This Picture?, As You Like It, Love! Valour! Compassion!, The Compleat Works of Wllm Shkspr (Abridged), Holiday Heart, A Tuna Christmas, Sylvia, Word of Mouth, Some People, Family Business* and *Him* (which speculated about what Elvis Presley would look like after a sex change operation). Not all of these works were generated by gay writers or directors, but the increase of these elements indicates the degree to which gay artists have unburdened themselves of the inhibitions of earlier eras.

Even the shows offering generous glimpses of skin require clothes for the actors to shed, and the multitude of cross-dressers need dresses to don, so the costume designers had no cause to worry about redundancy. The splashiest displays of the costumers' art were, as usual, in large period pieces. Florence Klotz traced the development of several decades of fashion for *Show Boat.* William Ivey Long put scores of Londoners and the ghosts and spirits that haunted them on display in *A Christmas Carol.* I was particularly taken with the specificity of Jane Greenwood's designs for *A Month in the Country* (she similarly blessed *The Heiress*), and Eduardo Sicangco's work on *Das Barbecü* provided a large percentage of that show's laughs (he also was responsible for the cartoon-like scenery).

The big shows had more financial resources to knock their audiences' eyes out with scenery. Tony Walton's work on *A Christmas Carol,* lit by Jules Fisher and Peggy Eisenhauer, was calculated to awe and succeeded. John Napier and his lighting designer Andrew Bridge excited much comment with *Sunset Boulevard,* particularly with Norma Desmond's staircase. Another staircase to be climbed by another lonely woman was an element of John Lee Beatty's elegant set for *The Heiress;* the lighting by Beverly Emmons brilliantly reinforced the action of the play. Stephen Brimson Lewis (scenery and costumes) and Mark Henderson (lighting) also dazzled with *Indiscretions* (Henderson also was represented by flashy work for *Hamlet*). The scenery by Loy Arcenas and lighting by Brian MacDevitt for *Love! Valour! Compassion!* were subtler but as impressive.

As noted here every season, these artists wouldn't have the opportunity to impress us with their visions onstage, were it not for the interior visions of the dramatists who first conceived the events the designers support and augment. Again this annual reaffirms its mission—to honor new work with citations for Best Plays. To quote Otis L. Guernsey Jr. in past volumes, "The choice is made without any regard whatever to the play's type—musical, comedy or drama—or origin on or off Broadway, or popularity at the box office, or lack of same.

"We don't take the scripts of bygone eras into consideration for Best Play citation in this one, whatever their technical status as American or New York 'premieres' which didn't have a previous production of record. We draw the line between adaptations and revivals, the former eligible for Best Play selection but the latter not, on a case-by-case basis." The choices of the Best Plays primarily reflect the editors' taste; and in any event, plays that win the major prizes are almost invariably included as definers of a season's character.

Our choices for the Best Plays of 1994–95 are listed below in the order in which they opened in New York (a plus sign + with the performance number signifies that the play was still running on June 1, 1995).

Love! Valour! Compassion!
   (Off B'way, 72 perfs.)
   (B'way, 122+ perfs.)

Sunset Boulevard
   (B'way, 222+ perfs.)

Hapgood
   (Off B'way, 129 perfs.)

A Tuna Christmas
   (B'way, 20 perfs.)

The Young Man From Atlanta
   (Off Off B'way, 24 perfs.)

After-Play
   (Off B'way, 59+ perfs.)

Camping With Henry & Tom
   (Off B'way, 88 perfs.)

Arcadia
   (B'way, 72+ perfs.)

The Cryptogram
   (Off B'way, 62 perfs.)

Night and Her Stars
   (Off B'way, 39 perfs.)

LONDON SUITE—Kate Burton, Paxton Whitehead, Jeffrey Jones and Brooks Ashmanskas in a scene from *The Man on the Floor* segment of Neil Simon's off-Broadway program of one-acts

Plays

Tom Stoppard's *Arcadia* is set in the same room of an English country estate at two different times—1809 and today. The characters in the scenes set today are engaged in research attempting to piece together what went on in 1809. As they seize on one clue after another and reach seemingly logical deductions, Stoppard juxtaposes 1809 scenes to reveal how far off the mark the contemporary researchers are. As ever, Stoppard has much on his mind. Maybe too much.

Several of the critics remarked that with *Arcadia* Stoppard engaged both the mind and the heart. Mine is apparently a minority heart. Despite an extremely attractive cast, the characters rarely achieved human dimension for me. Mostly they were nimble and articulate mouthpieces for the author's speeches on chaos theory, intellectual adventurism and the relationship between fashion and history. When Bernard Nightingale, an unscrupulous academic played by Victor Garber, made a play for principled feminist critic Hannah Jarvis, played by the stern but beguiling Blair Brown, I had no idea where the supposed sexual impulse came from. When mathematics wiz Valentine Coverly (played by Robert Sean Leonard) regaled Hannah with a long speech on his area of expertise, again I had no idea why it was there except that Stoppard wanted to communicate theoretical material to his audience.

The 1994–95 Season Off Broadway

PLAYS (32)

First Night
Young Playwrights
Playwrights Horizons:
  A Cheever Evening
  Police Boys
Public Theater:
  Blade to the Heat
  Simpatico
  Him
  Silence, Cunning, Exile
  Dancing on Moonlight
  A Language of Their
    Own
  Dog Opera
The Cover of Life
Manhattan Theater Club:
  LOVE! VALOUR!
    COMPASSION!
  Durang Durang
  AFTER-PLAY
  Holiday Heart
  Three Viewings
NIGHT AND HER
  STARS
Sylvia
The Truth Teller

Me and Jezebel
You Should Be So Lucky
THE YOUNG MAN
  FROM ATLANTA
The Old Lady's Guide to
  Survival
CAMPING WITH
  HENRY & TOM
Circus Life
Death Defying Acts
London Suite
THE CRYPTOGRAM
Party
Fortune's Fools

SPECIALTIES (6)

Woyzeck on the Highveld
Alive, Alive Oh!
Encores!:
  Call Me Madam
  Out of This World
  Pal Joey
Coming Through

MUSICALS (9)

Faith Journey
Two Hearts Over Easy
Ram in the Thicket
Swingtime Canteen
Jack's Holiday
The Petrified Prince
Nunsense 2: The Sequel
Inside Out
Das Barbecü

REVUES (3)

That's Life!
*The Compleat Works of
  Wllm Shkspr (Abridged)*
Loose Lips

FOREIGN-LANGUAGE
PLAYS (2)

Brooklyn Academy:
  Gorodish
  Fleischer

SOLO SHOWS (8)

Jelly Roll!
Laughing Matters
Public Theater:
  Some People
  The Diva Is Dismissed
Mother of All the Behans
The Truman Capote
  Talk Show
Dylan Thomas: Return
  Journey
The Only Thing Worse . . .

FOREIGN PLAYS
IN ENGLISH (6)

Public Enemy
The Professional
Vita & Virginia
HAPGOOD
The Man Who
Travels With My Aunt

REVIVALS (10)

Shakespeare Marathon:
  The Merry Wives
    of Windsor
  The Two Gentlemen
    of Verona
  The Merchant of Venice
Brooklyn Academy:
  As You Like It
  The Mountain Giants
  The Winter's Tale
Uncommon Women &
  Others
Three Postcards
The Acting Company:
  A Doll's House
  Othello

Categorized above are all the shows listed in the Plays Produced Off Broadway section of this volume.
Plays listed in CAPITAL LETTERS have been designated Best Plays of 1994–95.
Plays listed in *italics* were still running June 1, 1995.

I have heard from a number of people who have read *Arcadia* (at this writing I have not done so) that it is a very satisfying literary experience. That's not a small achievement, but the first responsibility of a play is to *play*—to offer a company of actors the opportunity to create characters that fascinate and whose relationships and contests intrigue. At first acquaintance, I found *Arcadia* lacking in this regard. Also, when one reads the text of a play, one sets one's own pace, and a dense passage may be examined at leisure. Presented on the stage, however, the same passage goes by at a rate determined by the actor in consultation with the director. Some of the speeches in *Arcadia* are very densely written; and, under Trevor Nunn's direction, they went by with such speed that I found them impossible to follow. I frequently felt as if I had been left at the station just as a train of logic had departed.

But this, as I say, is apparently a minority opinion. The play has won a number of awards and was a critical success both in New York and in London. It would be inappropriate for me to let my difficulties with it deny it a place as one of the season's Best Plays.

I preferred Stoppard's other Best Play, the less-enthusiastically-received meditation on espionage, *Hapgood.* For the first act, it's Stoppardian business as usual. This time, particle physics is embraced as a metaphor for human interaction, and there is much clever writing about mathematics and double agents and such. Then, toward the end of the first act, a child's life is endangered. Theoretical gambols take a back seat to human stakes, and what has been amusing suddenly acquires dramatic urgency. The child in question is the illegitimate son of Hapgood, the woman who is one of the master players in the spy war between British intelligence and the Soviets (the play was written and premiered in London before the fall of the Iron Curtain). Now Hapgood must act both as a biological mother and as Mother, the nickname she bears as an intelligence agent. During the course of the action of the second act, she must explore other dualities in her nature and those of the people around her. She is surprised both by what has previously gone unexamined in her own character and in theirs. Most interestingly, a colleague turns out to be simultaneously politically treacherous and personally honorable. As in *Arcadia,* the data at hand does not readily coalesce into the truth, but unlike in *Arcadia,* I found that the fates of characters in *Hapgood* mattered to me. Of course, it helped that the title character was played by the remarkable Stockard Channing.

Mark St. Germain's Best Play *Camping With Henry & Tom* is derived from a footnote in history—President Warren Harding did indeed venture into the wilds with such captains of industry as Henry Ford and Thomas Edison. St. Germain's script springs from the idea that the three get lost in the woods and have to occupy themselves with conversation while awaiting rescuing. The conceit is deceptively simple, for, though the play touches on familiar factoids about the famous threesome, its impact is not based so much on what it reveals about the private sides of these three men as on the underlying question of the qualities of leadership.

In *Coriolanus,* Shakespeare suggests that the very abilities that make his leading character a superb general are drawbacks for a politician. St. Germain is dealing with similar matters. Harding is a palpable mediocrity, thrust into a job he never sought. Ford, on the other hand, is a technological visionary whose leadership in making and marketing the Model T has profoundly transformed the American landscape. Ford believes that his abilities in industry are prima facie evidence of his potential as President.

The argument that what one needs in the Presidency is an able manager is one that continues to have appeal (witness the candidacy of Ross Perot). The action of St. Germain's play suggests something different. Yes, Ford is a visionary and a genius. He is also an anti-Semite, however, and an autocrat willing to resort to blackmail to impose his vision on others. Edison, also a visionary captain of industry, is revealed to be a not much more savory character than Ford, but he has sufficient insight into himself and the country's needs to block Ford's plans. Better to have as President a mediocrity with some genuine human sympathies than a tycoon who has never let petty ethical considerations stall the pursuit of his objectives.

Aside from its intellectual matter, the play provides meaty roles for three veteran actors. Under Paul Lazarus's direction, John Cunningham was steely and exasperated as Ford, Ken Howard found a touching dignity in Harding's pedestrian intellect and Robert Prosky was canny and ironic as Edison. (Prosky has a habit of playing power politics in a thicket; he was the wily Soviet diplomat in Lee Blessing's *A Walk in the Woods.*)

I was also impressed by another work spun from American history, Richard Greenberg's Best Play *Night and Her Stars,* which tells the story of the scandal that erupted in the 1950s when it became known that a popular TV quiz show was fixed. Who won and who lost was determined by the show's producers, based on their hunch as to which contestants would draw the largest viewing audience. The two key contestants introduced are Herb Stempel, a young New York Jewish husband and father whose intensity and awkwardness the producers consciously exaggerated, and Charles Van Doren, the Columbia University teacher whose WASP good looks and grace made him an intellectual matinee idol and to whom Stempel was ordered to lose.

Night and Her Stars had the misfortune of opening in the wake of *Quiz Show,* a well-received feature film based on the same events. But though the play and the film share some of the same story elements and characters, their emphases are very different. The film mostly concerns itself with a breakdown of faith between a large American institution and the public, and it clearly suggests a link to Watergate and other instances of the abuse of public trust. Greenberg, on the other hand, chooses to use the story as a meditation on the tenuous relationship between intelligence and morality.

Van Doren is indeed very smart; but, as depicted here, he becomes unmoored from his moral anchor by Dan Enright, the quiz show's fast-talking producer. Enright persuades Van Doren to be party to the deception in the name of making higher education attractive to a mass public. Enright is smart, too, but instead of using his intelligence to find a good path, he marshals it to defend unscrupulous choices, all the while protesting his integrity. His wonderfully telling line: "We have done nothing wrong, and we have done it in secret," could have come out of Feiffer's

The White House Murder Case or Mamet's *Glengarry Glen Ross,* other tales in which characters offer passionate and principled justifications for their corruption. Herb Stempel exemplifies another kind of intelligence. "I know more things than you!" he cries out in protest to Van Doren, and indeed he is a repository of huge quantities of data. But data by itself is of little value without an awareness of how to employ facts in the service of larger purposes.

At the end of Greenberg's play, a bewildered Van Doren is discovered in the country visiting his celebrated father, author Mark Van Doren. Charles mentions that the reason he was never asked botanical questions on the show is that botany is one of the areas in which he is ignorant. Gently, the senior Van Doren begins to teach his son the names of the trees and other plants around them. This act of putting the true names to things holds the promise of helping the younger man find his way back to a world where language is intended to correspond to reality rather than distort it. It is an act of healing and love and one of the most poignant scenes of the season.

The Manhattan Theater Club production, directed by David Warren, was sensitive to both the satiric wit and the wistfulness in Greenberg's remarkable script. In a strong ensemble, the versatile Peter Frechette was fine as the appalling, hypnotic and hilarious Enright. This production was one of the season's underestimated jewels.

As many observers have noted, A.R. Gurney often mines similar territory as did John Cheever (in fact, Gurney has adapted Cheever for the stage and TV), so the challenge of fashioning a dramatic "tapestry" out of 17 Cheever stories would seem to be a natural for him. The task brings to mind *Short Cuts,* which the film director Robert Altman fashioned out of several Raymond Carver stories. The effect of the Altman picture was to overwhelm the audience with the simultaneity of so many lives in sometimes unwitting intersection. In contrast, in *A Cheever Evening* Gurney chose to organize the material into three movements keyed to geography—beginning with episodes from the city, moving to the suburbs and ending in the country. Expert craftsman that he is, Gurney gave his talented company of six—John Cunningham, Jack Gilpin, Julie Hagerty, Mary Beth Peil, Robert Stanton and Jennifer Van Dyck—many opportunities to impress in individual moments; but, skipping from story to story and introducing another set of characters every few minutes, he offered no emotional focal point to carry the audience through the evening. The result was a lack of cumulative effect.

Having adapted Cheever, Gurney turned to territory most famously explored by James Thurber, another *New Yorker* writer—the triangle among man, wife and dog. The conceit of *Sylvia* is that the title dog is played by an actress who talks. One gradually gets the idea that what she says is a projection of the thoughts of her owner and his wife. Most of the charm of the piece is in the audience mentally translating the actress's behavior into dog behavior. This is engaging for a while—especially given the fact that Sarah Jessica Parker as Sylvia is personally so engaging—but it isn't engaging enough to disguise the fact that there is very little by way of story here. What could have made a beguiling diversion for one act is too slight to sustain two, even with the considerable compensation of the cast playing the humans in the story—Charles Kimbrough, Blythe Danner (who not so many years ago would have been an adorable Sylvia herself) and Derek Smith, who tripled in three roles—one male, one female and a "Leslie" of indeterminate gender.

All four of the actors in Giles Havergal's adaptation of Graham Greene's novel *Travels With My Aunt* also played multiple roles. They also jointly played aspects of the same role of Henry Pulling, the narrator. Pulling is a middle-aged bachelor who has settled for a quiet, unemotional life tending his garden, when his free-spirited aunt Augusta appears and gets him embroiled in various international misadventures. The tale is played as a romp, but I found it disquieting. Aunt Augusta is not a good-hearted soul violating the rules of a repressive society in the pursuit of higher humanistic values. She is relentlessly selfish and casually destructive, and the man whose love she holds precious is a lower-grade war criminal. I find it difficult to believe that the only choice Henry has to make is between being a plodding, reclusive soul and living a life of cheerful cynicism. The work's obliviousness to other alternatives makes it ethically off-putting.

On the other hand, under Havergal's direction, the performances of the quartet of actors—Jim Dale, Brian Murray, Martin Rayner and Tom Beckett—were a joy. Dale contrasted Henry's reserve with Aunt Augusta's explosiveness. Many of Murray's most vivid moments were in playing characters distant from his literal presence, particularly his interpretation of a giddy teenage girl. Martin Rayner had some of his most affecting moments as the tall, mysterious black man who is Augusta's sometimes consort. And Tom Beckett made an hilarious impression as a doomed dog named Wolf (another actor playing a dog!).

The Best Play *A Tuna Christmas* offered another opportunity to enjoy the transformational abilities of actors. Under Ed Howard's direction, Joe Sears and Jaston Williams played 22 citizens (men, women and children) of the small Texas town of Tuna in a script co-written by the three of them. Much of the material is flat-out funny, chronicling the small-mindedness and parochial character of a little world where there is not enough to do to distract people from minding each other's business too closely. (My Texas friend, dramatist Jay Presson Allen, assures me that, as funny as it is, the play is almost a documentary.) Underneath all of the humor, though, is a sadness that gives the evening weight. Sears, Williams and Howard have created a vision of a community's underside as disturbing as Sherwood Anderson's Winesburg.

Sears and Williams were followed in their tenancy of the Booth Theater by another two-person vehicle, *Having Our Say,* Emily Mann's theatrical distillation of the book about Sarah L. Delany and A. Elizabeth Delany, written by them with Amy Hill Hearth. The Delany sisters have both lived over a hundred years; and, as a pair of black women who pursued professional careers at a time when the system didn't open its arms to professionals who were either black or women, they have witnessed and participated in a large chunk of 20th century history. I hesitate to call *Having Our Say* a play in the normal sense of the term—there is no outstanding question the audience waits to have settled between the two women. The evening offers the illusion of spending extended time in their home, listening to their stories and marvelling at their ability to synthesize wisdom from experience. Play or not, it was a constantly engaging evening. If Mary Alice had a showier part as the mercurial Bessie, Gloria Foster (who has played her share of mercurial parts in her time) was equally impressive as the steady, determined Sadie. It is no mean feat to make a two-person show comprised mostly of talk hold the stage with such grace; Mann served the Delany sisters well, both as writer and as director.

The Old Lady's Guide to Survival by Mayo Simon introduced another pair of elderly ladies. Netty is a smart, self-sufficient elderly woman who avoids Shprintzy, a needy neighbor whose mind goes in and out of focus. Comes the day that Netty's sight gives out on her, she finds that her only way of managing is to take the annoying and intellectually infirm Shprintzy as a roommate. Simon doesn't avoid all of the easy sentimentality in the situation, but there is a surprising amount of toughness in the script as well. June Havoc's performance was tight, detailed and rigorous—a model of the actor's craft.

Two more model performances were featured in another two-hander for women, *Vita & Virginia,* Eileen Atkins's adaptation of the correspondence between Vita Sackville-West and Virginia Woolf. Atkins has not been as successful as Emily Mann in transforming written material to the stage. Perhaps the difference in their success is that Mann's source material began in a conversational mode, while Atkins's originated as literary material. Truth to tell, I was less interested in Vita and Virginia than I was in Atkins and Vanessa Redgrave who played them. Atkins's voice was dry and ironic, in contrast to the effusiveness of Redgrave. The evening was most satisfying as verbal chamber music for two superb instruments. I had the pleasure of seeing Atkins in a real play later in the season; I look forward to seeing Redgrave take the stage again in a vehicle that makes full use of her talents.

In R.T. Robinson's *The Cover of Life,* a tough-talking, cigarette-smoking *Life* photojournalist named Kate Miller arrives in a small Southern town to get the story on three sisters-in-law living with their mother-in-law while their servicemen husbands are overseas fighting in World War II. The three wives are three representative types—Sybil, the flashy fast one, Weetsie, the religious submissive one, and Tood, the one with stirrings of proto-feminist awareness. Robinson seems to be setting up a dramatic exploration of the Heisenberg Principle; a visitor in the household, Miller goes beyond being an observer and becomes a catalyst for Tood's declaration of liberty from her chauvinist husband. But the destruction Sybil meets is entirely coincidental to Miller's visit, and Weetsie seems to be there simply to fill in the picture. Under Peter Masterson's direction, Carlin Glynn played the mother-in-law with an admirable no-nonsense manner, and Kerrianne Spellman projected the necessary naive raunchiness to make Sybil something more than a sketch, but it was easier to admire the script's intentions than its formulaic execution.

Sam Shepard's *Simpatico* reminds me a good deal of David Rabe's play of last season, *Those the River Keeps.* Both concern a former criminal trying to cope with a troubling past that won't stay dead, both were directed by their authors and both would be much better if they were cut to their promising cores. Fifteen years ago,

DEATH DEFYING ACTS—Paul Guilfoyle, Linda Lavin, Gerry Becker and Debra Monk in Woody Allen's one-act *Central Park West*

Shepard's Vinnie was Carter's partner in a horse racing scandal that enriched Carter but devastated the life of a fellow named Simms. After years of subsisting in motels, Vinnie is motivated to try to square things with Simms and confront the moral consequences of his transgressions. It is an ambition that isn't calculated to make Carter happy.

The most original stroke in the play is Simms's refusal to accept whatever restitution Vinnie wants to make, or even explicitly to admit any restitution is owed to him. After his fall, Simms has remade his life. The clean breast Vinnie offers him holds no promise of satisfaction. Rather, it threatens to disrupt Simms's life yet again, and he wants no part of it. The idea of a man's moral redemption constituting a threat to his former victim is a wonderfully ironic and comic one, and the scene played between Fred Ward as Vinnie and James Gammon as Simms was the high point of the play.

Unfortunately, that scene is surrounded by a good deal of superfluous fiddling. Shepard has written long stretches that seem to be there simply because they are

amusing to the author. These detours are usually characterized by the absolute refusal of anybody to respond to a direct question with an answer that is to the point.
Ultimately this rhetorical gambit becomes tiresome and drains the play of much of
its energy.

But, again as with *Those the River Keeps,* I believe there is a strong and valuable
piece hidden within the text's ungainly size. At three hours, it tried the patience.
With the fat trimmed and with an eye on its original take on the disruptive potential
of a reformed character, I think it could rank with Shepard's more provocative plays.
The strong cast—which also included Ed Harris, Beverly D'Angelo and Marcia Gay
Harden—helped keep even the weaker passages of interest.

Given that Christopher Durang has often expressed his exasperation with drama
critics, it is amusing to see him join their number in *Durang Durang,* a bill of six of
his one-acts, three of which must be regarded as theater criticism. First comes a
piece in which a woman with illusions of culture offers a short and blissfully unre-
liable guide on how to appreciate the stage. Then Durang lets fly at two of his
colleagues—Tennessee Williams and Sam Shepard. (In fact, *Durang Durang* opened
within days of the openings of the revival of *The Glass Menagerie* and the premiere
of Shepard's *Simpatico.*)

Much has been made over the years of the idea that gay playwrights in the past
had to recast events and themes from their lives into heterosexual terms in order to
cater to a heterosexual theater audience. Durang's *For Whom the Southern Belle
Tolls* is *The Glass Menagerie* if Williams had written it as an openly gay play and
were annoyed by his characters. Instead of a Laura who collects glass animals, for
instance, he offers us Lawrence and his glass swizzle stick collection. The Gentleman
Caller is transformed into a lesbian ill-suited to the task of courtship. And so on.
Throughout, one can sense Durang's affection for Williams under the parody. Little
affection seems evident, however, in *A Stye of the Eye,* a thoroughly jaundiced take
on Shepard's *A Lie of the Mind* complete with battling brothers, strained symbolism
and empty macho posing.

The most effective of the remaining pieces is *Wanda's Visit,* about how a suburban
couple's kneejerk sympathies are put to the test by a visit from a woman from the
husband's past—a walking, wailing catalogue of disasters and disorders.

If *Durang Durang* doesn't offer the deeper satisfactions of the author's best writing—*The Marriage of Bette and Boo* and *Sister Mary Ignatius Explains It All for
You*—it still is a happy diversion with more than its share of quotable lines. Walter
Bobbie directed a nimble cast, getting especially pointed work out of three of the
women—Lizbeth Mackay as Amanda Wingvalley, Becky Ann Baker as the appalling Wanda and Patricia Elliott cheerfully uttering nonsense as the would-be expert
in drama, Mrs. Sorken.

Neil Simon offered another off-Broadway bill of one-acts, *London Suite,* a follow-
up to previous evenings of one-acts located in hotels—*Plaza Suite* and *California
Suite.* The first piece, *Settling Accounts,* a confrontation between a flamboyant Welsh
author and his cheating accountant, is the most satisfying. Marked with some virtuoso prevarication, it is marred only by a perfunctory conclusion. I was less taken

with *Going Home,* a mother-daughter piece lacking much of a compelling dramatic question. The fourth playlet, *The Man on the Floor,* is a sketch about a number of people in physical pain unable to help each other. The audience around me howled.

The playlet that attracted the most attention, *Diana & Sidney,* is a sequel to a one-act from *California Suite.* In the earlier piece, the title characters were an Oscar-nominated British character actress and the mostly gay husband she adored. *Diana & Sidney* takes place years after their divorce. She has gone on to become the wealthy and artistically-unchallenged star of a TV mystery series. He has ended up on an island with a male lover whose future security concerns him, particularly since he (Sidney) is facing his own death. There are affecting moments here, but the piece is a touch facile, and the writing for Sidney confers upon him nobility by virtue of his homosexuality, equivalent to the automatic nobility conferred upon Sidney Poitier in the Sixties by virtue of his being black. My hope is that some day Simon will choose to revisit Diana and Sidney, draw from the two pieces he's already written, compose some new episodes, dig more deeply and make of it the chronicle of a relationship it could be.

If I have reservations about the bill, I have none about the playing. Paxton Whitehead reaffirmed his status as one of our most versatile comic actors as the thieving accountant, as Sidney and as a blithely unhelpful doctor. Carole Shelley's Diana was an affectionate send-up of Angela Lansbury, and she did well with the less rewarding roles of a mother and a hotel functionary. Jeffrey Jones's best moments came as the indignant author. Kate Burton offered subtle work as Diana's lesbian assistant but otherwise was given little to show her gifts.

Jeffrey Hatcher's *Three Viewings* is a triple bill of monologues set in a funeral home. I was less enthusiastic about them than many of my colleagues. I found the ironies and reversals a shade too easy, but they gave the three performers opportunities to shine. As an undertaker who ends up having to employ his professional services on someone he's loved from afar, Buck Henry gave a performance of such detail and understatement that I thought I was watching an American Alec McCowen.

With her Best Play *After-Play,* actress-comedienne Anne Meara adds "playwright" to her string of hyphen-linked identifications. Her experience as one half of the comedy team of Stiller and Meara has given her a solid knowledge of how to build laughs. Her work as an actress (most recently her Tony-nominated performance in *Anna Christie*) has given her a sense of what actors need for a playable scene. *After-Play* is both funny and playable. It is also an impressive playwriting debut, a double portrait of a pair of couples in their late middle age who somehow maintain their friendships despite the continent that separates their homes and the differences in their philosophies and temperaments. The differences come to light as, over a late dinner in a mysterious restaurant, they discuss the play they have just seen. Terry and Marty Guteman, the sentimental New Yorkers, have been deeply moved by the show, which apparently depicted the immigrant experience of their parents' generation. Renee and Phil Shredman express appreciation for the efficient way the play pushed the audience's emotional buttons, but themselves were not touched by it much. The conversation moves on from the play to subjects closer to home—children, careers, sex and, always, illness and death.

Meara does not pretend to offer any great philosophical insights, rather this is a piece about how people manage as the options of life begin to close down around them. More than anything, it is a play about the courage required for even those comfortably off to stave off despair. It also offers the opportunity for two older actresses to cut loose, an opportunity that Rue McClanahan (as the heart-on-her-sleeve Terry) and Barbara Barrie (as the acerbic Renee) made the most of, well supported by Merwin Goldsmith and Larry Keith as their spouses. Rochelle Oliver and John C. Vennema are also featured in a brief but memorable scene of a couple who, in the wake of their son's death from AIDS, are not able to sustain the composure the Gutemans and the Shredmans are able to project. David Saint directed. (When the play transferred to a commercial run, McClanahan was unavailable, owing to a prior engagement, so the author stepped into the role of Terry, which she played with her customary panache.)

Like Anne Meara, Woody Allen and Elaine May (two of the three authors of the triple bill *Death Defying Acts*) began their careers as comic performers. Like Meara, they possess sure senses of how to provide actors with material that will get laughs out of an audience. Both Allen and May have written successfully for the stage and screen in the past, which makes their contributions to this bill all the more disappointing. In commenting on the chemistry of his partnership with Elaine May when they were one of the most successful comedy teams of the Sixties, Mike Nichols has said, "She could go on and on in a character." Describing himself as a more limited improviser, he suggested his key contribution to their classic sketches was editorial. "I was always very concerned with beginning, middle and end, and when it's time for the next point to be made and when it's time to move because, after all, we're telling a story." In a sense, May generated the cloth and he was the tailor.

In *Hotline,* a piece about a suicidal hooker with a vicious tongue and the good-hearted hotline volunteer who tries to help her, May did indeed come up with page after page of splendid comic cloth for the hooker (a part she originated in the play's first production at Chicago's Goodman Theater). Linda Lavin brought her considerable gifts to bear on it, making vivid the character's loneliness and pain without taking the edge off her essential disagreeableness. Unfortunately, there seems to have been no tailor of Nichols's mettle present in the revision of the script. May offers the merest excuse of a story to contain the character, and the play does not end so much as exhaust itself—a shame, because there is potential for more here.

Central Park West is the title of Woody Allen's piece, and can it be any coincidence that it is also the address of the woman from whom Allen had such a public and acrimonious separation? In the living room of an apartment overlooking the park, two couples who have pretended friendship for years attack each other for newly-revealed betrayals. Adultery has frequently figured in Allen's works, but the tone here is markedly different from anything seen from him before. The moral sense supporting such works as *Husbands and Wives, Crimes and Misdemeaners* and *Hannah and Her Sisters* is nowhere to be found in this piece. In contrast to the artist who has consistently explored human weakness with bemused compassion, the writer of *Central Park West* seems to be full of loathing for his characters, willing to have them do or say anything for a laugh, including indulging in a numbing series of withering sexual insults. Some of the lines are indeed funny, but the nastiness of the enterprise is unappealing. Debra Monk, Linda Lavin, Paul Guilfoyle and Gerry Becker could not be faulted, however, for the brio with which they served Allen's intentions under Michael Blakemore's direction.

The Mamet contribution to *Death Defying Acts, An Interview,* the least consequential of the evening, is essentially a laborious 15 minute setup for a pretty good lawyer joke. Mamet's more significant entry this season is his full-length one-act Best Play *The Cryptogram.* A woman named Donny learns that her husband has left her and further that her friend, a gay man named Del, has been complicit in her husband's deceptions. The focus of the play is on the effect these betrayals have on the way Donny deals with her son, John. Her anger at the way her husband and Del have abused her trust leads her to interpret an innocent act of John's as yet another betrayal and to browbeat the boy into making an unwarranted apology. The action of the play is a vivid examination of the ecology of pain—how suffering is passed along down the path of least resistance and results in the scarring of the innocent. Donny tells her distraught son, "Everyone has a story. This is yours." The understated callousness of her statement stops the heart. The matter of *The Cryptogram* is compelling and disturbing, and Mamet's portrait of Donny is the most successful writing for a woman since his remarkable father-daughter one-act, *Reunion.*

I have some reservations, however, about some of the execution. Mamet has written much of the script in his trademark style—short declarative statements and sentence fragments diced with repeated phrases and incomplete clarifications. Unfortunately, here this trademark style is so front-and-center that it inhibits belief in the characters having separate and specific lexicons and rhythms of their own. I never forgot for a second I was watching a written piece and consequently never succumbed to the illusion that I was being engaged by human beings in spontaneous behavior. The problem was aggravated by Mamet's direction, which called for deliberately flat and uninflected readings of the lines. All of the prescribed actions were taken and assigned lines were uttered with authority and precision, but I was reminded of nothing so much as what you get from a MIDI synthesizer connected to a computer reading a symphonic score—notes are hit in the proper sequence and relationship, but the texture and the soul of the music is missing. Every now and then a human sound escaped from the palpably talented actors, and the contrast was startling. I hope to encounter the play again in a production that doesn't feature the actors on such short leashes.

Alexandra Gersten's *My Thing of Love* offers another view of a betrayed wife. Gersten's script seems to have two aspects—one is raw and honest material about the gulf between intimates, the other yields to the temptation of setting up mechanical misunderstandings and coincidences and pushing characters to behave outlandishly just to whip up cheap excitement on the stage. (Though well-played by Mark Blum, a scene with an hysterical school guidance counselor is written with such self-conscious outrageousness as to seriously derail much of the second act.) If Gersten had not been distracted from her main task of detailing the chemistry of a dissolving marriage, and if the play had opened, say, at Manhattan Theater Club's second stage, I think the author would have been received with encouraging words. Laurie Metcalf, as the ferociously overwrought and betrayed wife, gave a virtuoso performance; something has to be present in the script for such a performance to be possible. What this show with an off-Broadway soul was doing plunked in a big musical house like the Martin Beck is beyond me, but whoever made the decision to engage this venue did serious damage to the play's chances.

Fortune's Fools presented one of the season's rare views of happy heterosexual coupledom. Concerning a pair who meet and ultimately get together in the wake of the marriage of friends, Frederick Stroppel's script is essentially an amiable situation comedy; but, within its limited ambitions, it provided a welcome contrast to much of the gloomy news about human relations in the rest of the season.

Set in Belgrade after the fall of Communism, *The Professional*'s ambitions were greater but less realized. A publisher named Teya is confronted by Luke, a mysterious man with a pile of manuscripts. It soon becomes evident that the mysterious man is a former member of the secret police and that he once had been assigned to shadow and record the actions of the publisher. At first, the policeman had been hostile to Teya, itching for the assignment to dispose of him. But he gradually became Teya's surreptitious guardian, saving his life more than once. The manuscripts he has brought are made up of edited transcripts of the surreptitious recordings of Teya; Luke has converted Teya's life into literature. I wish I could report that this provocative premise was fulfilled in the play's development, but writer Dusan Kovacevic doesn't go much farther than introducing it. A pity. The piece had the opportunity to give dramatic form to the quest for identity that is torturing many in the former Communist states.

Director Peter Brook and his collaborators used Oliver Sacks's *The Man Who Mistook His Wife for a Hat* as the basis of a new theater piece, *The Man Who.* Accompanied by a solo musician proficient on a number of instruments, four actors take turns playing doctors and patients. The patients are all suffering from neurological disorders, and it is the business of the evening to highlight the variety of these disorders. One man has no memory, another cannot stop Japanese music from playing continuously in his head, another cannot distinguish between people and inanimate objects, another suffers from Tourette's Syndrome, and so forth.

The individual scenes are played with an understated grace that is sometimes deeply affecting. My problem is with the collection of these scenes as an evening. Every scene is about the same thing—a new patient is introduced and, through interaction with a doctor, his particular symptoms are displayed, and we in the audience are invited to discern the parameters of this patient's affliction. Yes, this does invite speculation as to the degree to which each of us is subject to our personal operative logic, but monotony sets in.

I also felt a little queasy about these subjects and their symptoms being paraded to elicit sympathy or laughter. Though doctors are represented in the piece, there is little sense that they can *do* anything to improve the lives of their patients. If they can do nothing, then in the service of what are they displaying these unhappy people imprisoned in malfunctioning minds? I don't believe that Brook put on this piece to entertain audiences with suffering, but if Brook's objective is to have the audience muse on how the patients' conditions compare with our presumably "normal" conditions, I think he accomplished it within the first half hour. Though beautifully acted by David Bennent, Sotigui Kouyate, Bruce Myers and Yoshi Oida, the piece struck me as being attenuated.

Adapting a movie to the stage is a good idea only if the transition adds to the piece. Usually what is added are songs; many successful musicals have found their source material on the screen. (Billy Wilder alone has contributed to scripts that were the sources of *Sunset Boulevard, Promises, Promises, Sugar* and *Silk Stockings).* *On the Waterfront* would seem to have promise as a musical theater piece; hints of its potential can be heard in the famous film score by Leonard Bernstein. But the version that landed on Broadway this year had no songs, nor much else that could be called an enhancement of or improvement on the film. Not that the performances weren't in the main admirable, and the tableaux that director Adrian Hall managed to whip up in concert with Eugene Lee's shuttling industrial scenery and Peter Kaczorowski's lighting constantly gave the eye employment. But the best chunks of the script are those that the audience already has access to for the price of a video rental (and played by legendary actors). The new material Budd Schulberg and his collaborator Stanley Silverman introduced mostly consisted of speeches filled with redundant moralizing for the fighting priest. The effort was not deserving of the easy derision heaped on it, but it had no compelling reason to claim a Broadway stage.

Works exploring gay themes and images continued to be a large subset of the new plays; three—*Dog Opera, A Language of Their Own* and *Blade to the Heat*— were produced by the Public Theater.

Constance Congdon's *Dog Opera* concerns a woman named Madeline and a gay man named Peter who are best friends and share the problem of loneliness in the big city. The sad irony of the piece is that their mutually exclusive sexual identities keep them from providing each other with the kind of company they seek. The piece is made up of dozens of short scenes of varying effectiveness. Many of the most engaging involve the various supporting characters, played in the Public's production by Sloane Shelton (most vivid as the heroine's mother and the object of her experiment in lesbianism) and Richard Ramos (as a straight, conservative father doing his best to relate to the son he loves but doesn't pretend to understand). Wandering through the action is a young gay hustler named Jackie who is intended to provide poetic comment but struck me as an intruder from another play. At the end of the piece, in a dramatic development that seems as if it has been introduced just to bring the script to a conclusion, Peter reveals he has just been diagnosed HIV-positive.

AIDS again figures in Chay Yew's *A Language of Their Own,* which deals with the gay scene from the Chinese-American perspective. I thought its dialogue about the nature of emotional commitment was so generic that much of it could have been spoken by characters of almost any gender, sexuality or ethnicity. B.D. Wong and

Francis Jue gave performances of almost breathtaking precision, however, under Keng-Sen Ong's direction.

The third of the Public's gay-themed plays, Oliver Mayer's *Blade to the Heat*, is set in 1959, making it the rare contemporary gay play that doesn't deal with AIDS imagery. The central figure is a Chicano boxer simultaneously coping with his ethnicity and his homosexuality. Mayer has seized on an interesting juxtaposition—the image of a man whose private sexual identity is in conflict with his public identity as a champion in a sport which seemingly is the epitome of the masculine image. To raise an interesting juxtaposition is not the same as investigating it, however, and once Mayer establishes his dramatic turf, he does little to explore it. Director George C. Wolfe staged the piece with melodramatic intensity—most of the action was accompanied by a percussive sound track that telegraphed the urgency of the evening's intentions, and the fight sequences (choreographed by former boxer Michael Olajide Jr.) were vivid and persuasive—but the effect was of sound and fury for their own sakes.

The title character of Cheryl West's *Holiday Heart* is a large black drag queen who takes under his wing the teenage daughter of his junkie neighbor. The play intends to dramatize the idea that the impulse to family values is not the exclusive province of those physically and sexually capable of building traditional families, but West is so heavy-handed in the attempt to make Holiday endearing that the unintended effect is to make him tiresome. The saving graces of the production were the uncompromising performances by Maggie Rush and Afi McClendon as the mother and daughter.

Christopher, the gay electrolysist of *You Should Be So Lucky* is befriended by a wealthy Mr. Rosenberg who sees in the young man qualities he wished he saw in his own daughter. When Rosenberg dies and leaves a substantial portion of his fortune to Christopher, the daughter attempts to wrest it away from Christopher. Rosenberg returns (as a ghost only Christopher can see) to coach the young man on how to hold on to what is rightfully his.

The play is lackadaisically constructed, and in the second act resorts to what has become a comedic cliche—a scene set in a tabloid talk show run by a posturing moderator. Still, in production its sheer good nature went a long way toward ingratiating the audience. Author Charles Busch, usually seen in drag roles, played Christopher with great charm, Stephen Pearlman radiated generosity and determination as Mr. Rosenberg, and Julie Halston was brashly hilarious as Rosenberg's overbearing daughter Lenore.

Whenever I hear a character onstage say, "Let's play a game," my heart sinks. It is usually a sign that the playwright cannot figure out an organic way to manage exposition or whip up some kind of a dramatic event. Virtually all of *Party* consists of seven gay men playing a game in which they challenge each other to tell intimate secrets or enact fantasies. This is intercut with standard-issue jokes based on their obsession with musical comedy stars. The author-director, David Dillon, should be sharing his royalties with a dozen or so members of the Dramatists Guild, as a substantial percentage of the material is quotes from old shows. What little suspense

YOU SHOULD BE SO LUCKY—Stephen Pearlman,
Charles Busch and Nell Campbell in Busch's comedy

there is in the proceedings revolves around in what order the cast will disrobe. This was evidently enough to keep the audience around me very happy. (If a straight author had written this, I think the piece would be attacked for pandering to stereotypes.) At any rate, this play was obviously not meant for a general audience.

That it is possible to write a play about a community of gay men that reaches an audience beyond the community of gay men was proved this season by Terrence McNally with *Love! Valour! Compassion!* McNally continues to confound the common idea that dramatists tend to do their most significant work early in their careers. He arrived on the scene as part of the wave of iconoclastic young playwrights nurtured by off off Broadway in the Vietnam era, but it is recently, in his 50s, that he has grown most impressively. I wonder if it is by conscious choice that the plays of this period—*Lips Together, Teeth Apart, A Perfect Ganesh* and now *Love! Valour! Compassion!*—all center on characters supposedly at leisure. *A Perfect Ganesh* concerns two Connecticut matrons on vacation in India, and *Lips Together, Teeth Apart* and *Love! Valour! Compassion!* feature their dramatis personae on weekends in the country. All three plays, too, deal with isolation. The Connecticut ladies are culturally isolated from the world they are visiting, *Lips*'s two heterosexual couples find themselves in the middle of a homosexual colony where they feel ill at ease, and much of *L!V!C!* addresses the need for a retreat from the predominantly straight world toward and from which eight gay men feel hostility.

As in Chekhov, whose work clearly is a model for McNally, there is very little by way of story, but a great deal by way of illuminating incident, and the three hours of its length speed by as the many sides of its eight characters (two—a pair of morally dissimilar twins—played by the same actor) are revealed through a kaleidescope of scenes placing them in different combinations. I suspect that part of McNally's intention is to challenge straights' tendency to reduce all homosexuals to one "type." Despite the sexual preference they share, and the fact that their lives revolve around the relatively narrow world defined by the dance troupe their host runs, his characters embrace a variety of distinct philosophies, *modi vivendi* and survival tactics.

I have a minor reservation. McNally writes with such facility that here and there he doesn't avoid being facile. For instance, it is entirely too easy and coincidental that one of the characters happens to turn on the television just in time to see a news story about a gay-bashing that in turn licenses a big speech about straights' violence against gays. It is the occasional "easy" moment such as this that keeps the play from feeling quite finished.

But this doesn't obscure McNally's achievement—the creation of a community of vivid characters with a lot on their minds and in their hearts. Nathan Lane attracted a great deal of attention with the flashy part of Buzz, who tries to distract himself from his impending death from AIDS with musical comedy fantasies. If this character seems a little familiar, it's because McNally wrote a similar part for Lane as the opera-obsessed Mendy in *The Lisbon Traviata* a few seasons back. John Glover had the show's other flashy role as the twins. Usually I am a little put off by such self-conscious platforms for versatility, but Glover managed to pull off this tour de force with a becoming modesty. Stephen Bogardus provided a solid moral backbeat as the host of the weekends. Working with Loy Arcenas's impressionistic set and Brian MacDevitt's lighting, director Joe Mantello (who was so impressive as an actor in the two parts of *Angels in America)* offered a subtly modulated evening, a feat not so much of staging as conducting.

It is one of the oddities of the theater that a director who can do so well by one writer can damn near do in another. As fine as Mantello's work was in *Love! Valour! Compassion!,* he seemed to be thoroughly at sea staging Donald Margulies's *What's Wrong With This Picture?* I have had the opportunity to see Margulies's play in several stages of development, from a reading at New Dramatists, to an abortive and unreviewed early production at the Manhattan Theater Club, to the warmly-received off-off-Broadway production at the Jewish Repertory Theater which led to its being optioned for commercial presentation.

Here is another play that should not have been produced in a Broadway-sized house. In the more intimate space of the Jewish Rep, an understated performing style helped unify a script that mixes elements of naturalistic comedy with fantasy. Whereas the smaller theater allowed for a gentle, unforced playing style, the much larger Brooks Atkinson Theater demanded to be filled with larger gestures and voices pitched higher and louder. Lines that had once snuck up on the audience with their subtle humor, in the new space were batted out in a manner appropriate for *The Sunshine Boys.*

The play begins by showing how a Brooklyn Jewish family attempts to cope in the aftermath of the absurd death of wife and mother Shirley from choking on Chinese food. The loss is most difficult for her husband Mort, who cannot conceive of existence without her. His profound sense of disorientation and bewilderment is the focus of most of the first act with their teenaged son, Artie, as he unconsciously pressures the boy to fill the void his wife has left (even to the point of getting Artie to don one of his mother's dresses). Apparently his need has been felt as far as the grave. There is a knock at the door. When it is opened, in sails Shirley, grubby from her long walk from the cemetery and eager for a shower.

It is very much the point of the play that she has not returned to life. She is dead and cold to the touch, but even death cannot keep her from the family she knows needs her. Mort is willing to wall himself up in his apartment with his reanimated dead wife, but Artie realizes that neither he nor his father can move forward if Shirley doesn't return to the grave. By the play's end, Shirley understands through her son that it is a larger act of love to make it possible for those she leaves behind to mourn and assimilate her death and re-engage life.

This is delicate, poetic material, but somebody forgot to clue Mantello in. From the start, the show was staged as if it were a situation comedy. There is nothing in this approach that prepares one for the darker colors to come, so the piece seemed to lurch back and forth in a schizoid manner.

The shame of it is that—with the exception of David Moscow, an able actor too old to be a believable teenager—given the right house and the appropriate director, the cast assembled probably could have given a fine account of this difficult but rewarding script. Faith Prince has all the warmth and spirit necessary to make Shirley's reappearance credible, and Aaron Rosenberg, who played Mort, has often displayed a gift for portraying haplessness without looking pathetic. Florence Stanley, a veteran of other productions, held a true course as Mort's determined mother, and Jerry Stiller was both touching and funny as her husband. In a scene in which Stiller took Prince into his arms to dance with her and told the cold Shirley how warm she was, one realized with a shudder he could only say that because he was halfway to the grave himself.

Ultimately, what was wrong with *What's Wrong With This Picture?* was the production. Between misguided direction, an inappropriate venue, and an advertising campaign that led the audience to believe they were in for a laugh-riot Broadway comedy, a valuable play by one of our more talented writers was inadvertently sabotaged.

A number of other works passed this way without achieving the acceptance for which their producers had hoped. *Dancing on Moonlight* by Keith Glover was an earnest but unpersuasive attempt to superimpose the pattern of Greek tragedy on a tale of black gangsters. *Moonlight*'s director, Marion McClinton, was himself represented as a playwright with *Police Boys,* a harsh and insufficiently coherent treatment of a police unit assigned to deal with young gang members. Jack Neary's *First Night,* a comedy about a flirtation between a nun and the night manager of a video store, played a brief run off Broadway after a reportedly successful engagement in Boston.

Suzi, the Diane Arbus-like photographer who is the subject of Stuart Greenman's *Silence, Cunning, Exile,* makes a disturbing journey through the landscape of the Fifties and Sixties in a series of disquieting scenes, but the inner logic of her compulsion to chronicle the bizarre and alienated and, finally, to commit suicide, remains obscure. Elizabeth Marvel, however, was one of the season's finds in the lead. Joyce Carol Oates's *The Truth Teller,* the story of how a Jewish intellectual's tense visit with his girlfriend to her rich, conservative family upsets the household, floundered through the facile use of stereotypes. Still, the memory of her brilliant comedy *The Perfectionist* keeps me hopeful about what she will offer the stage in the future.

Here's where we list the *Best Plays* choices for the outstanding straight play achievements of 1994–95 in New York, on and off Broadway. In the acting categories, clear distinction among "starring," "featured" or "supporting" players can't be made on the basis of official billing, which is as much a matter of contracts as of esthetics. Here in these volumes we divide acting into "primary" or "secondary" roles, a primary role being one which might some day cause a star to inspire a revival in order to appear in that character. All others, be they vivid as Mercutio, are classed as secondary. Furthermore, our list of individual standouts makes room for more than a single choice when appropriate. We believe that no useful purpose is served by forcing ourselves into an arbitrary selection of a single best when we come upon multiple examples of equal distinction.

PLAYS

BEST PLAY: *Love! Valour! Compassion!* by Terrence McNally; *Night and Her Stars* by Richard Greenberg

BEST REVIVAL: *The Heiress* by Ruth and Augustus Goetz; *Indiscretions* by Jean Cocteau, translated by Jeremy Sams; *As You Like It* by William Shakespeare

BEST ACTOR IN A PRIMARY ROLE: Philip Bosco as Dr. Austin Sloper in *The Heiress;* Anthony LaPaglia as Alvaro Mangiacavallo in *The Rose Tattoo;* Brian Murray as Henry Pulling, Richard Pulling, A Vicar, Miss Keene, Tooley, Italian Girl, Frau General Schmidt, O'Toole and Yolanda in *Travels With My Aunt*

BEST ACTRESS IN A PRIMARY ROLE: Mary Alice as Dr. Bessie Delany in *Having Our Say;* June Havoc as Netty in *The Old Lady's Guide to Survival;* Cherry Jones as Catherine Sloper in *The Heiress;* Helen Mirren as Natalya Petrovna in *A Month in the Country*

BEST ACTOR IN A SECONDARY ROLE: F. Murray Abraham as Ignaty Illich Shpigelsky in *A Month in the Country;* Byron Jennings as Arkady Sergeich Islaev in *A Month in the Country;* John Glover as John and James Jeckyll in *Love! Valour! Compassion!*

BEST ACTRESS IN A SECONDARY ROLE: Francesca Annis as Gertrude in *Hamlet;* Aideen O'Kelly as Lizzy Sweeney in *Philadelphia, Here I Come!;* Rochelle Owens as Emily Paine in *After-Play*

BEST DIRECTOR: Declan Donnellan for *As You Like It;* Gerald Gutierrez for *The Heiress;* Giles Havergal for *Travels With My Aunt;* Joe Mantello for *Love! Valour! Compassion!*

BEST SCENERY: Stephen Brimson Lewis for *Indiscretions*

BEST COSTUMES: Jane Greenwood for *A Month in the Country*

BEST LIGHTING: Beverly Emmons for *The Heiress;* Brian Nason for *A Month in the Country*

Brenda Braxton, B. J. Crosby, DeLee Lively and Pattie Darcy Jones in a scene from the musical whose title appears above them, featuring the songs of Jerry Leiber and Mike Stoller

Musicals and Revues

With the death of his father, Samson, the title character of *The Petrified Prince* is in line to inherit the throne of Slavonia, a 19th century Ruritanian country. The obstacles he faces are his psychologically-based muteness and the designs such other political forces as Napoleon, a band of rebels and the Pope have on the kingdom. The show's plot concerns how the true love of a sweet prostitute awakens Samson from his condition, and how he bests his political rivals and achieves his birthright, but the tale doesn't hold together.

If you're going to center your plot around the question of who is going to rule a country, at some point you have to deal with the question of who, indeed, is best *suited* to rule. But Edward Gallardo's book (based on an unfilmed screen play by

Ingmar Bergman) never addresses this. The Prince is presumed to be the most qualified because he is the title character and he is to be played by an attractive performer, but it seems never to have occurred to Gallardo, composer-lyricist Michael
John LaChiusa or director Harold Prince that someone who has spent much of his
life in virtually an autistic state might not have the social skills, education or wisdom
to run a country. For that matter, nothing we see of the prince offers any persuasive
reason for the good-hearted young leading lady to fall in love with him.

Lacking both a credible love story and the intellectual rigor necessary for an
effective political parable, *The Petrified Prince* falls apart. Having been staged by
one of the musical theater's most imaginative directors, the production at the Joseph
Papp Public Theater offered the expected parade of intriguing elements—a unit set
by James Youmans that was ever spinning itself into new configurations, a chorus
of singing animals played by puppets, a series of arrestingly-lit and elaborately-
costumed tableaux. But all of this registered as dazzling icing on an unbaked cake.
The piece never engaged either the heart or the mind. Precisely because one goes
to any Harold Prince effort with high expectations, *The Petrified Prince* was a particular disappointment, not the least because Michael John LaChiusa's score seems
a step backward after the promise he displayed in last season's *Hello Again.*

A number of accomplished musical theater hands collaborated to attempt an
epic-sized version of Dickens's *A Christmas Carol* in the hopes that it will be an
annual holiday offering. Featuring a dazzling Tony Walton set made up to resemble
an advent calendar and special effects that would make George Lucas smile, the
show was a constant treat to behold. The score, by composer Alan Menken and
lyricist Lynn Ahrens, was a mixed effort. The sight of a bunch of tap-dancing chorus
girls pretending to be fruit in a song called "Abundance and Charity" suggested
nothing so much as a production number cut from Jackie Gleason's old TV variety
show and did little to support the tale's Victorian flavor. Most of the other songs
managed a neat balancing act between the literate and the accessible.

Ahrens and director Mike Ockrent collaborated on the book, which was less
successful. Perhaps the task of trying to cram so many special effects and production
numbers into 90 minutes dictated that the script would necessarily suffer. Perhaps
the authors figured that everybody knows the story so well that it was unnecessary
to give the narrative full weight. Whatever the reason, one of the great fail-safe
dramatic stories of literature had little emotional impact. The show seemed to be
less about Scrooge's redemption than pictures of Victorian London. There was some
rumor that the authors may continue to tinker with it. There is more than enough
there already to justify further effort.

Das Barbecü is Jim Luigs's and Scott Warrender's retelling of the Ring Cycle
using a country-Western score. There is a certain amount of fun to be had in seeing
Wagner's giants and gods and Rhine maidens and dwarves turned into various
strains of caricatured Texas types, but my hunch is it's probably sufficient to justify
a sketch, not a two-act musical. Despite the many clever touches in Christopher
Ashley's staging and the hard work and high spirits of a talented cast playing a

variety of parts, the show exhausted the comic possibilities of its premise long before the finale.

The Jack in *Jack's Holiday* is Jack the Ripper. The musical, featuring book and lyrics by Mark St. Germain and music by Randy Courts, hypothesizes the mysterious killer's visit to New York at the turn of the century. St. Germain and Courts are primarily interested in exploring parallels between the yellow journalism of the time and the media circuses made of criminal cases today. This point is made rather swiftly, though; and, despite earnest and crafty work on the part of the authors and a resourceful production, none of the characters is sufficiently intriguing to compel much investment in their dilemmas or fates. But St. Germain and Courts are clearly a talented team, and I look forward to their next piece with eagerness.

Smokey Joe's Cafe is a revue drawing its songs from the catalogue of Leiber and Stoller, the songwriting team who wrote many of the hits of the Fifties. The songs continue to be infectious, but Jerry Zaks, one of the ablest directors in New York, was unable to make a case for why this evening belonged in a Broadway house as opposed to playing in a briefer form in a night club.

Jelly Roll! is another entertainment built on a catalogue of pre-existent material, in this case the songs of Jelly Roll Morton. Vernel Bagneris, who conceived the piece, played Morton in a mellow mood, recalling the circumstances that led to his music. These reminiscences were punctuated frequently by Morton's songs. Bagneris is a master of elegant interpretation, his sly dance in perfect counterpoint to the vocals. He was accompanied by a Norwegian ragtime pianist named Morten Gunnar Larsen who matched Bagneris in his well-deserved self-assurance.

That's Life! is a revue about the Jewish-American experience, particularly the opposing impulses to assimilate and to celebrate and keep alive the culture. The topics engaged—nose jobs, Jewish kids feeling isolated in a Christian-dominated society, adjusting to retirement—are familiar stuff, but then the intent of this show is not to challenge but to be pleasant and affirming company. It accomplishes what it intends.

Writing about *Party,* I mentioned my dislike of the use of party games to cue the revelation of character. I think the use of group therapy situations is a similarly lazy device, which brings me to *Inside Out.* Six women meet regularly to hash out their problems, discuss their differences and find what they have in common. As well-intentioned as this piece undoubtedly is, it has nothing to say that hasn't been articulated dozens of times before in other works. Its production did offer the opportunity to make the acquaintance of six talented actresses who one hopes soon will be offered more satisfying employment.

Swingtime Canteen gave employment to another five actresses. A struggling movie star with a passing resemblance to Greer Garson and four other ladies are performing for the Eighth Air Force in London in 1944 as the first leg of a U.S.O. tour. This licenses authors Linda Thorsen Bond, William Reppici and Charles Busch to recycle a lot of showbiz jokes and simultaneously invoke and mock World War II nostalgia. The production was most successful when the plot was put aside and the ensemble was allowed to sing. The score is a collection of songs from the era

JELLY ROLL!—Vernel Bagneris as Jelly Roll Morton

arranged with wit and taste by Bob McDowell, and he had the good fortune to have a company with the voices to do them justice.

The leading figure of a show, let's say, is reclusive, prone to obsessive attachment and has access to a big staircase for dramatic moments. It's a combination that worked for *The Phantom of the Opera, Beauty and the Beast* and *Passion.* It was on view again this year in *Sunset Boulevard,* based on the classic film. The story of the ill-fated relationship between the has-been silent movie queen Norma Desmond and a down-on-his-luck young screen writer named Joe Gillis is a natural for musical treatment. Norma is an extravagant, oversized, self-dramatizing figure who justifies the long, romantic lines in which composer Andrew Lloyd Webber specializes. Between the cannily-constructed story, the frequent flashes of Lloyd Webber's special talents for lush melody, John Napier's equivalently lush set design and Glenn Close's deliciously over-the-top performance, there was more than enough to engage the eye and the ear.

As good as it was, I think it should have been better. In between the tuneful ballads, Lloyd Webber's music has extended passages that are either banal or disturbingly reminiscent of others' work. (He had the misfortune to open *Sunset Boulevard* within days of the revival of *Wonderful Town;* the setting of *Boulevard*'s drug store scene reminded a number of theatergoers of the Leonard Bernstein tune,

"What a Waste.") The book, too, is a bit of a disappointment. Co-librettist Christopher Hampton has earned a reputation for brilliant and witty dialogue, but I could detect little of his voice in the new material in the script. Most of the best lines are straight out of the original screen play. The lyrics are a mixed bag. "As If We Never Said Goodbye," the ballad Norma sings during her visit to the movie studio where she used to reign, is cannily conceived and raises the intended chills. The title song, however, which aspires to be a slashing indictment of the moral bankruptcy of Hollywood, plays instead as a childish and unfocussed tamper tantrum. "Too Much in Love to Care," a duet for the story's younger lovers, suffers from a lack of specificity—it could as easily be plugged into any of a number of other shows.

If the writing is erratic, the execution was first class. In addition to Glenn Close's commanding and pathetic Norma, the production benefitted from assured work by Alan Campbell as Joe Gillis and the rock-solid strength of George Hearn as Max, Norma's mysterious butler. (One wished there had been more for Hearn to sing.) Alice Ripley did her best with the blandly-conceived role of the girl Joe should have ended up with.

The program's credits note that *Sunset Boulevard* is based on the film Billy Wilder directed, but nowhere is it mentioned that Wilder co-wrote the screen play with Charles Brackett in collaboration with Leonard Marshman Jr. Given that many of the best lines cannibalized from the film for the musical's book were undoubtedly written by Brackett, not to mention the hand he had in shaping the story, it is a little distasteful that a show that claims to decry the callous and contemptuous treatment of artists should itself abuse the memory of a great screenwriter and another collaborator by failing to credit them for their contributions.

Here's where we list the *Best Plays* choices for the musical, revue and special-attraction bests of 1994–95.

MUSICALS, REVUES AND SPECIAL ATTRACTIONS

BEST MUSICAL OR REVUE: *Sunset Boulevard*

BEST REVIVAL: *Show Boat*

BEST ACTOR IN A PRIMARY ROLE: Matthew Broderick as J. Pierrepont Finch in *How to Succeed in Business Without Really Trying*

BEST ACTRESS IN A PRIMARY ROLE: Glenn Close as Norma Desmond in *Sunset Boulevard*

BEST ACTOR IN A SECONDARY ROLE: George Hearn as Max in *Sunset Boulevard*

BEST ACTRESS IN A SECONDARY ROLE: Elaine Stritch as Parthy in *Show Boat*

BEST DIRECTOR: Hal Prince for *Show Boat*

BEST CHOREOGRAPHY: Susan Stroman for *Show Boat*

BEST SCENERY: Eugene Lee for *Show Boat;* Tony Walton for *A Christmas Carol*

BEST LIGHTING: Richard Pilbrow for *Show Boat;* Jules Fisher and Peggy Eisenhauer for *A Christmas Carol*

BEST COSTUMES: Florence Klotz for *Show Boat;* William Ivey Long for *A Christmas Carol*

THE COMPLEAT WORKS OF WLLM SHKSPR (ABRIDGED)—Peter Jacobson, Christopher Duva and Jon Patrick Walker in a scene from their revue based on Shakespeare's writings

Special Presentations and Solo Shows

The trend of multiple role-playing I noted in the new plays was echoed this season in three solo shows by three gifted performers. Danny Hoch explored a neighborhood for its variety of voices in *Some People*. Dan Butler depicted many aspects of the gay world in *The Only Thing Worse You Could Have Told Me . . .*, from the frivolous and extravagant to the self-loathing. The organizing principle of James Lecesne's *Word of Mouth* off off Broadway was less evident than in Hoch and Butler's shows, but he, too, managed to bring to full and persuasive life a wide range of contemporary characters.

Rob Becker, on the other hand, played only himself in *Defending the Caveman,* an ingratiating combination of stand-up routines and easy-going pop anthropology designed to persuade the audience that many of the reasons men and women miscommunicate is because their brains and bodies were wired differently in order to cope with the problems of the pre-industrial world. His was a genial, healing evening, and one that offered the hope of joyful co-existence between the sexes.

Jennifer Lewis played herself to the imperious hilt in the self-mocking *The Diva*

Is Dismissed. In between her program of numbers unabashedly designed to show off her powerful voice, Lewis recounted her adventures as self-proclaimed un-crowned royalty in show business. The show was a very popular attraction at the Public Theater.

In *The Flying Karamazov Brothers Do the Impossible!,* the greying hippie jugglers redressed old bits with new patter and earned their usual high score of laughs. The respect the Karamazovs show to Dostoyevsky (none) is on a par with the respect a trio of young clowns show the Bard in *The Compleat Works of Wllm Shkspr (Abridged).* Irving Thalberg had the inspiration of setting the Marx Brothers loose on the world of grand opera. In a similar spirit, Adam Long, Daniel Singer and Jess Winfield run amok through the *oeuvre* of theater's greatest icon. At one point or another, all of the works are at least referred to, though it falls to *Hamlet* and *Romeo and Juliet* to be worked over the most. The puns are excruciating and the slapstick exuberant. No stage offered more purely entertaining silliness.

Revivals

Show Boat is commonly acknowledged to be a watershed in the development of the American musical. In addition to featuring the glorious Jerome Kern-Oscar Hammerstein II score, it deals with more serious themes than musicals had previously engaged, specifically the divisiveness of race, which Hammerstein would continue to explore in his partnership with Richard Rodgers.

For this production, director Harold Prince wove together material from various different stage and film versions of *Show Boat* as well as invented new sequences to solve dramatic problems. Most happily, he and choreographer Susan Stroman have created montages to make the passing of the years in the second act play more fluidly. "Ol' Man River" is reprised a number of times, reinforcing the idea that the river in question is not only the Mississippi but the river of time.

For all the fine work, though, *Show Boat* continues to be plagued with the structural infelicities that have been with it from the start. Most of the characters are maddeningly passive, being swept along by the current of events rather than taking action. The courtship between Ravenal and Magnolia is charming, but there is little material to sustain interest in the relationship once they have married. (Hammerstein had a similar problem with Billy Bigelow and Julie Jordan in *Carousel.*) Of all the characters, the one with the most depth is Julie, the show boat's black leading lady passing for white. But she is hustled off the stage midway through the first act. She makes a brief reappearance in the second act; then, after a gesture of self-sacrifice, has no part in the subsequent dramatic action. The question of what becomes of her is never answered. This lack of follow-through about the piece's most compelling character frustrates.

It didn't have to. In *Getting to Know Him: A Biography of Oscar Hammerstein II,* Hugh Fordin quotes Hammerstein as saying that John Lee Mahin, the writer of the 1951 M-G-M version, licked what Hammerstein knew was a problem. In this version, Julie reappears toward the end of the story and persuades the errant Ravenal to return to Magnolia, the show boat and the river. In the film's final scene, having orchestrated a happy ending for others, Julie stands on the dock watching the world she can no longer be a part of sail away.

Given what Prince had to (and chose to) work with, he has delivered a handsome production. If the central characters' journeys are less than compelling, the evocation of 45 years of Americana casts a spell. Here is where the production touches glory—in the evolving sets by Eugene Lee, the parade of fashions by Florence Klotz and the changing language of popular dance charted by Stroman.

And, if the characters as written are mostly an uncompelling lot, the performers were as fine an ensemble of musical theater pros as one could desire. John McMartin and Elaine Stritch added their particular sparkle to the stock figures of the cheerful, liberal father and his henpecking wife with a heart of gold. Rebecca Luker and Mark Jacoby sang the daylights out of their duets. Cast in the most complex role, Lonette McKee was a hypnotic Julie. Our historian, Thomas T. Foose, notes: "The last previous New York City revival of *Show Boat* was at this same theater on April 24,

Above, Philip Bosco as Dr. Sloper; *right,* Cherry Jones as Catherine Sloper and Jon Tenney as Morris Townsend

1983 and had the same actress, Lonette McKee, as in the current production. Miss McKee was said to be the first black actress to play the mulatto role of Julie."

The most arresting moment in the present production occurred when, to an understated accompaniment, McKee gave a simply perfect rendition of "Bill." Were it not for the fact that she had played this part on Broadway in the earlier production, and thus was ineligible for a Tony nomination, she would certainly have been a contender.

On the subject of *Show Boat,* Mr. Foose further reminds us that it was first produced by Florenz Ziegfeld at his Sixth Avenue theater on December 27, 1927, and "Several of the original actors stayed with their roles until the 1936 Irene Dunne film version. These were Charles Winninger as Andy, Helen Morgan as Julie and Sammy White as Frank. One cannot repeat often enough that the original Joe was not Paul Robeson, it was Jules Bledsoe; further, the original Magnolia was not Irene Dunne, it was Norma Terris."

With a pleasantly reedy voice and a ruthless charm, Matthew Broderick gave a superb comic performance as J. Pierrepont Finch in *How to Succeed in Business Without Really Trying.* Unfortunately, much of what played as satire in the early Sixties barely raises an indulgent smile today. Two of Frank Loesser's big comic numbers, "Coffee Break" and "Paris Original," don't have the punch they had in more innocent times, despite the invention and energy of Wayne Cilento's choreography. The high-tech scenic design, featuring the relentless projection of video images on large screens upstage, was dizzying and distracted from the good work of the performers they dwarfed. Though the physical production was ill-judged, and much of the material has lost its punch, the cast was a strong one. Megan Mullally was a trimly ironic Rosemary, Jeff Blumenkrantz explored the outer reaches of hysteria and paranoia as the villainous Bud Frump, Ronn Carroll was touchingly insecure with his power as the boss, J.B. Biggley, and Lillias White gave a fine account of the gospel-inspired "Brotherhood of Man" at the show's climax.

The story of fortune-hunting blonde Lorelei Lee, her brunette buddy Dorothy Shaw and their dealings with a variety of malleable men, *Gentlemen Prefer Blondes,* also suffered from the change in satiric tastes. Though the book was something to sit patiently through, many of the songs by Jule Styne and Leo Robin held up fine. The production, which was originally designed for the intimate Goodspeed Opera House, seemed misplaced in the Lyceum Theater. (Unfortunately, this was the only production sponsored this year by the National Actors Theater, the company Tony Randall built and championed.)

If I hadn't seen a delightful production of *Wonderful Town* starring Maureen Lipman in London's West End in the late Eighties, the New York City Opera's revival would make me skeptical about the viability of this work today. Granted, the size of the house overwhelmed the modesty that is one of the attributes of this celebration of Bohemian life in Greenwich Village. Kay McClelland and Crista Moore are both solid musical theater veterans and they played the Sherwood sisters with the requisite spunk and sass, but Richard Sabellico's production was distressingly flat and unfunny, sapping much of the energy from the tuneful Comden, Green and Bernstein score.

Having been a big fan of the original production of *Three Postcards* at Playwrights Horizons (in which form it was named a Best Play), I was dismayed by the version that was presented this season by Circle Rep. Reportedly under the influence of director Tee Scatuorchio, Craig Lucas substantially rewrote the book. In the original version, directed by Norman Rene, the show began with the gathering of three women, lifelong friends, in an upscale restaurant. As the meal progressed, the past, present and future of their relationships were revealed, as well as the interior lives to which the others were not privy. This revised version tacks on an extended verbal overture in which it is laboriously signalled that this show is about friendship. The effect is to turn what had been wistful and implicit into something thumpingly obvious. Craig Carnelia's music and lyrics are still impressive, particularly the brilliant song "Picture in the Hall," but this is a case in which a lovely work has been improved to death.

Another work focussing on the bonds between a group of women, *Uncommon Women and Others,* the 1977 play which served as Wendy Wasserstein's introduction to the New York stage, was also given an unsatisfying revival, and again it may be that the charms of this portrait of students muddling through a year at a women's college have been overwhelmed by time. Certainly, Wasserstein has progressed from this pleasant sketch pad of a play to more substantial achievements.

Under the direction of Sean Mathias, *Indiscretions* (a/k/a *Les Parents Terribles* and *Intimate Relations*) was great flamboyant fun. If it weren't for this book's policy of not citing revivals as Best Plays (our Mr. Foose assures us it played New York's Mermaid Theater in the Charles Frank translation as *Intimate Relations* for 76 performances beginning November 1, 1962), this piece would certainly be my choice for the year's best foreign work in the modern style. Similar to last season's *An Inspector Calls,* the production was fitted out with a set to provoke gasps. But, whereas I thought the design for *An Inspector Calls* was at war with the play Priestley wrote, here the design supports and amplifies the outrageousness of Cocteau's script. Most spectacular was a floor-to-flies circular staircase which provided the opportunity for acrobatics that mirrored the moral acrobatics of the characters.

As spectacular as the scenic elements were, this was not a production out of which you emerged humming the sets. Kathleen Turner, Roger Rees and Jude Law made for a gloriously extravagant and dysfunctional family, their grand gestures offering the perfect inflated balloons for Eileen Atkins (playing Turner's sister) to prick with ironic detachment. Cynthia Nixon was very affecting as the young woman who finds herself about to be swallowed up by these entertaining monsters. This was as raucously entertaining an evening as Broadway had to offer.

The Broadway revival of Brian Friel's 1980 play *Translations* was almost universally battered by critics who treasured the memory of the first New York incarnation at the Manhattan Theater Club. I didn't have the pleasure of seeing that production, so I came to the play fresh. Perhaps in a smaller, more intimate space, the personal values had more impact. In this production, however, the tale of the English suppression of the Irish tongue set in the town of Ballybeg in 1833 struck me as overly schematic. Characters appeared to exist as vehicles to represent different philosophies and political positions and only secondarily smacked of humanity. I didn't feel this was for want of casting. Several observers commented that Brian Dennehey was too robust for the role of the aging teacher, but his robustness served to accentuate the degree of his fall by the end of the play. I happen to be a particular Dana Delany fan and was delighted by the opportunity to finally see this gifted actress onstage, though the Irish girl she played must be counted a supporting role. The scene in which she and Michael Cumpsty (as an English lieutenant) courted despite a language barrier had a moment-to-moment life that the rest of the evening lacked.

Friel and his Ballybeg were better served by Joe Dowling's clear and unforced production of *Philadelphia, Here I Come!* at the Roundabout Theater. The play is based on a gimmick: two actors play Gareth O'Donnell, one his public face, the other his private. The meat of the play lies in the contrast between the explosive inner self (played by Robert Sean Leonard) and the guarded front he presents to the world (played by Jim True) and the trouble both sides have in making the gesture that would bridge the gulf with his reserved father (played by Milo O'Shea) as the boy prepares to move out of the house to a new life in America. Aideen O'Kelly shone as the aunt to whose house Gareth is moving, by turns an embarrassingly loud drunk and a woman trying to cope with deep pain.

The Roundabout generally had a good year. Though its production of *Hedda Gabler* (featuring Kelly McGillis in the title role) was a disappointment, its production of *The Molière Comedies,* a pair of one-acts featuring Brian Bedford in sharply contrasting roles, was one of the hottest tickets of the season. There was much disagreement over Scott Ellis's production of Turgenev's *A Month in the Country,* but I enjoyed every second of it and returned for a second helping. As Natalya Petrovna, the landowner's wife whose romantic obsession with her son's tutor disrupts the lives of everyone in the vicinity, Helen Mirren was especially successful in charting Natalya's abrupt shifts in attitudes—one second self-pitying and aspiring to tragic stature, the next impatient and self-mocking, and the next inspired to romantic hyperbole. Byron Jennings was also fine as her confused husband, in such a frenzy to be fair as to be ineffectual, and Ron Rifkin lent his dependable ironic voice to Natalya's longsuffering and overlooked admirer. There seems to be no middle ground between those who embraced F. Murray Abraham's performance as the self-seeking doctor and those who were put off by it. I declare myself to be in the former group. I thought the resolutely unromantic courtship scene Abraham played with Gail Grate an undiluted comic delight. I had some reservations about the steep incline set designer Santo Loquasto contributed to the exterior scenes, but the interplay of the colors in Jane Greenwood's costumes and Brian Nason's lighting design made the production a visual treat as well.

The Roundabout also offered a solid if unexciting 50th anniversary production of Tennessee Williams's *The Glass Menagerie* featuring Julie Harris as Amanda under the direction of Frank Galati. Calista Flockhart distinguished herself as Laura. Williams was better served by Robert Falls's staging of *The Rose Tattoo* for Circle in the Square. Anthony LaPaglia invested truckdriver Alvaro Mangiacavallo with an infectious clownishness. Mercedes Ruehl played Serafina with a nearly operatic intensity. I can't think of another actress who can so vividly project sheer joy.

She was also the chief asset of Circle in the Square's revival of Michael Cristofer's Pulitzer Prize-winning look at a hospice for terminal cancer patients, *The Shadow Box.* The company's version of *Uncle Vanya* had two strikes against it: Louis Malle's filmed record of Andre Gregory's version played in rehearsal clothes, *Vanya on 42nd Street,* was released to great and justifiable acclaim a short time before, and it was used as a club to batter Braham Murray's staging. And the part of Astrov was calamitously miscast with James Fox. Astrov is supposed to be a galvanizing presence, but Fox, who has distinguished himself in many other productions, played him so dryly as to create doubt that he possessed any bodily fluids. Tom Courtenay was a boiling teakettle of a Vanya, and Amanda Donohoe's combination of beauty and misdirected intelligence made her the perfect object of the men's rescue fantasies.

Outstanding
1994–95 Designs

Left, top to bottom: Kathleen Turner, Jude Law, Eileen Atkins, Cynthia Nixon and Roger Rees on Stephen Brimson Lewis's staircase in Jean Cocteau's *Indiscretions. Below,* Alessandro Nivola and Helen Mirren wearing Jane Greenwood's costumes in Ivan Turgenev's *A Month in the Country*

The two New York Shakespeare Festival offerings in the park were of lesser plays. *The Two Gentlemen of Verona* was most memorable for its ingenious setting by Eugene Lee including its own waterways in which the cast boated and swam. Set by director Daniel Sullivan in the old West, *The Merry Wives of Windsor* was at its best when Tonya Pinkins and Margaret Whitton (as the title characters) were busy at their plots against Falstaff, or when Andrea Martin, with her sure comic sense, whipped up shtick as Mistress Quickly. These two productions continued the Shakespeare Marathon Joseph Papp launched a few years before his death. Another in the Marathon, a production of *The Merchant of Venice* at the Public, featured Ron Leibman as a ferocious Shylock.

Ralph Fiennes won the Tony for his performance in *Hamlet,* and several of the critics were effusive in their praise of him. His was a turbo-charged prince, the rapidity of his speech suggesting a racing mind. Though there was no denying the intelligence and passion of the interpretation, I wish it had been more modulated. The strongest elements of Jonathan Kent's production were Francesca Annis and Tara FitzGerald as Gertrude and Ophelia. Though Gertrude is numbered one of the great Shakespearean roles for women, one gets the impression that Shakespeare didn't think much about her as he was writing the play. Certainly, we never get a peek at her interior life such as we get of Hamlet and Claudius, and she spends much of her time tossing in the odd addendum in group scenes. Annis somehow managed to connect the very scattered dots and create a full and complex woman subject to mutually exclusive impulses that threaten to tear her apart.

"What interests me about this *Hamlet* is that it is an independent production," our historian Mr. Foose comments. In listing for his own edification all the New York *Hamlet*s from John Barrymore's in 1922 to Fiennes's in the current Dodger-Almeida presentation, he finds that the last independent Broadway production of Shakespeare's play took place about 25 years ago, in 1969, starring Nicol Williamson. Other independently-produced *Hamlet*s have been Richard Burton's in 1964, Maurice Evans's in 1938, Leslie Howard's and John Gielgud's in 1936, Walter Hampden's in 1935 and 1925 and Barrymore's. Organizations which have provided New York *Hamlet*s during those decades were the City Center, Donald Wolfit's repertory, the French Government (with Jean-Louis Barrault), the Old Vic, the Phoenix, New York Shakespeare Festival at the Delacorte, the Beaumont and the Public, A.P.A., Roundabout, Carnegie Hall, Circle Rep and BAM.

The most successful Shakespeare this year was the Cheek by Jowl company's *As You Like It* featuring an all-male cast at BAM. After a while, the novelty of seeing men play Rosalind and Celia wore off, and one could appreciate the clarity and intelligence of their work. The whole evening was about the transformational power of theater—not only to accept the device of cross-gender casting without the condescension of camp, but to see an essentially bare stage constantly redefined by Declan Donnellan's nearly balletic blocking.

One of the surprise hits of the season was Ruth and Augustus Goetz's *The Heiress,* an adaptation of Henry James's short novel, *Washington Square.* Some of the press wrote of Gerald Gutierrez's production as if he had magically transformed a chestnut. Nonsense. He paid the script the compliment of taking it as seriously as it deserves. For a period piece, it is startlingly modern in its writing; many of the play's passages are as rich in malice dressed in manners as vintage Pinter, and its tale of the crippling relation between a parent and child is as psychologically violent as *The Cryptogram*. The Goetzes had the added advantage of writing for characters who are more comfortable with language than are many of our stammering contemporaries.

And the cast assembled for this production was more than equipped to fly with this language. Philip Bosco has long struck me as America's answer to Ralph Richardson (who played Dr. Sloper in William Wyler's extraordinary film adaptation). Richardson was brilliant in the role, but Bosco added a distinctly American note of Yankee hard-headedness. Frances Sternhagen expertly revealed the canniness under the surface silliness of a widowed aunt. Jon Tenney's suitor was solid, but there is more to be mined in the suitor's capacity for self-delusion than was evident the night that I saw it.

The role of Catherine, the good-hearted, not very attractive, awkward girl who ultimately blossoms through pain into bittersweet self-possession, was played by Cherry Jones, who herself blossomed this season into a full-fledged star. At the beginning, her lack of guile made her every thought and impulse register uncensored on her face. In the stunning sequence in which Catherine is stood up on the evening she expected to elope, she retreated into the darkest shadows of the stage (courtesy of lighting designer Beverly Emmons). When she re-emerged into the light, she was reborn as something harder, sadder. It was a moment to take the breath away.

This revival reaffirmed the play's place as a classic of the American stage. But this place has not always been secure. When the play premiered on Broadway in 1947, Brooks Atkinson concluded his review for the *Times* by saying, "The heroine cannot be acted; she can only be acted against. The story cannot be dramatized." In those days, there were enough other newspapers with other, credible critics to overcome the obstacle of a misguided *Times* pan. Enough said.

Offstage

Fewer new shows opened on Broadway (35 by our count as opposed to last season's 42), and, as mentioned earlier, many of the artists commonly associated with Broadway chose to work in smaller venues. Despite the shrinking number of offerings and the exodus by many of its leading artists, Broadway attendance increased. According to the League of American Theaters and Producers, more than 9 million tickets were sold (at an average price of $43.87) and the receipts jumped 14 percent above last year's all-time record gross $356,034,160 to $406,306,661. (Touring receipts were up slightly, too, from about $687.7 million to a shade less than $694.6 million.)

Go figure.

The big musicals accounted for much of the income and attendance. According to the *Times, Sunset Boulevard* opened with a $37 million advance and *Show Boat* regularly pulled in approximately $900,000 a week. Of course, part of the appeal of these offerings is spectacle, and spectacle costs a lot of money to put up in the first place. The record capitalization for the year, though, was for a show that didn't play in the traditional theater district but in Madison Square Garden—the $12 million *A Christmas Carol* which its producers hope will ultimately recoup its investment after years as an annual attraction. Expensive productions translate into expensive tickets. Seeing Vanessa Williams (Chita Rivera's replacement) in *Kiss of the Spider Woman* could cost you $70. *Sunset Boulevard,* too, had a $70 top. *Show Boat* charged $75 for the best seat in the house.

Among Broadway's non-musical offerings, the most expensive mounting was *On the Waterfront,* which required $3 million to open. Its swift closing made it reportedly the most costly straight-play flop in history.

There was some good news, however: After several unsuccessful productions under the Broadway Alliance contract (the special deal offering breaks on union minimums to the producers in exchange for lower ticket prices and other concessions), *Love! Valour! Compassion!* became the first show produced under the agreement to achieve the status of a hit. The transfer from Manhattan Theater Club to the Walter Kerr cost $675,000. (The season's other Broadway Alliance show, *My Thing of Love,* failed.)

New York Magazine devoted a cover story to the question "Can Broadway Be Saved?" Writer Michael Goldstein offered a series of suggestions which included finding a public figure who would act as a kind of theater czar, facing down the *Times* on the cost of theater advertising, encouraging producers to disenthrall themselves from unnecessary and overly expensive sets, negotiating reality-based contracts with the stagehands and musicians unions, and getting tax breaks for the production of new work. Goldstein also suggested taking a leaf from professional sports and charging more for the wealthy who can afford it. An underground economy supplies rich people with last-minute tickets to the biggest hits for much-inflated prices. Goldstein suggests that if producers themselves set aside, say, 40 tickets a night to the biggest hits and offered them to the Dom Perignon set for hundreds of dollars, the extra money would go to repay investors rather than enrich scalpers.

Though no comprehensive figures for off Broadway are available, between the continuing runs of *Three Tall Women, Stomp,* and *Tubes* (not to forget the ongoing phenomenon of *The Fantasticks,* which celebrated its 35th birthday this year), the record-breaking box office of *Death Defying Acts* (capitalized at $650,00, the show sold almost $130,000 of tickets the day Vincent Canby's supportive review was published), the strong initial showing of *London Suite* and the successes of *Travels With My Aunt* and *The Compleat Works of Wllm Shkspr (Abridged),* several of the commercial houses were profitably occupied. The off-Broadway limited 20-week run of *Vita & Virginia* also did well, returning $600,000 on the $400,000 capitalization.

As mentioned earlier, the off-Broadway production of a Neil Simon play attracted a lot of attention. The reasons cited for Simon's decision to abandon the Times Square environs were economic. Producer Emanuel Azenberg calculated that only $660,000 was required to open off Broadway, about two-fifths of what it would cost on Broadway; and, not being subject to some of the Broadway union schedules, the operating costs were lower. The *Times* quoted him as saying, "Off-Broadway, 400 seats at $40 makes me a smash. On Broadway, 400 seats at $55 closes me down. You tell me—what makes sense?"

The fact that Simon and some of his Broadway peers moved off Broadway and pulled in substantial grosses did not escape the notice of some of those they left behind. Many in the community are anticipating that the unions will indeed attempt to follow and introduce new labor contracts into these smaller venues. This would surely have the effect of making off-Broadway productions more expensive and less adventurous.

Continuing on the subject of unions, the musicians' union agreed to allow the Broadway producers of *Smokey Joe's Cafe* to invoke a "special circumstances" clause (negotiated in 1993 between the League of American Theaters and Producers and Local 802 of the American Federation of Musicians) and, for the first time, break the practice of requiring some musicians to be paid even if they weren't playing. Under the old system, booking specific theaters involved hiring a minimum number of musicians, so a theater that was slated for 26 musicians and required only eight would pay an additional 18 (known in the trade as "walkers"). *Smokey Joe's Cafe,* a show featuring rock music, required a band of only seven, and the union let the show go forward without requiring nine walkers who would ordinarily have been on the payroll at the Virginia Theater. In related news, at season's end, the League was preparing to negotiate with Local 1, the stagehands' union, whose contract was scheduled to expire in the summer.

With the election of Republican majorities in the U.S. House and Senate, the shrinking or elimination of the National Endowment for the Arts seems certain. There is a long tradition of reactionary politicians reinforcing the solidarity of their constituencies through demonizing some "other." With the collapse of the Soviet Union, figures such as Senator Jesse Helms and House Speaker Newt Gingrich appear to need some new "other" against which to rally their supporters. The group selected: artists, many of whom, oh so incidentally, are gay, liberal and/or from some ethnic minority not commonly found outside cosmopolitan urban areas. Past attacks on funding for the arts have been based on moral objections to some of the art funded. The move to balance the federal budget provided an additional rationale to cutting back on such "inessential" items as arts funding.

In these tight financial times, state and city budgets also were looking to slim down. New York being a theater center, the policies of the state and city governments have the potential of having major impacts on the quality and volume of the work done here. There is little in the election of Republican George Pataki to the Governorship and of Republican Rudolph Giuliani to the Mayorship to encourage false hope about energetic support for state or city arts programs. The question is not whether funding for the theater will be cut, but by how much.

The Nederlander Organization seemed inclined to pick up a little of the slack in the area of playwright support. It announced a program in association with the

Roundabout Theater Company under which four playwrights a year will be given $15,000 commissions for new plays.

Having clocked about a year as first-string critic at the New York *Times,* David Richards abruptly departed for the Washington *Post,* for which he had previously written. Reportedly he was dissatisfied by a policy that compelled him to focus only on the theater. He was replaced by longtime *Times* film critic Vincent Canby (who is himself a playwright). Margo Jefferson took over Canby's berth as the Sunday *Times* critic.

Josephine Abady, who in the spring of 1994 was so unceremoniously dumped by the board of the Cleveland Play House (where she had served as artistic director to acclaim), moved to Circle in the Square (uptown) as co-artistic director with founder Ted Mann. This season, she satisfied the outstanding obligation to subscribers to offer them two productions—*The Shadow Box* and *Uncle Vanya*—and went on to produce a third, *The Rose Tattoo.*

Another Circle—Circle Rep—went through a tumultuous period. It began the season by moving from its home of 17 years, the Sheridan Square Theater, to the larger downtown Circle in the Square (making it the Circle-in-the-Circle-in-the-Square?). Early in 1995, the board turned over artistic directorship to the team of actress Lynne Thigpen and actor-writer-director Austin Pendleton. When the new team cancelled the announced production next season of William H. Hoffman's *Riga* and dismissed Michael Warren Powell as the director of Circle Rep's lab, Circle's co-founders—Tanya Berezin, Marshall W. Mason and Lanford Wilson—resigned from the company in protest.

More conflict arose off-Broadway at the Westside Theater when the house's management evicted the commercial transfer of Charles Busch's *You Should Be So Lucky.* The mechanism for eviction was a stop-clause in the contract between the Westside and Rhoda Herrick, the show's producer. According to the terms, the show could be given the gate if its gross fell below one-third of the box office potential two weeks in a row. It did so, and, despite the fact that Herrick offered to make up the difference herself, Peter Askin on behalf of the Westside opted to force the closing. This made the desirable venue available for the New York premiere of David Mamet's *The Cryptogram* fresh from its acclaimed run in Boston. Herrick published an open letter to Mamet in the *Times, Variety* and the New York *Observer* that began, "As one of America's premier playwrights, you have been an acute observer of contemporary society, consistently exposing the deceit, the greed and the unethical behavior that increasingly affect this society, undermining its ethical standards and dehumanizing its citizenry." After detailing her version of the events, she concluded by writing: "WHAT'S GOING ON HERE? DOES THIS SCENARIO SEEM REMINISCENT OF ONE OF YOUR PLAYS?" There is no evidence that Mamet ever responded directly to Herrick. *The Cryptogram* did, however, open at the Westside for what turned out to be a brief run.

At season's end, both the Signature Theater and the Ridiculous Theatrical Company were looking for new homes. At first, the Signature seemed to have found a berth at the Provincetown Playhouse, but the Playhouse's landlord, New York Uni-

PAULS GRAVEYARD.

A CHRISTMAS CAROL—The sumptuous production at Madison Square Garden based on Dickens's classic was one of 1994–95's outstanding musical designs, described by Jeffrey Sweet as "a constant treat to behold." *Above* is one of Tony Walton's sketches for the scenery; *below* are two of William Ivey Long's costume sketches. The Jules Fisher-Peggy Eisenhauer lighting of the show was also cited among the year's best

versity, scuttled the deal over disagreements over the kind of seating to be installed (NYU wanted the facility to double as a lecture hall) and the length of the lease. Where the Signature's next home will be is still in doubt as this is being written. In the case of the Ridiculous, the landlord's refusal to renew the lease after a 17-year residency means that the company will have to leave the facility that bears the name of the Ridiculous's founder, the late writer-director, Charles Ludlam. The Ridiculous, too, doesn't know where it will produce next.

Sunset Boulevard composer-producer Andrew Lloyd Webber must sometimes wish he'd never undertaken the project. After having settled a lawsuit brought against him by the original London star, Patti LuPone, for $1 million when he reneged on his agreement to have her open the show in New York, he faced another lawsuit filed by Faye Dunaway when he closed the Los Angeles production of the show rather than have her replace star Glenn Close there. The reported reason— Dunaway couldn't sing well enough. Dunaway's action was based on the damage she believed this did to her reputation; this suit was settled, too.

His troubles with leading ladies were not over. The New York production opened successfully with Close, but when Close went on vacation, the New York office of Lloyd Webber's Really Useful Company issued figures that indicated only a modest dip in the box office take when understudy Karen Mason substituted for her. The figures turned out to be fudged upward to the tune of $150,000 a week. Close was furious that the company would misrepresent her value at the box office. Her "private" correspondence to Lloyd Webber expressing her outrage somehow found its way into the press. Apologies were issued, and public displays of reconciliation between the two were staged. Betty Buckley, who succeeded LuPone in London to acclaim, was scheduled to assume the role when Close completed her contract at the end of June.

It had been widely assumed that *Love! Valour! Compassion!* had the inside track on the Pulitzer Prize. Among those who assumed this was Horton Foote, whose win for *The Young Man From Atlanta* was widely viewed as a long-overdue acknowledgment of this fine dramatist's lifelong career.

In any case, *Love! Valour! Compassion!* won its share of honors, including the Tony, the Obie, the Drama Desk, and the Outer Critics Circle Awards as well as the New York Drama Critics Circle Award for best American play. (The Critics Circle gave its best play award to Stoppard's *Arcadia.*) *Sunset Boulevard* won the Outer Critics Circle Award and the Tony. The New York Drama Critics Circle declined to give an award to a musical this year, and the Drama Desk chose to honor the revival of *Show Boat* as the year's best musical production.

There was the usual chorus of objections to the Tony nominations, particularly over those who had not been nominated. Nathan Lane had been thought a shoo-in for a nomination for *Love! Valour! Compassion!,* and so he probably would have been if he'd been nominated in the featured acting category. But somehow, distinct from the others in the play's ensemble, he was ruled eligible to compete in the best actor category and didn't gather sufficient votes from the nominating committee to make it to the final slate. (Lane did win a Drama Desk award as a featured actor.)

I would add my surprise that Philip Bosco and Anthony LaPaglia weren't nominated. Ralph Fiennes picked up the Tony and Drama Desk Awards for *Hamlet,* and Matthew Broderick picked up Tony, Drama Desk and Outer Critics Circle Awards for *How to Succeed in Business Without Really Trying.* Glenn Close walked away with virtually every prize for which she was eligible, for *Sunset Boulevard.*

The most heavily-contested category was, predictably, for best actress in a play. In addition to the four palpably worthy nominees, good cases could have been made for Kathleen Turner, Gloria Foster, Laurie Metcalf and Mercedes Ruehl (for her performance in *The Rose Tattoo*). Cherry Jones won for *The Heiress* and picked up a slew of other honors as well.

The embarrassing lack of eligible musicals led to Tonys being given without competition for the book and score of *Sunset Boulevard.* There was also the odd sight of Jean Cocteau's *Indiscretions* (original and superior title, *Les Parents Terribles*) being nominated in the category for best new play, despite the fact that it premiered in Paris before World War II and was produced in New York in 1962 under the title *Intimate Relations.*

The Tony Committee also awarded a special award to Harvey Sabinson, who this season resigned as executive director of the League of American Theaters and Producers after a long and admirable tenure in that office.

The Tony broadcast itself went fairly smoothly, with Nathan Lane getting solace for his lack of a nomination by having co-hosts Glenn Close and Gregory Hines feed him setup lines all evening. In a reprise of a widely-criticized practice initiated last year, the broadcast's producers had the orchestra begin to play when the winners' speeches went past 30 seconds. Nobody got a chance to hear Terrence McNally's acceptance speech. Not only did the rising volume of the orchestra keep him from giving the speech, the broadcast switched to a commercial. On behalf of the Dramatists Guild, Peter Stone threatened a boycott of next year's proceedings if the authors of the productions that make the show possible aren't guaranteed greater respect.

Every year, death takes from us another round of precious talents. Without meaning to slight the contributions of any of the others who left us, I'd like to make special mention of a woman who never had a New York credit as a performer, writer or director yet whose work had a profound effect on the American theater—Viola Spolin. Through her pioneering work in creating theater games, she laid the theoretical foundation of literally hundreds of improvisational theater companies around the country and the world. Some of these troupes played notable engagements in New York (including Chicago's The Second City, San Francisco's The Committee, and Boston's The Proposition), and one, The Premise, made its home here. In addition, literally hundreds of major actors, writers and directors began their careers in one of these troupes and carried the disciplines they learned there into their work onstage and in film and television. Though not widely known to the general public, her influence on 20th century theater theory approaches that of Stanislavski.

A GRAPHIC GLANCE

1994–95
Drawings
By Hirschfeld

Ralph Fiennes in the title role of *Hamlet*

Julie Harris as Amanda in *The Glass Menagerie*

Andrew Lloyd Webber *(above)* with a scene from his latest creation, *Sunset Boulevard (left),* with Glenn Close *(foreground)* as Norma Desmond accompanied by Alice Ripley, Alan Campbell *(on phone),* George Hearn and Alan Oppenheimer

Matthew Broderick as J. Pierrepont Finch *(in foreground)* in the revival of the musical *How to Succeed in Business Without Really Trying* is surrounded by Jonathan Freeman, Gerry Vichi *(wearing glasses)*, Megan Mullally, Ronn Carroll *(on phone)*, Jeff Blumenkrantz, Luba Mason, Victoria Clark and Lillias White

Dorothy Loudon with puppet in *Comedy Tonight*

Patrick Stewart in his solo performance of *A Christmas Carol*

A Masque of Producers?

On opposite page, George Weissman, vice chairman of the Lincoln Center board of directors; *above,* Arthur Cantor

Jerry Lewis as Applegate in *Damn Yankees*

Below, the authors of the one-acts on the program *Death Defying Acts:* Elaine May *(Hotline),* David Mamet *(An Interview)* and Woody Allen *(Central Park West)*

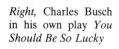

Left, Mary Alice and Gloria Foster as Bessie and Sadie Delany in *Having Our Say*

Right, Charles Busch in his own play *You Should Be So Lucky*

Davis Gaines as the Phantom in *The Phantom of the Opera*

Shirl Bernheim and June Havoc in *The Old Lady's Guide to Survival*

Marcia Gay Harden *(foreground)* with Ed Harris, Beverly D'Angelo and Fred Ward in Sam Shepard's *Simpatico*

Clockwise from upper left, Lonette McKee (Julie), Mark Jacoby (Gaylord Ravenal), Rebecca Luker (Magnolia), Michel Bell (Joe), Elaine Stritch (Parthy), John McMartin (Cap'n Andy), Michel Bell with Gretha Boston (Queenie), Dorothy Stanley (Ellie) and Joel Blum (Frank) in Harold Prince's version of the Jerome Kern-Oscar Hammerstein II musical *Show Boat*

Mercedes Ruehl in *The Rose Tattoo*

Laurie Metcalf in *My Thing of Love*

David Alan Grier (Ford), Tonya Pinkins (Mistress Ford), Margaret Whitton (Mistress Page), Miguel Perez (Page), Andrea Martin (Mistress Quickly) and Brian Murray (Falstaff) in New York Shakespeare's *The Merry Wives of Windsor* in Central Park

Jere Shea, Donna Murphy and *(at top)* Marin Mazzie in last
season's Stephen Sondheim-James Lapine musical *Passion*

Kelly McGillis in *Hedda Gabler*

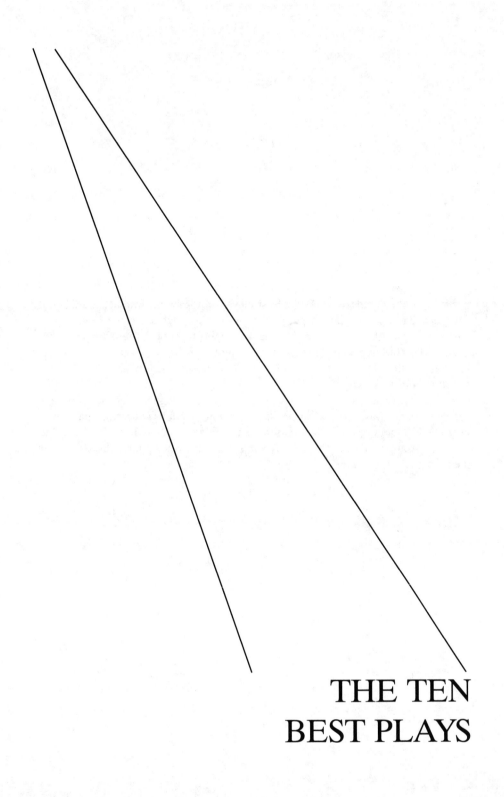

THE TEN
BEST PLAYS

Here are the details of 1994–95's Best Plays—synopses, biographical sketches of authors and other material. By permission of the playwrights, their representatives, publishers, and others who own the exclusive rights to publish these scripts in full, most of our continuities include substantial quotations from crucial/pivotal scenes in order to provide a permanent reference to style and quality as well as theme, structure and story line.

In the case of such quotations, scenes and lines of dialogue, stage directions and descriptions appear *exactly* as in the stage version or published script unless (in a very few instances, for technical reasons) an abridgement is indicated by five dots (. . . . .). The appearance of three dots (. . .) is the script's own punctuation to denote the timing of a spoken line.

Critics and Tony Awards

LOVE! VALOUR! COMPASSION!

A Play in Three Acts

BY TERRENCE McNALLY

Cast and credits appear on pages 322–323, 351–352

TERRENCE McNALLY was born in St. Petersburg, Fla., November 3, 1939 and grew up in Corpus Christi, Texas. He received his B.A. in English at Columbia where in his senior year he wrote the varsity show. After graduation he was awarded the Harry Evans Travelling Fellowship in creative writing. He made his professional stage debut with The Lady of the Camellias, *an adaptation of the Dumas story produced on Broadway in 1963. His first original full-length play,* And Things That Go Bump in the Night, *was produced on Broadway in 1965 following a production at the Tyrone Guthrie Theater in Minneapolis.*

McNally's short play Tour *was produced off Broadway in 1968 as part of the* Collision Course *program. In the next season, 1968–69, his one-acters were produced all over town;* Cuba Si! *off Broadway in the ANTA Matinee series;* Noon *on the Broadway program* Morning, Noon and Night; Sweet Eros *and* Witness *off Broadway that fall, and in early winter* Next *with Elaine May's* Adaptation *on an off-Broadway bill that was named a Best Play of its season.*

McNally's second Best Play, Where Has Tommy Flowers Gone?, *had its world premiere at the Yale Repertory Theater before opening on Broadway in 1971. His third,* Bad Habits, *was produced OOB in 1973 by New York Theater Strategy, directed then and in its off-Broadway and Broadway phases in the 1973–74 season by Robert Drivas. His fourth,* The Ritz, *played the Yale Repertory Theater as* The Tubs *before opening on Broadway January 20, 1975 for a run of 400 performances. His fifth,* It's Only a Play, *was produced in a pre-Broadway tryout under the title* Broadway, Broadway *in 1978 and OOB under the new title by Manhattan Punch Line in 1982. It finally arrived in the full bloom of an off-Broadway production—and Best Play designation—January 12, 1986, for 17 performances at Manhattan Theater Club, which also produced his sixth Best Play,* Lips Together, Teeth Apart, *June 25, 1991 for 406 performances.*

McNally's seventh Best Play, the book for the musical Kiss of the Spider Woman *with a John Kander-Fred Ebb score, took a circuitous route to Broadway acclaim. After a 1990 tryout in the short-lived New Musicals Program at SUNY Purchase, N.Y. and a Toronto production, it went on to an award-winning London staging in 1992 before reaching Broadway May 3, 1993, just in time to win that season's Critics best-musical award and the Tonys for book, score and show. His eighth Best Play,* A Perfect Ganesh, *was put on by Manhattan Theater Club June 27, 1994 for 124 performances. McNally's ninth Best Play,* Love! Valour! Compassion! *was produced by MTC November 1, 1994 for 72 performances, then moved to Broadway February 14 for a continuing run, and received the Tony for best play and the Critics Award for best American play.*

Other notable McNally presentations in one of the most active and successful play-writing careers in his generation have included Whiskey *(1973, OOB); the book for the John Kander-Fred Ebb musical* The Rink *(1984, Broadway);* The Lisbon Traviata *(1985, OOB; 1989, off Broadway at MTC);* Frankie and Johnny in the Clair de Lune *(1987, off Broadway at MTC for 533 performances); sketch material for MTC's musical revue* Urban Blight, *1988; in 1989,* Prelude and Liebestod *and* Hope *OOB and* Up in Saratoga *in regional theater at the Old Globe in San Diego; and in 1990, a revival at MTC of his* Bad Habits. *McNally adapted his own* The Ritz *and* Frankie and Johnny *for the movies and is the author of a number of TV plays, including the 1991 Emmy Award-winning* Andre's Mother. *He has been the recipient of Obies, Hull-Warriner Awards (for* Bad Habits *and* The Lisbon Traviata*); fellowships from CBS, Rockefeller and two from the Guggenheim Foundation; and a citation from the American Academy of Arts and Letters. He lives in Manhattan and has served as vice president of the Dramatists Guild, the organization of playwrights, composers, lyricists and musical book writers, since 1981.*

The following synopsis of Love! Valour! Compassion! *was prepared by Sally Dixon Wiener.*

Time: **The present, Memorial Day, 4th of July and Labor Day weekends, respectively**

Place: **A remote house and wooded grounds by a lake in Duchess County, two hours north of New York City**

ACT I

SYNOPSIS: A slope of greensward descends from center stage right to center stage left, and near the downstage edge there is a miniature Carpenter Gothic house with porches upstairs and down and with a welcoming golden glow shining from its windows. Tall square pillars rise on each side of the stage and passageways are to the left and right of the greensward. There is a good-sized downstage playing area. Behind the greensward, which doubles as the upstairs of the house, is a scrim of blue sky that conceals a lake area seen periodically during the play. Props are minimal.

Characters often address the audience directly and also take turns as narrator.

As the play begins, seven men are singing "Beautiful Dreamer." They are Gregory Mitchell, a choreographer with a minor speech impediment, the oldest of the group and the host; Arthur Pape, an accountant, slender and conservative; Perry Sellars, a lawyer, even more slender and conservative and Arthur's lover of many years; John Jeckyll, Gregory's rehearsal pianist, a tall, saturninely handsome Englishman now a U.S. citizen, a master of the putdown; Buzz Hauser, costumer for Gregory's company and the quintessential musical theater buff, short, bouncy and beefy; Bobby Brahms, Gregory's young lover, calm and controlled—and blind; and Ramon Fornos, a dancer from Puerto Rico, a young hunk, a bit on the defensive as the outsider who has arrived with John. It is Memorial Day weekend. The song ends, and Gregory turns and addresses the audience.

GREGORY: Um. I love my. Um. House. Everybody does. I like to fill it with my friends. Um. And walk around the grounds at night and watch them. Um. Through the lighted windows. It makes me happy to see them inside. Um. Our home. Mine. Um. And Bobby's. Um. I'm sorry. Um. I don't do this. Um. On purpose. Um.

ARTHUR: It's okay, Gregory.

GREGORY: It was built in 1915 and still has most of the. Um. Original roof. The wall paper in the dining room. Um. Is original, too. So is. Um. A lot of the cabinet work. You'd have to be a fool. Um. To change it. This sofa is my pride. Um. And joy. It came with the house. It's genuine. Um. Horsehair. It's itchy, but I don't care. I love it.

PERRY: Tell them about the sled.

GREGORY: Jerome Robbins gave me this sled.

PERRY: Mutual admiration, he said. One master choreographer to another.

GREGORY: It's flat here, I said. No hills. Um. What am I going to do with a sled? It's not a sled, Gregory, he told me. It's an antique.

JOHN: It's not an antique, Gregory. It's a piece of junk.

GREGORY: I hope you. Um. Appreciate detail. That. Um. Wainscotting there. This finial here. The main stairs. Um. Have a very gentle rise. Everyone comments how easy it is to. Um. Climb them.

BUZZ: I love your stairs, Gregory. They're so easy.

ARTHUR: Don't tease him like that.

BUZZ: Who's teasing? I wasn't teasing!

GREGORY: They don't build houses like this any more. Um. The golden age. Um. Of American housebuilding.

BUZZ: Is this going to be pick-on-Buzz weekend!

GREGORY: Not architecture, mind you, but housebuilding. This house. Um. Was meant. To stand. Welcome. Make yourself at home.

Everyone has been drifting off to the bedrooms except Ramon and Bobby, while Perry recalls (as though in a flashback being acted out) an incident during the weekend in which Ramon, despite Bobby's protestations, began kissing Bobby. Bobby had gone downstairs for milk and cookies (Perry reports), and Ramon had either followed him or was waiting for him. There is the sound of glass breaking. Bobby, being blind, isn't sure who is with him. Ramon whispers something in Bobby's ear, and (Perry continues) after they "achieved some sort of satisfaction," Ramon went back upstairs and got into bed with John again.

In a continuation of this incident, Arthur joins Perry in the kitchen and finds that Bobby has cut his foot on the shards from a broken milk bottle. Arthur wants to help but remembers having read an article stating that blind people hate being helped. They hate being patronized, Bobby corrects him. Being blind is not the most terrible thing that can happen, Bobby assures him. Perry is disdainful of Arthur's Mother Theresa attitude. The episode ends as Bobby is insisting that he is really fine.

"Americans confuse sentimentality with love," John interjects, and Perry explains that John has a fundamentally hateful nature as compared to Arthur's loving nature. It seems John wrote a musical that wasn't liked over there or over here, although John insists some people liked it. In any event, John stayed here and, in addition to being Gregory's rehearsal pianist, he is working on a new musical theater project of his own.

The conversation between John and Perry is annoying Ramon, who is trying to sleep. But mention of a musical has awakened Buzz.

BUZZ: Did somebody say something about musicals? I distinctly heard something about musicals. Somebody somewhere is talking about musicals.

He sits up with a start. Perry holds him.

I was having a musical comedy nightmare. They were going to revive *The King and I* for Tommy Tune and Elaine Stritch. We've got to stop them!

PERRY: Buzz liked John's musical.

BUZZ: It had a lot of good things in it.

PERRY: Buzz likes musicals, period.

BUZZ: I'm just a Gershwin with a Romberg rising in the house of Kern.

PERRY (*to us*): He's off.

BUZZ: I was conceived after a performance of *Wildcat* with Lucille Ball. I don't just love Lucy, I owe my very existence to her. For those of you who care but don't know, *Wildcat* was a musical by Cy Coleman and Carolyn Leigh with a book by N. Richard Nash. It opened December 16, 1960 at the Alvin Theater and played for one hundred and seventy-two performances. Two of its most remembered songs are "Hey, Look Me Over!" and "Give a Little Whistle." For those of you who care but know all that, I'm sorry. For those of you who don't know and don't care, I'm really sorry. You're going to have a lot of trouble with me.

Buzz's attention span for anything except musicals is the size of "a very small moth," Perry snipes, then admits he's not being fair. Buzz is not well. In addition to being the costumer for the company, Buzz is a volunteer at an AIDS clinic in Chelsea and "is going to find the cure for this disease all by himself and save the world for love and laughter." Buzz thinks Perry makes that sound ridiculous, and Perry apologizes, kisses Buzz on the head and returns to bed.

Arthur, finished bandaging Bobby's foot, tells Bobby he ought to realize he has an obvious stain on his pajamas. He had sort of an accident, Bobby says. Bobby doesn't want Gregory to know, but he admits it was Ramon. He shouldn't have, he chides himself, and he wonders if Ramon is attractive. And he also wonders if Arthur has been unfaithful to Perry. Arthur admits he was but doesn't recommend it. Arthur told Perry, and after that things have never been quite the same. Ramon is hot, but not that hot, Arthur tells Bobby.

Back in bed with Perry, Arthur admits to wanting to hold Bobby. "Desire is a terrible thing" he muses. "I'm sorry we're not young any more."

John is wandering around, driven by curiosity and "an unfaithful bedfellow." He wants to know who people really are, wants to know their secrets, and he sees and hears things he shouldn't. He notices Buzz asleep in a pool of sweat—Buzz's medication has been increased again. "And for what? He's dead." John's heard Arthur's admission of "inappropriate desire." And he reads words he was not meant to see, in Gregory's journal, as follows.

JOHN: "Memorial Day Weekend, Manderlay. Out here alone to work on the new piece. We've invited a full house, and they're predicting rain. We'll see if Fred Avens has fixed that leak on the north side porch this time. Thought he would never get around to taking down the storm windows and putting up the screens. The garden is late. Only the cukes will be ready. Everything else will have to come from the A&P." This isn't quite what I had in mind.

Buzz appears. He is carrying a knapsack.

BUZZ: Where is everybody?

JOHN: Did you know Gregory has only three places he feels safe? His work, in Bobby's arms and in his journal.

BUZZ: That's disgusting.

JOHN: What is? The weather? Or the startling unoriginality of naming your house Manderlay after a kitsch-classic movie?

BUZZ: Reading someone's journal.

JOHN: Did you just get here?

BUZZ: Yes. Where's Gregory?

JOHN: Down by the lake. Are you alone?

BUZZ: No, I have Michael J. Fox in here. Are you?

JOHN: No. "I've rounded up. Um. The usual suspects. Um."

BUZZ: That's not funny. You're a guest in his home.

JOHN: "I think I'll make my special ginger soy vegetable loaf Sunday night." You see why I do this? Gregory's cooking. There's still time to buy steaks.

BUZZ: If I thought you'd ever read anything I wrote when we were together, I'd kill you. I mean it.

JOHN: "I'm stuck on the new piece. Maybe the Webern was a bad choice of music."

BUZZ: I hate what you're doing.

He grabs the journal from John.

John is curious about the statement Gregory is making by being a choreographer who lives with a blind person, but Buzz points out that it isn't a statement, it's a relationship. Buzz is jealous that John's weekend companion, Ramon, is a dancer he's known for only three weeks. Buzz's last relationship has ended because Buzz was too intense.

Unable to keep from glancing at Gregory's journal, Buzz is surprised to find that Perry's work for Gregory is pro bono, as is Buzz's work for the clinic. Both arts advocacy and AIDS are in, John reminds him, and Buzz insists John pay up five dollars to the kitty for mentioning AIDS, a summer rule Buzz has instituted. John is convinced people with journals expect them to be read, and he goes back to reading Gregory's, reporting on the gift that's been purchased for Buzz's upcoming birthday. It's an out-of-print recording of a musical Buzz recently purchased at a higher price. Buzz rants on a bit, then addresses the audience.

BUZZ: You may wonder why I fill my head with such trivial-seeming information. First of all, it isn't trivial to me, and second, I can contain the world of the Broadway musical. Get my hands around it, so to speak. Be the master of one little universe. Besides, when I'm alone, it gives me great pleasure to sing and dance around the apartment. I especially like "Big Spender" from *Sweet Charity* and "I'm Going Back (Where I Can Be Me)" from *Bells Are Ringing.* I could never do this with anyone watching, of course. Even a boy friend, if I had one, which I don't. I'd be too inhibited. So, when I'm not at the clinic thinking I am single-handedly going to find the cure for this fucking scourge (It doesn't sound ridiculous when I say it, not to me!), I am to be found at my place in Chelsea doing "Rose's Turn" from *Gypsy*. I can't think of the last time I didn't cry myself to sleep. Hey, it's no skin off your nose .....

Gregory and Ramon have come back from swimming in the lake. Ramon drops the towel he's wearing and claims his "fabulous nuts" are gone. It's just the cold water, he's assured. Buzz is infatuated with Ramon, both as a dancer and as a person. It seems Gregory has also seen Ramon dance and been impressed. Ramon reveals his company is broke. Gregory claims every company is. They need a Diaghilev, Buzz points out, "a rich older man who in return for certain favors funds an entire ballet company."

When Ramon points out that the only thing an artist should do for nothing is make love, John interrupts crudely by suggesting they go upstairs and fuck. Ramon resents John's remark, and John retorts he hadn't appreciated Ramon "flapping his dick in everybody's face."

Perry is at the wheel of a car, driving Arthur and Bobby through heavy traffic on the way to Gregory's. He is using gratuitously bad language referring to another driver. Bobby is going along with it, but Arthur is disgusted. Does blind Bobby wonder what Gregory looks like? Perry asks. He knows what he looks like, Bobby assures him—in his mind's eye he sees things others take for granted. Perry wonders what he and Arthur "look like" to Bobby. Bookends, it seems, more alike as the years go by. Bobby envisions them as holding hands, that when Perry needs his hand to steer, he puts it back in Arthur's as soon as possible. That's how they drive, he believes, and that's how they live. As to the color of Perry's hair, Bobby thinks he's bald. He's wrong, Perry says. Bobby wanted to be wrong. He's uncomfortable with the game, and Perry apologizes.

Then Bobby wants to know what John looks like. Somehow, he can't get a picture of him. Perry describes him as Satanic. Arthur admits Perry has a problem with John. Gregory apparently told Arthur (but Arthur decided not to tell Perry) that John was coming for the weekend and bringing someone. "One of the Menendez brothers," Perry guesses. No, "Ramon something"—it sounds Latino to Perry, who thinks John has gone PC with a Third World boy friend. Puerto Rico doesn't qualify as Third World, Arthur points out.

Later, after everyone at Manderlay has been introduced and the new arrivals are settling in, Bobby stays outside for a bit as he always does when he comes from the city. Ramon, in the driveway area, is watching Bobby.

John confides to Perry he's been on the phone to London with his brother, James. "A twin brother. We're like *that*." (*He opens his arms wide.*) It seems James isn't well. Perry sympathizes, but John draws their attention back to Bobby and Ramon.

BOBBY: Thank you, God.
RAMON: Excuse me?

BOBBY: Who's that?

RAMON: I'm sorry.

BOBBY: You startled me.

RAMON: It's Ramon. I'm sorry. I thought you said something.

BOBBY: I was thanking God for all this. The trees, the lake, the sweet, sweet air. For being here. For all of us together in Gregory's house.

RAMON: I didn't mean to interrupt or anything.

BOBBY: I'm not crazy. I'm happy.

RAMON: I understand.

Their conversation is interrupted. But a little later, Ramon still has not taken his eyes off Bobby.

BOBBY: You're still there, aren't you? What are you doing? What do you want? Don't be afraid. Tell me. All right. Don't. Stay there. I'll come to you. Just tell me, should I fall (which I don't plan to), what color are my trousers? I think I put on white. I hope so. It's Memorial Day.

PERRY: I don't know why, but I'm finding this very painful.

BOBBY: Children play at this and call it Blind Man's Bluff. Imagine your whole life being a children's birthday party game!

JOHN: Painful, erotic and absurd.

BOBBY: I can feel you. I can hear you. I'm getting warm. I'm getting close. I like this game. I'm very good at it. I'm going to win. You haven't got a chance.

PERRY: Bobby didn't see the rake.

     Bobby trips and falls. He hurts himself. There will be a gash on his forehead.

RAMON: Oh!

BOBBY: He speaks! The cat has let go his tongue. I wouldn't say "no" to a hand.

     Ramon goes.

(*After him.*) At least tell me, what color are my trousers?

But it's Perry who answers him, moved. He assures Bobby they're white. Bobby admits he can get tired of behaving like a grown-up and calls for Gregory. Everyone gathers around, and after some discussion Ramon returns, claiming to have been down by the lake, and asking what happened. When Ramon wonders if Bobby's all right, he says he fell, that he does it often. He doesn't, Gregory insists. Gregory tries to pick up Bobby, can't manage and puts him down, to the embarrassment of the others.

When they've gone off, John again admits to being upset about his brother, whom he calls "the National Theater seamstress." He doesn't know how to cope with his feelings about him, never has. His brother needs him, wants to come over here from London, but John doesn't like him. "A tough order," Arthur comments before going off canoeing, leaving Perry and John alone.

PERRY: I work with quite a few AIDS organizations.

JOHN: Thank you.

PERRY: They can help him find a doctor.

JOHN: Thank you.

PERRY: It never ends.

JOHN: No.

PERRY: How does Buzz look to you?

JOHN: I don't know. How does he look to you?

PERRY: I can't tell any more.

JOHN: He wouldn't tell me if things were worse.

PERRY: I can't look at him sometimes.

JOHN: Anyway.

PERRY (*pleasantly*): You got that from me, you know.

JOHN: Got what?

PERRY: The "anyway."

JOHN: It's a word in the dictionary. Page 249. You can't copyright the English language, duck.

PERRY: Hey, I'm trying! Fuck you.

    He goes.

JOHN: Anyway. *En tout cas!* The weekend had begun. Everyone was in place. Old wounds reopened. New alliances forged. For fifteen minutes, while I helped Arthur wash their car, he was my best friend in the entire world. Later that afternoon, after too much picnic, when I came upon him and Perry all cozy in a hammock on the porch, he barely gave me the time of day. The hours until dinner seemed endless.

That evening, after dinner, Gregory has been trying to get the group to commit to an AIDS benefit performance of *Swan Lake.* He wants six men, non-dancers, in tutus. Perry says he won't even get one. They won't make fools of themselves dressing like women, and besides, they've done enough for AIDS.

Buzz sings a few lines from *The King and I,* then wonders why he's giving a Gertrude Lawrence imitation when nobody's heard of her. They have, but they don't care, John retorts, and a sarcastic round of name-dropping begins, with frequent references as to who was or is gay. "Who's anybody?" Buzz sums up. He longs for the day when people will ask "Who's Madonna?" The state of the American musical is upsetting him, but it should be the state of America upsetting him, Perry insists. "It's a metaphor" Buzz claims. He begins talking about the picture over his desk at the clinic, the photograph of a starving Somalian child with the vulture in the background. They've all seen the picture, Perry interrupts (except Bobby, who mentions this quietly), but what is the point Buzz is trying to make? He doesn't have one, Buzz admits. Why does he have to? Would it make it "comfortable"?

PERRY: I think the point is we're all sitting around here talking about something, pretending to care.

Top row, John Glover as John and James, Randy Becker as Ramon, Justin Kirk as Bobby, Anthony Heald as Perry and John Benjamin Hickey as Arthur, and *at bottom,* Nathan Lane as Buzz and Stephen Bogardus as Gregory in Terrence McNally's *Love! Valour! Compassion!*

ARTHUR: No one's pretending.

PERRY: Pretending to care, when the truth is there's nothing we can do about it. It would hurt too much to really care. You wouldn't have a stomach ache, you'd be dead from the dry heaves from throwing your guts up for the rest of your life. That kid is a picture in a newspaper who makes us feel bad for having it so good. But feed him, brush him off and in ten years he's just another nigger to scare the shit out of us. Apologies tendered, but that's how I see it.

ARTHUR: Apologies not accepted.

GREGORY: Don't, you two.

ARTHUR: I hate it when he talks like that.

PERRY: You'd rather I dissembled, sirrah? (I wasn't an English major at Williams for nothing!)

ARTHUR: Yes. I'd rather you would. Rather the man I shared my life with and loved with all my heart, rather he dissembled than let me see the hate and bile there.

PERRY: The hate and bile aren't for you, love.

ARTHUR: That's not good enough, Perry. After a while, the hate and bile are for everyone. It all comes around.

PERRY: Anyway.

ARTHUR: I hate that word. You use it to get yourself out of every tight corner you've ever found yourself in . . . . .

Arthur, somewhat miffed, goes off to the kitchen to rinse and stack. The problem, as Ramon sees it, begins "right here" with the way they relate to each other as gay men—they don't love one another because they don't love themselves. He wants to know where the love is at this table. Bobby and Gregory confirm they love each other. Perry claims to love Arthur, Gregory, Bobby and Buzz, and, at the moment, Ramon, for his righteous anger. Buzz doesn't love anyone there at this time, except Bobby and Gregory, a bit, because they are his hosts. John loves Queen Elizabeth ("She's been through hell lately"), his Aunt Olivia, in a pensioner's villa in Brighton, his Welsh corgie that died 11 years ago, and his job.

Asked if he's satisfied, Ramon remarks "None of you said yourself." Then how does Ramon love himself? John wonders. He loves himself when he dances. "I become all the best things I can be." And he loves himself when he makes love or eats good food or swims in the nude, but most of all when he's dancing well. John asks if this is as a gay dancer. Ramon replies, "Fuck you, John." John observes that Americans use that expression too frequently.

JOHN: In England we think it nearly as often as you do, but we don't actually say it to someone's face. It would be too rude. Half the people who are being knighted at the Palace every year are thinking "fuck you" as they're being tapped with that little sword, but they don't come right out and say it, the way an American would, which is why we don't knight Americans, the only reason, you're too uncouth.

ALL: Fuck you.

JOHN: What do you mean when you tell another person fuck you?

RAMON: Fuck you, John. And don't you ever call me Chiquita again.

BUZZ: This is good.

JOHN: I think you mean several things. Mixed signals, I believe they're called in therapeutic circles. I hate you. Get out of my life. At least, I hate you, get out of my life for the moment.

RAMON: Fuck you.

JOHN: I love you but you don't love me. I want to kill you, but I can't, so I will hurt you instead. I want to make you feel small and insignificant, the way you've made me feel. I want to make you feel every terrible thing my entire life right up until this moment has made me feel. Ah, there's the link! I knew we'd find it. The common bond uniting this Limey and the Yanks. The resolution of our fraternal theme.

RAMON: I said fuck you.

JOHN: But until we recognize and accept this mutual fuck you in each of us, with every last fibre of my fading British being, every last ounce of my tobaccoed English breath, I say fuck you right back. Fuck you, Ramon. Fuck you, Perry. Fuck you, Buzz. Fuck you, Gregory. Fuck you, Bobby. Fuck all of you. Well, I think I've said my piece.

His diatribe ended, John moves pretentiously away from the rest at the table and goes off to play the piano. Buzz hopes he'll play something gay—gay music by a gay composer. Hearing from Perry there's no such thing as gay music, he thinks there should be. Buzz is sick of straight people. . . ."Too goddam many of them." He'd been in a bank yesterday—they were everywhere. "Writing checks, making deposits," even applying for a mortgage. "They're taking over. No one wants to talk about it, but it's true," he warns. John is playing Tchaikovsky for Buzz. "All those dominant triads are so, so gay!" He wasn't fooling anybody, John assures Buzz.

Perry goes off to find Arthur. John switches to the "Pas des Cygnes" from *Swan Lake,* and Gregory begins dancing, *"as physically fluent as he is verbally inhibited."* He persuades Buzz to join him. Arms linked, they dance out onto the grounds.

Perry has found Arthur and apologized. Inside, John has apologized to Ramon and then gone back to playing the piano.

BUZZ: Arthur and Perry lay on blankets and looked at the heavens and talked things out. Gregory danced on by a couple of times. John played a melancholy piano until the wee small hours of the morning. Bobby and Ramon sat quietly talking across the deserted dining table—empty glasses, soiled napkins between them. All in all, there was a lot of love in Gregory and Bobby's house that first night of the first holiday weekend of the summer. It didn't start raining till the next morning. It didn't stop until the drive back home on Monday night. It rained all weekend.

BOBBY: It was raining when Buzz started crying in the middle of a movie on AMC and couldn't stop.

RAMON: It was raining when Gregory sat alone in his studio for six hours listening to a piece of music and didn't move from his chair.

BUZZ: It was raining when Ramon waited for Bobby by the refrigerator and he dropped the bottle.

ARTHUR: It was raining when John wanted Ramon to fuck him the next afternoon anyway.

PERRY: Anyway! There's that word again. And he's wrong, this once. I don't say "anyway" when I'm cornered. I say it when I'm overcome. I love you, Arthur Pape.

> *He kisses Arthur on the lips. Gregory and Buzz will dance by again. They are having a wonderful time. Bobby and Ramon remain at the dining table. John is playing a Chopin nocturne. The lights fade. The music swells. Curtain.*

ACT II

The men are singing "In the Good Old Summertime." As they move apart, we see Ramon lying naked on the wooden float at a distance from the lake shore. *"One by one, they stop singing, turn around and take a long look back at Ramon splayed on the raft. Even Bobby."* The others move away till only John and Ramon remain, then John turns aside, takes out Gregory's journal and starts reading it. It is the 4th of July weekend, high noon. The journal reveals Perry has already dubbed John and his twin brother John the Foul and James the Fair.

Perry, Arthur, Gregory and Buzz are playing tennis. There's also some internecine sniping going on when Perry finds Arthur staring off at Ramon, despite the fact they are to celebrate their anniversary this weekend. They've been together 14 years and find being role models stressful. Buzz is clowning around and wishes Gregory had a twin brother. What's the matter with his? John asks. Buzz claims James looks too much like John and acts too much like he (Buzz) does. "Where are all the men?" he bellows. John, going off, says he'll send James down with iced tea.

> *John is heard playing the piano off. Ramon raises up and looks around.*
> *He shields his eyes with his hand, scans the horizon and lies back down.*
> *Bobby appears. He is wearing a robe. He will advance to the stage apron.*

BOBBY: When Gregory told me he thought that John and Ramon were over and was surprised that John would be bringing him again, I didn't tell him that they were and that Ramon was coming with him because of me. I didn't tell him that when the phone rang Monday night, and then again Thursday, and there was no one there and he kept saying, "Hello? Hello? Who is this?", I didn't tell him it was Ramon on the other end.

> *Bobby falls off the stage.*

Don't anyone touch me. I don't want help.

> *He climbs back onto the stage.*

And I didn't tell him what Ramon's mouth felt like against my own. I didn't tell him the last time we made love I thought of it. I didn't tell him Ramon whispered to me this morning. He would be waiting for me on the raft when I swam out there.

Bobby drops his robe and goes into the lake, as James Jeckyll, a sweet and tender version of John (played by the same actor) appears with a serving cart. "It's not who you think," he assures the audience shyly. When his twin brother John stops playing the piano, "You can start getting nervous again," he confides.

James has a book John has given him—"Outing America: from A to Z," and he's fascinated. It lists the names of all the gay men and lesbians from before the Revolutionary War up to the present. He finds it impressive that for a young nation we've had a great many "poufters," and he's stunned by some of the extraordinary names as well.

Gregory, tiring at tennis, is worried about Bobby out in the lake. To his relief, Bobby shows up at the side of the raft. While Bobby joins Ramon, Gregory hurts himself running for a ball. The others call Bobby back to shore and help Gregory to his studio. Bobby and Ramon have arranged a rendezvous for that evening, and they kiss passionately before Bobby returns to shore.

Buzz, with James now, calls Ramon to come in also, but Ramon remains on the raft. Both James and Buzz find Ramon appealing. James's brother John has always had some good-looking man around, James comments, and Buzz accepts that as a compliment, revealing that he and John were together for a few months when John first came to this country. What happened then was that Buzz was too needy and John wasn't needy enough. James doesn't believe John's capable of loving anyone. And neither of them feels they are Ramon's type, but James admits to enjoying looking, however. And neither Buzz nor James has a boyfriend any more, it seems.

JAMES: I can't honestly say I'm minding. Last acts are depressing and generally one long solo.

BUZZ: They don't have to be.

Buzz finally looks at James.

How sick are you?

JAMES: I think I'm in pretty good nick, but my reports read like something out of Nostradamus.

He looks at Buzz.

I should have died six months ago.

BUZZ: Try eighteen. Do you have any lesions?

JAMES: Only one, and I've had it for nearly a year.

BUZZ: Where is it?

JAMES: In a very inconvenient spot.

BUZZ: They're all inconvenient. May I see it?

JAMES: It's. All right.

James pulls up his shirt and lets Buzz see the lesion.

I have a lesbian friend in London who's the only other person who's ever asked to see it. I was quite astonished when she did. Touched, actually. Mortified, too, of course. But mainly touched. Somebody loves me, even if it's not the someone I've dreamed of. A little love from a woman who works in the box office at the Lyric Hammersmith is better than none. Are you through?

Buzz kisses the lesion.

Gwyneth didn't go that far. It doesn't disgust you?

BUZZ: It's going to be me.

JAMES: You don't know that.

BUZZ: Yes, I do.

JAMES: You learn to make friends with them. Hello, little lesion. Not people you like especially but people you've made your peace with.

BUZZ: You're very nice, you know.

JAMES: Frankly, I don't see how I can afford not to be.

BUZZ: No, I mean it.

JAMES: So are you.

Buzz offers to bring James a real drink. For an ice-cold martini, dry, with a twist, James vows to "snitch a frock" from the National Theater storage for him, something of Dame Edith Evans's. James supposes she was gay, too; but Buzz, some sort of self-appointed expert, claims that she, and he thinks Deborah Kerr, actually aren't.

As Arthur tends to Gregory's leg, Perry looks at his legs and feet, appalled. "Doesn't everything hurt?" he wonders. Gregory concedes it does, but he keeps on because he doesn't know what he'd do if he didn't. His body is the scars of his dancing, and Gregory points out the Philip Glass scars, the Bach-Schoenberg, etc. But as for the Webern pieces, there aren't any scars yet, although the contracts are signed.

A phone call comes for Bobby, who learns from someone at the American consulate in Jaipur that his sister, two years older than he, has been killed in a freak accident. "Something to do with a faultily-installed ride at a funfair at a religious festival celebrating the god Shiva," Perry reports. Nobody knows whether they should stay here for the rest of the weekend or discretely leave. "It's all so fucking fragile. So fucking arbitrary," Bobby thinks, but he wants them to stay.

Later, Perry is livid as Buzz makes an entrance with more refreshments in an apron, high heels and nothing much more than high spirits. It isn't a nudist colony, and nobody wants to look at "that," Perry lectures, hoping Arthur will back him up. Arthur won't.

BUZZ: Thank you, Arthur. I'm glad Isadora Duncan and Sally Kirkland did not live entirely in vain.
PERRY: Please, Buzz.
BUZZ: No. Close your eyes. Take a walk. Drop dead.
PERRY: What brought this on?
BUZZ: Nothing brought it on. Some people do things spontaneously. It's a beautiful day. The sun feels good. I may not be around next summer. Okay? This is what I look like, Perry. Sorry it's not better. It's the best I can do. Love me, love my love handles.
ARTHUR: That's what I keep telling him!
PERRY: None of us may be around next summer.
        Arthur starts undressing.
What do you think you're doing?
ARTHUR: Come on, I'll race you out to the raft.
PERRY: Go to hell.

Perry is listening to a Bob Dylan tape when Ramon, out on the raft with Arthur, smacks Arthur on his bare bottom, explaining that there'd been a fly on him. He has a nice ass for somebody his age, Ramon remarks.

It seems Bobby's sister's body will not be arriving in Dallas until Tuesday, and he'll fly down Monday. Gregory will stay to finish his work, Bobby insists. Bobby takes this opportunity to make a confession to Gregory of his having made love with

Ramon on Memorial Day weekend. Does he want to again? Gregory finally splutters out. Bobby says he doesn't. Gregory wants Bobby to leave for Texas tonight. He doesn't want him in their home.

Out on the raft, Ramon plays a trick on Arthur, jumping off and sitting on the bottom of the lake until Arthur jumps in to investigate. Gregory appears and replaces them on the raft. Arthur and Ramon join Buzz and Perry onshore, Ramon irritating the others with a story about a chance meeting and sexual episode in Greece with one of the group's celebrity idols.

In the room John and Ramon share, Perry has talked Buzz into hiding in the closet, planning "to leap out at the moment of maximum inopportunity and embarrassment." John and Ramon, unknowing, lock the door and begin acting out a bondage routine in which Ramon, seated in a chair, is pretending to be a "beautiful bound prisoner." Ramon wants to know whom John is imagining. John admits it's Padraic Boyle: "He was 17 years old. I was 19." Padraic was "a fierce-looking ginger Irishman with big powerful shoulders and arms with muscles with big veins in them." Padraic and his father worked for John's father, who owned a fleet of busses. Padraic liked John, they were friends.

RAMON: Cut to the chase.

JOHN: Cut to what chase? There wasn't any chase.

RAMON: It's a movie expression. Get to the good part.

JOHN: It's all good part.

RAMON: Get to the sex. One night . . . !

JOHN: One day we started wrestling. It was summer. He was washing a coach (that's a bus), and.

RAMON: I know what a coach is. I've been to London.

JOHN: And Padraic squirted me with a hose, and I got him with a bucket of water, and then we started fooling around, and one thing led to another, and we started wrestling, we were in the garage now, and suddenly Padraic put his hand down there, and he could feel I was hard, and he said, "What is this? What the bloody hell is this, mate?"

RAMON: What did you do?

JOHN: I put my hand on him down there, and he was hard, and I said, "And what the bloody hell is that, mate?", and we both laughed, but we didn't move.

PERRY: Even from the closet, we were beginning to share Ramon's impatience.

PERRY and BUZZ: Cut to the fucking chase!

JOHN: He stopped laughing. "Do you know what we're doing?" I had no idea, so I nodded, "Yes." He took off my belt and wrapped it around my wrists. He raised my arms over my head and hung them to a hook along the wall. I probably could have freed myself. I didn't try. He took out a handkerchief and gagged me with it. Then, and this frightened me, he ripped open my shirt. It was a violent gesture, and it frightened me. Then he unfastened my trousers and let them drop to my ankles. Then he undressed himself and took a chair, very like this one, and sat in it, maybe five feet away from me. He had some rope. He wrapped it around his wrists like he was tied to the chair. He'd gagged himself, too, with his own knickers. He looked right at me. He didn't move. Not even the slightest undulation of his hips, and then he came and all he'd let out was this one soft "oh." After a while, he opened his eyes, asked me how I was doing and cleaned himself up. Then he stood up and kissed me lightly on the lips. No man had ever kissed me on the lips before. I wanted to kiss him back, but I didn't dare. He moved to whisper something in my ear. My heart stopped beating. He was going to tell me he loved me! Instead, he said, "I've doused this place with petrol. I'm lighting a match. You have three minutes to get out alive. Good luck, 007." And then he laughed and walked out whistling. He never wanted to play again. The last time I saw him he was overweight, the father of four and still washing our coaches. But that's who I still see there. Every time. And that's why we hate the bloody Irish!

As John finishes speaking, Gregory calls from outside the door. He needs a suitcase from the closet in the bedroom. When he opens the closet door, Perry signals Gregory to be silent. Wrong closet, Gregory tells John. Buzz manages to escape with Gregory without being seen. Ramon wants to go and tell Bobby goodbye, and John agrees to go with him. But John doesn't feel dressed without his wallet and going to get it discovers Perry in the closet. He is furious and accepts no apology or excuse. John wants to know what he's heard. Perry claims nothing, then promises he will never tell. John spits in his face, telling Perry he hopes he will get what James has and die of it. When he finds out Perry has caught it, then he'll forgive him.

Perry can't decide which is worse, John's words or the saliva, he tells Arthur shortly thereafter. They reminisce about when they first met, 14 years ago in Greenwich Village, where Perry had an apartment and Buzz was his roommate. Perry and Arthur met the same night Buzz and John met, but "We lasted, they didn't," Arthur notes.

Buzz and James come in and again try to persuade Perry to be fitted for a tutu for the benefit performance, but Perry steadfastly refuses, even though there is a tape measure around his waist and Buzz is draping him in tulle.

The rain has stopped. Bobby is waiting outside for the taxi. It is night. Ramon has come to say goodbye. He expresses his sympathy and claims he has a sister that he loves very much. When Ramon takes his hand, Bobby asks him not to. Ramon says he is sorry and Bobby admits, "A part of me is, too. I can't." When Gregory comes out, Ramon goes inside. Bobby explains he's still waiting for the taxi.

GREGORY: We both need time to think.

BOBBY: I don't. I'm sorry. I love you.

GREGORY (*he is angry*): Are any of you. Um. Gardeners? I'm especially. Um. Proud of what I've done here. Um. It's a. Um. Seasonal garden. Always something blooming. Um. Just as another dies. That's a. Um. Bobby knows the names of everything. Dianthus barbatus. That's the Latin name. Um. I can't think of the. Um. Common one.

BOBBY: Sweet William. It's Sweet William. And this one is rue. Bitter. Very bitter. Buzz says I would make a great Ophelia if I wouldn't fall off the stage.

GREGORY: He shouldn't. Um. Say things like that. Um. To you.

He is crying.

BOBBY: And this is. Wait. Don't tell me.

GREGORY: It's a rose.

BOBBY: I know it's a rose. Connecticut Pride Morning Rose.

GREGORY: I'll never understand it. The will to know the names of things you'll never see.

BOBBY: It's one way of feeling closer to you.

Gregory embraces Bobby, but they don't kiss.

GREGORY: Hurry back to me.

Gregory goes back into the house where the others are switching television channels and chatting. Buzz is opining there will be a gay President one day. Ramon gives a signal of sorts by asking if they are having dessert. Assured they are not, Buzz, James and Ramon go off to the kitchen. While they're gone Perry and Arthur and Gregory witness gay rights demonstration violence in a TV program from Seattle until finally they turn it off as the anniversary cake with its candles ablaze is brought in and "Happy Anniversary" is sung. Perry responds with a brief conventional speech, and Arthur sums up his sentiments by saying, "Ditto."

PERRY: Ditto? That's it? Ditto?

They begin a slow dance together.

JAMES: That's nice.

BUZZ: You don't have to go all Goody Two Shoes on us.

ARTHUR: Everybody dance. All lovers dance.

BUZZ: What about us single girls? (*To James.*) You know you're dying to ask me.

He starts dancing with James. There are two couples dancing now.

PERRY: So what was your wish?

Arthur whispers something in his ear.

No fucking way, Jose. He still thinks you're going to get me into one of those fucking tutus.

Perry now leads Arthur. They dance very well together. Buzz and James are dancing closer and closer in a smaller and smaller place. Pretty soon they're just standing, holding on to each other, their arms around each other. Gregory sits apart. Ramon watches them all.

Arthur, look.

ARTHUR: What?

PERRY: Answered prayers.

The two couples dance. Ramon and Gregory sit staring at each other. The lights fade swiftly. Curtain. The music continues until the house lights are up.

ACT III

It is Labor Day weekend. At dawn Gregory is in his studio, alone. Perry and Arthur are asleep. James and Buzz are taking a walk by the lake. Ramon and Bobby are awake, and Ramon is calling to Bobby, trying to get his attention, then goes to the kitchen to make coffee.

Perry tells us that Gregory's still stuck on his Webern project. He's so stubborn—and so is Ramon, Perry adds. As Gregory plays the same passage repeatedly, Bobby tells us it isn't stubbornness on Gregory's part. It's that he's scared. He's been saying the new work is nearly complete, and there isn't anything. Bobby would like to try to get him to "stay in the moment." The work doesn't have to be about "everything," Bobby believes, but Gregory's not receptive to his ideas and still bitter at Bobby's betrayal.

John comments on the wilted gardens, the brown lawns, the change in the air—but he hasn't changed. "Still hung up on Ramon and our rituals," he confesses. And still reading Gregory's journal: " . . . . . Who could not love James? We have all taken him to our hearts. It will be a sad day when that light goes out." In the studio, Gregory is in a rage and smashes a chair over and over again until it is in pieces, then begins to cry. Perry is upset at the sound, but Arthur advises him to leave other people alone—he's as bad as John. Perry protests that nobody is. He smells coffee and gets out of bed.

James confesses he is very cold, although hours ago he was drenched in sweat. They're a fine pair, he bemoans. "Loverly," Buzz agrees.

BUZZ: How are you feeling?

JAMES: Not sexy.

BUZZ: How are you feeling, really?

JAMES: "We defy augury."

BUZZ: What does that mean?

JAMES: I don't know. It's from a Shakespearean play we did at the National. The actor who played it tossed his head and put his hand on his hip when he said it. I think he was being brave in the face of adversity.

BUZZ: Would this have been Lady Derek Jacobi or Dame Ian McKellen?

JAMES: I believe I have the floor! So, whenever I don't like what's coming down, I toss my head, put my hand on my hip and say, "We defy augury."

BUZZ: Shakespeare was gay, you know.

JAMES: You're going too far now.

BUZZ: Do you think a straight man would write a line like "We defy augury"? Get real, James. My three-year-old gay niece knows Shakespeare was gay. So was Anne Hathaway. So was her cottage. So was Julius Caesar. So was Romeo and Juliet. So was Hamlet. So was King Lear. Every character Shakespeare wrote was gay. Except for Titus Andronicus. Titus was straight. Go figure.

JAMES: People are awake.

BUZZ: I'll get us some coffee.

John Glover, Anthony Heald and Nathan Lane in *Love! Valour! Compassion!*

Ramon is doing a Diana Ross diva imitation when Gregory enters the kitchen. Ramon greets him but goes on with his singing and dancing. This is how he won his high school talent contest, doing Diana Ross, he reveals, and then going into a tribute to Elvis. His singing and dancing is electrifying.

RAMON: I was turning the whole school on. Girls, boys, faculty. I loved it. If I ever get famous like you, Greg, and they ask me when I decided I wanted to be a dancer—no, a great dancer, like you were—I am going to answer, I remember the exact moment when. It was on the stage of the Immaculate Conception Catholic High School in Ponce in the Commonwealth of Puerto Rico when.

He slows down but keeps dancing.

What's the matter? What are you looking at? You're making me feel weird. Come on, don't. You know me, I'm goofing. "Great dancer you *are.*" I didn't mean it, okay?

He dances slower and slower, but he has too much macho to completely stop.

Fuck you then. I'm sorry your work isn't going well. Bobby told me. But don't take it out on me. I'm just having fun. Sometimes I wonder why we bother, you know? Great art! I mean, who needs it? Who fucking needs it? We got Diana. We got Elvis.

As Ramon dances himself almost into Gregory, Gregory grabs his wrist and takes him to the sink and throws on the switch for the dispose-all. Ramon tells Gregory to let go of him. Gregory turns off the switch but grabs Ramon's other arm and twists it behind Ramon's back before letting go of the wrist he was holding. He keeps insisting Ramon put his hand down the drain. Ramon knows why and finally says, "Because of Bobby". Gregory keeps this up against Ramon's will until Perry and Buzz come on, shocked, and try to make Gregory stop. Finally, Ramon puts his hand down the drain, daring Gregory to cut his fingers off, and then Gregory lets go of his arm.

Within the seemingly benign context of the ensuing coffee scene, Ramon makes it very clear to Gregory that the incident had not been about Bobby and himself, that it had been about Gregory and himself. Gregory is old and frightened and doesn't know what to do, and Ramon is young and not frightened and coming after him. And he knew Gregory would not turn on the switch. The incident wasn't ever mentioned again, Perry muses: "Funny, the things we sit on, stuff down." Gregory, in the end, finally asks Ramon to take coffee up to Bobby and then goes back out to his studio, turns on the music and sets to work.

By late afternoon, the rain having stopped, Arthur is out canoeing with Perry, and they wax philosophical. Arthur mentions AIDS and Perry claims he'll have to pay up five dollars. Arthur thinks they're not playing that game any more. When Perry asks who won, Arthur replies, "Not Buzz and James." They feel fortunate, and Arthur asks if Perry ever feels guilty. On the contrary, Perry feels grateful. Arthur at first was merely scared, then felt guilt, massive guilt. He looks at Buzz and James and realizes they won't be there, sooner or later. "None of us will be," is Perry's answer, and "Why not *not* you?" It's a question Arthur can't answer.

James and Buzz come into view, in another canoe, but each couple prefers to keep their own company. If the fellow next to him with his shoulder to the same wheel isn't as lucky as he is, Arthur ponders, and he becomes sick and I don't, why is that? "I think we should both go together." But he wonders if that's gay solidarity or a death wish. Perry doesn't want him to talk that way, but Arthur claims he'll always feel somewhat guilty, will always feel as if he's "a bystander at the genocide of who we are." He isn't a bystander, Perry assures him, but Arthur believes anyone who doesn't save the human race is one.

Meanwhile, James is not feeling well and asks Buzz to take him back. James confesses that he thinks he's "soiled" himself. Perry addresses himself to the audience, "Anyway. Anyway. That evening. I'm sorry," but he can't go on with what he was planning to tell us, and James picks it up, saying that it had rained harder than ever. He'd merely had a minor case of the runs but is all right now, he assures Perry: "The best is yet to come. The real horror." Buzz says they don't know that's so. James says they do. "I'll draw your bath, luv," Buzz announces. James wonders if that was "luv" or "love"? Buzz claims people who spell valor with a "u" and use words like "lorry" and "lift" are lucky our immigration is lenient.

JAMES: Anyway. (If I'm going to fill in for Perry here, I might as well try to sound like him. Bloody unlikely!) After my bath, Buzz (and I never remotely thought in my wildest imaginings that I would be making love to someone called Buzz and saying things like "I love you, Buzz," or "How do you take your tea, Buzz?") this same, wonderful Buzz wrapped me in the biggest, toastiest bath sheet imaginable and tucked me safely into that lovely big chair by the window in the corner of our room. I fell asleep listening to my brother play Rachmaninoff downstairs. I would wake up to one of the most unsettling, yet strangely satisfying, conversations of my long/short life. And I will scarcely say a word.

> *He closes his eyes. The piano music stops. He stands up and looks down at the chair. He is John.*

JOHN: There's no point in pretending this isn't happening. You're dying, aren't you? There are so many things I've never said to you, things we've never spoken about. I don't want to wait until it's too late to say them. I've spent my life waiting for the appropriate moment to tell you the truth. I resent you. I resent everything about you. You had mum and daddy's unconditional love, and now you have the world's. How can I not envy that? I wish I could say it was because you're so much better looking than me. No, the real pain is that it's something so much harder to bear. You got the good soul. I got the bad one. Think about leaving me yours.

> *Buzz appears.*

BUZZ: You're supposed to be resting. I'm sorry. I thought you were James. What are you doing in here?

JOHN: We're talking. Please, Buzz.

BUZZ: You sure you want to do this, honey?

> *He kisses James's figure in the chair.*

Five minutes, John. I mean it.

> *He goes.*

JOHN: They have names for us, behind our back. I bet you didn't know that, did you? James the Good and John the Bad, the Princes of Charm and Ugly. Gregory keeps a journal. We're all in it. I don't come off very well in there either. So what's your secret? The secret of unconditional love? I'm not going to let you die with it. My brother smiled wanly and shook his head, suggesting he didn't know, dear spectators. And just then a tear started to fall from the corner of one eye. This tear told me my brother knew something of the pain I felt of never, ever, not once, being loved. Another tear. The other eye this time. And then I felt his hand on mine. Not only did I feel as if I were looking at myself, eye half-open, deep in a winged back chair, a blanket almost to my chin, in the twilight of a summer that had never come, and talking to myself (who else could this mirror image be but me?), both cheeks wet with tears now, but now I was touching myself. That hand taking mine was my own. I could trace the same sinews, follow the same veins. But no! It brought it to other lips and began to kiss it, his kisses mingling with his tears. He was forgiving me. My brother was forgiving me. But wait!—and I tried to pull my hand away. I hated you. He holds tighter. I. More kisses. I. New tears. I wished you were dead. He presses his head against my hand now and cries and cries and cries as I try to tell him every wrong I have done him, but he just shakes his head and bathes my hand with his tears and lips. There have never been so many kisses, not in all the world, as when I told my brother all the wrongs I had done him and he forgave me. Nor so many tears. Finally we stopped. We looked at each other in the silence. We could look at each other at last. We weren't the same person. I just wanted to be the one they loved, I told him.

John sits in the chair.

JAMES: And now you will be.

Gregory has been working, through the night and into the following day, with Bobby shuttling food from the house to the studio and keeping the others at bay. But this time it's as if Gregory wanted to be watched. Arthur and Ramon are surreptiously watching. Ramon is impressed. He'd give his "left nut" to work with Gregory. Arthur mentions that Gregory's said Ramon is a "magnificent dancer." Ramon was unaware of this.

Gregory's work is finally finished. Beginning, middle, end and an epilogue. And he knew he couldn't ever dance it, not the way he wanted it to be danced, Perry tells us. It isn't just the legs. It's everything.

Gregory calls for Ramon. He *had* wanted Ramon to watch. Ramon would give his life to dance something like that solo, he ventures. Here was a 43-year-old man looking at a 22-year-old dancer, Perry notes. Ramon is better than he was at his age, Gregory admits, but he should be better. Ramon knows that. Surprising even himself, Gregory asks Ramon to do the solo at the premiere in New York in early December. Ramon is ecstatic. He wants to know if he can tell his mother. "She'll shit. She won't know what I'm talking about, but she'll shit." He runs off screaming with enthusiasm. "We always said I would stop when it's time," Gregory proclaims, "It's time, Bobby." Bobby concedes Gregory has done the right thing.

Later, Gregory comes on wondering who's using all the hot water. Buzz says he's sorry, he's running a tub for James, who's like ice. He'll shower later, Gregory shrugs, "Really, Buzz, it's fine."

BUZZ: If this were a musical that would be a great cue for "Steam Heat." "Really, Buzz, it's fine." "I've got Ding! Ding! Steam Heat!" Of course, if this were a musical there would be plenty of hot water, and it would have a happy ending. Life and Gregory's plumbing should be more like a musical: today's Deep Thought from Buzz Hauser.

PERRY: Musicals don't always have happy endings either.

BUZZ: Yes, they do. That's why I like them, even the sad ones. The orchestra plays, the characters die, the audience cries, the curtain falls, the actors get up off the floor, the audience puts on their coats, and everybody goes home feeling better. That's a happy ending, Perry. Once, just once, I want to see a *West Side Story* where Tony really gets it, where they all die, the Sharks and the Jets, and Maria while we're at it, and Officer Krupke, what's he doing sneaking out of the theater?, get back here and die with everybody else, you son of a bitch! Or a *King and I* where Yul Brynner doesn't get up from that little Siamese bed for a curtain call. I want to see a *Sound of Music* where the entire Von Trapp Family dies in an authentic Alpine avalanche. A *Kiss Me, Kate* where she's got a big cold sore on her mouth. *A Funny Thing Happened on the Way to the Forum* where the only thing that happens is nothing, and it's not funny, and they all go down waiting, waiting for what? Waiting for nothing, waiting for death, like everyone I know and care about is, including me. That's the musical I want to see, Perry, but they don't write musicals like that any more. In the meantime, gangway, world, get off my runway!

PERRY: You're my oldest friend in the world and, next to Arthur, my best.

BUZZ: It's not enough sometimes, Perry. You're not sick. You two are going to end up *On Golden Pond* in matching white wicker rockers. "The loons are coming, Arthur. They're shitting on our annuities."

PERRY: That's not fair. We can't help that.

BUZZ: I can't afford to be fair. Fair's a luxury. Fair is for healthy people with healthy lovers in nice apartments with lots of health insurance, which, of course they don't need, but God forbid someone like me or James should have it.

Buzz is afraid that he will not be there for James when he needs him, and he's angry that James will not be there for him when he needs James. "I wasn't going to do this again," Buzz insists, not lose anyone else. He had just been going to stay healthy, work at the clinic and complete the cataloging of his cast albums. "They're worth something to someone, some nut like me somewhere." It was all he thought he could handle, and now this has happened. Perry commiserates, but reminds him that what's happened is wonderful. But who will be there for him when it is his turn? Buzz wonders. Perry assures him they all will be. Buzz wishes he could believe it. James calls from off for Buzz to check on the bathtub.

BUZZ: Can you promise me you'll be holding my hand when I let go? That the last face I see will be yours?

PERRY: Yes.

BUZZ: I believe you.

PERRY: Mine and Arthur's.

BUZZ: Arthur's is negotiable. I can't tell you how this matters to me. I'm a very petty person.

PERRY: No, you're not.

BUZZ: I've always had better luck with roommates than lovers.

PERRY: I think this time you got lucky with both.

JAMES *(off)*: Buzz, it's running over.

BUZZ: I adore him. What am I going to do?

Gregory has given a five-minute call for a dress rehearsal of the *Swan Lake* "Pas des Cygnes," and Buzz, Arthur, Ramon and Gregory are putting on tutus and toe shoes and kidding each other. Perry is on the sidelines, and John, off, is ready to start playing. When the rehearsal actually begins, the dancers show considerable improvement since the last rehearsal. Bobby wonders how they look. Perry admits they look as if they're having fun. James comes on, in his tutu, links arms and joins in, though the others are apprehensive about his participating. The kidding goes on, and Perry is envious and can't believe his "button-down, plodding Arthur" is dancing with them. And then James collapses. He's fine, he pleads, just wants to lie down for a while. They should go on rehearsing without him, they need it. He goes off. Ramon goes to tell John to stop playing and comes back to report that John's gone up to James.

Buzz wants to put the record on and continue. He begins to take charge to cover up his concern about James. Buzz wonders if anyone objects to him calling them "ladies." Perry does. Buzz reminds him he is not in this piece. Perry confesses he did want to be up there dancing with the rest of them, but he just could not. Gregory urges him again. He's needed.

> *As the dance proceeds, one by one the men will stop dancing, step forward and speak to us.*

PERRY: I have twenty-seven years, eight months, six days, three hours, thirty-one minutes and eleven seconds left. I will be watching *Gone With the Wind,* of all things, again on television. Arthur will be in the other room fixing me hot cocoa and arguing with his brother on the phone. He won't even hear me go.

ARTHUR: You insisted on keeping the TV on so loud. Wouldn't buy a hearing supplement.

PERRY: I hate that word, supplement. They're aids. Hearing aids. They're for old men.

ARTHUR: Three years later, it's my turn. On the bus. The M-9. Quietly. Very quietly. Just like my life. Without him, I won't much mind.

GREGORY: You're getting behind, Arthur, catch up!

BUZZ: I don't want to think about it. Soon. Sooner than I thought, even. Let's just say I died happy. They'd reissued *Happy Hunting* on CD, and I'd met Gwen Verdon at a benefit. She was very nice, and I don't think it was because she knew I was sick. Perry and Arthur said, "You know what Ethel Merman is going to do to you, telling everyone she was a big dyke?"

GREGORY: On the beat, Buzz, on the beat.

> *James appears.*

JAMES: I wasn't brave. I took pills. I went back home to Battersea and took pills. I'm sorry, Buzz.

> *He goes.*

RAMON: I don't die. I'm fucking immortal. I live forever. Until I take a small plane to Pittsfield, Massachusetts. I was late for a concert. Nobody else from my company was on it. Just me and a pilot I didn't bother to look at twice.

Bobby is not so forthcoming. He doesn't know, doesn't want to. Gregory informs Bobby he won't be with him, Bobby will have someone else named Luke. Bobby wonders about Gregory. Gregory admits there wasn't anyone else for him. Bobby was the last. It was his age, Bobby admits it. But Bobby still doesn't want to know, even though he says he isn't afraid.

BOBBY: I'm sorry I couldn't stay with you.

GREGORY: I. Um. Bury every one of you. Um. It got. Um. Awfully lonely out here.

John appears.

JOHN: I didn't change. And I tried. At least I think I tried. I couldn't. I just couldn't. No one mourned me. Not one tear was shed.

The rehearsal resumes, but a thunderstorm causes a power failure. The music stops, and lights go off. Candles are lit, but "There will be no performance of ze *Red Shoes* tonight," Buzz announces. John comes on to say that James is sleeping. John wants to thank them—"You've all been so . . ." He wants to know if he can give anyone a hand.

It's clearing up outside. There's a moon "you could practically read by," according to Ramon. He wants Bobby to go outside with him, and the dishes can wait. The moonlight's wasted on him, Bobby claims, and the others should go on ahead down to the lake. Perry, Ramon, Arthur, Buzz and Gregory go upstage and sit facing the moonlight on the lake. They begin to sing "Shine On, Harvest Moon". Bobby is still clearing up when James comes in, wearing a robe. He's looking at Bobby.

BOBBY: Who's there? Somebody's there.

JAMES: It's me. Forgive me for staring. You looked very handsome in the moonlight. Very handsome and very graceful. You took my breath away. I'm going to remember you like that. It's James.

BOBBY: I know. Are you supposed to be down here?

JAMES: No. And neither are you. There's a full moon, and everyone's down by the lake. I saw them from my window. Come on. I'll go with you.

He takes Bobby by the arm.

I have a confession to make. I've never been skinny-dipping in the moonlight with a blind American. You only live once.

BOBBY: If you're lucky. Some people don't live at all. I thought you were scared of that snapping turtle.

JAMES: I'm terrified of him. I'm counting on you.

BOBBY: Let's go, then.

JAMES: I have another confession to make. I'm English. I've never been skinny-dipping in the moonlight with anyone.

BOBBY: I knew that.

They leave. The front of the stage and main playing area are bare. Everyone is taking off their clothes to go swimming now. One by one we see the men at the rear of the stage undress and go into the lake. As they go into the water and swim out, the sound of their voices will fade away. Silence. Empty stage. John enters. He looks back to the lake. He looks up at the sound of a plane overhead. He looks out to us.

JOHN: Anyway.

He looks straight ahead. He doesn't move. The lights fade. Curtain.

Tony Award

○ ○ ○
○ ○ ○
○ ○ ○
○ ○ ○
○ ○ ○
○ ○ ○   SUNSET BOULEVARD

A Musical in Two Acts

BOOK AND LYRICS BY DON BLACK
AND CHRISTOPHER HAMPTON

MUSIC BY ANDREW LLOYD WEBBER

BASED ON THE BILLY WILDER FILM

Cast and credits appear on page 314

DON BLACK (book and lyrics) was born in East London in 1939 and was educated there at the Hackney School. He began his onstage life as a standup comedian and made his West End debut as a lyricist with composer John Barry on the musical Billy *starring Michael Crawford. In the course of his lyric-writing career he has worked*

107

with Jule Styne, Henry Mancini, Elmer Bernstein and Charles Strouse and has won five Academy Award and three Tony nominations, five Ivor Novello Awards and one Golden Globe, plus many other citations, and his songs have been recorded by Barbra Streisand, Frank Sinatra, Bing Crosby, Sammy Davis Jr. and Ray Charles.

Black's first collaboration with Andrew Lloyd Webber was the song cycle "Tell Me on a Sunday" in 1979, later developed into the musical Song & Dance, which opened on Broadway in 1985 with Black's Tony-nominated lyrics. With Charles Hart, he supplied the Tony-nominated lyrics for Lloyd Webber's Aspects of Love in 1990. Since he and Christopher Hampton are credited with both book and lyrics of Sunset Boulevard, his third collaboration with Lloyd Webber is his first as a book writer. Based on Billy Wilder's celebrated movie in which Gloria Swanson played Norma Desmond, a faded silent-film superstar, the stage musical version of Sunset Boulevard opened in London June 29, 1993 (with Patti LuPone as Norma), in Los Angeles on December 2, 1993 (with Glenn Close as Norma) and on Broadway November 16, 1994. Besides being Black's first Best Play citation, it won him his share of the 1995 Tonys for best book and score.

Black's first major work of record for the American stage was The Little Prince and the Aviator, based on Saint-Exupery's The Little Prince, in 1982, for which he and John Barry wrote the score. It closed in previews, but Black had better luck the following year with Tony-nominated lyrics to Elmer Bernstein's music in Merlin. At present, Black is the vice president of the British Academy of Songwriters, Composers and Authors and chairman of the Vivian Ellis Prize encouraging young people to write for the musical stage. He is married and lives in London.

CHRISTOPHER HAMPTON (book and lyrics) was born in the Azores, at Fayal, on January 26, 1946 and finished his education with an M.A. in modern languages at New College, Oxford in 1968. Before he left college his first play, When Did You Last See My Mother?, was put on by the Royal Court Theater (where Hampton later served as resident dramatist, 1968–70) in London in June 1966, transferring to the West End and then to New York at the Sheridan Square Playhouse in January 1967. His first Best Play, The Philanthropist, opened in London in 1970 (winning the Evening Standard and London Theater Critics Awards) and came to Broadway March 15, 1971 for 72 performances during which its author was cited as most promising playwright in that season's Variety poll.

Hampton's second Best Play, Les Liaisons Dangereuses, adapted from the 18th-century novel of pre-Revolution French manners and mores by Choderlos de Laclos, was produced by Royal Shakespeare Company January 8, 1986 in London, where it won the Laurence Olivier, Evening Standard and London Theater Critics Awards. That RSC production transferred to Broadway April 30, 1987 for 148 performances, receiving the New York Drama Critics Award for best foreign play, a Tony nomination, and later in the film version the 1988 Academy and Writer's Guild Awards for Hampton's screen adaptation.

Hampton receives his third Best Play citation and first Tony awards for his collaboration with Don Black on the book and lyrics of the musical Sunset Boulevard. His

other works produced in the U.S. through the years have included new versions of
Henrik Ibsen's A Doll's House *and* Hedda Gabler *(Broadway, 1971),* Total Eclipse
(London, 1968; off Broadway at Chelsea Theater of Brooklyn, 1974), Savages *and*
Treats *(London Theater Critics Award, 1973; Los Angeles Theater Critics Award,*
1974; OOB at the Hudson Guild Theater, 1977), a translation of Odon Von Horvath's
Don Juan Comes Back From the Wars *(off Broadway, 1979 at Manhattan Theater*
Club) and Tales From Hollywood *(London Evening Standard Award, 1982; OOB*
1993 at Cafe LaMama), not to mention the many cross-country productions of his
works. In addition to the above, his plays produced in London have included The
Portage to San Cristobal of A.H. *(1982),* White Chameleon *(1990),* Alice's Adventures Under Ground *(1994) and translations/adaptations of two more Ibsen plays,*
three Molière plays, two more Odon Von Horvath plays and Chekhov's Uncle Vanya,
and he is also the author of a long list of film and TV scripts. He is married, with two
children, and lives in London.

ANDREW LLOYD WEBBER (music) was born in London, March 22, 1948. He
attended Westminster School as a Queen's Scholar and went on to Magdalen College,
Oxford and the Royal College of Music. His early work includes a suite for the theater
at age 9 and, in 1965, the unproduced musical The Likes of Us *with lyrics by Tim*
Rice. The Lloyd Webber-Rice collaboration flared forth on an international scale with
Joseph and the Amazing Technicolor Dreamcoat *(1968; off Broadway 1976 and*
1981; Broadway 1982 in Tony-nominated revival), Jesus Christ Superstar *(1970;*
Broadway 1971 with Tony-nominated score; Broadway 1995) and Evita *(1976;*
Broadway 1979 in Tony-winning production, book and score, and awarded the
Drama Critics citation as the season's best musical).

Evita *(which eventually played 1,567 performances) was still running when* Cats
(which is still running), with Lloyd Webber music put to T.S. Eliot words and addi-
tional lyrics by Trevor Nunn (and for one number by Richard Stilgoe), produced in
England in 1981, opened on Broadway Oct. 7, 1982 and was named a Best Play and
won Tonys for best production, score and lyrics. Lloyd Webber's Variations *(1978)*
and Tell Me on a Sunday *(1979), with lyrics by Don Black, were then combined into*
a show called Song & Dance *(Broadway 1985, with additional lyrics by Richard*
Maltby Jr.). Lloyd Webber's Starlight Express *(1984; Broadway 1987), with lyrics by*
Stilgoe, was still running alongside Cats *when* The Phantom of the Opera *came upon*
the Broadway scene on Jan. 26, 1988, as Webber's second Best Play, and 1987–88's
best-musical Tony winner, following a 1986 London production which won the Laur-
ence Olivier and London Standard awards.

Lloyd Webber wrote both the music and the book, adapted from the David Garnett
novel, for Aspects of Love, *with lyrics by Black and Charles Hart. Its Broadway run*
beginning April 8, 1990 was only 61 performances. But his next 1990s musical, Sunset
Boulevard, *gives him the unique distinction of having four musicals (*Cats, Phantom,
Starlight, Sunset*) running in London and three in New York (*Cats, Phantom, Sunset*)*
at the same time—and he previously had three running in each place in 1982 and

1988. Sunset Boulevard *is Lloyd Webber's third Best Play and his 1995 winner of the Tonys for best musical and score.*

Lloyd Webber's other major compositions are the score for the musical Jeeves *(1974), the movie scores for* Gumshoe *and* The Odessa File *and the Latin requiem mass for* Requiem, *for which he won a 1986 Grammy in the category of best classical contemporary composition. His Really Useful Company produces his own shows and has produced other major works like* Shirley Valentine, Lend Me a Tenor *and* La Bête. *He was knighted by Queen Elizabeth II in 1992 for services to the arts, is a fellow of the Royal College of Music and the first recipient of ASCAP'S Triple Play Award. Lloyd Webber (for the record, his name is listed under the Ls, not the Ws, in* Who's Who) *is married to his third wife (they have one son and he has a son and daughter by his first wife) and lives in London.*

Time: 1949/50
Place: Los Angeles

ACT I

Scene 1: The house on Sunset (exterior)

SYNOPSIS: Through the magic of stagecraft, the image is established of a swimming pool in which *"floating . . . . . fully clothed, face down, is the body of a young man."* The voice of Joe Gillis over this explains that it is 5 a.m. and a murder has been reported to the police, a murder that will make headlines because a silent film superstar is involved.

Joe Gillis—*"a handsome, broad-shouldered man in his early 30s"*—comes forward to address the audience directly in song, stating that he is one who knows all the facts of this situation. A blue light flashes and Los Angeles policemen approach the house, *"an Italianate Hollywood mansion, not more than 20 years old, but already shabby from neglect."*

Scene 2: Paramount Studios

The front of the Paramount lot takes shape, with young hopefuls gathering in the forecourt and Joe continuing his narration. Six months ago (as in this scene) he was an aspiring writer just fired by 20th Century-Fox and desperately hoping for a job at Paramount. He joins the other young hopefuls including Myron (a director), Mary (a young actress, *"blonde and beautiful, artificially disheveled"*) and Joanna (a writer, *"dark and intense"*) in the song "Let's Have Lunch."

MARY *(sings):*
>Don't forget me when you're casting

JOE *(sings):*
>We should talk

MARY *(sings):*
>Gotta run

BOTH *(sing):*
>Let's have lunch

JOE *(sings):*
>Morning, Joanna

JOANNA *(sings):*
>Who are you meeting?

JOE *(sings):*
>Sheldrake, but do I need it?

JOANNA *(sings):*
>I'm handing in my second draft

JOE *(sings):*
>I'd really love to read it

JOANNA *(sings):*
>We should talk

JOE *(sings):*
>Gotta run

BOTH *(sing):*
>Let's have lunch

MARY *(sings):*
>Hi there, Myron

MYRON *(sings):*
>You look great

MARY *(sings):*
>I've spent the last month fasting

MYRON *(sings):*
>I'm shooting a Western
>Down at Fox

MARY *(sings):*
>Don't forget me when
>You're casting

MYRON *(sings):*
>We should talk

MARY *(sings):*
>Gotta run

BOTH *(sing):*
>Let's have lunch

Before Jones, an elderly guard, can pass Joe through the Paramount gate, two men from the finance company accost Joe and try to repossess his car. But Joe has hidden it a few blocks away and manages to escape from them into the Paramount lot, where a group of extras from Cecil B. DeMille's *Samson and Delilah* dances across the scene.

On the lot, Joe encounters his agent, Morino, who can't find work for him, and a friend, Artie, who lends him $20 (he needs $300 to keep his car). He makes his way to his appointment with Sheldrake, who is *"a mournful, dyspeptic figure"* seated at his desk behind a battery of phones. Joe is trying to sell Sheldrake a baseball script entitled *Bases Loaded,* when Betty Schaefer, *"a clean-cut, bright-looking girl in her 20s,"* enters the office with a copy of Joe's script and doesn't hesitate to declare that she finds it pointless.

JOE: What sort of material do you suggest? James Joyce? Dostoevsky?

BETTY: I think pictures should at least try to say a little something.

JOE: I see, you're one of the message kids. I expect you'd have turned down *Gone With the Wind.*

SHELDRAKE: No, that was me.

ENSEMBLE *(sings):*

Gotta run

BETTY: And I guess I was disappointed. I've read some of your other work, and I thought you had some real talent.

JOE: That was last year. This year I felt like eating.

BETTY: Well, I'm sorry, Mr. Gillis . . . . .

ENSEMBLE *(sings):*

We should talk

Gotta run

Let's have lunch.

The ensemble continues to sing in overlapping lines in "*a nightmarish cacophony of phony greetings.*" Betty tries to encourage Joe by praising a story of his called *Blind Windows,* suggesting he offer it to Sheldrake, but Joe remains discouraged. Betty is suggesting they meet at Schwab's Drug Store this coming Thursday. The Financemen catch up with Joe again and demand the keys to his car. Betty helps Joe elude them.

Scene 3: On the road

A car chase ensues, and Joe is putting distance between himself and his pursuers on Sunset Boulevard, when he blows a tire. He ducks into the nearest driveway, and the Financemen roar past without spotting him.

Scene 4: The garage on Sunset

Joe pushes his car past a weedy garden and a covered pool into an open garage beside "*an insanely elaborate 1932 Isotta-Fraschini with speaking tubes, running boards, glass partitions and leopard-skin upholstery.*" A woman's voice calls out, "Why are you so late?" French doors are opened by Max von Mayerling, "*a 60-year-old butler in black tail coat, striped trousers, stiff-collar shirt and white cotton gloves.*" Max points the way inside the house and orders Joe to wipe his feet "*in some mitteleuropaisch accent.*"

Scene 5: The house on Sunset

The drawing room into which Joe steps is large and gloomy, despite lavish gilding. "*The floor is tiled and the the ceiling supported with dark heavy beams. There are framed photographs everywhere and musty hangings. The breeze moans through the pipes of a built-in organ . . . . . a black marble staircase leads up to a broad gallery.*"

Max departs with the cryptic remark, "If you need my help with the coffin, call me." Norma Desmond enters on the gallery and "*proceeds in stately fashion down the stairs.*" She's wearing dark glasses and is "*dressed in black loose pajamas and black high heel pumps. She looks younger than her age, which is probably somewhere in the vicinity of 50, and, despite a sickly pallor, she's extremely striking and was evidently once a great beauty. Her hair is encased in a leopard-pattern chiffon scarf.*"

Norma sings "Surrender": "Let them send their armies/I will never bend/I won't see you now till I surrender/I'll see you again when I surrender." Then she picks up the corpse of a chimpanzee which has been lying on a table under a shawl and presses its face to hers. She intends to bury her beloved pet in the garden, and both she and Max have mistaken Joe for the undertaker, whom they're expecting.

Joe recognizes Norma Desmond as a silent film star who "used to be big." "I *am* big," Norma insists, "It's the pictures that got small." Joe identifies himself as a writer, and Norma, in the song "With One Look," "*summons up before him the essence of her vanished stardom.*"

NORMA *(sings):*
> With one look
> I can break your heart
> With one look
> I play every part
> I can make your sad heart sing
> With one look you'll know
> All you need to know . . . . .
>
> No words can tell
> The stories my eyes tell
> Watch me when I frown
> You can't write that down . . . . .
>
> Yes, with one look
> I put words to shame
> Just one look
> Sets the screen aflame
> Silent music starts to play
> One tear in my eye
> Makes the whole world cry
> With one look
> They'll forgive the past . . . . .
>
> With one look
> I'll ignite a blaze
> I'll return to my glory days
> They'll say Norma's back at last
>
> This time I am staying
> I'm staying for good
> I'll be back
> Where I was born to be
> With one look

I'll be me.
> *She comes to herself suddenly, aware once again of Joe's presence.*

Now go.

JOE: Next time I'll bring my autograph album.
> *Joe nods good-naturedly, turns and sets off toward the French doors. He's almost out of them, when Norma speaks again.*

NORMA: Just a minute.
> *Joe stops in the doorway, half-turns back.*

Did you say you were a writer?

JOE: That's what it says on my guild card.

NORMA: And you've written pictures?

JOE: Sure have. Would you like to see my credits?

NORMA: Come over here, I want to ask you something.
> *Joe hesitates; but his curiosity gets the better of him, and he begins to move back into the body of the room.*

What sort of length is a movie script these days?

JOE: Depends.
> *Standing by the sofa, next to the gold grand piano covered in photographs, is an immense manuscript, several bundles, each wrapped in a red ribbon, standing about two feet high.*

NORMA: I wrote this. It's a very important picture.

JOE: Looks like six very important pictures.

NORMA: It's for DeMille to direct.

JOE: Oh, yeah? And will you be in it?

NORMA: Of course. What do you think?

JOE: Just asking. I didn't know you were planning a comeback.

NORMA: I hate that word. It's a return.

JOE: Well . . . fair enough.

NORMA: I want you to read it.

Joe is reluctant to get involved, but Norma orders him to sit and Max to bring him a drink, while she takes the ribbon off one of the bundles and goes "*off into a world of her own.*" She describes the script in the song "Salome": "Salome, what a woman, what a part!/Innocent body and a sinful heart,/Inflaming Herod's lust/But secretly loving a holy man./No one could play her like I can."

While Norma goes on about the "boiling cauldron of love and hate" in her script, Joe, in lyrics to the same song, describes the situation to the audience: "It sure was a real cheery setup/The wind wheezing through that organ/Max shuffling around and a dead ape dumped on a shelf/And her staring like a Gorgon." The real undertaker arrives at last and, with Max, removes the dead animal in a baby coffin. Joe finally interrupts the song to ask Norma, "Just how old is Salome?" "Sixteen," Norma replies and "*doesn't bat an eyelid.*"

Joe suggests that the script is a good start for a beginner, but needs dialogue. Impulsively, Norma asks him to work on it for her and, again, doesn't bat an eyelid when Joe tells her he gets $500 a week. Joe pretends to hesitate but is obviously going to take the job. Norma insists that he stay here while doing it, in a room over the garage.

Scene 6: Norma's guest house

Max escorts Joe across the dark patio and "*up an outside wooden staircase to an austere, small room above the garage.*" When Joe remarks that Norma is "quite a character," Max somewhat stiffly reminds him of her importance in the song "The Greatest Star of All."

MAX *(sings):*
    Once,
    You won't remember,
    If you said Hollywood, hers was the face you'd think of.
    Her face on every billboard,
    In just a single week she'd get ten thousand letters . . . . .

    She's immortal.
    Caught inside that flickering light beam
    Is a youth which cannot fade.

    Madame's
    A living legend;
    I've seen so many idols fall.
    She is the greatest star of all.

Max departs, leaving Joe impressed. Looking out his window, Joe sees Norma and Max come out and prepare to bury the chimpanzee. *Slow fade to black.*

Scene 7: Schwab's Drugstore

A crowd of Hollywood's young hopefuls are gathered at one of their favorite spots, Schwab's, exchanging news and views about their screen careers in the song "Every Movie's a Circus."

MARY *(sings):*
    Can't get a screen test,
    Don't you hate it
    When a yes-man says no?
GIRL *(sings):*
    Good part?
BOY *(sings):*
    I'm a policeman
    "Hands up, punk"
    That's all I say.

ACTOR *(sings):*
    First time
    You've worked on the lot there
ACTRESS *(sings):*
    I must say R.
    K.O. are OK.
ALL *(sing):*
    Movies.
BOY *(sings):*
    Then what?
GIRL *(sings):*
    He pressed a button.
    Out of the wall
    Fell a four-poster bed . . . . .
ALL *(sing):*
    Every
    Movie's a circus
    On the wire
    Without a net . . . . .

Joe comes in and joins Artie, who is newly engaged to be married. Artie's fiancee comes in—it's Betty. When Artie is called to the phone, Joe and Betty move to a table. Betty still believes Joe's story *Blind Windows* might make a good movie. Joe gives her permission to adapt it herself. She'd hoped they could collaborate, but now Joe is all tied up. Joe offers her some advice about writing screen plays in the song "Girl Meets Boy."

JOE *(sings):*
    Write this down
    I'll give you some ground rules.
    Plenty of conflict
    But nice guys don't break the law.
    Girl meets boy
    Gives herself completely
    And though she loves him
JOE & BETTY *(sing):*
    She keeps one foot on the floor.
BETTY *(sings):*
    No one dies except the best friend
    No one ever mentions communists
    No one takes a black friend to a restaurant.
JOE *(sings):*
    Very good.
    Nothing I can teach you

We could have had fun
Fighting the studio. . . . .

Artie joins them, and Betty goes off with him. *"Joe is the last customer in the drugstore, staring ruefully into his cup of coffee."*

Scene 8: The terrace on Sunset

Joe is walking across the patio in the moonlight, when Max intercepts him.

MAX: Madame is quite agitated. Earlier this evening, she wanted you for something and you could not be found.
JOE: Well, that's tough.
MAX: I don't think you understand, Mr. Gillis. Madame is extremely fragile. She has moments of melancholy. There have been suicide attempts.
JOE: Why? Because of her career? She's done well enough. Look at all the fan mail she gets every day.
MAX: I wouldn't look too closely at the postmarks if I were you.
JOE: You mean you send them?

The question answers itself. Joe is angry because Max doesn't seem to realize that he intends to have a life of his own, apart from this place. Max warns him that he must abide by Norma Desmond's rules if he wants to keep the script-writing job.

Scene 9: The house on Sunset

Joe is working on Norma's script with Norma looking over his shoulder to make sure her character, Salome, is in every scene. Joe realizes it's going to take him weeks, not days, to finish this job. Meanwhile, Max sets up the projector and starts to show "One of madame's enduring classics/*The Ordeal of Joan of Arc.*" As Norma watches herself on the screen she is entranced by her own performance and sings "New Ways to Dream."

NORMA *(sings):*
This was dawn
There were no rules,
We were so young.
Movies were born;
So many songs
Yet to be sung.
So many roads
Still unexplored;
We gave the world
New ways to dream.

Glenn Close (Norma) and Alan Campbell (Joe) in *Sunset Boulevard*

> Somehow we found
> New ways to dream . . . . .

"She smelled of faded roses," Joe comments in the song, touched by Norma's reliving her stardom. He takes Norma's hand as the scene fades to black.

Scene 10: The house on Sunset

Joe is sitting alone in the huge drawing room, playing solitaire and telling his troubles to the audience: he's finished the script but hasn't seen any money for it yet; the finance company has found and repossessed his car; the December rains leaked into his garage room, so he has been moved by Max into "the room of the husbands" in the main house.

Norma makes an entrance down the stairs, holding a typescript and announcing that today's the day Max is going to deliver the finished script to DeMille. Max departs on his errand. "*Joe is steeling himself to broach a difficult subject.*"

JOE: I want to thank you for trusting me with your baby.
NORMA: Not at all, it's I who should thank you.
JOE: Will you call and let me know as soon as you have some news?
NORMA (*frowns; turns to him, her expression bewildered*): Call where?
JOE: My apartment.
NORMA: You can't possibly think of leaving now, Joe.

JOE: The script is finished, Norma.

NORMA: No, Joe, it's just the beginning, it's the first draft. I couldn't dream of letting you go, I need your support.

JOE: Well . . .

NORMA: You'll stay on full salary, of course . . .

JOE: It's not the money.

>*Norma now has a look of genuine panic on her face, and Joe sees that some reassurance is essential.*

Of course, I'll stay until we get some sort of word back from Paramount.

>*He's on his feet now, and Norma grips his hand tightly for a moment.*

NORMA: Thank you, Joe.

>*She releases his hand and moves off, leaving him a little shaken by this turn of events . . . . .*

Max ushers in a men's outfitter and his many assistants. They are Norma's surprise for Joe's birthday—she's had them shut down the store for the day and come here to fit Joe for an entirely new wardrobe with accessories. The title of their song as they show Joe their wares says it all—"The Lady's Paying." Norma, impatient at the slowness of their progress, picks out a few items for Joe herself. She even insists on white tie and tails, though Joe can't imagine when he'll ever wear them. To her New Year's Eve party, Norma suggests. Joe tries to tell her that he's going elsewhere on New Year's Eve—to Artie's—but Norma insists. This largesse is beginning to appeal to Joe, and he agrees to change his plans and come to Norma's party.

The salesmen surround Joe, and when they move away from him he's in full evening dress. They sing "Gracefully accept the role you're playing/You will earn every cent the lady's paying/So why not have it all?" and the scene blacks out.

Scene 11: The house on Sunset

Max has caused the house to be lavishly decorated for New Year's Eve. As Joe observes, "It looks like gala night aboard S.S. Titanic," with streamers, flowers and candles, a small orchestra striking up a tango and Max readying the drinks tray. Norma enters at the top of the stairs "*in a dazzling diamante evening gown with long black gloves and bird of paradise feathers in her hair.*" She presents Joe with a gold cigarette case inscribed "Mad About the Boy" and pulls him onto the dance floor, tiled at Rudolph Valentino's suggestion, "It takes tiles to tango." As they move into the dance, they sing "The Perfect Year," Joe voicing some misgivings.

JOE: *(sings):*
Before we play
Some dangerous game;
Before we fan
Some harmless flame,
We have to ask

If this is wise
And if the game
Is worth the prize . . . . .
NORMA *(sings):*
It's New Year's Eve
And hopes are high,
Dance one year in
Kiss one goodbye.
Another chance,
Another start,
So many dreams
To tease the heart.

We don't need a crowded ballroom
Everything we want is here
And face to face
We will embrace
The perfect year.

Norma kisses Joe lightly at the end of the number, and they move to pick up their glasses of champagne. Joe wonders what time the other guests are due to arrive.

NORMA: There are no other guests. Just you and me.
          She leans in to kiss him again, this time more seriously. Max half turns
          away, averting his eyes.
I'm in love with you. Surely you know that.
JOE *(terribly startled by this)*: Norma . . . . .
NORMA: We'll have a wonderful time next year. I'll have the pool filled for you. I'll open up my house in Malibu, and you can have the whole ocean. I have enough money to buy us anything we want.
JOE: Cut out that "us" business.
NORMA: What's the matter with you?
JOE: What right do you have to take me for granted?
NORMA: What right? You want me to tell you?
JOE *(out of his depth now; all he can do is bluster)*: Norma, what I'm trying to say is that I'm the wrong guy for you; you need a big shot, someone with polo ponies, a Valentino . . .
NORMA: What you're trying to say is that you don't want me to love you. Say it! Say it!
          Joe doesn't answer; he looks away, avoiding her eye. Thus, it takes him
          completely by surprise when she slaps his face. And before he can react,
          she's turned and run all the way up the stairs to vanish into her bedroom.
          Joe finds himself standing face to face with Max.
JOE: Max. Get me a taxi.

Scene 12: Artie Green's apartment and the house on Sunset

Joe, in vicuna coat and full evening attire, feels a bit overdressed as he joins the New Year's Eve party of young people at Artie's, including all those doing walk-ons in *Samson and Delilah*. Artie and Betty both greet Joe warmly, and the others sing their optimistic outlook on how it's going to be "This Time Next Year." Artie's dream is a wife and child in "A rambling old house with a big apple tree/With a swing for the kid and a hammock for me." The girls *"dance a kind of parody Middle Eastern bump and grind."* Back at the house on Sunset, Norma can be seen drinking champagne and listening to the orchestra, alone with Max.

Betty's part of the New Year's song is good news: Sheldrake likes Joe's story *Blind Windows*, and Betty is doing the screen play.

> *At the house, Norma drifts upstairs with her glass of champagne. Max watches her leave, very concerned.*

BETTY *(to Joe, sings):*

I love *Blind Windows*
But I can't write it on my own
Can't we speak on the telephone?
All my evenings are free.

ARTIE *(sings):*

Hey, just a minute
I'm the fellow who bought the ring

BETTY *(sings):*

Artie, this is a business thing
It's important to me
You'll be on location in Clinch, Tennessee.
> *She turns to Joe . . . . . with real intensity.*
Please make this your New Year's resolution for me.
> *The chorus starts up again.*

ALL *(sing):*

By this time next year
I will get my foot in the door
Next year I know I'm going to score
An amazing success

Cut to the moment
When they open the envelope
Pass the statuette to Bob Hope
And it's my name you hear . . . . .

We'll have nothing to fear
Contracts all signed
Three-picture deal
Yellow brick road career

Hope we're not still saying these things
This time next year.

At the house on Sunset, Max, in sudden alarm, runs upstairs.

At Artie's, Joe has decided not to go back to Norma's, and Artie offers to put him up for a couple of weeks. Joe calls Norma's house. When Max answers, Joe tries to ask him to pack and send his belongings, but Max cannot talk to him now, except to say, "Madame found a razor in your room. And she cut her wrists." To everyone's astonishment, Joe grabs his coat and runs off.

Scene 13: The house on Sunset

The scene in Artie's apartment dissolves. Max has helped Norma, her wrists heavily bandaged, to a sofa in the living room and is bathing her forehead with ice water, when Joe comes in, agitated, telling Norma her attempted suicide was "a silly thing" to do. Norma threatens to do it again.

JOE: Attractive headline: great star kills herself for unknown writer.
NORMA: Great stars have great pride.
> *She turns away from him. Max, still anxious, is moving back, melting into the background.*

You must have some girl; why don't you go to her?

JOE (*kneels beside Norma and speaks to her with great gentleness*): I never meant to hurt you, Norma. You've been good to me. You're the only person in this stinking town that's ever been good to me.

NORMA: Then why don't you say thank you and go? Go, go!
> *Joe goes to the stairs as if to leave, then goes to Norma. He sits near her on the sofa, leans forward and kisses her.*

JOE: Happy New Year.

NORMA (*reaches up and wraps her bandaged arms around his neck*): Happy New Year, darling.
> *They kiss. Norma pulls Joe down onto the sofa . . . Slow fade to black. Curtain*

ACT II

Scene 1: Norma's Swimming Pool

Joe, wearing sunglasses, sits on a chaise lounge sipping a drink and addressing the audience in the song "Sunset Boulevard," explaining that he's lost some of his original ambition to make good in the movies after a year of penury and frustration. He's now of a mind to "do whatever pays the wages."

JOE *(sings)*:
> Sunset Boulevard
> Frenzied boulevard
> Swamped with every kind of false emotion.
>
> Sunset Boulevard
> Brutal boulevard
> Just like you we'll wind up in the ocean.
>
> She was sinking fast
> I threw a rope
> Now I have suits
> And she has hope
> It seemed an elegant solution.
>
> One day this must end,
> It isn't real
> Still, I'll enjoy
> A hearty meal
> Before tomorrow's execution.
>
> Sunset Boulevard
> Ruthless boulevard
> Destination for the stony-hearted.
>
> Sunset Boulevard
> Lethal boulevard
> Everyone's forgotten how they started
> Here on Sunset Boulevard.

Norma comes in, excited, because she's received a call from Paramount. They want to see her right away (she sings, in the form of a reprise of "The Perfect Year"), but since it was only an assistant who called and not C.B. himself, she'll let them wait till she's ready. Joe can't believe they really like the script but doesn't want to discourage her. Three days later (Joe sings) "She dressed up like a Pharaoh/Slapped on a pound of makeup/And set forth in her chariot . . . . . "

Scene 2: Paramount Studios

At the studio gate, Norma, chauffeured by Max in her vintage Isotta-Fraschini, is recognized by Jones, the elderly guard, who opens the barrier and lets her car in but also phones to warn DeMille on Stage 18 that she is coming.

> *A scene change reveals the cavernous interior of Sound Stage 18, where the stand-ins for Victor Mature and Hedy Lamarr are in position, in a blaze of light, on the grandiose* Samson and Delilah *set. Mr. DeMille*

> . . . . . *confers with his director of photography. He's interrupted by one*
> *of his assistants, Heather, who approaches with some trepidation.*

HEATHER: Mr. DeMille?

DEMILLE: What is it?

HEATHER: Norma Desmond is here to see you, Mr. DeMille.

DEMILLE: Norma Desmond?

HEATHER: She's here at the studio.

DEMILLE: It must be about that appalling script of hers. What shall I say?

HEATHER: Maybe I could give her the brush.

DEMILLE: Thirty million fans have given her the brush. Isn't that enough? Give me a minute.

Norma, Max and Joe have arrived outside the sound stage, and Heather comes to bring Norma inside (Joe wishes her luck but declines to accompany her). DeMille greets her, and Norma complains that it was an assistant who phoned her and asked her to come to the studio, and she feels DeMille himself should have called her. DeMille has absolutely no idea what she's talking about but takes her onto his set, where an elderly electrician, Hog-Eye, recognizes Norma, calls a greeting to her and fixes a spotlight on her. Technicians, extras, stagehands gather round Norma as she sings "As If We Never Said Goodbye."

NORMA *(sings):*
    I don't know why I'm frightened
    I know my way around here
    The cardboard trees,
    The painted seas,
    The sound here.
    Yes, a world to rediscover
    But I'm not in any hurry
    And I need a moment . . . . .

    I've spent so many mornings
    Just trying to resist you
    I'm trembling now
    You can't know how
    I've missed you,
    Missed the fairy-tale adventures
    In this ever-spinning playground,
    We were young together.

    I'm coming out of makeup
    The lights already burning
    Not long until
    The cameras will
    Start turning

And the early morning madness
And the magic in the making
Yes, everything's as if we never said goodbye . . . . .

When Norma finishes the song, "We taught the world new ways to dream," the people on the sound stage applaud.

Outside, Betty encounters Joe and reminds him, before hurrying off, that *Blind Windows* is on hold until he can find time to work with her.

Sheldrake comes by, sees the Isotta and informs Max that he was looking out of the window the other day and saw the car, unique outside a museum, perfect for the Bing Crosby film he's planning. Sheldrake is the assistant who's been phoning Norma. It's not her script he wants, it's her car, and he'll pay her $100 a week to rent it for his picture.

Max is outraged at this development and refuses to pass on Sheldrake's offer to Norma.

On the sound stage, DeMille can no longer ignore Norma and the crowd around her. He joins her in a reprise of the song "Surrender" about the good old days. But DeMille's scene is now ready, and he ushers Norma to the door with encouraging but noncommittal parting words. Believing she is just about all set for a comeback, Norma gets into her car, and Max drives it off, having already told Joe that it's the car they want, not Norma or her script. As Norma leaves, Betty joins a reflective DeMille on the set.

DEMILLE *(sings):*
    If you could have seen
    Her at seventeen
    When all of her dreams were new,
    Beautiful and strong,
    Before it all went wrong;
    She's never known the meaning of
    Surrender;
    Never known the meaning of
    Surrender.
        Slow fade to black.

Scene 3: Betty's office at Paramount

Betty is sitting while Joe, in shirtsleeves, is pacing, trying to think of a good way for Boy to meet Girl in their script. Betty comments on Joe's gold cigarette case inscribed with Norma's name and "Mad About the Boy." Joe counters with "How's Artie?" Betty replies, "I'm missing him something fierce." They get back to work, discussing plot possibilities in a reprise of the song "Girl Meets Boy" and are becoming more and more enthusiastic about this script's potential.

Scene 4: The house on Sunset

An army of beauticians is working on Norma, and a masseur and an astrologer are also in attendance, getting her ready, as she believes, to go back before the cameras. Joe sits reading while the astrologer advises about the best time to begin shooting and the others work their magic, all singing "Eternal Youth Is Worth a Little Suffering."

When the team finally departs, Joe is looking around the living room for something which (it turns out after the others have gone) Norma has hidden under her towel and now produces: the script Joe is writing with Betty. Norma is curious about it, but it's her bedtime under her new, strict regime.

NORMA: Are you coming up?

JOE: I think I'll read a little longer.

NORMA: You went out last night, didn't you, Joe?

JOE: I went for a walk.

NORMA: You took the car.

JOE: I drove to the beach

NORMA: Who's Betty Schaefer?

    Silence. Eventually Joe shakes his head.

JOE: Surely you don't want me to feel I'm a prisoner in this house?

NORMA: You don't understand, Joe. I'm under a terrible strain. It's been so hard I even got myself a revolver. The only thing that stopped me from killing myself was the thought of all those people waiting to see me back on the screen. How could I disappoint them? All I ask is a little patience, a little understanding.

JOE: Norma, there's nothing to worry about, I haven't done anything.

NORMA: Of course you haven't. Good night, my darling.

She kisses him and disappears upstairs. After she's gone, Joe picks up his script and explains to the audience that he probably should have stayed there, but he and Betty wanted to finish the script. Max enters and, his expression troubled, sees Joe exit through the French doors on his way to Betty's.

Scene 5: Betty's office and the Paramount back lot

At Paramount, at night, Joe and Betty write "The End" on the script, then stroll from her office through a Manhattan street setting on the lot, "*and the flimsy struts holding up the substantial set are gradually revealed.*" Betty explains that as a child she played on this street; she is third-generation Hollywood—her grandmother was a Pearl White stunt girl, her father an electrician—and she was expected to become a star, not a writer.

Joe notices that Betty is upset about something and gets her to admit that she's received a telegram from Artie asking her to join him in Clinch, Tennessee, and get married—but Betty is no longer in love with Artie. "What happened?" Joe asks her. "You did," she replies. This brings on a long kiss and the song "Too Much in Love to Care."

JOE *(sings):*
     . . . . . If you were smart,
     You would keep on walking
     Out of my life
     As fast as you can.
     I'm not the one
     You should pin your hopes on,
     You're falling for
     The wrong kind of man.
     This is crazy.
     You know we should call it a day.
     Sound advice, great advice,
     Let's throw it away.
     I can't control
     All the things I'm feeling,
     I haven't got a prayer
     If I'm a fool, well, I'm too much in love to care.

BETTY *(sings):*
     . . . . . I thought I had
     Everything I needed.
     My life was set,
     My dreams were in place.
     My heart could see
     Way into the future.
     All of that goes
     When I see your face.
     I should hate you,
     There I was, the world in my hand
     Can one kiss kiss away
     Everything I planned?
     I can't control
     All the things I'm feeling,
     I'm floating in mid-air.
     I know it's wrong, but I'm too much in love to care . . . . .

        They fall into each other's arms and embrace passionately. Then Joe leads Betty by the hand back into the office. They kiss again, and it's obvious that they're about to make love.

Scene 6: The house on Sunset (exterior)

When Joe drives the Isotta back into the garage, Max is waiting to tell him he's worried about the effect these nightly excursions of Joe's may have on Norma. Max

George Hearn as Max von Mayerling in *Sunset Boulevard*

reveals that he is the famous director—Max von Mayerling—who made Norma a star, and he means to protect her now. As they move from garage to patio, Max explains further in a reprise of "New Ways to Dream."

MAX *(sings):*
> When we met
> She was a child,
> Barely sixteen;
> Awkward and yet
> She had an air
> I'd never seen.
> I knew I'd found
> My perfect face.
> Deep in her eyes,
> New ways to dream,
> And we inspired
> New ways to dream.
>
> Talkies came;
> I stayed with her,
> Took up this life,
> Threw away fame.
>> *He hesitates before steeling himself to go on.*
> Please understand
>> *A beat.*
> She was my wife.
>> *Pause. Joe is staggered. Max is fighting back a wave of emotion.*
> We had achieved
> Far more than most
> We gave the world
> New ways to dream.
> Everyone needs
> New ways to dream.

So, Max continues in song, he has become "the keeper of the flame" and will never allow Norma to surrender to a demeaning fate.

Scene 7: The house on Sunset

Norma, looking tormented, dressed in a white negligee, dials the phone and reaches Betty Schaefer. Norma taunts Betty with Betty's ignorance of Joe's real circumstances, living with and on Norma. Joe enters, hears what is going on, grabs the phone angrily and challenges Betty to come on over to Sunset Boulevard and see for herself how he's living.

Norma begs Joe not to hate her for calling Betty—Norma is so upset she's "wasting away." Joe turns his back on her, and she disappears upstairs.

Outside, a storm brings lightning and torrential rain, and, inside, a storm is brewing with Joe slumped on the sofa and Norma, unseen by Joe, emerging from her room holding a revolver and concealing herself on the balcony.

Betty arrives, impressed with the surroundings but mystified by Joe's place in them. In a reprise of "Sunset Boulevard" Joe informs Betty that this is Norma Desmond's house and the situation is the usual one: "Older woman/Very well-to-do/Meets younger man/A standard cue/For two mechanical performers."

Betty's reaction is, "Just pack your things and let's go." Joe pretends that he could never leave all this luxury and go back to his dreary existence in one room with a Murphy bed, finishing, "You should go back to Artie and marry the fool/ And you'll always be welcome to swim in my pool." Betty can't stand any more of this and runs off through the French doors into the storm.

Norma comes down the stairs, the revolver now out of sight, grateful that Joe seems to have chosen to stay with her: "Thank you, thank you, Joe, thank you." But Joe disappears upstairs and then reappears carrying his battered old typewriter. He starts down the stairs, on his way to leaving Norma and everything she has given him, as he makes clear to the music of "Sunset Boulevard."

JOE *(sings):*
　　It's been a bundle of laughs
　　And thanks for the use of the trinkets.
　　　　He takes the gold cigarette case out of his pocket and hands it to her.
　　A little ritzy for the copy desk
　　Back in Dayton.
　　　　He starts to move on, then turns back to her, his expression serious.
　　And there's something you ought to know.
　　I want to do you this favor:
　　They'll never shoot that hopeless script of yours.
　　They only wanted your car.
　　　　During this, Max has entered below. He looks on, helpless.
NORMA *(sings):*
　　That's a lie! They still want me!
　　What about all my fan-mail?
JOE *(sings):*
　　It's Max who writes you letters.
　　Your audience has vanished.
　　They left when you weren't looking.
　　Nothing's wrong with being fifty
　　Unless you're acting twenty.
　　　　He sets off down the stairs.
NORMA: I am the greatest star of them all.
JOE: Goodbye, Norma.
　　　　*He's spoken without looking back; so he doesn't see Norma fetch the
　　　　revolver out of her pocket and point it at him.*
NORMA *(sings):*
　　No one ever leaves a star.

She fires. Joe looks extremely surprised, but carries on walking, for the moment apparently unaffected. At the bottom of the stairs, he lets go of the typewriter, which crashes down onto the tiles. He staggers slightly, but carries on, out through the French doors. Norma hurries after him. Outside the door, she fires twice more. A flash of lightning is followed by a drum roll of thunder. Max moves forward to the center of the stage, aghast, for once completely at a loss. Slow fade to black.

Scene 8: The house on Sunset

Outside the house, Joe's body floats face-down in the swimming pool, while the inside is crowded with reporters, police and newsreel crews with portable lights. Norma emerges from her room on the landing, dressed *"in some strange approximation of a Salome costume"* and starts down the stairs with all eyes fixed on her. She's still holding her revolver, which causes one of the policemen to draw his, in case it's needed. But Norma is disoriented, singing broken phrases of songs, exclaiming, "Mad about the boy!"

Max takes charge, gesturing at the policemen to keep clear, and announces to Norma that the cameras are ready to film her dance. The music of "The Greatest Star of All" and "Surrender" is a background for Norma's performance as she starts to descend the stairs after Max exclaims, "You are the greatest star of all!"

> *Max cups a hand to his mouth and springs into action.*
MAX: Lights!
> *The portable lights flare up. In addition, there's the flash of countless flashbulbs. Norma reacts, her eyes widen, she drapes the scarf around her shoulders.*
Cameras!
> *The whirr and grind of the old-fashioned Movietone cameras.*
Action!
> *And so, as the music swells, Norma descends the staircase, waving her arms in some strange rendition of Salome's approach to the throne. However, halfway down, she suddenly comes to a halt and begins to sing.*
NORMA *(sings):*
When he scorned me I
Knew he'd have to die
Let me kiss his severed head.
Compromise or death
He fought to his last breath
He never had it in him to surrender
Just like me he never could surrender.

I can't go on with the scene; I'm too happy. May I say a few words, Mr. DeMille? I can't tell you how wonderful it is to be back in the studio making a picture. I promise you I'll never desert you again. This is my life. It always will be. There is nothing else. Just us and the cameras and all you wonderful people out there in the dark. And now, Mr. DeMille, I'm ready for my closeup.

> *She continues down the staircase as the music of "With One Look" swells to a climax.*

(Sings):
This time I'm staying
I'm staying for good
I'll be back
Where I was born to be
With one look
I'll be me.

> *Darkness. Curtain.*

Best Play Citation

○○○
○○○
○○○
○○○
○○○
○○○ HAPGOOD

A Play in Two Acts

BY TOM STOPPARD

Cast and credits appear on page 358

TOM STOPPARD, the author of Hapgood, *is also the author of* Arcadia *in a rare and possibly unique instance of two unrelated plays by the same author being cited as Best Plays in the same season. A biographical sketch of Stoppard appears following the title of the* Arcadia *synopsis on page 219 of this volume.*

Time: 1989
Place: London

ACT I

Scene 1

SYNOPSIS: "*We are looking at part of the men's changing-room of an old-fashioned municipal swimming-baths. It is 10 o'clock in the morning. The cubicles are num-*

133

bered, and they have doors which conceal occupancy although they don't meet the ground. There is a wash-basin or two, a place to shave facing front. Four of the cubicles have to 'work.' There are four ways of coming and going: 'Lobby,' 'Pool,' 'Showers' and, for the sake of argument, 'Upstage.' "

The word "Men" is seen in reverse on the glass doors which give entrance from the lobby. We can hear one of the showers in use, and Wates—a black American shabbily dressed—is using the shaving area. At the same time, we can hear a man and a woman talking on short wave radio. There is some kind of clandestine surveillance project in progress, of which Wates is a part.

A man enters carrying a rolled-up towel—*"We call this man Russian One because he is Russian and because there are going to be two of them"*—and enters Cubicle One, closing the door. Ridley, a man in his mid-30s, enters, walks around among the cubicles. Russian One exits his cubicle dressed to swim and exits, leaving his towel hanging on the cubicle door. Ridley then pushes a briefcase under the door of Cubicle One, takes the towel off it and enters Cubicle Two and closes the door (*"As a matter of interest, the Ridley who posts the briefcase is not the same Ridley who entered with it"*) and throws the towel over the door of Cubicle Two.

The shower is still running and Wates still shaving as Kerner, 40-ish, enters carrying a briefcase and towel, pushes the briefcase under the door on which the towel is showing, pulls the towel off the door and throws it over the door into the cubicle, enters Cubicle Three, closes the door behind him and hangs his towel over it.

Ridley leaves Cubicle Two carrying both towel and briefcase, hangs the towel on Cubicle One and disappears toward the swimming pool, from which a soaking wet Russian One soon appears, carrying the briefcase. He reenters Cubicle One.

"Russian Two enters from the lobby. He is the twin of Russian One and dressed like Russian One. He carries a similar rolled-up towel. However, he also carries a briefcase. He glances round briefly and notes the towel on Kerner's door (Cubicle Three). He posts his briefcase under Kerner's door. He enters a cubicle, Cubicle Four."

Merryweather, *"a boyish 22-year-old in sports jacket and flannels"* enters, obviously prepared to take some part in this caper. Merryweather follows Russian One when the latter departs, carrying his rolled-up towel but not the briefcase. Kerner leaves Cubicle Three with the briefcase that had been dropped there. Russian Two appears, collects the briefcase from Cubicle One and departs, followed by Ridley.

"The shower stops running. There is a pause, and then the occupant of the shower, Hapgood, a woman aged 38, approaches, somewhat encumbered by a briefcase (Kerner's original), a leather rectangular clutch handbag with a shoulder strap and an umbrella which she is at the moment taking down and shaking out. From her appearance, the umbrella has been an entire success." She is obviously the agent in charge of this operation, and Wates reports to her on Merryweather's actions: "Followed the man in, followed the wrong man out, meanwhile Merryweather's man turns around and leaves with the goods."

Ridley enters, calling Hapgood "Mother," reporting that Russian Two, whom he followed, has left in a Peugeot. Hapgood looks in her briefcase, finds a box containing a computer disc but shows no interest in it. Merryweather appears and reports to "Mother" that he lost his man, Russian One—but Russian One's cab is apparently under surveillance. On her short wave radio, Hapgood issues orders for the Peugeot to be apprehended and the Russian and his briefcase seized.

"I guess we took our eye off the ball," Wates comments, but Hapgood, preparing to leave, thanks him for his help and assures him he'll be brought in again later. Merryweather returns from the pool area, where he has found nothing. He is directed by Hapgood to drain the pool, as she exits.

Wates, alone, prepares to talk on his radio but hears a sound that changes his manner to one of extreme alertness. He draws his revolver and stands listening, "*While a figure comes out of the dark upstage between the cubicles.*" It is Paul Blair, "*probably 20 years older than Hapgood, but in good shape,*" wearing hat, tweed overcoat and a colorful scarf.

> *Wates does not move until the downstage light falls across Blair's face. Blair comes to a halt. Wates puts his gun away, gets the radio back into his hand and resumes.*

WATES *(to radio):* Wates—I need the sweeps. (*He nods at Blair.*) Paul.

BLAIR *(greets him back):* Ben.

RADIO: Sweeps coming up.

WATES *(to radio):* Thank you.

> *He puts the radio in his pocket and, in leaving, speaks to Blair without reproof, just information.*

She blew it.

> *He goes out through the lobby doors. Blair takes a radio from his pocket. The scene begins to change.*

BLAIR *(to radio):* Ridley.

RIDLEY *(on radio):* Ridley.

BLAIR *(to radio):* I want Kerner in Regent's Park, twelve o'clock sharp.

> *He puts the radio away and looks at his wrist watch. The next time he moves, it is twelve o'clock, and he is at the zoo.*

Scene 2

Blair dismisses Ridley and informs Kerner that he is blown as their agent, and if he is a double he is blown both ways, as a Russian agent, too: "*Which* way is perhaps an academic question." Kerner, in a Russian accent, launches into a philosophical discussion about the difference between the path of bullets and of light, of waves as opposed to particles, but Blair persists, "Joseph, I want to know if you're ours or theirs, that's all." Kerner replies enigmatically.

KERNER: . . . . . Somehow light is continuous and also discontinuous. The experimenter makes the choice. You get what you interrogate for. And you want to know if I'm a wave or a particle. Every month at the Pool, I and my friend Georgi exchange material. When the experiment is over, you have a result. I am your joe. But they also have a result: because you have put in my briefcase enough information to keep me credible as a Russian sleeper activated by my KGB control; which is what Georgi thinks he is. So naturally he gives me enough information to keep me credible as a British joe. Frankly, I can't remember which side I'm supposed to be working for, and it's not in fact necessary for me to know.

       Pause.

BLAIR: It wasn't Georgi today.

KERNER: No?

BLAIR: No, it was different today.

KERNER: Today you decided to look. Why was that?

BLAIR: Some of your research has turned up in Moscow. Real secrets, not briefcase stuff.

KERNER: Tsk, tsk, tsk.

BLAIR: That's what the Americans said, roughly . . . . .

KERNER: What happened at the Pool?

BLAIR: Wates wanted us to abort the meet and put you through the mangle. But Mrs. Hapgood insisted you were straight. And she wanted to keep the channel open. She made Wates an offer. She duplicated the contents of your briefcase. So now we had everything twice, in two briefcases. Ridley showed up before you at the Pool—

KERNER: What is a mangle?

BLAIR: I'm trying to tell you what happened at the Pool.

KERNER: You already did. Your Mr. Ridley delivered to my Russian control, and I delivered where Ridley put his towel. Quite nice. If I'm putting something extra in my briefcase, you get it all back.

BLAIR: That sort of thing.

KERNER: And was there something extra in my briefcase?

BLAIR: No. There was something missing. The computer disc was there but the films were gone.

Wates had sprayed Kerner's suitcase with some substance that can be detected by a Geiger counter. Kerner tests negative for this, so he didn't touch the contents. There was also a transmitter in the briefcase, but its bleep died and the transmitter is missing, so obviously "Mr. Nobody" interfered with the drop. Blair notes one other thing: "It wasn't Georgi today, it was twins . . . . . Give it some thought."

Kerner exits, signalling Ridley to accompany him. When Blair moves, "*He is on the touch-line of a rugger pitch.*"

Scene 3

Blair is watching a rugby match between 11-year-olds. Hapgood is cheering for her son, who is playing on one of the teams. Blair informs Hapgood that the Americans want them to take Kerner out of play: "If they're going to spend a hundred million dollars over here on Kerner's SDI research, they'd rather he didn't continue swapping briefcases with the high dive champion of the Russian Embassy." Kerner's work concerns an "anti-particle trap" (something to do with release of energy). Hapgood pleads that Kerner is the star of her disinformation operation.

It seems that the fact of twins working for the KGB has been rumored for years, and at the Pool there they were—but the twins were expendable, and everything went as the Russians had planned. And adding to the puzzle (Blair reveals), it was Hapgood herself who was holding the briefcase when the transmitter went off the air. Hapgood goes over the events at the Pool and remembers that it was Ridley, finally, who came to her and said, "You didn't tell me it was twins." Hapgood concludes, "He was expecting twins. I think it's Ridley, Paul. I've left my own back door open."

Hapgood's son Joe, muddy, with boots a size too large, comes on, and Hapgood gives him a clean tracksuit to put on. Joe is accustomed to losing—his team always loses, he tells the grownups—but somewhat embarrassed because his mother is the only person who comes to watch the 11-year-olds play. His boots are oversized because he bought them from an older boy; he had been playing in his running shoes, but apparently one of these was tossed onto the roof. Joe has "borrowed" the key to a master's garage to get a ladder to retrieve the shoe, but now he has lost the key. Hapgood advises him in his search to "Do the grid—five minutes for every square," and then phone her if he hasn't found the key.

Joe runs off. Blair had noticed that at one point in the conversation Joe had thanked his mother for a post card from Vienna. Hapgood apologizes for this obvious breach of security, but then decides, "If I can't send him a rotten postcard, you can take Vienna and stick it up your—" and Blair settles for "Fair enough." Then he wonders what they are to do about Ridley.

BLAIR: We could reel him in for a hostile interview, but I'd rather catch him at it.

HAPGOOD: Yes, that's right. We missed our chance today, we'll have to make him do it all again.

BLAIR *(surprised):* He won't come back to the well, it's been poisoned.

HAPGOOD: I know. It's difficult. I'll think about it. Do you want some tea? They lay it on for parents, and he's entitled to two.

BLAIR *(shakes his head):* I think I'd better get the search going in back numbers. Perhaps you could organize a relief team from eight o'clock.

HAPGOOD: I've done that.

BLAIR: And someone should tell Downing Street we're standing by Kerner.

HAPGOOD: I've done that too.

BLAIR: Well . . . *(He nods goodbye at her.)* Don't pack it in yet, I need you.

HAPGOOD: I was calling you at the Pool this morning.

BLAIR: I was there.

HAPGOOD: I needed *you.*

BLAIR: No, no, that was only personal. But you're going to need me now.

HAPGOOD: I'll see you tomorrow. I'll be twenty minutes late in, there's something I have to do.

Hapgood departs. The scene around Blair changes to Hapgood's office.

Scene 4

Blair hands his hat and coat to Maggs, Hapgood's secretary, in his 20s, "*young, calm professional.*" The centerpiece of the office is a long desk fully equipped with electronic communications devices, including two phones, one of them a red one which promptly rings. As Maggs answers, Wates enters, greeting Blair. It's not Downing Street on the phone, it's Hapgood's son Joe having trouble finding the lost key.

When Maggs leaves, Wates questions Blair about Hapgood. She is the only woman on the Defense Liaison Committee. She is not married but is called Mrs. Hapgood out of courtesy. Blair refuses to answer Wates's direct question about who Joe's father was. Then the American complains that Hapgood calls him "Wates" instead of the more friendly "Ben."

Wates has come to talk about Ridley. In Ridley's past, there was a caper in Athens in which a Russian target was missed and an American operative killed. Then, in Paris, a Bulgarian named Ganchev was killed while trying to meet with Ridley, who has an alibi for this death—he was caught in a traffic jam in a taxi with Hapgood. As for Kerner's bleep having gone off the air during the Pool caper, Wates has since checked with a radio-finder and heard the bleep loud and clear. He pinpointed its origin and found it is coming from right here in Hapgood's office. Wates suggest they proceed cautiously, give Hapgood a little room for now.

But when Hapgood enters, carrying shopping bags, Blair comes right out with, "Guess what—Kerner's bleep came alive in the night, it seems to be coming from your office." Maggs enters with the morning batch of papers, etc. for Hapgood to process. She sits and goes over them while talking to Wates about the bleep, reviewing what seems to have happened: The bleep went dead a little after 7 and was on the air again when Wates checked at 2 a.m. with a receiver capable of identifying that particular bleep. Wates has diagramed last night's complicated activity on a sheet of pink paper. He wants Hapgood to open her safe for inspection; instead, she calls in Merryweather to ask if he drained the swimming pool last night as ordered. "Right down to the filter," Merryweather replies, and he left an envelope on her desk. Hapgood finds and opens this envelope, takes from it a poker-chip-sized transmitter and tosses it to Wates, commenting, "Ten hours dead in the water. It only drowns the signal, when Merryweather fished it out it was back on the air."

Maggs brings in a tea tray. Hapgood gives him the next move in a chess game she's playing with someone in Ottawa, then gives Merryweather detailed orders for a meet. He listens intently, repeating her instructions, as she orders him to proceed to a school called St. Christopher's at precisely 1:50 and ask the first boy he meets, "Do you know Hapgood? I have a message from Mother." The message is, "The garage key is on Roger's hutch," Roger being a pet hamster. Hapgood has deduced that the animal and the missing key are together. Merryweather leaves on his assignment.

Wates suggests that they now must look into everything Ridley ever touched. Wates is again chagrined to learn a second time that Hapgood and Blair are ahead of him. Blair has been up all night doing just that.

HAPGOOD *(to Wates):* Do you remember Ganchev, our Bulgarian? Paul and I think that's one which needs looking at, did he tell you?

WATES *(that's three times; he is suddenly angry):* You guys!

HAPGOOD: Wates—

WATES: My friends call me Ben!

HAPGOOD: I don't care what your friends call you, I want to tell you something— I will not be tagged by your people in my own *town!* I took them all round Lilly-whites, and I can number them off, don't think I can't, I've been followed by marching bands that did it better, and if they're not pulled by the time I go to lunch, you're off the bus. Is that entirely clear?

WATES: It's clear.

HAPGOOD: Good . . . . . Where are we, Paul?

> *Blair passes her Wates's pink diagram.*

BLAIR: Where we are is that when the bleep died it was no longer in the briefcase, it was in the water, and Ridley was by the pool. We're no further than that. But it's really quite attractive: every month, Ridley helps to pack Kerner's briefcase. That's his job. Kerner's job is handing the briefcase over to the Russians.

WATES: It's made in heaven.

BLAIR: Yes. The opposition don't care which way Kerner is bent, either way he's a channel for Ridley. Yesterday it nearly came apart, but only because of the leak in Moscow. Ridley had to remove the evidence.

WATES: Why did he remove your films?

BLAIR *(smoothly):* Obviously because he put *in* a roll of film, and they all look the same.

WATES: And the bleep?

BLAIR: Oh, you know, pass-the-parcel . . . did you ever play that? The object is not to be the one holding the parcel when the music stops. Ridley drowned the signal when . . . someone else was holding the . . .

WATES *(deflecting):* Yes, all right. *(Pause.)* And he did all that without opening the briefcase?

BLAIR: Ah, yes. That's the bit we're still working on.

WATES: I'd say you have a problem.

BLAIR: We have a hypothesis.

WATES: A *hypothesis?*

BLAIR: Mmm. Actually, it's Mr. Kerner's hypothesis.

> *Blair and Hapgood are complicitly wary of Wates, not secretive but slightly embarrassed, expecting his derision.*

WATES: And is this *hypothesis* a hypothesis you can share?
HAPGOOD: It's twins.
WATES: It's twins?
HAPGOOD: Two Ridleys.
> *Long pause. Blair and Hapgood watch him nervously.*
WATES *(evenly):* Yeah . . . that would do it.
> *Hapgood and Blair relax . . . . .*

Scene 5

At an indoor shooting range, Ridley fires his six-shot firearm at six targets without doing very well—two misses and a hit on a blue target that is supposedly friendly. Ridley reloads, and next time he lets a blue go by before firing at all five other targets, missing only one.

Hapgood enters, as she is putting a small automatic into her handbag. She wants to talk to Ridley privately. The gallery operator discreetly withdraws. Ridley puts the gun he's been firing into a holster in his waistband and wonders what the problem is. Hapgood tells Ridley that he and she are suspected of "playing dirty," using Kerner to pass along secret information. In explaining why they are suspected, she goes over the events at the Pool: the disappearing bleep and—she tells him—radioactive traces on her hands. And Wates is looking into events that transpired in Athens and with Ganchev in Paris. Blair thinks it might be Kerner who is betraying them, but Hapgood refuses to believe it, unless Kerner was turned by a uniquely Russian and powerful form of homesickness.

Ridley thinks that might be it, Kerner might have a family in Russia. When he processed Kerner after the meet, he found a tiny photograph of a boy in a football uniform in Kerner's wallet. In any case, Ridley and Hapgood have been suspended.

RIDLEY: God almighty. What do we do now?
HAPGOOD: You do what Blair tells you. In my office, seven o'clock, and you're there to listen, don't talk out of turn. By the way, we're not telling the Americans.
RIDLEY: Trust me. (*Then a flat challenge.*) Why don't you, as a matter of fact.
HAPGOOD: You're not safe, Ridley. You're cocky and I like prudence, you're street smart and this is a boardgame. In Paris you bounced around like Tigger, you thought it was cowboys and Indians. In Athens you killed a man, and it was the best time of your life, you thought it was sexy. You're not my type. You're my alibi, and I'm yours. Trust doesn't come into it.
RIDLEY: Well, go and fuck yourself, Hapgood . . .
> *He now takes his lighter out and lights his cigarette with deliberate, insolent defiance.*
. . . since we're on suspension. You come on like you're running your joes from the senior common room and butter wouldn't melt in your pants, but you operate like a circular saw, and you pulled me to watch your back because when this is a street business I'm your bloody type all right, and in Athens if you could have got your

David Lansbury as Ridley and Stockard Channing in the title role of Tom Stoppard's *Hapgood*

bodice up past your brain you would have screwed me and liked it. (*He starts to leave.*)

HAPGOOD: Ridley. (*He stops.*) Safety.

RIDLEY: I didn't reload.

HAPGOOD: You saved on the blue.

RIDLEY: That's true.

   He takes his gun from the holster, checks it and puts it back.

This is all right.

HAPGOOD: What is?

RIDLEY: I like it when it's you and me.

Ridley leaves. Kerner enters, coming towards her out of the dark and into the light. She sees him and is not surprised. She takes her radio out of her bag.

HAPGOOD *(to radio):* Is he clear?

RADIO: Green.

HAPGOOD: I'm here to be told.

She puts the radio back into her bag.

(To Kerner.) Do you mean there's another one like him?

KERNER: It's a hypothesis.

HAPGOOD: So where's the other one?

KERNER: Maybe that was the other one.

HAPGOOD: Joseph!

Kerner, chatting amiably with Hapgood, explains that he has studied Wates's diagram of the activities at the Pool and concluded that these complicated movements couldn't have been accomplished by a single person—they required two people, twin Ridleys to match the twin Russians. Kerner muses on the subject of spy stories: "I like them. Well, they're different, you know. Not from each other, naturally. I read in hope, but they all surprise in the same way. Ridley is not very nice: he'll turn out to be all right. Blair will be the traitor: the one you liked. This is how the author says, 'You see! Life is not like books, alas!' They're all like that. I don't mind. I love the language . . . . . Safe house, sleeper, cover, joe . . . I love it."

When Kerner learns all the words, he'll write his own book and turn the usual formula upside down; he will expose the traitor from the beginning—no surprises. He likens the world of spying to particle physics, where an electron "can be here or there at the same moment . . . . . It defeats surveillance." That's what he means about the twins. The mystery of life (he elaborates) is a missing rung between the atom and the grain of sand, "the join between things which are distinct and yet continuous, body and mind, free will and casualty, living cells and life itself; the moment before the foetus. Who needed God when everything worked like billiard balls? What were you going to say?"

Hapgood was going to say that Kerner's spying career will be ended after this operation—though not, of course, his career as a scientist.

HAPGOOD: . . . . . I won't need you any more, I mean I'll need you again—oh, sugar!—you *know* what I mean—do you want to marry me? I think I'd like to be married. Well, don't look like that.

KERNER: What is this?—because of a photograph in my wallet? It is not even necessary, I never look at it.

HAPGOOD: Won't you want to meet him now?

KERNER: Oh, yes. "This is Joe." "Hello, young man."

HAPGOOD *(defiantly):* Well, I'm going to tell him, whether you marry me or not.

KERNER: I'm not charmed by this. If I loved you, it was so long ago I had to tell you in Russian, and you kept the tape running. It was not a safe house for love. The spy was falling in love with the case-officer, you could hear it on the playback. One day you switched off the hidden microphone and got pregnant.

HAPGOOD: That's uncalled for. I loved you.

KERNER: You interrogated me. Weeks, months, every day. I was your thought, your objective . . . If love was like that, it would not even be healthy.

HAPGOOD *(stubbornly):* I loved you, Joseph.

KERNER: You fell in your own honeypot—

HAPGOOD *(flares):* That's a damned lie! You unspeakable *cad!*

KERNER: —and *now* you think you'd like to be married, and tell Joe he has a father after all, not dead after all, only a secret, we are all in the secret service!— no, I don't think so. And suppose I decided to return.

> *That brings her up short.*

HAPGOOD: Where? Why would you do that?

KERNER: *Toska po rodine.*

HAPGOOD: You mustn't say that to me, Joseph. Please don't say it.

KERNER: You would not tell.

HAPGOOD: I might. Take it back.

> *Kerner comforts her.*

KERNER: *Milaya moya, rodnaya moya* . . . it's all right. I am your Joe.

> *She suffers his embrace, then softens into it.*

Cad is good. I like cad.

HAPGOOD: Honeypot . . .

KERNER: Is that wrong?

HAPGOOD: Honey*trap.* And anyway, that's something else. You and your books.

KERNER: I thought you would marry Paul.

> *Wrong. Hapgood stiffens, separates herself.*

HAPGOOD: I'll see you tonight. And let Paul do the talking. Keep your end of it as simple as you can.

KERNER: Worry about yourself. I will be magnificent.

> *Curtain.*

ACT II

Scene 1

In the evening, in Hapgood's office, Blair is sitting at the desk, with Ridley and Hapgood seated to right and left. Kerner enters and sits on the opposite side of the desk from Blair, who explains that this is a friendly rather than a hostile interview. Blair shows Kerner some photos of Kerner's reports that were obtained in Moscow by an American agent. What Kerner wants most to know is, why is Blair sitting in Hapgood's chair? Blair enlightens him: "Mrs. Hapgood isn't here. Mr. Ridley isn't here either. They are on paid leave, which is why they can't be with us this evening, and which is why this is a friendly interview." Kerner's research program will also be temporarily interrupted—he'll be notified of his suspension by messenger.

Kerner suggests that there must be a great number of people who might be able to get their hands on this photographed material one way or another. Paul believes otherwise; because of its nature, it probably had a circulation of only three. Kerner finally confesses that he passed this along to the Russians. Hapgood perceives that Kerner is saying this only to protect her, but Kerner insists he gave it away because it was his to give.

KERNER: ..... Whose did you think it was? Yours? Who are you? You and Blair? Dog-catchers. And now you think I am your dog—be careful the dog didn't catch you.

HAPGOOD: Don't give me that! (*To Blair.*) He's straight, you know damn well he's straight—he's my joe!

KERNER (*laughs, not kindly*): Pride. And your certainty is also amusing—you think you have seen to the bottom of things, but there is no bottom. I cannot see it, and you think you are cleverer than me?

HAPGOOD (*heatedly*): He's a physics freak and a maverick, the Russians picked him for this because he had a good defector profile and he didn't fool us, he fooled them, he despises the Soviets, he'd never play ball, and he has no reason to. *He has no reason*—give me his reason.

KERNER: They found out about Joe.

    Pause. Hapgood poleaxed, as it were. Blair stays level.
Sorry.

BLAIR: How?

KERNER: I don't know.

BLAIR: When?

KERNER: More than a year. They came to me and said, "Well, so you have a child with your British case-officer, O.K.—congratulations, we were stupid, but now it is time to mend the damage. For the sake of the boy."

BLAIR: What did they mean by that?

KERNER: What do *you* think, Paul? I didn't ask. (*To Hapgood.*) I had to, Lilya.

HAPGOOD: Joseph. All you had to do was tell me.

KERNER: That is naive.

So, Kerner says, he passed along information on a disc about how the particle trap works. Blair's immediate reaction is to summon Maggs and ask him to check on Hapgood's son at the school. Maggs tells them Merryweather has reported back: the boy is not at the school, he left with a driver apparently sent by his mother to pick him up, and Merryweather has left Hapgood a note in an envelope (which Maggs delivers). Kerner protests that there's no conflict—he delivered what the Russians asked. Blair informs him, "We intercepted your delivery, they never got your disc," so seizing the boy must be their counter-move.

They are shouting at each other until Ridley suggests they turn over the disc in exchange for the kidnapped boy: "What has Kerner got? (*Derisively.*) The solution to the anti-particle trap! Since when was the anti-particle trap a problem?" It is just a physics stunt, useless even in strategic defense, "Instructions for one go on a bil-lion-dollar train set . . . . . All the particle accelerators on earth produce no more anti-matter in a year than will make a bang like twenty pounds of dynamite." He decries the military usefulness of Kerner's physics, finishing, "It's a joke. I'd trade it for my cat if I had a cat."

Hapgood opens her safe and hands Blair a disc-box. Blair exits, followed by Kerner. Alone with Ridley, Hapgood reveals that she gave Blair a dummy disc, and she has her own plans as to how to proceed from here. She orders Ridley to stay in touch with her on a radio she takes from her handbag and gives him. When Ridley exits, Hapgood takes another radio from a drawer, places it on her desk and asks it, "Is he clear?" "Green," the radio replies.

Maggs comes in and out to say goodnight. Hapgood then picks up the red phone, calls the school and is waiting for her son to come to the phone when Blair enters and remonstrates, "You know, you're going to get into such trouble one day . . . I *mean, that's the Downing Street one-to-one red line*—what are they supposed to think when they pick it up and it's *busy*? . . . . . You use the security link with Ottawa to play chess, you arrive in Vienna after dog-legging through Amsterdam on a false passport and then proceed to send postcards home as if you're on bloody holiday . . . . . For someone who's so safe you're incredibly, I don't know, there's a little anarchist inside you."

But Blair also reassures Hapgood that he's assigned an operative to keep watch over her son at the school until this business is finished, and he warns her, "You know it's going to be tricky doing the swap without a boy to swap."

Kerner enters with vodka and three cups, as Joe comes on the line. His mother was right—the key was in the hamster's hutch. Kerner borrows the phone for a moment or two to hear his son's voice. Then Hapgood tells her son she'll be away for a day, but to phone her the morning of the day after that: "Yes, Joe, I'm here to be told."

Scene 2

In mid-morning, the doorbell rings in what is obviously a photographer's work-plus-living space. Hapgood comes running to answer it. *"We haven't seen her like this. She is as different from her other self as the flat is different from her office; the office being rather cleaner, tidier and better organized."* She opens the door to Ridley, who addresses her as "Mrs. Newton." She takes one look at him, tells him, "You're not what I want." Ridley ignores this, puts down some parcels he has brought and wanders around as though inspecting the premises, as Hapgood uses the phone: "Hello, darling, you're losing your grip—I said a Roman soldier, not an Italian waiter, and also he looks queer to me . . . Don't tell me what I mean, you're gay, he's queer, he's got a queer look about him . . . . ." Ridley comes back, orders Hap-good to hang up, and, when she doesn't, disconnects the call.

HAPGOOD: What do you think you're doing? . . . . . (*He looks at her. She goes from fear to relief.*) You're Betty's friend. God, I am sorry, darling, I'm Celia, don't be offended, being rude about models is the house style, it saves a lot of nonsense about being paid for the reshoot. And anyway, you do look like an Italian waiter. What does Betty want?—I don't owe her any favors, she never does me any, I mean there must be lots of photographic work going in the spy racket. She says I won't keep my mouth shut—can you believe it? Can you smell burning?—Oh, sod!

> *She leaves the room in a hurry. Ridley has been looking at her like somebody looking at a picture in a gallery. He reaches into his jacket and produces his radio.*

RIDLEY *(on radio):* Mother.

HAPGOOD *(on radio):* Ridley.

RIDLEY: You're out of your fucking mind.

HAPGOOD *(on radio):* What's the matter?

RIDLEY: She may be your twin, but there the resemblance ends. She's a pothead, it reeks, she's growing the stuff in the window-box, she won't stop talking, she picks her nose, she looks like shit, I mean it doesn't *begin* . . .

HAPGOOD *(on radio):* Where is she?

RIDLEY: In the kitchen burning things.

HAPGOOD *(on radio):* I'm signing off.

RIDLEY: No, listen—

Hapgood cuts the connection. Ridley unloads the shopping bags he's brought with him containing *"one outfit, suitable for the office."* "Hapgood's twin" comes in, and Ridley reminds her that she's been told by Hapgood to do as he says. They have an appointment in three hours. This Hapgood tries to phone her sister Betty, but Ridley pulls the phone cord from the wall. This infuriates her, but she is mollified by the sight of two batches of bank notes, 2,000 pounds in each, which will be hers when the job is completed, but he warns her that he'll deduct 50 pounds every time she uses foul language. "Fuck yourself," she replies, trying him, and Ridley extracts a 50-pound note and sets fire to it with his cigarette lighter before her eyes.

Hapgood claims she's only doing this because her sister needs her help. Years ago, she says, they were both interviewed for the service, and they took Betty but not Celia. Ridley sends her off to bathe and change into the clothing he's brought. He stays where he is as the scene changes, and *"the next time he moves, he's somebody else."*

Inter-Scene

When the previous set disappears, Ridley is in some transportation center like a railroad station or airport. *"The main thing is that he is a man arriving somewhere. He carries a suitcase. He is a different Ridley. It's like a quantum jump. And now we lose him. Perhaps he walks out. Perhaps the scene change has been continuous and he is now erased by its completion."*

Stockard Channing (Hapgood), David Strathairn (Kerner),
David Lansbury (Ridley) and Josef Sommer (Blair) in *Hapgood*

Scene 3

Blair, with the pink diagram, and Kerner are at the zoo discussing the situation. The scene with the photographs they staged for Ridley's benefit was slightly flawed, Paul notes: Here was Kerner suddenly admitting responsibility for the same kind of pictures—but not the identical ones—Ridley had been sending to Moscow. "We can't have Ridley sitting there wondering why you're owning up to his pictures," Paul comments. And Paul wonders why Kerner wasn't surprised that the photos had different cyclotron numbers on them, "pulled together from different sets, the way somebody might do it at the Moscow end."

KERNER: . . . . . Poor Paul. Everybody is a suspect. (*Reminded.*) Explain something to me. I forgot to ask Elizabeth. Prime suspect: it's in nearly all the books. I don't understand. A prime is a number which won't divide nicely, and all the suspects are prime. It's the last thing to expect with a suspect. You must look for *squares.* The product of twin roots. Four, nine, sixteen . . . what is the square root of sixteen?

BLAIR: Is this a trick question?

KERNER: For you, probably.

BLAIR: Four, then.

KERNER: Correct. But also minus four. Two correct answers. Positive and negative. (*Pause.*) I'm not going to help you, you know. Yes—no, either—or . . . You have been too long in the spy business, you think everybody has no secret or one big secret, they are what they seem or they are the opposite. You look at me and think: *Which is he?* Plus or minus? If only you could figure it out like looking into me to find my root. And then you still wouldn't know. We're all doubles. Even you. Your cover is Bachelor of Arts first class, with an amusing incomprehension of the sciences, but you insist on laboratory standards for reality, while I insist on its artfulness. So it is with us all, we're not so one-or-the-other. The one who puts on the clothes in the morning is the working majority, but at night—perhaps in the moment before unconsciousness—we meet our sleeper—the priest is visited by the doubter, the Marxist sees the civilizing force of the bourgeoisie, the captain of industry admits the justice of common ownership.

BLAIR: And you—what do you admit?

KERNER: My estrangement.

BLAIR: I'm sorry.

KERNER: I'm thinking of going home, perhaps you know.

Blair thinks that going back to Russia might present some special difficulties for Kerner. And Blair still believes "the West is morally superior," and a person is either one thing or the other—and if Kerner is playing a double game at Hapgood's expense, "I'll feed you to the crocodiles." Kerner's reply is, "*You* would betray her before I would." Blair is satisfied, and he asks Kerner, "Is the sister thing going to work?" Kerner had his doubts about it, but he is convinced that it will work with Ridley.

Scene 4

Ridley and Hapgood—as the photographer, Celia, dressed in the clothes Ridley brought her—enter spymaster Hapgood's empty office. Ridley takes an envelope from the desk and extracts a key which he hands to Hapgood so that she can open the middle drawer of the desk and take out an electronic key to the safe. From the safe she takes a disc-box—"a new one, i.e. a sealed once-only box"—and gives it to Ridley. Ridley puts the box together with the envelope and a note that came with it into his bag. He is ready to insert a listening device into the red phone, when Maggs enters with a question from Sydney requiring a yes or no. Ridley starts to put Maggs off, but Hapgood readily peruses the paper and gives Maggs a yes. And Maggs gives her the latest chess move from her Ottawa opponent.

> *The red phone rings. Maggs lifts it up.*
> MAGGS (*to phone*): Mrs. Hapgood's office . . . just a moment.
> *He gives the phone to Hapgood.*

RIDLEY: Shit!

HAPGOOD: What do I do?

RIDLEY: Talk!

HAPGOOD *(to phone):* Hello . . . yes, it's her, it's me . . .

RIDLEY: *"I want to talk to Joe"* . . . *"I want to talk to Joe!"*

HAPGOOD *(covering the phone):* I can't hear! *(Into phone.)* Yes . . . Eleven-thirty . . . *(To Ridley.)* Someone wants a meeting.

RIDLEY: Where? Keep them talking, ask for Joe . . .

HAPGOOD: Yes . . . Where? . . . Right . . .

Ridley is nowhere near ready when she puts the phone down.

RIDLEY: I'll kill you for this!—Eleven-thirty where? *Where?*

Hapgood is still contemplating the phone wearily.

HAPGOOD: Ten Downing Street.

RIDLEY: *What?* Oh, Jesus.

Obviously this was not the call Ridley expected. He continues to work on the red phone while they discuss the sisters' relationship, Hapgood explaining, "She was always the scholarship girl, and I was the delinquent. Having the kid was good for her, she always thought the delinquents had the bastards and the scholarship girls had the weddings. It shook up her view of the world, slightly."

Hapgood starts to light up one of her home-made cigarettes, and Ridley takes it away from her. When Hapgood lapses into a vulgarity, Ridley burns another 50-pound note. When the red phone rings again, Ridley tells Hapgood quickly that these are Joe's kidnappers calling. He orders her to answer the phone and tell the caller she wants to talk to Joe. To give Hapgood's voice an edge of distress, he *"chops her hand across the knuckles with cooly judged force"* with the edge of his own hand.

> *He lifts the red phone now and puts it into her right hand, meanwhile putting the extra earpiece in his ear. Hapgood is whimpering and disoriented.*

HAPGOOD *(into phone):* Hello, where's Joe, I want to talk to Joe—I—Yes—yes—yes—Yes. I heard—can I talk to—

> *Ridley relaxes. He takes the phone from her gently and replaces it. The phone call has taken perhaps fifteen seconds. Hapgood springs away from the desk, from him, crying, comforting her injured hand.*

RIDLEY: You were very good!

HAPGOOD: You bloody maniac!

> *Ridley is disconnecting his eavesdrop, replacing everything into his bag.*

Where's Betty? Is it true about Joe?

RIDLEY: Yes, it's true. But we'll get him back. Eight hours to kill.

> *Ridley retrieves her cigarette from his pocket, lights it and puts it in her mouth. Hapgood draws on the cigarette, still shocked, trembling, settling down.*

You were fine. We can go now. Me first. Count twelve, and I'll see you outside.

> *Ridley picks up his bag. Carefully he takes away her cigarette, takes a drag himself and keeps the cigarette. He opens the door.*

Welcome to the firm.

> *Ridley leaves. Left alone, Hapgood relaxes, although her hand is still painful. Maggs enters, anxious.*

MAGGS: Is everything all right, Mrs. Hapgood?

HAPGOOD: Yes, Maggs—everything's fine. (*She heads through the open door.*) Queen to king one.

MAGGS (*following her out*): Queen to king one.

Scene 5

In a cheap hotel room, Hapgood is resting on the bed while Ridley is trying to raise Mother on his radio, without success. Ridley ignores Hapgood when she asks, "I hardly dare ask you this, but is your mother in the secret service too?"

Ridley checks his gun, while complaining that somebody, maybe Betty, may be lying to him, but he'll try to get her son back for her, if only as a personal favor.

HAPGOOD: You're potty about her, Ernest. I'm disappointed in you. You don't know if you're carrying a torch for her or a gun, no wonder you're confused. You're out on a limb for a boy she put there while she was making the world safe for him to talk properly in and play the game. What a pal, I should have a friend like you.

RIDLEY: It's not her fault. Do you think you cracked it taking snaps of fancy junk? She's all right. Anyway, I like kids, and you never know, now and again someone is telling the truth.

HAPGOOD: You're all right, Ernest. You're just not her type.

RIDLEY: Yeh, she says I'm not safe. Too damned right I'm not. If I was safe I wouldn't be in a whore's hotel with somebody's auntie waiting for a meet that smells like a dead cat.

HAPGOOD: Where would you be?

RIDLEY: Anywhere I like, with a solid gold box for a ticket.

HAPGOOD: You can walk away, Ernie, it's only skirt.

RIDLEY: Shut up.

HAPGOOD (*cranking up*): You'd better be sure, she plays without a board. You haven't got a prayer.

RIDLEY: *Shut up!*

HAPGOOD: If you think she's lying, walk away. If you think bringing back her son will make you her *type,* walk away. You won't get in the money, women like her don't pay out—take my advice and open the box.

RIDLEY (*grabbing her*): *Who the hell are you?*

HAPGOOD: I'm your dream girl, Ernie—Hapgood without the brains or taste.

> *She is without resistance, and he takes, without the niceties; his kiss looks as if it might draw blood.*

Scene 6

> *The Pool. Night. Empty. A towel hangs over the door of Cubicle One (any cubicle). It is dark. Ridley (Two) enters from the lobby carrying a large flashlight. He looks around with the help of the flashlight. He moves upstage. We see only the flashlight now. The flashlight-beam comes back toward us. Ridley (One) walks into the beam . . . . . He carries the sports bag. He approaches the flashlight. The two men embrace briefly. Our Ridley remains; the one with the flashlight retires. (The flashlight, of course, changed hands upstage—here and subsequently we only clearly see, and only hear, the actor who plays Ridley.)*
>
> *Ridley now opens his holdall, takes out a disc-box and posts it under the door with the towel on it. He removes the towel and enters Cubicle Two. He hangs the towel over that door.*
>
> *Hapgood enters from the lobby. She pauses. Timid.*

HAPGOOD: Ernest . . . ?

> *Ridley, with the flashlight, reveals himself.*

RIDLEY: It's O.K. Call the boy.

> *Hapgood hesitates.*

Call the boy.

HAPGOOD: Joe . . .

JOE *(out of sight):* Mummy . . . ?

> *He appears from upstage in the cubicle area. Hapgood moves to where she can see him.*

HAPGOOD: Hello, darling. It's all right.

RIDLEY: Stay there, Joe.

> *Joe halts.*

Do it.

> *Hapgood opens her bag, takes the disc-box from it and posts it under the door of Cubicle Two (where the towel hangs). She pulls the towel down and tosses it over the door into the cubicle. She comes back to Joe and takes his hand.*

HAPGOOD: Off we go.

> *Hapgood takes Joe out through the lobby doors, followed by Ridley. When they have gone, Ridley (Two) comes out of Cubicle Two holding the towel and the disc which Hapgood had posted. He takes the towel to Cubicle One, where it had originally hung, and tosses it over the door. The door of the cubicle opens. Wates is inside. Wates has a gun.*

WATES *(just conversation):* Hey, Ridley. Here's what you do. You walk, you don't talk.

> *Wates walks Ridley upstage into the dark cubicle area. Pause. Blair comes from upstage and approaches Cubicle One. He takes from the cubicle the disc which had been posted there. Blair moves out towards the lobby, but before he gets there Ridley comes in. Ridley is amused.*

BLAIR *(greeting):* Ridley.

RIDLEY *(laughs):* It never smelled Russian, not for a minute. It smelled of private profit. No wonder the kidnap was so clean. Uncle Paul. What a breeze.

BLAIR: Except . . . surely . . .

RIDLEY: Except, the boy will tell. I'm thinking.

BLAIR: I should.

RIDLEY: There was no kidnap.

BLAIR: Better.

RIDLEY: There never was any kidnap. You and Hapgood.

BLAIR: Much better.

RIDLEY: You and Hapgood. Make it look right, make a mug of me and the sister, and afterwards both of you back in place like china dogs on the mantelpiece.

BLAIR: Now you've lost me. Something about a sister.

RIDLEY: The sister is perfect. I know about this. She's here and she's not here.

BLAIR: I keep thinking you said sister.

Hapgood now comes in quietly from the lobby.

Surely you know Mrs. Hapgood?

RIDLEY: I know her sister better. *(To Hapgood.)* Don't I? *(She gives nothing away.)* Give me a minute, I'm slow.

A radio talks softly, briefly. It is in Hapgood's hand. She raises it to her mouth.

HAPGOOD: Mother.

The radio mutters and stops. She puts the radio in her bag.

RIDLEY: Listen, be yourself. These people are not for you, in the end they get it all wrong, the garbage cans are gaping for them. Him most. He's had enough out of you, and you're getting nothing back, he's dry and you're the juice. We can walk out of here, Auntie.

HAPGOOD: You should have opened the box.

RIDLEY: I could have walked away with it any time and let the boy take his chances. This way you got both, my treat.

HAPGOOD: There was nothing in there except a bleep.

Pause.

RIDLEY: Well, now I don't know which one you are. One of them fucks and one of them—

HAPGOOD: Don't, Ridley—

Ridley is going to kill her . . . . . Everything goes into slow motion, beginning with and including the sound of Hapgood's gun, lasting probably five seconds. Ridley has got as far as taking his gun out when Hapgood shoots him. Meanwhile, Wates is leaning into view, upstage, slightly late, gun in hand . . . . . Blair doesn't move.

With strobe lighting, the scene changes from the cubicle area to the lobby outside it, with Ridley's body on a stretcher. Ridley Two, in handcuffs, looks sadly at the face under the blanket before being led away under arrest. Bearers carry off the body; Wates shakes hands with Hapgood and departs. Hapgood tells Blair firmly that she'll never forgive him for actually bringing her son Joe into the caper, which they'd planned and he'd promised to execute without the boy being present. Blair shrugs this off, convinced that she'll get over it.

HAPGOOD: No.

BLAIR: What about your network?

HAPGOOD: *What network?!* Ridley's blown it inside out! Christ, Paul, I must have been buying nothing but lies and chickenfeed since Joe was in his pram!

BLAIR: One has to pick oneself up and carry on. We can't afford to lose. It's them or us, isn't it?

HAPGOOD: What is? What exactly? The game has moved on. Read the signs. It's over.

BLAIR: Try telling that to the opposition.

HAPGOOD: Oh, the KGB! The opposition! Paul, we're just keeping each other in business, we should send each other Christmas cards—oh, f-f-fuck it, Paul!

> *So that's that. Blair turns away, hesitates and leaves. The next time Hapgood moves, she is standing by the rugby pitch.*

Scene 7

Hapgood is watching the boys practice, when Kerner approaches her. He has completed all his plans for leaving, and he's come to say goodbye, telling Hapgood, "Paul thinks I was a triple, but I was definitely not, I was past that, quadruple at least, maybe quintuple."

Joe comes to say hello to Hapgood, wearing a tracksuit which he takes off and gives to his mother, leaving himself in his clean rugby uniform. Hapgood introduces Kerner to him. Joe greets Kerner politely, then runs off to his game.

KERNER: Very nice. Very English. *(Pause.)* Of course, he *is* half English, one forgets that. Well . . . good.

HAPGOOD: Do you want to stay for tea? They lay it on for parents.

KERNER: Better not, I think.

HAPGOOD: Oh, Joe.

> *She breaks down. He holds her, awkwardly.*

Prosty, Josef (I'm sorry, Joseph).

KERNER: *Da nyet—vyet u menya byl vybar, Lilichka* (No, no. I had a choice too, Lilichka).

HAPGOOD: *Nyet tagda u tibya nye bylo vybora—*(You had no choice then).

KERNER: *Da—mu ya pashol . . . ya napishu kagda dayedu . . .* (Yes, I'd better go. I'll write when I get there).

> *Kerner kisses her and starts to leave.*

HAPGOOD: How can you go? *How can you?*

She turns away. The game starts. Referee's whistle, the kick. After a few moments, Hapgood collects herself and takes notice of the rugby. When the game starts, Kerner's interest is snagged. He stops and looks at the game.

Come on, St. Christopher's—we can win this one! Get those tackles in!

She turns and finds that Kerner is still there. She turns back to the game and comes alive.

Shove!—heel!—well heeled!—well out!—move it!—*move it,* Hapgood!—that's good—that's better!

Curtain.

Best Play Citation

○○○
○○○
○○○
○○○
○○○
○○○ # A TUNA CHRISTMAS

A Play in Two Acts

BY JASTON WILLIAMS, JOE SEARS AND ED HOWARD

Cast and credits appear on page 320

JASTON WILLIAMS is, like the characters in his play, a Texan, raised in Crosbyton and educated at San Jacinto College in Houston. He became acquainted with his co-author Joe Sears 20 years ago when both were members of San Antonio's First Repertory Company. The majority of their credits to date are acting credits in both classics and new plays far and wide across the spectrum of American production. Williams also directed a new musical, Bad Girls Upset by the Truth, *at the Alliance Theater in Atlanta.*

In 1979 Williams co-founded the Production Company of Atlanta and Austin with his other collaborator, Ed Howard. Sears joined them in the creation of Greater Tuna, *whose early stagings took place in Atlanta and Austin. It finally arrived off Broadway at Circle in the Square Downtown October 21, 1982 for 501 performances. This was the authorship trio's only New York credit prior to the arrival on Broadway this season of their sequel to* Greater Tuna, A Tuna Christmas, *on December 15 for a limited engagement of 20 performances as a stopover on their lengthy national tour, picking up their first Best Play citation in passing.*

Williams is a recipient of the Texas Governor's Award for contribution to the arts, and he performed at Gov. Ann Richards's inauguration and Kennedy Center's Texas Festival in 1990, and at the Austin salute to the late writer and folk hero John Henry

Faulk, to whom A Tuna Christmas *is dedicated. His work on the* Tunas *has been honored with Helen Hayes Award nominations in Washington and a Los Angeles Drama-Logue Award for writing and acting. He has finished a new play entitled* Romeo and Thorazine *and plans to do* The Merry Wives of Windsor *with Sears next season. Williams resides in Austin.*

JOE SEARS came from Bartlesville, Oklahoma and Northeastern State University in Tahlequah to team up with Jaston Williams two decades ago portraying half of the dozens of Texas characters onstage in Greater Tuna *and* A Tuna Christmas, *as well as co-authoring them. His acting career has included a year with Performing Arts Repertory Theater in New York, appearances in summer stock, TV, outdoor drama, eight Shakespeare plays and the successful national tours and other manifestations of the two* Tunas, *stopping in such places as the Hartford, Conn. Stage Company, Houston's Alley Theater, the American Spoleto Festival, Kennedy Center and the White House in a command performance for President and Mrs. George Bush, and as far afield as the Edinburgh Festival in Scotland. He of course shared with his co-authors the acting and writing accolades of Helen Hayes nominations in Washington and Drama-Logue in Los Angeles, as well as this 1994–95 Best Play citation in New York. He is making his movie debut this year in the Western* The Good Old Boys. *He is now a Texan, residentially speaking, living in Austin.*

ED HOWARD, director of the Best Play A Tuna Christmas *as well as its co-author, is an Alabaman hailing from Tuscumbia. He received a B.A. in religion and philosophy from Birmingham-Southern College and his M.A. in stage directing from the University of Alabama before joining forces with Jaston Williams in the founding of the Production Company of Atlanta in 1979 and the creation with Williams and Joe Sears and staging of* Greater Tuna *and* A Tuna Christmas *in all of their tours and other presentations. Howard's career has included acting and design as well as directing and playwriting (he staged Romulus Linney's* Laughing Stock *in New York and, more recently,* Love Arnette *written and performed by Dianne Murray at the Hyde Park Theater in Austin). At present he is writing* The Tempest Tossed, *a Caribbean musical about Shakespeare, and* Daisy Faye and the Miracle Man, *a dramatization of Fannie Flagg's novel about growing up in Alabama. Howard now lives in Doraville, Georgia.*

Time: Christmas Eve
Place: Tuna, third smallest town in Texas

A Tuna Christmas consists of 22 characters (both men and women played by Joe Sears and Jaston Williams) in two acts and seven scenes depicting events and confrontations in and around a small Texas town on Christmas Eve, with many of the

characters appearing in more than one scene. In order to present this comedy in full
flavor, we represent it in these pages with three of its scenes in their entirety, bringing
in seven of the characters.

ACT I

Scene 3: Didi's Used Weapons

> *We hear an instrumental version of "Away in a Manger." The Christmas
> tree of the previous scene is replaced with a scruffy prefab tree which is
> strung with ornaments made out of shell casings, bullets and other instru-
> ments of violence. We are in Didi Snavely's used weapons shop. There is
> a customer counter, and . . . . . tables and chairs and radio complete the
> set. Every time someone enters or leaves the shop from the outside door,
> we hear a cowbell ring offstage.*
>
> *As the music fades, Didi Snavely enters singing her own version of a
> popular Christmas song . . . . . She is smoking an imaginary cigarette and
> is carrying a box of tree ornaments of the same types as those already on
> the tree. Didi puts the box on the table, hangs a grenade ornament on the
> tree and looks around for her husband.*

DIDI *(sings):*

Frosty the Snowman

Was a jolly, happy soul

With a . . .

> *She takes a long puff off her cigarette, then picks up the song without
> missing a beat.*

. . . out of coal.

Frosty the Snowman

Had a broomstick up . . .

(Calls to her husband): R.R.? R.R. . . damn you, get in here.

> *R.R. Snavely enters.*

R.R.: Yeah, Didi. I'm right here.

DIDI: Right here, my rear. What'd you do with those dud grenades? I need a few
more to finish trimming that tree.

R.R.: The last time I saw them, your mama was going through them in the powder
room.

DIDI: Where?

R.R.: In the powder room.

DIDI: The powder room! God—damn it, R.R., how many times have I warned
you about that gun powder?

R.R.: You said they were duds.

DIDI: Poor Mama's confused again. She thinks those grenades are pineapples
that Dottie and Clyde sent out from California. Well, don't just stand there like a
government employee, get in that powder room and find those grenades . . .

R.R. exits and changes to Pearl Burras.

God, I'm not even comfortable smoking in there. I live in fear that Mama's gonna walk into the kitchen to fix a fruit salad and blow us all the way to Tierra del Fuego.

We hear the sound of bullets dropping offstage where R.R. has just exited.

Hey! Hey! Hey! Sweep up whatever you spilled in there, R.R. Pathetic. I thought when the sky turned black on my wedding day that it was just Texas weather. Mama swore it was an omen, but I wouldn't listen. Well, it's too late now.

We hear the cowbell ring, and Pearl Burras enters.

C'mon in, Pearl.

PEARL: Merry Christmas, Didi.

DIDI: Be right with you, Pearl. (*Toward R.R.*) R.R., don't break up those shell casings. I'm shipping those off to Little Rock. (*Back to Pearl.*) Pearl, I've been meaning to call you. Why didn't you do a yard display this year?

PEARL: I've thrown in the towel, Didi. Vera Carp wouldn't let go of that trophy if you sprayed her with mustard gas.

DIDI: Well, maybe she will and maybe she won't. That giant Christmas tree of mine out there is gonna be hard to top. But I really thought you had a contender last year with that Christmas at Colonel Sanders'.

PEARL: Oh, it took me too long to get all those chickens in their little elf costumes. No, Didi, I'm here looking for something to kill bluejays with.

DIDI: Oh, Pearl, have I got a gun for you. Now, this here is a Canadian hummingbird derringer. It's light, easy to handle, you can keep it in your purse, and it'll blow the fuzz off a gnat's ass at thirty-five yards.

PEARL: I, I can't use a gun. It's too loud. My hens won't lay.

DIDI: No problem. R.R., see if we've got any poisoned bird seed in there.

PEARL: Oh, no. Poison's out. I quit using that after I killed Henry's bird dog.

DIDI (*toward R.R.*): Never mind, R.R. But fix me a cup of hot chocolate while you're in there, and try not to scald the milk. Pitiful. Well, let me think.

Pearl opens a drawer.

PEARL: Oh, Didi! There's snakes in your drawers!

DIDI: Oh, don't worry, Pearl, those snakes are rubber. Hey now, they're great for scarin' off pests. You sprinkle a few of these babies around the yard, and those bluejays won't slow down till they hit Oklahoma.

PEARL: I don't know, Didi. I can't be around anything that don't have feet.

DIDI: Some people are funny that way. You know, I left one of those rubber snakes in my sister's mailbox one time.

PEARL: You know, she screamed like white trash at a tent meeting.

DIDI: She sure did. She claimed it sped up her hair loss. But Dottie's hair has always been so thin you could count it.

PEARL: Oh, I've seen better hair on anchovies.

DIDI: . . .but back to your bird problem. I guess the only thing left is the old sling shot and ball bearing routine. Now, a sling shot is not as enjoyable as a gun—to me. But there is nothing like a sling shot for nostalgia.

Didi puts down her cigarette to get out a sling shot which she wraps and gives to Pearl.

PEARL: Oh, yeah. And I've got all those marbles I've had at home for years. I got 'em for Bertha's kids when they were little, but Charlene swallowed so many I put 'em away. But I still got 'em.

DIDI: That's smart, Pearl. One person's clutter can be another person's weapon. My mama always taught me that.

PEARL: Oh, how is your mama? Is Mimi feeling better? Dixie said she tried to cut off all her hair.

DIDI: Oh hell, she did. Poor Mama's just goin' down hill every day. She nearly gassed us twice last week. Twice! Tried to fry Rice Krispies the other day. We're lookin' for a home for her now. I tell ya, it just damn near kills me. And this morning she hops outta bed, says she's the Phantom.

PEARL: Oh, you need to find her a home, quick.

DIDI: Ah hell, it gets worse. She says you and Dixie Deberry put her up to it.

PEARL (*laughing it off*): Oh, no!

DIDI: I tell ya, Pearl, the mind is the first thing to go. Let me get her out. She'd love to see ya. Mama.

Didi opens the door.

PEARL: Oh, Didi, don't disturb her.

DIDI: Mama. Mama. Oooh, Mama! Now you're gonna mop that up.

Pearl exits and changes to R.R.

Mama. Pearl Burras is here. You remember Pearl, Mama . . . Pearl . . . Pearl! Ahhh, never mind.

Didi closes the door, then turns around and sees that Pearl is gone.

Well, what scared her off? Oh, hell, I'll just put that on her bill.

Didi picks up her cigarette, then goes to the ornament box, picks out an ornament and hangs it on the tree. As she does so, she sings a Christmas carol.

Sleigh bells ring, are you listenin'?

In the . . .

She takes another long puff off her cigarette and again picks up the song without missing a beat.

. . . glistenin'.

A beautiful sight, we're happy tonight . . .

(*Calls offstage.*) R.R.? R.R. . . did you find them?

R.R. (*voice*): Find what?

DIDI: The grenades. God—damn it. That's what I sent you in there for.

R.R. enters.

R.R.: Oh, I forgot. But I found that old *National Geographic* back there that we'd thought . . .

DIDI (*cuts R.R. off*): Yeah. I'll bet. Useless, God, I'll do it myself. You stay here, look after the customers. Don't cross that line. God, if you were a cat I'd have you fixed.

Didi exits and changes to Petey. R.R. watches her go, then shuffles about aimlessly. The cowbell rings as Petey Fisk enters with Fresno, an imaginary coyote on a leash.

PETEY: Hey, R.R.

R.R.: Hi, Petey, Hi, Fresno. Don't let Didi see Fresno. She shoots coyotes on sight.

PETEY: He's only half coyote, and I've nearly turned him into a vegetarian.

R.R.: Well, she shoots coyotes and vegetarians, so watch out. What happened to your finger?

PETEY: Oh, Fresno regressed. I think he was just a little low on protein. I was wondering, do you sell muzzles?

R.R.: No. Didi says they're a waste of shelf space. Why have a guard dog if he can't bite? She'll be right back.

PETEY: I gotta run. Oh, you see any U.F.O.s lately?

R.R.: Not any big ones.

PETEY: Me neither. Bye, R.R.

Fresno pulls Petey off, and the cowbell rings. Petey changes to Didi. R.R. takes an ornament from the box and hangs it on the tree. From offstage we hear Didi's voice.

DIDI (*voice*): R.R. R.R. God—damn it. I want you to get back into this mace and tear gas department and put everything back into alphabetical order.

R.R. takes a grenade ornament from the tree and mimes tossing it in Didi's direction, then mimes an explosion.

God, this is no way to run a business.

R.R.: I'm right on it, Didi.

Didi enters, carrying a single hand grenade ornament.

DIDI: And that milk's boiling over.

R.R.: Uh oh.

He runs off and changes to Sheriff.

DIDI: Mama told me I was marrying the original missing link, but I wouldn't listen. Oh, well. Too late now.

Didi crosses to the tree and hangs up the grenade. As she does, she sings another of her own carols.

All I want for Christmas is a Bowie knife,
A Bowie knife, just a Bowie knife.
All I want for Christmas is a Bowie knife,
So I can stab my ignorant husband.

She is interrupted by the cowbell, as Sheriff Buford Givens appears at the counter.

SHERIFF: Hey, Didi. How you?

DIDI: I was fine 'til just now. Whatever you want, we're out of.

SHERIFF: You should have been a comedian, you know that?

DIDI: I'll accept that as a compliment coming from the town joke. Some sheriff. You've been wagging that gun around for years, and not one notch on it. You're an example of wasted tax dollars.

Joe Sears as Bertha in *A Tuna Christmas*

SHERIFF: Well, what do you think about this? I'm requisitioning all your book-keeping records and receipts.

DIDI: Now don't tell me someone went and taught you how to read.

SHERIFF: I'm doing some undercover work trackin' down that Christmas Phantom.

DIDI: I'm not showin' my records to nobody.

SHERIFF: You might as well cooperate, Didi. If you make me come back, I'll bring a subpoena.

DIDI: If you think you're gonna come in here and snoop in my bookkeeping, you'd better bring a Chinese dinner for six.

SHERIFF *(hurt)*: You make it damn hard for me to do my job, Didi.

   The cowbell rings, as Sheriff exits and changes to Ike. Didi yells after him.

DIDI: Hey! Hey! You lay a finger on my filing cabinet, and you'll scratch your ass with a stump for the rest of your life!

Didi starts to pick out an ornament from the box. The cowbell rings, and Ike Thompson appears at the counter.

IKE: Hey, Didi, you gotta minute?

DIDI: Maybe. That depends on what you're buying.

IKE: Now, I've been a good customer, you know that.

DIDI: Yeah, the last thing you bought from me was a quarter's worth of b.b.s for that delinquent kid of yours.

IKE: He never had any problems 'til he ate all that plant food. Say, Didi, have you seen Hank Bumiller?

DIDI: You know, Ike, I was in such a rush to get to work this morning I didn't even have time to check the gutters.

IKE: That ain't funny, Didi. I just talked to Bertha. I gotta find Hank, or it's gonna be a blue Christmas for a whole lotta folks.

DIDI: Boo, hoo, hoo. I repeat, are you here to buy anything?

IKE: I'll be back for that later. Right now I've got to find Hank.

DIDI: Well, Bertha's parking her car across the street right now. Why don't you ask her?

IKE: *Adios amigos.*

Ike exits and changes to Bertha as the cowbell rings. Didi calls after him.

DIDI: You'd better find Hank Bumiller, or it'll be *vaya con Dios.*

The telephone rings. Didi sings another carol while she crosses to answer it.

Good King What's-his-name went down . . .

(*Picks up the phone*): Didi's Used Weapons. If we can't kill it, it's immortal . . . Hello, Dottie . . . Well, it's usually bad news when you call, Dottie. What's the matter, is your plane late, or what? . . . What do you mean, you're not comin'? . . . Well, great. Why? . . . Ah, hell . . . Ah, hell . . . Ah, hell, he's always had that . . . Well. Don't they have anti-fungal creams in California, Dottie? . . . Well, you still gotta come get Mama . . . No. No. I had her last Christmas . . . I know you took her for Easter, Dottie. She's still got egg dye in her hair and under her nails and God knows where else. We can't even take her to church . . . Oh, yeah? Well, I've got a Christmas wish for you, too, Dottie. Yeah, well, I hope Santa Claus craps down your chimney.

Didi hangs up the phone.

God, it is hell being a twin.

The cowbell rings, and Bertha enters.

BERTHA: Hi, Didi. Are you busy?

DIDI: Come on in, Pickles. Have a cup of coffee. I'm never too busy to chat with you.

BERTHA: Well, I thought you might be frazzled with the last-minute rush.

DIDI: Business is always brisk when the Phantom is on the loose. You be sure to thank Stanley for me.

BERTHA: I hope to God the cops don't catch him.

DIDI: Oh, Sheriff Givens couldn't catch a cold in the Klondike.

BERTHA: Well, Didi, I really stopped by to see if you have any burglar alarms left.

DIDI: I sold my last one yesterday. Are you having a problem with prowlers?

BERTHA: No, nothing like that. I just wanted something to wake me up when my worthless husband comes sneaking in late at night.

DIDI: Has Hank been out tom-cattin' again?

BERTHA: It's so embarrassing. I tell you, Didi, it's hard to hold up when the whole town knows my husband's as useless as ice trays in hell.

DIDI: Don't get me started. R.R.'s been on a wandering binge lately. You know, Bertha, I often wonder how such well brought-up girls like you and me could have married so bad.

BERTHA: It's a mystery.

DIDI: R.R.'s drinkin' has only gotten worse. He wanders off so much, I decided I'd better find out something about safe sex.

BERTHA (flustered): Oh, Didi! I swear!

DIDI: Can you imagine how depressed I got when I found out that's what we'd been doin' all along?

BERTHA: Well, I suppose some things are better left unknown.

DIDI: Amen, hallelujah.

BERTHA: Was that Ike Thompson I saw sneakin' away?

DIDI: Yeah. There's another one just as worthless as titties on a boar hog. But back to your Hank problem. I can order that burglar alarm for you.

BERTHA: No, That 's all right, Didi. I'll just do what I've always done.

DIDI: What's that?

BERTHA: Rearrange all the furniture and unscrew all the light bulbs.

Bertha and Didi both laugh.

DIDI: Pickles, Pickles, Pickles. We sure knew what we were doing back in high school when we voted you the class wit.

BERTHA: Sometimes you have to laugh to keep from cryin'. Well, I'd better get home. It'll take me a while to move that sofa.

She laughs. Didi laughs too.
Merry Christmas, Didi.

DIDI: Merry Christmas, Bertha.

We hear the cowbell as Bertha exits . . . . . Didi calls after her.
Don't strain your back.

Didi crosses to the radio while she sings another carol.
Just hear that ring, ring, ring-l-ing,
Jing, jing, jing-l-ing, too,
Because it's . . .

She takes a drag on her cigarette and comes back into the song right on the beat.
. . . with you.

Didi turns on the radio. The voice of Leonard Childers comes over it.

LEONARD (*radio tape*): Okay, folks, we're back with Leonard's Let-the-Stops-Out Radio Shopping Spree. Now folks, I haven't sold anything in weeks. I'm so desperate, I'll take hot checks. Where's your Christmas spirit? We've got great merchandise here. C'mon now, gimme a call.

> *During the above speech Didi picks up the phone and dials. She turns down the radio.*

DIDI: Leonard? Didi Snavely. No, I didn't call to buy nothin'. I called to talk to you about that egg separator I bought from you last March. It had a ten-month guarantee . . . It broke in nine and a half . . . What do you mean you don't want to talk about it on the air? Well, maybe you'd rather talk about that red-headed bank clerk from Sand City that you go bowling with every other Friday night . . . Yeah, I know your wife could be listening, I hope to God she is. Can you hear me, Reba? Reba? Can you hear me? . . . Don't talk to me about ruining your Christmas, Leonard. My husband's a drunk who sees flyin' saucers. My mama's lost what's left of her mind. My sister, Dottie, had to call up and show her butt. My Christmas has been ruined. I just thought I'd ring you up and ruin yours.

> *We hear a car speed by.*

Well, I just saw Reba heading that way in her Land Rover. If I were you, Leonard, and I wanted to see New Year's in one piece, I'd start dashing through the snow.

> *Didi hangs up the phone. She starts to sing another carol as she crosses to pick up the box of ornaments.*

Jingle bells, jingle . . .

> *She puffs again.*

. . . the way . . .

> *The lights fade, and an instrumental tag of "Jingle Bells" swells over Didi's last phrase as she exits.*

ACT II

Scene 3A: Petey's backyard

> *We hear Petey Fisk calling from the distance. He enters to a stage that is empty, save for table and chairs. All around him is a vast, starlit sky. Petey is heavily bandaged and is using a crutch and is accompanied by his imaginary pets—Paula, Fresno and Vera's runaway sheep. He carries a small evergreen tree with its roots in a burlap ball.*

PETEY: Fresno! Fresno! Fresno, sit. Stay. Now, Fresno, I know you're half coyote and you're not used to being stampeded by hostile sheep. But if you bite me one more time you're going to be making the call of the wild. And you sheep stay over by the gate. Don't stampede the coyote. This natural enemy thing is about to kill me. I'm down to my last arm and leg. One more injury and we'll all starve to death. And Paula, I know iguanas are prone to depression—but you're gonna end up with a zipper and a snap if you don't lighten up. You all ought to be ashamed of your-

Jaston Williams as Petey Fisk, with stand-ins for his
imaginary pets, in a scene from *A Tuna Christmas*

selves. Where's your Christmas spirit? Hey, hey, stay calm! Stay calm! Stay calm!
Stay calm! . . . Just stay calm. Let me look for the star . . . There it is. Fresno . . .
     He beckons to Fresno.
There it is, shining like the very first Christmas. We were all a part of it. Shepherds
were watching their flocks of sheep by night—obviously there was a coyote prob-

lem—when they saw that star. And Joseph and Mary found no room at the inn, but the innkeeper said they could stay in the stable, and that's where the baby was born, among the cattle and the sheep—and the iguanas. Look at it shine. You know, the light from that star left before there was even anybody here to see it. It's like looking at eternity. Shining down on everything—joy and sorrow, man and nature, hatred and forgiveness. Peace on earth, good will to everybody. I never get tired of hearing that. Well, that's something to wish for.

> *He motions to his pets.*

Come on now, Fresno. Paula, let's go inside. Girls, stay calm. We all need our rest. Tomorrow's Christmas Day.

> *Petey exits and changes to Didi, as the lights fade and music swells, a choral of "Hark the Herald Angels Sing."*

Scene 3B: Didi's backyard

> *The music fades out, and lights fade to a dim night scene. The stage is bare except for the table and chairs. We are in Didi's and R.R.'s yard. R.R. enters pulling one end of a long, tangled, orange extension cord. He is whistling "We Wish You a Merry Christmas." As he finishes the tune, he hears an eerie sound effect. He drops the cord and exits to investigate the sound. Didi enters with her cigarette and picks up the end of the cord. As she crosses, she sings a Christmas carol.*

DIDI *(sings):*

Oh, holy night, the stars so brightly shining.

It is the . . .

> *She takes a drag from her cigarette, then picks up the tune right on beat.*

. . . birth.

> *At the other side of the stage she pulls out another cord and plugs the two together. The stage is illuminated from offstage by the blinding lights of her aluminum display tree. She steps back to admire it a moment, then continues singing.*

Now that is one heavenly light! (*Sings.*)

Fall on your knees,

Oh, hear the angel . . .

> *R.R. enters whistling "We Wish You a Merry Christmas." Didi stops singing.*

R.R., where in the hell have you been?

R.R.: Merry Christmas, Didi.

DIDI: Is it? God—damn you, you did it again.

R.R.: You weren't supposed to peek at your Christmas present, Didi.

DIDI: Shut up. I have put up with your drinkin' . . .

R.R.: I've been getting better . . .

DIDI: Your tardiness . . .

R.R.: I've been trying . . .

DIDI: Your U.F.O. sightings . . .

R.R.: I can't help it.

DIDI: And God knows the books never balance. But this Christmas is the topper, R.R. I have dropped hints for two months that all I wanted for Christmas was Sal Mineo's Greatest Hits, and what do you give me? . . . . . A Clue game!

R.R.: We can take it back . . .

DIDI: We can't return it now. Mama's already swallowed half the pieces.

R.R.: I'm sorry, Didi.

DIDI *(screaming)*: God—damn it. If I could have one Christmas wish, it would be that one of your U.F.O.s would pick you up tonight and haul your dead weight off to kingdom come!

(*Sings*): Fa la la la la la la la la . . .

> *Didi exits singing . . . . . R.R. sighs. He starts to whistle "We Wish You a Merry Christmas" again. Three lines into the tune, a U.F.O. with massive lights and sound effects travels across the stage above R.R. He looks off-stage, and a high-tech, illuminated ramp lets down from the stage wing. R.R. looks in wonder, then exits up the ramp as the U.F.O. plays a huge, symphonic ". . . And a Happy New Year." The ramp closes, and the lights fade to black with only stars remaining as we hear the sound of the U.F.O. leaving.*

Pulitzer Prize

THE YOUNG MAN
FROM ATLANTA

A Full-Length Play in One Act

BY HORTON FOOTE

Cast and credits appear on page 359

HORTON FOOTE was born in Wharton, Tex. March 14, 1916 into a family with deep, multigenerational roots in that Gulf Coast town. His father ran a local clothing store, and his mother was a gifted pianist. He left home at 16 for an acting apprenticeship at the Pasadena Playhouse and later studied with a Stanislavski protegée, Tamara Daykarhanova, in New York City. His acting career merged with a writing career at the turn of the decade, as he joined American Actors Theater and that group put on his one-act Wharton Dance *in the fall of 1940 and his full-length* Texas Town *the following spring.*

Foote's playscripts produced in New York in the 1940s and 1950s at various levels have included Only the Heart *(1942),* Two Southern Idylls *(Miss Lou and* The Girls, *1943),* The Lonely *and* Goodby to Richmond *(1944),* Daisy Lee *(1944),* Celebration *(1948),* The Chase *(1952),* The Trip to Bountiful *(1953) and* The Traveling Lady *(1954). His parallel career of distinguished authorship for the large and small screen (and the novel, for that matter) has taken in more than a dozen major works for Fred Coe, "Playhouse 90" and others in TV's golden age and numerous screen plays including the Academy Award-winning* To Kill a Mockingbird *and* Tender Mercies.

169

Foote withdrew from the fray to a farm in New Hampshire for most of the 1970s. There he began writing the nine-play cycle The Orphans' Home, *based on stories his father had told him about the family, beginning in 1902 with his father's leaving home at age 12 and ending with the death of Foote's maternal grandfather in 1928, set against the background of the decline of the cotton plantations and the rise of the mercantile class in the Gulf Coast area. The nine, some already produced on the stage and screen and all to be published by Grove Press in sets of three, are* Roots in a Parched Ground, Convicts, Lily Dale *(produced off Broadway November 20, 1986 for 112 performances),* The Widow Claire *(also produced off Broadway December 17, 1986 for 150 performances and Foote's first Best Play citation),* Courtship, On Valentine's Day, 1918, Cousins *and* The Death of Papa.

This season, off off Broadway's Signature Theater devoted its entire schedule to four Foote plays: Talking Pictures *(September 23),* Night Seasons *(November 4),* The Young Man From Atlanta *(January 27) and* Laura Dennis *(March 10). This limited 26-performance engagement of* The Young Man From Atlanta *was its world premiere, and it is cited here as Foote's second Best Play and was awarded the 1995 Pulitzer Prize (see Mel Gussow's review in the Plays Produced Off Off Broadway section of this volume).*

Foote has been active on New York and cross-country stages in the 1980s and 1990s. His The Man Who Climbed the Pecan Trees *was presented in the 1st New York International Festival of the Arts in the summer of 1988, and his program of three one-acts* The Roads to Home (A Nightingale, The Dearest of Friends, Spring Dance) *was produced off Broadway in the fall of 1992. In regional theaters there were his* Dividing the Estate *(Princeton 1989, Cleveland 1990),* Talking Pictures *(Sarasota 1990, Houston 1991) and* Night Seasons *(Teaneck, N.J. 1993). And in April 1989 he traveled to Independence, Kansas to receive the William Inge Foundation's prestigious award for lifetime achievement in the American theater.*

Foote is a widower, with two sons and two daughters, and lives in Wharton, Tex.

Time: Spring 1950
Place: Houston, Texas

Scene 1

SYNOPSIS: Will Kidder, in his late 50s, is seated at his desk at the Sunshine Southern Wholesale Grocery, with a telephone nearby. Tom Jackson, 35, who also works at this company, enters, and the two have a friendly discussion of their personal affairs. Will has just moved into his new $200,000 house which has been stocked with new furniture. Seeking to cover this expense with an increase in life insurance, Will went for a routine physical the day before, and the doctor found a slight heart condition—nothing serious.

Will, dirt poor when he was a boy, now wants only the best—the best house in the best city in the best country of the world, with the best wife and working for "the best wholesale produce company." Tom's comment, referring to the company, is "Was." "Will be again," asserts Will, who's worked here nearly 40 years and thrives on aggressive competition: "I'm a competitor, son."

Will shows Tom Jackson a photo of his son Bill, whom Tom has never met. Bill liked math and loved to study. During World War II he volunteered for the Air Force and afterwards he decided not to settle in Houston—Will doesn't know why—and moved to Atlanta, where he got a job traveling for an Atlanta company.

WILL: He was in Florida for his company, and he stopped at this lake to go for a swim. He couldn't swim. Never learned, and I never remember hearing of him going swimming before. Anyway, that's what he did this day. The man that owned the lake was there alone, and he said it never occurred to him to ask him if he could swim. He said he went into the bath house and changed his clothes and came out and waved to him as he walked into the lake. He said he just kept walking until he was out of sight. The man got concerned when he couldn't see him any longer, and he yelled to him, and when he got no answer he got his boat and rowed out to where he had last seen him and found his body. He had drowned. He was thirty-seven—thirty-seven. Drowned. Our only child. I wanted to have more, but my wife had such a difficult time when he was born that we never had any more.

JACKSON: I wonder why if he couldn't swim?

WILL: That's what everyone asked. It was the middle of the day. Why in the middle of the day in a lake in Florida out in deep, deep water if you can't swim.

   A pause.

Everyone has their theories, and I appreciate their theories, but I'm a realist. I don't need theories. I know what happened. He committed suicide. Why, I don't know.

JACKSON: Oh, that's terrible.

WILL: I know. I know. I've never told anybody that before. But that's what I think. I always have. I feel close to you, son. I suppose I shouldn't be saying these things, even to you. But I have no one else I feel I can confide in.

JACKSON: Did he leave children?

WILL: No. He never married. If he even went with a girl, we never knew about it. I've never told my wife what I thought happened. We never discuss that part of it. We talk about how much we miss him and what a fine man he was and what a considerate son, and he was certainly that. A fine and considerate son. My wife has become extremely religious since his death. She was always interested in religion, but now that's all she thinks about. God this and God that.

JACKSON: Was your son religious?

WILL: No more than I am. I can take it or leave it. He joined the Episcopal Church as a young man. Your job was the one I hoped would interest him here in the company, but it didn't.

Miss Lacey, Will's secretary, comes in to tell her boss "that same young man" is on the phone, but Will won't talk to him. Miss Lacey exits, and Will explains to Tom that the caller was Bill's roommate in Atlanta, ten years younger than Bill. The Kidders first met the young man when he came here for Bill's funeral, during which "he got hysterical and cried more than my wife." He told the Kidders that their son had become very devout in the year before his death and prayed often and loudly. Sam Curtis, Will's oldest friend, sized the young man up as "a phoney" looking for money. Will agreed and got rid of him, but now he calls Will once a week: "God knows what he wants. Money, I suppose. Although he tells my secretary he just wants to stay in touch with Bill's dad."

Miss Lacey brings a slip of paper with a phone number the young man asked Will to call back. Will doesn't intend to do so—he has even instructed his wife not even to answer the young man's occasional letter. But when he looks at the number he sees it's a Houston number—the downtown YMCA—not an Atlanta number. He dials it and asks for the young man by name (Randy Carter), but he's not in.

Will further confides in Tom that his wife's stepfather, Pete Davenport, is living with them at this time. Pete is from Atlanta—he didn't move to Houston till he was 20—but he doesn't identify Randy Carter as anyone connected to anybody Pete knew back there. Will hopes their new house will distract them from sad memories of the past, and he is buying his wife a new car to celebrate the move.

Tom warns Will that their company has just lost three major accounts. He learned this from the head of the company, Ted Cleveland Jr., 44, who is in his office today. Will's answer is, "It doesn't worry me at all. We went through the Depression with flying colors, when the rest of Houston was on its knees. Begging for mercy—not us. Not us. We were prospering."

Ted Cleveland Jr. enters, and Will reminisces about his friendship and business association with Ted's father: "Your father was a hell of a man, Ted. They don't make them like that any more." Ted asks Tom to excuse them, and Tom exits. Ted sympathizes with Will about the loss of his only son. And they both agree that Tom Jackson is a fine young man.

WILL: I hired him, you know. I trained him.
TED: Yes, I'm aware of that.
    A pause.
The company is going through a bad patch, Will. We've just lost three more accounts. Including Carnation.
WILL: You don't say. When did you hear this?
TED: Yesterday.
WILL: I wish you would have told me this right away. You know I've handled the Carnation account from its beginning with the company. They respect me over there. We've done business together now for over thirty years. And if I do say so myself . . .
TED: May I be frank, Will?
WILL: Yes sir.
TED: You're the reason they're giving for leaving us.
WILL: Me?

TED: Yes. You. They feel you're not with it any longer, as they say.

WILL: Who says? Not Cochran Judd, why he and I . . .

TED: No, not Cochran Judd. He's been fired.

WILL: My God. When?

TED: As of yesterday. There have been a lot of replacements there, I believe. It's a new age, Will. My father wouldn't recognize business as it's done today. Very competitive.

WILL: Shoot. That doesn't scare me. I thrive on competition, Ted. When I started with this company, when your dad and I were young men, that's what made us the success we became. Our competitive spirit. Your dad said to me one day, "Will, I've always thought of myself as a competitive man, but you're the most competitive man I've ever known or seen. The most." That is what he said. And he called me into his office just before he died, and he said, "Will, I'm going to die soon, I know, but I'm going with peace of mind knowing you are here to help my son run the company. The company we built together, Will."

   A pause.

TED: It's a different ball game, Will. What worked forty years ago, or twenty, or ten doesn't work any more. I'm going to have to replace you, Will. You'll have three months notice beginning today.

"This is the house I built," Will protests, but Ted has no choice. The company needs younger leadership. Will indicates he might try to start his own company if he can raise sufficient capital, in which case he'll be leaving immediately. Ted wishes him luck and exits.

The first thing Will does is cancel the order for a new car; the second is to summon Tom into his office and tell him what has happened: "I won't lie to you. It's quite a blow to my pride." But Will means to survive by starting his own company with the help of "friends in every bank in Houston," even though almost all his savings have gone into the new house. He wants Tom to join his new company when he gets it on its feet, but Tom confesses that it is he, Tom, who is the "younger man" who is to take over Will's job. Tom tries to apologize, but Will understands, wishes Tom luck and picks up the phone to start trying to find financing for his new venture.

Scene 2

The next evening, Will is sitting on a couch in his den at home and is joined by his wife Lily Dale, her stepfather Pete Davenport and the cook, Clara, who comes in with the coffee service and then exits.

LILY DALE: It was a lovely supper, wasn't it? I tell you, I believe Clara is the best cook we've ever had. During the war, you know, Mrs. Roosevelt got all the maids in Houston to join the Disappointment Club.

PETE: Did she? I never heard about that.

LILY DALE: You didn't? It was just awful. A maid would say they were going to work for you. You would arrange the hours and the salary, and she would be so nice and polite, then the day she was supposed to start work she wouldn't show up, and that meant she was a member of the Disappointment Club whose purpose was to disappoint white people.

WILL: And you think Mrs. Roosevelt was behind that?

LILY DALE: I know she was. Everybody in Houston knows she was. She just hated the South, you know. She took out all her personal unhappiness on the South.

WILL: Shoot. Somebody sold you a bill of goods, Lily Dale. I never cared much for either of the Roosevelts, as you know, but I don't think Mrs. Roosevelt organized the maids in Houston into anything.

LILY DALE: Well, she did.

WILL: All right, she did.

Lily Dale, who often calls her husband "Daddy," wonders when the new car is to arrive. Will explains that he wants to pay off the house and furniture before he assumes any more debt. Lily Dale wishes Bill had lived to see the new house—"I miss Bill so much, Daddy"—and remembers that when Bill would come home for a visit, the first thing he'd do would be to ask his mother if she had composed any new pieces of music. If so, he'd ask her to sit right down and play them for him. Lily Dale hasn't touched the piano since Bill died.

Will, tired, starts in the direction of bed but pauses to tell Lily Dale that their son's former Atlanta roommate is now in Houston and has tried to get in touch, but they are to have nothing to do with him. After Will exits, Lily Dale tells Pete she can't understand why Will is so against the young man, whom he seemed to like very much at first. Lily Dale thinks him "a very sweet boy" and appreciated very much hearing from him how her son had taken to religion and prayer. An Atheist friend of hers, Alice Temple, upset Lily Dale by challenging her to explain why God let Bill commit suicide. Lily Dale insisted it was an accident but, deeply disturbed, phoned the roommate in Atlanta, directly against her husband's orders, for reassurance. The roommate told Lily Dale he'd talked to Bill on the phone from Florida the night before his death. Lily Dale was happy to learn, "the whole time they talked about God. So, I felt very relieved after that, and I thanked God, got on my knees and thanked God for sending this sweet friend of Bill's to tell me once again of Bill's faith in God."

Pete promises never to tell Will about Lily Dale's disobedience to Will in getting in touch with the young man. Lily Dale further acknowledges that she calls her son's former roommate every time she feels depressed, and she's been helping him from time to time.

LILY DALE: Loaning him money. Well, not loaning it to him exactly. Although he says that's how he feels about it. You know he's been so blue and depressed since Bill died that he couldn't keep his mind on his job, and he got fired, and so I sent him five thousand dollars until he could get himself together, and then . . .

PETE: Is that all you sent him, Lily Dale?

LILY DALE: No, not all.

PETE: How much have you given him, Lily Dale?

LILY DALE: I don't know exactly. I've got it written down somewhere. His mother got sick and needed an operation, and I sent him ten thousand for her, and his sister's husband deserted her and she has three small children, and so I sent . . .

PETE: Lily Dale.

LILY DALE: It's my money, Pete. I prayed about it, and God said that's what Bill would want me to do, and Randy, that's the name of Bill's friend, said he was sure it was, because he said Bill was going to make him the beneficiary of his life insurance, and that's another reason he knew he didn't commit suicide, because he hadn't had time to change his life insurance making him the beneficiary.

PETE: Lily Dale.

LILY DALE: It's my money, Pete. Will gave me the money every Christmas, and he always said spend it like you want to, and I never spent any of it because there was nothing I needed or wanted, and I kept it all untouched, just in case one day Bill might need something to buy a house when he got married . . .

Lily Dale is worried that Will seems so depressed, and she asks Pete about it. Pete knows what's wrong but can't tell her. Will asked him not to, but no doubt Will will tell Lily Dale when he thinks the time is right. This leaves Lily Dale more worried than ever, and she is additionally troubled because she knows that Bill's friend Randy is in Houston. She has seen him twice—he's looking for a job and hopes that Will can take him on in the company. Randy never had a father. Bill was a surrogate father to Randy, who feels that perhaps Will might take Bill's place in this capacity. Lily Dale has invited Randy to visit her here in the afternoons when Will is at work, and she asks Pete to keep all this to himself until Will has a change of heart about Randy, which Lily Dale believes will take place.

Will enters in robe and pajamas, unable to sleep and resolved to tell Lily Dale about the turn of events: "I've been fired" from the company and replaced by a younger man, Tom Jackson. Will is determined to start his own company and needs every cent he can find, including what has mounted up from the Christmas checks he has been giving Lily Dale.

WILL: I'll just need to borrow it back for a month or so.

LILY DALE: Well—and then you have Bill's money that you gave him that you were going to give me after he died—

WILL: That money was all spent.

LILY DALE: Spent?

WILL: Yes.

LILY DALE: How? Bill never spent money on anything that I knew of. He spent no money on clothes, you gave him his car. He didn't even have an apartment—he lived in a boarding house.

WILL: That's perfectly true.

LILY DALE: Then how did he spend it, Will?

WILL: I don't know how he spent it. There was nothing in his room.

LILY DALE: I don't understand it.

WILL: Neither do I. But that's how it is. His life insurance barely paid the funeral expenses. Would you mind going down in the morning and getting your money? I gave you five thousand for fifteen Christmases, so you should have at least seventy-five thousand unless you've spent some of it. *(A pause.)* Have you spent any of it?

LILY DALE: Not that I remember.

Will promises to get this situation straightened out and goes off to bed, feeling somewhat relieved. Alone with Pete, a distressed Lily Dale confesses that she has less than $25 thousand left and asks Pete to lend her the $35 thousand he has from the sale of the duplex that Pete and Lily Dale's late mother owned. It's all Pete has except for his Social Security, but he promises to get it for Lily Dale in the morning.

Will comes back, still not able to sleep, admitting that he will need help from Pete too and learning about the $35 thousand that Pete has accumulated. With Lily Dale's $75 thousand, Pete's $35 thousand and the new house as security, Will thinks he can raise the $300 thousand he needs to start a new company.

Lily Dale begins to weep and begs Pete to disclose the true state of affairs to Will, which she can't bear to do herself. Pete explains that Lily Dale has given away as much as $35 thousand of her money. Will doesn't understand, and Lily Dale tries to explain: "You told me, Will, the money was mine to do what I wanted to with it." Will wants to know where the money went, and Pete insists that Lily Dale, who is still crying, be the one to tell him.

WILL: Will you please stop crying, Lily Dale, and tell me who you gave the money to? *(A pause.)* Lily Dale—

LILY DALE: That sweet young friend of Bill's.

WILL: Oh, my God. I told you not to go near him. Ever again.

LILY DALE: I know you did.

WILL: What the hell do you mean giving him my money?

LILY DALE: You said it was my money. You said when you gave it to me I could do with it like I wanted to.

WILL: Not to throw it away on bums, I didn't.

LILY DALE: I don't think he's a bum, Will.

WILL: Well, I do. B-U-M—bum . . . Get it back from him. He's at the YMCA. Call him up and get it back. Tell him if he doesn't give it back, I'll have him arrested. I'm going down there right now and get it from him. I'll break his neck. You lied to me, Lily Dale. God damn it. You told me you hadn't been near that boy. You lied to me. God damn it. Why did you lie to me? Why? Why? Why?

    A pause.

LILY DALE: I don't know. I felt sorry for him. He lost his job because he was so upset over Bill's death, and then his mother got sick and needed a serious operation, and then his sister had three small children, and her husband deserted her.

WILL: Bull.

LILY DALE: That's the truth. That's what he told me.

WILL: Bull. You've been taken for a fool, woman. All right. I'm going to sell this God damn house and use the money in my business. We'll live in a tourist court. I'm firing Clara tomorrow. You can do the housework for a change. I'm sick of working myself to death for you to give my good money to dead beats. *(He goes.)*

LILY DALE: Oh, Pete. Go to him. He's all upset. Calm him down. Go to him, Pete.

PETE: Maybe you should go to him, Lily Dale.

LILY DALE: No, he doesn't want to see me. He hates me now. Go to him, Pete. Please.

> *Pete goes. Lily Dale puts her head in her hands. She is trying to control her crying. Pete comes back in.*

PETE: Call his doctor, Lily Dale. He thinks it's his heart.

LILY DALE: My God, my God.

> *She goes to the phone as the lights fade. Curtain.*

Scene 3

A week later, Clara is dusting and Lily Dale is still distraught over what has happened. She confides to Clara all the details culminating in the heart attack which almost killed Will and from which he is now recovering. What's more, a relative of Pete's from Atlanta came to visit Pete the day before. The relative—Carson—knew Bill in Atlanta, liked him but didn't think much of his friend Randy. Furthermore, Randy was an only child, he has no living mother, and Carson—who had a room in Bill's boarding house—never heard Bill pray or carry on about religion. And Lily Dale adds, "Will can't work now even if he wanted to, and we have no money except what I have left from my Christmas gifts."

Clara tries to help Lily Dale look on the bright side, commenting, "God is going to take care of you." Pete enters with Carson and introduces him as his great nephew. Carson informs Lily Dale that Bill's friend Randy was "a big talker, always bragging" and "He never worked, as far as I know."

Will enters, dressed in pajamas and robe and meets Carson. Lily Dale asks Clara about the Disappointment Clubs, but Clara has never heard of them and goes to answer the front doorbell. Tom Jackson enters with a bouquet of flowers and meets the others. Lily Dale brings up the subject of Will's having been fired, but Will makes her drop it: "The doctor says I'm not supposed to dwell on all of that," and Tom had nothing to do with the firing, anyway.

Clara comes in to get the flowers to put in a vase and, in passing, mentions that a friend of hers has heard of Disappointment Clubs. As she exits, Will comments that the Houston bankers have been one big Disappointment Club as far as he is concerned. Tom suggests, "When you get stronger I wish you'd come down to the company. I was talking to Ted last night. He thinks he may be able to find something for you to do, less responsibility, I suppose." But Will has no intention of ever going back after the way he's been treated.

The doorbell rings, and Clara comes in to announce that the young man from Atlanta is here. Lily Dale directs Clara to send him away and tell him not to return. Carson makes a disparaging comment about Randy, and Lily Dale exits in tears. "He is nothing but a four-flusher," Carson insists. Tom wishes Will a swift recovery and takes his leave, then Will explains to Pete and Carson who Tom is.

WILL: He was the one took my job. I brought him into the company and trained him, and they gave him my job. I didn't think I felt any hard feelings toward him, but I do. God help me. I do. I gave my life for that company, you know.

PETE: Now, Will—

WILL: Of course, I realize now I've been foolish. I spent too much on this house, I should have saved more. But I'm still comparatively a young man, you know. Sixty-four ain't old.

CARSON: Who's sixty-four?

PETE: Will.

CARSON: How old are you, Great Uncle Pete?

PETE: None of your business. I don't tell my age.

CARSON: I'm twenty-seven.

PETE: Well, I'm older than you are. I'll tell you that much.

WILL: I gave Bill a hundred thousand dollars, at least, over the years, and I thought as frugal as he was he was saving every penny of it, investing it. I don't know what he made on his job. I don't think a whole lot—that is why I gave him money every year, so he would have a nest egg, and he squandered it.

PETE: Now that's water over the dam, Will.

WILL: And Lily Dale giving money behind my back.

PETE: Come on, Will. You're getting all exercised. That's not good for your heart.

Lily Dale enters, followed by Clara with the flowers ("Take them home with you," Will tells Clara, rejecting Tom's gift). Will recalls how he joined Ted Cleveland Sr. at age 26 and helped built up the company. He states his belief that Ted Jr. will run the company into the ground, and all the 20- and 30-year-olds he can find won't prop it up. And he admits, "I was foolish too, you know. I should have seen this coming. I should have saved money. I don't need luxuries or fine cars and fine houses. I'm a simple man at heart. I'm a country boy at heart, and all I want to do is work, and now they tell me I can't work. They've taken my work away from me."

Lily Dale has put all her remaining money in Will's account. Pete has a check for Will, too, but Will turns it down until later, maybe, when he's well enough to think about starting a business. Clara delivers a letter that Tom left for Will—it contains a check for three months salary, all he now has to show at age 64 for devoting himself to the company for 38 years (Will wishes he could afford to tear it up). Will remembers how he prospered, and how Houston grew, causing Carson to comment that his home town of Atlanta is going to be the South's largest metropolis.

Carlin Glynn as Lily Dale and Ralph Waite as Will Kidder in *The Young Man From Atlanta* by Horton Foote

WILL: It is like hell. Houston is the largest city in the South, and I tell you what, I give it ten years, fifteen, twenty, it will be the largest city in America, the largest and the richest. If I were only a young man again— *(A pause.)* But I'm not a young man. I'm sixty-four years old, and I have been fired, and I have to keep reminding myself of that.

LILY DALE: Will, sixty-four isn't old. I'm sixty, and I don't feel old at all. I don't—
He gives her a look. She shuts up.
I guess you don't want to hear my opinion.

WILL: I guess I don't.
He gets up slowly and leaves the room.

LILY DALE: Carson, go see he gets back to his room safely.

CARSON. Yes, Ma'm.

LILY DALE: My God, Pete. He's still mad at me—
Carson goes.

PETE: He'll get over it, Lily Dale. Give him time.
Carson comes back in.
Did he get to his room all right?

CARSON: I don't know. He told me to stop following him around, he wasn't a God damned baby. Do you really think Houston is going to be the largest city in America?

PETE: I don't know, son.

Will comes back in.

WILL: I've got some pride left. I'm not going to take Ted Jr.'s God damn check.

He hands it towards Lily Dale.

Here, Lily Dale, give it to your boy friend from Atlanta.

Lily Dale cries and leaves the room. He tears the check up. He throws it in the wastebasket as the lights fade.

Scene 4

Lily Dale is sitting on the sofa. She has her Bible and is chatting with Clara about a friend named Etta Doris who used to work for Lily Dale a long time ago. Etta remembers how well Lily Dale used to play the piano, and how lively a little boy her son was.

Will is still in bed (Clara reports) but got up to eat his breakfast. Carson stayed overnight with Pete. They come in to greet Lily Dale and tell her they stayed up half the night talking about Atlanta, and Pete has decided to return to his native city with Carson for a visit: "I think I want to see it one more time before I die." Pete used to work for the railroad, and he still has his railroad pass.

The doctor has told Will he can't work for six months, and Pete is ready to lend Will at least $25,000 when he needs it ($5,000 of his money is going for an operation for Carson's sister, at whose home Carson sleeps on the living room couch because the bedrooms are filled with children). And Pete will also help Carson to go on to the University of Georgia to finish his education.

Will comes in, and Pete tells him of his plan to visit Atlanta. Will asks for Carson (he's having breakfast) and requests that Carson drive him downtown to visit a bank that seems to want to discuss a loan. And Will now has use for that $25,000 that Pete insists he accept. Will goes to get dressed. Lily Dale goes to phone the doctor to see if it's all right for Will to leave the house.

Carson has seen a photograph of Bill in the other room and remarks to Pete that it doesn't look like the Bill he knew, who was "very thin and stooped shoulder and he was getting bald." Lily Dale returns.

LILY DALE: The doctor says he shouldn't go. He should stay in his bed and rest for at least two more weeks. Will you tell him that, Pete?

PETE: You tell it to him, Lily Dale.

CARSON: I met Bill's roommate at the YMCA yesterday. He said he'd seen me out here when he came by the other day. He asked how I know you all, and I told him I was kin in a way, and he said did I know why you all had turned against him, and—

Will comes in. He is dressed,

WILL: Let's go, Carson.

CARSON: Yes, sir.

He and Will start out.

LILY DALE: Will. I called your doctor. He said you shouldn't go, not for two weeks. He said you must stay in bed and rest.

WILL: The hell with the doctor. I'm going. Come on, Carson.

CARSON: Yes, sir.

They continue on out.

PETE: I think he's going to be all right, Lily Dale. It may be the best thing for him. Particularly if it's good news. That will cheer him up and give him something to think about.

Clara brings in Etta Doris who greets Lily Dale warmly, admires her well-preserved looks and commiserates with her on the deaths of her mother and her son. Etta Doris finally leaves with Clara. When Pete goes to pack for his two- or three-day trip, Lily Dale calls Clara back to ask her to check with Etta Doris on Mrs. Roosevelt and the Disappointment Clubs.

Pete returns and hears that Lily Dale is going downtown for a while. Before she leaves, Clara comes back in to report that Etta Doris has never heard of Disappointment Clubs either.

Scene 5

In late afternoon, Will and Carson join Pete in the den. They bring somewhat disappointing news. The young man at the bank was polite and friendly and wanted to tell Will in person, rather than over the phone, that "They had a real interest in me and valued me as a customer and hoped one day to do business with me, but he had to be candid and say this was not, in his opinion, the best time to start a new business, but not to be discouraged and to come back, if I hadn't found another bank interested, in six months, and perhaps the climate would have changed by then, and I said, 'Do you know you got me out of a sick bed to tell me this?', and he began again about how he felt the telephone was too unpersonal, and he personally wanted to meet me and make me feel they were interested in me."

Will ran into Ted Cleveland Jr. while he was downtown. Ted had sent Will a get-well card and repeated to him what Tom told him previously: they might be able to find a spot for him at the company and added, "In the meantime, don't be a stranger."

Will wonders why Lily Dale went downtown. He guesses she might be going to give more money to that young man, and he admits to Pete that he has been mean to Lily Dale on that subject. Reflecting on his meeting with Ted, Will comments, "I can't believe I thanked Ted Cleveland Jr. for offering me a lousy job . . . . . It's one I'll never take. I'll go on relief first."

Pete and Carson leave Will to rest on the sofa. Clara brings in Etta Doris, who wants to say hello to the man of the house she used to work in. Etta Doris remembers that Will loved baseball, and she brings up the ailments of age, from which they both suffer, and the fact that the old house has been torn down like everything else in Houston.

ETTA DORIS: . . . . . I was sorry about your boy.

WILL: Thank you.

ETTA DORIS: You were bound and determined to make him a baseball player, too. Did he take to it?

WILL: No, he never did.

ETTA DORIS: Well, I declare. He was a sweet boy. Blond, blue eyed.

WILL: Yes.

ETTA DORIS: Pretty.

WILL: Yes.

ETTA DORIS: And the friendliest little boy I ever saw. Never knew a stranger.

WILL: Yes, he was very friendly.

ETTA DORIS: Did he keep on that way?

WILL: I think so. More or less.

ETTA DORIS: I went back to see your wife a year or two after I had stopped working for you all, and he had just come in from school. She said he was smart. Made good grades.

WILL: Yes, he was.

ETTA DORIS: And I said to him, "You remember me, little boy." "Yes, Ma'm," he said. "I remember you well." *(She laughs.)* That's what he said. "I remember you well." *(A pause.)* That was a long time ago. I'm sorry I never got to see him again.

> *She and Clara go. Will is left alone. He goes to the phone. He dials.*

WILL: Tom, this is Will Kidder. Pretty fair. Look, I hope you didn't tell Ted about our conversation, because I've been thinking it over, and maybe when I'm stronger I will come in and talk to him. Do you have any idea what he has in mind? Oh, I see. All right. Yeah. I'll see you soon.

Pete and Carson come in to say goodbye, and Will asks Carson to help him to his bed, which Carson does.

Scene 6

Later that same day, in the den, Clara is telling Lily Dale that another friend of hers has heard nothing about Mrs. Roosevelt having anything to do with Disappointment Clubs, though she remembers that the President's wife did visit Houston at one time.

Will is resting, and Pete and Carson have gone. Lily Dale confesses to Clara that she's seen the young man again. He was standing in the driveway, and she had either to stop and talk to him or run over him. The young man wanted to know why the Kidders had turned against him, and Lily Dale told him what Carson had said. The young man called Carson a liar. Carson made the whole thing up because he was jealous of him. Lily Dale asked, "Why was he jealous of him?", and he said, "Because I was Bill's friend, and he wasn't." He said, "If I'm so terrible, why did he try to get me to room with him at the YMCA?", and Lily Dale said, "Did you room with him?", and he said, "No, I wouldn't be caught dead in the same room with him." Furthermore, the young man insisted that he *does* have "a precious mother and a precious sister," and Bill *did* pray a good deal, adding, "Pete's nephew is known as a notorious liar all over Atlanta."

Will comes in, and Lily Dale asks him how it went at the bank.

WILL: Not too well. It was just a courtesy thing. *(A pause.)* I've lost my spirit, Lily Dale. I know I've been cross with you, and I'm sorry. But I have to tell you, I am worried. I've just lost my spirit.

LILY DALE: Please, please don't keep saying that, honey.

WILL: For the first time in my life I don't know where to turn or what to do. Here I am in the finest city in the greatest country in the world, and I don't know where to turn. I'm whipped. I'm whipped.

LILY DALE: Will, please.

WILL: I'm not mad at you any more, Lily Dale.

LILY DALE: I'm glad of that, Daddy.

WILL: But please answer me this one thing.

>*He sees Clara.*

Clara, would you mind leaving us alone?

CLARA: No, sir. *(She goes.)*

WILL: Why did you give that boy money, Lily Dale? Behind my back after I had asked you not to see him again or go near him. Didn't I ask you that?

LILY DALE: Yes, you did.

WILL: Then why, Lily Dale? Why?

LILY DALE: I don't know. I felt sorry for him. He had a sick mother, he lost his job, his sister was deserted with three small children.

WILL: All lies, as we know now. But even if they were true, after I had asked you—

LILY DALE: I know, I know. I have never deceived you before, Daddy, except for one time.

Lily Dale tells Will of an incident that took place while Will was in Chicago on a business trip 20 years ago. Lily Dale's cousin Mary Cunningham persuaded her to let two men come to the house. Will came home from the trip sooner than expected, and the men ran out the back door. They did nothing wrong, but the escapade has been on Lily Dale's conscience all these years. She often gets lonely now, with Will at work so much and Bill dead and her piano music lost to her, so that the young man's sweetness was a comfort to her. When a friend told Lily Dale everyone was saying Bill committed suicide, she was afraid it would upset Will too much if she went to him with this story, so she phoned Randy in Atlanta to be comforted by his belief that Bill did not kill himself. "That boy is a liar," Will insists, but even so, to Lily Dale he is a great comfort.

Will tells Lily Dale he believes Bill *did* commit suicide, there is no other logical explanation for his having walked into the lake like that. But he can't understand why Bill did it: "I failed him, Lily Dale. Someway I failed him. I tried to be a good father, but I just think now I only wanted him to be like me, I never tried to understand what he was like. I never tried to find out what he would want to do, what he would want to talk about. Life goes so fast, Lily Dale. My God. It goes so fast. It seems like yesterday he was a baby, and I was holding him in my arms, and before I turned around good he was off to school, and I thought when he comes back he'll come into the business, and I'll be close to him."

But that didn't happen, and too soon Bill was gone and sorely missed by both father and mother. Lily Dale confesses that she has seen Randy only today, here in the driveway. When she told him about Carson (she explains to Will, who closes his eyes), "He said that Carson was jealous of his friendship with Bill."

And then Lily Dale goes on to confess that she and her cousin Mary had never been properly introduced to those two men but flirtatiously picked them up while riding along in Mary's car. The men asked the women up to their apartment, but Mary (without asking Lily Dale's permission) asked them to the Kidder house. Lily Dale has stopped seeing Mary because Mary once told her that Pete had tried to kiss her when Lily Dale's mother was out of the room. In the case of Carson vs. Randy, "Who are we to believe, Daddy?" After a pause, Will changes the subject.

WILL: I ran into Ted Jr. at the bank, Lily Dale. He said they would like to find something for me to do at the company again, and I wanted to say, "Go stuff it," but I didn't. I thanked him, and I have to tell you I may have to swallow my pride and go back there and see what they'll dole out to me.

LILY DALE: Whatever you think best, Will. And you know what I've been thinking, maybe I could start teaching music and that would help us out too.

WILL: If you like. It might give you something to think about.

A pause.

LILY DALE: Will?

WILL: Yes?

He takes her hand.

We're going to make it, Lily Dale. We always have.

LILY DALE: I know. *(A pause.)* Will?

WILL: Yes.

LILY DALE: Would you do me one last favor.

WILL: What is it?

LILY DALE: Would you speak to Bill's friend. Let him tell you his side of the story. That is all he asks. Then he says he'll go away and leave us alone forever if you want him to. Would you see him, Will? He's outside in my car.

WILL: No.

LILY DALE: Will.

WILL: No.

LILY DALE: Why, Will? Why can't you just talk to him?

WILL: Because I don't want to, Lily Dale. Because there are things I'd have to ask him, and I don't want to know the answer.

LILY DALE: Like what?

WILL: You know the money I gave Bill at Christmas?

LILY DALE: Yes, and that he spent.

WILL: And I told you I didn't know how he spent it. Well, I didn't tell you the truth. In his safety box there were some canceled checks totalling a hundred thousand dollars, and they were all made out to his friend.

LILY DALE: Will, maybe there was a reason.

WILL: Maybe so. But I don't want to know what it is. Ever. So tell him that for me. That I know my son gave him a hundred thousand dollars, and maybe it was for his sick mother, too, or his sister, but I don't believe it. And I don't believe— anyway, whatever the reasons, I don't want to know. There was a Bill I knew and a Bill you knew, and that's the only Bill I care to know about.

LILY DALE: What will I tell him?

WILL: Just tell him to please go away and leave us alone.

LILY DALE: All right, Will.

She goes. Will goes to the phone. He dials.

WILL: Tom? How about my coming in tomorrow. Early afternoon—all right. I'll be there. Thank you.

He hangs up the phone. Lily Dale comes in.

LILY DALE: I told him, Will. He cried, Will, when I told him. He said Bill insisted on giving him the money, for buying nice things. He said he was like a father to him and he'd never known his father, and that—and he'd go back to Atlanta now and not bother us any more, and he was sorry if he had upset us in any way. He is a sweet boy, Will, I don't care what anybody says. *(A pause.)* He said, too, that he wished he could have gone down in the water that day with Bill. That's how much he loved him and missed him. *(She's crying.)* Oh, my God, Will, oh my God.

WILL: Don't cry, Lily Dale. Everything is going to be all right. If I go back to work and you start teaching, everything will be all right. Everything will be all right.

He holds her as the lights fade. Curtain.

Lortel Award

○○○
○○○
○○○
○○○
○○○
○○○

CAMPING WITH
HENRY & TOM

A Play in Two Acts

BY MARK ST. GERMAIN

Cast and credits appear on page 363.

MARK ST GERMAIN was born in 1955 in Newark, where his father was a mechanical engineer. He received his B.A. from Seton Hall in 1976 and his M.A. in drama from Villanova in 1978 and set out on a teaching career at the college level. His first produced play, Out of Gas on Lover's Leap, *emerged off off Broadway April 23, 1985 for 28 performances at the WPA Theater. At this time, his musical collaboration with Randy Courts had already borne fruit in the form of* Gifts of the Magi *at the Lamb's Theater Company December 3, 1984 for 34 performances, and it was repeated by the Lamb's in the Christmas seasons of 1988 and 1992. St. Germain and Courts contributed material to the revue* A ... My Name Is Still Alice *at the Old Globe Theater in San Diego in 1992, and they have since had two full off-Broadway musical productions (books by St. Germain, music by Courts, lyrics by St. Germain and Courts):* Johnny Pye and the Foolkiller *October 31, 1993 for 49 performances at the Lamb's and* Jack's Holiday *this season, March 5, for 25 performances at Playwrights Horizons.*

St. Germain's first full off-Broadway production of a straight play, Camping With Henry & Tom, *also opened this season on February 20, played 88 performances and won its author his first Best Play citation in addition to the Lucille Lortel and Outer Critics Circle Awards as the year's best off-Broadway play. It had premiered in 1993 in Stockbridge, Mass. Other St. Germain works presented in regional theater have included the play* Forgiving Typhoid Mary *at the O'Neill in 1988 and the book for the musical* Just So *in Allentown, Pa. in 1984.*

St. Germain is the author of several motion picture and TV plays, is a frequent participant in the New Harmony Project and is a member of New Dramatists, the Dramatists Guild and Writer's Guild East. He is married, with two children, and lives in Rutherford, N.J.

Time: *July 24, 1921*

Place: *The woods outside Licking Creek, Maryland*

ACT I

SYNOPSIS: In early evening, the sound of a Model T Ford can be heard approaching a clearing, followed by a thud (as the car hits an unseen deer) and a series of crashes during which the car appears and comes to a stop against a tree, jostling its occupants: Henry Ford (the driver), President Warren G. Harding and Thomas Edison. The men aren't hurt, but the deer (Harding finds) seems to be laid out gasping for breath but still alive, and the car (Ford finds, after inspection) is out of commission with a cracked block. They consider putting the animal out of its misery. Harding, more deeply affected than the others, rushes off into the bushes to be sick.

FORD *(shouts after Harding):* Don't worry about the deer! He's coughing blood! He won't last long!

EDISON: You're a comfort, Henry.

FORD: Don't blame this on me! I wasn't driving five miles an hour.

EDISON *(settles down on a log):* Your mouth was doing twice that.

FORD: Somebody had to make conversation! Not all of us can pretend we're stone deaf rather than make small talk. You can't ignore him all weekend! He's the President, for God's sake!

EDISON: I didn't vote for him. I didn't invite him. And I won't call him "Mr. President."

FORD: Call him anything! But at least try to be sociable.

EDISON: How can I undo you crashing him into a tree? Beat him awhile with a stick, maybe? I'm seventy-four years old; I don't have much "sociability" left.

FORD: All I'm asking you is, go easy on him.

EDISON *(hand to ear):* Say again?

FORD *(serious):* Go easy on him. For my sake.

Edison brushes him off.

I'm asking you as a personal favor.

EDISON *(studying him):* What are you after, Henry?

FORD: Don't you worry.

EDISON: I'm not. He should be.

    Harding returns.

HARDING: Colonel Starling has a gun. *(Ford and Edison stare at him.)* My Secret Service man. As soon as he gets here, he can put the poor brute out of his misery.

EDISON: Be interesting to see who he shoots.

HARDING *(confused):* The deer. *(Realizes.)* Oh, I see, you were making a joke?

EDISON: That's all right. Most of my inventions don't work either.

The Secret Service man saw them leave and will attempt to follow—but he can't, because (Ford confesses) Ford pulled the battery wires out of his car. They wanted to get away from the mob of press and photographers back at their luxurious campsite, so Ford has made it possible for them to have a real outing by themselves: "An opportunity for all of us to put our feet up and get to know each other."

Edison has brought a book; Ford considers that the nearby stream might run a power plant; Harding just wants to "bloviate" and has brought a flask which he offers, but the others decline. Ford accuses Edison of having read a newspaper all during Bishop Anderson's sermon, and Edison explains, "I would have napped, but I'd never get to bed later. Used to sleep two-three hours at night, now I barely do that in a week. When I was younger, I used to like it; it gave me more time to think. The older I get, I hate it; it gives me more time to think. There's your divine retaliation, Henry. I'll be dead and no one will know it, I'll still be awake."

The sound of a bird reminds Ford of home—he and his wife greet each other with bird calls (he demonstrates) when he comes into the house. And Ford recalls that Edison and his wife communicate in Morse code while holding hands (Mrs. Edison had been a telegraph operator).

Harding is beginning to enjoy this adventure.

HARDING: . . . . . I can't tell you how much I appreciate the invitation, Mr. Ford.

FORD: Henry. Call me Henry.

HARDING: Frankly, "Henry," I don't know if I can get used to calling a genius by his first name.

EDISON *(not looking up):* Call me Mr. Edison. Henry does. It suits me fine.

FORD: Never called him anything else from the first day we met. I was thirty-three years old, just sold my first car for two hundred dollars, and there I was at some mechanical convention face to face with my hero. Do you remember that, Mr. Edison?

EDISON *(turning a page):* I trust your memory, Henry.

FORD: I spit ideas at him, couldn't stop myself, and he said, "Son, that's the ticket! The self-contained unit carrying its own fuel! Keep at it!" That kept me going, don't you know.

HARDING: I would say so.

FORD: From then on, Mr. President, whenever I want anything, that's what I do. Keep at it, and keep at it some more. And don't stop until I get it.

HARDING: I have to say when I got your letter, the prospect of spending time with two such famous men was more than a little humiliating.

FORD: How can you say such a thing? You're President of the United States.

Edison looks over his book at Ford, raising his eyebrows; Ford shrugs.

HARDING: That's the voters' doing, not mine. But the man who gave us the automobile; who put this country on four tires? We've got more cars than streets; we can't build roads fast enough, ocean to ocean. *(To Edison.)* And you, sir; the man who gave us the light bulb, the phonograph! Mr. Edison, when I was a boy, you were no less a hero to me than Caesar or Napoleon.

EDISON: Dead heroes are always the safer choice.

Edison returns to his book while Harding tells Ford of a visit last week to see Charlie Chaplin's movie *The Kid.* Harding believes the moving picture to be another great Edison contribution to society, but Edison doesn't want to talk about it—he's harassed by lawsuits and patent problems. Edison goes off to relieve himself, and Ford mentions to Harding that Edison's work might fill a museum some day. Edison calls out that he doesn't want a museum ("He's got tricky ears," Ford comments). Edison comes on ranting about "The whole world sticks its hands in my pockets and robs me blind," then goes back off to finish his business.

The subject of Ford's son Edsel comes up, and Ford complains that the last time he left Edsel in charge by himself, he came back to find a new design and a new color—red. Ford tore the new model apart and left it scattered on the factory floor, commenting, "Boys, you can have any color you want, as long as it's black." Edsel swallowed the affront without saying anything, but it's Ford's hope that such aggravation will stimulate the best in Edsel that Ford knows is there.

Ford informs Harding that he knows all there is to know about him. Ford has what he calls a "Sociology Department" at the plant, a group of investigators whom Ford assigned to look into Harding's life and career. "They filled my ears, Warren," Ford remarks, "They filled them full."

Edison returns before Ford can elaborate any further on this subject, and the men try to figure out in which direction they should go if they tried to walk back. Edison suggests they'd better take stock of their situation here while the light lasts, and they find that the car's trunk contains a lantern, a case of Pounded Carrots (healthful but not very appetizing) and an Edison Vitaphone in mint condition, intended as a surprise gift for the inventor, together with music cylinders to play on it.

Ford thinks they ought to start a fire. While he and Edison debate the relative merits of rubbing sticks together vs. flint striking steel, Harding produces some matches and—after Ford tries unsuccessfully to light the fire with them until they're down to their last match—suggests that they light the lantern first and then the fire from it, which with great effort they accomplish.

Ford picks up Edison's book and sees that it is Conan Doyle's *The World of the Supernatural.*

EDISON: It's a mystery why he wrote it. Sherlock Holmes couldn't find one clear thought in it so far.

HARDING: Then why are you reading it?

EDISON: It's the only kind of human folly I still enjoy. The kind I can toss across the room whenever I'm sick of it.

FORD *(excited):* You're building it, aren't you?

EDISON: I didn't say that, Henry.

FORD: You're thinking about it, then. Admit it!

HARDING: Building what?

FORD: I've been after Mr. Edison for years to invent a machine to contact the dead.

HARDING *(taken aback):* Well. Good luck to you.

EDISON: We can't build a fire, and the man thinks I can find an afterlife.

FORD: If anybody can do it, you can.

HARDING: I don't know which would be more terrifying, finding it, or not finding it.

EDISON: That all depends on who's waiting for you when you get there.
        Harding smiles; Ford turns on him.

FORD: You're not a believer, I take it.

HARDING: I certainly am. I most definitely am . . . well, yes and no.

EDISON: Good God . . . is there politics after death?

FORD *(burrowing in):* You believe in the human soul? The indestructible, eternal, all-knowing human soul?

HARDING *(pause):* Well, sure.

FORD: You'd better! You've got one right there under your vest. Some of us have old souls, some have young souls. But we've all got one. Standard equipment. Me; now I know I've been here before. I died once in the Civil War, and that's a fact. Why do you think I hate war so much? I've been there. I was born July 30, 1863, right after the Battle of Gettysburg. And one of those dead boys slipped me the soul I've been using ever since.

Ford explains further that not all souls are strong enough to get back into a body and are just left wandering around. He is interrupted when Harding's flask falls into the fire and makes it flare up. Harding's concern has been aroused—he confesses that a fortune teller who predicted his election to Congress and the Presidency has told him he has only two years to live. Ford comments, "That's grade-A cowcrap. Gypsy Hoo-ha. Pay her more, and she'll swear you'll live forever."

But Harding remembers that only two weeks ago a bolt of lightning hit the White House lawn where he had just been standing, shaking hands with people in a daily ritual that he has found to be "The most pleasant part of the job. I love to meet people. I have fun talking with them, even if it's just, 'Well, look who's here!' and that kind of thing. And they seem to enjoy it. I bring Laddie out, my Airedale. The day of the storm, we had a whole lawn filled with Girl Scouts in uniform. And the Duchess, too, she put hers on; her cap and kneesocks. So, frankly, I wasn't too upset when it started to rain. But when I saw that lightning! It scorched a hole in the ground, right where I'd been standing. It was like an explosion, like a white hot finger from the sky. The staff was scared to death, made me move my desk clear across the room. But I knew I was safe. Somehow, when the end does come, I don't think I'll go as quickly as a bolt of lightning. I have never been what you'd call a lucky man."

They hear the deer thrashing around and realize they ought to put the animal out of its misery. Ford offers Harding a tire iron for the job, but the others argue that Ford was driving when they hit the deer, so Ford ought to finish him. Ford—a self-described "Michigan farmboy"—is not at all reluctant to kill the animal, but before he can do so, Harding remarks, "Mr. Ford, why don't we get this over with," and he's not talking about the deer's fate.

HARDING: . . . . . I'm talking about the reason I was invited here. *(To Ford.)* You want the Muscle Shoals Hydroelectric Plant. And you expect me to convince Congress to sell it to you at a bargain rate. Isn't that what you want? Henry?

FORD: You know what I want? I want this country to learn to harness its own energy. I want to give jobs to every man and woman who need one. I want the farmers of the Tennessee Valley to be able to plant the richest farmland since the Garden of Eden. That's what I want.

HARDING: And your price?

FORD: This isn't about money, can't you see that? You've got a half-built plant sitting there like a dead stump, no use to anybody! If Wilson didn't give up on it when the war ended it could be in full swing by now! Have you ever *seen* the Tennessee River, Harding? Do you have any idea how much energy we could collar down there?

HARDING: I've read the figures . . .

FORD *(interrupting):* I wrote them! We could be running three to four hundred nitrate factories on that land! Three to four hundred! We could be stockpiling the largest supply of fertilizer and gunpowder on this planet. Enough for every crop and bomb this country could ever use. We can take the Tennessee Valley and turn it into another Detroit!

　　　Edison takes up his book.

EDISON: Where was I . . . ?

HARDING: I understand the possibilities—

FORD: These aren't "possibilities!" These are facts, just waiting for us to open our eyes! We're sitting on unlimited power! And the next time we've got ourselves a war, we don't have to go with our hat in our hands to every nancy boy in Europe begging for firepower! We can drop bombs over the whole damn planet! And they'll know it, and line up begging for vegetables instead! Don't you see what this means,

Harding? We can do an epochal thing here! An epochal thing! We can eliminate war from the world!

EDISON *(closing book):* How's that, Henry? Blow us all to bits and then scrape us up for fertilizer?

The people of Tennessee Valley support Ford's plan enthusiastically. Harding declares that the government is considering Ford's proposal, but it isn't as simple to implement as Ford seems to think. Ford argues, "The truth is, Mr. President, that the reason for all the foot-dragging is that none of your boys can figure out yet how they can carve their own slice of the pie." Ford warns Harding that anyone who is not with him is against him, which might make Harding his enemy—then he picks up the tire iron and goes off to dispatch the deer.

Edison refuses to support Harding in this matter—all his life he's shunned politics—and when Ford returns, Edison makes it clear that he's not on Ford's side either. Harding decides that he's the odd man out and makes a move to walk back by himself, until Ford apologizes for his outburst and agrees that the subject of Muscle Shoals is now closed.

Edison urges the others to build up the fire and accepts the loan of Ford's jacket. He recalls setting fire to his father's barn at age 4 to see how fire worked and getting whipped in front of the whole village. And his mother believed Edison lacked normal emotions.

EDISON: There was a boy I played with when we lived in Milan. He was six or seven, older than I was. His father owned the general store. I remember he always had a good suit of clothes. Not like mine. I wore hand-me-downs from my older brother, Carlile. Carlile died when he was six, but till I got there, his clothes fit me fine. One day this boy and I went for a swim in the creek. Outside of town it was, in the woods. We took off our clothes and jumped right in; nobody else was there. And we played together, whatever boys play in the water. Dunking and hiding and holding our breath. But after awhile I didn't see him. I waited for him to come up, but it got dark, so I put on my clothes and went home.

HARDING *(pause):* What happened then?

EDISON: I ate dinner. We had chicken stew. And then I went to bed. Until sometime in the middle of the night my mother shook me awake. The whole town was out with lanterns looking for the boy. And someone mentioned me. I told them how we swam, and how I waited, and they went off to drag the creek for his body. Which they found. And that was that.

HARDING: Why didn't you tell anyone?

EDISON: I did, when they asked.

HARDING: Before that, at dinner, when you got home.

FORD: He must have been terrified! Seeing a boy killed like that! No wonder you didn't say anything, you probably felt it was your fault somehow!

EDISON: I don't remember. I remember standing in the water. I remember how cold it was. And I can remember thinking, "He's not coming up. He must be drowned.'' And I was hungry, so I went home. To this day I can't remember his name. There's a good reason for that, and I hope I never understand what it is.

Edison adds to the fire. They wonder whether Edsel or the Secret Service man will come looking for them, and how soon. Ford gets an idea: if they put the music on the player, as loud as possible, maybe somebody will hear it. They choose "Alexander's Ragtime Band," which leads to a comment by Ford on the health benefits of dancing and Harding's demonstration of a dance called The Newport. When Ford is told that the song's author, Irving Berlin, is not a German but an American Jew, he pulls the cylinder off the machine and substitutes "Turkey in the Straw." Harding immediately becomes furious, taking this as an insinuated reference to the rumor that he has negro blood in his veins, circulated as a political ploy: "I don't have to stand for the poisonous slander of a contemptible bigot!" He moves to depart.

FORD: Are you calling me a bigot?

HARDING: Yes!

FORD (stops Harding): Do you have any idea how many colored men I have working for me? Negro workers *and* negro bosses, do you have any idea?

HARDING: No I don't, and I don't care either.

FORD: Then you're the bigot! Because I do care! And I don't have anything but respect for the negro! They're good men and good workers, and if you're the first black President, hip hip hooray! It's just a pity you're so ashamed of it.

HARDING (pause): Perhaps I misunderstood what you were saying.

FORD: Perhaps you did.

HARDING: I hope we can forget all about this.

FORD: I hope so too.

HARDING: I don't see any purpose to holding a grudge—

FORD: There is none! I'm agreeing with you! And I'll work at it. Because I've got one of those memories that's like a curse; it holds on like bad teeth. Now you take most people, they don't have that problem. I envy them. You take that rumor about you being partial to the Dark Continent? Right or wrong, true or false, it didn't matter, they forgot long before election day. You know it doesn't matter to me! I told you that! But Mr. President, between us? If you ever want to know for sure? And I admit, I'm a man who doesn't like to leave a cow half-milked. If you're ever curious, I can turn my Sociology boys loose on it. And they'll find out. (Snaps fingers.) Quicker than that.

HARDING (pause): So what's your offer, Mr. Ford? How much for Muscle Shoals?

Ford offers $5 million for an installation that has already cost the taxpayers over $80 million, might be worth $10 million in its present condition and would cost another $50, $60 million to restore to working condition before Ford would be willing to take it on. "Your proposal makes no sense!" is Harding's reaction, angering

Ford enough so that he launches into vilification of Harding's henchman Harry Daugherty and the Wall Streeters who now call the shots for the President.

HARDING: Ford, I don't care what you think about me. You can say anything you want about Warren Harding. But I won't stand for you abusing the office of the Presidency.

FORD: Abusing the office? You beat me to it!

HARDING: I'm walking back.

FORD: Abusing the office and the office closet! *(Harding stops.)* Nice thing about White House closets, they're nice and roomy. Don't you think so, "Wurren"? Big enough to fit two people, even. Especially if one of them's just an itty-bitty thing. Say sixteen years old.

HARDING: You're a liar.

FORD: You're right, she was sixteen when you met her. My mistake. Nan's nineteen, now, isn't she? All grown up. I know she's old enough to be a Mommy. Cute little thing, her baby girl, Elizabeth Ann. Fat little cheeks, big blue eyes, just like yours. You should see her, "Wurren." You really should.

HARDING: She is none of your business.

FORD: I think she is. I think it's everybody's business when the President turns the White House into a cat house. Don't you think so, Mr. Edison?

EDISON: I'm not listening, Henry.

FORD *(approaches Harding):* Flopping around on the floor of his coatroom, rolling over the galoshes with a girl young enough to be his daughter, the President of the United States, with his whore and his bastard baby—

Harding goes to hit him; Ford ducks it, assumes fighting pose.

HARDING: You keep away from them, do you hear me?

FORD: Don't threaten me, Harding.

EDISON: STOP IT! Both of you. You're a couple of old jackasses.

Both men pull back.

HARDING *(to Ford):* You are a vicious, twisted man.

FORD: I'm a man who knows the truth and how to use it.

HARDING: You're not getting Muscle Shoals, no matter what you do. You can take me down, but you're not getting your greedy hands on that. I'll stop you any way I can.

Ford intimates that he'll use anything he can against Harding, and Edison advises the President to "Give him the damn factories." Ford goes on about wanting to reform the government and give it back to the people, finally shocking the other two by revealing his true aim: "I'm going to be the thirtieth President of the United States."

They are interrupted by a sound in the bushes. It's the deer, still alive. Ford grabs the tire iron and goes to finish him off (he had thought he was already dead the last time he approached the animal) but returns with his mission unfulfilled, complaining, "He keeps looking at me" and won't stay still. Harding goes off with Ford to help him, and the sound of their voices trying to cope with the animal is drowned out when Edison slips a Caruso cylinder onto the Vitaphone. Harding's and Ford's cries of distress are drowned out by "Ridi, Pagilacci," as Edison covers his ears and the lights fade. *Curtain.*

ACT II

Twenty minutes later, Harding is lying down with his eyes closed, and Ford—a bloody bandage around his head and walking with a slight limp—is heating a can of carrots over the fire and expounding on their health value. The deer clearly won this round, having knocked the wind out of Harding in addition to the damage done to Ford. Edison believes the animal has a broken hind leg. Ford offers carrot patties all around. The others refuse, but Harding gets up and takes one to the deer who, it seems, startled Ford into running head first into a tree.

Edison advises Ford that he shouldn't run for President, he's not a good enough speaker to carry on a campaign. Ford is determined to do it, however, buying what he needs for the job, and he wants to know where Edison stands, with him or against him. "Think of me as Switzerland," Edison replies, "cold and neutral."

Harding comes back to report that the deer at least licked at the carrot patty. Ford returns to the subject foremost on his mind. He claims to be the most popular man in the country at this moment, more popular than Harding or even Edison, and he proposes that Harding hand over Muscle Shoals to him immediately, whisking it past Congress, and then support Ford in 1924 instead of running for a second term.

FORD: . . . . . It's your call. We can work on the same team, or I can hunker down with our newspaper boys. And by the time I'm through with you, you won't be able to swing a vote in Sodom or Gomorrah. *(Pause.)* What'll it be?

HARDING: You've given me a lot to think about. I was trying to do that before, laying here. Much too much to think about. So after awhile I thought I should listen to my heart—

FORD: "Listen to your heart." Talk like a man, Harding, don't throw flowers at me.

HARDING: I've been a politician most of my life, Henry. Saying what I really think, well, that's not a skill I've had to develop. But here it is: I think you should go to the press.

FORD: What?

EDISON: Don't be a damn fool!

HARDING: No, no; I think if anybody ever rescues us from this wilderness, you should grab a reporter and give him the story of his life. Henry Howard at the *Post* is a favorite of mine; he can even write. Why don't you tell him?

FORD: Did you get kicked in the head?

HARDING: Maybe I did. Maybe he kicked some sense into me.

EDISON: You know, we've got the timber here. Maybe you should just hammer a cross together and take a shortcut.

Ken Howard as President Warren G. Harding, Robert Prosky as Thomas Edison
and John Cunningham as Henry Ford in a scene from Mark St. Germain's *Camping With Henry & Tom*

HARDING: You don't understand—

EDISON: It's self-pitying nonsense! If you don't want to fight him for the damn office you can just step aside!

FORD: Don't you realize what this would do to you? They'll be all over you, swinging their hatchets! You'll have no job and no marriage! Why do that to yourself?

HARDING: Because I don't want to be President. Or married. I never did. If you want the job, go ahead and take it. I wish you could do the same with my wife.

EDISON: But he doesn't have to "take it."

FORD: I can run in the next election! I told you that!

HARDING: I know what you told me. And I know myself, much better than you gentlemen do. When I walk out of these woods, all I'll ever decide to do is procrastinate. You said it yourself, and you were right. Other people will decide for me. But here, I can make the decision I know is right. Go to the press. Tell them what I am. They'll boot me out the front door, and so will my wife. You'll be the President, and I'll be the happiest man on earth.

Harding is convinced that his wife knows about that affair already, and about an earlier one Ford doesn't even know about. He never wanted the Presidency, he'd have preferred to remain in the Senate, but he looked like a President, and Daugherty made him run. Also, Harding had suffered five nervous breakdowns (Ford doesn't know about them either) and Wilson knew about them but wouldn't use them in the campaign. And Daughetry told Harding, "There's no first-raters out there now, and you're the best of the second-rate. So you're it. You're going to run, and you're going to win."

Ford's reaction to all this is, "You're not dumping all your dirty work on me, Harding. I am not going to tell the newspapers that you have a ladyfriend, a love child, a cabinet full of crooks and chiselers, and you're crazy as a loon to boot! What would I look like? Some kind of cripple kicker!"

Harding has never even seen his baby daughter. Overcome with emotion, he wanders off, leaving Ford to accuse Edison of being a nay-sayer when somebody wants to do something positive. Edison believes that mankind is basically "unfixable" and declines in advance any of the posts Ford might offer him if Ford were elected.

Harding comes back to report that something big is moving out there in the woods. When they hear its movements, Ford pretends in a loud voice to be carrying a gun and hands the tire iron to Harding and a stout branch to Edison. A low growl is heard. Edison sees a pair of wolves, attracted no doubt by the wounded deer. To the others' surprise, Harding utters a loud wolf cry and goes off, still howling loudly, to chase the animals away. Harding comes back, still doing his wolf calls (after all, he had to listen to Ford's bird calls) and feeling proud of himself.

They continue trying to attract rescuers with noise, Ford shouting for help, Harding howling, Edison pressing the car horn until the battery dies. Harding dreams of going back into the newspaper business when he retires. Edison challenges Ford to name "one great thinker who has changed the world." Ford immediately names Jesus Christ. Edison concedes, "He said some very pretty things, all suitable for embroidery. But did he improve the world?" Edison thinks not.

EDISON: We're toymakers, Henry. That's all we are.

FORD: If you want to spit in your own soup, fine, but leave mine alone. I've made the world a better place, and I'm proud of it.

EDISON: Oh yes. We can hop in your Model Ts after working all day and drive home to our families who we can stare at all night, thanks to my light bulb. Or we can all hop back into our cars and drive to our movie house where we won't have to talk at all. And when somebody finally steals even more of my patents and makes projectors cheap enough for every home, we won't even need to get out of our easy chairs to ignore each other. Where's your "better" world, Henry?

FORD: Every kind of knowledge benefits mankind.

EDISON: Don't get noble on me, Henry. Nobody cares about mankind, not even you. We're not devised to comprehend the notion; we've got the survival skill of selfishness built into our core.

FORD: Not mine.

EDISON: No? You want to save the country because *you* want the gratification of that dubious achievement. You want to benefit mankind, but I've never heard you say one kind word to your own son since I've known you. I'm no better! I gave up on my own children as soon as I realized they weren't me, and even worse, they didn't wish they were.

FORD *(seething):* Edsel loves the car business.

EDISON: Edsel loves you, and what's that gotten him? A bleeding ulcer and shoes he'll never fill, because whenever he tries to, you slip them back on! Henry, it makes me want to scream when I hear people talk about loving "humanity." It's such a bald-faced excuse to climb over everybody's back so the crowd can get a better look at you.

HARDING: I think you're right.

FORD: Well isn't that nice; Mister Five Time Mentally Broken to Pieces thinks you're right. You know what I think, Edison? I think you think too much!

EDISON: And I think most folks will go to any extreme not to think at all.

Harding states his preference for the traditional smoke-filled room over the staff of political science experts with conflicting opinions, for getting things done. Edison complains that the new "Modern Age" scientists like young Einstein are working merely on "Thoughts conceived for their own sake! Nothing we can build or touch." Ford calls the others "crybabies," insisting, "We *are* the Modern Age!"

A voice in the woods startles them. Col. Edmund Starling of the Secret Service, *"a lean and exacting military man,"* enters on foot. The car he borrowed from Edsel Ford (because the battery on his own was disconnected) has run out of gas. The three tell Starling what happened to them, and the Colonel gravely informs them, "You've endangered the President and the entire country." So far, however, the episode is known to no one except Edsel and his mother. And Mrs. Harding has been trying to get ahold of her husband on the phone but has been told he's sleeping.

Ford sets Starling to siphoning gas out of the wrecked car, while Edison and Harding stare at the full moon and speculate about Jules Verne's stories. The other car is half a mile away, so Harding tells Starling to fetch it and come for them. Starling wants to protect the President and tells him, "You must come with me," but Harding sends him off with a sharp order. Ford promises to replace the Secret Service with a private force when he becomes President, and he's ready to make his announcement immediately (Harding wants to radio Washington first, to give his aides, especially Coolidge, notice that he'll be resigning). Ford promises, "We'll give them a country they can afford for once. Get our hands back on our own treasury. So the first thing we've got to do is get rid of the Jews."

This statement startles Harding and Edison. Ford continues his condemnation of the Jews, with reference to the spurious "Protocols of Zion," and the others protest vigorously. Over Edison's protests, Ford continues to denigrate unions, schools and even Harding: "The man doesn't have a thought in his head." Edison counters, "He's smart enough to know he can't do the job. And he hates himself for it. But that's better than blaming a whole race of people for no other reason than your own ignorance." Finally, Edison warns Ford that he will not permit Ford to become President.

EDISON: Do you really think this hate talk of yours will look pretty in the headlines?

FORD: It might not look pretty, but it will help get me elected. There's plenty of people out there who think just like I do.

EDISON: Maybe there are. I don't want to find out. But Henry, if you make one move to announce your candidacy, I'll make an announcement of my own. And I can promise you that once you've given Harding the heave-ho for moral degeneracy, the country will be in the mood for yours.

Sound of car getting closer.

FORD *(furious and hurt):* You son of a bitch. Anything I ever said to you was private conversation. Private!

EDISON: Then don't make me say more.

FORD: Nobody will believe you! Not over me! Some half-deaf dinosaur who can't remember his own name half the time—

EDISON: "Agnes." Was that her name? The servant girl you sent back to Finland. Or was that the other one? The stenographer you gave the car to, and the boat, and the farm. "Evangeline." Wasn't that her name? Or was that the baby.

Sound of car stopping.

STARLING *(offstage):* Men!

EDISON: I don't want to remember, Henry, but I will.

HARDING: Mr. Edison, Henry; we all need to do some thinking . . .

Starling appears, annoyed.

STARLING: Sir!

HARDING: Wait in the car, Colonel.

STARLING: Sir, it's almost—

HARDING: *Wait in the car!*

Starling exits.

Henry, listen to me. Henry! I see two separate issues here. Two different decisions. Now what you decide to do about yourself, that's your business. But what about my situation? You're still going to the press, you're still going to tell them—

FORD: Tell them yourself! Can't you even do that much? Stand up for yourself for once in your life!

There is a shot, then Starling enters, explaining that he put the deer out of its misery—much to Harding's annoyance. Harding goes off with Starling, leaving Ford to ask Edison, "That's what you want for your President?" Edison allows as how democracy produces neither the best nor the worst leadership, and maybe that's how it should be; and maybe Harding's feeling of pity for the deer is a plus. In any case, Ford may be a great businessman, but he's not a leader, Edison tells him directly: "A leader's got to know where he's going. And he's got to have somebody behind him when he gets there." Seeing how upset Ford has become with the turn of events, Edison changes the subject.

EDISON: You know what, Henry? I am working on that machine to contact the dead. I want to prove you wrong about reincarnation.

FORD: What if I'm right?

EDISON: Then I'll probably come back as a deer. And you'll be back as a tire. *(They start to go: Edison stops.)* Billy.

FORD: What?

EDISON: Billy Eagan. That's his name. My friend who was drowned.

> *Harding enters.*

HARDING: Gentlemen. I wanted to let you know I won't be here tomorrow morning. I'll be leaving early.

> *Sound of car horn.*

They need me in Massachusetts to dedicate Plymouth Rock. They moved it.

FORD: Why would they move Plymouth Rock?

HARDING: Well, it was never all that close to the water. And it's high. The only way any Pilgrims could have really landed on it is if they were dropped by balloon. This way, all the people who come to see it will be happier.

FORD: Aw, shit!

> *Ford exits. Harding looks at Edison, who gestures for Harding to go ahead of him.*

EDISON: Mr. President.

> *Edison and Harding exit. Slow blackout. Curtain.*

Best Play Citation

AFTER-PLAY

A Full-Length Play in One Act

BY ANNE MEARA

Cast and credits appear on pages 351–353

ANNE MEARA married Gerald (Jerry) Stiller on September 14, 1954, and together they have made the comedy team of Stiller & Meara renowned on stage, screen and radio. Individually, too, their acting careers have flourished. Meara, born in Brooklyn, was studying at the Herbert Berghof Studio at the time of her marriage. In the four decades since then, her dozens and dozens of roles have won her stage citations in Maedchen in Uniform *(1995, Show Business Off-Broadway Award) and* Anna Christie *(1993, Tony nomination); movie accolades in such as* The Boys From Brazil, Fame, Awakenings *and* Through an Open Window; *and four Emmy nominations in the course of her appearances on TV as a guest and series star. And even in the field of writing Meara is no stranger to special distinction. She and her collaborator Lila Garrett won a Writers Guild Outstanding Achievement Award in 1983 for CBS's* The Other Woman. *Now she joins the ranks of Best Play authors with* After-Play, *one of Manhattan Theater Club's three Best Play productions this season, which opened at MTC on January 31 and then moved to a continuing off-Broadway run May 16, at which time Meara took over from Rue McClanahan the role of Terry in her own play.*

Stiller & Meara are almost as well known for their award-winning radio commercials as for their more formal appearances, which included more than 35 stints on the

Ed Sullivan Show. "*Anne thanks Jerry, Amy and Ben for all the good things in her life,*" *Meara commented in the* After-Play *Playbill, Amy and Ben being the couple's two children.*

The following synopsis of After-Play *was prepared by Jeffrey Sweet.*

Place: A restaurant somewhere in Manhattan

Scene 1

SYNOPSIS: Raziel, an etherial-looking black waiter, prepares a table, then turns to the window and makes "a sweeping gesture." Snow begins to fall. There is the sound of a car crash, but it doesn't seem to startle Raziel. He looks at the door in anticipation, then exits as Marty and Terry Guteman and Renee and Phil Shredman enter the restaurant.

The two couples are agitated. A "cabdriver from hell" nearly crashed them into a truck. In reaction, Marty is having an attack of back pain, and he takes to the floor hoping to loosen it up. As the four debate whether they should pursue some kind of legal action against the driver, Raziel appears. Terry says they have a reservation.

As Raziel escorts them to their table, he tells them how much he likes her and Marty's work. (Apparently the Gutemans are actors who have done everything from "Shakespeare to sitcoms.") "You were the golden couple," he says, taking the party's coats offstage. Marty is flattered to be recognized. Phil, Renee and Terry think there's something familiar about Raziel. In fact, he looks a lot like the cabdriver. When Raziel returns, they ask if he has a driver for a brother. Raziel says no, but he may be a distant relation.

Everybody sits and starts thinking about drink orders. Renee comments on Terry's having ordered a spritzer. "I've reformed," says Terry. Phil is going to have a double. Renee is cold; she asks Raziel to bring her coat back. Terry vividly describes the torture the minks who made Renee's coat must have endured. "Terry, my guilt list is so long, this mink isn't even a contender," says Renee.

It has been more than three years since these couples have seen each other. Tonight they rendezvoused at a play and then hopped a cab together to this restaurant, which, according to Terry, is supposed to be the new "in" place.

PHIL: Boy, we all go back together, don't we?

RENEE: A hundred years.

PHIL: Whoever thought we'd end up being the alta-cockers.

TERRY: I keep looking behind me. What was that? What was that stuff all about?

RENEE: We're not going to get melancholy, are we?

MARTY: What stuff?

TERRY: All that carrying on. All that stuff.

PHIL: I think they call that Life.

RENEE: My philosopher. Who knew he was so deep.

TERRY: It's like this morning I was nine years old. It's now ten p.m., and I've gone through menopause.

RENEE: Join the crowd, sweetheart. I had my last tampax bronzed ages ago.

PHIL: Renee, that's a little rough.

RENEE: You have no idea, darling.

The drinks arrive and the two couples toast each other. And now they start to discuss the play they saw this evening. Terry and Marty loved it. They wept, they identified. The play was filled with images that reminded them of their pasts, their childhoods. "That whole family, that was my family," says Marty. Phil's opinion: "The guy's a craftsman, no question." Phil and Renee were obviously unmoved. Oh, they appreciate the technical aspects of the play, but . . . Terry is offended by their analytical language. Phil insists that he and Renee appreciate the play's virtues, but that doesn't blind them to how it is put together.

More low-level friction occurs when Terry lights up a cigarette over Renee's objections. Terry asks Marty to switch chairs with her so that the smoke will be farther away from Renee. In making the move, Marty's back acts up again. We learn that Phil used to smoke until a multiple bypass broke him of the habit.

Terry brings up the subject of the play again. She was particularly moved by "that scene with the mittens." Renee doesn't even remember the scene. This cues Marty and Terry to go into a detailed description. But Phil and Renee continue to react in an analytic, unemotional way.

RENEE: It was very well done, but I'm aware when my strings are being pulled.

MARTY: I didn't get that at all.

TERRY: You're saying you weren't moved?

RENEE: Medium.

MARTY: Medium?

RENEE: Medium moved.

PHIL: Renee's got a Richter scale for emotional involvement.

RENEE: Cute. I was aware I was being moved, so when I'm aware that I'm being moved, I'm only medium moved.

TERRY: I guess that makes me a pushover, according to you.

RENEE: You have your opinion. I have my opinion.

MARTY: I bought the whole thing, what do I know.

In response to a compliment from Renee, Terry tells her that the change for the better is caused by getting her teeth done and going into therapy. Renee is apparently not a big fan of therapy. At this point, she realizes she's lost one of her earrings. Everybody starts to look for the earring on the floor. No luck.

While the search goes on, the two couples continue to express their very different perspectives on the play. As Marty talks about the show, it becomes apparent that much of it was very close to his personal history. He gets more and more emotional. Terry gets Marty a glass of water from Raziel to help him calm down.

RENEE: We've all done things when we were kids. He struck a nerve, that's all.
TERRY: How can you be so blasé?
PHIL *(to Renee):* Ease up.
TERRY: Stop making us feel like we've been had.
     Phil signals to Raziel.
RENEE: I'm just separating the wheat from the chaff. People get fooled by shtick!
TERRY: Shtick! There was no shtick.
     Raziel comes over.
RAZIEL: Yes, sir?
PHIL: Bring us another round. Give it a rest, Renee.
     Raziel goes.
RENEE: Please. I've been in this business for half my life, and I know shtick when I see it. Funny shtick or sad shtick. Tonight I saw sad shtick.
TERRY: You are unbelievable.
PHIL: C'mon, we're getting silly. Renee doesn't mean to offend your . . .
RENEE: Guilty with an explanation—thank you, Phil.
MARTY: It's not your fault. It's me.
TERRY: Are you okay, honey?
RENEE *(to Phil):* I don't need you to defend me.
MARTY: I'm okay.
PHIL: I wasn't defending.
RENEE: Worse. Explaining. Don't explain me, please.
PHIL: By me you're the Rosetta Stone.
MARTY: I'm sorry, everybody.
RENEE: What's that supposed to mean? Rosetta Stone?
TERRY: Don't be sorry. You have nothing to be sorry about.
RENEE: Cryptic. That's what it means, cryptic.
TERRY: You saw a play, and you were deeply moved. You have no reason to apologize to anyone.
RENEE: I'm a very direct person. I've never been cryptic. You're all full of shit.
MARTY: I'm sorry, I've got a very low threshold tonight.
     Raziel brings another round.
PHIL: Hey, this is what the theater is supposed to do, right? Stimulate controversy.
RENEE: Friends argue, no big deal. Here's to us.
     Renee toasts and everyone drinks. Marty gags on his drink.
MARTY: Going to the Men's, back in a minute.

Terry explains that Marty's been going through a rough time since his last surviving cousin died. Phil identifies with the loss. His own family situation hasn't been the greatest—he hasn't seen his father since he was young, when the old man ran away with his aunt; and, though he pays her bills, he hasn't talked to his schizo-phrenic sister in years. Terry tells them that Marty's parents died in a car accident in Florida two years ago. Phil is surprised to hear that they were still driving. "Just Marty's mother," says Terry. "She was behind the wheel, his father was crossing the street." At that point, they had just been divorced a month, though they were living in the same neighborhood.

This blow is what got Terry and Marty to go into therapy—that and the need to address their daughters' anger at them for having spent so much of their time con-centrating on career as opposed to family. Renee affirms that they were wonderful parents, but Terry insists otherwise—she was hot-tempered and frequently smashed. Renee is not thrilled to be on the receiving end of these revelations and confessions. Besides, kids aren't the only ones who have pain. At one point, Renee had two kids, two ex-husbands, no money. That was no picnic.

Marty returns to the table with apologies. Phil and Renee tell him he owes no apologies for reacting strongly to a play that was put together that well. Terry con-tinues to complain about Phil and Renee's harping on the writer's techniques and use of devices: "I resent that elitist attitude." Phil tries to play the diplomat, sug-gesting that Renee's comments aren't meant to be as harsh as they sound. Renee is not pleased that Phil is presuming to interpret or apologize for her.

Raziel arrives to take their food order. The couples continue to argue over the play as they query the waiter about the specials. When Renee orders the veal, Terry is ready with a graphic description about what is done to the baby calves to get veal. Renee surrenders and orders pasta instead. And then it's back to arguing about the play some more, particularly a phrase "the veins of the world." Terry and Marty find it poetic and profound. Renee thinks it was "a lot of airy-fairy shit."

TERRY (*mumbling*): Typical. Pearls before swine.
RENEE: What's that?
MARTY: The play meant a lot to us, Renee.
RENEE: Well, there's no need to be rude.
TERRY: Yes there is. There's a definite need to be rude.
PHIL: We're all tired.
  Lights fade down to black and up again.

Scene 2

A minute or two later, Marty and Terry are upset to learn that their old friend Toby Fenner died the week before. They are also upset that nobody bothered to phone and tell them. Phil and Renee insist that it was somebody else's goof-up, not theirs. Yet another of their circle of friends gone—Terry goes over some of the names of the recently deceased. And now it is Renee and Phil's turn to be surprised about the news of a death, that of a woman named Lillian Mossman. The hospital is being sued. Lillian went in to have her varicose veins dealt with, and the anesthetist

Anne Meara (*left*) as Terry in her own
After-Play, with Barbara Barrie as Renee

made a little fatal mistake. "Everything's falling apart," says Marty. Phil, determined to be upbeat, insists that the four of them are doing fine, right? As the saying goes, "It ain't over 'till the fat lady sings."

The food arrives. Well, some of it does. Renee's order has been mixed up. Raziel apologizes and promises to correct the situation. Phil makes a joke that leads the four of them into a discussion about changing fashions in comedy. It was the comedians who made Phil want to go into the business. The guys wax nostalgic. Renee continues to gripe about the non-appearance of her food, and she will not be assuaged by Terry's offer to share what she ordered. Wrapping her fur around her, Renee wanders off to the Ladies.

Terry and Marty ask Phil how Renee is doing. Well, it could be easier, says Phil as he gets another of his ongoing series of refills on his drink. One of her ex-husbands committed suicide when he got caught up in a savings-and-loan scandal, but the son from that marriage, Brian, is O.K. In fact, "Both of those little shits are doing just fine." The kids have been nothing but heartache to Renee. Renee's daughter Heather hasn't been appreciative despite the fact her mom rescued her from some crummy apartment and set her up in a new condo. In the meantime, Brian has left his wife and children for a Swedish actress (who happens to be a particular favorite of Marty's). Despite the fact that Renee is now supporting the abandoned wife and the kids, she's been forbidden to see her own grandchildren. Terry sympathizes. Mother is a tough gig. "From the first tremor in the womb, to the day they put you on a respirator, it's a series of aftershocks." The lights go down and bump up again.

Scene 3

Renee returns to the table and is irritated to learn that Phil has told Terry and Marty about her problems with the kids. During the course of this, it comes out that Renee has had a mastectomy, too (which Phil blames on the kids). Renee tells her friends not to worry, she's "squeaky clean" now, and she's had reconstruction surgery. "You look great," says Terry. Renee replies, "Not really. But my new breast looks better than my face."

And now Renee begins to open up about her kids. Terry and Marty suggest that maybe a good heart-to-heart talk with them . . . No, says, Renee, the kids aren't interested in hearing anything that the people who raised and supported them (and, in some cases, still support them) have to say. Phil's son is another handful, bubbling with blame about his parents' divorce and his mother's death from cancer.

PHIL: The boy has deep emotional problems . . .

RENEE: Boy! Adam is over thirty.

PHIL: They think it's, whaddya call . . . ? Manic depression.

RENEE: Bipolar. They call it bipolar now.

TERRY: We all have issues with our parents that go back to childhood, Renee . . .

PHIL: Could be a chemical-imbalance thing.

RENEE: I have no issues! My mother was a saint! She washed, cleaned and cooked for all of us and my father who thought he was artistic. He was so artistic he died of cirrhosis of the liver. She broke her fingers sewing brassieres in a sweatshop while I took care of my little brothers.

PHIL: Don't upset yourself, honey. . . .

RENEE: I took care! I was responsible! And I'm still taking care. I took care of my kids. Who else was going to do it? Both of their fathers were losers. I was the one who had to buy Brian the car for high school. I was the one who scrimped to give Heather the acrobatic, ballet and tap! I picked up the tab for everyone. Phil, get me a drink!

Raziel appears. Renee cancels her food order and asks for a vodka Gibson. She continues to rail against the injustices visited upon her. Her daughter-in-law poisons her grandchildren's minds against her. Her daughter Heather thanks her for her kindness and generosity by hitting her, just because Renee re-did Heather's kitchen to her (Renee's) taste rather than Heather's. Heather wanted avocado for the color scheme, but Renee knew that stainless was better. "After they installed everything she said that she had wanted the avocado but that I didn't listen to her, that I never listened to her, and I said I did listen to her and that avocado was Valley-tacky, that stainless had more class and would last longer, and that she really had no color sense and would one day thank me. Then she hit me with the colander."

Marty and Terry sympathize. Phil (echoing the words he used earlier about his son) says Heather has "deep emotional problems . . . . . We're talking Menendez here," he adds, referring to the defendants in a notorious case in which two boys were accused of killing their parents. The lights go down and bump up again.

Scene 4

Terry and Renee wistfully sing a song they learned in girls' camp. Marty and Phil head for the Men's.

Alone, the two women talk about the things they couldn't talk about with the men around. We learn more about their joint pasts, such as the fact that when they were young they had roomed together in the Village and that Marty had started off as Renee's boyfriend before Terry took him away "in your shiksa goddess net." Or at least that's Renee's version. As Terry remembers it, she picked Marty up after Renee had pretty much finished with him. Renee always had a wild side, one that Terry envied. Still does.

RENEE: Envy! Be serious. My body parts are slowly disintegrating, my children are candidates for the Hitler Youth, and I have moments of despair that would terrify you. If it weren't for Phil . . . I'd be dead.

TERRY: You're strong, you're resilient—you're everything I wanted to be . . .

RENEE: Don't do that to me. Don't put me in some superwoman box . . . I'm a quivering custard, like everyone else. I just talk loud. I never had my fifteen minutes. I skirted the area, but I never had my fifteen minutes.

TERRY: You had ardor, you had lustiness, you had desire . . .

RENEE: Oh, that. We were young. I didn't know what the hell I was doing . . . screwing my brains out . . .

TERRY *(emotional):* I never had that . . .

RENEE: It's exhausting. Why? You and Marty are fine, aren't you? You're his life, you know.

TERRY: Yes, yes, he's wonderful. I love him, I'm just getting to know him. He's such a sensitive . . . we're learning so much about each other in thera . . .
        She breaks down.
I'm sorry.

RENEE: Give yourself a break.

TERRY *(emotional):* Passion! I never had passion! Now it's too late.

RENEE: Don't be an ass. If Marty's slowing down, do what everyone does, get a vibrator.

TERRY: It's not Marty—it's me. Toxic nuns, sins of impurity. I'm strangling in ancient rosary beads, trapped in some eternal Lent.

Terry wishes there were more animal passion in the relationship. Renee counsels the use of costumes and other fantasy devices. Soon the two women are howling with laughter. They are still laughing as Marty and Phil re-enter. Phil has been telling Marty about his near-death experience during an operation. They don't quite understand why the women are laughing.

Lights go to black and bump up again.

Scene 5

Phil tells a raunchy joke about sex and death. They all laugh. Now Terry sees Emily and Mathew Paine rise from a table in the back. They are old friends who last year lost their 39-year-old son to leukemia. Marty isn't sure what to say, but when the couple arrive, Terry invites them to join. It quickly becomes apparent that Emily has had too much to drink and Mathew isn't thrilled that Emily is about to have another.

Introductions are made. Emily and Mathew, too, have just been to the theater, an alleged black comedy that they thought was a bomb. Terry tells them they'd have better luck with the show they saw, *Jamie, We Hardly Knew You.* As soon as she has said the title she realizes that Jamie was the name of the Paines' son. She begins to apologize for her gaffe. The drinks arrive.

Renee tells the Paines that she knows how hard leukemia is. That's what her brother died of. He probably contracted it because of living in Nevada where all that nuclear testing was done. Emily cuts through Renee's talk by saying that her son didn't die of leukemia. That's just what they let people think. It was AIDS.

MATHEW: He was diagnosed HIV two years before he died.

TERRY: Two years. My God, to carry that burden around for . . .

EMILY: It wasn't a burden, it was my son.

TERRY: No, no, of course. I meant . . .

MATHEW: Our son.

EMILY: Matt's been overcompensating lately.

MATHEW: I'm not overcompensating.

EMILY: He's really been great about it. He even wears his little red ribbon . . . don't you, Matt. Show them your little red AIDS ribbon.

     She goes through his pockets.

Where's your little red ribbon? Oooh, he forgot his little red ribbon.

MATHEW *(pushing her hands away roughly):* You had to have that second Irish coffee.

TERRY: Emily, I wish I'd known.

EMILY: Really—why?

TERRY: I could've been there for you, I could've . . . I don't know.

MATHEW: Nobody knows.

EMILY *(singing loudly):* De trouble ah seen, nobody knows my sorrow. Nobody knows de trouble ah seen . . .

MATHEW *(loudly):* Shut up!

EMILY: Oops! Sorry, I get carried away. So, what exactly would you have done, Terry? Send me books, like my sister-in-law did? She sent me cartons of books: Louise Hay, Kubler-Ross. Courses upon courses in fucking miracles.

RENEE: Are there any groups that you can go to?

PHIL: Renee . . .

EMILY: Excuse me?

PHIL: Renee.

RENEE: Stop saying "Renee" like that. You're treating me like an outpatient.

EMILY: Groups? Like what? Community theater? PAC groups? What?

MATHEW: Give it a rest, will you?

RENEE: I'm sorry.

EMILY: Me too. No, we do. We go to groups. Matt drags us to every goddamn grieving gay group there is.

MATHEW: It helps.

EMILY: Who? Matt loves these groups. He gets to give testimony. He gets to make it up to Jamie and openly "share." "My name is Mathew, and I am the father of a dead gay boy who had AIDS."

MATHEW (emotional): Christ, will you stop . . .

EMILY: Aw, look, he's so bereaved . . . the star mourner!

MARTY: Emily . . .

EMILY: They love him, all those lost infected men. He's their aging macho champion.

TERRY: How about a cup of coffee, Emily.

EMILY: Sounds great. Irish, if you don't mind.

MATHEW: Time to go, I think.

EMILY: You get off on it. Instant redemption for years of living on a distant planet.

TERRY: Em, c'mon, come to the Ladies with me.

EMILY: I don't have to go, okay? I'm happy here with my Irish. You should appreciate that, Terry. You're Irish, aren't you? As I remember, you used to toss a few back in the old days. Right, Matt? Remember those New Year's parties with Marty and Terry when she'd sing old Catholic girls school hymns, while her kids would try to get her to stop?

> Laughing.

Your kids were so embarrassed, trying to pick you up off the floor, dragging you into the bedroom. God, I'll never forget the look on Marty's face. Remember that, Marty? Remember those drunken parties, where Terry used to humiliate you in front of all of us? God, it was hilarious.

MARTY: Don't do this, Em.

MATHEW: Sorry, Terry, it hasn't been easy.

TERRY: It's okay. I understand.

EMILY: You don't understand shit! None of you understand anything! When I buried my boy, he weighed sixty-five fucking pounds.

MATHEW: I'll get our coats.

> (Mathew goes)

EMILY (really losing it): Yeah, get the coats. Bastard! Where was he when Jamie wanted to talk to him? Shoving him into sadistic Little League games. Jamie wanted to go to Pratt, he says, sure, Jamie, but go to Babson first. Get that MBA, then you can paint all you want. Is that a riot! Now my husband is the Gay Men's Health

Crisis poster boy! (*Screaming after Mathew.*) Aren't you, Matt! Aren't you the understanding straight-father fantasy of every queen in town!

Emily falls to the floor. Raziel helps her up, and Emily pushes him away. She knows what he is—another gay boy. Raziel tries to soothe her, but Emily will not be soothed. "Goddamn fag! You all killed my boy, you hear me?!"

Apologetically, Mathew tells Raziel that the Paines lost their son. Raziel seems to know. Mathew leads Emily to the door. Raziel tells them that everything's going to be all right now.

The Paines exit. Terry and Marty apologize to Raziel for their friends. Raziel tells them it's not a problem. "It happens all the time." "All the time?" Renee asks. "More and more," Raziel replies. Marty suggests that at this point coffee might be a good idea.

The encounter with the Paines has upset Phil deeply. Here's another example of the way a kid has destroyed his parents. "Those people, those friends of yours? They're finished. They bought the farm because of that schmuck kid of theirs." Yes, the kid died. But the kid was like so many kids, filled with unjustified anger, drugs and diseases. When Terry suggests that parents have to accept some responsibility for the way their kids turn out, Phil gets angrier. Renee defends her husband. Phil's son, Adam, always manages to have an overdose or some other crisis just when his father is about to be honored with an award or something. It's a kind of sabotage.

Terry says it's a cry for help, and she tries to tell a parallel story about their girls. Marty tries to restrain her, but Terry is determined to demonstrate her empathy.

TERRY: I know your pain, Phil—I've been there. It's important to get in touch with these feelings, no matter how . . .

RENEE: Please. Stop with this pain business. We all know pain. Who are you, the martyr of the universe?

TERRY: You can't bury all this emotion under a scab. It's still there, festering . . .

RENEE: A scab is scar tissue. People our age have a lot of scar tissue. If we didn't have scabs, we'd bleed to death.

MARTY: You can't force therapy on people.

TERRY: Stop undermining me!

MARTY: Stop trying to convert him.

RENEE: Once a gentile, always a gentile.

PHIL: What are we doing here? I'm sorry, let's get off this stuff. Old news.

TERRY: I was just letting Phil know that I care . . .

PHIL: I know that, kid, it's okay. It's over. We move on.

TERRY: Just sharing my feelings with people I love . . .

RENEE: Do us a favor—don't love us so much.

PHIL: Listen, it's my fault. Going into that whole megillah . . .

TERRY: Just trying to help, to show some empathy for Phil's upset . . .

MARTY: Teresa, enough already!

RENEE: You know, you're addicted to suffering. You're a "pain" junkie.

Merwin Goldsmith (Marty, *on floor*), Anne Meara (Terry),
Larry Keith (Phil) and Barbara Barrie (Renee) in *After-Play*

TERRY: Thank you, Renee, for being so understanding.

RENEE: This whole evening is turning into an extended root canal.

   Silence.

PHIL: What we all need is a good laugh. Better than your therapy, Terry.

RENEE: Phil's right. Who needs tragedies? We get enough of that every day.

MARTY: Laughter is healing. That guy wrote a book about it. He laughed himself right out of a hospital bed.

TERRY: The man who wrote that book died.

RENEE: Well, before he died he had a few laughs. Which is better than picking at scabs.

And now Phil tells a very funny joke which gets Marty and Renee howling with him. Terry, though, insists on telling an anecdote about an Asian actress who was shooting a scene in a movie which turned out to be similar to an incident in her (the actress's) real life—a scene involving children being separated from their mother. Terry remembers it being a Chinese actress. Renee is sure she read the same article and the actress was Vietnamese. The nationality isn't what's important, says Terry, it's the universal tragedy of loss. "The woman could be anything: Chinese, Vietnamese, Siamese . . . whatever." Trying to relieve the tension, Phil jokes, "Sure, just have the shirts back by Thursday." Terry is offended by the implied racism of the joke. Renee and Marty try to get her to lighten up. The joke wasn't a political statement, it was just a dumb quip to cheer everyone up. Phil tries to apologize, but Terry blasts on about her theme: "The pain of separation, the gaping void that can never be filled!"

Renee doesn't understand. What gaping void? What's all this talk been about how wonderful therapy has been for Terry and Marty and their daughters? Terry runs to the Ladies. Renee and Phil turn to Marty for an explanation. What Terry was talking about wasn't her relationship with her kids but with her mother; specifically, all the unresolved stuff from her suicide. The information that Terry's mother committed suicide comes as shocking news to Phil and Renee. Marty amplifies. Terry and her father found the mother when they returned from getting take-out from a Chinese restaurant. This upsets Phil more. Instead of the laundry joke, he came *that* close to making a joke about "one from column A, one from column B." Phil heads for the Men's, as Renee explains to Marty, "Comedy is his life."

Lights go down and come up again.

Scene 6

Renee complains about the chilliness of the restaurant. Raziel says there's something wrong with the heat tonight, but he can offer them each a complimentary drink by way of compensation.

Phil muses on how different the world today is from when they were young, particularly the generational tastes in humor. "We had jokes. Set-up, rhythm, punch line. They just dribble on." Renee says the kids are laughing at *them*, their tastes and humor. The idea galls Phil.

Marty remembers the stage shows that accompanied the movies of their child-hood. Orchestras and curtains and comedians who knew their trade. Marty and Phil resurrect some of the old-style jokes, about over-endowed ladies and lecherous doc-tors, and so forth. They crack each other up with the old gags, as Renee shakes her head. Marty and Phil both know that the world those stage shows introduced them to—show business—is what made it possible for them to go on. Terry returns and, being cued in on the topic, rhapsodizes about the old picture palaces. She loved it all, except for the comedians.

As Raziel returns to offer them dessert, Marty thinks about what he's left undone. He's never made any organized attempt to make sense of his life. "What sense?" Phil challenges. "There's no sense. Everyone does their turn and gets off, so the next slob can screw up." "Thank you, Phil," says his wife, "for giving meaning to my life."

Terry tells them she believes she encountered Nellie Kramer recently. Nellie apparently was a wonderful actress Terry and Marty worked with once. Now? She's a bag lady. She said, "How's it going, kid?" to Terry and cried when Terry gave her a twenty. None of them has an answer for how someone who used to get raves from the *Times* could end up on the street. Did other generations manage better? Renee doubts it.

TERRY: Why can't we all just grow old and accept the seasons of life? . . . . .

RENEE: "Seasons of Life," "Ages of Man"—whatever you call it, we all end up with a tag on our toe.

TERRY: How can you be so negative? Three quarters of the world believes in an afterlife.

RENEE: Naturally. They're starving in deserts, brushing flies from dead babies, waiting for Allah to save them.

TERRY: Not only Third World people believe in . . .

RENEE: If you want to believe in some cosmic Disneyland, go ahead. Let all the mothers of all the dead kids from all the wars believe that their little boys are up there, doing a hora with Buddha, or Christ . . . or . . . Shirley. Whoever.

MARTY: How can you be so sure you're right?

RENEE: Who's sure? I expect nothing.

TERRY: I know there's something more . . .

PHIL: I'm leaving my eyes.

MARTY: Even on PBS, they had a show about reincarnation.

RENEE: God, you mean I get to do this again?! No thank you, I'd rather live in Cleveland.

Phil and Marty laugh.

MARTY: "Cleveland" is funny—the "k" sound, right?

PHIL: Not if you've played there.

TERRY: There is more, there's some other . . . something.

RENEE: You think when your friend Nellie what's her name dies, she's going to get a feathery hug from compassionate angels? You think her life of misery and despair is going to be made up to her? I . . . don't . . . think so.

Raziel brings the drinks.

MARTY: You know, my mother and father died in a car accident in Florida. And right after we got the phone call telling us they died . . .

TERRY: Two pigeons flew onto our apartment balcony . . .

MARTY: They just circled around us and then flew away!

RENEE: In opposite directions, I bet.

MARTY: What . . .?

TERRY: It's okay, honey.

PHIL: This is getting depressing.

RENEE: Brushing my teeth is depressing.

MARTY: At least you *have* teeth.

RENEE: That's what you think.

The lights go down and come up again, as Marty lies on the floor in reaction to a back spasm.

Scene 7

Renee tells Marty that he missed something special when he passed up the chocolate dessert.

Raziel appears to announce last call for drinks. Phil comments on the height of the snow drifts. It turns out that this neighborhood is unfamiliar to all of them.

Raziel offers to help Marty with his back. Whatever Raziel does, it works. Marty's pain is completely gone. He is spry and nimble and even able to pull Terry into a dance. It's been some night, hasn't it? Terry suddenly wants to call her daughters, but Marty tells her it's too late. "I know," says Terry. An elegiac mood overtakes the four. Terry apologizes to Renee for being overbearing. Renee tells her it's O.K. They all turn to each other to say how much fun it's been to be together.

Phil decides he's in the mood to order more drinks. But Raziel appears to say that the restaurant is closing. It isn't a drink Renee wants, exactly. Raziel produces the missing earring.

RENEE: My earring. I thought it was lost.

RAZIEL *(laughing):* Nothing is lost, ma'am . . . . .
>   *Raziel has handed out the coats and hats by now. He is still holding Terry's cape. Renee has her coat with her.*

MARTY: I really loved that play.

TERRY: So sad . . . but happy parts, too . . .

RENEE: The old sweet and sour . . .

PHIL: I didn't get all of it . . .

RENEE: We got what we got.
>   *Raziel is holding Terry's cape. She takes it and puts it on.*

TERRY: Well. "Our revels now are ended."
>   *Terry turns to Raziel.*

Aren't they?

> *Raziel smiles.*

RENEE: Oh yeah. Dream stuff, that's us. "Rounded with a sleep ..." C'mon, Phillie.

PHIL: No, not yet.

RENEE *(to Raziel):* We weren't too awful, were we?

RAZIEL: You were perfect.

> *Raziel takes Renee's hands and kisses them.*

MARTY *(to Raziel):* Could I have just a taste of that chocolate cake?

RAZIEL: I'm afraid the kitchen is closed.

> *Marty goes to the service table where dessert dishes are piled and takes a plate with some cake crumbs.*

MARTY: Just a taste, okay?

RAZIEL: Help yourself.

MARTY *(savoring the crumbs):* Good. This is so good.

RENEE: C'mon, Phillie, it's over—time to go.

PHIL: Not yet. I didn't hear the fat lady ...

RENEE: He never knows when to get off ...

> *We hear a rich deep soprano voice singing ..... "Je veux vivre dans ce reve," from Gounod's "Romeo et Juliette."*

PHIL: Now, that's an exit.

> *Phil takes Renee's arm, and they go out the door. Marty dips his finger into the chocolate and holds his finger out to Terry. She licks the chocolate from Marty's finger.*

MARTY *(to Raziel):* Thank you for everything. I hope we weren't too demanding.

RAZIEL: No more than anyone else. You were fine.

TERRY: Thank you, Raziel.

RAZIEL: Safe trip. See you next time.

TERRY: You're kidding ... ?

MARTY *(still licking his fingers from the cake crumbs):* Really ... ?

RAZIEL *(takes the cake plate from Marty):* Absolutely.

TERRY: —Yes!

> *Raziel smiles. Terry and Marty go out the door. Raziel waves them good-bye, then picks up a drink from the table, toasts the departing guests and drinks as the deep soprano voice fills the room. Lights fade to black.*

Critics Award

ARCADIA

A Play in Two Acts

BY TOM STOPPARD

Cast and credits appear on pages 323–324

TOM STOPPARD was born in 1937 in Zlin, Czechoslovakia, where his family name was Straussler. When he was 18 months old his father, a physician, moved the family to Singapore, and from that time on Stoppard was brought up within the English-speaking culture. During World War II the doctor sent his wife and son to India for safety, and the boy attended an American school in Darjeeling. His father was killed in Singapore by the invading Japanese.

After the war Stoppard, age 9, and his mother (remarried to an English army major) moved to England, where Stoppard attended school until age 17 and then entered upon a writing career, first as a journalist and then as a free-lance whose credits included several TV and radio plays. His first stage play, A Walk on the Water *was produced in Hamburg and Vienna in 1964, after appearing on BBC-TV in 1963; then, under the new title* Enter a Free Man, *it was done in London in 1968 and off off Broadway in 1974. The first Stoppard play to appear on Broadway began as a one-act verse burlesque written in Berlin on a Ford Foundation Grant in 1964,* Rosencrantz and Guildenstern. *The full-length version with the full-length title* Rosencrantz and Guildenstern Are Dead *was produced by the Oxford Theater Group at the 1966 Edinburgh Festival before moving on to London and then to New York October 16, 1967 for a year's run, Stoppard's first Best Play citation and the Critics and Tony awards for the best play of the season.*

Stoppard's The Real Inspector Hound *was produced in London in 1969, and his* After Magritte *appeared there the following year. Combined on a single program, these two short plays were produced off Broadway for 465 performances, followed by a national U.S. tour under the auspices of Kennedy Center. His* Albert's Bridge, *a version of a Prix Italia-winning drama, was produced in London in 1971. A year later his* Jumpers *appeared at London's National Theater and, in the words of the critic Ossia Trilling, "introduced, unless I'm much mistaken, full frontal nudity for the first time on this august stage in the shape of the shapely Diana Rigg."* Jumpers *was produced in Washington in February, 1974 by Kennedy Center and came to Broadway April 22, 1974 for 48 performances and a Best Play citation.*

Stoppard's playwriting career continued with a new English version of Lorca's The House of Bernard Alba, *staged in Greenwich, England. His* Travesties *was produced by the Royal Shakespeare Company June 10, 1974 for 39 performances in repertory and crossed the Atlantic to Broadway October 30, 1975 for 155 more performances, another Best Play citation and the Drama Critics and Tony awards for the best play of the season. Subsequent Broadway productions of Stoppard works were* Dirty Linen & New-Found-Land *January 11, 1977 for 159 performances;* Every Good Boy Deserves Favour *(written with Andre Previn) July 30, 1979 for 8 performances;* Dogg's Hamlet, Cahoot's Macbeth *October 3, 1979 for 31 performances;* Night and Day *November 27, 1979 for 95 performances; and* The Real Thing, *which came in from London January 5, 1984 to win its author's fourth Best Play citation and the Critics and Tony awards for the best play of the season. During the ensuing decade, his only major New York production of a new work was the short-lived* Artist Descending a Staircase, *presented on Broadway November 30, 1989 for 37 performances. But this season he was a resounding presence on New York stages with* Hapgood *December 4 at Lincoln Center's off-Broadway facility and* Arcadia *March 30 on its Broadway mainstage, his fifth and sixth Best Play citations and his third Critics Award as the season's best (for* Arcadia).

Off off Broadway and in U.S. regional theater, Stoppard continues to be one of the most frequently produced modern playwrights. The list of his other stage works includes a translation of Arthur Schnitzler's Undiscovered Country; *an adaptation from Johann Nestroy,* On the Razzle; *and* Rough Crossing, Dalliance *and* Tango. *He has also written extensively for both large and small screens and the radio (and in the process has received the Venice Film Festival's Prix d'Or, the BAFTA Award, the Italia Prize and the Giles Cooper and Sony Awards to go with the Tonys and six Evening Standard Awards for his stage offerings). The novel* Lord Malmquist and Mr. Moon *is also a product of his pen. Stoppard, a Royal National Theater board member, lives near London with his wife, Dr. Miriam Stoppard (a writer and broadcaster) and four sons.*

Time: April 1809 and the present

Place: A room on the garden front of a very large country house in Derbyshire

ACT I

Scene 1

SYNOPSIS: The setting in both time periods is identical, a spacious room, high-ceilinged, with an upstage wall of uncurtained windows through which can be glimpsed suggestions of a vast estate. There are doors right and left to other parts of the house, plus French windows leading out to the garden.

In 1809 the room is serving as a schoolroom sparsely furnished with table, straight-backed chairs and a reading stand. This estate is Sidley Park, the country seat of Lord and Lady Croom, whose daughter, Thomasina Coverly, age 13, is seated at the table with an open mathematics textbook before her. Present also is Septimus Hodge, age 22, her tutor, whose pet tortoise, Plautus, serves as a docile paperweight among the collection of books and papers on the table.

Thomasina questions Septimus, not about mathematics, but about the meaning of the phrase "carnal embrace." Septimus immediately replies, "the practice of throwing one's arms around a side of beef," but is soon shamed by his pupil's request for the truth.

THOMASINA: If *you* do not teach me the true meaning of things, who will?

SEPTIMUS: Ah. Yes, I am ashamed. Carnal embrace is sexual congress, which is the insertion of the male genital organ into the female genital organ for the purposes of procreation and pleasure. Fermat's last theorem, by contrast, asserts that when x, y and z are whole numbers each raised to the power of n, the sum of the first two can never equal the third when n is greater than 2.
> *Pause.*

THOMASINA: Eurghhh!

SEPTIMUS: Nevertheless, that is the theorem.

THOMASINA: It is disgusting and incomprehensible. Now when I am grown to practice it myself I shall never do so without thinking of you.

SEPTIMUS: Thank you very much, my lady. Was Mrs. Chater down this morning?

THOMASINA: No. Tell me more about sexual congress.

SEPTIMUS: There is nothing more to be said about sexual congress.

THOMASINA: Is it the same as love?

SEPTIMUS: Oh no, it is much nicer than that.

At the moment, the situation at Sidley Park is as follows: Ezra Chater, a poet, age 31, is visiting the manor with his wife. Richard Noakes, a middle-aged landscape architect is redesigning the graceful acres and structural accoutrements of Sidley Park into the currently fashionable Gothic style (the gazebo, for example, is to be replaced by a hermitage, though no hermit is at present a prospective tenant). Lady Croom's brother, Capt. Brice of the Royal Navy, is also a guest, as is a college classmate of Septimus—Lord Byron, beginning to establish his reputation.

It becomes clear that Thomasina has learned the expression "carnal embrace" from gossip after the butler, Jellaby, enters with a note from Chater demanding Septimus's presence in the gun room; and Chater, not waiting for a response to this demand, bursts into the schoolroom and demands satisfaction from Septimus for having insulted his wife by making love to her (Thomasina is sent off to spare her hearing the details of this). Septimus doesn't deny the adventure but distracts Chater, playing on his literary vanity by telling him, "There are no more than two or three poets of the first rank now living, and I will not shoot one of them dead over a perpendicular poke in a gazebo with a woman whose reputation could not be adequately defended with a platoon of musketry deployed by rota." Soon they are discussing Chater's latest work, *The Couch of Eros* (a copy of which has been sent to Septimus for review), instead of his wife's infidelity. Septimus heaps praise upon it, and soon Chater is inscribing the copy, "To my friend Septimus Hodge, who stood up and gave his best on behalf of the Author—Ezra Chater, at Sidley Park, Derbyshire, April 10th, 1809."

The landscape architect, Noakes, enters with a sketch book full of his drawings, followed by Lady Croom and her brother Capt. Brice. Thomasina returns from the music room to hear her mother criticize Noakes's plans.

LADY CROOM: . . . . . Where there is the familiar pastoral refinement of an Englishman's garden, here is an eruption of gloomy forest and towering crag, of ruins where there was never a house, of water dashing against rocks where there was neither spring nor a stone I could not throw the length of a cricket pitch. My hyacinth dell is become a haunt for hobgoblins, my Chinese bridge, which I am assured is superior to the one at Kew, and for all I know at Peking, is usurped by a fallen obelisk overgrown with briars—

NOAKES (*bleating*): Lord Little has one very similar—

LADY CROOM: I cannot relieve Lord Little's misfortunes by adding to my own. Pray, what is this rustic hovel that presumes to superimpose itself on my gazebo?

NOAKES: That is the hermitage, madam.

LADY CROOM: I am bewildered.

BRICE: It is all irregular, Mr. Noakes.

NOAKES: It is, sir. Irregularity is one of the chiefest principles of the picturesque style—

LADY CROOM: But Sidley Park is already a picture, and a most amiable picture too. The slopes are green and gentle. The trees are companionably grouped at intervals that show them to advantage. The rill is a serpentine ribbon unwound from the lake peaceably contained by meadows on which the right amount of sheep are tastefully arranged—in short, it is nature as God intended, and I can say with the painter, "*Et in Arcadia ego!*" "Here I am in Arcadia," Thomasina.

THOMASINA: Yes, Mama, if you would have it so.

Guns are heard popping in the distance, in the pursuit of game, which is an almost continuous activity at Sidley Park. Lady Croom looks out and sees that Septimus's friend and house guest (Lord Byron) has bagged a pigeon. Septimus believes it must have been either Lady Croom's husband or son (Augustus, age 15) who shot it, because "My schoolfriend was never a sportsman." Lady Croom and her entourage exit, leaving the schoolroom once again to teacher and pupil, with the architectural sketches remaining on the reading stand.

THOMASINA: Pop, pop, pop . . . I have grown up in the sound of guns like the child of a siege. Pigeons and rooks in the close season, grouse on the heights from August, and the pheasants to follow—partridge, snipe, woodcock and teal—pop—pop—pop, and the culling of the herd. Papa has no need of the recording angel, his life is written in the game book.

SEPTIMUS: A calendar of slaughter. "Even in Arcadia, there am I!"

THOMASINA: Oh, phooey to Death!

> *She dips a pen and takes it to the reading stand.*

I will put in a hermit, for what is a hermitage without a hermit? Are you in love with my mother, Septimus?

SEPTIMUS: You must not be cleverer than your elders. It is not polite.

THOMASINA: Am I cleverer?

SEPTIMUS: Yes. Much.

THOMASINA: Well, I am sorry, Septimus.

> *She pauses in her drawing and produces a small envelope from her pocket.*

Mrs. Chater came to the music room with a note for you. She said it was of scant importance, and that therefore I should carry it to you with the utmost safety, urgency and discretion. Does carnal embrace addle the brain?

SEPTIMUS (*taking the letter*): Invariably. Thank you. That is enough education for today.

THOMASINA: There. I have made him like the Baptist in the wilderness.

SEPTIMUS: How picturesque.

> *Lady Croom is heard calling distantly for Thomasina who runs off into the garden, cheerfully, an uncomplicated girl. Septimus opens Mrs. Chater's note. He crumples the envelope and throws it away. He reads the note, folds it and inserts it into the pages of The Couch of Eros.*

Scene 2

In the same room, it is immediately obvious that the time has changed to the present (although the furnishings are the same) because its sole occupant, Hannah

Peter Maloney as Richard Noakes, Lisa Banes as Lady Croom and David Manis as Capt. Brice in a scene from Tom Stoppard's *Arcadia*

Jarvis, is wearing modern clothing. "*The action of the play shuttles back and forth between the early 19th century and the present day, always in this same room. Both periods must share the state of the room, without the additions and subtractions which would normally be expected. The general appearance of the room should offend neither period. In the case of props—books, paper, flowers, etc.—there is no absolute need to remove the evidence of one period to make way for another. However, books, etc. used in both periods should exist in both old and new versions . . . . . During the course of the play the table collects this and that, and where an object from one scene would be an anachronism in another (say a coffee mug) it is simply deemed to have become invisible. By the end of the play the table has collected an inventory of objects.*" There is even a pet tortoise in both periods—in the present his name is Lightning.

Hannah, in her late 30s, is the author of a book about Byron's mistress Caroline Lamb and is now researching a book on Sidley Park, and in particular its hermit. Hannah disappears on an errand before Chloe Coverly, age 18, enters with Bernard Nightingale, a don in his late 30s who has come to seek information about Byron. Among those in residence at this time are Valentine Coverly, a mathematician age

25–30, and his brother Gus, age 15, who never speaks. And Sidley Park is in a turmoil of preparation for the annual costume ball given for those who live in this district.

Chloe leaves in search of Hannah, who soon enters and finds herself in a discussion with Bernard about Ezra Chater. Bernard produces from his bag the copy of *The Couch of Eros* with Chater's inscription "To my friend Septimus Hodge, etc." Bernard informs Hannah that the British Library knows of only one Chater, a botanist who died in Martinique, yet he feels the author of this book deserves at least a monograph of attention. Hannah mistrusts academics, who criticized her book sharply, but she explains to Bernard who Septimus Hodge was and his position here. But she has found nothing so far on Chater. She points to the drawing of the hermit (Thomasina's) which has survived along with Noakes's papers and tells Bernard that much of what she knows was learned from an 1860 letter written by Thomas Love Peacock and published in a magazine.

HANNAH: The point is, the Crooms, of course, had the hermit under their noses for twenty years so hardly thought him worth remarking. As I'm finding out. The Peacock letter is still the main source, unfortunately. When I read this *(The magazine in her hand.)* well, it was one of those moments that tell you what your next book is going to be. The hermit of Sidley Park was my . . .

BERNARD: Peg.

HANNAH: Epiphany.

BERNARD: Epiphany, that's it.

HANNAH: The hermit was *placed* in the landscape exactly as one might place a pottery gnome. And there he lived out his life as a garden ornament.

BERNARD: Did he do anything?

HANNAH: Oh, he was very busy. When he died, the cottage was stacked solid with paper. Hundreds of pages. Thousands. Peacock says he was suspected of genius. It turned out, of course, he was off his head. He'd covered every sheet with cabalistic proofs that the world was coming to an end. It's perfect, isn't it? A perfect symbol, I mean.

BERNARD: Oh, yes. Of what?

HANNAH: The whole Romantic sham, Bernard! It's what happened to the Enlightenment, isn't it? A century of intellectual rigor turned in on itself. A mind in chaos suspected of genius. In a setting of cheap thrills and false emotion. The history of the garden says it all, beautifully. There's an engraving of Sidley Park in 1730 that makes you want to weep. Paradise in the age of reason. By 1760 everything had gone—the topiary, pools and terraces, fountains, an avenue of limes—the whole sublime geometry was ploughed under by Capability Brown. The grass went from the doorstep to the horizon and the best box hedge in Derbyshire was dug up for the ha-ha so that the fools could pretend they were living in God's countryside. And then Richard Noakes came in to bring God up to date. By the time he'd finished it looked like this. *(The sketch book.)* The decline from thinking to feeling, you see.

BERNARD *(a judgment)*: That's awfully good. *(Hannah looks at him in case of irony but he is professional.)* No, that'll stand up.

HANNAH: Thank you.

BERNARD: Personally, I like the ha-ha. Do you like hedges?

HANNAH: I don't like sentimentality.

BERNARD: Yes, I see. Are you sure? You seem quite sentimental over geometry. But the hermit is very, very good. The genius of the place.

HANNAH (*pleased*): That's my title!

BERNARD: Of course.

HANNAH (*less pleased*): Of course?

BERNARD: Of course. Who was he when he wasn't being a symbol?

HANNAH: I don't know.

BERNARD: Ah.

HANNAH: I mean, yet.

BERNARD: Absolutely. What did they do with all the paper? Does Peacock say?

HANNAH: Made a bonfire.

Casually, Bernard inquires whether Hannah has come across any reference to Byron in her progress through Sidley Park's voluminous papers. He suggests that he might look over the ones Hannah's already been through. At this moment Chloe drifts across the room carrying an armful of old ledgers (the Park's game books) and addresses Bernard as "Mr. Nightingale," a name which Hannah recognizes as that of a Byron scholar.

Now Bernard must admit that it's Byron he's looking into, not Chater. His copy of *The Couch of Eros* came from Byron's own library. It is Septimus's former copy with passages underlined for quotation in an unfavorable review which Bernard jumps to the conclusion that Byron might have written. Within its leaves three Chater notes have survived the centuries: first, Chater's demand to meet someone who has offended him; second, a warning from Mrs. Chater that her husband has ordered pistols; and third, a challenge from Chater: "Sidley Park, April 11, 1809. Sir—I call you a liar, a lecher, and a slanderer in the press and a thief of my honor. I wait upon your arrangements for giving me satisfaction as a man and a poet. E. Chater, Esq."

We know from the previous scene that it was Septimus who was challenged and who reviewed Chater's poem, but Bernard clings to the assumption that it must have been Byron. In his scholarly pursuit of the past, Bernard further deduces that since nothing more was heard of Chater after *The Couch of Eros,* when he was only 31 years of age, and that in 1809 Byron suddenly departed from England for the Continent, Byron must have killed Chater in a duel here at Sidley Park.

Hannah doubts that Bernard will find anything in the Sidley papers to suggest that Byron ever visited here. But when she discloses that Byron and Hodge had been classmates at Trinity, Bernard is elated and resolves to remain in this neighborhood until he can prove his dramatic scholarly point.

Chloe comes back as Barnard exits into the garden. She informs Hannah that she's attracted to Bernard (Hannah is not) and that her older brother Valentine is in love with Hannah. Chloe exits. Her younger brother Gus comes in and offers Hannah an apple "*with a leaf or two still attached,*" as the scene ends.

Scene 3

Back in 1809, Thomasina is translating a Latin description of Cleopatra, Jellaby is delivering a third note to Septimus, who places it in his volume of *The Couch of Eros,* and there is talk of Lord Byron's attentions to Lady Croom. Chater's anger at Septimus has evidently been refueled by an incident at breakfast in which Byron, unwittingly, revealed to Chater that it was Septimus who wrote the scathing review of Chater's book.

While finishing writing a letter of his own, Septimus criticizes Thomasina's translation of the Cleopatra passage for a lack of poetry. He then tosses her a mathematics exercise which he has just graded.

THOMASINA: . . . . . Alpha minus? Pooh! What is the minus for?

SEPTIMUS: For doing more than was asked.

THOMASINA: You did not like my discovery?

SEPTIMUS: A fancy is not a discovery.

THOMASINA: A gibe is not a rebuttal.

> *Septimus finishes what he is writing. He folds the pages into a letter. He has sealing wax and the means to melt it. He seals the letter and writes on the cover, Meanwhile—*

You are churlish with me because Mama is paying attention to your friend. Well, let them elope, they cannot turn back the advancement of knowledge. I think it is an excellent discovery. Each week I plot your equations dot for dot, x's against y's in all manner of algebraical relation, and every week they draw themselves as commonplace geometry, as if the world of forms were nothing but arcs and angles. God's truth, Septimus, if there is an equation for a curve like a bell, there must be an equation for one like a bluebell, and if a bluebell, why not a rose? Do we believe nature is written in numbers?

SEPTIMUS: We do.

THOMASINA: Then why do your equations only describe the shapes of manufacture?

SEPTIMUS: I do not know.

THOMASINA: Armed thus, God could only make a cabinet.

SEPTIMUS: He has mastery of equations which lead into infinities where we cannot follow.

THOMASINA: What a faint-heart! We must work outward from the middle of the maze. We will start with something simple.

> *She picks up the apple leaf.*

I will plot this leaf and deduce its equation. You will be famous for being my tutor when Lord Byron is dead and forgotten.

> *Septimus completes the business with his letter. He puts the letter in his pocket.*

SEPTIMUS (*firmly*): Back to Cleopatra.

THOMASINA: Is it Cleopatra?—I hate Cleopatra!

SEPTIMUS: You hate her? Why?

THOMASINA: Everything is turned to love with her. New love, absent love, lost love—I never knew a heroine that makes such noodles of our sex. It only needs a Roman general to drop anchor outside the window, and away goes the empire like a christening mug into a pawn shop. If Queen Elizabeth had been a Ptolemy, history would have been quite different—we would be admiring the pyramids of Rome and the great Sphinx of Verona.

SEPTIMUS: God save us.

THOMASINA: But instead, the Egyptian noodle made carnal embrace with the enemy who burned the great library of Alexandria without so much as a fine for all that is overdue. Oh, Septimus!—can you bear it? All the lost plays of the Athenians! Two hundred at least by Aeschylus, Sophocles, Euripides—thousands of poems— Aristotle's own library brought to Egypt by the noodle's ancestors! How can we sleep for the grief?

SEPTIMUS: By counting our stock. Seven plays from Aeschylus, seven from Sophocles, *nineteen* from Euripides, my lady! You should no more grieve for the rest than for a buckle lost from your first shoe, or for your lesson book which will be lost when you are old. We shed as we pick up, like travellers who must carry everything in their arms, and what we let fall will be picked up by those behind. The procession is very long and life is very short. We die on the march. But there is nothing outside the march, so nothing can be lost to it. The missing plays of Sophocles will turn up piece by piece, or be written again in another language. Ancient cures for diseases will reveal themselves once more. Mathematical discoveries glimpsed and lost to view will have their time again. You do not suppose, my lady, that if all of Archimedes had been hiding in the great library of Alexandria, we would be at a loss for a corkscrew? I have no doubt that the improved steam-driven heat-engine which puts Mr. Noakes into an ecstasy that he and it and the modern age should all coincide, was described on papyrus. Steam and brass were not invented in Glasgow . . . . .

Septimus redirects Thomasina's attention to the Latin text and after a moment or two of thought sets to translating it himself, putting Thomasina's stumbling efforts to shame in a vividly poetic description of Cleopatra's barge—which he is reciting from Shakespeare, not sight-reading from the schoolbook. "Cheat! Cheat! Cheat!" cries Thomasina and runs off in tears of rage.

Chater and Capt. Brice enter, determined to arrange a duel with Septimus, who is not so inclined. Lady Croom enters in search of a copy of *The Couch of Eros* for Lord Byron, spies Septimus's copy (containing the three letters) and makes off with it, after commanding Septimus to take charge of Byron's pistols so that the poet won't go charging off to the Continent in search of adventure. Septimus takes Chater somewhat aback by promising to meet him and Capt. Brice at 5 a.m., pistols in hand.

Scene 4

In the present, Hannah and Valentine are looking through the 1809 schoolroom material, and Hannah is reading from Thomasina's mathematics lesson book: "I,

Thomasina Coverly, have found a truly wonderful method whereby all the forms of nature must give up their numerical secrets and draw themselves through number alone. This margin being too weak for my purpose, the reader must look elsewhere for the New Geometry of Irregular Forms discovered by Thomasina Coverly."

Apparently this is the "discovery" for which Septimus graded Thomasina A minus. Valentine, himself a mathematician, explains to Hannah that it is an "iterated algorithm," i.e.: "The left-hand pages are graphs of what the numbers are doing on the right-hand pages. But all on different scales. Each graph is a small section of the previous one, blown up. Like you'd blow up a detail of a photograph, and then a detail of the detail, and so on, forever. Or in her case, till she ran out of pages . . . . . Like a feedback. She's feeding the solution back into the equation, and then solving it again. Iteration, you see." This technique is similar to the one Valentine is using in a project involving Sidley Park's game books.

VALENTINE: When your Thomasina was doing maths, it had been the same maths for a couple of thousand years. Classical. And for a century after Thomasina. Then maths left the real world behind, just like modern art, really. Nature was classical, maths was suddenly Picassos. But now nature is having the last laugh. The freaky stuff is turning out to be the mathematics of the natural world.

HANNAH: This feedback thing?

VALENTINE: For example.

HANNAH: Well, could Thomasina have—

VALENTINE (*snaps*): No, of course she bloody couldn't!

HANNAH: All right, you're not cross. What did you mean you're doing the same thing she was doing? (*Pause.*) What *are* you doing?

VALENTINE: Actually, I'm doing it from the other end. She started with an equation and turned it into a graph. I've got a graph—real data—and I'm trying to find the equation which would give you the graph if you used it the way she's used hers. Iterated it.

HANNAH: What for?

VALENTINE: It's how you look at population changes in biology. Goldfish in a pond, say. This year there are x goldfish. Next year there'll be y goldfish. Some get born, some get eaten by herons, whatever. Nature manipulates the x and turns it into y. Then y goldfish is your starting population for the following year. Just like Thomasina. Your value for y becomes your next value for x. The question is: what is being done to x? What is the manipulation? Whatever it is, it can be written down as mathematics. It's called an algorithm.

Valentine is working on his game books, which go back even beyond Thomasina's time, trying to express the changes in grouse population in an algorithm that he intends to publish if he finds it. He assures Hannah that you could even make a picture of the apple leaf, "If you knew the algorithm and fed it back, say, ten thousand times, each time there'd be a dot somewhere on the screen. You'd never know where to expect the next dot. But gradually you'd start to see this shape, because every dot will be inside the shape of this leaf. It wouldn't *be* a leaf, it would be a mathematical object. But yes. The unpredictable and the predetermined unfold together to make everything the way it is. It's how nature creates itself, on every scale, the snowflake and the snowstorm. It makes me so happy. To be at the beginning again, knowing almost nothing. People were talking about the end of physics. Relativity and quantum looked as if they were going to clean out the whole problem between them. A theory of everything. But they only explained the very big and the very small . . . . . The future is disorder. A door like this has cracked open five or six times since we got up on our hind legs. It's the best possible time to be alive, when almost everything you thought you knew is wrong."

The piano is heard offstage—it is Gus playing music he makes up as he goes along. He is a sort of genius, with advanced intuitive skills. He did speak until age 5, after which he has remained silent.

Bernard comes in, and Hannah presents him with a letter she has found—Lady Croom writing from London to her husband in 1810 that Mrs. Chater married Capt. Brice. From this and other information, Bernard elatedly deduces that Byron visited here in 1809, promptly seduced Chater's wife, was challenged to a duel, killed Chater and departed for the Continent, leaving Mrs. Chater a widow free to marry Capt. Brice a year later.

Hannah reminds Bernard that they don't really know how or where or why Chater died, nor can they prove there was any duel. But Bernard means to take the bull by the horns and put his theory into writing. And he is rendered speechless with excitement when Valentine, who has overheard this conversation about Byron, remarks that the poet indeed visited Sidley Park. How does he know? Byron is recorded in the 1809 game book as having shot a hare.

Bernard goes off to find Chloe and tell her the news, leaving Valentine and Hannah to resume their discussion of mathematics.

HANNAH: What I don't understand is . . . why nobody did this feedback thing before—it's not like relativity, you don't have to be Einstein.

VALENTINE: You couldn't see to look before. The electronic calculator was what the telescope was for Galileo.

HANNAH: Calculator?

VALENTINE: There wasn't enough time before. There weren't enough *pencils.*
    He flourishes Thomasina's lesson book.
This took her I don't know how many days, and she hasn't scratched the paintwork. Now she'd only have to press a button, the same button over and over. Iteration. A few minutes. And what I've done in a couple of months, with only a *pencil* the calculations would take me the rest of my life to do again—thousands of pages—tens of thousands! And so boring!

Valentine admits that in addition to the boredom, you'd have had to be crazy to attempt it without the calculator. He leaves with Gus to look for costumes for the forthcoming ball, leaving Hannah with her thoughts.

ACT II

Scene 5

In the present, Bernard is reading his proposed lecture about Byron's hitherto undiscovered adventure at Sidley Park to an audience of Valentine, Chloe and Gus. Hannah joins them, bringing a holograph copy of the Peacock letter. Bernard continues with closely argued, scholarly conjectures about what happened and why (and since we saw and know what happened in the 19th century scenes, we can see how far Bernard's deductions—based on the copy of *The Couch of Eros* and its three letters—have led him from the actual facts). Bernard goes on reading his account of Byron's supposed dalliance, duel, victory and flight to the Continent, much impressed by his own perspicacity. He anticipates the renown this new Byronic tale will bring him in academic circles. He describes it for his listeners as "probably the most sensational literary discovery of the century."

Hannah, herself a scholar and writer, remains skeptical: "Bernard, I don't know why I'm bothering—you're arrogant, greedy and reckless. You've gone from a glint in your eye to a sure thing in a hop, skip and a jump. You deserve what you get, and I think you're mad. But I can't help myself, you're like some exasperating child pedalling its tricycle towards the edge of a cliff, and I have to do something. So listen to me. If Byron killed Chater in a duel I'm Marie of Romania. You'll end up with so much *fame* you won't leave the house without a paper bag over your head." This touches off a scholars' quarrel between Bernard and Hannah until Valentine brings them to an abrupt halt by calling their concerns "trivial."

VALENTINE: The questions you're asking don't matter, you see. It's like arguing who got there first with the calculus. The English say Newton, the Germans say Leibnitz. But it doesn't *matter*. Personalities. What matters is the calculus. Scientific progress. Knowledge.

BERNARD: Really? Why?

VALENTINE: Why what?

BERNARD: Why does scientific progress matter more than personalities?

VALENTINE: Is he serious?

HANNAH: No, he's trivial. Bernard—

VALENTINE (*interrupting, to Bernard*): Do yourself a favor, you're on a loser.

BERNARD: Oh, you're going to zap me with penicillin and pesticides. Spare me that, and I'll spare you the bomb and aerosols. But don't confuse progress with perfectability. A great poet is always timely. A great philosopher is an urgent need. There's no rush for Isaac Newton. We were quite happy with Aristotle's cosmos. Personally, I preferred it. Fifty-five crystal spheres geared to God's crankshaft is my idea of a satisfying universe. I can't think of anything more trivial than the speed of light. Quarks, quasars—big bangs, black holes—who gives a shit? How did you people con us out of all that status? All that money? And why are you so pleased with yourselves?

CHLOE: Are you against penicillin, Bernard?

BERNARD: Don't feed the animals. *(Back to Valentine.)* I'd push the lot of you over a cliff myself. Except the one in the wheelchair, I think I'd lose the sympathy vote before people had time to think it through . . . . . If knowledge isn't self-knowledge it isn't doing much, mate. Is the universe expanding? Is it contracting? Is it standing on one leg and singing "When Father Painted the Parlor"? Leave me out. I can expand my universe without you. "She walks in beauty, like the night/Of cloudless climes and starry skies/And all that's best of dark and bright/Meet in her aspect and her eyes." There you are, he wrote it after coming home from a party.

Valentine declares himself "not against poetry" and reveals that he's given up on the grouse project. "There's just too much *bloody noise!*" he exclaims, upset, as he departs, followed by sympathetic Chloe and Gus.

Bernard has a twinge of regret that he contended so forcefully with a non-professional like Valentine; but he immediately goes after Hannah with the information that the drawing, supposedly of Byron and Caroline Lamb, that Hannah used on the dust jacket of her book, is not of them at all. He offers documentation but then suggests this matter is "trivial" anyway and invites Hannah to come with him to London—not for the lecture, but for sex. Hannah declines and bids him "Cheerio," but he's coming back here for the dance at Chloe's ardent invitation. In the meantime, Bernard has found an entry about Sidley Park in a small travel book, written in 1832, that should be of particular interest to Hannah because it mentions her project, the hermit.

BERNARD: "Five hundred acres including forty of lake—the Park by Brown and Noakes has pleasing features in the horrid style—viaduct, grotto, etc.—a hermitage occupied by a lunatic since twenty years without discourse or companion save for a pet tortoise, Plautus by name, which he suffers children to touch on request."
>   *He holds out the book for her.*

A tortoise. They must be a feature.
>   *After a moment, Hannah takes the book.*

HANNAH: Thank you.
>   *Valentine comes to the door.*

VALENTINE: The station taxi is at the front . . .

BERNARD: Yes . . . thanks . . . Oh—did Peacock come up trumps?

HANNAH: For some.

BERNARD: Hermit's name and CV?
>   *He picks up and glances at the Peacock letter . . . . . He puts the letter down.*

Well, wish me luck—*(Vaguely, to Valentine.)* Sorry about . . . you know . . . *(And to Hannah.)* And about your . . .

VALENTINE: Piss off, Bernard.

BERNARD: Right. *(Goes.)*

HANNAH: Don't let Bernard get to you. It's only performance art, you know. Rhetoric. They used to teach it in ancient times, like PT. It's not about being right, they had philosophy for that. Rhetoric was their chat show. Bernard's indignation is a sort of aerobics for when he gets on television.

VALENTINE: I don't care to be rubbished by the dustbin man. *(He has been looking at the letter.)* The what of the lunatic?

Hannah reclaims the letter and reads it for him.

HANNAH: "The testament of the lunatic serves as a caution against French fashion . . . for it was Frenchified mathematick that brought him to the melancholy certitude of a world without light or life . . . as a wooden stove that must consume itself until ash and stove are as one, and heat is gone from the earth."

VALENTINE *(amused, surprised)*: Huh!

HANNAH: "He died aged two score years and seven, hoary as Job and meagre as a cabbage-stalk, the proof of his prediction even yet unyielding to his labors for the restitution of hope through good English algebra."

VALENTINE: That it?

HANNAH *(nods)*: Is there anything in it?

VALENTINE: In what? We are all doomed? *(Casually.)* Oh yes, sure—it's called the second law of thermodynamics.

HANNAH: Was it known about?

VALENTINE: By poets and lunatics from time immemorial.

HANNAH: Seriously.

VALENTINE: No.

HANNAH: Is it anything to do with . . . you know, Thomasina's discovery?

VALENTINE: She didn't discover anything.

HANNAH: Her lesson book.

VALENTINE: No.

HANNAH: A coincidence, then?

VALENTINE: What is?

HANNAH *(reading)*: "He died aged two score years and seven." That was in 1834. So he was born in 1787. So was the tutor. He says so in his letter to Lord Croom when he recommended himself for the job. "Date of birth—1787." The hermit was born in the same year as Septimus Hodge.

VALENTINE *(pause)*: Did Bernard bite you in the leg?

HANNAH: Don't you see? I thought my hermit was a perfect symbol. An idiot in the landscape. But this is better. The Age of Enlightenment banished into the Romantic wilderness! The genius of Sidley Park living on in a hermit's hut!

VALENTINE: You don't *know* that.

HANNAH: Oh, but I do. I do. Somewhere there will be *something* . . . if only I can find it.

Scene 6

In 1809, the sound of a pistol shot is followed by Jellaby's voice offstage calling, "Mr. Hodge!" and then, almost immediately, the entrance of Septimus followed by

In *Arcadia*, in 1809 (*above*), Thomasina (Jennifer Dundas) and Septimus (Billy Crudup) review her lesson book; and, in the present (*below*), Hannah (Blair Brown) reads to Bernard (Victor Garber, *left*) and Valentine (Robert Sean Leonard)

Jellaby. It is 5:30 A.M., and the former is carrying Lord Byron's pistols and a rabbit which he has just shot and presents to the latter, for Lady Croom. Septimus spent last night in the boathouse, and it seems that Capt. Brice departed in a carriage with Mr. and Mrs. Chater long before the proposed time of the duel. Lord Byron's horse was brought for his departure at 4 A.M. Septimus asks about the book he had loaned his classmate, who has apparently taken it with him. And apparently the ladies had encountered each other on the threshold of Lord Byron's room in the middle of the night, Mrs. Chater leaving and Lady Croom entering.

Jellaby exits as Lady Croom enters bearing two opened letters which Septimus had written the night before, in the event of his death in this morning's scheduled duel. One is a love letter to Lady Croom. The other is addressed to Thomasina but was also opened by Lady Croom, who characterizes it as "full of rice pudding."

Jellaby enters with an elaborate "infusion" ordered by Lady Croom and a letter to Septimus from Lord Byron, who left it with the valet. After Jellaby exits, Septimus pours Lady Croom a cup of tea.

LADY CROOM: I do not know if it is proper for you to receive a letter written in my house from someone not welcome in it.

SEPTIMUS: Very improper, I agree. Lord Byron's want of delicacy is a grief to his friends, among whom I no longer count myself. I will not read his letter until I have followed him through the gates.

LADY CROOM (*considers this for a moment*): That may excuse the reading but not the writing.

SEPTIMUS: Your Ladyship should have lived in the Athens of Pericles! The philosophers would have fought the sculptors for your idle hour!

LADY CROOM (*protesting*): Oh, really! . . . (*Protesting less.*) Oh really . . .
> *Septimus has taken Byron's letter from his pocket and is now setting fire to a corner of it, using the little flame from the spirit lamp.*

Oh . . . really . . .
> *The paper blazes in Septimus's hand, and he drops it and lets it burn out on the metal tray.*

SEPTIMUS: Now there's a thing—a letter from Lord Byron never to be read by a living soul. I will take my leave, madam, at the time of your desiring it.

LADY CROOM: To the Indies?

SEPTIMUS: The Indies? Why?

LADY CROOM: To follow the Chater, of course. She did not tell you?

SEPTIMUS: She did not exchange half a dozen words with me.

LADY CROOM: I expect she did not like to waste the time. The Chater sails with Captain Brice.

SEPTIMUS: Ah. As a member of the crew?

LADY CROOM: No, as wife to Mr. Chater, plant-gatherer to my brother's expedition.

SEPTIMUS: I knew he was no poet. I did not know it was botany under the false colors.

LADY CROOM: He is no more a botanist. My brother paid fifty pounds to have him published, and he will pay a hundred and fifty to have Mr. Chater picking flowers in the Indies for a year while the wife plays mistress of the Captain's quarters. Captain Brice has fixed his passion on Mrs. Chater, and to take her on voyage he has not scrupled to deceive the Admiralty, the Linnean Society and Sir Joseph Banks, botanist to His Majesty at Kew.

SEPTIMUS: Her passion is not as fixed as his.

LADY CROOM: It is a defect of God's humor that he directs our hearts everywhere but to those who have a right to them.

SEPTIMUS: Indeed, madam. *(Pause.)* But is Mr. Chater deceived?

LADY CROOM: He insists on it and finds the proof of his wife's virtue in his eagerness to defend it. Captain Brice is *not* deceived but cannot help himself. He would die for her.

SEPTIMUS: I think, my lady, he would have Mr. Chater die for her.

LADY CROOM: Indeed, I never knew a woman worth the duel, or the other way about. Your letter to me goes very ill with your conduct to Mrs. Chater, Mr. Hodge. I have had experience of being betrayed before the ink is dry, but to be betrayed before the pen is even dipped, and with the village noticeboard, what am I to think of such a performance?

SEPTIMUS: My lady, I was alone with my thoughts in the gazebo, when Mrs. Chater ran me to ground, and I being in such a passion, in an agony of unrelieved desire—

LADY CROOM: Oh . . .!

SEPTIMUS: —I thought in my madness that the Chater with her skirts over her head would give me the momentary illusion of the happiness to which I dared not put a face.

    Pause.

LADY CROOM: I do not know when I have received a more unusual compliment, Mr. Hodge. I hope I am more than a match for Mrs. Chater with her head in a bucket. Does she wear drawers?

SEPTIMUS: She does.

LADY CROOM: Yes, I have heard that drawers are being worn now. It is unnatural for women to be got up like jockeys. I cannot approve. *(She turns with a whirl of skirts and moves to leave.)* I know nothing of Pericles or the Athenian philosophers. I can spare them an hour, in my sitting room when I have bathed. Seven o'clock. Bring a book.

    She goes out. Septimus picks up the two letters, the ones he wrote, and starts to burn them in the flame of the spirit lamp.

Scene 7

Valentine and Chloe, dressed in Regency costumes for the ball, and Gus, trying on costumes from a large hamper, are discussing Bernard's lecture on Byron and the duel at Sidley Park, prominently reported in the newspapers: "Byron Fought

Fatal Duel, Says Don." Hannah comes in with a tabloid which headlines it as "Bonking Byron Shot Poet." Gus follows Chloe off, and Hannah and Valentine speculate on whether the Byron episode will be proven either way, true or false. Then they take their places at the table, Hannah researching Lady Croom's "garden books," Valentine at his computer. It's not long before Hannah breaks the silence by asking Valentine what he is doing, then pursuing some of the subjects they'd previously raised between them.

HANNAH: ..... It's *all* trivial—your grouse, my hermit, Bernard's Byron. Comparing what we're looking for misses the point. It's wanting to know that makes us matter. Otherwise we're going out the way we came in. That's why you can't believe in the afterlife, Valentine. Believe in the after, by all means, but not the life. Believe in God, the soul, the spirit, the infinite, believe in angels if you like, but not in the great celestial get-together for an exchange of views. If the answers are in the back of the book I can wait, but what a drag. Better to struggle on knowing that failure is final. *(She looks over Valentine's shoulder at the computer screen. Reacting.)* Oh! but . . . how beautiful!

VALENTINE: The Coverly set.

HANNAH: The Coverly set! My goodness, Valentine!

VALENTINE: Lend me a finger.

He takes her finger and presses one of the computer keys several times.
See? In an ocean of ashes, islands of order. Patterns making themselves out of nothing. I can't show you how deep it goes. Each picture is a detail of the previous one, blown up. And so on. For ever. Pretty nice, eh?

HANNAH: Is it important?

VALENTINE: Interesting. Publishable.

HANNAH: Well done!

VALENTINE: Not me. It's Thomasina's. I just pushed her equations through the computer a few million times further than she managed to do with her pencil.

From the old portfolio he takes Thomasina's lesson book and gives it to Hannah. The piano starts to be heard.
You can have it back now.

HANNAH: What does it mean?

VALENTINE: Not what you'd like it to.

HANNAH: Why not?

VALENTINE: Well, for one thing, she'd be famous . . .

HANNAH: No, she wouldn't. She was dead before she had time to be famous . . .

VALENTINE: She died?

HANNAH: . . . burned to death.

VALENTINE *(realizing)*: Oh . . . the girl who died in the fire!

HANNAH: The night before her seventeenth birthday. You can see where the dormer doesn't match. That was her bedroom under the roof. There's a memorial in the Park.

VALENTINE *(irritated)*: I know—it's my house.

> *Valentine turns his attention back to his computer. Hannah goes back to her chair. She looks through the lesson book.*

HANNAH: Val, Septimus was her tutor—he and Thomasina would have—

VALENTINE: You do yours.

As Valentine and Hannah concentrate on their work, there is a pause after which Lord Augustus *"bursts into the room and dives under the table,"* chased by Thomasina. For the first time in the play, the present-day and 19th-century characters share their presence on the stage, eventually interweaving but never touching. Some time has passed among the latter since 1809, because Thomasina is now 16 years old.

Septimus enters carrying book, decanter and glass and quelling the youngsters' roughhousing before pouring himself a glass of wine. He invites Augustus to join Thomasina in drawing geometrical models, but Augustus declines.

> *From the portfolio Septimus takes Thomasina's lesson book and tosses it to her, returning homework. She snatches it and opens it.*

THOMASINA: No marks? Did you not like my rabbit equation?

SEPTIMUS: I saw no resemblance to a rabbit.

THOMASINA: It eats its own progeny.

SEPTIMUS (*pause*): I did not see that.

> *He extends his hand for the lesson book. She returns it to him.*

THOMASINA: I have not room to extend it.

> *Septimus and Hannah turn the pages doubled by time. Augustus indolently starts to draw the models.*

HANNAH: Do you mean the world is saved after all?

VALENTINE: No, it's still doomed. But if this is how it started, perhaps it's how the next one will come.

HANNAH: From good English algebra?

SEPTIMUS: It will go to infinity or zero, or nonsense.

THOMASINA: No, if you set apart the minus roots they square back to sense.

> *Septimus turns the pages. Thomasina starts drawing the models. Hannah closes the lesson book and turns her attention to her stack of "garden books."*

VALENTINE: Listen—you know your tea's getting cold.

HANNAH: I like it cold.

VALENTINE (*ignoring that*): I'm telling you something. Your tea gets cold by itself, it doesn't get hot by itself. Do you think that's odd?

HANNAH: No.

VALENTINE: Well, it is odd. Heat goes to cold. It's a one-way street. Your tea will end up at room temperature. What's happening to your tea is happening to everything everywhere. The sun and the stars. It'll take a while, but we're all going to end up at room temperature. When your hermit set up shop nobody understood this. But let's say you're right, in 18-whatever nobody knew more about heat than this scribbling nutter living in a hovel in Derbyshire.

HANNAH: He was at Cambridge—a scientist.

VALENTINE: Say he was. I'm not arguing. And the girl was his pupil, she had a genius for her tutor.

HANNAH: Or the other way around.

VALENTINE: Anything you like. But not *this!* Whatever he thought he was doing to save the world with good English algebra, it wasn't this!

HANNAH: Why? Because they didn't have calculators?

VALENTINE: No. Yes. Because there's an order things can't happen in. You can't open a door till there's a house.

HANNAH: I thought that's what genius was.

VALENTINE: Only for lunatics and poets.

> *Pause.*

HANNAH: "I had a dream which was not all a dream.

> The bright sun was extinguished, and the stars
> Did wander darkling in the eternal space,
> Rayless, and pathless, and the icy earth
> Swung blind and blackening in the moonless air . . ."

VALENTINE: Your own?

HANNAH: Byron.

> *Pause. Two researchers again.*

THOMASINA: Septimus, do you think that I will marry Lord Byron?

AUGUSTUS: Who is he?

THOMASINA: He is the author of *Childe Harold's Pilgrimage,* the most poetical and pathetic and bravest hero of any book I ever read before, and the most modern and the handsomest, for Harold is Lord Byron himself to those who know him, like myself and Septimus. Well, Septimus?

SEPTIMUS (*absorbed*): No.

> *Then he puts her lesson book away into the portfolio and picks up his own book to read.*

THOMASINA: Why not?

SEPTIMUS: For one thing, he is not aware of your existence.

THOMASINA: We exchanged many significant glances when he was at Sidley Park. I do wonder that he has been home almost a year from his adventures and has not written to me once.

SEPTIMUS: It is indeed improbable, my lady.

AUGUSTUS: Lord Byron?!—He claimed my hare, although my shot was the earlier! He said I missed by a hare's (sic) breadth. His conversation was very facetious. But I think Lord Byron will not marry you, Thom, for he was only lame and not blind.

SEPTIMUS: Peace! Peace until a quarter to twelve. It is intolerable for a tutor to have his thoughts interrupted by his pupils.

AUGUSTUS: You are not *my* tutor, sir. I am visiting your lesson by my free will.

SEPTIMUS: If you are so determined, my lord.

> *Thomasina laughs at that, the joke is for her. Augustus, not included, becomes angry.*

AUGUSTUS: Your peace is nothing to me, sir. You do not rule over me.

THOMASINA (*admonishing*): Augustus!

SEPTIMUS: I do not rule here, my lord. I inspire by reverence for learning and the exaltation of knowledge whereby man may approach God. There will be a shilling for the best cone and pyramid drawn in silence by a quarter to twelve *at the earliest.*

AUGUSTUS: You will not buy my silence for a shilling, sir. What I know to tell is worth much more than that.

> *And throwing down his drawing book and pencil, he leaves the room on his dignity, closing the door sharply. Pause. Septimus looks enquiringly at Thomasina.*

THOMASINA: I told him you kissed me. But he will not tell.

SEPTIMUS: When did I kiss you?

THOMASINA: What! Yesterday!

SEPTIMUS: Where?

THOMASINA: On the lips!

SEPTIMUS: In which county?

THOMASINA: In the hermitage, Septimus!

SEPTIMUS: On the lips in the hermitage! That? That was not a shilling kiss! I would not give sixpence to have it back. I had almost forgot it already.

THOMASINA: Oh, cruel! Have you forgotten our compact?

SEPTIMUS: God save me! Our compact?

THOMASINA: To teach me to waltz! Sealed with a kiss, and a second kiss due when I can dance like Mama!

SEPTIMUS: Ah yes. Indeed. We were all waltzing like mice in London.

THOMASINA: I must waltz, Septimus! I will be despised if I do not waltz! It is the most fashionable and gayest and boldest invention conceivable—started in Germany!

SEPTIMUS: Let them have the waltz, they cannot have the calculus.

Thomasina then becomes so absorbed in a new science book from France that she doesn't notice that the sound of piano music from the other room is now competing with the "*distant regular thump*" of a steam engine being used by Noakes in his landscaping project; nor that Lady Croom has now entered the room and is silently watching her.

Chloe comes in asking Valentine and Hannah for Gus's whereabouts—he's needed for a group photo. Chloe exits with Valentine.

Lady Croom is annoyed by the sound of the steam engine and wishes Noakes would turn it off. She notices the pot of dwarf dahlias on the table, and her comment is a clue to what may have happened in consequence of Capt. Brice's botanical expedition to the Indies: "For the widow's dowry of dahlias I can almost forgive my brother's marriage. We must be thankful the monkey bit the husband. If it had bit the wife the monkey would be dead and we would not be the first in the kingdom to show a dahlia."

Lady Croom's remarks had been recorded in the "garden book" which Hannah is studying for her researches. Hannah rises and exits, carrying the book with her, and Thomasina speaks emphatically as she thumps her French science book onto the table: "Well! Just as I said! Newton's machine which would knock our atoms from cradle to grave by the laws of motion is incomplete! Determinism leaves the road at every corner, as I knew all along, and the cause is very likely hidden in this gentleman's observation about 'the action of bodies in heat'."

Lady Croom asks Thomasina how old she is. "Sixteen years, eleven months and three weeks," the girl replies, leading her mother to decide it's time she should be married.

Noakes enters, and Lady Croom complains about the noise his steam engine is making.

NOAKES (*pleased and proud*): The Improved Newcomen steam pump—the only one in England!

LADY CROOM: That is what I object to. If everybody had his own I would bear my portion of the agony without complaint. But to have been singled out by the only Improved Newcomen steam pump in England, this is hard, sir, this is not to be borne.

NOAKES: Your lady—

LADY CROOM: And for what? My lake is drained to a ditch for no purpose I can understand, unless it be that snipe and curlew have deserted three counties so that they may be shot in our swamp. What you painted as forest is a mean plantation, your greenery is mud, your waterfall is wet mud, and your mount is an opencast mine for the mud that was lacking in the dell. (*Pointing through the window.*) What is that cowshed?

NOAKES: The hermitage, my lady?

LADY CROOM: It is a cowshed.

NOAKES: Madam, it is, I assure you, a very habitable cottage, properly founded and drained, two rooms and a closet under a slate roof and a stone chimney—

LADY CROOM: And who is to live in it?

NOAKES: Why, the hermit.

LADY CROOM: Where is he?

NOAKES: Madam?

LADY CROOM: You surely do not supply a hermitage without a hermit?

NOAKES: Indeed, madam—

LADY CROOM: Come, come, Mr. Noakes. If I am promised a fountain I expect it to come with water. What hermits do you have?

NOAKES: I have no hermits, my lady.

LADY CROOM: Not one? I am speechless.

NOAKES: I am sure a hermit can be found. One could advertise.

LADY CROOM: But surely a hermit who takes a newspaper is not a hermit in whom one can have complete confidence.

NOAKES: I do not know what to suggest, my lady.

Thomasina has been busy drawing a "diagram" which she tears out of her exercise book and hands to Septimus, while needling Noakes: "Bad news from Paris! It concerns your heat engine. Improve it as you will, you can never get out of it what you put in." Septimus admits that he doesn't understand what Thomasina is saying. Noakes departs, followed by Lady Croom, and Thomasina continues, to Septimus, "Newton's equations go forwards and backwards, they do not care which way. But the heat equation cares very much, it goes only one way. That is the reason Mr. Noakes's engine cannot give the power to drive Mr. Noakes's engine."

"Everybody knows that," Septimus observes, and Thomasina replies, "Yes, Septimus, they know it about engines!" Septimus assigns her this week's essay: explain her "diagram." Thomasina admits she can't, she doesn't know the mathematics for it. She hands Septimus a drawing she's done of him and Plautus and exits.

Augustus enters, apologizes for his previous rudeness, sees Thomasina's drawing and obtains Septimus's permission to keep it. Augustus has noticed that Thomasina has some strange ideas about sex and asks Septimus to counsel him on the subject so that he can set Thomasina straight. Septimus agrees, and the two men leave as Bernard, Hannah and Valentine enter.

Bernard is extremely upset about how the new evidence about the dahlia will reflect on his scholarship. "You're fucked," Valentine warns him. Hannah explains that the Indies dahlia, raised under glass during the voyage home, was named "Charity" by Capt. Brice in honor of his new bride, the former Charity Chater: "It means that Ezra Chater of the Sidley Park connection is the same Chater who described a dwarf dahlia in Martinique in 1810 and died there, of a monkey bite." It means that Chater was not killed in a duel with Byron. It means that Bernard did not leave well enough alone—finding a new episode in Byron's life in the Sidley Park records—but had to persuade himself on very flimsy evidence not only that a duel took place, but that it resulted in a fatality. And now he's committed his erroneous deductions to the scholarship record, and what's worse, to a public appearance on The Breakfast Hour.

BERNARD: . . . . . If only I hadn't somehow . . . made it all about *killing Chater.* Why didn't you stop me?! It's bound to get out, you know—I mean this—this *gloss* on my discovery—I mean how long do you think it'll be before some botanical pedant blows the whistle on me?

HANNAH: The day after tomorrow. A letter in the *Times.*

BERNARD: You wouldn't.

HANNAH: It's a dirty job, but somebody—

BERNARD: Darling. Sorry. Hannah—

HANNAH: —and, after all, it is my discovery.

BERNARD: Hannah.

HANNAH: Bernard.

BERNARD: Hannah.

HANNAH: Oh, shut up. It'll be very short, very dry, absolutely gloat-free. Would you rather it were one of your friends?

BERNARD (*fervently*): Oh God, no!

HANNAH: And then in *your* letter to the *Times*—

BERNARD: Mine?

HANNAH: Well, of course. Dignified congratulations to a colleague, in the language of scholars, I trust.

BERNARD: Oh, eat shit, you mean?

HANNAH: Think of it as a breakthrough in dahlia studies.

Chloe comes in to fetch Bernard for the group picture. Bernard exits with both the Coverlys after selecting a hat from the costume box that covers his face and his shame in a photo that will run in the local paper.

Piano music from the next room can be heard, as Septimus enters carrying an oil lamp and his pupil's algebra notebook and essay, soon followed by Thomasina in nightgown and carrying a candle, which she puts on the table and blows out. "Tomorrow I will be seventeen!" she exclaims, then kisses Septimus on the lips in advance recompense for teaching her the waltz here and now. Party music can be heard offstage, too slow for a waltz. Septimus is reading her essay and demands her silence while he is doing so, pouring himself some wine.

Hannah enters with Valentine who is also drinking wine and is somewhat under its influence. He roots around among the old papers and pulls out Thomasina's "diagram."

Septimus and Valentine study the diagram doubled by time.

VALENTINE: It's heat.

HANNAH: Are you tight, Val?

VALENTINE: It's a diagram of heat exchange.

SEPTIMUS: So, we are all doomed!

THOMASINA (*cheerfully*): Yes.

VALENTINE: Like a steam engine, you see—

Hannah fills Septimus's glass from the same decanter and sips from it.

She didn't have the maths, not remotely. She saw what things meant, way ahead, like seeing a picture.

SEPTIMUS: This is not science. This is story-telling.

THOMASINA: Is it a waltz now?

SEPTIMUS: No.

The music is still modern.

VALENTINE: Like a film.

HANNAH: What did she see?

VALENTINE: That you can't run the film backwards. Heat was the first thing which didn't work that way. Not like Newton. A film of a pendulum, or a ball falling through the air—backwards, it looks the same.

HANNAH: The ball would be going the wrong way.

VALENTINE: You'd have to know that. But with heat—friction—a ball breaking a window—

HANNAH: Yes.

VALENTINE: It won't work backwards.

HANNAH: Who thought it did?

VALENTINE: She saw why. You can put back the bits of glass, but you can't collect up the heat of the smash. It's gone.

SEPTIMUS: So the Improved Newtonian Universe must cease and grow cold. Dear me.

VALENTINE: The heat goes into the mix.

He gestures to indicate the air in the room, in the universe.

THOMASINA: Yes, we must hurry if we are going to dance.

VALENTINE: And everything is mixing the same way, all the time, irreversibly . . .

SEPTIMUS: Oh, we have time, I think.

VALENTINE: . . . till there's no time left. That's what time means.

SEPTIMUS: When we have found all the mysteries and lost all the meaning, we will be alone, on an empty shore.

THOMASINA: Then we will dance. Is this a waltz?

SEPTIMUS: It will serve. *(He stands up.)*

THOMASINA *(jumping up)*: Goody!

Septimus takes her in his arms carefully, and the waltz lesson, to the music from the marquee, begins. Bernard, in unconvincing Regency dress, enters carrying a bottle.

BERNARD: Don't mind me, I left my jacket . . .

VALENTINE: Are you leaving?

Bernard is stripping off his period coat. He is wearing his own trousers, tucked into knee socks, and his own shirt.

BERNARD: Yes, I'm afraid so.

HANNAH: What's up, Bernard?

BERNARD: Nothing I can go into—

VALENTINE: Should I go?

BERNARD: No, *I'm* going!

Valentine and Hannah watch Bernard struggling into his jacket and adjusting his clothes. Septimus, holding Thomasina, kisses her on the mouth. The waltz lesson pauses. She looks at him. He kisses her again, in earnest. She puts her arms round him.

THOMASINA: Septimus . . .

Septimus hushes her. They start to dance again, with the slight awkwardness of a lesson. Chloe bursts in from the garden.

CHLOE: I'll kill her! I'll *kill* her!

BERNARD: Oh dear.

VALENTINE: What the hell is it, Chloe?

CHLOE (*venomously*): Mummy!

BERNARD (*to Valentine*): Your mother caught us in that cottage.

CHLOE: She snooped!

BERNARD: I don't think so. She was rescuing a theodolite.

CHLOE: I'll come with you, Bernard.

BERNARD: No, you bloody won't.

CHLOE: Don't you want me to?

BERNARD: Of course not. What for? *(To Valentine.)* I'm sorry.

CHLOE (*in furious tears*): What are you saying sorry to *him* for?

BERNARD: Sorry to you too. Sorry one and all . . . . . Sorry, sorry, sorry, now can I go?

CHLOE (*stands stiffly, tearfully*): Well . . .

> *Thomasina and Septimus dance.*

HANNAH: What a bastard you are, Bernard.

CHLOE (*rounds on her*): And mind your own business! What do you know about anything?

HANNAH: Nothing.

CHLOE (*to Bernard*): It *was* worth it, though, wasn't it?

BERNARD: It was wonderful.

> *Chloe goes out through the garden door, towards the party.*

HANNAH (*an echo*): Nothing.

VALENTINE: Well, you shit. I'd drive you, but I'm a bit sloshed.

> *Valentine follows Chloe out and can be heard outside calling "Chlo! Chlo!"*

BERNARD: A scrape.

HANNAH: Oh . . . *(She gives up.)* Bernard!

BERNARD: I look forward to *The Genius of the Place*. I hope you find your hermit. I think out front is the safest.

> *He opens the door cautiously and looks out.*

HANNAH: Actually, I've got a good idea who he was, but I can't prove it.

BERNARD (*with a carefree expansive gesture*): Publish!

> *He goes out, closing the door. Septimus and Thomasina are now waltzing freely. She is delighted with herself.*

THOMASINA: Am I waltzing?

SEPTIMUS: Yes, my lady.

> *He gives them a final twirl, bringing them to the table, where he bows to her. He lights her candlestick. Hannah goes to sit at the table, playing truant from the party. She pours herself more wine. The table contains the geometrical solids, the computer, decanter, glasses, tea mug, Hannah's research book, Septimus's books, the two portfolios, Thomasina's candlestick, the oil lamp, the dahlia, the Sunday papers . . .*

> *Gus appears in the doorway. It takes a moment to realize that he is not Lord Augustus; perhaps not until Hannah sees him.*

Take your essay, I have given it an alpha in blind faith. Be careful with the flame.

THOMASINA: I will wait for you to come.

SEPTIMUS: I cannot.

THOMASINA: You may.

SEPTIMUS: I may not.

THOMASINA: You must.

SEPTIMUS: I will not.

> *She puts the candlestick and the essay on the table.*

THOMASINA: Then I will not go. Once more, for my birthday.

> *Septimus and Thomasina start to waltz together. Gus comes forward, startling Hannah.*

HANNAH: Oh!—you made me jump.

> *Gus looks resplendent. He is carrying an old and somewhat tattered stiff-backed portfolio fastened with a tape tied in a bow. He comes to Hannah and thrusts this present at her.*

Oh . . .

> *She lays the folio down on the table and starts to open it. It consists only of two boards hinged, containing Thomasina's drawing.*

"Septimus holding Plautus." *(To Gus.)* I was looking for that. Thank you.

> *Gus nods several times. Then, rather awkwardly, he bows to her. A Regency bow, an invitation to dance.*

Oh, dear, I don't really . . .

> *After a moment's hesitation, she gets up and they hold each other, keeping a decorous distance between them, and start to dance, rather awkwardly.*
>
> *Septimus and Thomasina continue to dance, fluently, to the piano. Curtain.*

Best Play Citation

THE CRYPTOGRAM

A Full-Length Play in Three Scenes

BY DAVID MAMET

Cast and credits appear on pages 365–366

DAVID MAMET was born November 30, 1947 in Chicago. He graduated from God-dard College in Vermont with a B.A. in English literature in 1969, after observing creative theater at close quarters as a busboy at Chicago's theater group Second City and having studied it at a professional school in New York. From 1971 to 1973 he was artist-in-residence at Goddard. In 1974 he became a member of the Illinois Arts Council faculty, and in 1975 he helped found and served for a time as artistic director of St. Nicholas Theater Company in Chicago, which mounted some of the first pro-ductions of his scripts including Reunion, Squirrels, Duck Variations *and* Sexual Perversity in Chicago.

Mamet's first experience in the New York theater was as usher, house manager and assistant stage manager of The Fantasticks *at the Sullivan Street Playouse in 1967. His first New York production was* Duck Variations *off off Broadway at St. Clements in May 1975, followed by* Sexual Perversity *at the same group in September 1975. His* American Buffalo *moved from its world premiere at Chicago's Goodman Theater in October 1975 to St. Clements in January 1976. Mamet received the 1975–76 Obie Award as best playwright for these OOB productions, but his career on the wider*

247

New York stages began officially with the off-Broadway program of Duck Variations *and* Sexual Perversity *at the Cherry Lane Theater for 273 performances beginning June 16, 1976. Later that season, on February 16, 1977, his* American Buffalo *was produced on Broadway, ran 135 performances, was named a Best Play of its season, won the Critics Award for best American play and established its author in the front rank of contemporary American playwrights with productions all over the world. It has been revived in New York June 3, 1981 for 262 performances off Broadway and October 27, 1983 for 102 performances on Broadway.*

Mamet's second Best Play, A Life in the Theater, *was presented off Broadway October 20, 1977 for 288 performances. His third,* Glengarry Glen Ross, *premiered January 27, 1984 at the Goodman Theater and opened on Broadway March 25, 1984, running for 378 performances and winning the Critics Award for best American play and the Pulitzer Prize (for its original staging in Chicago). Tony nominations that year included* Glengarry Glen Ross *for best play and* American Buffalo *for best revival, an unusual instance of an author with two different plays cited in two different categories in the same season.*

Mamet's fourth Best Play was Speed-the-Plow, *produced on Broadway May 3, 1988 just in time for a Tony nomination and minority representation in the Critics Award voting. It ran for 278 performances.* Oleanna *was his fifth Best Play, presented under Mamet's direction in the Back Bay Theater production, which had premiered May 1, 1992 at the American Repertory Theater in Cambridge, Mass. before arriving off Broadway October 25, 1992 for 513 performances, Mamet's longest New York run to date. It has been followed by his sixth Best Play,* The Cryptogram, *which opened off Broadway April 13, also under Mamet's own direction, after a world premiere in London and an American premiere at the American Repertory Theater. And it was not the only new Mamet work to have a successful run in New York this season. His one-acter* An Interview *was the curtain raiser for the three-play program* Death Defying Acts *which opened off Broadway March 6.*

Off-Broadway productions of works by this prolific and versatile playwright have included The Water Engine *(1977, transferred to Broadway with the curtain-raiser* Mr. Happiness); The Woods *(1979, a program of one-acts comprising* The Sanctity of Marriage, Dark Pony *and* Reunion; Edmond *(1982);* Prairie du Chien *and* The Shawl *(1985);* Vint *(1986, from a translation by Avrahm Yarmolinsky);* Where Were You When It Went Down *(1988, a sketch for the Manhattan Theater Club revue* Urban Blight); *and the one-act* Bobby Gould in Hell *on the Lincoln Center program* Oh, Hell! *(1989). He directed the popular magic show* Ricky Jay & His 52 Assistants *off Broadway last season. For the theater Mamet is also the author of* Lakeboat, The Revenge of the Space Pandas, The Spanish Prisoner, The Frog Prince *(staged OOB in 1985);* Two War Scenes: Cross Patch and Goldberg Street *(staged OOB in Ensemble Studio Theater's 1990 Marathon),* The Old Neighborhood *and translations/adaptations of Pierre Laville's* Red River *and Anton Chekhov's* The Cherry Orchard, Uncle Vanya *and* Three Sisters *(the latter presented OOB by Atlantic Theater Company in 1992–93).*

Mamet's screen plays have included The Postman Always Rings Twice, The Verdict, The Untouchables, House of Games *(writer-director),* Things Change *(co-author-director),* Homicide *(writer-director)* and Hoffa. *His work for the printed page includes* Warm and Cold *(a children's book);* Writing in Restaurants, Some Freaks *and* The Cabin *(essays);* On Directing Film; The Hero Pony *(poems); and* The Owl *(a children's book co-authored with his first wife, Lindsay Crouse).*

Mamet's long list of honors features many Joseph Jefferson Awards for distinguished Chicago offerings and grants from New York State Council on the Arts Plays for Young Audiences, Rockefeller (as playwright-in-residence) and CBS at Yale. He has taught acting and directing at NYU and the University of Chicago as well as at Yale Drama School. His activities often extend to Vermont, New York, Los Angeles and beyond, but home base for his wife (the actress Rebecca Pidgeon) and himself is Cambridge, Mass.

Time: 1959
Place: Donny's living room

Scene 1: One evening

SYNOPSIS: Del, a man in his 30s, is seated on the sofa in a sparsely-furnished living room whose major feature is a right-angled staircase upstage leading to the bedrooms on the floor above. A door to the kitchen is up left. John, a boy of about 10, comes down the stairs barefoot, in his pajamas. He has been looking for his slippers but can't find them, he must have packed them (he tells Del) for the forthcoming trip. Del doesn't believe John will need them. John produces a pair of socks and puts them on while explaining to Del that he's taking the slippers along to keep his feet warm in the cabin.

JOHN: I know I couldn't wear them in the woods.
DEL: No. No. That's right. Where were we?
JOHN: Issues of sleep.
DEL: ... is ...
JOHN: Issues of sleep.
DEL: No. I'm sorry. You were quite correct. To take your slippers. I spoke too quickly.
JOHN: That's all right.
DEL: Thank you. *(Pause.)* Where were we? Issues of sleep.
JOHN: And last night either.
DEL: Mm ... ?

JOHN: ... I couldn't sleep.
DEL: So I'm told.
> *Pause.*
JOHN: Last night, either.
DEL: Fine. What does it mean "I could not sleep"?
JOHN: ... what does it mean?
DEL: Yes. It means nothing other than the meaning you choose to assign to it.
JOHN: I don't get you.
DEL: I'm going to explain myself.
JOHN: Good.
DEL: A "Trip," for example, you've been looking forward to.
JOHN: A trip. Yes. Oh, yes.
DEL: ... absolutely right.
JOHN: ... that I'm excited.
DEL: ... who wouldn't be?
JOHN: *Anyone* would be.
DEL: That's right.
JOHN: ... to go in the *Woods* ... ?
DEL: Well. You see? You've answered your own question.
JOHN: Yes. That I'm excited.
DEL: I can't blame you.
JOHN: You can't.
DEL: No. Do you see?
JOHN: That it's natural.
DEL: I think it is.
JOHN: Is it?
DEL: I think it absolutely is. To go with your *father* ... ?
JOHN: Why isn't he home?
DEL: We don't know.

Even grownups feel so excited about such a trip, thinking about what they're leaving and what they're going toward, that they can't sleep either, Del assures John.

There is a crash offstage. Donny—John's mother, in her late 30s—is heard exclaiming that she's broken the teapot and spilled the tea. Del points out that this accident is probably an example of grownup excitement before a trip. Donny isn't going to the woods, "But," Del continues to John, "*you* are. And your father is. It's an upheaval." "It's a minor one," John observes and wants to know what Del felt when Del took a trip last week. Del felt no pressure, he says, "Because people differ."

Donny comes in to explain that the tea is delayed because she dropped the pot. She's surprised to find that John is downstairs instead of up in bed.

JOHN: I want to wait till my father comes home.
DONNY: Well, yes, I'm sure you do. But you need your sleep. And if you don't get it, you're not going on the trip.

JOHN: Will he be home soon?

DONNY: Yes. He will.

JOHN: Where is he?

DONNY: I don't know. Yes, I do, yes. He's at the Office. And he'll be home soon.

JOHN: Why is he working late?

DONNY: I don't know. We'll find out when he comes home, John. Must we do this every night?

JOHN: I only want . . .

DEL: Do you know what?

JOHN: I didn't want to upset you. I only . . .

DEL: . . . could I? . . .

JOHN: I only . . .

DEL: Could I make a suggestion? *(To John.)* John. Why don't you busy yourself?

DONNY: He has to sleep.

DEL: . . . but he's not *going* to sleep. He's . . .

JOHN: That's right.

DONNY: . . . one moment.

JOHN: . . . If I had something to *do* . . .

John suggests that since his father isn't packed for the trip, he might get a start on the packing for him. Donny tells John to go neaten up the attic (which is in some disarray after Donny's "rummaging"), at the same time looking for things John and his father might need on their trip. John goes upstairs on this mission, leaving the grownups to discuss his sleeplessness. Donny complains that it's the same every night, with a new excuse for staying awake. Sending him up to the attic is the answer, Del observes.

Donny shows Del a small photo she found during her rummaging. As Del studies the photograph, puzzled, wondering when it could have been taken, John returns from the attic. He forget to pack a coat and wonders which one he should take (the blue fabric one, Donny finally decides). Then John wants to know where his sweaters are, and where he can find the fishing equipment.

DONNY: The fishing stuff. They brought back. Last week, John. It's all . . .

JOHN: . . . they brought it back.

DONNY: Yes. It's up in the attic . . .

JOHN: You should have left it at the Cabin.

DONNY: It's in the attic. You'll see it up there.

DEL: . . . we were afraid . . .

DONNY: . . . they didn't want it to Get Stolen.

JOHN: And the fishing line. Do we have that good line?

DEL: . . . we were afraid it would get taken.

JOHN: . . . that good heavy line . . . ?

DONNY: . . . I'm sorry, John . . . ?

JOHN: The fishing line.

DONNY: I'm sure you. Yes. Fishing line. In the same box.

John indicates his father wants him to bring the special line, very strong. Donny sends him back to the attic to look for it, also telling him to put some clothes on.

DEL (*of photo*): ... when was this taken?
DONNY: I swear. He's ...
DEL: What? Well, he's having difficulty sleeping.
DONNY: It's all such a mystery.
DEL: Do you think?
DONNY: Yes. All our good intentions ...
DEL: Big thing. Going in the Woods. Your Father ...
DONNY: ... mmm.
DEL: ... big thing.
DONNY: Is it?
DEL: Hope to tell you.
DONNY (*pause*): It goes so quickly.
DEL: Certain things remain.
DONNY: Yes?
DEL (*pause*): Friendship ... (*Pause.*) Certain habits.
DONNY: It goes so quickly ...

Sometimes Donny wishes she were an old man, a monk who simply sits and gazes out at "his domain." Donny pursues her "fantasy of rest," but Del is preoccupied with the photograph, noting that the absence of a tree in it could give them a clue as to when it was taken. Del wonders what Donny is planning to do this weekend with her son and husband away and offers to keep her company when she replies, "I'm going to sit."

John comes down wrapped in a plaid stadium blanket, which isn't what Donny meant when she told him to put some clothes on. He confesses that he pulled it out too quickly, heard it rip on a nail or something and now the blanket has a tear in it (which he shows). Donny corrects John: the blanket was torn long ago.

John is somewhat upset because the tackle box is tied up with twine, and he cannot untie it. Del takes out a knife and offers it to John to cut the twine, if Donny will give John permission to use it. Donny thinks it's all right for John to use it, and John agrees that his father would permit it.

DEL: Then there you go.
      Hands John the knife.
JOHN: Where did you get the knife, though?
DONNY: Good *Lord,* please ... calm *down* tonight.
JOHN: No.
DONNY: What?
JOHN: I can't.

Ed Begley Jr. as Del and Felicity Huffman as Donny in a scene from *The Cryptogram,* written and directed by David Mamet

DONNY: ... why not?

JOHN: The Tea, the Blanket ... ?

DONNY: I don't understand.

JOHN: I'm *waiting* for it.

DEL: You're waiting for what?

JOHN: "The Third Misfortune."

DEL: "The Third Misfortune."

DONNY: Third ... ?

JOHN: I'm waiting to see "What is the Third Misfortune?"
   Pause.

DONNY: What does he mean?

JOHN: It's in the book.

DEL: Misfortunes come in threes.

DONNY: Where *is* that book, by the way?

JOHN: Misfortunes come in threes.

DONNY: The third misfortune. I remember. Yes.

JOHN: It's in the book.

The two present misfortunes (John informs his mother) are the breaking of the teapot and the tearing of the blanket. The latter doesn't count, Donny insists, because it happened so long ago. John *thought* he tore it just now, but Del tells him, "Because we *think* a thing is one way does not mean that this is the way that this thing must be."

John now wonders whether Del noticed his grey hat hanging on a peg at the cabin. Del doesn't remember seeing it there "Because I wasn't looking for it." This leads Del to suggest a game that John and his father can play, to sharpen their skills—maybe John's father already knows the game, maybe not. At the end of the day they must write down everything they've observed, then compare to "see whose recollection was more accurate." It could be things they decided in advance to observe, or decided later to remember. And, John remarks, perhaps something that happened a long time ago could be the Third Misfortune.

DEL: How could that be?

JOHN: It could be if the Third Misfortune happened long ago. If, when it *happened,* no one *noticed,* or . . .

DEL: "at the *time* . . ."

JOHN: Yes, or neglected to *count* it . . .

DEL: . . . I . . .

JOHN: . . . until we recognized it *now* . . . And also, what could we pick? To observe, beside the Cabin?

DEL: What? *Anything.* The *pond,* the . . .

JOHN: . . . where did you get the knife?

DEL: The knife.

JOHN: Yes.

DEL: I told you. Your father gave it to me.

JOHN: He gave you his war knife.

DEL: Yes.

JOHN: His *pilot's* knife . . . ?

DEL: Yes.

> *Pause.*

JOHN: But we couldn't choose the pond.

DEL: Why not?

JOHN: Because it's changing. *(Pause.)* When?

DEL: . . . when what?

JOHN: Did he give it to you?

DEL: Aha.

JOHN: When?

DEL: Last week. When we went camping.

JOHN: Oh.

DEL: Does that upset you?

JOHN: No.

When Donny comes back with tea mugs, Del asks her about the photo—he knows it's of the lake, but he doesn't remember it being taken. Del is grinning, John observes, which isn't like him. From the photo's details, Del deduces that it was taken "before the War." Del is wearing Robert's (Donny's husband's) shirt in the photo but can't recall why, or when the picture could have been taken.

John has fallen asleep, giving Del the opportunity to tell Donny, "I believe that this trip has a 'meaning' for him." Del also feels that John is jealous of the trip his father went on last week with Del. Donny replies, "*Let* him be jealous. What if he was? Yes. I think he needs to spend more time with his father; and, yes, I think that he has to learn the world does not revolve around him." After a pause she confesses to Del that she feels consumed with guilt.

Returning to the photo with which he's preoccupied, Del has noticed that they are all in it, and so he wonders who could have snapped it. Donny doesn't remember, but she is amazed at the amount of stuff from the past, including the stadium blanket, which has accumulated in the attic. Del also finds himself filling the hotel room in which he lives with a collection, mostly of papers, which he must clean out every so often.

DONNY: I went to the Point.

DEL: You did?

DONNY: I walked down there. Yes.

DEL: Recently?

DONNY: Yes. *(Pause.)* And I remembered. When the Three of us would go. Late at night. Before the war.

DEL: I remember.

DONNY: And *Robert* and I. Would make love under a blanket. And I wondered. After all this time, why it never occurred to me. I don't know. But I wondered. Did you *hear* us; and if you did. If it upset you.

> *Pause.*

DEL: And you've thought about it all this time.

DONNY: That's right.

DEL: Oh, Donny.

DONNY: Did it upset you?

DEL: Aren't you sweet . . . aren't you sweet to worry.

DONNY: Did it?

DEL: Well. I . . .

But their conversation breaks off when John awakens, wondering whether his father has come home yet. John is told again that he didn't tear the blanket, it happened a long time ago, but he doesn't remember it. John wants to know what it was used for (a coverlet), where his mother got it (in London, at an arcade) and whether his father was with her at the time (no, he was away at war). They used the blanket to cover John when he was little but put it away after it was torn.

Once again Donny tells John to go to bed, but John wants to talk about voices and singing he hears either in his head or outside his room as he is going to sleep. And he still wants to know how the blanket got torn, and where his father is, and he plans to play the game Del suggested: "So, I'll ask my Dad, first thing, 'You tell me the name of an *object*. Or a collection of things' . . . you know what I mean." As John starts upstairs, he picks up a white envelope and Donny gives him the blanket.

> DONNY (*of envelope*): What have you got?
> JOHN: Goodnight.
> DONNY: . . . what is that?
> JOHN: It's a letter . . . it's a note for you.
> > *Donny takes it, opens it.*

And it could be something . . . it would have to be something *new* . . . something that would . . .

> DONNY: . . . that's right . . .
> JOHN: . . . *surprise* us.
> DONNY: . . . when did this get here . . . ?
> JOHN: . . . you see?
> DONNY: John. Go to bed. Now. Yes.
> JOHN: Do you see?
> DONNY: Go to bed.
> JOHN: All right. I understand. I'm going.
> DEL: Goodnight, John.
> > *John exits.*

What is it?

> DONNY: It's a letter to me.
> > *Pause.*
> DEL: A letter. *(Pause.)* What does it say?
> DONNY: My husband's leaving me.
> DEL: He's leaving you. *(Pause.)* Why would he want to do that?

Scene 2: The next night

Donny is listening to John, in his bathrobe, conjecturing that maybe everything is a void—no real thoughts in his head, no people in the buildings, no real cities or places where that map of the world says they are. Or, on the contrary, maybe everything is real.

Del enters and indicates at once that he hasn't been able to find John's father. He pours some medicine into a spoon and tries to give it to John to make him sleep, but John refuses: "Every time I go to sleep I see things." Donny conjures words like "hospital" and "doctor," but John still says no.

> JOHN: No one understands. You think that I'm *in* something . . . You don't know what I'm feeling.
> DEL: What are you feeling?
> > *Pause.*

Are you afraid to go to bed?

JOHN: Yes.

DONNY: Why?

DEL: What are you afraid of in there?

JOHN: I don't know.

DONNY: I . . . I . . . I know it *frightens* you . . .

JOHN: I don't want to go to sleep.

DEL: All right, all right, I'm going to *promise* you . . . look at me. John. I'm going to *promise* you if you take this and . . . you take this and go upstairs, then you won't be afraid. I promise. *(Pause.)* I promise you.

>   Pause.

JOHN: I sweat through the sheets . . .

DEL: We'll change . . .

JOHN: . . . the *bed* is wet.

DEL: We'll change, we'll change the sheets, you don't have to worry.

DONNY: You go lie down in my bed.

DEL: . . . you lie down in your mother's bed. *(Pause.)* You go lie down there.

JOHN: I'm going to sweat them.

DEL: That's all right. Do you hear what I'm telling you . . . ?

>   Pause.

JOHN: Maybe I'll just . . . maybe I'll just go there . . . maybe I'll just go there and lie down.

DONNY: Yes. You go and lie down now. You take this, now.

>   *Del gives John his medicine.*

John admits he's tired and that he doesn't feel quite right (he has a fever, his mother tells him), and he disappears upstairs.

Del apologizes to Donny for not having been able to find her husband and suggests a game of gin or casino, but Donny opts for a drink. Del opens a new bottle with his knife, gets two glasses from the kitchen and pours two drinks. They work out a toast between them: May they always be as close to each other as they are now. Maybe the answer to everything (Del proposes) is getting drunk and reviewing the memories now dulled by time. Del offers to check on John, but Donny is sure he's all right. Del again apologizes for not finding Robert, commenting, "I suppose I thought that . . . . . it wasn't a good *idea* to have him come here. But what business is that of *mine?* . . . . . None. None, really."

Donny admits Robert's leaving her is a shock, but she and Del should have seen it coming because Robert's giving Del his German knife was what Donny calls an "Odd Gesture" of parting, a going-away present. The knife, Donny reminds Del, is a pilot's knife with a specific purpose.

DONNY: If he was forced to *parachute* . . .

DEL: Yes.

DONNY: The pilot would use it to cut the *cords*. If his parachute snagged.

DEL: Huh. If it snagged. On, on what?

DONNY: On a tree.

DEL: Oh, you mean when he landed.

DONNY: Yes.

DEL: Huh.

> *Pause.*

DONNY: And that's the meaning.

> *Pause.*

DEL: ... yes ...

DONNY: When he was forced to abandon ...

DEL: Yes. *(Pause.)* When he was forced to *abandon* his ... *(Pause.)* He looked for *safety,* and the knife, it cut ... it "released" him.

DONNY: Yes. That's right.

DEL: ... as *any* tool ...

DONNY: And he gave it to you.

DEL: He can be very generous. Is that all right? To ...

DONNY: Yes. No. He can *(Pause.)* ... what am I going to do? You tell me. Yes. He could be generous. *I* don't know.

DEL: ... he was opening a can. With it. And I said ... actually, he saw me looking at the knife. And he wiped it. And gave it to me.

> *Pause.*

DONNY: When you were at the Camp. Last week.

DEL: That's right—

Donny wants to know what they talked about there in the woods. Robert seemed to be happy and (Del says) gave no hint that he planned to leave Donny. Once again, Donny gets Del to tell her that Robert gave him the knife on last week's camping trip, then informs him that, on the contrary, the knife was upstairs in the attic—she saw it when she put the other camping things away last week.

Del suggests that maybe Robert went upstairs to put it back before Donny put back the equipment. "You said he gave it to you when you were camping," Donny finishes, "How could he give it to you when you were *camping,* when it was here in the trunk when you both came back?"

Del tries to sell the idea that maybe there were two knives, or Robert came to get it from the trunk instead of giving it to Del at the cabin, but Donny isn't buying. In fact, she now doubts that they ever went camping at all. She wants to know the truth about why Robert gave Del the knife.

DEL: You don't want to know.

DONNY: I do.

DEL: *Believe* me, you don't. *(Pause.)* To shut me up. All right? There. Are you *happy?* I told you you wouldn't be.

DONNY: To shut you up about what?

> *Pause.*

DEL: Because we didn't go.

DONNY: What?

DEL: We didn't *go!* Do I have to *shout* it for you. . . ? We stayed *home.* What do you *think?* He'd traipse off in the *wilds* . . . with *me* . . . ? To talk about *life?* Are you *stupid?* Are you *blind?* He wouldn't spend a *moment* with me. Some poor geek . . . "Here's my Old Friend Del . . ." You're *nuts,* you're *stupid* if you think that's what went on. *(Pause.)* He used my *room,* all right? He said, "Del, can I Use Your Room?" Is that so weird? There. Now I've told you. Now you can sleep easier. I *told* you not to ask. Don't tell me I didn't tell you.

    Pause.

DONNY: He used your room.

DEL: That's absolutely right.

DONNY: Why?

    Pause.

DEL: To go there with a woman. *(Pause.)* And now, and now you know the truth, how weak I am. How "Evil" I am. He said, "I have some things to do," "I want it to seem like I'm gone." *I* spent the week, *I* slept in the, in my, my nook in the *library.* In *fishing* clothes . . . and don't you think *that* looked stupid! *(Pause.)* I . . . I actually, I've been waiting for this. I knew that I should tell you. This is the only bad thing I have ever done to you. I'm sorry that it came out like this. Indeed I am. *(Pause.)* But we can't always choose the, um . . .

    Pause.

DONNY: Get out. *(Pause.) GET OUT.*

    Del exits.

Donny starts to cry. John appears on the stairs in his bathrobe, asking, "Are you dead?" but not explaining to his mother why he asked that particular question.

JOHN: I heard voices . . .

DONNY: . . . you should go back to bed.

JOHN: . . . and I thought they were you.

    Pause.

DONNY: It was me.

JOHN: And so I said, ". . . there's someone troubled." And I walked around. Did you hear walking?

DONNY: No.

JOHN: . . . and so I went outside. I saw a candle. In the dark.

DONNY: Where was this?

JOHN: In my room. It was burning there. I said, "I'm perfectly alone." This is what I was saying to myself: "I'm perfectly alone." And I think I was saying it a long time. Cause I didn't have a pen. Did that ever happen to you?

DONNY: I don't know, John.

JOHN: So I came downstairs to write it down. I know that there *are* pens up there. But I don't want to look for them.

    Donny goes to him and cradles him.

Do you think that was right?

DONNY: Shhh.

JOHN: Do you think that I was right?

DONNY: Go to bed.

JOHN: Mother?

   Pause.

DONNY: What?

JOHN: Do you think that I was right?

DONNY: I don't know, John.

JOHN: I saw a candle in my room.

Scene 3: One month later, evening

The room now contains packing boxes instead of furniture, and obviously the movers are expected. John asks his mother, "Do you ever wish that you could die?" Donny answers him by asserting that the events of life have meaning, even though that meaning may be obscure. John persists with the question, but Donny is unable to answer it directly.

DONNY: At some point . . . there are things that have occurred I cannot help you with . . . that . . .

JOHN: I can't sleep.

DONNY: Well. It's an unsettling time.

JOHN: . . . I want . . .

DONNY: Yes?

JOHN: I would like to go to the Cabin.

DONNY: . . . well . . .

JOHN: I want to go to the Lake.

DONNY: Well, no, John, we can't. You know we can't.

JOHN: I don't know that.

DONNY: No. We can't.

JOHN: That's why I can't sleep.

DONNY: What do you want me to do? John? I am not God. I don't control the World. If you could think what it is I could do for you . . . If I could help you . . . *(Sound of kettle offstage.)*

JOHN: Did you ever wish you could die? *(Pause.)* It's not such a bad feeling. Is it?

DONNY: I know that you're frightened. I know you are. But at some point, do you see . . . *(Pause. Exits. Speaks offstage.)* John, everyone has a story. Did you know that? In their lives. This is yours.

   Del enters.

And finally . . . finally . . . you are going to have to learn how you will deal with it. You understand? I'm going to speak to you as an adult. At some point . . . At some point, we have to learn to face ourselves.

Shelton Dane as John with Ed Begley Jr.
and Felicity Huffman in *The Cryptogram*

Del came to see John, he says, but John avoids him and disappears upstairs, as Donny comes in with mugs of tea. She asks after Robert. Del doesn't see Robert, he assures her; he has come here to see her and the boy, bringing a book of Donny's he's had for years and the pilot's knife for John. The boy should have it as a memento of his father's service in the war. But Robert did not capture it in the fighting, Donny declares and adds, "Could he capture the knife from the other man in the air? You fool." He bought it in London.

Del believes that Donny is telling him this to hurt him, to reveal that the knife he prizes as a gift from his friend Robert has no real or important war association for that friend. Del continues, "Oh, if we could speak the truth, do you see, for one instant. Then we would be free. *(Pause.)* I should have chucked it anyway. *(Pause.)* How could a knife be a suitable gift for a child? No, but we know it can't. We bring our . . . our little 'gifts.' And take your book. It's your goddam book. I've had it at the hotel. All these years. I borrowed it and never brought it back. How about that. Eh? Years ago. That's how long I've had it. Was ever anyone so false? Take it. I hate it. I hate the whole fucking progression. Here. Take the cursed thing."

Donny shows Del that it's really not her book but his—it has his name in it. "I'm pathetic. I know that. You don't have to tell me. The life I lead is trash," Del says, but there are still things he wants to talk to Donny and John about. John appears on the stairs—he is chilly and afraid—"I know I should not *think* about certain things"—but Donny doesn't see that there is anything she can do about this. John wants the stadium blanket, but it's in the attic, Donny has already packed it in a box for the movers. Donny gives John permission to unpack it if he will promise to then go to sleep. John promises and exits.

After John has disappeared, Donny complains bitterly to Del that she has never found any man who wouldn't betray her. This sets Del to apologizing for his own recent betrayal of Donny.

DONNY: Isn't that sweet. Aren't you sweet. How could one be miffed with you? The problem must be *mine.*

DEL: I'm sorry I betrayed you.

DONNY: Just like the rest of them. All of you are.

DEL: I'm sorry.

DONNY: Can you explain it to me, though? Why? *(Pause.)* You see? That's what baffles me. I try to say "human nature" . . .

DEL: . . . I know . . .

DONNY: I don't know what our nature is. If I do, then it's bad.

DEL: . . . I know . . .

DONNY: If I do, then it's filthy. No, you don't know. You have no idea. All the men I ever met . . .

DEL: And I'm so sorry. To have added one iota, in my stupid . . .

DONNY: In this cesspool.

DEL: Could I . . .

DONNY *(pause)*: No. I don't care any more.

DEL: Could I talk to you? Who am I? Some poor Queen. Lives in a hotel. Some silly old Soul Who loves you.

DONNY: Oh, please.

DEL: No. I need you to forgive me.

Del tries to get Donny to face up to whatever reason these betrayals take place—whether it's pure chance or, possibly, whether Donny provokes them. The idea that it might be her own fault startles Donny.

Del has observed Donny and John closely for quite a while. He's about to continue with his conclusions and advice based on this close relationship, when John appears on the stairs. Donny refuses to listen to any excuses from John for breaking his promise to go to bed, telling him, "I love you, but I can't like you," because breaking his solemn promise is a sort of lie.

Del intercedes, trying to calm the boy and giving him the book to take to bed with him. Finally John manages to get in the explanation that he was given permission to take the blanket out of the box; but the box is tied up with twine, and John needs a knife to cut it. Since the kitchen knives are all packed now, John will have to do without the blanket, even though he was told he could have it.

John starts to exit without replying to Del's "Goodnight," which fans the flames of Donny's anger: "I'm speaking to you. Come back here. John? The man said goodnight to you. Come back down and tell the man you're sorry." When John remains silent, Donny asks him, "What must I do that you treat me like an animal?" When Del tries to calm the waters by telling her it's all right, Donny turns on him.

DONNY: . . . . . Don't you *dare* to dispute me.

DEL: The child . . .

DONNY: Don't you *dare* to dispute me in my home. How, I'm *speaking* to you, John. Don't stand there so innocently. I've asked you a question. Do you want me to go mad? Is that what you want? Is that what you want?

DEL: Your mother's speaking to you, John.

DONNY: Is that what you want?

DEL: She asked you a question.

DONNY: Can't you see that I need comfort? Are you blind? For the love of God . . .

JOHN: I hear voices.

DEL: John. Your mother's waiting for you to . . .

JOHN: Before I go to sleep.

DEL: Your mother's waiting, John. What does she want to hear?

JOHN: . . . before I go to sleep.

DEL: What does she want to hear you say?

JOHN: I don't know.

DEL: I think that you do. *(Pause.)* What does she want to hear you say?

     Pause.

JOHN: "I'm sorry."

DEL: What?

JOHN: I'm sorry.

DEL: All right, then.

JOHN: You told me I could have the blanket.

DONNY: Goodnight, John.

JOHN: You told me I could have the blanket.

DEL: Yes. You can.

JOHN: It's wrapped up.

DEL: Take the knife. When you're done . . .

> *Hands the boy the knife.*

JOHN: I can't fall asleep.

DEL: That's up to you, now.

JOHN: I hear voices. They're calling to me.

> *Pause.*

DONNY: Yes I'm sure they are.

JOHN: They're calling me.

DEL: Take the knife and go.

JOHN: They're calling my name. *(Pause.)* Mother. They're calling my name.

> *Curtain.*

Best Play Citation

NIGHT AND HER STARS

A Play in Two Acts

BY RICHARD GREENBERG

Cast and credits appear on pages 351, 353

RICHARD GREENBERG was born in 1958 in East Meadow, Long Island, the son of an executive of a film theater chain. He was educated in local schools and went to college at all of the Big Three: Princeton (B.A. 1980), Harvard (in a Ph.D. course in English literature, abandoned after less than a year) and Yale (M.F.A. from the Drama School in 1985, where he won the Molly Kazan Playwriting Award). He began writing fiction at Princeton, including a novel for his thesis; but it was his first play, started after the Harvard experience and later submitted to Yale, that won him a place in the playwriting program under Oscar Brownstein.

Greenberg's first New York production took place while he was still at Yale: The Bloodletters *off off Broadway November 17, 1984 at Ensemble Studio Theater. It won him the 1985 Oppenheimer Award for best new playwright. His one-acter* Life Under Water *was produced by the same OOB group later that season and was published in the* Best Short Plays *volume of its year. Ensemble also mounted his one-acters* Vanishing Act *(1986) and* The Author's Voice *(1987, also a Best Short Plays selection). Also in 1987, his adaptation of a Martha Clarke performance work based on Kafka writing,* The Hunger Artist, *appeared OOB as a Music Theater Group/ Lenox Arts Center showcase.*

Greenberg's first full off-Broadway production was The Maderati *at Playwrights Horizons February 19, 1987 for 12 performances. His first Best Play,* Eastern Standard, *opened October 27, 1988 at Manhattan Theater Club (after a run the previous season at Seattle Repertory Theater), played 46 off-Broadway performances, transferred to Broadway January 5, 1989 for 92 additional performances and was twice cited among the Outer Critics Circle nominees for the bests of the season. Greenberg's second Best Play,* The American Plan, *was produced at Manhattan Theater Club December 16, 1990 for 37 performances. For the third season in a row he provided the New York stage with a a Best Play,* The Extra Man, *which opened a 39-performance run May 19, 1992 at Manhattan Theater Club. (Things were happening in threes at MTC;* The Extra Man *was not only their third Greenberg play but their third 1991-92 Best Play, with* Lips Together, Teeth Apart *and* Sight Unseen.*) Still at MTC, his fourth Best Play is this season's* Night and Her Stars *which opened April 26 after a production a year before in March at South Coast Repertory in Costa Mesa, Calif. (and it too is one-third of an MTC triple: MTC's* Love! Valour! Compassion! *and* After-Play *are also Best Plays of this season).*

Greenberg is also the author of Neptune's Hips *(1988, Ensemble Studio Theater OOB),* Jenny Keeps Taking, *a solo play written for Leslie Ayvazian, at MTC for 30 performances April 8, 1993, under the nom de plume Lise Erlich and the TV scripts* Trying Times *and the adaptation of his own* Life Under Water. *He is a member of the Dramatists Guild and Ensemble Studio Theater, lives in New York City and almost always starts a new play while in rehearsal for the previous one.*

The following synopsis of Night and Her Stars *was prepared by Sally Dixon Wiener.*

ACT I

SYNOPSIS: The play, the title of which is taken from Ralph Waldo Emerson's *The American Scholar,* is set in various locales, and the action is fluid. An old-fashioned morality play with a relentlessly high-tech setting, it is performed in two acts, and the audience is frequently addressed. The upstage wall is comprised of panels, some or all of which are lit up periodically, sometimes as television screens, or, at other times, as a background (such as a diagonally-placed article deploring television, or the raised keys of an old-fashioned standard typewriter). At numerous points in the play titles also appear. Sound is taped and/or live. There are two elevated booths, stage right and left; and, as the play begins, downstage center is a 1950s television set with rabbit-ear antennae facing upstage—a centerpiece, so to speak. Nine cast members play the more than three dozen roles.

The play, the author notes in the Playbill "is based in history, has much in common with history, must not be mistaken for history. Facts have been shifted, eliminated, re-combined, and invented . . . . . And while the characters of the play have far too much in common with their (well-known) real world counterparts for changing names to have been an option . . . . . they have been freely imagined and should be considered virtually fictional."

In the dark we hear an announcer doing a Revlon commercial; then we see coves of light before three television fans watching The Sixty-Four Thousand Dollar Question. Each hopes the contestant will win and is disappointed when the contestant's answer is wrong. A young fan comes on, wondering what life was like before television. Up above, a title informs us that the quiz shows are the rage of 1956. The lights go up on Dan Enright, suave, unctuous, slickly-tailored and groomed, and smiling. The Machiavellian television executive (who also plays the announcer) is addressing the audience.

ENRIGHT:
  But are we satisfied?
  Remember: I was there for radio.
  Radio was fine,
  but radio, listen:
  with radio, there was an out,
  a margin for error,
  a crack for the imagination.
  That was its weakness,
  the fatal flaw—
  but flaws are for mending
  and now we have these Boxes of Light,
  Boxes of Light
  speeding one vision through the land.
  Now when Ma Perkins is on,
  she's not "my" Ma Perkins,
  she's just, "Ma Perkins"—
  the absolute, uncontested, no-room-for-doubt Ma Perkins.
  Maybe I'm crazy, but that gives me a little thrill.

The run's been good enough with "these little quiz things," he admits, The Sixty-Four Thousand Dollar Question, The Big Payoff, Tic-Tac-Dough, Name That Tune, Top Dollar, et cetera, and his "masterpiece"—Twenty-One. Television's perfect for right now when society's a machine that's nearly perfect. The only job is to make television make people happy. But Enright's afraid of the days ahead—the days being past when a nation could be mesmerized by a test pattern. People are ungrateful to technology as they are to God.

ENRIGHT:
  And can we blame the people, can we?
  When week after week
  on our little show
  it might as well be the butcher
  carrying off the prize,
  might as well be the neurasthenic auntie

or Cousin Homer with the problem—
Might as well?
Hell, it is!
Too many weeks of commonness . . . . .
The time has come,
we need a hero.
We need the tall man,
the tall, graceful, brilliant, virile
and undeflectably *deserving* man—
We need a hero
and I'll make a hero
and I'll make him *now*
because, cliche:
There's no time like the present
and no time to waste.
Good evening.

A new title assures us that people at night across America are watching Twenty-One, and we see two contestants in the lit booths and Jack Barry. He's a large fair man, a little heavy, old-boy, but boyish. Downstage, watching the show on television are Enright, and Al Freedman (youngish, dark-haired, horned-rimmed-glasses-wearing, intense). Also present are a network person and a sponsor. The sponsor is unhappy. As a contestant in a booth is stumped and silent, the sponsor wants to know what he's watching. Enright explains it's concentration, suspense. The sponsor's not buying it. He likes silence, but in its place. In church, when he's praying. The network person reports talking's about to begin, just as Barry cuts a contestant off with a "Sorry—your time is up—".

The sponsor is livid. He's been promised Einsteins, and the people in the isolation booths filing their nails and failing to recall what the nuns taught them are not filling the bill. The sponsor must appeal to the geriatric market, and when he watches this (he's seeing another contestant stumped) he can only think that 80-year-old ladies will not love this.

Enright tries to defend the talent he's recruited, but the sponsor expects better. Enright promises him there is somebody—somebody who scored higher on the test than anybody ever has, but he is a little peculiar. He's "vivid" though, Enright insists. He's Herb Stempel, almost sure to be a champion. The sponsor, relieved, leaves, and Freedman wonders if Enright's concerned. But Enright is onto a theory that there's some kind of fuse that links unlikely people, like Hitler and Ghandi, for instance, or Marilyn Monroe and Douglas MacArthur.

FREEDMAN: The point of this bullshit being . . .
ENRIGHT:
    The point of this bullshit being
    Twenty-One is not going down the toilet—

it's not my destiny.
I've been thinking ...
FREEDMAN: ... Now?
ENRIGHT: Yes, now, I think. Whose idea was it?
FREEDMAN: Who remembers?
ENRIGHT *(to us through this section):* The contestants have to have charisma—
FREEDMAN: —to attract the viewers—
ENRIGHT: They have to have brains—
FREEDMAN: —to be persuasive in interviews—
ENRIGHT: They have to keep secrets well—
FREEDMAN: —to save our asses.

Enright calls Stempel, and it is revealed he is at home in Forest Hills, baby-sitting while his wife is at the movies.

Enright is now in Forest Hills in Stempel's home. Herb Stempel is a decent-enough-looking young man, but something about him is just a little off-kilter.

ENRIGHT *(reading from cards):*
  This unfinished church
  is one of the landmarks of Barcelona, Spain—
STEMPEL:
  Say no more—
  I've got it, I've got it:
  The Church of the Holy Family
  actually commenced by Francesco del Vilar in 1882,
  but taken over by the famed genius Antonio Gaudi
  the following year and continued by him
  until 1926 when he was run over by a Barcelona streetcar.
  And killed.
  Needless to say.
  So he stopped.
  Shall I describe its lineaments?
  Thirteen tubular towers were planned,
  pillars that swayed,
  very peculiar—
ENRIGHT:
  No, no no—
  not necessary.
  You've answered the question.
STEMPEL:
  After his death,
  his friends and assistants—
ENRIGHT: Herb—
STEMPEL: —continued work to finish—

ENRIGHT:
> Herb.
> Done.

STEMPEL:
> Oh, oh, sure.
>> *Beat.*
> Because only one of the tubes and one transept
> were completed when he—

ENRIGHT: Moving on—

STEMPEL:
> —kicked it.
> Gotcha.
> Go.

Asked the capital of Nepal, Stempel remarks "Oh, please," but answers "Katmandu" when Enright informs him they do not pay for "Oh, please." Again Stempel wants to go on with the same topic, but Enright cuts him off. Stempel finds it hard to control himself because he is so knowledgeable that he's "bursting." But he also would like to know if Enright thinks being on the program will help his career. It seems Stempel wants to be an actor. He's been told he has a lot of potential but tends to be miscast. Now he thinks it's the right time for him with the "new vogue for kitchen sink realism," because he regards himself as the realistic type. Enright hedges but assures Stempel being on the program won't reduce his chances.

Enright asks Stempel another question from his cards (about the national anthem of South Africa), and Stempel is hard put to come up with the answer. This upsets him and even makes him wonder if he didn't suffer some kind of momentary physical lapse. He wants to know whether the questions on the program will be like these. Enright maneuvers around answering him directly.

ENRIGHT:
> . . . . . We do sometimes say, don't we?
> that a person is behaving in a way that's so *like* himself?
> Don't we?
> Or so *unlike* himself?

STEMPEL: . . . Uh . . . yes . . .

ENRIGHT:
> So, I suppose by that logic, yes—
> These questions are very "like" the real ones.

STEMPEL: Oh . . . Oh!

ENRIGHT:
> Memorize this:
> You'll begin by asking for a nine point question.
> You'll answer that correctly.
> You'll stutter a little, as you do.

We'll turn off the air in the isolation booth
to make you sweat.
You'll follow that question with another nine point question.
Another correct answer.
Stuttering.
Sweating.
Then—

STEMPEL:
Excuse me—!
Is this really how it works?

ENRIGHT:
Yes.
This is how it works.

STEMPEL:
Because I thought
the points and all—
I thought that was my choice.

ENRIGHT:
It is.
Of course it is.
You'll *choose* a nine point question.
Then you'll *choose* another.
Those will be your choices.
What's the problem?

STEMPEL:
. . . No.
Nothing . . .
No . . .

ENRIGHT:
Of course
you'll mention this to no one.
> *Beat. They look at each other.*
'Cause, you know, this could cause
me a whole lot of *tsuris.*
But when we met
I had this instinct . . .
I mean, I *think* I know I can trust you.
> *Beat. Stempel smiles tentatively.*

Enright goes off to poke into Stempel's closet—to dress him for the show. Stempel had thought his clothes from Brooks Brothers would be suitable. Enright demurs and brings out a shiny suit for Stempel to try on, actually Stempel's father-in-law's suit, smaller than his own clothes and representing Pitkin Avenue taste. Stempel is not happy. He wants to make a good impression, but Enright insists.

Stempel goes on, worrying about having failed the anthem question, and talking about his "eidetic" memory (like photographic but he prefers "eidetic" because it's not as well-known a word), and he's still concerned about his appearance. Enright feels it's perfectly in character and sums up his image of Stempel: ex-serviceman, goes to City College at night, a Brooklynite (Stempel protests he's from Queens), married, with a baby boy, limited resources (his in-laws help out, Stempel emphasizes).

Enright asks Stempel to give him his watch. It ticks very loudly. Enright asks Stempel to wear it for that very reason, the closer to the microphone the better. Stempel will sweat and stutter and tick and look poor, as Enright envisions him in the isolation booth.

ENRIGHT:
> . . . . . Can this man put bread on the table?
> Will his child perish
> of some poor-person's disease
> in terrible Brooklyn?
> Tune in next week.
> Hypnotic.
> Splendid.
> We'll all make a lot of money . . .
>> *Pause.*

STEMPEL *(suddenly, almost in a rage):*
> Look—
> I just want you to know—
> If this isn't how it's done—
> If I'm a special case—
> You know, "Good for the Jews" or something—
> I don't need it—
> I'm a fantastic answerer—
> I know all the answers—
> I can do it myself!
> I can do it myself.
> These clothes . . . Jeez.
> My wife thinks I'm attractive.

ENRIGHT:
> This *is* how it's done—
> I can assure you.
> Herb—really—you're about to be a champion.

STEMPEL:
> . . . Yes.
> Very true.
> In that case, I'm happy to oblige.

Stempel's wife Toby—a sweet, baffled-seeming, overstuffed baked potato of a woman, arrives as Enright is about to leave. He'll be talking with Herb, Enright states as he exits. Stempel explains to Toby that Enright is "good news," but Toby wonders why her husband is wearing that ill-fitting suit.

As we see *The Christian Century* editorial on the upstage panels, we hear aloud the condemnation of not just television itself, but now the quiz programs as well, and then Stempel is making his debut on the program. Barry introduces him, not forgetting to ask if that tree is still growing there in Brooklyn. Stempel goes into the booth and puts on the headphones. The category is national anthems. He chooses a nine point question. It's the one Stempel had trouble with when Enright questioned him previously. This time he knows the answer. Barry congratulates the smiling Stempel. But a housewife complains to the producers that their new champion makes her nervous, want to shower, to scratch herself. If she's crackers, as Enright suggests, they can't all be, the sponsor argues. There have been other letters. It's the "fascination of the abomination" Enright explains.

It is late evening at the Stempel home. Toby, who can't sleep, is awake when her husband arrives home. He's had dinner in the Village with friends and then was thrilled, at a jazz concert afterward, to be recognized. He was sorry she hadn't come to meet him. (Her mother would have sat with the baby.) He tells Toby she's pretty. Toby confesses she's tense. Stempel, it seems, has told Enright their financial situation, and Enright has given Stempel an advance on his winnings. But suppose he doesn't win? Toby points out. Stempel brushes that aside. The advance is a considerable amount of money, and Stempel wants to give Toby a present, not just to pay the bills, but a luxury. "How would you like a little analysis?" Stempel suggests, and Toby protests that she may get a little nervous sometimes, but it's Stempel who chronically overreacts: "Every good comes thirteen-to-the-dozen bad with you." "I'm not the one who's terminally morose," Stempel replies and offers to hold Toby to help her fall asleep.

Charles Van Doren, handsome, impeccable, to the manner born, enters, explaining his lateness for an appointment with Enright. There was a theological dispute in the freshman American Lit class he teaches at Morningside Heights, and he had to clear it up, and then there followed the sudden rainstorm, lost umbrella, subway breakdown, mistaken address, stalled elevator. He's apologetic and rather damp. Enright asks if he may call him Charles, then does.

ENRIGHT:
Charles,
what was that theological dispute about,
if you don't mind my—
CHARLES:
Oh God—
I was trying to explain to them
the idea of grace.

ENRIGHT:

   I see—

   and they couldn't follow the idea of grace?

CHARLES:

   No, they could follow it well enough

   but they seemed to resent its implications.

   You see,

   I kept insisting that

   what defines grace is

   it's God's will and has nothing to do with how people act;

   and *they* kept insisting

   that means you can behave like a jerk and still be saved,

   and that offends them as, I don't know, Americans or someth—

ENRIGHT: I can see you love to teach, Charles.

CHARLES:

   It's all right.

   Well . . . you know . . .

   "Youth."

ENRIGHT: You don't care for "Youth"?

CHARLES:

   They're fine.

   It's just

   I'm too old to *be* Youth

   and too young to *crave* it

   which means I'm mostly irritated by it

   when it comes to me *en masse,* at least,

   as it does every single

   . . . I love to teach, yes.

Getting to the point, Enright tells him they want him on the program, starting next week, revealing that Charles's test grades were among the highest. Charles questions the "among the highest" and apologizes for being indecisive about whether or not he can do it. He knows nothing about TV, doesn't even own a TV set. Enright wonders if he is making Charles nervous, or is he just "a brooder"? His family regards him as happy-go-lucky, according to Charles—although that may mean being a dummy.

Enright scoffs at the idea of Charles being dumb, citing his many accomplishments: Doctorate in Mathematics, a year at the Sorbonne, Astronomy major, Doctorate in Literature, accomplished clarinet player—in fact, a Renaissance man. And Enright knows about Charles's background.

Consulting more cards, Enright reels off facts about Charles's father, Mark Van Doren: Pulitzer for poetry, definitive biography of Hawthorne, prominent critic, short story writer and teacher, at Columbia, of Lionel Trilling, Thomas Merton, Allen Ginsberg (this gives Enright pause), Whittaker Chambers. Charles interrupts, and Enright feels he's upsetting him. Was his father loved in class and cold at home? Charles demurs. He was "exceptionally warm . . . . . as monuments go," then adds, "No, very warm." Enright, knowing who Charles's father, mother, uncle and aunt are, feels he knows what made Charles and says he can imagine what's holding Charles back. He urges Charles not to let it, to go on television and make a lot of money and then take a sabbatical and perhaps write a novel. Charles has written a novel, it seems, and is not inclined to write another. It was about patricide, Charles admits, but he doesn't want Enright to get the wrong idea—Charles has always had an interest in classical ideas.

ENRIGHT: Did your father like it?
CHARLES:
    Very much.
    He always likes everything I do—it's a sort of a mania in him—
    but my *point* is
    I'm a teacher now.
    And that's a tricky sort of business
    and terribly old-fashioned, so
    I
    can't be on a quiz show, I'm afraid.
ENRIGHT: . . . Huh!
CHARLES: . . . I just don't think I can probably do it.
ENRIGHT: . . . I'm wondering—
CHARLES: What?
ENRIGHT:
    The obvious frustration you feel—
    is it *because* you're so young
    and what you do is so nearly archaic?
CHARLES: . . . I'm sorry?
ENRIGHT: Well, you just said so yourself—
CHARLES: I did? When was that?
ENRIGHT:
    And in a way
    I guess I have to agree with you
    because
    well
    who are the Van Dorens
    really
    these days?
    This somewhat fading tradition in American letters,
    yes?
    Holdovers from the nineteenth
    the *best* of the nineteenth century—
    I remember reading your father in college

and it was lovely
but I always pictured him on a hilltop somewhere,
chatting with the Oversoul,
experiencing Immediate Truth—
CHARLES *(overlapped):*
You're supposed to be wooing me;
decimating my forbears is a pretty odd way to go about it—
ENRIGHT *(overlaps):*
I overstepped.
Forgive me.
CHARLES: No, that's fine, it's just you're so . . . depressingly on-target.

Enright is still stinging from Charles's earlier revelation that he doesn't even have a television set—but he will, everybody will, and everybody will be watching a vast amount of something. Enright confides that his strategy is to take the lowly quiz show and put everything he values and doesn't want to see disappear from the world into it. That's why he needs Charles's egghead quality, his superior misfittedness, his "every-mother's-daughter-should-marry-it" sex appeal.

Charles feels uncomfortable. But he isn't sure, is he? Enright goes on. He sees Charles as winning thousands and thousands—don't tell him what Columbia instructors make—and he sees Americans poring over encyclopedias, learning things, because of Charles. Using the medium to subvert the medium is irony—wouldn't Charles call it literary irony? Charles wonders if Enright was trained by Jesuits. He's nearly won him over, Charles admits, but he has big gaps in his knowledge. If he were asked, "What's that flower?" he'd be at a loss. What if he didn't win? Charles asks. Enright suggests they discuss that in a few days.

Toby, alone, muses about a suggestion a neighbor made to her recently: maybe they should invest Stempel's winnings in a Florida home and move there. Toby acknowledges, "I don't like it here."

At the same time, Charles is writing to his father about the possibility of going on television: "It's filled with wonderfully intelligent people who are also somehow mindless." He wonders what his father would think about Charles getting involved and senses that he would all too readily agree that Charles should do it.

Two days after their last meeting, Enright, with his cards, is having Charles repeat over and over the names of the four Balearic Islands. Charles wonders if his voice and his posture are all right. Assured he's doing well, he can't understand why they keep at it. "I mean, it's not as though I'm suppose to—" He suddenly grasps what's happening, takes it in for a minute, then crosses to get his coat.

CHARLES: I won't say anything to anyone.
ENRIGHT: It's how things are done—
CHARLES: Not the way I do them.
ENRIGHT: I just want you to succeed—

Peter Frechette as Dan Enright and John Slattery as Charles Van
Doren in a scene from Richard Greenberg's *Night and Her Stars*

CHARLES:
    I know that:
    Are you expecting me to fail?
ENRIGHT:
    I'm expecting you to *triumph!*
    But, Charles,
    you've said it yourself—
    Somewhere on this spherical perplexity
    we call Earth
    there are some
    tidbits of information
    some *tiniest* facts
    that you haven't mastered—
CHARLES: That's the chance I was supposed to be—

ENRIGHT:
> We don't *take* chances here.
> Charles.

They are interrupted by Freedman calling from offstage to tell Enright that Jack Barry wants to talk to him. Enright hastily hides his cards in a drawer. Barry comes in looking for cigars, followed by Freedman. Barry and Charles are introduced. Barry greets Charles cheerily, hopes they can "improve his lot," but adds that that's up to Charles. Enright is out of cigars, and Barry leaves. Charles took note of the stashing of the cards out of Barry's sight and is shocked that Enright's own partner doesn't know what's going on.

ENRIGHT:
> Jack's . . .
> Not everyone is intelligent, Charles.
> Jack is a very sweet man,
> a very *dear* man,
> but things to him are what they are.

CHARLES: Is that how you define stupidity?

ENRIGHT:
> Oh, Charlie,
> this is not some big moral stand
> you're taking—
> this is a failure to grasp the medium.
> This is entertainment, Charles.
> Entertainment requires calculation.
> It's that simple.
> The other day you said
> you wanted to help preserve certain values with this
> —I thought that was the most important part of it for you—
> maybe I was wrong.
> But if I wasn't wrong,
> what can possibly *disturb* you here?
> We're not breaking any rules,
> it will be the best thing for *everyone*—
> so what is it that *scares* you here? . . .
> Is it just that it's likely
> to have an effect?
> > *Pause.*

CHARLES: Who would know?

ENRIGHT: The three of us.
> > *Beat.*

CHARLES: The guy you've got going now—

ENRIGHT: Mr. Stempel.

CHARLES:
    Mr. Stempel.
    Was he . . . arranged
    as well?
ENRIGHT: Obviously, I can't *tell* you that.
CHARLES: Would he know about . . . his successor?
ENRIGHT:
    He won't be a problem.
    Nobody will know anything.
    You'll come to our offices.
    You'll have your sessions
    of advice and encouragement
    usually, I think, with Mr. Freedman;
    you'll be . . .
    two people alone in a room.

Charles is dubious, and Enright suggests he think about it; take his time, but not too long. The choice is Charles's.

Charles leaves, and in his absence Enright imagines what is going on in Charles's mind. Charles must be obsessed with the need to come to a decision, he must be facing and thinking about the ordinary, materialistic, humdrum world and really looking at the city life moving around him for the first time.

ENRIGHT:
    . . . . . And at some moment he didn't notice,
    I suspect the question changed for him,
    became no longer what he would *do,*
    but how he was to *think* of it.
    And my guess is that this happened:
    He remembered what he'd been teaching with such difficulty
    the first time he'd come to see me.
    And from that enormous confusion,
    I think Charles was attracted to a single idea:
    You can behave any way at all in the world
    as long as God has whispered in your ear
    that you're one of the Elect.
    Because if you've been chosen
    what you do *must* be right—deep down, privately, obscurely right—
    no matter how it seems—it only follows—
    Anything can mean anything—how delightful! How free!
    What he said to himself was:
    "I will lie in service to the truth of the mind."
    He said to himself:
    "It's such a big paradox."

Charles, now with Enright, insists on one condition, however: He doesn't want to be given the answers, just the questions. He'd prefer to do the research, the work ... like school.

Charles makes his first appearance on Twenty-One, and his relationship to the well-known members of his family is touted. The program ends in a tie between Stempel and Charles, and the sponsor thinks it would be fine if they ended up with a "nice, wholesome champion" and not the "freak with a trick brain."

Stempel, in a coaching session with Enright, is being rather flip and wants to know if he is going to tie again this week—he's only asking so he would be able to be in character. He needn't worry, he's assured. Stempel is to be asked the name of the Academy Award winner of Best Picture of 1955. He knows it's *Marty,* but he's to reply incorrectly, saying it's *On the Waterfront.* Stempel is suspicious that this might be his ouster. Enright won't answer directly but reminds him he's had a good run. Stempel is incredulous that they are going to do it to him with *Marty.* It's his favorite movie, and he can't bear to "take a dive" on *Marty.* Change the year, he demands. That's not acceptable, Enright replies. Stempel doesn't see why not.

STEMPEL:

    I've been an exceptionally good champion!
    I've been very obedient to the situation.
    I was hoping to tell *stories* to my *son* about this—
    this is not the story I was hoping to tell
    but I've done everything you asked
    so how can you not—
ENRIGHT: Herb—
STEMPEL:

    I mean, I've worn these clothes.
    I've answered incorrectly
    innumerable answers I had at my fingertips.
    I've even pretended to people
    you actually pay as much as you say you do—no small thing—
ENRIGHT: Herb, listen—
STEMPEL *(continuous):*

    I mean, I've gone into that *booth*
    week after week
    I've sweated and I've stuttered
    and I've been deferential and I've never told a joke
    or smiled nicely or done anything but what you asked of me.
    I mean, I've done every single thing you asked of—
    I've done every—
    I've done
    I've done ...
    What have I done?
ENRIGHT: Herb.

STEMPEL: ... Let me play straight.

ENRIGHT: Christ!

STEMPEL:

> Scrap everything!
> One night—
> give me just one night—!
> I'll—whatever—I'll
> give back all the money
> but let me play for real
> because it can't
> I can't have it end like this—

ENRIGHT:

> We have established rules, Herb.
> Mr. Barry has *seen* these questions.
> What explanation
> what explanation
> do you propose we give Mr. Barry?
> I don't know how it is where you grew up
> but around here when a man gives his word
> we expect him to keep it.
> You gave your word, Herb.
> This little
> this sentimental explosion
> this *Marty* crap—
> it's crap.
> Now, I think a man *is* his word.
> The question is:
> are *you* that kind of man?
> Are you your word, Herb?
> When you're in that isolation booth
> can I expect cooperation?
> are you *contented* with this?
>> *Long pause.*

STEMPEL *(very softly):* I'm content.

Stempel having conceded, Enright tells him he and Barry are going to have a new panel show, and they are interested in having Stempel on it.

Stempel loses and leaves the show. Charles, in his fourth victorious week, is writing and rewriting a letter to his father. He is getting so much fan mail he's had to hire someone to answer it.

CHARLES *(continuing letter):*

> ..... Anyway, there's a lot more money now—would you like some money?—

and the world is moving in a different way
towards me—it's delightful and hectic and with any luck
I'll lose next week.
Maybe I'll throw the contest. Kidding.
Delete.
Finally, in answer to your question:
Yes, you're right.
The moment in the isolation booth when they ask you a question
is the academic's nightmare.
A number of times I've stood there,
uncertain how to respond,
everything hanging in the balance,
and the thought that's gone through my mind has been about you:
"Why didn't you teach me better?"
But that passes and the answer comes.
Don't be proud of my courage—I'm only doing what anyone would do,
after all.
Oh, listen, don't worry—
obviously, this isn't as dire as I'm making it sound—
You know what an *actor* I can be.
Best, Charles.

Stempel enters and rages at Enright, "You lied!" *Variety* has published the cast list for the new panel show, and Stempel is not on it. Enright offered Stempel's name for consideration, but he was overruled, he claims. Stempel is hell-bent on reparations, restitutions, but it isn't money he wants; he wants a rematch with Van Doren played straight. Not possible, Enright argues.

Stempel insists Enright give him what he asks for—"Because I possess information." But Stempel has difficulty getting anyone's attention. He has been telling friends the truth, and they've disregarded him. He's pursued other outlets and is now putting his faith in the press. He gets in touch with Warren Corso (of the New York *Post*) and Spats O'Brian (of the *Journal-American*). Both of the journalists are typical tough, eager reporters. O'Brian gets on the phone with Enright as Stempel and Corso continue talking. Stempel swears he'll stand by his story. "Cool," Corso remarks.

Both reporters talk to Enright about Stempel. When the reporters met Stempel, O'Brian noticed that he was drooling, and Corso noticed that his shoelaces were untied. They both decided there was no story in this obvious eccentric, but they thought Enright should know about what Stempel was telling the press. More in sorrow than in anger, Enright explains to the reporters that Stempel is a madman consumed with "Jewish self-hatred." The reporters, in unison, comment, "Sure."

The thing is, Enright continues, Stempel can't stand succeeding. He's trying to get back his "psychological equilibrium" by slandering, but what he wants is to slander himself. With the press calmed down, Enright reminds them he wouldn't interfere with their work any more than they would with his, but he asks their discretion. "I'm very protective of my own," he finishes.

It is late at night, and Charles, who has been on the program for seven weeks, comes into the office where Enright is having a drink. He makes one for Charles and wonders what he's there for. He did well tonight, he tells Charles. (The sweating was much improved.) Enright mentions the article in *The Atlantic Monthly* that claims Charles has "grown" over the weeks and has "taken on an aura of almost 'presidential density'." Charles gets to the point: he wants to stop. It's success that's making him miserable of course, Enright claims. He understands. Charles asks him to stop understanding and listen.

CHARLES:
    I'm sorry
    . . . but you have to know
    I'm not just being capricious here, Dan;
    this isn't some
    easy
    "crisis of conscience" I'm indulging . . .
    I'm finding it almost literally impossible
    to make my way through a day with this . . .
    Everything
    the most unimportant things
    require the most incredible calculation
    and I don't know how to manage it.
    . . . I can't figure what to say
    or what to conceal
    or which lies make sense
    and when I'm not lying at all
    it feels like an oversight . . .
ENRIGHT: On the show you're doing very—
CHARLES:
    On the show it's worse.
    . . . I'm asked these questions
    and even when I've known the stuff forever
    none of it is . . . familiar, somehow—
    You've seen it—
    there are times I can barely stammer out the answers . . .
ENRIGHT *(under):* That works.
CHARLES:
    . . . as though it's all become some other thing . . . do you see?
    Because I've *made* it that.
    And I can't stand it.
        Beat; quietly.
    Or any of it.

... The whole thing ... all the time ...
I feel as though I've violated some sort of
covenant
I never even knew I made
but without it,
I don't know how to go on.

Enright claims time will take care of everything. Charles's life is not that bad. There have been some "tough moments" in public, but he is famous. Even though there's not much money, there will be opportunities. He won't want them, Charles insists. What about that pretty girl he's seeing (the one answering his fan mail)? He can't talk to her, Charles admits, because of not being able to talk freely. He doesn't want to win any more, he insists. It's his fate, Enright declares, going on about the increased number of college applications that have been filed as a result of Charles's example. He reminds Charles he said he'd wanted to do some good. The good is just beginning, and does Charles want to take the honor out of this? How many covenants does he plan to break? If he's made it through this far, the next weeks will pass smoothly.

"Do you think we only recognize grace once we've fallen from it?" Charles asks. Enright doesn't know. He's going home to get some sleep. As the act ends, we hear Jack Barry's voice welcoming Charles Van Doren back to Twenty-One for "an all-time-record fifteenth consecutive appearance." *Curtain.*

ACT II

A brief look at the Today Show reveals that Charles, apparently a frequent guest, had "an unprecedented four-month run on the Twenty-One program not so many months ago." Charles is mentioning a new play he thinks will become a classic. Meanwhile, Toby is watching television, and Stempel, standing behind her, surmises it's Paddy Chayefsky's *Middle of the Night,* but Charles is referring to Archibald MacLeish's *J. B.*

Freedman has come into Enright's office bursting with some news he's picked up, but Doris, the plumpish, cheerful, carefully-coiffed secretary, enters with coffee and it must wait until she's finished her good mornings and departed. The news involves a contestant (whose name he can't get straight) on a quiz show called Dotto who was on the show at the same time as Marie Winn. It seems that Winn had a little notebook she left behind in the green room. This other contestant peeks at it, takes it and goes into the wings and discovers "he can *read* along with her." Realizing he's been tricked, he takes the page, the evidence, to some eager assistant D.A. Freedman is scared.

ENRIGHT:
It's Dotto
Dotto is not our show—

FREEDMAN:

The D.A.'s office has already called Top Dollar.

On The Sixty-Four Thousand Dollar Question,

they're handing over phone numbers of the contestants who—

ENRIGHT:

The people who've been on our show

are Pillars of their Communities

and they will do everything in their power

to avoid telling the truth—

FREEDMAN: Not every one of them.

> *Beat.*

ENRIGHT:

Oh, Christ, he's . . .

How can you be afraid of him?

He's this little *vahntz*—

He hasn't said anything in—

We haven't heard from him—*no*body's heard from him.

For all practical purposes, he's vanished.

FREEDMAN:

Not into the *Mists* of *Time.*

He has an address—he has a phone number.

We will have to hand over his phone number.

And this time, people will be *asking* what he knows.

ENRIGHT: Be calm.

FREEDMAN: Television is my *life.*

ENRIGHT: Don't be pathetic.

FREEDMAN: Dan—

ENRIGHT:

You have nothing to fear.

I will take care of you.

FREEDMAN:

It gives me the willies when you get nice.

What?

What are we gonna do?

> *Pause.*

ENRIGHT: Penance.

Enright telephones Stempel, who is suspicious and seems to be in bad shape. He's nervous about speaking to Enright because he's alone at home, just sitting there, and hasn't talked to many people of late. There have been "some reverses." He admits to having had a job, but he quit. Enright soothes him and claims he's calling him because he feels badly about what had happened between them. Enright wants to make amends. He has something for Stempel. Stempel isn't up to this. He's in analysis and on medication. He's given up "certain kinds of expectations," and it's been the better for him. Curiosity gets the better of him, though, and he asks what Enright has for him—then says he'll hang up before Enright can tell him. Enright won't tell him on the telephone anyway, and he tries to coax a reluctant Stempel to come to see him in his office. "Have you been feeling that nobody cares?" Enright asks. Stempel admits that he has. Enright points out that he, at least, must care because he has phoned Stempel and now wants to see him. Finally Stempel agrees to come to Enright's office.

At the office, Enright and Freedman greet Stempel. Today they'll tie up loose ends in their relationship and then discuss the promising future. Stempel knows he's capable of being a commercial entity, and, Stempel believes, Enright has finally realized that. Enright agrees, but first he needs Stempel to write out a statement that, contrary to anything he's said before, Dan Enright has never disclosed questions, answers, points or "anything like it." Stempel agrees. He begins to write while Enright goes on speaking (and later signs this paper). Enright confides to Stempel that his lawyer had suggested he go to the D.A. after Stempel's last visit to these offices, but he hadn't wanted to destroy Stempel. He had affection for him and wanted to help him.

Stempel admits he "flipped," he should have been grateful to Enright for giving him a break. But something he'd gotten involved with—he had come home one day and a man, a neighbor whom his wife had been fond of, had absconded with all his money. And Toby, always fearful, doesn't do anything now except watch television. "... She had some hopes of moving, of Florida ... and then: this." Enright soothes him again. Stempel can't believe that with what he knows, with all this information, why can't he "make the world move an inch" in his direction?

Enright wants to get a psychiatrist for Stempel, but Stempel already has one. Stempel hoped Enright had planned a re-match between him and Van Doren, but what Enright had in mind was another panel show on which Stempel would appear once every day and speak a few words. They'd exploit that mind, that talent. But what Stempel wants to know is, will they pay his bills? including one for the car he bought, a three-toned Packard.

STEMPEL *(becoming belligerent):*
    And why shouldn't I have a nice car?
    Why shouldn't I have all those things?
    I was supposed to.
    There were promises.
    Don't look at me like
    greed
    or or
    bad values . . .
    this sick world!
    sick
    criminal—!

I just want what's coming to me!

I—!

Oh, Dan, I'm sorry, I'm sorry, I'm so sorry—

It's my fault—

Everything's my fault.

> *He cries. Pause. Enright puts his arm around Stempel's shoulder.*

ENRIGHT:

This is not a day for whose fault it is.

The world is hard

and fame can be very harsh.

We opened that door for you

and then it closed

without warning.

I don't think you can cope with life at this stage, Herb.

And I say we have help.

STEMPEL: I'm perfectly willing to need help.

ENRIGHT:

Good boy.

Well.

This has been an excellent day.

We've made real progress.

The details we'll work out next time.

STEMPEL:

Dan—!

I

It's

People

So many people have

It's gotten to such a point

I

I need someone to trust

. . . so, don't laugh, I'm choosing you.

All right?

> *Beat.*

Is that all right?

ENRIGHT:

I'm

I'll be honored to be the one you trust, Herb.

> *Stempel nods, exits. Enright opens desk drawer, removes tape recorder,*
> *rewinds, plays. It plays back a portion of their conversation.*

VOICE OVER: "I'm perfectly willing to need help."

ENRIGHT: Excellent sound.

> *He turns off the machine.*

In Charles's case, fans continue their adoration, but he is being queried by an investigator to test the breadth of his knowledge. Unable to recall the fate of many of Henry VIII's wives, he claims he was never a fan of regicide. The investigator, not amused, remarks, "And yet when these questions were posed to you on Twenty-One, you had no problem." The investigator asks if Charles had a brain injury in the past two years. He's been watching more television, Charles admits, but his brain is the same. His explanation for the "staggering" information loss is that, once a question is asked, and therefore unlikely to be asked again, he "deleted" the answer from his memory bank to create room for information more liable to prove profitable. So the investigator has gathered from others on Twenty-One. "Trick minds think alike, too," Charles supposes. The investigator sums it up as a kind of "self-induced intellectual amnesia." "Well put," Charles notes.

The investigator wonders if Charles misses anything he's forgotten. Charles is surprised at the question—no one's ever asked. But could he ask something? He wants to know why this is happening—the grand jury thing and now Congress stepping in. The investigator explains that with the burgeoning of television, a new center of power in society, it's necessary to set proper restraints.

Charles understands that and is all for exposing corruption, but as far as Twenty-One goes, all they have are allegations of one man whom everyone agrees is mad—and he retracted them. The investigator reports that Stempel claims he was tricked into signing the statement; and, as for the tape, they believe it to be edited.

Charles refers to Stempel's apparent vendetta against him. Stempel does insist Charles be brought up before the committee, the investigator informs him. And it seems Stempel's not the only accuser. There's someone in Charles's department who's remarked, "Charlie couldn't have known all those things; Charlie barely knows his own subject."

Charles admits to the investigator that, yes, he does sometimes miss what he's forgotten. He also admits he doesn't know how he can go on much longer—"This thing has been pretty hellish." But he hasn't done anything wrong—unless going on television and teaching people about literature or inspiring them to continue their education is wrong. He doesn't like feeling the investigator mistrusts him. The mistrust is everywhere, even among those people nearest to him. He begins to talk about his wife, and the investigator tries to interrupt him.

CHARLES:
  I've done absolutely nothing wrong,
  why isn't that enough?
  And I don't mean simply the *facts* of the thing,
  that's part of it,
  but there's so much else besides the facts,
  so much else
  that no one ever seems to take into account—
  my *intentions*, my reasons,
  the . . . rightness

the rightness *beyond* rightness of my reasons,
nobody seems to ask about that or consider
what it may—
INVESTIGATOR *(from "seems to ask"):* What does that mean?
CHARLES: . . . What?
INVESTIGATOR:
    You just said something about
    "the rightness beyond rightness of your reasons"—
    I don't understand what that means.
        Pause.
CHARLES *(quietly):*
    Why should you?
    It's babble.
INVESTIGATOR: . . . Ah . . .
CHARLES:
    . . . I'm having trouble lately . . .
    matching words to my life.
        Pause. Charles smiles at Investigator. It's incredibly sad.
    This has been
    an unnecessary sneak preview of my breakdown.
    I'm sorry; I haven't been sleeping.
INVESTIGATOR: That's all right.
CHARLES:
    The time.
    . . . I'm sorry, I have to go.
    I need to get back to Columbia now and
    . . . natter things at sophomores—
INVESTIGATOR:
    That's all right;
    I'll be calling you again very soon.
CHARLES: Of course.
INVESTIGATOR: Mr. Van Doren—before you go—may I ask a favor of you?
CHARLES: What's that?
INVESTIGATOR: Would you say hello to your father for me?
CHARLES: . . . What?
INVESTIGATOR: He was my teacher centuries ago.
CHARLES: Is that right?
INVESTIGATOR:
    I don't know why I think he'd remember me
    except
    he has a talent for making the most unexceptional person
    feel memorable,
    doesn't he?
CHARLES:
    Yes

    Beat. On the verge of something, then, quietly.
I don't know who you've been talking to, but
I *do* know my subject.
. . . I really do.

Toby and Stempel, Freedman and Enright enter, *"their scenes crossing before sorting themselves out."* Stempel is trying to get Toby's attention, but she wants to go to the store. Freedman is insisting that he and Enright must talk, but if Freedman is going to do his "end-of-the-world number" Enright needs coffee.

    Stempel is still trying to get Toby to listen to him. He's found, in the cluttered drawer of the credenza, something important. It's a photostat. Toby wants to leave because the store will be crowded later.

STEMPEL:
    No—no—no—
    you *must* listen—you don't understand what this *is*—
    That time on the show when I got an advance—
    Well
    you know me—my *mishegas*—
    I made a *photostat* of the check.
    On the check I made a notation:
    "Advance on Future Winnings!"
    Do you *see?*
        No response.
    Toby?
    I show this check
    and this time they will have to believe me
    because this time
    it's not *me,*
    it's a piece of *paper.*
    Do you understand?
TOBY:
    . . . Mama's coming back with the baby
    in half an hour.
    She can't stay;
    if you have to go out,
    Mrs. Abresch upstairs will—
STEMPEL:
    Don't do this!
    . . . Look,
    I know this has been difficult.
    I know life of late
    has been the thing after terrible

but I'm just saying, please *listen.*
It's not like I'm asking something *hard*
like you should *love* me or something
just that, just that . . .
TOBY: You think I don't . . .
STEMPEL: . . . Just that you *listen* when I tell you—
TOBY: You don't think I—
STEMPEL: This is good news!
TOBY *(shuts eyes; hands over ears): Please! God! No more good news!*

Freedman thinks people are starting to doubt Stempel's insanity, not his sanity, he warns Enright. Enright explodes, and Freedman wants him to lower his voice—there are people with subpoenas in the hall. Freedman is disgusted. They've been lucky for quite a while, but they "screwed up," and they are now vulnerable.

ENRIGHT:
    We've broken no law—
    what have we done?
            Beat.
FREEDMAN: Look—
ENRIGHT:
    Violated some principle?
    A principle that finds expression
    in not a single statute
    or, or edict
    or regulation?
    That is at best a *perception* of *wrongdoing*
    And I *control* the perceptions?
FREEDMAN: Um . . . Dan . . .
ENRIGHT:
    Do you see, Al?
    Do you understand?
    This investigation is going to collapse.
    It is going to collapse
    from a lack of inner *necessity.*
FREEDMAN: I think you've lost your mind, so listen to me.
ENRIGHT:
    No. *You.*
    In the first place, we have done nothing wrong.
    In the second place, we have done it in *utmost* secrecy.
    Third, we have performed a fa—
    a very great and delicate favor for people of enormous pow—
    sponsors, a *network*—
    enormously powerful people:

We have managed to inform them of everything
without *in any way* compromising their ignorance.
A certain gratitude comes with that.
certain protections—
Has almost everyone gone along with us till now? . . . . .
Do you think, what, I don't understand people any more?
Do you think I've lost my touch or something?
Jesus, Al, you're my partner,
my *friend*—
don't you believe in *anything?*
FREEDMAN *(quietly):*
I believe in little pieces of paper
with writing on them, Danny.
> *Beat; almost wistful.*
I have no other talents—
could you at least have the courtesy
to panic along with me?
Stempel has that check.
He will show them that check,
a check drawn against winnings
that were not yet won.
Face it, Dan:
What can that possibly *mean?*
ENRIGHT: . . . Give me a minute.

Stempel is making his statement to Congress. Pleased to be addressing "this august body," he claims he has nothing new to say, but the annotated document attests to his remarks. He was coached for each appearance on Twenty-One by Dan Enright, he states, both for content and performance. Nor was his grooming his own. As for any knowledge of his successor, Stempel was informed when he himself would lose, so he can only presume that it was previously ascertained that his successor would win. Stempel believes if his successor were called before this body and tells the truth, it would serve to make his own "true remarks truer." And they do have the check, in addition to Stempel's Bible oath.

Enright, while Stempel is still making his statement, has come on and is speaking to the press. He concedes that he gave Stempel the money but doesn't term it "an advance." The situation was, he tells the press, that Stempel had threatened to leave the show while he was still winning. Enright hadn't wanted to disappoint the viewers and could only appease Stempel with money. He claims there are two reasons for the accusations. One: Stempel's hatred for Van Doren (Stempel's had considerable psychoanalytical care, but Enright hopes that's off the record) and two: (this is hard for him, Enright pleads) Stempel's father died when Stempel was very young, and he began to look upon Enright as a replacement father figure.

Charles Van Doren (John Slattery, *center*) in the Congressional Committee scene in *Night and Her Stars*

Meanwhile, Jack Barry and network and sponsor spokesmen reaffirm their faith in Van Doren and their innocence and ignorance of any wrongdoing.

> *Charles in his office at Columbia. A radio plays.*

RADIO: ... has not yet responded personally to the charges although a Today Show spokesman this evening said that Mr. Van Doren is completely ...

> *Charles flicks off the switch. He picks up a book, tries to read. Turns radio back on.*

RADIO: ... Meanwhile, Mr. Van Doren has continued to teach his ...

> *Charles quickly turns to another station.*

OTHER STATION: ... while Dave Garroway has given his personal assurance that his Today Show colleague is as ...

> *Charles turns station again.*

THIRD STATION: ... Twenty-One producer Dan Enright meanwhile is ...

> *Charles starts flicking among stations; it has a grizzly fascination for him, an inundating horror he's almost exhausted enough to enjoy.*

STATION BABBLE: . . . be allowed to continue on the Today Show while . . . son of Mark Van Doren, Pulitzer prize-winning author of . . . was implicated by . . . although Mr. Stempel's charges were effectively refuted by . . . he has, surprisingly, remained silent on the issue and . . .

Charles turns off radio.

Charles is writing something, then crumples up the page of paper, tossing it onto his desk. He begins to read a book. It is midnight, and Stempel appears in Charles's office doorway, just looking at his back for a while before he speaks his name. Charles doesn't recognize him at first. Stempel looks different. It's his clothes, Stempel points out: they fit.

Charles wonders why Stempel is here. He couldn't sleep, so he took a walk, Stempel explains. But Stempel lives in Brooklyn, Charles recalls. Queens, Stempel corrects him. Actually he'd come on the subway. Then he'd seen a sign "This Way to the Smartest Man in the World" and assumed it was Charles. Charles's students had put it up the previous year, it seems.

Stempel felt the need to talk. Hasn't Charles read the papers and seen that Enright is telling lies to the press? Charles wonders, since Stempel had taken "a good slice" out of him in front of the committee, if Stempel's here to get the rest. Nobody's going to believe him, Stempel insists, until Charles speaks. Charles acknowledges Stempel's hatred, but it won't get him anywhere, he claims. Why would he hate him? Stempel wonders, he doesn't even know Charles. Stempel can't understand why this all has to be about Charles and not him: "Am I your shadow? Is my life some sort of *afterthought* to yours?"

Stempel is sorry he's been shrill. It's lack of sleep. Stempel had thought things would be sorted out once he'd announced he had the check. Now people who had thought him "off-balance" regard him as psychotic, and Enright has told the world "the specific *kind* of lunatic I am . . ." Charles was the only one he could think of to talk to, because Charles is obliged to believe him.

Stempel apologizes for trespassing. Charles admits he doesn't sleep either—because he's been accused—"that's all." He's stayed in his office the past two nights, waiting here for "the catastrophe that never completely happens." He's tried to replace the world with books, and it hasn't worked. The world comes in anyway.

CHARLES:
.....You're right, you know—
I finally read some of the letters—
everyone *does* believe me.
STEMPEL: I know.
CHARLES:
It's amazing—it's a riot!
They believe me—what a thing!
STEMPEL: Yes.

CHARLES:
>It's ... horrible.
>I want part of my life to be over
>but I'm too scared to say what I have to
>to bring it to an end.

STEMPEL:
>What are you going to tell them when they call you?
>what will you say when—

CHARLES *(overlaps):*
>I don't think they're going to call me.
>I don't think they want to—

STEMPEL:
>It doesn't have to be their decision!
>You can *go* before them, you can *choose* to—

CHARLES: I know.

STEMPEL:
>... for someone to glean the right values
>to bring this part of our
>of your life to an end—you *want* that—

CHARLES: Yes.

STEMPEL: Then will you—

CHARLES: I don't know.

STEMPEL: But—

CHARLES: I don't know.

STEMPEL: But you've just told me—you've told *me.*

CHARLES: We're two people alone in a room here.

STEMPEL:
>... Oh ... oh ...
>Well then
>that's that ...

Stempel hesitates, unsure of whether or not to leave, and wonders what Charles was reading when he came in. It was *Creve-Coeur*. Stempel bets he remembers it better than Charles because he never forgets. He wishes he could. They each admit they are glad they have talked and wish each other good luck. As Stempel leaves, he again asks Charles to tell the truth.

After he's gone, Charles picks up the paper he crumpled earlier and reads aloud: "Respectfully request you read following statement into the record of the proceedings before your committee, quote: 'Mr. Van Doren has made himself available to members of the committee's staff. He is available to speak to the committee directly.'" He almost seems as if he might tear it in two, then he signs it.

Charles is going before the five-member committee, which is upstage. Toby and Stempel are seated downstage. Charles shakes hands with the head of the committee and makes his statement. He wishes he could change the course of his life in the past few years. He can't, but he has learned a good deal—about life, about himself, about good and evil, which aren't always what they seem to be. He admits he was deeply involved in the deception. He's been acting a role, not just recently, but for years, perhaps all his life. He does not ask forgiveness—it would be inappropriate—but he hopes one day to earn forgiveness. He regrets deceiving his friends.

There is a pause, and we hear Stempel's "And now it comes . . ." All stops out, each member of the committee in turn commends Van Doren for his "soul-searching fortitude," declaiming "the measure of a man is best taken not when he's aloft but when he's returned to human reach." Forgiveness is his.

CONGRESSMAN FOUR: What you have been to people . . .
CONGRESSMAN THREE: What people have asked you to be . . .
CONGRESSMAN TWO: No man should bear the burden . . .
CONGRESSMAN FIVE: No man can possibly . . .
CONGRESSMAN TWO: Only one Man ever has . . .
CONGRESSMAN FOUR: The world today . . .
CONGRESSMAN FIVE: This country . . .
CONGRESSMAN THREE: This abundant . . .
CONGRESSMAN TWO: This perilous country . . .
CONGRESSMAN ONE: With so much on offer . . .
CONGRESSMAN TWO: With everything on offer . . .
CONGRESSMAN FOUR: With everything on offer to you . . .
CONGRESSMAN TWO: A man of your talents . . .
CONGRESSMAN FIVE: A man of your appeal . . .
CONGRESSMAN THREE: This story was inevitable . . .
CONGRESSMAN TWO: This story was undeniable . . .
CONGRESSMAN ONE: This story was waiting for its hero . . .

Charles's gallantry and bravery in testifying freely to the committee are praised, and the "God blesses" flow freely as the session ends. Stempel looks at Toby and begins to laugh. The laughter increases in volume. Then Charles is laughing as well. When Charles's laughter fades, Stempel's laugh becomes dry, then almost inaudible before it stops.

Freedman and Enright are clearing out Enright's office when Barry comes in and out looking for his putter, declaring that he didn't lie or cheat. Freedman wonders what he and Enright will do now. Enright doesn't know. It's been quite a setback, but fortunately his reputation is intact, Enright muses. Freedman would prefer not to think about what they've done, and not to wonder why he's been indicted and Enright hasn't. And he keeps trying to recall what life was like before television.

The upstage wall of panels separates vertically and we see a tall tree upstage center. We are in a clearing in the woods at Charles's parents' home in West Cornwall, Connecticut. Charles and his handsome elderly father, Mark Van Doren, come on with a wooden table and benches. A picnic seems to be in the offing, with guests due to arrive in a half hour or so. There are bugs, Charles notes. He'd like to be inside, but Mark wants to stay outside. Charles is nervous about the prospect of being with people, even though they are people he has liked, but he's agreed to make an effort to socialize, it seems.

The senior Van Dorens have become "devoted to the monotony" of the place. Less happening seems to mean more experiencing. It's "good for poets," Mark believes, but not for conversation. It suits them, however. Charles wonders if finding a house to sit and read in might—but Mark cuts him off. He doubts it's possible for Charles. Mark, having been born in the last century, finds it natural, but "that sort of rhythm" is finished. Charles has to live in his own time.

Mark remembers he *has* been doing something—making lists. One was a list of every poem he means to write during the rest of his life, "things I would celebrate." When he finished making the list, he realized it was a poem. Maybe Charles will read it.

Mark urges Charles to talk to him, about anything. Charles doesn't see the need. He does, however, tell his father that two of his students collected about six hundred signatures on a petition to demand his re-instatement. Five hundred showed up at a rally, in the middle of which a student from a dorm shouted, "Hey, Charlie's in the quad handing out the answers to the Comparative Lit final." A group had applauded, and then others joined in. "Columbia isn't the world," Mark remarks, but Charles thinks it is. Again he wants to go inside. He has said he'd loved this spot, Mark reminds him. Not now, Charles claims. He feels nothing now. Well, one thing. Shame.

MARK: I'd like to help you, Charlie.
CHARLES:
    But you can't.
    You of all people.
    We're opposites, you and I;
    you love the world
    and I think I've come to hate it.
MARK: Don't say that to me.
CHARLES:
    But it's true!
    I've betrayed
    everything
    and
    I . . . hate it
    I hate
    the sound of my own voice.
    I wish I never had to speak
    another word—
    all the words have broken in me.
    I want . . . to be rid of them,
    if I could just be rid of them
    but it's not possible.

I started out as nothing much
and then I became *this*
and now it's the only thing I ever can be.
I want to start over
but how.
I don't know how.
I can't imagine where
I
can't imagine it ... I ... can't ... I
> *He's in tears now. Mark holds him; he allows it. A long moment.*

MARK:
Charlie, you're right.
The world's a terrible place
... and the worst things seem to happen toward the end ...
But
the list ... you know ...
So many ... things ...
> *Pause.*

Tell me what to say, Charlie.
I can't have got to this point
and have nothing useful to say.
> *Beat.*

CHARLES: I'm sorry for what I've done to you.

MARK:
... Thank you for that,
but you're mine.

Charles notices that an important old tree has been cut down (because it was interfering with the plumbing, Mark explains). Charles grew up here but doesn't know the names of any of the trees. Mark informs him the big tree they cut down was an oak.

CHARLES:
... That one over there, then,
that must be another oak, yes?

MARK: That's a maple.

CHARLES: Oh ... it looks the same as—

MARK:
And next to it is a cedar.
... and a paper birch, tamarack ... black birch ... black pine ...

CHARLES:
Hm.
Maple, cedar, paper birch, tamarack, black birch, black pine—

MARK: You're a quick study.

CHARLES:
  I know that.
  Maple, cedar, tamarack, paper birch—
MARK: . . . paper birch, tamarack—
CHARLES: . . . paper birch, tamarack, black birch . . . black pine.
MARK: That's it.
        Beat.
CHARLES: The names.
MARK: Yes.
        Beat.
CHARLES: . . . That one over there?
MARK:
  Charlie,
  Why don't you look in the branches?
  I think you can figure it out for yourself.
CHARLES:
  Oh!
  Right.
  Apple.
  . . . And that's another tamarack, isn't it?
MARK: Yes.
        Lights begin slowly to fade.
CHARLES:
  . . . and a paper birch
  another cedar . . .
MARK: Yes.
CHARLES:
  . . . and a maple
  and another
  . . . and a black birch
  and a row of them
  and a tamarack
  a black pine
  another apple
  another cedar
  and a . . . . .
        Fade out. Curtain.

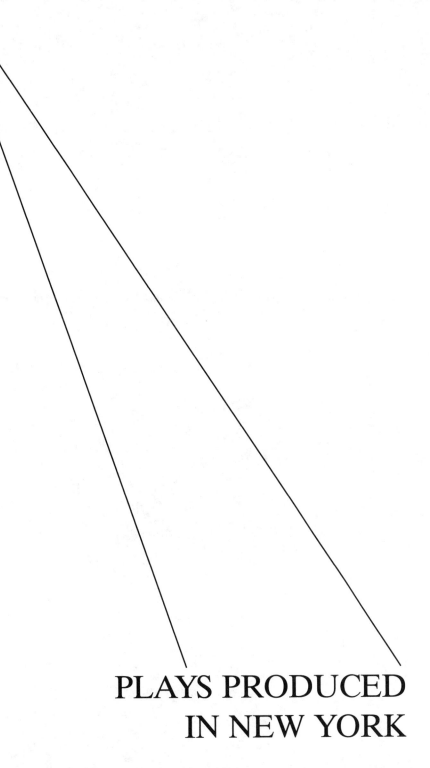

PLAYS PRODUCED
IN NEW YORK

PLAYS PRODUCED ON BROADWAY

Figures in parentheses following a play's title give number of performances. These figures do not include previews or extra non-profit performances. In the case of a transfer, the off-Broadway run is noted but not added to the figure in parentheses.

Plays marked with an asterisk (*) were still in a projected run June 1, 1995. Their number of performances is figured through May 31, 1995.

In a listing of a show's numbers—dances, sketches, musical scenes, etc.—the titles of songs are identified wherever possible by their appearance in quotation marks (").

HOLDOVERS FROM PREVIOUS SEASONS

Plays which were running on June 1, 1994 are listed below. More detailed information about them appears in previous *Best Plays* volumes of appropriate years. Important cast changes since opening night are recorded in the Cast Replacements section of this volume.

*Cats (5,281). Musical based on *Old Possum's Book of Practical Cats* by T.S. Eliot; music by Andrew Lloyd Webber; additional lyrics by Trevor Nunn and Richard Stilgoe. Opened October 7, 1982.

*Les Misérables (3,368). Musical based on the novel by Victor Hugo; book by Alain Boublil and Claude-Michel Schönberg; music by Claude-Michel Schönberg; lyrics by Herbert Kretzmer; original French text by Alain Boublil and Jean-Marc Natel; additional material by James Fenton. Opened March 12, 1987.

*The Phantom of the Opera (3,074). Musical adapted from the novel by Gaston Leroux; book by Richard Stilgoe and Andrew Lloyd Webber; music by Andrew Lloyd Webber; lyrics by Charles Hart; additional lyrics by Richard Stilgoe. Opened January 26, 1988.

*Miss Saigon (1,725). Musical with book by Alain Boublil and Claude-Michel Schönberg; music by Claude-Michel Schönberg; lyrics by Richard Maltby Jr. and Alain Boublil; additional material by Richard Maltby Jr. Opened April 11, 1991.

*Crazy for You (1,370). Musical with book by Ken Ludwig; co-conceived by Ken Ludwig and Mike Ockrent; inspired by material (in the musical *Girl Crazy*) by Guy Bolton and John McGowan; music by George Gershwin; lyrics by Ira Gershwin. Opened February 19, 1992.

Guys and Dolls (1,144). Revival of the musical based on a story and characters by Damon Runyon; book by Jo Swerling and Abe Burrows; music and lyrics by Frank Loesser. Opened April 14, 1992. (Closed January 6, 1995)

The Sisters Rosensweig (556). Transfer from off Broadway of the play by Wendy Wasserstein. Opened October 22, 1992 off Broadway where it played 149 performances through February 28, 1993; transferred to Broadway March 18, 1993. (Closed July 16, 1994)

*The Who's Tommy (928). Musical with book by Pete Townshend and Des McAnuff; music and lyrics by Pete Townshend; additional music and lyrics by John Entwistle and Keith Moon. Opened April 22, 1993.

Blood Brothers (839). Musical with book, music and lyrics by Willy Russell. Opened April 25, 1993. (Closed April 30, 1995)

*Kiss of the Spider Woman (868). Musical based on the novel by Manuel Puig; book by Terrence McNally; music by John Kander; lyrics by Fred Ebb. Opened May 3, 1993.

Angels in America, Part I: Millennium Approaches (367). Opened May 4, 1993 and was joined in repertory November 23, 1993 by **Part II: Perestroika** (216). By Tony Kushner. (Both plays closed December 4, 1994)

She Loves Me (355). Revival of the musical based on a play by Miklos Laszlo; book by Joe Masteroff; music by Jerry Bock; lyrics by Sheldon Harnick. Opened June 10, 1993. (Closed August 1, 1993) Reopened October 7, 1993. (Closed June 19, 1994)

Laughter on the 23rd Floor (320). By Neil Simon. Opened November 22, 1993. (Closed August 27, 1994)

*Damn Yankees (449). Revival of the musical based on Douglas Wallop's novel *The Year the Yankees Lost the Pennant;* book by George Abbott and Douglas Wallop; music and lyrics by Richard Adler and Jerry Ross. Opened March 3, 1994. Suspended performances December 31, 1994. Reopened March 12, 1995.

Carousel (337). Revival of the musical based on the play *Liliom* by Ferenc Molnar, as adapted by Benjamin F. Glazer; book and lyrics by Oscar Hammerstein II; music by Richard Rodgers. Opened March 24, 1994. (Closed January 15, 1995)

Jackie Mason: Politically Incorrect (347). Solo performance by Jackie Mason; created and written by Jackie Mason. Opened April 5, 1994. (Closed June 4, 1995)

Medea (83). Revival of the play by Euripides; translated by Alistair Elliot. Opened April 7, 1994. (Closed June 26, 1994)

Twilight: Los Angeles, 1992 (72). Transfer from off Broadway of the solo performance by Anna Deavere Smith; conceived and written by Anna Deavere Smith. Opened off Broadway March 23, 1994 where it played 13 performances through April 3, 1994; transferred to Broadway April 17, 1994. (Closed June 19, 1994)

*Beauty and the Beast (474). Musical with book by Linda Woolverton; music by Alan Menken; lyrics by Howard Ashman and Tim Rice. Opened April 18, 1994.

Broken Glass (73). By Arthur Miller. Opened April 24, 1994. (Closed June 26, 1994)

An Inspector Calls (454). Revival of the play by J.B. Priestley. Opened April 27, 1994. (Closed May 28, 1995)

Sally Marr . . . and Her Escorts (50). By Joan Rivers, Erin Sanders and Lonny Price; suggested by the life of Sally Marr. Opened May 5, 1994. (Closed June 19, 1994)

Passion (280). Musical based on the film *Passione D'Amore* by Ettore Scola and the novel *Fosca* by I.U. Tarchetti; book by James Lapine; music and lyrics by Stephen Sondheim. Opened May 9, 1994. (Closed January 7, 1995)

*Grease (424). Revival of the musical with book, music and lyrics by Jim Jacobs and Warren Casey. Opened May 11, 1994.

PLAYS PRODUCED JUNE 1, 1994-MAY 31, 1995

*Roundabout Theater Company. Schedule of seven revivals. **Hedda Gabler** (33). By Henrik Ibsen; translated by Frank McGuinness. Opened July 10, 1994. (Closed August 7, 1994) **Philadelphia, Here I Come!** (52). By Brian Friel. Opened September 8, 1994. (Closed October 22, 1994) **The Glass Menagerie** (57). By Tennessee Williams. Opened November 15, 1994. (Closed January 1, 1995). **The Molière Comedies** (61). Program of two plays by Molière, English verse translation by Richard Wilbur: *The School for Husbands* and *The Imaginary Cuckold*. Opened February 2, 1995. (Closed March 26, 1995) ***A Month in the Country** (43). By Ivan Turgenev; translated by Richard Freeborn. Opened April 25, 1995. And *The Play's the Thing* by Ferenc Molnar, scheduled to open 7/6/95. Produced by Roundabout Theater Company, Todd Haimes artistic director, Gene Feist founding director, Ellen Richard general manager, at Criterion Center Stage Right.

HEDDA GABLER

Miss Julie Tesman .... Patricia Conolly	Thea Elvsted .... Laura Linney
Berte .... Bette Henritze	Judge Brack .... Keith David
Jorgen Tesman .... Jeffrey DeMunn	Eilert Lovborg .... Jim Abele
Hedda Gabler .... Kelly McGillis	

Directed by Sarah Pia Anderson; scenery, David Jenkins; costumes, Martin Pakledinaz; lighting, Marc B. Weiss; music, Dan Moses Schreier; sound, Douglas J. Cuomo; production stage manager, Jay Adler; press, Boneau/Bryan-Brown, Adrian Bryan-Brown, Susanne Tighe.

The last major New York revival of *Hedda Gabler* was by Classic Stage Company off Broadway 9/20/75 for 48 performances. The play was presented in two parts.

PHILADELPHIA, HERE I COME!

Madge .... Pauline Flanagan	Lizzy Sweeney .... Aideen O'Kelly
Gareth O'Donnell in Public .... Jim True	Con Sweeney .... James Murtaugh
Gareth O'Donnell in	Ben Burton .... Robert Stattel
Private .... Robert Sean Leonard	Ned .... Joel James Forsythe
S.B. O'Donnell .... Milo O'Shea	Tom .... Timothy Reynolds
Kate Doogan .... Miriam Healy-Louie	Joe .... Gregory Grene
Sen. Doogan .... Peter McRobbie	Canon Mick O'Byrne .... Leo Leyden
Master Boyle .... Jarlath Conroy	

Understudies: Misses Flanagan, O'Kelly—Robin Howard; Messrs. True, Reynolds, Grene—Sean Dougherty; Messrs. Leonard, Forsythe—Jay Snyder; Messrs. O'Shea, Leyden—Robert Stattel; Miss Healy-Louie—Catherine Walsh; Messrs. McRobbie, Conroy, Murtaugh, Stattel—Philip LeStrange.

Directed by Joe Dowling; scenery, John Lee Beatty; costumes, Catherine Zuber; lighting, Christopher Akerlind; sound, Philip Campanella; casting, Pat McCorkle/Richard Cole; production stage manager, Lori M. Doyle.

Time: The early 1960s, the night before and on the morning of Gar's departure for Philadelphia. Place: The small village of Ballybeg in County Donegal, Ireland. The play was presented in three parts.

Philadelphia, Here I Come! opened on Broadway, following its Dublin production, 2/16/66 for 119 performances and was named a Best Play of its season. This is its first major New York revival.

THE GLASS MENAGERIE

Tom .... Zeljko Ivanek	Laura .... Calista Flockhart
Amanda .... Julie Harris	Jim .... Kevin Kilner

THE IMAGINARY CUCKOLD—Brian Bedford and
Suzanne Bertish in the Molière comedy at the Roundabout

Understudy: Miss Harris—Martha Randall.

Directed by Frank Galati; scenery, Loy Arcenas; costumes, Noel Taylor; lighting, Mimi Jordan Sherin; sound, Richard R. Dunning; projection design, John Boesche; original music, Miriam Sturm; casting, Pat McCorkle, Richard Cole; production stage manager, Jay Adler; stage manager, Charles Kindl; press, Boneau/Bryan-Brown, Adrian Bryan-Brown, Susanne Tighe.

Act I: Preparation for a gentleman caller. Act II: The gentleman calls.

The last major New York revival of *The Glass Menagerie* took place on Broadway 12/1/83 for 92 performances, with Jessica Tandy in the role of Amanda. This is its 50th anniversary revival (its first staging was at Chicago's Civic Theater 12/26/44).

THE MOLIERE COMEDIES

PERFORMER	"THE SCHOOL FOR HUSBANDS"	"THE IMAGINARY CUCKOLD"
David Aaron Baker	Ergaste	Lelie
Brian Bedford	Sganarelle	Sganarelle
Suzanne Bertish	Lisette	Sganarelle's Wife
Patricia Dunnock	Isabelle	Celie's Maid
Cheryl Gaysunas	Leonor	Celie
Malcolm Gets	Valere	Mme. Sganarelle's Brother
Denis Holmes	Notary	Villebrequin
Remak Ramsay	Ariste	Gorgibus
Reg Rogers	Magistrate	Gros-Rene
Jeff Stafford	Attendant	Servant

Understudies: Mr. Bedford—Reg Rogers; Mr. Ramsay—Denis Holmes; Misses Dunnock, Gay-sunas—Elizabeth Rainer; Miss Bertish—April Black; Messrs. Gets, Holmes, Stafford—Daniel Travis; Messrs. Baker, Rogers—Nick Sullivan, Jeff Stafford.

Directed by Michael Langham; scenery, Douglas Stein; costumes, Ann Hould-Ward; lighting, Richard Nelson; sound, Douglas J. Cuomo & One Dream Sound; casting, Pat McCorkle; production stage manager, Lori M. Doyle; stage manager, Jana Llynn.

Time: Late 17th century. Place: *The School for Husbands,* Paris; *The Imaginary Cuckold,* in a small French town. The program was presented in two parts.

The last major New York revival of *The School for Husbands* was by the Theater Guild on Broadway 10/16/33 for 116 performances. The last major New York revival of *The Imaginary Invalid (Sganarelle)* was by Yale Repertory Theater off Broadway 6/7/78 for 15 performances.

A MONTH IN THE COUNTRY

Schaaf ....Rocco Sisto	Matvei ....Dan Moran
Anna Semenova .... Helen Stenborg	Ignaty Ilich Shpigelsky ..... F. Murray Abraham
Lizaveta Bogdanova ....Gail Grate	Verochka .... Kathryn Erbe
Natalya Petrovna ....Helen Mirren	Arkady Sergeich Islaev ....Byron Jennings
Mikhailo Aleksandrovich Rakitin .... Ron Rifkin	Katya ....Patricia T.A. Ageheim
Kolya .... Benjamin N. Ungar	Afanasy Ivanovich
Aleksei Nokolaevich	Bolshintsov ....John Christopher Jones
Belyaev .... Alessandro Nivola	

Standby: Miss Mirren—Suzanna Hay; Messrs. Rifkin, Abraham, Jennings—Julian Gamble; Messrs. Sisto, Jones—Dan Moran; Misses Erbe, Ageheim—Jennifer Garner; Mr. Ungar—Paul F. Dano; Miss Stenborg—Patricia Baxter; Messrs. Nivola, Moran—Ezio Cutarelli.

Directed by Scott Ellis; scenery, Santo Loquasto; costumes, Jane Greenwood; lighting, Brian Nason; sound, Tony Meola; casting, Pat McCorkle; production stage manager, Jay Adler.

Time: The 1840s. Place: On the Islaev Estate in Russia. Act I: The drawing room, afternoon. Act II: The garden, the following day. Act III: The drawing room, the following day. Act IV: A portico, the same evening. Act V: The drawing room, the following day. The play was presented in two parts with the intermission following Act III.

The last major New York revival of *A Month in The Country* was by Roundabout in the Ariadne Nicolaeff translation 12/11/79 for 135 performances.

Ian McKellen: A Knight Out at the Lyceum (5) Solo performance by Ian McKellen; devised by Ian McKellen for The Cultural Festival of Gay Games IV, which produced it at the Lyceum Theater. Opened June 21, 1994; see note. (Closed June 25, 1994)

Scenery, Norbert U. Kolb; lighting, Richard Winkler; sound, Cynthia J. Hawkins; assistant to Ian McKellen, Mig Kimpton; technical supervisor, Christopher C. Smith; production stage manager, Patrick Horrigan; press, Cromarty & Company, Peter Cromarty.

One-man demonstration of classical acting, gay activism, editorials, etc., including material credited to Armistead Maupin, Martin Sherman, Peter Shaffer, Tony Blair and Tennessee Williams.

Note: Within this short limited engagement, 6/22/94 was the official opening night.

*Show Boat (275). Revival of the musical based on the novel *Show Boat* by Edna Ferber; book and lyrics by Oscar Hammerstein II; music by Jerome Kern. Produced by Livent (U.S.) Inc. at the Gershwin Theater. Opened October 2, 1994.

Steve ....Doug LaBrecque	Frank .... Joel Blum
Queenie .... Gretha Boston	Julie .... Lonette McKee
Pete; Drunk ....David Bryant	Gaylord Ravenal .... Mark Jacoby
Parthy ....Elaine Stritch	Vallon ....Jack Dabdoub
Windy ....Ralph Williams	Magnolia ....Rebecca Luker
Cap'n Andy ....John McMartin	Joe ....Michel Bell
Ellie .... Dorothy Stanley	Dealer; Jake .... Bob Walton

Jeb ....David Earl Hart
Backwoodsman; Jim ....Mike O'Carroll
Young Kim ....Larissa Auble
Ethel ....Danielle Greaves
Landlady ....Lorraine Foreman

Mother Superior; Old Lady (on the
Levee) ....Sheila Smith
Charlie; Radio Announcer ....Michael Scott
Lottie ....Louise-Marie Mennier
Dottie ....Karen Curlee
Kim .... Tammy Amerson

The *Show Boat* Ensemble: Van Abrahams, Timothy Albrecht, Derin Altay, Kevin Bagby, Hal Beasley, Timothy Robert Blevins, David Bryant, Joseph Cassidy, Roosevelt Andre Credit, Karen Curlee, Jack Dabdoub, Debbie de Coudreaux, Lorraine Foreman, Jose Garcia, Ron Gibbs, Steve Girardi, Danielle Greaves, Jeff Hairston, Lorna Hampson, Linda Hardwick, Pamela Harley, David Earl Hart, Richard L. Hobson, Michel LaFlèche, Karen Lifshey, Kim Lindsay, Jesse Means II, Louise-Marie Mennier, Kiri-Lyn Muir, Panchali Null, Mike O'Carroll, Amy Jo Phillips, Catherine Pollard, Jimmy Rivers, Michael Scott, Jill Slyter, Bob Walton, Laurie Walton, Cheryl Warfield, Jo Ann Hawkins White, Dathan B. Williams, Gay Willis, Lonel Woods, Darlene B. Young.

Children: Larissa Auble, Kimberly Jean Brown, Joran Corneal, Edwin Hodge, Imani Parks.

Band on the Cotton Blossom: Derin Altay cymbals, Bob Walton glockenspiel, Paul Gallo clarinet, Dan Levine trombone, Michael Scott bass drum, Nathan Durham tuba, Brian Miller flute.

Swings: Dennis Daniels, David Dannehl, Tari Kelly, Richie McCall, Kimberley Michaels, Louise St. Cyr.

Show Boat Orchestra: Jeffrey Huard conductor; David Holcenberg, Catherine Matejka associate conductors; Yuval Waldman concertmaster; Joel Pitchon, Mara Milkis, Lesa Terry, Christopher Cardona, Nina Simon, Byong Kwak, Christine Sunnerstam violin; Susa Follari, Katherine Sinsabaugh viola; David Calhoun, Ellen Hassman cello; Jeffrey Levine bass; Brian Miller flute, piccolo; Vincent Della Rocca flute, clarinet, soprano sax; Paul Gallo clarinet; Dale Kleps clarinet, bass clarinet, alto sax; George Morera bassoon, tenor sax; Marsha Heller oboe, English horn; Robert Millikan, Richard Kelley trumpet; Dan Levine tenor trombone; Nathan Durham tuba, bass trombone; Katie Dennis, Jeffrey Scott, French horn; Hank Jaramillo drums; Richard Fitz percussion; Pattee Cohen harp; Scott Kuney banjo, guitar; David Holcenberg piano.

Standbys: Mr. McMartin—Ralph Williams; Miss Stritch—Sheila Smith; Mr. Bell—Andre Solomon-Glover.

Understudies: Mr. McMartin—Mike O'Carroll; Miss Stritch—Lorraine Foreman; Miss Luker—Kim Lindsay, Gay Willis; Mr. Jacoby—Doug LaBrecque, Joseph Cassidy; Miss McKee—Derin Altay, Debbie de Coudreaux; Miss Boston—Pamela Harley, Jo Ann Hawkins White; Mr. Bell—Richard L. Hobson, Jose Garcia; Mr. LaBrecque—Michael Scott, David Earl Hart; Mr. Blum—Bob Walton, Steve Girardi, Ron Gibbs; Miss Stanley—Karen Curlee, Tari Kelly; Miss Amerson—Kiri-Lyn Muir, Karen Lifshey; Miss Auble—Kimberly Jean Brown; Messrs. Williams, Bryant—David Dannehl, David Earl Hart; Messrs. O'Carroll, Dabdoub—Michael Scott, David Dannehl; Messrs. Walton, Hart, Scott—David Dannehl, Dennis Daniels; Miss Greaves—Kimberley Michaels, Louise St. Cyr; Miss Foreman—Panchali Null; Miss Smith—Lorraine Foreman, Panchali Null; Misses Mennier, Curlee—Laurie Walton, Tari Kelly.

Directed by Harold Prince; choreography, Susan Stroman; scenery, Eugene Lee; costumes, Florence Klotz; lighting, Richard Pilbrow; sound, Martin Levan; musical supervisor, Jeffrey Huard; orchestrations, Robert Russell Bennett, William David Brohn; dance music arrangements, David Krane; assistant to Mr. Prince, Ruth Mitchell; special effects, Gregory Meeh; production stage manager, Randall Buck; stage manager, Betsy Nicholson; press, Mary Bryant, Wayne Wolfe.

The last major New York revival of *Show Boat* took place on Broadway in the Houston Grand Opera production 4/24/83 for 73 performances. A program note by the director of this 1994–95 production states, "This version of *Show Boat* is culled from the original 1927 production, the subsequent London script, the 1946 Broadway revival and the 1936 film. It owes a great deal to the scholarship and boundless enthusiasm of two men: John McGlinn, who produced and recorded a version of all the music and lyrics written for *Show Boat* (annotating every major production) and Miles Kreuger, who published his exegesis on *Show Boat,* the classic."

ACT I

Overture ....Orchestra
Scene 1: The levee at Natchez on the Mississippi River, 1887
    "Cotton Blossom" .... Stevedores, Gals, Townspeople

"Cap'n Andy's Ballyhoo" .... Cap'n Andy, Parthy, The Show Boat Troupe, Stevedores, Gals,
Townspeople
"Where's the Mate for Me?" ....Ravenal
"Make Believe" .... Ravenal, Magnolia
"Ol' Man River" ....Joe, Stevedores
Scene 2: Kitchen pantry of the Cotton Blossom
"Can't Help Lovin' Dat Man" ....Julie, Queenie, Joe, Magnolia, Ensemble
Scene 3: Natchez. Outside a riverfront gambling saloon
"Till Luck Comes My Way" .... Ravenal, Pete, Frank, Townsmen
Scene 4: Auditorium of the Cotton Blossom
"Mis'ry's Comin' Aroun'" ....Queenie, Stevedores, Gals
Scene 5: The windows of Magnolia's cabin and Ravenal's room
"I Have the Room Above Her" .... Ravenal, Magnolia
Scene 6: Fort Adams. Box office on the foredeck of the Cotton Blossom
"Life Upon the Wicked Stage" .... Ellie, Townswomen
"Queenie's Ballyhoo" ....Queenie, Stevedores, Gals
Scene 7: Auditorium and stage of the Cotton Blossom
Scene 8: Upper deck of the Cotton Blossom
"You Are Love" .... Ravenal, Magnolia
Scene 9: The levee in Natchez
Finale: The Wedding Celebration .... Company

ACT II

Entr'acte ....Orchestra
Scene 1: The levee in Natchez. Exterior of the Cotton Blossom, 1889
Scene 2: Magnolia's room on the Cotton Blossom
"Why Do I Love You?" .... Parthy, Company
Scene 3: Montage I. Chicago, 1889
"Dandies on Parade" .... City Folk
On the dock at Natchez, 1899—Chicago, outside the Palmer House Hotel, 1899
Scene 4: Chicago, a room in a boarding house
Scene 5: Chicago, St. Agatha's Convent
"Alma Redemptoris Mater" .... Choir
"Ol' Man River" (Reprise) ....Joe
Scene 6: Chicago, rehearsal at the Trocadero Night Club
"Bill" .... Julie
lyrics by P.G. Wodehouse, revised by Oscar Hammerstein II
"Can't Help Lovin' Dat Man" .... Magnolia
Scene 7: Entrance to the Palmer House Hotel, New Year's Eve 1899
Scene 8: Trocadero Night Club
"Goodbye, My Lady Love" ....Frank, Ellie
music and lyrics by Joseph E. Howard
"After the Ball" .... Magnolia, Ensemble
music and lyrics by Charles K. Harris
Scene 9: Montage II, 1900–1921. The levee at Natchez
"Ol' Man River" (Reprise) ....Joe
The streets of Chicago. The revolving door of the Palmer House Hotel.
Scene 10: The levee at Natchez, 1927
"Dance Away the Night" .... Magnolia
Scene 11: Later on the levee
"Kim's Charleston" .... Kim, Parthy, Company
Finale ....Joe, Company
Additional music sources: "I Might Fall Back on You," "It's Getting Hotter in the North," "Ah
Still Suits Me," "How'd You Like to Spoon With Me?" (by Jerome Kern but not originally in *Show
Boat*), "Dance Away the Night," "Hey, Feller!", "The Washington Post" (by John Philip Sousa).

SHOW BOAT—Elaine Stritch (Parthy) and John McMartin (Cap'n Andy) in the revival directed by Harold Prince

New York City Opera. Schedule of two stage musical revivals. **Wonderful Town** (14). Musical based on the play *My Sister Eileen* by Joseph Fields and Jerome Chodorov; book by Joseph Fields and Jerome Chodorov; music by Leonard Bernstein; lyrics by Betty Comden and Adolph Green. Opened November 8, 1994. (Closed November 20, 1994) **The Merry Widow** (7). Musical with original German text by Victor Leon and Leo Stein; English book adaptation by Robert Johanson; music by Franz Lehar; English lyrics by Albert Evans. Opened March 26, 1995. (Closed April 22, 1995) Produced by New York City Opera, Christopher Keene general director, Mark J. Weinstein executive director, Donald Hassard managing director of artistic administration, at the New York State Theater.

WONDERFUL TOWN

Tour Guide; Chef; Associate Editor .... William Ledbetter	Robert Baker .... Richard Muenz
Appopolous .... Larry Block	Danny .... Jeffrey Weber
Lonigan .... Don Yule	Party Guest .... Marilyn Armstrong
Helen .... Meghan Strange	Trent; Waiter .... Daniel Shigo
Wreck .... Timothy Warmen	Mrs. Wade .... Susan Browning
Violet .... Amanda Green	Frank Lippencott .... Don Stephenson
Speedy Valenti .... Carlos Lopez	Delivery Boy; 1st Cadet .... Larry Sousa
Eileen Sherwood .... Crista Moore	Chick Clark .... Stephen Berger
Ruth Sherwood .... Kay McClelland	Shore Patrolman .... Ron Hilley
Fletcher; Rexford; Ruth's Escort ..Gary Jackson	Brazilian Ambassador; Solo Policeman .... John Lankston
Drunk; Eskimo Pie Man; 2d Cadet .... Mason Roberts	Flower Sellers .... Paula Hostetter, Melissa Maravell
Drunk; Mr. Mallory .... Louis Perry	Customer .... Beth Pensiero

Policemen: Ron Hilley, Louis Perry, William Ledbetter, Jeffrey Weber. Children: Zoe Startz Barton, Simon Behr, Dov Lebowitz-Nowak, Sebastian Perez, Jacqueline Rosenfield, Rachel Rosenfield.

Standbys: Miss McClelland—Dorothy Kiara; Miss Moore—Michele McBride; Mr. Muenz—Patrick Boll.

Directed by Richard Sabellico; conductor, Eric Stern; choreography, Tina Paul; scenery, Michael Anania; costumes, Gail Baldoni; lighting, Jeff Davis; sound, Abe Jacob; chorus master, Joseph Colaneri; press, Susan Woelzl.

Time: August 1939. Place: In and around Greenwich Village, New York City.

The last major New York revival of *Wonderful Town* took place on Broadway by New York City Center Light Opera Company 5/17/67 for 17 performances. The list of scenes and musical numbers in *Wonderful Town* appears on page 389 of *The Best Plays of 1966–67*.

THE MERRY WIDOW

Baron Mirko Zeta .... George S. Irving	Hanna .... Jane Thorngren
Valencienne .... Elizabeth Futral	Count Danilo Danilovitch .... Michael Hayes
Kromov .... Joseph McKee	Lolo .... Jean Barber
Olga .... Beth McVey	Dodo .... Stephanie Godino
Bogdanovich .... John Lankston	Jou-Jou; Young Hanna .... Christiane Farr
Sylviane .... Suzanne Ishee	Frou-Frou .... Kathy Meyer
Njegus .... Robert Creighton	Clo-Clo .... Debbi Fuhrman
Camille de Rosillon .... Carlo Scibelli	Margot .... Joan Mirabella
Vicomte Cascada .... Jeffrey Lentz	Young Danilo .... John MacInnis
Raoul de St. Brioche .... James Bobick	

Directed by Robert Johanson; conductor, Eric Stern; choreography, Sharon Halley; scenery, Michael Anania; costumes, Gregg Barnes; lighting, Mark W. Stanley; sound, Abe Jacob; chorus master, Joseph Colaneri; assistant stage director, Paul L. King; musical preparation, Susan Woodruff-Versage.

Time: Early 1900s. Place: Paris. Act I: The Marsovian Embassy. Act II: The garden of Madame Glawari's villa, outside Paris. Act III: Chez Maxim.

This is a new New York City Opera production of *The Merry Widow*, created for the Paper Mill Playhouse, Millburn, N.J. The last major New York revival of this operetta was by Light Opera of Manhattan (English lyrics by Alice Hammerstein Mathias) off Broadway 9/10/80 and 1/7/81 for 35 performances.

At list of musical numbers in *The Merry Widow* appears on pages 365-6 of *The Best Plays of 1956–57*.

Radio City Music Hall. Schedule of two programs. **Radio City Christmas Spectacular** (193). Spectacle originally conceived by Robert F. Jani. Opened November 11, 1994. (Closed January 8, 1995) **Radio City Easter Show** (24). Spectacle including *The Glory of Easter* pageant originally produced by Leon Leonidoff. Opened April 8, 1995. (Closed April 22, 1995). Produced by Radio City Music Hall Productions, J. Deet Jonker executive producer, Howard Kolins producer, Penny DiCamillo producer/director of Rockettes, at Radio City Music Hall.

RADIO CITY CHRISTMAS SPECTACULAR

Santa; Scrooge; Narrator .. Charles Edward Hall
Clara; Sarah Cratchit .... Lori Bennett
Bob Cratchit .... Tim Santos, Arte Phillips
Scrooge's Nephew ......Russell Garrett, Michael Berglund
Marley's Ghost .... Paul Cole, Jeff Elsass
Ghost of Christmas Past ....Melanie Malicote, Tina Ou
Ghost of Christmas Present .....John R. Corella, Troy Magino
Mrs. Cratchit; Mrs. Claus .... Mylinda Hull, Corinne Melançon

Belinda Cratchit ....Suzanne Phillips, Linda Bowen
Peter Cratchit .. Anthony Manganiello, Joey Cee
Tiny Tim .... Corey Ballman, Jeffrey Force
Poultry Man ..Raymond C. Harris, Peter Moore
Tinker .... Michael J. Gilden
Thinker .... Kristoffer Elinder
Tannenbaum .... Tricia Ann Bonomo
Bartholomew ....Dwayne Wiseman
Thumbs .... Leslie Stump
Swings .... Steven Babiary, Marty Klebba

Skaters: Laurie Welch & Randy Coyne, Karen Courtland & David Goodman.

Rockettes: Dottie Belle, Kiki Bennett, Heather Berman, Linda Bloom, Stephanie Chase, Eileen Collins, Lillian Colon, Helen Conklin, Mary Lee DeWitt, Susanne Doris, Rebecca Downing, Dottie Earle-DeLuca, Pamela Everett, Debi Field, Jennifer Frankel, Ganine Giorgione, Eileen Grace, Prudence Gray, Leslie Guy, Susan Heart, Cheryl Hebert, Ginny Hounsell, Connie House, Stephanie James, Jennifer Jiles, Debby Kole, Anne Kulakowski, LuAnn Leonard, Ashley Listro, Judy Little, Setsuko Maruhashi, Mary Frances McCatty, Patrice McConachie, Julie McDonald, Mary McNamara, Lori Mello, Laraine Memola, MarQue Munday, Rosemary Noviello, Michelle O'Steen, Carol Toman Paracat, Renee Perry-Lancaster, Madeline J. Reiss, Laureen Repp-Russell, Linda Riley, Louise Ruck, Laura Sambol, Jereme Sheehan, Trina Simon, Jane Sonderman, Terry Spano, Leslie Stroud, Karyn Tomzak, Marilyn Westlake, Kristin Willits, Rose Ann Woolsey, Beth Woods.

Ensemble: Barbara Angeline, Robert Armitage, Todd Bailey, James Allen Baker, Michael Berglund, Linda Bowen, Michael Clowers, Paul Cole, John R. Corella, Karen Courtland, Randy Coyne, Kyle Craig, John Dietrich, Carolyn Doherty, Mamie Duncan-Gibbs, Byron Easley, Jeff Elsass, Ivy Fox, Russell Garrett, Kevin Gaudin, Aldrin Gonzalez, David Goodman, Raymond C. Harris, Jamie Harris, Lonnie Henderson, Mylinda Hull, Devanand Janki, Jennifer Krater, Tom Kosis, Ray Leeper, Michele Lynch, Mary MacLeod, Troy Magino, Melanie Malicote, Michelle Mallardi, Joanne Manning, Michael McCaskey, Marty McDonough, Hannah Meadows, Corinne Melancon, Stephanie Michels, Joan Mirabella, Peter Moore, Brad Musgrove, Tina Ou, Suzanne Phillips, Arte Phillips, Wendy Piper, Tim Santos, Vikki Schnurr, Kathleen Swanson, David Michael Underwood, Laurie Welch, Kelly Woodruff.

Radio City Music Hall Orchestra: Don Pippin conductor; Bryan Louiselle associate conductor; Mary L. Rowell concertmaster; Andrea Andros, Carmine DeLeo, Joseph Kowalewski, Julius J. Kuntsler, Nannette Levi, Susan Lorentsen, Samuel Marder, Holly Ovenden violin; Barbara H. Vaccaro, Richard Spencer viola; Frank Levy, Sarah Carter cello; Dean Crandall bass; Kenneth Emery flute; Gerard J. Niewood, Richard Oatts, John M. Cipolla, Joshua Siegel, Kenneth Arzberger reeds; George Bartlett, Nancy Schallert, French horn; Richard Raffio, Zachary Shnek, Hollis Burridge trumpet; John D. Schnupp, Thomas B. Olcott, Mark Johansen trombone; Andrew Rodgers tuba; Thomas Oldakowski drums; Mario DeCiutiis, Maya Gunji percussion; Anthony Cesarano guitar; Susanna Nason, Henry Aronson piano; Jeanne Maier harp; George Wesner, Fred Davies organ.

Directed by Robert Longbottom; musical direction and vocal arrangements, Don Pippin; choreography, Linda Haberman, Violet Holmes, Robert Longbottom, Scott Salmon, Marianne Selbert; original choreography and staging restaged by Violet Holmes, Linda Lemac; scenery, Michael Hotopp, Charles Lisanby; costumes, Gregg Barnes, Pete Menefee, Frank Spencer; lighting, Ken Billington; assistant choreographers, John Dietrich, Tom Kosis, John MacInnis; assistant musical director, Bryan Louiselle; associate lighting designer, Jason Kantrowitz; production stage manager, Andrew Feigin; stage managers, Mimi Apfel, Travis DeCastro, Doug Fogel, Janet Friedman, Hollie Hopson, Arturo Porazzi, Robin Rumpf, Mary Tynan; press, Annie Fort.

Special Credits: Writing—*Charles Dickens' A Christmas Carol* (play) by Charles Lisanby. Original Music: "Santa's Gonna Rock and Roll" and "I Can't Wait Till Christmas Day" lyrics by Bill Russell, music by Henry Krieger arranged by Bryan Louiselle; "What Do You Want for Christmas" music by Larry Grossman, lyrics by Hal Hackady; "Christmas in New York" by Billy Butt. Original Orchestrations—Elman Anderson, Michael Gibson, Don Harper, Arthur Harris, Phillip J. Lang, Dick Lieb, Don Pippin, Danny Troob, Jonathan Tunick, Jim Tyler. Dance Music Arrangers—Marvin Laird, Peter Howard, Mark Hummel. Musical Routines—Tony Fox, Bob Krogstad, Don Pippin, Don Smith.

62d edition of the Music Hall's Christmas show, starring the Rockettes and including one new number (Santa's Gonna Rock and Roll) and the traditional Nativity Pageant, presented without intermission.

SCENES AND MUSICAL NUMBERS: Overture—Radio City Music Hall Orchestra. Scene 1: Santa's Gonna Rock and Roll—Santa, Rockettes. Scene 2: *The Nutcracker,* A Little Girl's Dream. Scene 3: The Parade of the Wooden Soldiers—Rockettes. Scene 4: *Charles Dickens' A Christmas Carol.* Scene 5: Christmas in New York—Rockettes, Orchestra, Ensemble. Scene 6: Ice Skating in the Plaza. Scene 7: Santa's Toy Fantasy—Santa, Mrs. Claus, Elves. Scene 8: Carol of the Bells—Rockettes, Ensemble. Scene 9: The Living Nativity with One Solitary Life ("Silent Night," "O Little Town of Bethlehem," "The First Noel," "We Three Kings," "O Come All Ye Faithful," "Hark, the Herald Angels Sing")— Company. Jubilant, "Joy to the World"—Organ.

RADIO CITY EASTER SHOW

Rabbit .... Gregg Burge

Rockettes: Dottie Belle, Kiki Bennett, Julie Branam, Eileen Collins, Lillian Colon, Susanne Doris, Rebecca Downing, Joyce Dwyer (dance captain), Pamela Everett, Eileen Grace, Prudence Gray, Susan Heart, Cheryl Hebert, Vicki Hickerson, Ginny Hounsell, Stephanie James, Jennifer Jones, Dee Dee Knapp-Brody, Debby Kole, Anne Kulakowski, Judy Little, LuAnn Leonard, Ashley Listro, Michele Lynch, Setsuko Maruhashi, Lori Mello, Laraine Memola, Patrice McConachie, Mary McNamara, Carol Toman Paracat, Angela Piccinni, Kerri Quinn, Laureen Repp-Russell, Linda Riley, Jereme Sheehan, Trina Simon, Karyn Tomzak, Natalie Willes, Deborah Yates (Rockettes appear in various roles throughout the show).

Ensemble: Robert Armitage, Todd Bailey, Michael Berglund, Pam Bradley, Raquelle Chavis, Eric Christian, Kim Culp, Lea Carmen Dellecave, Geralyn Del Corso, Carolyn Doherty, Mamie Duncan-Gibbs, Jeff Elsass, Jennifer Frankel, Kevin Gaudin, Lonnie Henderson, Lenny Juliano, David Kent, Keri Lee, Carol Lee Meadows, Gregory Reuter, Josh Rhodes, Vincent Sandoval, Rebecca Sherman, Kristin Willits. Swings: Barbara Angeline, Jim Osorno.

Brackney's Madcap Mutts: Tom Brackney, Bonnie Brackney.

Radio City Music Hall Orchestra: Don Pippin conductor; Bryan Louiselle associate conductor; Mary L. Rowell concertmaster; Andrea Andros, Carmine DeLeo, Joseph Kowalewski, Julius J. Kunstler, Nannette Levi, Susan Lorentsen, Samuel Marder, Holly Ovenden violin; Barbara H. Vaccaro, Richard Spencer viola; Frank Levy, Sarah Carter cello; Dean Crandall bass; Kenneth Emery flute; Gerard J. Niewood, Richard Oatts, John M. Cipolla, Joshua Siegel, Kenneth Arzberger reeds; George Bartlett, Nancy Schallert, French horn; Richard Raffio, Zachary Shnek, Hollis Burridge trumpet; John D. Schnupp, Thomas B. Olcott, Mark Johansen trombone; Andrew Rodgers tuba; Thomas Oldakowski drums; Mario DeCiutiis, Maya Gunji percussion; Anthony Cesarano guitar; Jeanne Maier harp; Susanna Nason piano; Robert Wendel keyboard; George Wesner organ.

Directed and choreographed by Linda Haberman; assistant choreographer, Dennis Callahan; musical direction and vocal arrangements, Don Pippin; associate musical director, Bryan Louiselle; Gershwin scenery and costumes, Erté; additional scenery, Eduardo Sicangco; costumes, Eduardo Sicangco, Jose Lengson; lighting, Ken Billington, Jason Kantrowitz; orchestrations, Michael Gibson, Dick Lieb, Glenn Osser, Jim Tyler; dance music arrangements, Mark Hummel, Marvin Laird; *The Glory of Easter* lighting, Billy B. Walker, restaging, Linda Lemac, vocal solo recording, Marilyn Horne; Honey Bunny costumes, Pete Menefee; additional costumes, Pete Menefee, Bob Mackie; Dancing in Diamonds staging, Violet Holmes, costumes, Bob Mackie; original production directed and choreographed by Scott Salmon; production stage manager, Andrew Feigin.

Original Music Credit: "Put a Little Spring in Your Step" music and lyrics by Jeffrey Ernstoff.

Special Music Credits: "Put on Your Sunday Clothes" music and lyrics by Jerry Herman; "La Cage aux Folles" music by Jerry Herman, arranged by Gordon Lowry Harrell; "There Are No Girls Like Showgirls" music by Don Pippin, lyrics by Sammy Cahn; "Encore" music by Stan Lebowsky, lyrics by Fred Tobias, arranged by Tom Bahler, orchestrated by Robert Freedman.

ACT I, Prologue: *The Glory of Easter.* Overture—Radio City Music Hall Orchestra. Scene 1: Pure Imagination—Rabbit. Scene 2: "Put a Little Spring in Your Step"—Rabbit, Singers, Dancers, Rockettes in Happy Feet. Scene 3: I'd Rather Lead the Band—Rabbit, Orchestra. Scene 4: Dancing in Diamonds— Rockettes. Scene 5: With Gershwin—Singers, Dancers, Orchestra, Rockettes.

ACT II, Entr'acte—Radio City Music Hall Orchestra. Scene 1: Rockettes Easter Parade—Rabbit, Rockettes. Scene 2: Hats—Dancers. Scene 3: Brackney's Madcap Mutts—Tom Brackney, Bonnie Brackney, dogs. Scene 4: "Dancing in the Dark"—Rockettes (laser show). Scene 5: Yesteryear, Easter morning in the 1890s—Company.

*Sunset Boulevard (222). Musical based on the Billy Wilder film; book and lyrics by Don Black and Christopher Hampton; music by Andrew Lloyd Webber. Produced by The Really Useful Company at the Minskoff Theater. Opened November 17, 1994.

Norma Desmond	Glenn Close	Betty Schaefer	Alice Ripley
Joe Gillis	Alan Campbell	Cecil B. DeMille	Alan Oppenheimer
Max von Mayerling	George Hearn	Artie Green	Vincent Tumeo

Others: 1st Harem Girl, Beautician—Sandra Allen; Young Writer, Salesman, DeMille's Assistant—Bryan Batt; Heather, 2d Masseuse—Susan Dawn Carson; Cliff, Salesman, Young Guard—Matthew Dickens; 3d Harem Girl (Jean), Beautician, Hedy Lamarr—Colleen Dunn; Morino, Salesman, Hog Eye—Steven Stein-Granger; Lisa, Doctor—Kim Huber; 1st Financeman, Film Actor, Salesman—Rich Hebert; Katherine, Psychiatrist—Alicia Irving; 2d Harem Girl, Beautician—Lada Boder; Mary, 1st Masseuse—Lauren Kennedy; Sheldrake, Police Chief—Sal Mistretta; John, Salesman, Victor Mature—Mark Morales; Myron, Manfred—Rick Podell; 2d Financeman, Salesman, Party Guest—Tom Alan Robbins; Jonesy, Sammy, Salesman—David Eric; Choreographer, Salesman—Rick Sparks; Joanna, Astrologer—Wendy Walter.

Orchestra: Paul Bogaev conductor; James May assistant conductor; Sanford Allen concertmaster; Sylvia D'Avanzo, Myra Segal, Paul Woodiel, Kurt Coble, Avril Brown, Kurt Briggs violin; Richard Brice, Henry Kao viola; Francesca Vanasco cello; Douglas Romoff bass, electric bass; M. Bernard Phillips flute, piccolo, alto flute; Andrew Sterman alto sax, bass clarinet, clarinet; Edward Salkin tenor sax, flute, clarinet; Theresa MacDonnell-Hardison, Steve Zimmerman, French horn; Christian Jaudes trumpet, piccolo trumpet; Jeffrey Nelson bass trombone; James Saporito drums, percussion; David Boguslaw guitar; Robert Gustafson, Maggie Torre, James May keyboards.

Standby: Miss Close—Karen Mason. Understudies: Miss Close—Susan Dawn Carson; Mr. Campbell—Bryan Batt, Matthew Dickens; Miss Ripley—Kim Huber, Lauren Kennedy; Mr. Hearn—Steven Stein-Granger, Rich Hebert; Mr. Oppenheimer—Steven Stein-Granger, David Eric; Mr. Tumeo—Matthew Dickens, Darrin Baker; Others—Darrin Baker, Harvey Evans, Rosemary Loar, Darlene Wilson.

Directed by Trevor Nunn; musical staging, Bob Avian; musical supervision and direction, David Caddick; musical direction, Paul Bogaev; scenery, John Napier; costumes, Anthony Powell; lighting, Andrew Bridge; sound, Martin Levan; orchestrations, David Cullen, Andrew Lloyd Webber; casting, Johnson-Liff Associates; production stage manager, Peter Lawrence; stage managers, John Brigleb, Jim Wooley, Lynda J. Fox; press, Boneau/Bryan-Brown, Adrian Bryan-Brown, John Barlow.

Time: 1949/50. Place: Los Angeles.

Has-been silent screen superstar captures young writer in her gilded web and consumes him in an effort to make a comeback, per Billy Wilder's movie *Sunset Boulevard,* with scenes and musical numbers identified below, and in the program, as though in a movie script.

Karen Mason replaced Glenn Close 3/7/95. Glenn Close replaced Karen Mason 3/19/95.

A Best Play; see page 107.

ACT I

Overture
1. Exterior/dawn, the house on Sunset
    Prologue ....Joe
2. Ext/day, Paramount Studios
    "Let's Have Lunch" ....Joe, Ensemble
3. Ext/day, on the road
4. Ext/day, the garage on Sunset
5. Interior day & evening, the house on Sunset
    "Surrender" ....Norma
    "With One Look" ....Norma
    "Salome" ....Norma, Joe
6. Int/night, Norma's guest house
    "The Greatest Star of All" ....Max

7. Int/evening, Schwab's Drugstore
"Every Movie's a Circus" .... Joe, Betty, Artie, Ensemble
"Girl Meets Boy" .... Joe, Betty
8. Ext/night, the terrace on Sunset
9. Int/evening, the house on Sunset
"New Ways to Dream" .... Norma
10. Int/day, the house on Sunset
"The Lady's Paying" .... Manfred, Norma, Joe, Salesmen
11. Int/night, the house on Sunset
"The Perfect Year" .... Norma, Joe
12. Int/night, Artie Green's apartment
"This Time Next Year" .... Joe, Betty, Artie, Ensemble
13. Int/night, the house on Sunset

ACT II

Entr'acte
1. Ext/day, Norma's swimming pool
"Sunset Boulevard" .... Joe
"The Perfect Year" (Reprise) .... Norma
2. Ext/day, Paramount Studio
"As If We Never Said Goodbye" .... Norma
"Surrender" (Reprise) .... Cecil B. DeMille
3. Int/night, Betty's office at Paramount
"Girl Meets Boy" (Reprise) .... Betty, Joe
4. Int/day, the house on Sunset
"Eternal Youth Is Worth a Little Suffering" .... Norma's Consultants
5. Int/ext/night, Betty's office/ Paramount backlot
"Too Much in Love to Care" .... Betty, Joe
6. Ext/night, the house on Sunset
"New Ways to Dream" (Reprise) .... Max
7. Ext/int/night, the house on Sunset
"Sunset Boulevard" (Reprise) .... Joe, Betty
8. Ext/int/dawn, the house on Sunset
"The Greatest Star of All" (Reprise) .... Max, Norma
"Surrender" (Reprise) .... Norma

Circle in the Square. Schedule of three revivals. **The Shadow Box** (48). By Michael Cristofer. Opened November 20, 1994. (Closed January 1, 1995) **Uncle Vanya** (29). By Anton Chekhov; English version by Jean-Claude van Itallie. Opened February 24, 1995. (Closed March 19, 1995) ***The Rose Tattoo** (36). By Tennessee Williams. Opened April 30, 1995. Produced by Circle in the Square, Theodore Mann and Josephine Abady co-artistic directors, Robert Bennett managing director, at Circle in the Square Theater.

THE SHADOW BOX

Interviewer	Ron Frazier	Brian	Jamey Sheridan
Cottage One:		Mark	Raphael Sbarge
Joe	Frankie R. Faison	Beverly	Mercedes Ruehl
Steve	Sean Nelson	Cottage Three:	
Maggie	Mary Alice	Agnes	Marlo Thomas
Cottage Two:		Felicity	Estelle Parsons

Understudies: Messrs. Frazier, Faison—Charles Dumas; Miss Alice—Yvette Hawkins; Messrs. Sheridan, Sbarge—Grant Albrecht; Misses Ruehl, Thomas—Carol Locatell; Miss Parsons—Peggy Cosgrave.

Directed by Jack Hofsiss; scenery, David Jenkins; costumes, Carrie Robbins; lighting, Richard Nelson; sound, Aural Fixation; fight choreography, B.H. Barry; dance sequence choreography, Nora Kasarda; casting, Barbara Hipkiss; production stage manager, Wm. Hare; press, Jeffrey Richards Associates, Kevin Rehac, Irene Gandy.

THE ROSE TATTOO—Mercedes Ruehl (Serafina) and Anthony LaPaglia (Alvaro) in the Circle in the Square revival of the play by Tennessee Williams

The Shadow Box was first produced on Broadway 3/31/77 for 315 performances and was cited as a Best Play of its season and received the Pulitzer Prize. This is its first major New York revival, presented in two parts.

UNCLE VANYA

Maryina (Nanny) .... Bette Henritze
Mikhail Lvovich Astrov .... James Fox
Ivan Petrovich Voinitsky
  (Vanya) .... Tom Courtenay
Alexander Vladimirovich
  Serebryakov .... Werner Klemperer
Ilya Ilyich Telyegin .... Gerry Bamman
Sofya Alexandrovna (Sonya) ...... Kate Skinner
Yelena Andreyevna .... Amanda Donohoe
Maria Vasilyevna Voinitskaya .. Elizabeth Franz
Worker .... Richard Council

Understudies: Misses Henritze, Franz—Angela Thornton; Messrs. Fox, Klemperer—Richard Council; Messrs. Courtenay, Bamman, Council—Paul Hebron; Misses Skinner, Donohoe—Catherine Dent.

Directed by Braham Murray; scenery, Loren Sherman; costumes, Mimi Maxmen; lighting, Tharon Musser; sound, John Kilgore; music, Stanley Silverman; casting, Stuart Howard, Amy Schecter; production stage manager, Wm. Hare; stage manager, Cheryl Zoldowski.

Place: In and around the family estate. The play was presented in two parts and four acts with the intermission following Act II.

The last major New York productions of *Uncle Vanya* were 6/13/91 for 16 performances off Broadway in the Lithuanian language by the State Theater of Lithuania and, in English, 6/4/73 for 64 performances on Broadway by Circle in the Square.

THE ROSE TATTOO

Salvatore	Anthony Manganiello	Violetta	Fiddle Viracola
Vivi	Jackie Angelescu	Mariella	Elaine Bromka
Assunta	Antonia Rey	Father De Leo	Dominic Chianese
Rosa Delle Rose	Cara Buono	Doctor; Salesman	Philip LeStrange
Serafina Delle Rose	Mercedes Ruehl	Miss Yorke	Ellen Tobie
Estelle Hohengarten	Deborah Jolly	Flora	Catherine Campbell
The Strega	Irma St. Paule	Bessie	Kay Walbye
Giuseppina	Carol Locatell	Jack Hunter	Dylan Chalfy
Peppina	Suzanne Grodner	Alvaro Mangiacavallo	Anthony LaPaglia

Understudies: Messrs. Manganiello, Angelescu—Teddy Alvaro; Misses Tobie, Walbye, Campbell—Elaine Bromka; Messrs. LaPaglia, LeStrange—Kevin Geer; Miss Ruehl—Suzanne Grodner; Mr. Chianese—Philip LeStrange; Miss Rey—Carol Locatell; Misses St. Paule, Grodner, Locatell—Diane Martella; Misses Buono, Jolly, Viracola, Bromka—Elizabeth Rouse; Mr. Chalfy—Sam Trammell.

Directed by Robert Falls; scenery, Santo Loquasto; costumes, Catherine Zuber; lighting, Kenneth Posner; sound, John Kilgore; dialects, K.C. Ligon; casting, Stuart Howard/Amy Schecter; stage manager, Peggy Peterson; press, Jeffrey Richards Associates, Kevin Rehac, Irene Gandy.

Act I, Scene 1: Evening. Scene 2: Almost morning, the next day. Scene 3: Noon of that day. Scene 4: A late spring morning, three years later. Scene 5: Immediately following. Scene 6: Two hours later that day. Act II, Scene 1: Two hours later that day. Act III, Scene 1: Evening of the same day. Scene 2: Just before dawn of the next day. Scene 3: Morning.

The last major New York revival of *The Rose Tattoo* was by City Center Drama Company on Broadway 10/20/66 for 76 performances.

The Flying Karamazov Brothers Do the Impossible! (50). New Vaudeville performance piece devised by The Flying Karamazov Brothers. Produced by The Imagination Company, Ltd., Herb Goldsmith Productions, Inc. and Jujamcyn Theaters at the Helen Hayes Theater. Opened November 20, 1994. (Closed January 1, 1995)

Dmitri Karamazov	Paul Magid	Rakitin Karamazov	Michael Preston
Ivan Karamazov	Howard Jay Patterson	Smerdyakov Karamazov	Sam Williams

Kamikaze Ground Crew: Steve Bernstein trumpet, slide trumpet, percussion; Gina Leishman saxophone, bass clarinet, piccolo, accordion; James Pugliese drums, mallets; Marcus Rojas tuba; Doug Wieselman saxophone, clarinet, guitar, percussion.

Musical direction, Doug Wieselman; stage manager, Shannon Rhodes; press, Boneau/Bryan-Brown, Bob Fennell, Jamie Morris.

Fourth New York engagement of this group of agile and imaginative performers who combine physical and verbal humor in a show presented in two parts.

The segment called *The Gamble* has this footnote in the program: "Our Champ will juggle any three objects, supplied and chosen by the audience, which are heavier than an ounce, lighter than ten pounds and no bigger than a bread box. He gets three (3) tries to keep the objects in the air for at least ten (10) counts. . . . . The Champ is allowed three 'modifications' with which he may alter the objects in any way he chooses. The Champ will not juggle live animals or anything that might prevent the Champ himself from continuing to be a live animal."

A Christmas Carol (71). Musical based on the story by Charles Dickens; book by Mike Ockrent and Lynn Ahrens; music by Alan Menken; lyrics by Lynn Ahrens. Produced by Nickelodeon Family Classics and Madison Square Garden at the Paramount Madison Square Garden Theater. Opened December 1, 1994. (Closed January 1, 1995)

Punch and Judy Man; Marley as a Young Man; Undertaker	Christopher Sieber	Jack Smythe	Andy Jobe
Punch and Judy Woman	Donna Lee Marshall	Grace Smythe	Lindsay Jobe
Organ Grinder	Robert Ousley	Scrooge	Walter Charles
Grave Digger	Bill Nolte	Cratchit	Nick Corley
Mr. Smythe	Joseph Kolinski	Old Joe; Mr. Kent	Ken McMullen
		Match Girl	Arlene Pierret

Sandwich Board Man; Ghost of Christmas
  Present .... Michael Mandell
Fred .... Robert Westenberg
Jonathan .... Jason Fuchs
Lamplighter; Ghost of Christmas
  Past .... Ken Jennings
Blind Hag; Scrooge's
  Mother .... Andrea Frierson Toney
Mrs. Mops .... Darcy Pulliam
Ghost of Jacob Marley .... Jeff Keller
Judge .... Michael H. Ingram
Scrooge at 8 .... David Gallagher
Fan at 6 .... Mary Elizabeth Albano

Scrooge's Father;
  Undertaker .... Michael X. Martin
Scrooge at 12 .... Ramzi Khalaf
(Fan at 10) ...... Jacy De Filippo, Olivia Oguma
Fezziwig .... Gerry Vichi
Scrooge at 18 .... Michael Christopher Moore
Mrs. Fezziwig .... Mary Stout
Emily .... Emily Skinner
Tiny Tim .... Matthew Mezzacappa
Mrs. Cratchit .... Joy Hermalyn
Sally, Fred's Wife .... Natalie Toro
Ghost of Christmas Future ...... Theara J. Ward

(Parentheses indicate role in which performers alternated)

Charity Men: Robert Ousley, Martin Van Treuren, Walter Willison. Street Urchins and Children: Matthew F. Byrne, Jacy De Filippo, Justin Bartholomew Kamen, Olivia Oguma, Christopher Mark Petrizzo, P.J. Smith. The Cratchit Children: Mary Elizabeth Albano, Betsy Chang, David Gallagher, Sean Thomas Morrissey.

Angels and Children's Chorus: Blessed Sacrament Chorus of Staten Island, PS 26 Chorus, Righteousness Unlimited, William E. Halloran Vocal Ensemble-School 22.

Business Men, Ghosts, Gifts, People of London: Mary Elizabeth Albano, Joan Barber, Renee Bergeron, Christophe Caballero, Betsy Chang, Candy Cook, Madeleine Doherty, Mark Dovey, Donna Dunmire, Andrea Frierson Toney, David Gallagher, Melissa Haizlip, Joy Hermalyn, Michael H. Ingram, Don Johanson, Eric H. Kaufman, John-Charles Kelly, Ramzi Khalaf, David Lowenstein, Seth Malkin, Donna Lee Marshall, Michael X. Martin, Carol Lee Meadows, Michael Christopher Moore, Sean Thomas Morrissey, Ken McMullen, Karen Murphy, Bill Nolte, Robert Ousley, Tom Pardoe, Gail Pennington, Angela Piccinni, Arlene Pierett, Darcy Pulliam, Josef Reiter, Pamela Remler, Sam Reni, Eric Riley, Rommy Sandhu, Christopher Sieber, Emily Skinner, Erin Stoddard, Mary Stout, Tracy Terstriep, Natalie Toro, Martin Van Treuren, Gerry Vichi, Theara J. Ward, Walter Willison.

Orchestra: Paul Gemignani conductor; Mark C. Mitchell associate conductor; Aloysia Friedmann concertmaster; Karl Kawahara, Ann Labin, Sebu Sirinian violin; Monica Gerard, Adria Benjamin viola; Clay Ruede cello; Charles Bergeron bass; David Weiss, Daniel Willis, Al Hunt, Kenneth Dybisz, John Campo woodwinds; Ronald Sell, French horn; Stu Sataloff, Larry Lunetta, Dominic Derasse trumpet; Phil Sasson, Dean Plank trombone; Steve Tyler, Mark C. Mitchell keyboard; Jennifer Hoult harps, keyboard; Paul Pizutti drums; Glenn Rhian percussion.

Understudies: Mr. Nolte—Seth Malkin, David Lowenstein; Mr. Kolinski—James Judy, Michael Hayward-Jones; Mr. Jobe—Christopher Mark Petrizzo, P.J. Smith; Miss Jobe—Olivia Oguma, Jacy De Filippo; Mr. Charles—Michael X. Martin, James Judy; Mr. Corley—James Judy, John-Charles Kelly; Mr. McMullen—Billy Vitelli; Mr. Westenberg—James Judy, Michael Hayward-Jones; Mr. Fuchs—P.J. Smith, Christopher Mark Petrizzo; Miss Toney—Donna Lee Marshall, Whitney Webster; Miss Pulliam—Whitney Webster, Karen Murphy; Mr. Keller—James Judy, Michael Hayward-Jones: Mr. Jennings—Don Johanson, Billy Vitelli; Mr. Ingram—Billy Vitelli; Mr. Martin—Michael Hayward-Jones, Billy Vitelli; Mr. Gallagher—Justin Bartholomew Kamen, Matthew F. Byrne; Mr. Khalaf—Christopher Mark Petrizzo, P.J. Smith; Mr. Vichi—Michael Hayward-Jones, John-Charles Kelly; Mr. Moore—Christopher Sieber, Josef Reiter; Miss Stout—Joy Hermalyn, Whitney Webster; Miss Skinner—Natalie Toro, Donna Lee Marshall; Mr. Mandell—Bill Nolte, Michael Hayward-Jones; Mr. Mezzacappa—David Gallagher, Jason Fuchs; Miss Hermalyn—Whitney Webster, Cynthia Thole; Miss Ward—Donna Dunmire.

Directed by Mike Ockrent; choreography, Susan Stroman; musical direction, Paul Gemignani; scenery, Tony Walton; costumes, William Ivey Long; lighting, Jules Fisher, Peggy Eisenhauer; sound, Tony Meola; projections, Wendall K. Harrington; flying, Foy; orchestrations, Michael Starobin; dance arrangements and incidental music, Glen Kelly; executive producer, Dodger Productions (Michael David, Edward Strong, Sherman Warner); associate director and production stage manager, Steven Zweigbaum; associate choreographer, Chris Peterson; casting, Julie Hughes; stage manager, Clifford Schwartz; press, Boneau/Bryan-Brown, Suzanne Tighe, Jamie Morris, Patty Onagan.

Time: 1880. Place: London. The play was presented without intermission.

The Dickens Christmas tale as a modern musical spectacle.

MUSICAL NUMBERS

Scene 1: A graveyard near St. Paul's Cathedral, Christmas Eve
  "The Years Are Passing By" ....Grave Digger
Scene 2: The Royal Exchange
  "Jolly, Rich and Fat" ...... Three Charity Men, Smythe Family, Businessmen, Wives and Children
  "Nothing to Do With Me" .... Scrooge, Crachit
Scene 3: The street
  "Street Song (Nothing to Do With Me)" ... People of London, Scrooge, Fred, Jonathan, Sandwich
                                        Board Man, Lamplighter, Blind Hag, Jack Smythe
Scene 4: Scrooge's house
  "Link by Link" ....Marley's Ghost, Scrooge, Ghosts
Scene 5: Scrooge's bedchamber
  "The Lights of Long Ago" .... Ghost of Christmas Past
Scene 6: The law courts
  "God Bless Us, Everyone" .... Scrooge's Mother, Fan at 6, Scrooge at 8
Scene 7: The factory
  "A Place Called Home" .... Scrooge at 12, Fan at 10, Scrooge
Scene 8: Fezziwig's banking house
  "Mr. Fezziwig's Annual Christmas Ball" ....Fezziwig, Mrs. Fezziwig, Guests
  "A Place Called Home" (Reprise) ....Emily, Scrooge at 18, Scrooge
Scene 9: Montage
  "The Lights of Long Ago" (Part II) .... Scrooge at 18, Young Marley, Emily, People From
                                                                    Scrooge's Past
Scene 10: A starry night
  "Abundance and Charity" .... Ghost of Christmas Present, Scrooge, Christmas Gifts
Scene 11: All over London
  "Christmas Together" ....Tiny Tim, The Crachits, Fred, Sally, Scrooge, People of London
Scene 12: The graveyard
  "Dancing on Your Grave" ...... Grave Diggers, Ghost of Christmas Future, Monks, Businessmen,
                                        Mrs. Mops, Undertakers, Old Joe, Mr. Smythe, Cratchit
  "Yesterday, Tomorrow and Today" ....Scrooge, Angels, Children of London
Scene 13: Scrooge's bedchamber
  "The Years Are Passing By" (Reprise) ....Jonathan
Scene 14: The street, Christmas Day
  "Nothing to Do With Me" (Reprise) ....Scrooge
  "Christmas Together" (Reprise) ....People of London
  "God Bless Us, Everyone" (Finale) ....Company

What's Wrong With This Picture? (13). By Donald Margulies. Produced by David Stone, The Booking Office, Albert Nocciolino and Betsy Dollinger in association with Ted Snowdon at the Brooks Atkinson Theater. Opened December 8, 1994. (Closed December 18, 1994)

Artie	David Moscow	Sid	Jerry Stiller
Bella	Florence Stanley	Ceil	Marcell Rosenblatt
Mort	Alan Rosenberg	Shirley	Faith Prince

Standbys: Misses Prince, Rosenblatt—Emily Zacharias; Mr. Rosenberg—Paul Harman; Mr. Stiller—Stan Lachow; Miss Stanley—Rose Arrick; Mr. Moscow—Brad Stoll.

Directed by Joe Mantello; scenery, Derek McLane; costumes, Ann Roth; lighting, Brian MacDevitt; sound, Aural Fixation; wigs, Paul Huntley; original music, Mel Marvin; associate producer, Ruth Kalkstein; production stage manager, Michael Ritchie; stage manager, Barnaby Harris; press, Boneau/Bryan-Brown, Jackie Green, Bob Fennell.

Time: Some years ago. Place: A middle-class apartment in Brooklyn, N.Y. Act I: The living room, evening. Act II: The following day.

Produced by Manhattan Theater Club in 1984 but withdrawn before opening, by Back Alley Theater in Los Angeles in 1988 and OOB by Jewish Repertory Theater 6/21/90, *What's Wrong With This Picture?* is a comedy about a mother who returns from the grave to straighten out problems among the family members she left behind.

A CHRISTMAS CAROL—Walter Charles as Ebenezer Scrooge in the musical version of the Dickens tale at Madison Square Garden

A Tuna Christmas (20). Two-man performance by Joe Sears and Jaston Williams; written by Jaston Williams, Joe Sears and Ed Howard. Produced by Charles H. Duggan and Drew Dennett at the Booth Theater. Opened December 15, 1994. (Closed December 31, 1994)

CAST OF CHARACTERS: Thurston Wheelis, Elmer Watkins, Bertha Bumiller, Leonard Childers, R.R. Snavely, Pearl Burras, Sheriff Givens, Ike Thompson, Inita Goodwin, Phoebe Burkhalter, Joe Bob Lipsey—Joe Sears; Arles Struvie, Didi Snavely, Petey Fisk, Jody Bumiller, Charlene Bumiller, Stanley Bumiller, Vera Carp, Dixie Deberry, Fraley Burkhalter, Helen Bedd, Garland Poteet—Jaston Williams.

Understudies: Mr. Williams—Greg Currie; Mr. Sears—Tim Mateer.

Directed by Ed Howard; scenery, Loren Sherman; costumes, Linda Fisher; lighting, Judy Rasmuson; sound, Ken Huncovsky; producing associates, Joe Mac/Shyrl Ponder, Carla McQueen/Sean Ashley; production stage manager, Peter A. Still; press, the Pete Sanders Group, Ian Rand, Glenna Freedman.

Affectionate and broadly comic portrayals of 22 citizens of the fictional town of Tuna, Tex., and their eccentric ways and manners of keeping Christmas, a sequel to the Williams-Sears-Howard off-Broadway hit *Greater Tuna* which opened 10/21/82 and played 501 performances. The play, a touring attraction brought to New York for a limited holiday engagement, was presented in two parts.

A Best Play; see page 155.

Comedy Tonight (8). Performance program by and with four comedians: Joy Behar, Michael Davis, Dorothy Loudon and Mort Sahl. Produced by Alexander H. Cohen and Max Cooper at the Lunt-Fontanne Theater. Opened December 18, 1994. (Closed December 25, 1994)

Musicians: Peter Howard conductor, piano; Michael Keller drums; Vincent Bell guitar, banjo; Bruce Samuels bass.

Directed by Alexander H. Cohen; musical staging, Albert Stephenson; musical direction, Peter Howard; scenery, Ray Klausen; costumes, Alvin Colt; lighting, Richard Nelson; sound, Bruce D. Cameron; special material for Miss Loudon, Bruce Vilanch; music coordinator, John Monaco; associate producer, Hildy Parks; production stage manager, Bob Borod; press, Merle Debuskey, Susan Chicoine.

The four comedians in solo stints of a half hour each, presented without intermission. Previously produced in regional theater at Rich Forum, Stamford, Conn.

A Christmas Carol (18). Return engagement of the solo performance by Patrick Stewart; adapted by Patrick Stewart from Charles Dickens. Produced by Terri and Timothy Childs at the Richard Rodgers Theater. Opened December 22, 1994. (Closed January 8, 1995)

Directed by Patrick Stewart; lighting, Fred Allen; executive producer, Kate Elliott; press, Boneau/Bryan-Brown, Susanne Tighe, Bob Fennell.

Stewart's one-man version of the Dickens story was previously produced on Broadway 12/19/91 for 14 performances and 12/17/92 for 22 performances. The play was presented in two parts. A foreign play produced on a tour of the U.S. in 1988.

Jesus Christ Superstar (16). Revival of the musical based on the last seven days in the life of Jesus of Nazareth; conceived for the stage by Tom O'Horgan; music by Andrew Lloyd Webber; lyrics by Tim Rice. Produced by Landmark Entertainment Group, Magic Promotions & Theatricals and TAP Productions at the Paramount Madison Square Garden Theater. Opened January 17, 1995. (Closed January 29, 1995)

Jesus of Nazareth	Ted Neeley	Simon	Lawrence Clayton
Judas Iscariot	Carl Anderson	Pontius Pilate	Dennis DeYoung
Mary Magdalene	Syreeta Wright	Peter	Mike Eldred
Caiaphas	David Bedella	King Herod	Douglass Fraser
Annas	Danny Zolli	Maid by the Fire	Karen Byers
1st Priest	Mark Slama	Soldier by the Fire	Mark C. Reis
2d Priest	Michael Guarnera	Old Man by the Fire	Pressley Sutherland
3d Priest	Gary Bankston		

Tormentors: Carol Bentley, Shannon Falank, Kristen Young. Soul Sisters: Karen Byers, J. Kathleen Lamb, Hillary Turk.

Apostles, Their Women, The People of Bethany and Jerusalem: Gary Bankston, Carol Bentley, Kevin Bernard, Karen Byers, Phil Dominguez, Mike Eldred, Shannon Falank, Robert H. Fowler, Michael Guarnera, Vanessa A. Jones, Eileen Kaden, J. Kathleen Lamb, Mark C. Reis, Mark Slama, Pressley Sutherland, Hillary Turk, Kristen Young. Swings: Michelle DeJean, Jill B. Gounder, Hans Kriefall, Cindi Parise, Larry Vickers.

Orchestra: Craig Barna conductor; Keith Thompson associate conductor, keyboard I; James Laev keyboard II; J. Anthony DeAugustine drums; Brian Nakagawa guitar, banjo; Kevin Moore 1st trumpet; Dan Snurr 2d trumpet; Anthony Alms trombone; Robert Pawlo wind, reeds; Ed Shea percussion; Robert Hillebrecht bass; Richard Tremarello, French horn.

Standby: Mr. DeYoung—Jeffrey Watkins. Understudies: Mr. Neeley—Jeffrey Watkins, Danny Zolli; Mr. Anderson—Lawrence Clayton, Danny Zolli; Miss Wright—Vanessa A. Jones, Eileen Kaden, Hillary Turk; Mr. DeYoung—Lawrence Clayton, Pressley Sutherland; Mr. Eldred—Gary Bankston, Pressley Sutherland; Mr. Clayton—Gary Bankston, Robert H. Fowler; Mr. Zolli—Gary Bankston, Michael Guarnera; Mr. Bedella—Mark Slama, Jeffrey Watkins; Mr. Fraser—Kevin Bernard, Pressley Sutherland; Messrs. Slama, Guarnera, Bankston—Hans Kriefall, Pressley Sutherland; Mr. Reis—Hans Kriefall; Mr. Sutherland—Hans Kriefall, Mark Slama; Miss Byers—Michelle DeJean, Cindi Parise.

Directed and choreographed by Tony Christopher; musical direction, Craig Barna; scenery, Bill Stabile; lighting, Rick Belzer; costumes, David Paulin; sound, Jonathan Deans; special effects, Gregg Stephens; associate choreographer, Larry Vickers; executive producer, Forbes Candlish; casting, Peter Wise & Associates; production stage manager, Joe Cappelli; stage manager, Michael McEowen; press, The Jacksina Company, Judy Jacksina.

The last major New York revival of *Jesus Christ Superstar* took place on Broadway 11/23/77 for 96 performances. This touring production had previously played 112 cities in 23 months.

ACT I

Overture ....Company
"Heaven on Their Minds" .... Judas
Bethany, Friday night
　"What's the Buzz" .... Jesus, Mary, Apostles, Their Women
　"Strange Things Mystifying" ....Judas, Jesus, Apostles, Their Women
　"Everything's Alright" ....Mary, Judas, Jesus, Apostles, Their Women
Jerusalem, Sunday
　"This Jesus Must Die" ....Caiaphas, Annas, Priests, Company
　"Hosanna" ....Caiaphas, Jesus, Company
　"Simon Zealotes" ....Simon, Company
　"Poor Jerusalem" ....Jesus
Pontius Pilate's house, Monday
　"Pilate's Dream" .... Pilate
　"The Temple" .... Jesus, Merchants, Money Lenders
　"I Don't Know How to Love Him" ....Mary, Jesus
Tuesday
　"Damned for All Time" .... Judas, Annas, Caiaphas, Priests

ACT II

Thursday night
　"The Last Supper" .... Jesus, Judas, Apostles
The garden
　"Gethsemane" ....Jesus
　"The Arrest" ....Peter, Jesus, Apostles, Reporters, Caiaphas, Annas
　"Peter's Denial" .... Maid, Peter, Soldier, Old Man, Mary
Pilate's palace, Friday
　"Pilate and Christ" .... Pilate, Soldier, Jesus, Company
House of Herod
　"King Herod's Song" .... Herod
　"Could We Start Again, Please" ....Mary, Peter, Company
　"Judas' Death" ....Judas, Annas, Caiaphas
Pilate's palace
　"Trial Before Pilate" .... Pilate, Caiaphas, Jesus, Mob
　"Superstar" .... Voice of Judas, Company
Golgotha
　"The Crucifixion" ....Jesus, Company
　"John 19:41" ....Orchestra

*Love! Valour! Compassion! (122). Transfer from off Broadway of the play by Terrence McNally. Produced by Manhattan Theater Club, Lynne Meadow artistic director, Barry Grove managing director, by special arrangement with Jujamcyn Theaters, James H. Binger chairman, Rocco Landesman president, Paul Libin producing director, Jack Viertel creative director, at the Walter Kerr Theater. Opened February 14, 1995.

Gregory Mitchell	Stephen Bogardus	Buzz Hauser	Nathan Lane
Arthur Pape	John Benjamin Hickey	Bobby Brahms	Justin Kirk
Perry Sellars	Anthony Heald	Ramon Fornos	Randy Becker
John Jeckyll; James Jeckyll	John Glover		

　Understudies: Messrs. Heald, Lane, Hickey—Steven Skybell; Messrs. Glover, Bogardus, Heald—Kirk Jackson; Messrs. Kirk, Becker—David Noroña.
　Directed by Joe Mantello; scenery, Loy Arcenas; costumes, Jess Goldstein; lighting, Brian MacDevitt; sound, John Kilgore; choreography, John Carrafa; associate artistic director, Michael Bush; casting, Randy Carrig; production stage manager, William Joseph Barnes; press, Helene Davis, Kevin P. McAnarney.
　Time: The present, Memorial Day, 4th of July and Labor Day Weekends, respectively. Place: A remote house and wooded grounds by a lake in Duchess County, two hours north of New York City. The play was presented in three parts.

Eight gay men vacationing, having fun and occasionally experiencing emotional crises. Previously produced off Broadway by Manhattan Theater Club for 72 performances 11/1/94–1/1/95; see its entry in the Plays Produced Off Broadway section of this volume.

Mario Cantone replaced Nathan Lane 4/4/95.

A Best Play; see page 81.

*Smokey Joe's Cafe (102). Musical revue with words and music by Jerry Leiber and Mike Stoller. Produced by Richard Frankel, Thomas Viertel, Steven Baruch, Jujamcyn Theaters/Jack Viertel, Rick Steiner, Frederic H. Mayerson and Center Theater Group/Ahmanson Theater/Gordon Davidson at the Virginia Theater. Opened March 2, 1995.

Ken Ard	Pattie Darcy Jones
Adrian Bailey	DeLee Lively
Brenda Braxton	Frederick B. Owens
Victor Trent Cook	Michael Park
B.J. Crosby	

The Night Managers: Louis St. Louis conductor, piano; David Keyes associate conductor, synthesizer; Frank Canino bass; Brian Brake drums; Drew Zingg guitars; Chris Eminizer saxophones; Frank Pagano percussion.

Standbys: Messrs. Cook, Park—Bobby Daye; Misses Braxton, Lively—April Nixon; Messrs. Ard, Bailey, Owens—Kevyn Morrow; Misses Crosby, Jones—Monica Pege.

Directed by Jerry Zaks; musical staging, Joey McKneely; scenery, Heidi Landesman; costumes, William Ivey Long; lighting, Timothy Hunter; sound, Tony Meola; orchestrations, Steve Margoshes; arrangements, Louis St. Louis; music coordinator, John Miller; original concept, Stephen Helper, Jack Viertel, co-conception with additional musical staging, Otis Sallid; associate producers, Marc Routh, Rhoda Mayerson, Thomas Glaser; casting, Peter Wise & Associates; production stage manager, Kenneth Hanson; stage manager, Maximo Torres; press, Boneau/Bryan-Brown, Jackie Green.

Compendium of Leiber and Stoller songs, including Elvis Presley hits, from the 1950s and 1960s.

MUSICAL NUMBERS, ACT I: "Neighborhood"—Company; "Young Blood"—Adrian Bailey, Ken Ard, Victor Trent Cook; "Falling"—DeLee Lively; "Ruby Baby"—Michael Park, Bailey, Frederick B. Owens, Ard, Cook; "Dance With Me"—Ard, B.J. Crosby, Bailey, Owens, Cook; "Neighborhood" (Reprise)—Crosby, Brenda Braxton, Lively, Pattie Darcy Jones; "Keep on Rollin' "—Cook, Bailey, Ard, Owens; "Searchin' "—Cook, Bailey, Ard, Owens; "Kansas City"—Crosby, Jones, Park; "Trouble"—Lively, Braxton; "Love Me/Don't"—Bailey, Jones; "Fools Fall in Love"—Crosby; "Poison Ivy"—Ard, Bailey, Owens, Cook; "Don Juan"—Braxton; "Shoppin' for Clothes"—Cook, Owens, Bailey, Ard, Park; "I Keep Forgettin' "—Jones; "On Broadway"—Bailey, Owens, Ard, Cook; "D.W. Washburn"—Cook, Company; "Saved"—Crosby, Company.

ACT II: "That Is Rock & Roll"—Company; "Yakety-Yak"—Company; "Charlie Brown"—Company; "Stay a While"—Louis St. Louis, David Keyes; "Pearl's a Singer"—Jones; "Teach Me How to Shimmy"—Park, Lively, Bailey, Cook; "You're the Boss"—Owens, Braxton; "Smokey Joe's Cafe"—Owens, Company; "Loving You"—Ard, Company; "Treat Me Nice"—Cook; "Hound Dog"—Crosby; "Little Egypt"—Owens, Bailey, Ard, Park, Cook; "I'm a Woman"—Crosby, Braxton, Lively, Jones; "There Goes My Baby" and "Love Potion #9"—Bailey, Owens, Ken, Park, Cook; "Some Cats Know"—Crosby; "Jailhouse Rock"—Michael, Company; "Fools Fall in Love"—Crosby; "Spanish Harlem" (by Phil Spector and Jerry Leiber)—Ard, Braxton; "I (Who Have Nothing)"—Cook; "Neighborhood" (Reprise)—Jones; "Stand by Me"—Bailey, Company; "That Is Rock & Roll" (Reprise)—Company.

*Lincoln Center Theater. Schedule of three programs. ***The Heiress** (96). Revival of the play by Ruth and Augustus Goetz; suggested by Henry James's novel *Washington Square*. Opened March 9, 1995. ***Arcadia** (72). By Tom Stoppard. Opened March 30, 1995. And *Chronicle of a Death Foretold* adapted from the Gabriel Garcia Marquez novella by Graciela Daniele and James Lewis, with music by Bob Telson and lyrics and additional material by Michael John LaChiusa, scheduled to open 6/15/95. Produced by Lincoln Center Theater, Andre Bishop and Bernard Gersten directors, *The Heiress* at the Cort Theater, *Arcadia* at the Vivian Beaumont Theater.

THE HEIRESS

Maria	Katie Finneran	Arthur Townsend	Karl Kenzler
Dr. Austin Sloper	Philip Bosco	Marian Almond	Michelle O'Neill
Lavinia Penniman	Frances Sternhagen	Morris Townsend	Jon Tenney
Catherine Sloper	Cherry Jones	Mrs. Montgomery	Lizbeth Mackay
Elizabeth Almond	Patricia Conolly		

Understudies: Misses Finneran, O'Neill—Jenn Thompson; Mr. Bosco—William Cain; Misses Sternhagen, Conolly, Mackay—Amelia White; Miss Jones—Michelle O'Neill; Messrs. Kenzler, Tenney—Richard Thompson.

Directed by Gerald Gutierrez; scenery, John Lee Beatty; costumes, Jane Greenwood; lighting, Beverly Emmons; original music, Robert Waldman; sound, Aural Fixation; casting, Daniel Swee; production stage manager, Michael Brunner; stage manager, Christopher Wigle; press, Merle Debuskey & Associates, Susan Chicoine.

Time: 1850. Place: The front parlor of Dr. Sloper's house in Washington Square: Act I, Scene 1: An October evening. Scene 2: Two weeks later. Scene 3: The next morning. Act II, Scene 1: An April night six months later. Scene 2: Two hours later. Scene 3: A morning three days later. Scene 4: A summer evening almost two years later.

The Heiress was first produced on Broadway 9/29/47 for 410 performances and was named a Best Play of its season. Its major New York revivals have taken place 2/8/50 for 16 performances at New York City Center and 4/20/76 on Broadway for 23 performances in the American Bicentennial Theater program.

Donald Moffat replaced Philip Bosco 4/25/95.

ARCADIA

Thomasina Coverly	Jennifer Dundas	Capt. Brice	David Manis
Septimus Hodge	Billy Crudup	Hannah Jarvis	Blair Brown
Jellaby	Richard Clarke	Chloe Coverly	Haviland Morris
Ezra Chater	Paul Giamatti	Bernard Nightingale	Victor Garber
Richard Noakes	Peter Maloney	Valentine Coverly	Robert Sean Leonard
Lady Croom	Lisa Banes	Gus Coverly; Augustus Coverly	John Griffin

Musicians: Joshua Rosenblum musical director, piano; Lawrence Yurman synthesizer; Wally Kane saxophone.

Understudies: Messrs. Crudup, Leonard—Don Reilly; Messrs. Clarke, Giamatti, Maloney, Manis—Anderson Mathews; Misses Banes, Brown—Gloria Biegler; Messrs. Garber, Manis—Terrence Caza; Mr. Griffin—Josh Bromberg.

Directed by Trevor Nunn; scenery and costumes, Mark Thompson; lighting, Paul Pyant; sound, Charles Bugbee III; original music, Jeremy Sams; casting, Daniel Swee; production stage manager, Alan Hall; stage manager, Ruth E. Rinklin.

Time: April 1809 and the present. Place: A room on the garden front of a very large country house in Derbyshire. The play was presented in two parts.

Elaborate philosophical tapestry interweaving mathematics, art, environmentalism, sex and other similar concerns of two sets of characters in the same upper-class setting but separated in time by almost two centuries. A foreign play previously produced in London.

A Best Play; see page 219.

Note: *Gray's Anatomy*, a one-man show written and performed by Spalding Gray, was presented on Sunday and Monday evenings for 8 performances at the Vivian Beaumont Theater 6/5-6/27/95.

Translations (25). Revival of the play by Brian Friel. Produced by Noel Pearson in association with Joseph Harris at the Plymouth Theater. Opened March 19, 1995. (Closed April 9, 1995)

Manus	Rob Campbell	Hugh	Brian Dennehy
Sarah	Amelia Campbell	Owen	Rufus Sewell
Jimmy Jack	Donal Donnelly	Capt. Lancey	Geoffrey Wade
Maire	Dana Delany	Lt. Yolland	Michael Cumpsty
Doalty	David Herlihy	Soldier	Hugh O'Gorman
Bridget	Miriam Healy-Louie		

Standbys: Misses Campbell, Healy-Louie—Kerry O'Malley; Miss Delany—Mari Nelson; Messrs. Dennehy, Donnelly—Malachy McCourt; Messrs. Campbell, Sewell—Brian Mallon; Messrs. Wade, Herlihy, Cumpsty—Hugh O'Gorman.

Directed by Howard Davies; scenery, Ashley Martin-Davis; costumes, Joan Bergin; lighting, Chris Parry; sound, T. Richard Fitzgerald; special effects, Gregory Meeh; casting, Julie Hughes, Barry Moss; production stage manager, Susie Cordon; stage manager, Allison Sommers; press, Shirley Herz Associates, Sam Rudy.

Time: 1833. Place: A hedge-school in the townland of Baile Beag/Ballybeg, an Irish-speaking community in County Donegal. Act I: An afternoon in late August. Act II, Scene 1: A few days later. Scene 2: The following night. Act III: The evening of the following day. The play was presented in two parts with the intermission following Act II.

The first New York production of *Translations* took place off Broadway at Manhattan Theater Club 4/7/81 for 48 performances, when it was named a Best Play of its season. This is its first major New York revival.

*How to Succeed in Business Without Really Trying (80). Revival of the musical based on the book by Shepherd Mead; book by Abe Burrows, Jack Weinstock and Willie Gilbert; music and lyrics by Frank Loesser. Produced by Dodger Productions, Kardana Productions, the John F. Kennedy Center for the Performing Arts and the Nederlander Organization at the Richard Rodgers Theater. Opened March 23, 1995.

Voice of the Narrator	Walter Cronkite	Miss Krumholtz	Kristi Lynes
J. Pierrepont Finch	Matthew Broderick	Office Boy; Ovington; TV	
Milt Gatch; Toynbee	Tom Flynn	Announcer	Randl Ask
Jenkins	Jay Aubrey Jones	Security Guard	Kevin Bogue
Davis	William Ryall	Henchmen	Jack Hayes, Jerome Vivona
Bert Bratt	Jonathan Freeman	Miss Jones	Lillias White
Tackaberry	Martin Moran	Twimble; Wally Womper	Gerry Vichi
J.B. Biggley	Ronn Carroll	Hedy La Rue	Luba Mason
Rosemary Pilkington	Megan Mullally	Scrubwomen	Rebecca Holt,
Smitty	Victoria Clark		Carla Renata Williams
Bud Frump	Jeff Blumenkrantz	Dance Soloist	Nancy Lemenager

Wickets and Wickettes: Kevin Bogue, Maria Calabrese, Jack Hayes, Nancy Lemenager, Kristi Lynes, Aiko Nakasone, Jerome Vivona, Carla Renata Williams.

Ensemble: Randl Ask, Kevin Bogue, Maria Calabrese, Tom Flynn, Jack Hayes, Rebecca Holt, Jay Aubrey Jones, Nancy Lemenager, Martin Moran, Aiko Nakasone, William Ryall, Jerome Vivona, Carla Renata Williams.

Orchestra: Ted Sperling conductor; Todd Ellison associate conductor; Diane Monroe concertmaster; Michael Roth, Rob Shaw, Nam-Sook Lee violin; Adam Grabois, Susannah Chapman cello; John Babich bass; Chuck Wilson, Mike Migliore, Rick Heckman, Ken Hitchcock, Roger Rosenberg woodwinds; Byron Stripling, Glen Drewes, Larry Lunetta trumpet; Chris Korner, French horn; Keith O'Quinn, Herb Besson trombone; Scott Kuney guitar; Ray Marchicha drums; Bill Hayes percussion; Grace Paradise harp.

Understudies: Mr. Broderick—Randl Ask, Martin Moran; Mr. Vichi—Jay Aubrey Jones; Mr. Freeman—Tom Flynn; Misses Clark, White—Carla Renata Williams; Mr. Blumenkrantz—Randl Ask; Miss Mason—Pamela Gold, Rebecca Holt; Miss Mullally—Kristi Lynes; Mr. Carroll—William Ryall. Swings: Jeffry Denman, Tom Flagg, Pamela Gold.

Directed by Des McAnuff; choreography, Wayne Cilento; musical direction, incidental music arrangements and vocal arrangements, Ted Sperling; scenery, John Arnone; costumes, Susan Hilferty; lighting, Howell Binkley; video design, Batwin + Robin Productions; sound, Steve Canyon Kennedy; orchestrations, Danny Troob; additional orchestrations, David Siegel, Robert Ginzler; dance arrangements, Jeanine Tesori; music coordinator, John Miller; executive producer, Dodger Productions; associate producer, Whistlin' Dixie; casting, Julie Hughes, Barry Moss; production stage manager, Frank Hartenstein; stage manager, Diane DeVita; press, Boneau/Bryan-Brown, Adrian Bryan-Brown, John Barlow, Susanne Tighe.

Time: 1961. Place: The World Wide Wicket Company in New York City.

How to Succeed in Business Without Really Trying was first produced on Broadway 10/14/61 for 1,417 performances, was named a Best Play of its season and received the Critics Award for best musical and the Pulitzer Prize. It was revived on Broadway by New York City Center Light Opera Company 4/20/66 for 23 performances. The present production originated in regional theater at the La Jolla, Calif. Playhouse.

ACT I

Overture ....Orchestra
"How to Succeed" .... Finch
"Happy to Keep His Dinner Warm" .... Rosemary
"Coffee Break" ....Frump, Smitty, Company
"The Company Way" ....Twimble, Finch
"The Company Way" (Reprise) .... Frump, Company
"A Secretary Is Not a Toy" ....Bratt, Company
"Been a Long Day" ....Smitty, Rosemary, Finch
"Been a Long Day" (Reprise) .... Frump, Biggley, Hedy
"Grand Old Ivy" ....Biggley, Finch
"Paris Original" ....Rosemary, Krumholtz, Smitty, Jones, Company
"Rosemary" ....Finch, Rosemary
Finale—Act I .... Finch, Rosemary, Frump

ACT II

Entr'acte...Orchestra
"How to Succeed" (Reprise) .... Smitty, Krumholtz, Women
"Happy to Keep His Dinner Warm" (Reprise) .... Rosemary
"Love From a Heart of Gold" ....Biggley, Hedy
"I Believe in You" ....Finch, Men
"The Pirate Dance" ....Wickets, Wickettes
"I Believe in You" (Reprise) .... Rosemary
"Brotherhood of Man" .... Finch, Womper, Jones, Company
Finale ....Company

*__Defending the Caveman__ (56). Solo performance by Rob Becker; written by Rob Becker. Produced by Contemporary Productions, Inc. at the Helen Hayes Theater. Opened March 26, 1995.

Production stage manager, Jason Lindhorst; press, Frimark & Thibodeau Associates, Erin Dunn.
Exploring some of the differences between men and women, aimed at humor and performed without intermission.

*__Having Our Say__ (63). By Emily Mann; adapted from the book by Sarah L. Delany and A. Elizabeth Delany with Amy Hill Hearth. Produced by Camille O. Cosby and Judith Rutherford James at the Booth Theater. Opened April 6, 1995.

Miss Sadie Delany ....Gloria Foster
Dr. Bessie Delany .... Mary Alice

Standbys: Miss Foster—Frances Foster; Miss Alice—Novella Nelson.
Directed by Emily Mann; scenery, Thomas Lynch; costumes, Judy Dearing; lighting, Allen Lee Hughes; projection design, Wendall K. Harrington, Sage Marie Carter; original music, Baikida Carroll; associate producer, Dreyfuss/James Productions, Inc.; production stage manager, Martin Gold; stage manager, Ed De Shae; press, Boneau/Bryan-Brown, Andy Shearer.
Time: February 1993. Place: The living room, dining room and kitchen of the Delany home in Mount Vernon. N.Y. The play was presented in three parts.
Recollections of two sisters, both over 100 years old, whose father, a onetime slave, became America's first black Episcopal bishop. Previously produced in regional theater at the McCarter Theater, Princeton, N.J., Emily Mann artistic director.

__Gentlemen Prefer Blondes__ (24). Revival of the musical adapted from the novel by Anita Loos; book by Anita Loos and Joseph Fields; music by Jule Styne; lyrics by Leo Robin. Produced by National Actors Theater, Tony Randall founder and artistic director, in association with

HAVING OUR SAY—Mary Alice as Bessie Delany and
Gloria Foster as Sadie Delany in the play by Emily Mann

the Goodspeed Opera House, Michael P. Price executive producer, at the Lyceum Theater.
Opened April 10, 1995. (Closed April 30, 1995)

Dorothy Shaw	Karen Prunzik	Josephus Gage	Jamie Ross
Lorelei Lee	KT Sullivan	Steward; Mr. Esmond Sr.	Dick Decareau
Gus Esmond	Allen Fitzpatrick	Frank; Robert Lemanteur	Craig Waletzko
Lady Phyllis Beekman	Carol Swarbrick	George	Ken Nagy
Sir Francis Beekman	David Ponting	Mime	Joe Bowerman
Mrs. Ella Spofford	Susan Rush	Louie Lemanteur	John Hoshko
Henry Spofford	George Dvorsky		

Tango Couples: Paula Grider, Joe Bowerman, Lisa Hanna, Ken Nagy, Richard Costa, Lorinda Santos. Park Casino Trio: Angela Bond, John Hoshko, Craig Waletzko.

Ensemble: Angela Bond, Joe Bowerman, Richard Costa, Paula Grider, Lisa Hanna, Bryan S. Haynes, John Hoshko, Ken Nagy, Wendy Roberts, Lorinda Santos, Craig Waletzko.

Orchestra: Michael O'Flaherty musical director, keyboard; Andrew Wilder associate musical director, keyboard; Dennis Anderson, John Campo reeds; David Rodgers trumpet; Larry Farrell trombone; Greg Utzig guitar; Brad Flickinger percussion; Bill Meade musical coordinator.

Understudies: Misses Sullivan, Rush, Swarbrick—Angela Bond; Miss Prunzik—Lisa Hanna; Messrs. Fitzpatrick, Decareau—John Hoshko; Messrs. Ross, Ponting—Dick Decareau; Mr. Dvorsky—Craig Waletzko; Mr. Bowerman—Ken Nagy; Swings—Melissa Bell, Marty McDonough.

Directed by Charles Repole; choreography, Michael Lichtefeld; musical direction, Andrew Wilder; scenery and costumes, Eduardo Sicangco; lighting, Kirk Bookman; sound, T. Richard Fitzgerald; orchestrations, Douglas Besterman; musical supervision and vocal arrangements, Michael O'Flaherty; dance music, G. Harrell; executive producer, Manny Kladitis; associate producer, Sue Frost; casting, Warren Pincus; production stage manager, Donna Cooper Hilton; stage manager, Kathy J. Faul; press, Springer Associates, Gary Springer, John Springer.

Time: 1926.

Gentlemen Prefer Blondes was first produced on Broadway 12/8/49 for 740 performances, with Carol Channing as Lorelei Lee. This is its first major New York revival, previously produced in regional theater at Goodspeed Opera House.

ACT I

Overture .... Orchestra
Scene 1: Onstage and backstage at Club Purgatory, New York City
  Opening .... Dorothy, Men
  "It's High Time" .... Lorelei, Dorothy
Scene 2: The French Line Pier in New York, midnight sailing
  "It's High Time" (Reprise) .... Company
  "Bye Bye Baby" .... Gus, Lorelei, Company
Scene 3: Sun deck of the Ile de France, three days out
  "I'm Just a Little Girl From Little Rock" .... Lorelei
  "I'm Atingle, I'm Aglow" .... Gage, Lorelei, Dorothy, Mrs. Spofford
  "I Love What I'm Doing" .... Dorothy, Olympic Men
Scene 4: Lorelei's suite on the Ile de France, later that day
  "Just a Kiss Apart" .... Henry, Dorothy
  "It's Delightful Down in Chile" .... Sir Francis, Lorelei
Scene 5: Paris
  Sunshine Montage .... Mime, Company
Scene 6: Lorelei's suite at the Ritz in Paris, evening
  "I'm Atingle, I'm Aglow" (Reprise) .... Gage, Company
Finale Act I .... Lorelei

ACT II

Entr'acte .... Orchestra
Scene 1: Onstage at the Club Cocteau in Paris, the next evening
  "Mamie Is Mimi" .... Dorothy, Company
Scene 2: Dorothy's dressing room, immediately following
  "Diamonds Are a Girl's Best Friend" .... Lorelei
Scene 3: Streets of Paris, in front of the Cafe Rouge
  "A Ride on a Rainbow" .... Henry, Dorothy, Tango Couples
Scene 4: Lorelei's suite, 3 a.m.
  "Gentlemen Prefer Blondes" .... Lorelei, Gus
  "Homesick" .... Gus, Lorelei, Dorothy, Henry, Mrs. Spofford, Gage
Scene 5: The Central Park Casino, New York, ten days later
  "I Love What I'm Doing" .... Trio
  "You Say You Care" .... Trio
  "Keeping Cool with Coolidge" .... Company
Finale Act II .... Company

Indiscretions (Les Parents Terribles) (40). Revival of the play by Jean Cocteau; translated by Jeremy Sams. Produced by The Shubert Organization, Capital Cities/ABC, Roger Berlind and Scott Rudin in the Royal National Theater production at the Ethel Barrymore Theater. Opened April 27, 1995.

George	Roger Rees	Michael	Jude Law
Leonie (Leo)	Eileen Atkins	Madeleine	Cynthia Nixon
Yvonne	Kathleen Turner		

Standbys: Miss Turner—Leslie Hendrix; Miss Atkins—Sandra Shipley; Mr. Rees—Lewis Arlt; Mr. Law—Jim Stanek; Miss Nixon—Carrie Preston.

Directed by Sean Mathias; scenery and costumes, Stephen Brimson Lewis; lighting, Mark Henderson; sound, Jonathan F. Suffolk; music, Jason Carr; casting, Johnson-Liff Associates; production stage manager, Arthur Gaffin; stage manager, David J. O'Brien; press, Alma Viator, Michael Borowski, William Schelble.

Time: Sometime in the 1940s. Place: Paris. The play was presented in three parts.

Les Parents Terribles opened in Paris 11/14/38 and was produced as a film in 1948. This production was mounted by Royal National Theater 4/21/94. Its New York premiere of record took place at the Mermaid Theater 11/1/62 for 76 performances in the Charles Frank translation as *Intimate Relations*. The play concerns eccentric emotional relationships within a self-devouring family.

On the Waterfront (8). By Budd Schulberg with Stan Silverman. Produced by Mitchell Maxwell, Dan Markley, Victoria Maxwell, Pines/Goldberg, Michael Skipper, Harvey Klaris, David Young, Dina Wein-Reis, James L. Simon, Palmer Video Corporation and Workin' Man Films, in association with Fred H. Krones, Hugh Hayes and Alan J. Schuster at the Brooks Atkinson Theater. Opened May 1, 1995. (Closed May 7, 1995)

Terry Malloy	Ron Eldard	Pop Doyle	Brad Sullivan
Edie Doyle	Penelope Ann Miller	Charley Malloy	Michael Harney
Johnny Friendly	Kevin Conway	Father Vincent	George N. Martin
Father Barry	David Morse		

Company: Barry McEvoy, Jarlath Conroy, Robertson Carricart, Jerry Grayson, Michael Mulheren, Desmond Devenish, Skip Sudduth, Lance Davis, Afemo Omilami, Leon Addison Brown, Richard Pruitt, Alison Sheehy, David Warshofsky, Wayne Grace, Steve Ryan, Charlie Hofheimer, Lynn Eldredge, Kevin Hagan, Peter Linari.

Directed by Adrian Hall; music, David Amram; scenery, Eugene Lee; costumes, Ann Hould-Ward; lighting, Peter Kaczorowski; sound, Dan Moses Schreier; associate producers, Robert Brandes, Lauren Doll, Paula Heil Fisher, Follows Latimer Productions, Keith Hurd, Lesley Mazzotta, Wayne Nathan, Marcus Ticotin, TDI Inc.; casting, Jay Binder; production stage manager, Franklin Keysar; press, Peter Cromarty & Company.

A longshoreman's struggle against the mob, based on the Academy Award-winning motion picture of the same title. The play was presented in two parts.

*****Hamlet** (35). Revival of the play by William Shakespeare. Produced by Dodger Productions, Roger Berlind, Endemol Theater Productions, Inc., Jujamcyn Theaters, Kardana Productions, Inc., and Scott Rudin in the Almeida Theater Company production, Ian McDiarmid and Jonathan Kent artistic directors, at the Belasco Theater. Opened May 2, 1995.

Francisco; Lucianus	Gilly Gilchrist	Polonius	Peter Eyre
Barnardo	Colin Mace	Ophelia	Tara FitzGerald
Horatio	Paterson Joseph	Reynaldo	David Melville
Marcellus; Captain	Terry McGinity	Rosencrantz	James Wallace
Ghost; Player King;		Guildenstern	Nicholas Rowe
Gravedigger	Terence Rigby	Prologue; Gentleman	Peter Helmer
Hamlet	Ralph Fiennes	Player Queen	Caroline Harris
Laertes	Damian Lewis	Fortinbras	Rupert Penry-Jones
Claudius	James Laurenson	Priest	Gordon Langford-Rowe
Gertrude	Francesca Annis	Osric	Nicholas Palliser

Members of the Court: Melissa Chalsma, Denis Holmes, James Langton, Thomas Schall, Spence White.

Understudies: Mr. Gilchrist—Thomas Schall, David Melville; Mr. Mace—Peter Helmer; Mr. Joseph—Colin Mace; Mr. McGinity—Denis Holmes, Thomas Schall; Mr. Rigby—Terry McGinity; Mr. Fiennes—Rupert Penry-Jones; Mr. Lewis—James Wallace; Mr. Laurenson—Gilly Gilchrist; Miss Annis—Caroline Harris; Mr. Eyre—Gordon Langford-Rowe; Miss FitzGerald—Melissa Chalsma; Mr. Melville—Spence White; Mr. Wallace—Peter Helmer; Mr. Rowe—Nicholas Palliser; Mr. Helmer—James Langton, Spence White; Miss Harris—Melissa Chalsma; Mr. Penry-Jones—David Melville; Mr. Langford-Rowe—Denis Holmes; Mr. Palliser—David Melville.

Directed by Jonathan Kent; scenery, Peter J. Davison; costumes, James Acheson; lighting, Mark Henderson; music, Jonathan Dove; sound, John A. Leonard; fight direction, William Hobbs; executive producer, Dodger Productions; associate producers, The Durst Organization, Whistlin' Dixie; casting, Joyce Nettles (U.K.), Jay Binder (U.S.); production stage manager, Anne Keefe; stage manager, Frank Lombardi; press, Boneau/Bryan-Brown, Adrian Bryan-Brown, Bob Fennell.

Place: In and near Elsinore Castle in Denmark. The play was presented in two parts.

The last major New York revival of *Hamlet* was by Roundabout Theater Company on Broadway 4/2/92 for 45 performances. The present production was previously produced in London.

My Thing of Love (15). By Alexandra Gersten. Produced by Barry and Fran Weissler and Jujamcyn Theaters in association with Pace Theatricals at the Martin Beck Theater. Opened May 3, 1995. (Closed May 14, 1995)

Elly	Laurie Metcalf	Kelly	Jane Fleiss
Jack	Tom Irwin	Garn	Mark Blum

Voices: Kate—Erin Rice; Chris—Rebecca L. Rice.

Standby: Messrs. Irwin, Blum—Jim Abele.

Directed by Michael Maggio; scenery, John Lee Beatty; costumes, Erin Quigley; lighting, Howell Binkley; original music, Rob Milburn, Michael Bodeen; sound, Peter Fitzgerald; associate producer, Alecia Parker; casting, Stuart Howard, Amy Schecter; production stage manager, Jane E. Neufeld; press, the Pete Sanders Group, Pete Sanders, Glenna Freedman, Michael Hartman.

Time: Now. Place: A modest house in an American suburb. Act I, Scene 1: Now. Scene 2: One week later. Act II, Scene 1: Same time. Scene 2: That weekend. Scene 3: Several hours later.

A troubled marriage, its causes and results. Previously produced in regional theater at the Steppenwolf Theater, Chicago.

PLAYS PRODUCED
OFF BROADWAY

Some distinctions between off-Broadway and Broadway productions at one end of the scale and off-off-Broadway productions at the other are blurred in the New York Theater of the 1990s. For the purposes of the *Best Plays* listing, the term "off Broadway" is used to distinguish a professional from a showcase (off-off-Broadway) production and signifies a show which opened for general audiences in a mid-Manhattan theater seating 499 or fewer and 1) employed an Equity cast, 2) planned a regular schedule of 8 performances a week in an open-ended run (7 a week for one-person shows) and 3) offered itself to public comment by critics at designated opening performances.

Occasional exceptions of inclusion (never of exclusion) are made to take in visiting troupes, borderline cases and nonqualifying productions which readers might expect to find in this list because they appear under an off-Broadway heading in other major sources of record.

Figures in parentheses following a play's title give number of performances. These figures do not include previews or extra non-profit performances.

Plays marked with an asterisk (*) were still in a projected run on June 1, 1995. Their number of performances is figured from opening night through May 31, 1995.

Certain programs of off-Broadway companies are exceptions to our rule of counting the number of performances from the date of the press coverage. When the official opening takes place late in the run of a play's regularly-priced public or subscription performances (after previews) we sometimes count the first performance of record, not the press date, as opening night—and in each such case in the listing we note the variance and give the press date.

In a listing of a show's numbers—dances, sketches, musical scenes, etc.—the titles of songs are identified wherever possible by their appearance in quotation marks (").

HOLDOVERS FROM PREVIOUS SEASONS

Plays which were running on June 1, 1994 are listed below. More detailed information about them appears in previous *Best Plays* volumes of appropriate date. Important cast changes since opening night are recorded in the Cast Replacements section of this volume.

*The Fantasticks (14,518; longest continuous run of record in the American theater). Musical suggested by the play *Les Romanesques* by Edmond Rostand; book and lyrics by Tom Jones; music by Harvey Schmidt. Opened May 3, 1960.

Nunsense (3,672). Musical with book, music and lyrics by Dan Goggin. Opened December 12, 1985. (Closed October 16, 1994)

*Perfect Crime (3,334). By Warren Manzi. Opened October 16, 1987.

*Tony 'n' Tina's Wedding (2,461). By Artificial Intelligence. Opened February 6, 1988. (Editor's note: This show fits some but not all conditions of our off-Broadway category, in which it hasn't always been listed. We list it now for information purposes, recognizing the unique place it has made for itself on the New York theater scene.)

Forever Plaid (1,811). Musical by Stuart Ross. Opened May 20, 1990. (Closed June 12, 1994)

*Tubes (1,574). Performance piece by and with Blue Man Group. Opened November 17, 1991.

Blown Sideways Through Life (262). Solo performance by Claudia Shear; written by Claudia Shear. Opened September 21, 1993. (Closed December 5, 1993) Reopened January 13, 1994. (Closed July 17, 1994)

Family Secrets (458). Solo performance by Shirley Glaser; written by Shirley Glaser and Greg Howells. Opened October 6, 1993. (Closed January 1, 1995)

Manhattan Theater Club. Four Dogs and a Bone (271). By John Patrick Shanley. Opened October 31, 1993. (Closed June 26, 1994) Kindertransport (50). By Diane Samuels. Opened May 17, 1994. (Closed June 30, 1994)

All in the Timing (526). Program of six one-act plays by David Ives. Opened February 17, 1994. (Closed May 20, 1995)

*Stomp (523). Percussion performance piece created by Luke Cresswell and Steve Mc-Nicholas. Opened February 27, 1994.

Mort Sahl's America (73). Solo performance by Mort Sahl; written by Mort Sahl. Opened April 4, 1994. (Closed June 12, 1994)

*Three Tall Women (478). By Edward Albee. Opened April 5, 1994.

Moe's Lucky Seven (33). By Marlane Meyer. Opened May 15, 1994. (Closed June 12, 1994)

Hysterical Blindness (197). Musical with book by Leslie Jordan; music and lyrics by Joe Patrick Ward. Opened May 19, 1994. (Closed November 6, 1994)

SubUrbia (113). By Eric Bogosian. Opened May 22, 1994. (Closed September 28, 1994)

PLAYS PRODUCED JUNE 1, 1994–MAY 31, 1995

New York Shakespeare Festival Shakespeare Marathon. Schedule of revivals of plays by William Shakespeare. The Merry Wives of Windsor (28). Opened June 23, 1994; see note. (Closed July 24, 1994) The Two Gentlemen of Verona (22). Opened August 9, 1994; see note. (Closed September 4, 1994) The Merchant of Venice (48). Opened January 17, 1995; see note. (Closed February 26, 1995) Produced by New York Shakespeare Festival, George C. Wolfe producer, Jason Steven Cohen managing director (through 1994), Rosemarie Tichler and Kevin Kline associate producers, *The Merry Wives of Windsor* and *The Two Gentlemen of Verona* with the cooperation of the City of New York, Rudolph W. Giuliani Mayor, Peter F. Vallone Speaker of the City Council, Schuyler Chapin Commissioner of Cultural Affairs, Henry Stern Commissioner of Parks and Recreation, at the Delacorte Theater in Central Park; *The Merchant of Venice* at the Joseph Papp Public Theater's Anspacher Theater.

THE MERRY WIVES OF WINDSOR

Justice Shallow	George Hall	Mistress Quickly	Andrea Martin
Abraham Slender	Walker Jones	John Rugby	Kevin Orton
Parson Hugh Evans	Reggie Montgomery	Doctor Caius	Rocco Sisto
Master George Page	Miguel Perez	Fenton	Alec Phoenix
Sir John Falstaff	Brian Murray	Mistress Page	Margaret Whitton
Bardolph	Chris O'Neill	Mistress Ford	Tonya Pinkins
Pistol	Bray Poor	Master Frank Ford	David Alan Grier
Nym	Enrico Colantoni	Robin	Pedro James Vasquez
Simple	Kevin Dewey	John	John Ellison Conlee
Anne Page	Millie Chow	Robert	C.J. Wilson
Host of the Garter	Steve Ryan		

Ensemble: Candace Marie Bennett, Jennifer Carroll, Brian Coats, Shelton Dane, Jesse Ontiveros, Nick Sullivan, Collette Wilson.

The Premiere Brass: Anthony Giminez cornet; Jamie Hersch, French horn; Stephen R. Rawlings trombone; Michael S. Milnarik tuba.

Recorded Music: Martha Caplin violin; David Oei piano; Sam Pilafian tuba; Stanley Silverman guitar, banjo; Dr. John piano.

Understudies: Misses Whitton, Martin—Jennifer Carroll; Messrs. Jones, Montgomery, O'Neill—Brian Coats; Mr. Murray—John Conlee; Messrs. Dewey, Orton, Vasquez, Wilson, Conlee—Jesse Ontiveros; Messrs. Sisto, Poor, Colantoni—Kevin Orton; Messrs. Hall, Ryan—Nick Sullivan; Mr. Phoenix—Pedro James Vasquez; Messrs. Perez, Grier—C.J. Wilson; Misses Pinkins, Chow—Collette Wilson.

Directed by Daniel Sullivan; original music, Stanley Silverman; scenery, John Lee Beatty; costumes, Ann Hould-Ward; lighting, Allen Lee Hughes; sound, Tom Morse; animal trainer, William Berloni; violence choreographer, Jamie Cheatham; casting, Jordan Thaler; production stage manager, Jess Lynn; stage manager, Allison Sommers; press, Carol Fineman, Eugenie Hero, Terence Womble.

This version of Shakespeare's comedy has been transposed in time and place to the California Gold Rush. It was presented in two parts. The last major New York revival of *The Merry Wives of Windsor* was by New York Shakespeare Festival 7/25/74 for 24 performances.

THE TWO GENTLEMEN OF VERONA

In Verona:

		In Milan:	
Valentine	Joel De La Fuente	Duke of Milan	Jack Ryland
Proteus	Malcolm Gets	Silvia	Lisa Gay Hamilton
Speed	Robert Dorfman	Thurio	Steven Skybell
Launce	Peter J. Gerety	Host	Jerry Mayer
Crab	Bugsy	Sir Eglamour	Herb Foster
Julia	Nance Williamson	In a Forest Near Mantua:	
Lucetta	Camryn Manheim	1st Outlaw	Brett Rickaby
Antonio	Jerry Mayer	2d Outlaw	Marc Damon Johnson
Panthino	Thomas Ikeda	3d Outlaw	Daniel Mastrogiorgio

Ensemble: Brian Coats, John Ellison Conlee, Tracey Copeland, Christopher Duva, Jeff Stafford, Kristi Wedemeyer.

Musicians: William Schimmel accordion, Melodica, concertina; Gergory Uhtzig guitar, mandolin.

Understudies: Messrs. Foster, Rickaby, Johnson, Mastrogiorgio—Brian Coats; Messrs. Mayer, Skybell, Ryland—John Ellison Conlee; Misses Hamilton, Manheim—Tracey Copeland; Mr. Dorfman—

Christopher Duva; Mr. Ikeda—Marc Damon Johnson; Mr. Gerety—Daniel Mastrogiorgio; Mr. Gets—Brett Rickaby; Messrs. De La Fuente, Mayer (Host)—Jeff Stafford; Miss Williamson—Kristi Wedemeyer.

Directed by Adrian Hall; music, Richard Cumming; scenery, Eugene Lee; costumes, Catherine Zuber; lighting, Ken Billington; sound, Tom Morse; animal trainer, William Berloni; casting, Jordan Thaler; production stage manager, Lisa Buxbaum; stage manager, Buzz Cohen.

The last major New York revival of *The Two Gentlemen of Verona* was by New York Shakespeare Festival 7/24/87 for 21 performances. The play was presented in two parts.

THE MERCHANT OF VENICE

Antonio	Byron Jennings	Shylock	Ron Leibman
Bassanio	Jay Goede	Jessica	Nina Landey
Salerio	Paul Mullins	Tubal; Duke of Venice	Earle Hyman
Solanio	Billy Porter	Old Gobbo; Arragon; Stephano	Walker Jones
Gratiano	Peter Jay Fernandez	Morocco; Jailer	Robert Jason Jackson
Lorenzo	Willis Sparks	Lancelot	Tom Nelis
Portia	Laila Robins	Leonardo; Jailer	Cornell Womack
Nerissa	Gail Grate	Balthazar; Jailer	Peter Rini

Directed by Barry Edelstein; scenery, John Arnone; costumes, Catherine Zuber; lighting, Mimi Jordan Sherin; sound, Darren Clark; original music, Michael Torke; casting, Jordan Thaler, Heidi Griffiths; production stage manager, William H. Lang.

The last major New York revival of *The Merchant of Venice* was by the Peter Hall Company from England on Broadway 12/19/89 for 81 performances. the play was presented in two parts.

Note: Press date for *The Merry Wives of Windsor* was 6/30/94, for *The Two Gentlemen of Verona* was 8/18/94, for *The Merchant of Venice* was 2/5/95.

Note: New York Shakespeare Festival's Shakespeare Marathon is scheduled to continue through following seasons until all of Shakespeare's plays have been presented. *A Midsummer Night's Dream, Julius Caesar* and *Romeo and Juliet* were produced in the 1987–88 season; *Much Ado About Nothing, King John, Coriolanus, Love's Labour's Lost, the Winter's Tale* and *Cymbeline* were produced in the 1988–89 season; *Twelfth Night, Titus Andronicus, Macbeth* and *Hamlet* were produced in the 1989–90 season; *The Taming of the Shrew, Richard III* and *Henry IV, Part 1* and *Part 2* were produced in the 1990–91 season; *Othello* and *Pericles, Prince of Tyre* were produced in the 1991–92 season; *As You Like It* and *The Comedy of Errors* were produced in the 1992–93 season and *Measure for Measure, All's Well That Ends Well* and *Richard II* were produced in the 1993–94 season (see their entries in *Best Plays* volumes of appropriate years).

Faith Journey (193). Musical with book by Clarence Cuthbertson; music by George Broderick; lyrics by George Broderick and Clarence Cuthbertson. Produced by Elohim Unlimited in association with Jesse L. DeVore Jr. at the Lamb's Theater. Opened July 21, 1994. (Closed January 5, 1995)

Paul	Craig Anthony Grant	Sister Bell	Clarencia Shade
Lucille	Loreal Steiner	Brother	Robert L. Evans
Amos	Claude Jay	Traci	Claudette Evans
Ruby	Janet Weeden	Policeman; Jason	Jeff Benish
JP	Henry C. Rawls		

George Broderick acoustic piano; Ron Granger synthesizer.

Directed by Chuck Patterson; musical direction, George Broderick; choreography, Barry Carrington; costumes, Nancy Brous; visuals, Leon Oliver, Nelsena Burt Spano; visual producer, Elizabeth Bello; technical director, Marvin Devonish; creative manager, Ron McIntyre; stage manager, Kimberly K. Harding; press, David Rothenberg.

Evangelical influences on social progress in the era of Martin Luther King.

ACT I

Second Street Baptist Church, 1955
    Musical Prelude .... Company
    "Somebody's Knocking" .... Amos, Company
Church office, a few days later
    "I Made a Vow" .... Paul
    "Justice Is Knocking" .... Amos, JP, Brother
Church, a few hours later
    "Over My Head" .... Sis, Bell, JP, Ruby
    "The Best of Both Worlds" .... Ruby
    "Should I Wait" .... Lucille
    "Decide" .... Paul, Lucille, Brother, JP
    "Don't Take Your Love" .... Paul
    "One Day" .... Paul, Amos
    "We Got a Movement" .... Paul, Company
Church office, a few days later
    "By Any Means Necessary" .... Traci
    "We Got a Movement" (Reprise) .... Brother, Company
Church, later that day
    "To Be Loved for Who I Am" .... Lucille
Church, months later
    "Help Me Find a Way" .... Paul, Traci
    "I Wanna Be Ready" .... Paul, Company
City street, later that day
    "I Got to Go"/"I Just Wanna Be Loved" .... Lucille, Traci
Riot, 1961
    "Ain't Gonna Let Nobody Turn Me 'Round" .... Company

ACT II

Second Street Baptist Church
    "Woke Up This Morning" .... Amos, Jason, Company
Church office, June 1962
    "There's a War in Mississippi" .... Amos, Jason, Company
    "We Shall Overcome" .... Company
Washington, D.C., 1963
    "My Country Tis of Thee" .... Sister Bell
    "One Day" (Reprise) .... Ruby, Company
    "Freedom"/"Walk Together" .... Company
Traci and Lucille's home
    "I Find a Friend in You" .... Traci, Lucille
Paul's office, January 1964
    "I Miss You" .... Traci, Paul
    "By Any Means Necessary" (Reprise) .... JP, Company
    "Ain't Gonna Let Nobody Turn Me 'Round" (Reprise) .... Company

That's Life! (292). Musical revue conceived by Helen Butleroff; music by Rick Cummins, Dick Gallagher, Ben Schaechter and Carolyn Sloan; lyrics by Susan DiLallo, Dan Kael, Stacey Luftig, June Siegel, Glenn Slater, Carolyn Sloan, Cheryl Stern and Greer Woodward. Produced by Leahy Productions in association with Peter Breger in the Jewish Repertory Theater production, Ran Avni artistic director, Edward M. Cohen managing director, at Playhouse 91. Opened August 1, 1994. (Closed April 30, 1995)

      Robert Michael Baker   Cheryl Stern
          David Beach   Steve Sterner
         Lisa Rochelle

The Band: Christopher McGovern piano; Sande Campbell keyboards; Kerry Meads drums, percussion.

Directed and choreographed by Helen Butleroff; musical direction, Christopher McGovern; scenery, Fred Kolo; costumes, Gail Cooper-Hecht; lighting, Betsy Finston; sound, Robert Campbell; arrangements and orchestrations, Sande Campbell, Christopher McGovern; casting, Irene Stockton; production stage manager, D.C. Rosenberg; press, Shirley Herz Associates, Wayne Wolfe; press, Pete Sanders, Glenna Freedman following move to Theater East 9/13/94.

Vignettes of Jewish life in America, originally produced off off Broadway 6/4/94 by Jewish Repertory Theater.

MUSICAL NUMBERS, ACT I: "More Than 5700 Years" (music by Ben Schaechter, lyrics by Dan Kael)—Company; "It's Hard To Be a Patriarch Today" (music by Carolyn Sloan, lyrics by Glenn Slater)—Robert Michael Baker, Steve Sterner; "Endangered Species" (music by Dick Gallagher, lyrics by June Siegel)—Cheryl Stern, David Beach, Baker, Sterner; "It's Beyond Me" (music by Schaechter, lyrics by Kael)—Lisa Rochelle; "Tap My Potential" (music by Schaechter, lyrics by Susan DiLallo)—Beach, Baker, Rochelle, Sterner; Power Babies (monologue by Cheryl Stern)—Baker; "Rhinoplasty" (music by Gallagher, lyrics by Stern)—Stern; "In a Schoolyard in Brooklyn" (music by Schaechter, lyrics by Greer Woodward)—Baker; "My Calling" (music by Sloan, lyrics by Stacey Luftig)—Stern; "A Share of Paradise" (music by Rick Cummins, lyrics by Woodward)—Sterner; "Mama, I Want to Sit Downstairs" (music by Sloan, lyrics by Luftig)—Rochelle; "Gorgeous Kay" (music by Cummins, lyrics by Woodward), time and place: Christmas Eve, Akron, Ohio, 1966 and the present—David Beach, Company.

ACT II: "We All Could Be Jewish If We Tried a Little Harder" (music by Cummins, lyrics by Siegel)—Company; "Observant in My Way" (music by Cummins, lyrics by Kael)—Beach; "I Can Pass" (music by Sloan, lyrics by Sloan and Stern)—Stern, Beach, Baker, Rochelle; "The Geshrunken Meshuggena Rag" (music by Cummins, lyrics by Siegel)—Beach, Baker, Stern, Sterner; Jews in Groups (monologue by Luftig)—Rochelle; "Bei Mir Bist Du Rap" (music by Gallagher, lyrics by Stern)—Baker, Stern; "Fathers and Sons" (music by Sloan, dialogue and lyrics by Stern)—Baker, Rochelle, Sterner; "More Than 5700 Years" (Reprise)—Company.

*Jelly Roll! (319). Solo performance by Vernel Bagneris; book by Vernel Bagneris; music and lyrics by Jelly Roll Morton. Produced by Michael and Barbara Ross with Susan Melman at the 47th Street Theater. Opened August 9, 1994.

Accompanist: Morten Gunnar Larsen.

Choreography, Pepsi Bethel; production supervisor, Dean Irby; scenery, Mike Fish; lighting, John McKernon; sound, One Dream Sound, Darren Clark; associate producer, David Melman; production stage manager, Michael Chudinski; press, Shirley Herz Associates, Wayne Wolfe, Miller Wright.

Vernel Bagneris as Jelly Roll Morton in a musical revue about his life, subtitled the Music and the Man. The play was presented without intermission.

MUSICAL NUMBERS: "Mamie Desdoume's Blues" (Desdoume), "Pep," "Le Miserere" from *Il Trovatore* (Verdi), "Le Miserere" (jazz version), "Mr. Jelly Lord," "Aaron Harris," "Jelly Roll Blues," "Wolverines," "The Crave," "Winin' Boy," "If You Knew How I Love You" (Werac-Morton), "Don't You Leave Me Here"/"Alabama Bound," "Fingerbreaker," "Animule Ball," "Buddy Bolden's Blues," "Milneburg Joys" (Mares-Morton), "Ballin' the Jack" (Smith), "Tiger Rag" (LaRocca), Medley: "Someday Sweetheart" (Spikes-Morton), "My Home Is in a Southern Town," "Nearer My God to Thee," "Didn't He Ramble" (traditional), "Sweet Substitute," "Jelly Roll Blues" (Reprise).

Two Hearts Over Easy (39). Musical by Robert W. Cabell. Produced by Michael and Barbara Ross in association with Evette Stark and Marvin Gardens at Actor's Playhouse. Opened August 24, 1994. (Closed September 25, 1994)

CAST: Melanie Dimitri, Bill Ebbesmeyer, Randy Weiss, Maggie Wirth.

Directed by Robert W. Cabell; musical direction, Seth Osburn; choreography, Marvin Gardens; scenery, Tristan Wilson; costumes, Maggie Anderson; lighting, Bob Kneeland; press, Maya Associates, Penny M. Landau.

Loves and fantasies of a gay man and a divorced woman who meet every Sunday for brunch.

Ram in the Thicket (24). Musical with book by Bill Johnson and Michael Criss; music by Steve Rue; lyrics by Steve Rue and Michael Criss. Produced by Mid-America Artist Showcase, Inc. (MAASh) at the Judith Anderson Theater. Opened August 31, 1994. (Closed September 18, 1994)

God .... Robert C. Barnes	Female Pharisee .... Jerri L. White
Abraham .... Steve Frazier	David; Shadrach .... Chad Frisque
Woman .... Charleen Ayers	Sarah .... Julieanne Stapleton
Male Pharisee; Meshach .... Dennis Yadon	Isaac .... Stuart Gray

Dancers: Jamie Waggoner, Nicole-Capri Wallace, Anemoné White.
Musicians: Steve Rue piano; Laura Bergquist keyboard; Kevin Brightup percussion.
Directed by L. Keith White; musical direction, Steve Rue; choreography, Jamie Waggoner; costumes, Jerri L. White; production coordinator, Jennie Mitchell.
Time: Now. Place: The Bible.
Series of musical vignettes based on stories from the Bible and ancient Jewish history, juxtaposing Old and New Testament stories with contemporary issues like AIDS and abortion.

ACT I

Scene 1: Ritual
"Blood Religion"—Chad Frisque, Company; "Solitary Star"—Steve Frazier; "The Promise"—Robert C. Barnes
Scene 2: The Boat
"The Shadrach and Meshach Show"—Frazier, Dennis Yadon, Frisque, Dancers
Scene 3: In a whale
"The Jonah Cliche"—Barnes, Frazier
Scene 4: In Ninevah
"Let's Do the Confessional"—Frazier
Scene 5: In Sodom
"Trying to Get Back on My Feet Again"—Charleen Ayers; Reprise—Barnes, Ayers, Frazier
Scene 6: Old time revival
"Smelly Demon Swine"—Yadon, Jerri L. White, Company; "Who Is This Man?"—Ayers, Barnes
Scene 7: Ritual
"A Mother With Sons"—Company; "You Call This a Promise?"—Ayers, Barnes

ACT II

Scene 1: A TV show
"Together So Long"—Julieanne Stapleton, Frazier; "It's All in the Family"—Barnes, Company
Scene 2: The prodigal son
"Out on My Own"—Stuart Gray, Frazier; Sin Ballet—Gray, Jamie Waggoner, Anemoné White, Frisque; "Just as I Am"—Gray.
Scene 3: King David
"King David"—Company; "Lullaby"—Barnes; "Life of an Innocent Child"—Frisque; "The Promise Broken"—Yadon, White, Barnes, Ayers, Stapleton, Frisque, Frazier
Scene 4: Ritual/Crucifixion
"Trying to Get Back on My Feet Again" (Reprise)—Ayers, Barnes; "Blood Religion (reprise)—Frisque, Company; Finale—Company

Woyzeck on the Highveld (5). Puppet theater presentation based on the play by Georg Buchner. Produced by the Jim Henson Foundation in the Handspring Puppet Company of South Africa production at the Joseph Papp Public Theater (Estelle R. Newman Theater). Opened September 6, 1994. (Closed September 10, 1994)

Woyzeck .... Louis Seboko	Captain .... Basil Jones
Maria .... Busi Zokufa	Doctor .... Adrian Kohler
Miner; Margaret; Andries;	
Barker .... Tale Motsepe	

Directed by William Kentridge; design, Adrian Kohler, William Kentridge; animation, William Kentridge; assistant animator, Erica Elk; music production, Steve Cooks, Edward Jordan; sound, Wilbert Schoubel; lighting, Mannie Manim; costumes, Hazel Maree; press, Anne Dennin, Robert Boyd, Carol Fineman.

The action of the Buchner play is transposed from 19th century Europe to modern South Africa, in the drama of a black worker driven by racism to madness and murder. The last major New York revival of *Woyzeck* was by New York Shakespeare Festival 12/6/92 for 33 performances.

Note: This Handspring Puppet Company production was presented as part of the second international Festival of Puppet Theater which included performances by 16 puppet companies from around the world at the Joseph Papp Public Theater and at P.S. 122, 9/6/94–9/18/94.

Laughing Matters (34). Solo performance by Nick Ullett; written by Nick Ullett. Produced by Primary Stages, Casey Childs artistic director, in association with Arthur Cantor at Primary Stages. Opened September 8, 1994. (Closed October 2, 1994)

Directed by Rick Podell; scenery and lighting, Bruce Goodrich; associate producer, Seth Gordon; production stage manager, Liz Dreyer; press, Arthur Cantor.

Comedy presentation of the author's life as a child in England and as a performer in the United States.

First Night (48). By Jack Neary. Produced by Scottie Held and Ann Baker at the Westside Theater Upstairs. Opened September 11, 1994. (Closed October 29, 1994)

Danny ....Daniel McDonald
Meredith .... Lannyl Stephens

Understudies: Mr. McDonald—Jack Koenig; Miss Stephens—Patricia Dunnock.

Directed by Tony Giordano; scenery and lighting, Neil Peter Jampolis; costumes, David Murin; sound, Raymond D. Schilke; associate producers, Helene Wilson, Kirsten Wilson, Sara Wilson; casting, Judy Henderson, Alycia Aumuller; production stage manager, Tom Aberger; press, Cromarty & Company, Peter Cromarty, Michael Hartman.

Time: New Year's Eve. Place: A town outside of Boston. The play was presented without intermission.

Romantic comedy, two onetime parochial school classmates meet 17 years later and fall in love.

Brooklyn Academy of Music. Schedule of seven programs. **As You Like It** (14). Revival of the play by William Shakespeare in the Cheek by Jowl Company production, Declan Donnellan and Nick Ormerod artistic directors. Opened October 4, 1994. (Closed October 9, 1994 after 7 performances) Reopened December 6, 1994. (Closed December 10, 1994 after 7 performances) **The Man Who** (26). Performance piece inspired by *The Man Who Mistook His Wife for a Hat* by Oliver Sacks; written by Oliver Sacks with the collaboration of Marie-Hélène Estienne and the performers; adapted into English by Peter Brook; co-produced by Centre International de Créations Theatrales, Micheline Rozan and Peter Brook directors, with Roy A. Somlyo and William Wilkinson. Opened March 13, 1995. (Closed April 9, 1995) **The Mountain Giants** (I Giganti Della Montagna) (5). Revival of the play by Luigi Pirandello; the Piccolo Teatro di Milano-Teatro D'Europa production performed in the Italian language with simultaneous English translation by Marta Abba. Opened April 26, 1995. (Closed April 30, 1995)

Also repertory of two programs by the Cameri Theater of Tel Aviv, Noam Semel director general, Omry Nitzan artistic director, presented in the Hebrew language with simultaneous English translation by Miriam Shlesinger: **Gorodish** (3) by Hillel Mittelpunkt, opened May 17, 1995; and **Fleischer** (3) by Igal Even-Or, opened May 23, 1995. (Repertory closed May 25, 1995) Repertory of two revivals by the Royal Dramatic Theater of Sweden, Lars Lofgren artistic director, presented in the Swedish language with simultaneous English translation by Jennifer Forsberg and Tamara Carlin: **The Winter's Tale** (4). By William Shakespeare; Swedish translation by Britt G. Hallquist and Claes Schaar. Opened May 31, 1995. (Closed June 3, 1995). And *Madame de Sade* by Yukio Mishima scheduled to open 6/7/95. Produced by Brooklyn Academy of Music, Harvey Lichtenstein president and executive producer (*As You*

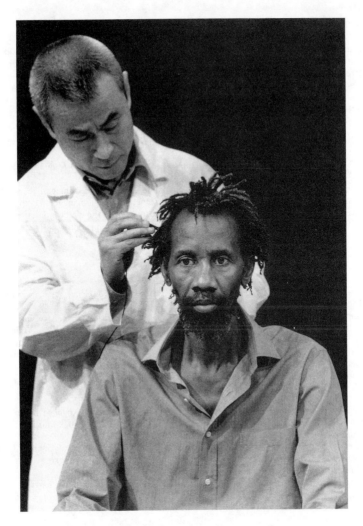

THE MAN WHO—Yoshi Oida and Sotigui Kouyate (*in front*)
in the play adapted and directed by Peter Brook at BAM

Like It and *The Man Who* at the Majestic Theater; *The Mountain Giants, Gorodish, Fleischer*
and *The Winter's Tale* at Brooklyn Academy of Music).

AS YOU LIKE IT

Orlando de Boys	Scott Handy	Rosalind	Adrian Lester
Oliver de Boys	Jonathan Chesterman	Touchstone	Peter Needham
Jacques de Boys; Le Beau	Sean Francis	Charles; Corin	Paul Kissaun
Adam; Audrey	Richard Cant	Jaques	Michael Gardiner
Dennis; Sir Oliver Martext	Steve Watts	Amiens; William	Rhashan Stone
Duke Frederick; Banished Duke	David Hobbs	Silvius	Gavin Abbott
Celia	Simon Coates	Phebe	Wayne Carter

Directed by Declan Donnellan; design, Nick Ormerod; music and musical direction, Paddy Cunneen; movement direction, Sue Lefton; lighting, Judith Greenwood; fight direction, John Waller; stage manager, Marcus Bray; press, Heidi Feldman.

Shakespeare's comedy imaginatively presented by a British company with an all-male cast, in two parts. The last major New York revival of *As You Like It* was the Public Theater's Shakespeare Marathon production 8/6/92 for 18 performances.

THE MAN WHO

CAST: David Bennent, Sotigui Kouyate, Bruce Myers, Yoshi Oida, Mahmoud Tabrizi-Zadeh (music).

Directed by Peter Brook; literary advisor, Jean Claude Carrière; video images, Jean-Claude Lubtchansky; technical director, Jean-Guy Lecat; lighting designer and stage manager, Philippe Vialatte.

Dramatic study of neurologists and their patients, in a style which the director describes as "a search for a new theatrical form," presented without intermission. A foreign play previously presented in Paris and London.

THE MOUNTAIN GIANTS

The Countess's Company:		Cotrone (The Magician)	Franco Graziosi
Ilse (The Countess)	Andrea Jonasson	The Unlucky:	
The Count	Giancarlo Dettori	Duccio Doccia	Gianfranco Mauri
Diamante	Anna Saia	La Sgricia	Giulia Lazzarini
Cromo	Ettore Conti	Quaqueo	Fabrizio Caleffi
Spizzi	Leonardo De Colle	Milordino	Maximilian Mazzotta
Battaglia	Enzo Tarascio	Mara-Mara	Giovanna Rotellini
Sacerdote	Francesco Cordella	Maddalena	Giorgia Senesi
Lumachi	Sante Calogero		

Human Puppets: Paola Benocci, Michele Bottini, Barbara Calbiani, Angelica Dettori, Francesco Montemurro, Paola Roscioli, Luca Scaglia, Giorgia Senesi, Maria Grazia Solano, Marina Sorrenti, Maria Egle Spotorno, Matteo Verona.

Directed by Giorgio Strehler; scenery, Ezio Frigerio; costumes based on designs by Ezio Frigerio and Enrico Job, revised by Luisa Spinatelli; simultaneous English translation read by Terry D'Alfonso; music, Fiorenzo Carpi; mime, Marise Flach; stage manager, Luciano Ferroni.

Time and place: Between fantasy and reality. The play was presented in two parts.

Imaginative and philosophical presentation of actors' lives, Pirandello's last play unfinished at his death in 1936, never before produced in New York under this title.

GORODISH

Gorodish	Igal Naor	Leon Cohen	Sassi Sa'ad
Epstein	Avi Kushnir, Icho Avital	Pachima	Rami Amit
Moshe Dayan	Yonathan Cherchi	Friedman	Dov Navon
Adam Baruch	Gal Zaid	Bardugo; Druze	Nir Erez
Dalia	Noa Arad-Brenner	Gilboa; Gen. Gudrian	Ami Traub
Nitza; Nurse	Debby Jovani	Um Nagi	Tchia Danon
Military Rabbi; Ulrich	Zare Vartanian	Golda	Elisheva Michaeli
Carmeli	Evyatar Lazar	Officer	Amnon Doyev

Soldiers & Officers: Elisha Nurieli, Ifat Garti, Boaz Zafrir, Yoram Ishmael, Eyal Sela, Eli Danker, Idan Antebi.

Directed by Hillel Mittelpunkt; music, Ori Vidislavski; scenery, Eitan Levy; costumes, Michal Laor; lighting, Benzion Munitz; narration, Reuma Eldar; simultaneous translators, Miriam Shlesinger, Johnny Phillips, Anthony Berris.

Gorodish, hero of the six-day war in 1967, becomes the scapegoat of the Yom Kippur War in 1973. A foreign play presented in two parts.

FLEISCHER

Arye Fleischer	Joseph Carmon	Hava	Naama Shapira
Berta Fleischer	Zaharirah Charifai	Shloymele	Eitan Naveh
Rosa	Miriam Gavrielli	Reeva	Aya Shva
Gershon	Albert Cohen	Rabbi Fuchs	Yossi Yadin
Hoond	Yossi Kantz		

Directed by Amit Gazit; music, Rafi Kadishson; scenery, Eli Sinai; costumes, Tzili Charney; lighting, Hanni Vardi; simultaneous translators, Miriam Shlesinger, Johnny Phillips, Anthony Berris; stage manager, Yossi Shiri.

Secular Israeli neighborhood inexorably changes into an ultra orthodox environment, with tragic results for an elderly family striving to maintain their lives there. A foreign play presented in two parts.

THE WINTER'S TALE

Songe	Irene Lindh	Paulina	Bibi Andersson
Carl Jonas Love Almquist;		Emilia; Dorcas	Monica Nielsen
Dion	Pierre Wilkner	Amalia; Mopsa	Anna von Rosen Sundelius
Leontes	Borje Ahlstedt	Archidamus; Warden	Oscar Ljung
Hermione	Pernilla August	Old Shepard	Tord Peterson
Mamillius	Anna Bjork	Clown	Per Mattson
Perdita	Kristina Tornquist	Judge	John Zacharias
Polyxenes	Krister Henriksson	Autolycus	Reine Brynolfsson
Florizel	Jakob Eklund	Gerontes; Judge; Lady at the Ball;	
Camillo	Gosta Pruzelius	Abbess	Gerd Hagman
Antigonus; Old Courtier	Ingvar Kjellson	Mariner	Jan Nyman
Cleomenes	Jan Blomberg	Time, as Chorus	Kristina Adolphson

Other Lords and Gentlemen, Ladies, Officers, Servants, Shepherds and Shepherdesses: Therese Andersson, Asa Edenroth, Johanna Johansson, Helen Hellquist, Sara Larsson, Susanne Renck, Virpi Pahkinen, Adriana Savin, Robin Alexander, Marten Andersson, Peter Engelfeldt, Michael Jason Uggeldahl, Jonas Malmsjo, Benny Saldemar, Urban Wedin, Max Winerdal, Danilo Bejarano, Ulph Bergman, Daniel Carter, Iwo Najdenowicz, Martin Nordstrom, Kristian Stahlgren.

Children: Wictor Waldenbrant, Alexandra Wennerlund.

Directed by Ingmar Bergman; scenery and costumes, Lennart Mork; lighting, Hans Akesson; choreography, Donya Feuer; songs and music, Carl Jonas Love Almquist; Almquist songs translated by Paul Britten Austin; musical direction, Jean Billgreb; producer, Sofi Lerstrom; pianist, Maria Wieslander; simultaneous translators, Harry G. Carlson, Paul Luskin, Tana Ross; stage manager, Tomas Wennerberg.

Time: The beginning of the 19th century. Place: The celebration of a young lady's birthday in a Swedish manor house where the guests are playing Shakespeare's *The Winter's Tale* as part of the celebration. Act I: Sicily. Act II: Sixteen years later in Bohemia and Sicily.

The last major New York revival of *The Winter's Tale* was by BAM 4/19/94 for 8 performances in the Royal Shakespeare production.

1994 Young Playwrights Festival (27). Program of three one-act plays: *The Basement at the Bottom at the End of the World* by Nadine Graham, *The Most Massive Woman Wins* by Madeleine George and *The Love of Bullets* by Jerome D. Hairston. Produced by Young Playwrights, Inc., Sheri M. Goldhirsch artistic director, Brett W. Reynolds managing director, at the Joseph Papp Public Theater. Opened October 4, 1994. (Closed October 29, 1994)

The Basement at the Bottom
at the End of the World

Daneen	Amber Kain
Paul	Mark Rosenthal

Directed by Gloria Muzio; dramaturge, Mick Casale; stage manager, Rick Steiger.

Black woman and white man, in a ruined world, try to close the distance between them.

The Most Massive Woman Wins

Sabine	Candace Taylor
Carly	Amy Ryder
Rennie	Elaina Davis

Cel. ....Suzanne Costallos
  Directed by Phyllis S.K. Look; dramaturge, Sarah Higgins; stage manager, Elise-Ann Konstantin.
  Four women share stories of their difficulties in growing up.

The Love of Bullets
Sydney ....Sandra Daley

Darius .... Harold Perrineau
Mattie ....Curtis McClarin
Evan .... Candace Taylor
Dick Banks ....Victor Mack
  Directed by Brett W. Reynolds; dramaturge, Morgan Jenness; stage manager, Elise-Ann Konstantin.
  Drug melodrama, pusher's girl friend is trying to kick the habit.

ALL PLAYS: Scenery, Alan Moyer; costumes, Karen Perry; lighting, Pat Dignan; sound, Raymond D. Schilke; casting, Alan Filderman, Michele Ortlip; production stage managers, Elise-Ann Konstantin, Rick Steiger.

Three plays by authors 18 years old or less at the time of submission in the 13th annual playwriting contest for young people run by Young Playwrights, Inc. The program was presented in three parts.

Playwrights Horizons. Schedule of four programs. **A Cheever Evening** (103). By A.R. Gurney; based on stories of John Cheever. Opened October 6, 1994. (Closed January 1, 1995) **Jack's Holiday** (25). Musical with book by Mark St. Germain, music by Randy Courts, lyrics by Mark St. Germain and Randy Courts. Opened March 5, 1995. (Closed March 26, 1995) **Police Boys** (13). By Marion McClinton. Opened May 14, 1995. (Closed May 26, 1995) And *The Springhill Singing Disaster* by Karen Trott, scheduled to open 6/22/95. Produced by Playwrights Horizons, artistic director Don Scardino, managing director Leslie Marcus, general manager Lynn Landis, associate artistic director Tim Sanford, at the Anne G. Wilder Theater.

A CHEEVER EVENING

John Cunningham	Mary Beth Peil
Jack Gilpin	Robert Stanton
Julie Hagerty	Jennifer Van Dyck

Directed by Don Scardino; scenery, John Lee Beatty; costumes, Jennifer Von Mayrhauser; lighting, Kenneth Posner; sound, Aural Fixation; casting, Janet Foster; production stage manager, Lloyd Davis Jr.; stage manager, Caroline Ranald; press, Philip Rinaldi, Barbara Carroll, Kathy Haberthur; James Morrison.

Time: The late 1940s to the early 1970s. Place: The East Side of Manhattan; the northern suburbs; the New England coast. The play was presented in two parts.

Material from 17 Cheever short stories interwoven, as stated in a program footnote by the author, into a complicated tapestry accommodated to the special demands of the stage.

JACK'S HOLIDAY

Swan's Players:
  Jennie (Female Ingenue) ....Lauren Ward
  Sarah (Actor Manager's
    Wife) .... Anne Runolfsson
  Spencer (Actor Manager) .... Herb Foster
  Elizabeth (Leading Lady) .... Alix Korey
  John (Male Ingenue) ....Mark Lotito
  Jack (General Utility Man) ..Allen Fitzpatrick
  Edward (Leading Man) .... Michael X. Martin
Will Bolger .... Greg Naughton
Snatchem Leese .... Henry Stram
Humpty Jackson .... Michael Mulheren

Gallus Mag ....Lou Williford
Max Pierce ....Nicolas Coster
Inspector Thomas Byrnes .... Dennis Parlato
Clubber Williams .... Mark Lotito
Shakespeare; Mrs. Parkhurst;
  Molly .... Alix Korey
Mary Healey ....Judy Blazer
Suzy; Edith .... Anne Runolfsson
Samuel Shine; Rev. Billis ..... Michael X. Martin
Servant; Daisy ....Lauren Ward
Rev. Parkhurst; Ameer Ben Ali;
  Sgt. Deehan .... Herb Foster

Musicians: Steve Tyler keyboard 1; Antony Geralis keyboard 2; Glenn Rhian percussion; John Benthal guitar; Lou Bruno bass; Jon Kass violin.

JACK'S HOLIDAY—Judy Blazer and Allen Fitzpatrick in
the Mark St. Germain-Randy Courts musical about Jack the
Ripper at Playwrights Horizons

Directed by Susan H. Schulman; musical staging, Michael Lichtefeld; musical direction, vocal arrangements and incidental music, Steve Tyler; scenery and projection effects, Jerome Sirlin; costumes, Catherine Zuber; lighting, Robert Wierzel; sound, Dan Moses Schreier; fight direction, J. Allen Suddeth; casting, Janet Foster; stage manager, Lloyd Davis Jr.; production stage manager, Perry Cline.

Time 1891. Place: New York City.

Jack the Ripper visits New York as a member of an acting company.

ACT I

"The Line" ....Byrnes, Jack
"What I Almost Said" ....Will, Mary
"The Hands of God" .... Revs. Parkhurst, Billis, Company
"Letter #3" ....Jack
"You Never Know Who's Behind You" ....Byrnes, Jack
"What Land Is This?" ....Will, Jack, Byrnes, Company
Act I Finale..Company

ACT II

"Stage Blood" ....Jack, Acting Company
"Letter #4" ....Jack
"If You Will Dream of Me" ....Mary
"Don't Think About It" ... Max, Gallus Mag, Humpty, Snatchem, Samuel Shine, Daisy, Edith, Molly
"Don't Think About It" (Reprise) ....Humpty, Snatchem
"All You Want Is Always" ....Will, Jack
"Pandarus' Song" ....Spencer
"Never Time to Dance" (Reprise) .... Jack, Mary
Act II Finale...Company

POLICE BOYS

The Signifying Monkey ....Larry Gilliard Jr.
Christopher "Comanche"
  Chileogus Cummings .... Richard Brooks
The Royal Boy .... Akili Prince
Teddy (The Lady in White);
  Meredith Fellows .... Judith Hawking

Capt. Jabali Abdul LaRouche ....Chuck Cooper
Sgt. Ruth "Babe Ruth" Milano ..... Nancy Giles
Cross "Superboy"
  Beauchamp .... Russell Andrews
Benjamin Santiago Bowie ....Leland Gantt

Directed by Donald Douglass; fight direction, David Leong; scenery, Riccardo Hernandez; costumes, Judy Dearing; lighting, Jan Kroeze; incidental music and sound, Don DiNicola; presented in association with the Pittsburgh Public Theater, Edward Gilbert artistic director; casting, Janet Foster; production stage manager, Andrea J. Testani; stage manager, Jane Rothman Ronis.

Time: A future you can touch with your hand. Place: The community affairs room, the captain's office and the holding cell of a police station. The play was presented in two parts.

Melodrama both realistic and symbolical in an inner city police station. Previously produced in regional theater at Center Stage, Baltimore.

New York Shakespeare Festival. Schedule of ten programs. **Some People** (45; see note), with Danny Hoch, written by Danny Hoch, opened October 18, 1994; and **The Diva Is Dismissed** (34; see note), with Jenifer Lewis, written by Jenifer Lewis and Charles Randolph-Wright, opened October 30, 1994; solo performances presented in repertory. (Repertory closed December 31, 1994). **Blade to the Heat** (38). By Oliver Mayer. Opened November 3, 1994. (Closed December 4, 1994) **Simpatico** (40). By Sam Shepard. Opened November 14, 1994. (Closed December 18, 1994) **The Petrified Prince** (32). Musical based on the screen play by Ingmar Bergman; book by Edward Gallardo; music and lyrics by Michael John LaChiusa. Opened December 18, 1994. (Closed January 15, 1995) **Him** (13). By Christopher Walken. Opened January 5, 1995. (Closed January 8, 1995) **Silence, Cunning, Exile** (25). By Stuart Greenman. Opened February 19, 1995. (Closed March 12, 1995) **Dancing on Moonlight** (24). By Keith Glover. Opened April 11, 1995. (Closed April 30, 1995) **A Language of Their Own** (46). By Chay Yew. Opened April 20, 1995. (Closed May 28, 1995) **Dog Opera** (15). By Constance Congdon. Opened May 10, 1995. (Closed May 21, 1995) Produced by New York Shakespeare Festival, George C. Wolfe producer, Jason Steven Cohen managing director (through 1994), Rosemarie Tichler and Kevin Kline associate producers, at the Joseph Papp Public Theater (see note).

SOME PEOPLE

Directed by Jo Bonney; lighting, David Castaneda; production stage manager, Sarah Sidman; press, Carol R. Fineman, Terence Womble, Eugenie Hero.

Characters: Caribbean Tiger, Madman, Kazmierczack, Floe, Bill, Toño, Blanca, Al Capón, Doris, Flex, César.

One-man portrayal of urban characters from all walks of life. The show was presented without intermission.

Note: *Some People* played 45 advertised performances in an irregular repertory schedule with *The Diva Is Dismissed.*

THE DIVA IS DISMISSED

Directed by Charles Randolph-Wright; musical direction, Michael Skloff; additional material, Mark Alton Brown; lighting, David Castaneda; production stage manager, Jim Ring.

One-woman performance—partly autobiographical, partly imaginary—by Jenifer Lewis of a diva in progress from Missouri to Broadway and Hollywood. The show was presented without intermission.

Note: *The Diva Is Dismissed* played 34 advertised performances in an irregular repertory schedule with *Some People.*

MUSICAL NUMBERS: "Climb" (music and lyrics by Jenifer Lewis), "Grandma Small" (music and lyrics by Jenifer Lewis), "Killer Cheer" (1971 music and lyrics by Jenifer Lewis, additional lyrics by Charles Randolph-Wright), "And I Was Fired" (music by Jenifer Lewis and Michael Skloff, lyrics by Mark Brown, Jenifer Lewis and Charles Randolph-Wright), Broadway Medley, "I Wanna Come Home" (music and lyrics by Jenifer Lewis, Michael Skloff and Charles Randolph-Wright), "Staring at the Moon" (music and lyrics by Jenifer Lewis).

BLADE TO THE HEAT

Garnet	Carlton Wilborn	Pedro Quinn	Kamar De Los Reyes
Three-finger Jack	Chuck Patterson	Reporter; Announcer; Referee	James Colby
Alacran	Jaime Tirelli	Sarita Malacara	Maricela Ochoa
Mantequilla Decima	Paul Calderon	Wilfred Vinal	Nelson Vasquez

Musicians: Ron McBee and Carlos Valdez, congas.

Directed by George C. Wolfe; scenery, Riccardo Hernandez; costumes, Paul Tazewell; lighting, Paul Gallo; sound, Dan Moses Schreier; fight choreography, Michael Olajide Jr.; casting, Jordan Thaler; production stage manager, Gwendolyn M. Gilliam; stage manager, Robert Castro.

Time: 1959. The play was presented in two parts.

The dark side of the sport of prizefighting as it was 35 years ago.

SIMPATICO

Carter	Ed Harris	Simms	James Gammon
Vinnie	Fred Ward	Kelly	Welker White
Cecilia	Marcia Gay Harden	Rosie	Beverly D'Angelo

Directed by Sam Shepard; scenery, Loy Arcenas; costumes, Elsa Ward; lighting, Anne Militello; sound, Tom Morse; original music, Patrick O'Hearn; production stage manager, Ruth Kreshka; stage manager, Anders Cato.

Act I, Scene 1: Cucamonga, morning. Act II, Scene 1: San Dimas, afternoon. Scene 2: Midway, Ky., late night. Scene 3: Cucamonga, later, same night. Act III, Scene 1: Lexington, Ky., next morning. Scene 2: Midway, Ky., that afternoon. Scene 3: Cucamonga, that evening.

Vengeful good vs. evil opposition, detective story style, set in the world of horse racing.

THE PETRIFIED PRINCE

Prince Samson ....Alexander Gaberman
King Maximilian; Abbe Sebastian; Fernando,
  King of the Gypsies ....Mal Z. Lawrence
Queen Katarina ....Candy Buckley
Franz .... Gabriel Barre
Cardinal Pointy .... Timothy Jerome
Judge Schied .... Robert Blumenfeld
Gen. Petschul ....George Merritt

Pope Pius VII ....Ralph Byers
Mama Chiaramonte .... Marilyn Cooper
Roberta .... Loni Ackerman
Gen. Montesquieu ....Geoffrey Blaisdell
Napoleon .... Alan Braunstein
Mme. Paulina ....Jane White
Elise ....Daisy Prince
Nursemaid ....Judith Moore

Ensemble: Wendy Edmead, Amy N. Heggins, Darren Lee, David Masenheimer, Dana Moore, Judith Moore, Troy Myers, Casey Nicholaw, Cynthia Sophiea, Mark Anthony Taylor, Sally Ann Tumas. Swings: Mindy Cooper, Nicholas Garr.

Orchestra: Jason Robert Brown conductor, piano; David Evans, assistant conductor, synthesizer; Carl Anderson trumpet; Diane Barrere cello; Steven Bartosik percussion; Jacqueline Henderson bassoon; Walter Kane woodwinds; Raymond Kilday bass; Mia Wu violin.

Directed by Harold Prince; musical staging, Rob Marshall; musical direction and arrangements, Jason Robert Brown; scenery, James Youmans; costumes, Judith Dolan; lighting, Howell Binkley; sound, Jim Bay; orchestrations, Jonathan Tunick; barge puppets, Jim Henson Productions, Inc.; assistant to Mr. Prince, Ruth Mitchell; musical coordinator, Seymour Red Press; line producer, Wiley Hausam; produced by arrangement with John Flaxman and Live Entertainment of Canada, Inc. and by permission of Warner Brothers; casting, Jordan Thaler/Heidi Griffiths and Donna DeSeta/David Cady; production stage manager, Bonnie Metzgar; stage manager; Lisa Buxbaum;

Time: 1807. Place: Slavonia.

Political satire, a physically handicapped prince inherits a troubled kingdom.

ACT I

Prologue: Slavonia, 1807
  "Move" ....Prince Samson, Company
Scene 1: The palace
  "There Are Happy Endings" .... Queen Katarina, King Maximilian
Scene 2: The throne room
  "His Family Tree" ....Cardinal Pointy, Judge Schied, Gen. Petschul, Courtiers
  "The Easy Life" ....Queen Katarina
  "Abbe's Appearance" .... Abbe Sebastian
  "Samson's Thoughts" .... Prince Samson
Scene 3: The Vatican
  "Pointy's Lament" .... Cardinal Pointy, Statues
Scene 4: Gypsy campsite, Bohemia
  "A Woman in Search of Happiness" ....Roberta, Fernando, Gypsies
Scene 5: Napoleon's tent near the Silesian front
  "Napoleon's Nightmare" ....Napoleon
  "Dormez-Vous" ....Gen. Montesquieu, Gen. Petschul
Scene 6: Vienna
  "One Little Taste" ....Mme. Paulina, Brothel Girls
Scene 7: On the road to Slavonia
  "Never Can Tell" .... Elise
Scene 8: The palace
  "Look Closer, Love" .... Elise
  "Stay" ....Prince Samson, Elise
  Finale: "Move" .... Queen Katarina, Company

ACT II

Scene 1: The palace
  "Move" (Reprise) .... Queen Katarina, Company
  "Without Me" ....Queen Katarina, Palace Guards

Scene 2: The animal barge to Bucharest
  "The Animal Song" .... Elise
  "Samson's Epiphany" .... Prince Samson
Scene 3: The Blue Forest
  "Fernando's Suicide" .... Fernando
Scene 4: The throne room
  "Easy Life" (Reprise) .... Queen Katarina
Scene 5: The family portrait gallery
  "Easy Life" (Reprise) .... Elise
Scene 6: The banquet room
  "Addio, Bambino" .... Mama Chiaramonte, Pope Pius VII
  "Roberta's Passion Play" .... Roberta, Fernando
Scene 7: The throne room
  "What the Prince Is Saying" .... Elise, Company
  "I Would Like to Say" .... Prince Samson, Elise
  Finale .... Company

HIM

Him	Christopher Walken	Joe; Mel	Barton Heyman
Bro	Rob Campbell	Al; Disappointed Fan; Stylagi	Peter Appel
Doc; Borden; Taxman; Stylagi	Larry Block	Nurse; Dolores; Journalist	Ellen McElduff

Musicians: Mike Evans drums; Annie Gosfield keyboards; Mike Nolan guitar, pedal steel guitar; Scott Williams bass.

Directed by Jim Simpson; scenery and lighting, Kyle Chepulis; costumes, Franne Lee; musical direction and sound, Mike Nolan, choreography, John Carrafa; casting, Jordan Thaler; production stage manager, Kristen Harris; stage manager, Cathleen Wolfe.

Satirical view of Elvis Presley and the pop culture which produced him. The play was presented without intermission.

SILENCE, CUNNING, EXILE

Suzie	Elizabeth Marvel	Transient; Boy Friend;	
Donald	Denis O'Hare	Inert Man	Matte Osian
Beryl	Margaret Whitton	Homely Transvestite	Michael Lynch
Frank	Tim Hopper	Fat Prostitute	Jerry Mayer
Kiki	Adina Porter	Acquaintance; Man at Party	Timothy Wheeler
Isaac	Rocco Sisto		

Directed by Mark Wing-Davey; scenery, Derek McLane; costumes, Catherine Zuber; lighting, Christopher Akerlind; sound, John Gromada; fight direction, Nels Hennum; casting, Jordan Thaler, Heidi Griffiths; production stage manager, Thom Widmann.

Self-described as "inspired by the life of Diane Arbus," the late photographer, in the 1950s and 1960s, with names changed. The play was presented in two parts.

DANCING ON MOONLIGHT

Anansi	Adina Porter	Eclipse	Badja Djola
Apollotis	Kevin Jackson	Sorry Charlie	Andre De Shields
Dady Jerry	Terry Alexander	La Ronda	Kim Yancy
Neptune	Anna Marie Horsford	Robber Lee	Ray Anthony Thomas

Directed by Marion McClinton; scenery, Riccardo Hernandez; costumes, Karen Perry; lighting, Paul Gallo; sound, Dan Moses Schreier; music, Max Roach; choreography, Donald Byrd; fight direction, David Leong; casting, Jordan Thaler/Heidi Griffiths; production stage manager, Jana Llynn; stage manager, Trevor Brown.

Prologue: Harlem, 1935. Act I: Harlem, 1959. Act II: Harlem, 1960. The play was presented in two parts.

Poetic drama of racketeering and civil rights ideals coexisting and colliding. The first of three plays offered at the Public under the portmanteau title American Identity: Does Context Determine Content?

A LANGUAGE OF THEIR OWN

Ming	B.D. Wong	Robert	David Drake
Oscar	Francis Jue	Daniel	Alec Mapa

Directed by Keng-Sen Ong; scenery, Myung Hee Cho; costumes, Michael Krass; lighting, Scott Zielinski; music, Liang-Xing Tang; fight direction, J. Steven White; casting, Jordan Thaler, Heidi Griffiths; production stage manager, Buzz Cohen; stage manager, Rick Steiger.

Verbal and physical communication among four young men in search of love, presented in two parts. The second of three plays offered at the Public under the portmanteau title American Identity: Does Context Determine Content?

DOG OPERA

Peter Szczepanek	Albert Macklin	Joe's Lover; Man on Street; Stavros; Paul;	
Madeline Newell	Kristine Nielsen	Arapahoe	Eduardo Andino
Jackie	Kevin Dewey	Charlie Szczepanek; Brad;	
Steven; Chris; David; Tim;		Sanny	Richard Russell Ramos
Hank	Rick Holmes		
Bernice; Ruby; Dale Williamson;			
Doris; Maureen	Sloane Shelton		

Directed by Gerald Gutierrez; scenery, John Lee Beatty; costumes, Toni-Leslie James; lighting, Brian MacDevitt; sound, Otts Munderloh; casting, Jordan Thaler, Heidi Griffiths; production stage manager, Marjorie Horne; stage manager, Anne Marie Paolucci.

High school friends, a man and a woman, supporting each other in their search for life partners, presented in two parts. The third of three plays offered at the Public under the portmanteau title American Identity: Does Context Determine Content?

Note: in the Joseph Papp Public Theater there are many auditoria. *Some People, The Diva Is Dismissed* and *A Language of Their Own* played the Susan Stein Shiva Theater, *Blade to the Heat* and *Dancing on Moonlight* played the Anspacher Theater, *Simpatico* played the Estelle R. Newman Theater, *The Petrified Prince, Silence, Cunning, Exile* and *Dog Opera* played Martison Hall, *Him* played LuEsther Hall.

Uncommon Women & Others (78). Revival of the play by Wendy Wasserstein. Produced by Second Stage Theater, Carole Rothman artistic director, Suzanne Schwartz Davidson producing director, by special arrangement with Lucille Lortel at the Lucille Lortel Theater. Opened October 26, 1994. (Closed January 1, 1995)

Kate Quin	Stephanie Roth	Muffet DiNicola	Haviland Morris
Samantha Stewart	Mary McCann	Susie Friend	Robin Morse
Rita Altabel	Jessica Lundy	Carter	Danielle Ferland
Mrs. Plumm	Rosemary Murphy	Leilah	Joan Buddenhagen
Holly Kaplan	Julie Dretzin	Narrator	Voice of Forrest Sawyer

Standby: Miss Murphy—Patricia O'Connell. Understudies: Misses Buddenhagen, Roth, Lundy, Morris—Annika Peterson; Misses Ferland, Dretzin, McCann, Morse—Tessa Auberjonois.

Directed by Carole Rothman; scenery, Heidi Landesman; costumes, Jennifer Von Mayrhauser; lighting, Richard Nelson; sound, Janet Kalas; associate producer, Carol Fishman; casting, Meg Simon; production stage manager, Roy Harris; stage manager, James FitzSimmons; press, Richard Kornberg, William Schelble.

Time and Place: A restaurant in 1978 and six years earlier at a college for women. The play was presented in two parts.

Left, James Gammon and Marcia Gay Harden in *Simpatico* by Sam Shepard; *above,* Mal Z. Lawrence and Loni Ackerman in *The Petrified Prince,* the Michael John LaChiusa-Edward Gallardo musical directed by Harold Prince

Uncommon Women and Others was originally produced off Broadway by the Phoenix Theater 11/17/77 for 22 performances. This is its first major New York revival.

Annabelle Gurwitch replaced Jessica Lundy 11/22/94.

The Cover of Life (29). By R.T. Robinson. Produced by T. Harding Jones Entertainment, Inc., Frederic B. Vogel, Herb Goldsmith Productions, Inc., Angels of the Arts and Snapshot Theatrical Productions at the American Place Theater. Opened October 27, 1994. (Closed November 20, 1994)

Kate Miller	Sara Botsford	Sybil	Kerrianne Spellman
Tood	Alice Haining	Addie Mae	Cynthia Darlow
Weetsie	Melinda Eades	Tommy	David Schiliro
Aunt Ola	Carlin Glynn		

Understudies: Misses Glynn, Darlow, Botsford—C.C. Loveheart; Mr. Schiliro—Bobby C. King.

Directed by Peter Masterson; scenery, Amy Shock; costumes, Lindsay W. Davis; lighting, Marc B. Weiss; sound, Jeremy Grody; original music, Randy Courts; associate producers, Joan Asher, Ron Cohen, Michael Lintecum; co-producer, Bakula Productions, Inc.; casting, Helyn Taylor; production stage manager, Marjorie Horne; stage manager, Bobby C. King; press, Richard Kornberg, William Schelble.

Time: September 1943. Place: New York City and at various locations in Sterlington, La. The play was presented in two parts.

Life photographer moves in with small-town war brides to cover their story.

The Irish Repertory Theater. Repertory of two plays: **Mother of All the Behans** (38), solo performance by Rosaleen Linehan, written by Peter Sheridan, adapted from the book by Brian Behan, with additional material by Rosaleen Linehan, opened October 27, 1994; and **Alive, Alive Oh!** (35), written and conceived by Milo O'Shea and Kitty Sullivan, opened October 31, 1994. Produced by Jim Sheridan, Peter Sheridan, the Irish Repertory Theater Company, Inc. and One World Arts Foundation, Inc., in association with Georganne Heller and Beverly Karp in the Irish Repertory Theater productions, Charlotte Moore artistic director, Ciaran O'Reilly producing director, at Theater Four. (Repertory closed December 18, 1994)

MOTHER OF ALL THE BEHANS

Directed by Peter Sheridan; scenery and costumes, Chisato Yoshimi; lighting, Tony Wakefield; production stage manager, Kathe Mull; press, Boneau/Bryan-Brown, Susanne Tighe.

Rosaleen Linehan in a biography of Kathleen Behan, Irish mother of six sons including Brendan Behan and a conspicuous presence in the Dublin of her time.

ALIVE, ALIVE OH!

CAST: Milo O'Shea, Kitty Sullivan, Michael Lavine (accompanist).

Scenery, David Raphel; lighting, Gregory Cohen; sound, Richard Clausen; production stage manager, Pamela Edington.

An evening of songs, poetry, vaudeville, drama and pantomime, including selections from the works of major Irish writers.

ACT I: Cockles and Mussels, Biddy Mulligan, Phil the Fluther (by Percy French), *Juno and the Paycock* (by Sean O'Casey), I Wish It Were So (by Marc Blitzstein), Selections From *Pygmalion/My Fair Lady* (by George Bernard Shaw, Alan Jay Lerner and Frederick Loewe), the Reillys, *The Playboy of the Western World* (by John Millington Synge), Goliath and the Leprechaun, Wee Hughie, *Waiting for Godot* (by Samuel Beckett), *Arms and the Man* (by George Bernard Shaw).

ACT II: *Waiting for Godot* (by Samuel Beckett), Seeing Things at Night, The Leprechaun, The Selfish Giant (by Oscar Wilde), *She Stoops to Conquer* (by Oliver Goldsmith) and An English Country Garden (by Percy Granger), The Lake Isle of Innisfree (by William Butler Yeats), Come Back Paddy Reilly (by Percy French), Fionnuala at the Films, Ach, I Dunno (by Percy French), I Know My Love, Bedtime Story (by Sean O'Casey), The Blackbird (by Fergus Linehan), *Ulysses* (by James Joyce).

Nunsense 2: the Sequel (149). Musical with book, music and lyrics by Dan Goggin. Produced by Twice Blessed Company, Inc. at the Douglas Fairbanks Theater. Opened October 31, 1994. (Closed February 26, 1995)

Sister Mary Regina	Sister Robert Anne .... Carolyn Droscoski
(Rev. Mother) .... Nancy E. Carroll	Sister Mary Leo .... Susan Emerson
Sister Mary Hubert .... Terri White	Sister Mary Amnesia ...... Semina De Laurentis

Musicians: Michael Rice conductor, piano; John Ogden synthesizer; David Nyberg drums, percussion.

Understudy: Teri Gibson.

Directed by Dan Goggin; musical staging and choreography, Felton Smith; musical direction, Michael Rice; scenery, Barry Axtell; lighting, Paul Miller; sound, Jim van Bergen; orchestrations, Michael Rice, David Nyberg; production stage manager, Paul J. Botchis; press, The Pete Sanders Group, Pete Sanders, Ian Rand, Glenna Freedman.

Time: The present, about six weeks after the Little Sisters of Hoboken presented their first benefit entitled *Nunsense.* Place: Mt. St. Helen's School auditorium.

Taking up where *Nunsense 1* left off, the *Nunsense 2* sisters make plans for another benefit.

Elizabeth Dargan Doyle replaced Susan Emerson 11/1/94. Julie J. Hasner replaced Nancy E. Carroll 12/20/94. Amanda Butterbaugh replaced Semina De Laurentis 1/1/95.

NOTE: *Nunsense 1* played 7 performances in repertory with *Nunsense 2* on Tuesdays and Thursdays 1/10–1/31/95.

ACT I

Overture ....The School Band
"Jubilatedo"...Company
"Nunsense, the Magic Word" ....Company
"Winning Is Just the Beginning" ....Company
"The Prima Ballerina"..Sr. Leo
"The Biggest Still Ain't the Best" ....Srs. Hubert, Leo
"I've Got Pizzazz" ....Sr. Robert Anne
"I've Got Pizzazz" (Reprise) ....Rev. Mother
"The Country Nun"..Sr. Amnesia
"Look Ma, I Made It" ....Rev. Mother
"The Padre Polka"...Srs. Hubert, Leo, Amnesia
"The Classic Queens" ....Rev. Mother, Sr. Hubert
"A Hat and Cane Song" ....Company

ACT II

"Angeline" ....Sr. Robert Anne
"We're the Nuns to Come To" ....Srs. Hubert, Robert Anne, Amnesia, Leo
"What Would Elvis Do?" ....Rev. Mother, Sr. Hubert
"Yes, We Can" ....Srs. Leo, Amnesia, Robert Anne
"I Am Here to Stay" ....Sr. Robert Anne
"What a Catastrophe" ....Srs. Hubert, Robert Anne, Amnesia, Leo
"No One Cared Like You" ....Sr. Amnesia
"Gloria in Excelsis Deo" ....Company
"There's Only One Way to End Your Prayers" ....Sr. Hubert, Company
"Nunsense, the Magic Word" (Reprise) ....Company

*Manhattan Theater Club. Schedule of eight programs. **Love! Valour! Compassion!** (72). By Terrence McNally. Opened November 1, 1994. (Closed January 1, 1995 and reopened on Broadway February 14, 1995; see its entry in the Plays Produced on Broadway section of this volume) **Durang Durang** (41). By Christopher Durang. Opened November 13, 1994. (Closed December 18, 1994) ***After-Play** (59). By Anne Meara. Opened January 31, 1995. (Closed March 5, 1995) Reopened May 16, 1995; see note. **Holiday Heart** (56). By Cheryl L. West. Opened February 21, 1995. (Closed April 9, 1995) **Three Viewings** (32). By Jeffrey Hatcher. Opened April 4, 1995. (Closed April 30, 1995) **Night and Her Stars** (39). By Richard Greenberg. Opened April 26, 1995. (Closed May 28, 1995) ***Sylvia** (10). By A.R. Gurney. Opened May 23, 1995. And *The Radical Mystique* by Arthur Laurents, scheduled to open 6/6/95. Produced by Manhattan Theater Club, Lynne Meadow artistic director, Barry Grove managing director, *Love! Valour! Compassion!*, *Holiday Heart* and *Sylvia* at City Center Stage I, *Durang Durang*, *After-Play* and *Three Viewings* at City Center Stage II, *Night and Her Stars* at American Place Theater.

LOVE! VALOUR! COMPASSION!

Gregory Mitchell	Stephen Bogardus	Buzz Hauser	Nathan Lane
Arthur Pape	John Benjamin Hickey	Bobby Brahms	Justin Kirk
Perry Sellars	Stephen Spinella	Ramon Fornos	Randy Becker
John Jeckyll; James Jeckyll	John Glover		

Understudies: Messrs. Bogardus, Hickey—David Phillips; Messrs. Becker, Kirk—David Noroña.

Directed by Joe Mantello; scenery, Loy Arcenas; costumes, Jess Goldstein; lighting, Brian Mac-Devitt; sound, John Kilgore; choreography, John Carrafa; associate artistic director, Michael Bush; casting, Randy Carrig; production stage manager, William Joseph Barnes; stage manager, Ira Mont; press, Helene Davis, Amy Lefkowitz.

Time: The present, Memorial Day, 4th of July and Labor Day Weekends, respectively. Place: A remote house and wooded grounds by a lake in Duchess County, two hours north of New York City. The play was presented in three parts.

Eight gay men vacationing, having fun and occasionally experiencing emotional crises.

A Best Play; see page 81.

DURANG DURANG

ACT I: Theater

Mrs. Sorken

Mrs. Sorken ...... Patricia Elliott

For Whom the Southern Belle Tolls; or,
The Further Adventures of Amanda and
Her Children

Amanda	Lizbeth Mackay
Lawrence	Keith Reddin
Tom	David Aaron Baker
Ginny	Patricia Randell

A Stye of the Eye

Jake	Marcus Giamatti
Ma	Becky Ann Baker
Dr. Martina	Patricia Elliott
Agnes; Beth	Keith Reddin
Meg	Lizbeth Mackay
Wesley	David Aaron Baker
Mae	Patricia Randell

ACT II: Everything Else

Nina in the Morning

Narrator	David Aaron Baker
Maid	Patricia Randell
Nina	Patricia Elliott
James; Robert; LaLa	Keith Reddin
Foote	Marcus Giamatti

Wanda's Visit

Jim	Marcus Giamatti
Marsha	Lizbeth Mackay
Wanda	Becky Ann Baker
Waiter	David Aaron Baker

Business Lunch at the Russian Tea Room

Chris	Keith Reddin
Margaret	Patricia Elliott
Waiter	Marcus Giamatti
Melissa Stearn	Patricia Randell

Directed by Walter Bobbie; scenery, Derek McLane; costumes, David C. Woolard; lighting, Brian Nason; sound, Tony Meola; production stage manager, Perry Kline; stage manager, Gregg Fletcher.

Program of short plays and commentary, billed as "A New Evening," includes takeoffs on Tennessee Williams (*For Whom the Southern Belle Tolls*) and Sam Shepard (*A Stye of the Eye*) and an adaptation of a PBS teleplay in the Trying Times series (*Wanda's Visit*).

AFTER-PLAY

Raziel	Lance Reddick	Renee Shredman	Barbara Barrie
Marty Guteman	Merwin Goldsmith	Emily Paine	Rochelle Oliver
Terry Guteman	Rue McClanahan	Mathew Paine	John C. Vennema
Phil Shredman	Larry Keith		

Directed by David Saint; scenery, James Youmans; costumes, Jane Greenwood; lighting, Don Holder; sound, John Gromada; casting, Randy Carrig; production stage manager, Lisa Iacucci.

Two show-biz couples, old friends, one from New York and one from L.A., enjoy a combative reunion at dinner after the theater. The play was presented without intermission.

Note: After 40 performances at Manhattan Theater Club, this production reopened 5/16/95 in independent off-Broadway production by Nancy Richards, Judith Resnick and Evangeline Morphos in association with Carol Ostrow at Theater Four.

Anne Meara replaced Rue McClanahan 5/16/95.

A Best Play; see page 203.

HOLIDAY HEART

Niki Dean	Afi McClendon	Silas Jericho	Ron Cephas Jones
Holiday Heart	Keith Randolph Smith	Ricky; Mark	Alimi Ballard
Wanda Dean	Maggie Rush		

Directed by Tazewell Thompson; scenery, Riccardo Hernandez; costumes, Tom Broecker; lighting, Jack Mehlar; sound, James Wildman; fight direction, Brad Waller; production stage manager, James FitzSimmons.

Comedy and melodrama, a drag queen tries to create a family by taking in a waif from the streets.

THREE VIEWINGS

Tell Tale
Emil .... Buck Henry

The Thief of Tears
Mac .... Margaret Whitton

Thirteen Things About Ed Carpolotti
Virginia .... Penny Fuller

Understudies: Mr. Henry—William Wise; Miss Whitton—Kate Skinner.

Directed by Mary B. Robinson; scenery, James Noone; costumes, Michael Krass; lighting, Pat Dignan; sound, Bruce Ellman; casting, Nancy Piccione; production stage manager, Tom Aberger.

Time: Now. Place: A parlor in a small midwestern town. The play was presented without an intermission.

Three monologues in a funeral parlor: a funeral director reveals his love for a real estate agent (*Tell Tale*), a granddaughter comes to town for the funeral of her grandmother (*The Thief of Tears*), a widow is left in debt by her mafia-connected husband (*Thirteen Things About Ed Carpolotti*).

NIGHT AND HER STARS

Herb Stempel	Patrick Breen	Jack Barry	David Andrew Macdonald
Mark Van Doren	Keith Charles	Warren Corso	Reese Madigan
Dan Enright	Peter Frechette	Doris	Linda Pierce
Toby Stempel	Ileen Getz	Charles Van Doren	John Slattery
Al Freedman	Jordan Lage		

Fans, Journalists, Contestants, Congresspeople, TV Personnel, etc.—Company.

Understudies: Misses Getz, Pierce—Jennifer Bill; Messrs. Frechette, Slattery, Macdonald—Charles Tuthill.

Directed by David Warren; scenery, Derek McLane; costumes, Walker Hicklin; lighting, Peter Kaczorowski; projection design, Wendall K. Harrington; original music and sound design, Michael Roth; casting, Randy Carrig; production stage manager, Ruth Kreshka; stage manager, K. Dale White.

The TV quiz show scandals of the 1950s. The play was commissioned and previously produced by South Coast Repertory, Costa Mesa, Calif. and presented here in two parts.

A Best Play; see page 265.

SYLVIA

Sylvia	Sarah Jessica Parker	Kate	Blythe Danner
Greg	Charles Kimbrough	Tom; Phyllis; Leslie	Derek Smith

Directed by John Tillinger; scenery, John Lee Beatty; costumes, Jane Greenwood; lighting, Ken Billington; sound, Aural Fixation; casting, Michael R. Moody; production stage manager, Roy Harris; stage manager, James FitzSimmons.

Time: The present. Place: New York City. The play was presented in two parts.

A romantic comedy in which a dog named Sylvia becomes the third side of an emotional triangle in a troubled marriage.

Public Enemy (133). By Kenneth Branagh. Produced by the Irish Arts Center, Nye Heron artistic director, Marianne Delaney executive director, at the Irish Arts Center. Opened November 3, 1994. (Closed February 26, 1995)

Thompson	George Coe	Kitty Rogers	Bernadette Quigley
Tommy Black	Paul Ronan	Ma	Patti Allison
Davey Boyd	Brian D'Arcy James	Robert Black	Neal Jones
Georgie Pearson	Tony Coleman	Kevin O'Donnell	James Beecher

Directed by Nye Heron; scenery, David Raphel; costumes, Mimi Maxmen; lighting, Susan Roth; choreography, Josephine McNamara; music and sound, Nico Kean; video design, Edwin Dennis; produced by Marianne Delaney and Don Kelly; associate producer, Georganne Heller; casting, Laura Richin; production stage manager, John Brophy.

Time: The mid-1980s. Place: A protestant, working-class neighborhood in Belfast. The play was presented in two parts.

Urban Irish toughs, in particular one of them infatuated with the James Cagney image. A foreign play previously produced by Renaissance Theater Company, London.

Inside Out (61). Musical with book by Doug Haverty; music by Adryan Russ; lyrics by Adryan Russ and Doug Haverty. Produced by Marc Routh, Richard Frankel, Randy Kelly, Carol Ostrow and George Tunick at the Cherry Lane Theater. Opened November 7, 1994. (Closed January 1, 1995)

Dena	Ann Crumb	Liz	Jan Maxwell
Grace	Harriett D. Foy	Chlo	Cass Morgan
Molly	Kathleen Mahoney-Bennett	Sage	Julie Prosser

Musicians: Frank Lindquist conductor, piano; Monica Kuligowski drums.

Understudies: Lisby Larson, Jennifer Naimo.

Directed by Henry Fonte; choreography, Gary Slavin; musical direction and vocal arrangements, E. Suzan Ott; scenery, Rob Odorisio; costumes, Gail Brassard; lighting, Douglas O'Flaherty; orchestrations, Ned Ginsburg; associate producers, Margot Ross London, Prima K. Stephen; casting, Alan Filderman; production stage manager, Craig Palanker; press, Boneau/Bryan-Brown, Chris Boneau, Andy Shearer.

Six women share their lives with each other in a series of weekly meetings. Previously produced by the Group Repertory Theater, the Village Theater Company (as *Roleplay*) and the Florida Studio Theater.

ACT I

"Inside Out"	Company
"Thin"	Molly, Sage, Chlo, Liz
"Let It Go"	Sage, Grace
"I Can See You Here"	Grace
"If You Really Loved Me"	Company
"Yo, Chlo"	Dena, Company
"If You Really Loved Me" (Reprise)	Chlo
"Behind Dena's Back"	Company
"No One Inside"	Dena
"Inside Out" (Reprise)	Company

ACT II

"Grace's Nightmare" .... Grace, Company
"All I Do Is Sing" .... Dena
"Never Enough" .... Chlo
"I Don't Say Anything" .... Sage
"The Passing of a Friend" .... Molly, Company
"Things Look Different" .... Liz, Grace
"Do It at Home" .... Liz, Company
"Reaching Up" .... Dena, Company

Das Barbecü (30). Musical with book and lyrics by Jim Luigs; music by Scott Warrender. Produced by Thomas Viertel, Steven Baruch, Richard Frankel, Jack Viertel, Dasha Epstein, Margery Klain, Leavitt/Fox/Mages and Daryl Roth at the Minetta Lane Theater. Opened November 10, 1994. (Closed December 4, 1994)

CAST: Narrator, Fricka, Erda, Needa Troutt, Back-Up Singer, Katsy Snapp, Valkyrie—Julie Johnson; Wotan, Gunther, Hagen, Giant—J.K. Simmons; Siegfried, Milam Lamar, Alberich, Giant—Jerry McGarity; Gutrune, Freia, Y-Vonne Duval, Valkyrie, Tambourine Girl—Carolee Carmello; Brünnhilde—Sally Mayes.

Norn Triplets—Carolee Carmello, Sally Mayes, Jerry McGarity; Dwarves—Carolee Carmello, Sally Mayes, J.K. Simmons; Rivermaidens—Carolee Carmello, Julie Johnson, Sally Mayes.

Musicians: Jeff Halpern conductor, keyboard; Ian Herman keyboard; Mike Levine acoustic, electric, peddle and steel guitars; Kenny Kosek fiddle, mandolin; Perry Cavari drums.

Understudy: Rick Crom.

Directed by Christopher Ashley; musical staging, Stephen Terrell; musical direction, Jeff Halpern; scenery and costumes, Eduardo Sicangco; lighting, Frances Aronson; sound, T. Richard Fitzgerald; musical supervision and dance arrangements, Michael Kosarin; orchestrations, Bruce Coughlin; music coordination, John Miller; associate producer, Marc Routh; co-producers, Mitchell Maxwell, Alan Schuster; casting, Jay Binder; production stage manager, Karen Moore; press, Boneau/Bryan-Brown, Chris Boneau, Andy Shearer, Bob Fennell, Jackie Green.

Time: the present. Place: Texas. the play was presented in two parts.

The drama of the Ring cycle transplanted to Texas and adapted to its country ways. Previously produced in regional theater at Seattle Opera (in 1991), Goodspeed Opera House and Center Stage, Baltimore.

ACT I

"A Ring of Gold in Texas" .... Company
"What I Had in Mind" .... Brünnhilde, Siegfried, Gutrune, Gunther
"Hog-Tie Your Man" .... Norn Triplets
"Makin' Guacamole" .... Needa Troutt, Milam Lamar, Gutrune
"Rodeo Romeo" .... Siegfried, Back-Up Singer, Gutrune
"County Fair" .... Brünnhilde
"Public Enemy Number 1" .... Texas Rangers

ACT II

"A Little House for Me" .... Freia
"River of Fire" .... Wotan
"If Not Fer You" .... Wotan, Alberich
"Slide a Little Closer" .... Siegfried, Brünnhilde
"Barbecue for Two" .... Brünnhilde, Gutrune
"After the Gold Is Gone" .... Rivermaidens
"Wanderin' Man" .... Siegfried, Fricka
"Turn the Tide" .... Brünnhilde, Erda, Wotan
Closing .... Company

Circle Repertory Company. Schedule of four programs. **Three Postcards** (31). Revival of the musical with book by Craig Lucas; music and lyrics by Craig Carnelia. Opened November 16, 1994. (Closed December 11, 1994) **The Truth Teller** (22). By Joyce Carol Oates. Opened February 9, 1995. (Closed February 26, 1995) **The Professional** (30). By Dusan Kovacevic; translated and adapted by Bob Djurdjevic. Opened May 11, 1995. (Closed June 4, 1995) And *Lonely Planet* by Steven Dietz, scheduled to open 6/28/95. Produced by Circle Repertory Company, Tanya Berezin artistic director, Milan Stitt executive director, Meredith Freeman managing director, at Circle in the Square Downtown.

THREE POSTCARDS

Bill	Steve Freeman	Little Jane	Amy Kowallis
Walter	David Pittu	K.C.	Amanda Naughton
Big Jane	Johanna Day		

Direction and musical staging by Tee Scatuorchio; musical direction, Steve Freeman; scenery, Derek McLane; costumes, Toni-Leslie James; lighting, Tom Sturge; production stage manager, Denise Yaney; press, Tom D'Ambrosio.

The first New York production of *Three Postcards* was by Playwrights Horizons off Broadway 5/14/87 for 22 performances and a citation as a Best Play of its season. It was presented without intermission.

The list of musical numbers in *Three Postcards* appears on page 337 of *The Best Plays of 1986–87*.

THE TRUTH TELLER

Hedda Culligan	Lynn Hawley	Maggie Culligan	Barbara Gulan
Saul Schwartz	Andrew Polk	Biff Culligan	Craig Bockhorn
"Tiny" Culligan	John Seitz	"Nelly" Rockefeller	Richard Seff
Nora Culligan	Kathleen Widdoes		

Directed by Gloria Muzio; scenery, Stephan Olson; costumes, Ellen McCartney; lighting, Peter Kaczorowski; sound, Janet Kalas; production stage manager, Denise Yaney.

Daughter upsets her parents' lives when she brings her boy friend home after a five-year absence. The play was presented in two parts.

THE PROFESSIONAL

Luke	Fritz Weaver	Martha	Jan Maxwell
Teya	Jonathan Hogan		

Directed by Peter Craze; scenery, Edward T. Gianfrancesco; costumes, Mary Myers; lighting, Brian Aldous; sound, Chuck London; produced by special arrangement with Simone Genatt, Marcy Drogin and Fred L. Carroll; casting, Alan Filderman; production stage manager, Karen A. Potosnak.

Secret policeman confronts a publisher with the details of his life, collected while on duty for the now defunct Communist regime. A foreign (Yugoslavian) play presented without intermission.

Vita & Virginia (129). Adapted from the correspondence between Vita Sackville-West and Virginia Woolf by Eileen Atkins. Produced by Lewis Allen, Robert Fox Ltd. and Julian Schlossberg with Mitchell Maxwell and Alan J. Schuster at the Union Square Theater. Opened November 21, 1994. (Closed March 19, 1995)

Vita Sackville-West	Vanessa Redgrave
Virginia Woolf	Eileen Atkins

Directed by Zoe Caldwell; scenery, Ben Edwards; costumes, Jane Greenwood; lighting, Rui Rita; original music and sound, John Gromada; associate producer, Meyer Ackerman; production stage manager, Diane Trulock; stage manager, John Handy; press, Bill Evans & Associates, Jim Randolph.

THE TRUTH-TELLER—Kathleen Widdoes (*foreground*) with Craig Bock-horn, Barbara Gulan, John Seitz, Lynn Hawley and Andrew Polk in the play by Joyce Carol Oates at Circle Rep

Portrayals of two noted women writers in a relationship that progressed from friendship to love. The play was presented in two parts. A foreign play previously produced in London.

The Truman Capote Talk Show (43), by Bob Kingdom, opened November 29, 1994; and **Dylan Thomas: Return Journey** (33), devised by Bob Kingdom from the writings of Dylan Thomas, opened November 30, 1994; repertory of two solo performances by Bob Kingdom. Produced by Eric Clapton, Paul Stuart Graham, Ethel Watt and PW Productions at the Perry Street Theater. (Repertory closed February 11, 1995).

The Truman Capote Talk Show directed by Kevin Knight; *Dylan Thomas: Return Journey* directed by Anthony Hopkins; both productions designed by Kevin Knight and Andrew Leigh; associate producer, Patricia Watt; production stage manager, Rupert Tebb; press, the Jacksina Company, Judy Jacksina.

The troubled life of Truman Capote and soaring poetry of Dylan Thomas remembered in two monologues, with Kingdom as each of the two characters.

Lincoln Center Theater. Schedule of two off-Broadway programs. **Hapgood** (129). By Tom Stoppard. Opened December 4, 1994. (Closed March 26, 1995) and *Twelve Dreams* by James Lapine, scheduled to open 6/8/95. Produced by Lincoln Center Theater under the direction of Andre Bishop and Bernard Gersten at the Mitzi E. Newhouse Theater.

HAPGOOD

Hapgood	Stockard Channing	Merryweather	Brian F. O'Byrne
Wates	Clifton Davis	Joe	Yaniv Segal
Ridley	David Lansbury	Blair	Josef Sommer
Radio Voices	Graeme Malcolm	Kerner	David Strathairn
Russian; Intern; Radio Voices	Boris McGiver	Maggs	Michael Winther

Standby: Miss Channing—Robin Moseley. Understudies: Messrs. Sommer, Strathairn—Graeme Malcolm; Mr. Segal—Brett Barsky; Messrs. Strathairn, Lansbury, McGiver, Malcolm—Jeffrey Hayenga; Messrs. Winther, O'Byrne, McGiver, Malcolm—Rick Holmes; Messrs. Lansbury, Winther, O'Byrne—Boris McGiver; Mr. Davis—David Wolos-Fonteno.

Directed by Jack O'Brien; scenery, Bob Crowley; costumes, Ann Roth; lighting, Beverly Emmons; projections, Wendall K. Harrington; sound, Scott Lehrer; original score, Bob James; casting, Daniel Swee; production stage manager, Jeff Lee; stage manager, J.P. Elins; press, Merle Debuskey, Susan Chicoine, Michael Levine.

Time: 1989. Place: London. The play was presented in two parts.

Female chief of a British spy agency copes with family problems as well as espionage intrigue salted with nuclear particle physics. A foreign play previously produced in London.

A Best Play; see page 133.

Me and Jezebel (15). By Elizabeth Fuller. Produced by Elliot Martin and Ron Shapiro in association with Robert R. Blume at the Actors' Playhouse. Opened December 7, 1994. (Closed December 18, 1994)

Bette Davis .... Louise DuArt
Herself .... Elizabeth Fuller

Understudy: Melissa Zriny.

Directed by Mark S. Graham; scenery and lighting, Gordon Link; casting, Marjorie Martin; production stage manager, Katie Rader; press, Jeffrey Richards Associates, Irene Gandy, Kevin Rehac.

Time: 32 days in spring 1985. Place: Various locales in and around Westport, Conn. The play was presented in two parts.

Two-character reminiscence of events when a writer, Elizabeth Fuller, invited Bette Davis to dinner, and the actress arrived with bag and baggage and stayed for a month.

You Should Be So Lucky (96). Transfer from off off Broadway of the play by Charles Busch. Produced by the Herrick Theater Foundation in the Primary Stages production, Casey Childs artistic director, at the Westside Theater Upstairs. Opened December 8, 1994. (Closed March 5, 1995)

Mr. Rosenberg	Stephen Pearlman	Walter	Matthew Arkin
Christopher	Charles Busch	Lenore	Julie Halston
Polly	Nell Campbell	Wanda Wang	Jennifer Kato

Directed by Kenneth Elliott; scenery, B.T. Whitehill; costumes, Suzy Benzinger; lighting, Michael Lincoln; sound, Aural Fixation; title song music and lyrics by Dick Gallagher, sung by Mary Cleere Haran; production stage manager, John Frederick Sullivan; press, Tony Origlio Publicity, Stephen Murray.

Time: The present. Place: A small apartment in Greenwich Village. The play was presented in two parts.

Antic comedy, a West Village electrologist progresses from rags to riches. Previously produced off off Broadway at Primary Stages.

Donald Berman replaced Matthew Arkin 12/20/94.

The Young Man From Atlanta (24). By Horton Foote. Produced off off Broadway in a limited engagement by Signature Theater Company, James Houghton founding artistic director, Thomas C. Proehl managing director, at the Kampo Cultural Center. Opened January 27, 1995. (Closed February 26, 1995)

Will Kidder	Ralph Waite	Pete Davenport	James Pritchett
Tom Jackson	Devon Abner	Clara	Frances Foster
Miss Lacey	Christina Burz	Carson	Michael Lewis
Ted Cleveland Jr.	Seth Jones	Etta Doris	Beatrice Winde
Lily Dale	Carlin Glynn		

Directed by Peter Masterson; scenery, E. David Cosier; costumes, Teresa Snider-Stein, Jonathan Green; lighting, Jeffrey S. Koger; casting, Jerry Beaver; production stage manager, Dean Gray; press, Philip Rinaldi, James Morrison.

Time: Spring 1950. Place: Houston. The play was presented without intermission.

Houston family suffers many setbacks including the death of an only child.

A Best Play (in our policy of citing certain special cases of OOB production); see page 169.

Encores! Great American Musicals in Concert. Schedule of three revivals presented in limited engagements. **Call Me Madam** (4). Book by Howard Lindsay and Russel Crouse; music and lyrics by Irving Berlin. Opened February 16, 1995. (Closed February 18, 1995) **Out of This World** (4). Book by Dwight Taylor and Reginald Lawrence; music and lyrics by Cole Porter. Opened March 30, 1995. (Closed April 1, 1995) **Pal Joey** (4). Book by John O'Hara; music by Richard Rodgers; lyrics by Lorenz Hart. Opened May 4, 1995. (Closed May 6, 1995). Produced by City Center, Judith E. Daykin executive director, and Encores, Walter Bobbie artistic director, at City Center.

ALL PLAYS: Musical direction, Rob Fisher; scenic consultant, John Lee Beatty; sound, Scott Lehrer; musical coordinator, Seymour Red Press; casting, Jay Binder; press, Philip Rinaldi, James Morrison, Kathy Haberthur.

The Coffee Club Orchestra (different ensembles made up from these musicians): Seymour Red Press, Harvey Estrin, Dennis Anderson, Lawrence Feldman, John Camo, Al Regni, Edward Zuhlke, Eugene Scholtens, Les Scott, Alva Hunt woodwinds; John Frosk, Lowell Hershey, Kamal Adilifu, Robert Millikan trumpet; Jack Gale, Dave Bargeron, Bruce Bonvissuto trombone; Roger Wendt, Kaitlin Mahoney, French horn; Bruce Doctor, Glenn Rhian, Sue Evans drums, percussion; Jay Berliner guitar; Joe Thalken, Robert Hirshhorn piano; Suzanne Ornstein, Alicia Edelberg concertmasters; Gayle Dixon, Maura Giannini, Joyce Hammann, Katherine Livolsi, Michael Roth, Belinda Whitney-Barratt, Paul Woodiel, Marilyn Reynolds, Masako Yanagita, Ashley Horne, Mia Wu violin; Barry Finclair, Jill Jaffe, Mitsue Takayama, Kathryn Kienke viola; Clay Ruede, Jeanne Le Blanc cello; John Beal, Dennis James bass; Lise Nadeau, Beth Robinson harp.

The 1995 *Encores!* season was dedicated to George Abbott, who was associated with the original productions of all of this season's shows.

CALL ME MADAM

Mrs. Sally Adams	Tyne Daly	Kenneth Gibson	Lewis Cleale
Mr. Gibson	John Leslie Wolfe	Sen. Brockbank	MacIntyre Dixon
Congressman Wilkins	Christopher Durang	Sen. Gallagher	Ken Page
Cosmo Constantine	Walter Charles	Princess Maria	Melissa Errico
Pemberton Maxwell	Peter Bartlett	Grand Duchess Sophie	Jane Connell
Sebastian Sebastian	Simon Jones	Grand Duke Otto	Gordon Connell

Singing Ensemble: Jamie Baer, John Clonts, Colleen Fitzpatrick, Michael Hayward-Jones, Dale Hensley, David Masenheimer, Beth McVey, Lori Brown Mirabal, Rebecca Spencer, Christianne Tisdale, Brent Weber, John Leslie Wolfe.

Dancers: Michael Berresse, Angelo Fraboni, Amy Heggins, JoAnn M. Hunter, Mary Ann Lamb, Darren Lee.

Directed by Charles Repole; concert adaptation, Bill Russell, Charles Repole; lighting, Richard Pilbrow, Dawn Chiang; choreography, Kathleen Marshall; apparel coordinator, Eduardo Sicangco; original orchestration, Don Walker; production stage manager, Clifford Schwartz.

Call Me Madam was first produced on Broadway 10/12/50 for 644 performances. This is its first major New York revival and the first complete *Best Plays* listing of its scenes and musical numbers.

ACT I

Overture .... Orchestra
Washington, D.C.
  "Mrs. Sally Adams" .... Company
  "The Hostess With the Mostes' on the Ball" .... Sally
  "Washington Square Dance" .... Sally, Company
The Grand Duchy of Lichtenburg
  Public Square
    "Lichtenburg" .... Cosmo, Company
  The Embassy
    "Can You Use Any Money Today" .... Sally
    "Marrying for Love" .... Sally, Cosmo
  Public Square
    "The Ocarina" .... Princess Maria, Company
    "It's a Lovely Day Today" .... Kenneth, Princess Maria, Ensemble
  The Embassy
    "It's a Lovely Day Today" (Reprise) .... Kenneth
    "The Best Thing for You" .... Sally, Cosmo
    "Can You Use Any Money Today?" (Reprise) .... Sally

ACT II

Entr'acte .... Orchestra
The Grand Duchy of Lichtenburg
  Public Square
    "Lichtenburg" .... Cosmo, Ensemble
  The Embassy
    "Something to Dance About" .... Sally, Company
    "Once Upon a Time Today" .... Kenneth
    "They Like Ike" .... Sen. Brockbank, Congressman Wilkins, Sen. Gallagher
    "It's a Lovely Day Today" (Reprise) .... Princess Maria, Kenneth
    "You're Just in Love" .... Kenneth, Sally
    "The Best Thing for You" (Reprise) .... Sally
Washington, D.C.
  "Mrs. Sally Adams" (Reprise) .... Company
  "You're Just in Love" (Reprise) .... Sally, Company

OUT OF THIS WORLD

Mercury	Peter Scolari	Night's Attendants	Blanche Hampton,
Jupiter	Ken Page		Noriko Naraoka
Helen	Marin Mazzie	Juno	Andrea Martin
Bartender	Francis Ruivivar	Chloe	La Chanze
Art O'Malley	Gregg Edelman	Niki Skolianos	Ernie Sabella
Night	Mary Ann Lamb		

Ensemble: Rachel Coloff, Andrea Green, Marc Heller, Dale Hensley, David Masenheimer, Chris Monteleone, Christiane Noll, Francis Ruivivar, John Scherer, Margaret Shafer, Dawn Spare, Elizabeth Walsh.

Directed by Mark Brokaw; concert adaptation, David Ives; lighting, Marc B. Weiss; choreography, John Carrafa; apparel coordinator, Jess Goldstein; original orchestration, Robert Russell Bennett; production stage manager, Michael F. Ritchie.

The last New York revival of record of *Out of This World* was by Equity Library Theater 11/30/62 for 9 performances. This is the first complete *Best Plays* listing of its scenes and musical numbers.

ACT I

Overture	Orchestra
"Prologue"	Mercury

Mt. Olympus
"I, Jupiter, I, Rex"	Jupiter, Male Ensemble

New York Bar & Mt. Olympus
"Use Your Imagination"	Helen, Mercury

Mt. Olympus
"Juno's Ride"	Ensemble
"I Got Beauty"	Juno, Ensemble

Arcadia Inn, Greece
"Maiden Fair"	Chloe, Female Ensemble
"Where, Oh, Where?"	Chloe
"They Couldn't Compare to You"	Mercury, Female Ensemble
"From This Moment On"	Art O'Malley, Helen
orchestration by Jonathan Tunick	
"What Do You Think About Men?"	Juno, Helen, Chloe
"Dance of the Long Night"	Night, Attendants
"You Don't Remind Me"	Jupiter
"I Sleep Easier Now"	Juno
"I Am Loved"	Helen

ACT II

Entr'acte	Orchestra

Mt. Olympus
"Climb Up the Mountain"	Juno, Ensemble
"Dance of the Dawn"	Night, Attendants

Arcadia Inn, Greece
"No Lover for Me"	Helen
"Cherry Pies Ought To Be You"	Mercury & Chloe, Juno & Niki
"Hark to the Song of the Night"	Jupiter
"Nobody's Chasing Me"	Juno

Arcadia Inn & Mt. Olympus
"From This Moment On" (Reprise)	Company

PAL JOEY

Joey Evans	Peter Gallagher	Vera Simpson	Patti LuPone
Mike Spears	Ron Orbach	Vera's Escorts	John Antony,
Gladys Bumps	Vicki Lewis		Christopher Sieber
The Kid	Lori Werner	Ernest (The Tailor); Victor	John Deyle
Terry	Mary Ann Lamb	Stage Manager; Hotel Manager	Jeff Brooks
Tilda	Dana Moore	Louis (The Tenor)	Arthur Rubin
Valerie	Mamie Duncan-Gibbs	Melba Snyder	Bebe Neuwirth
Diane	Nora Brennan	Ludlow Lowell	Ned Eisenberg
Janet	Lynn Sterling	Deputy Commissioner	
Linda English	Daisy Prince	O'Brien	Richard Council

Directed by Lonny Price; concert adaptation, Terrence McNally; lighting, Richard Pilbrow, Dawn Chiang; choreography, Joey McKneely; apparel coordinator, Gail Brassard; original orchestration, Hans Spialek; production stage manager, Perry Cline.

The last major New York revival of *Pal Joey* was by Circle in the Square on Broadway 6/27/76 for 73 performances.

Encores!

Left, Andrea Martin as Jur
in *Out of This World,* one
three Broadway musicals pr
sented this season in the Ci
Center's series of script-i
hand concert revivals

Above, Tyne Daly as Mrs.
Sally Adams with Walter
Charles as Cosmo in *Call Me
Madam; at right,* Patti LuPone
as Vera in *Pal Joey* at City
Center

The list of scenes and musical numbers in *Pal Joey* appears on pages 302–303 of *The Best Plays of 1951–52.*

The Old Lady's Guide to Survival (29). By Mayo Simon. Produced by Daniel Mayer Selznick at the Lamb's Theater. Opened February 16, 1995. (Closed March 5, 1995)

Netty...June Havoc
Shprintzy ....Shirl Bernheim

Directed by Alan Mandell; scenery, Douglas W. Schmidt; costumes, Marianna Elliott; lighting, Dennis Parichy; sound, Jim Capenos; production stage manager, Susan Slagle; press, Keith Sherman, Jim Byk, Stuart Ginsberg.

Comedy, the friendship of two elderly women mutually supporting each other. The play was presented in two parts.

Camping With Henry & Tom (88). By Mark St. Germain. Produced by Daryl Roth, Wind Dancer Theater Inc. and Randall L. Wreghitt in association with Lucille Lortel at the Lucille Lortel Theater. Opened February 20, 1995. (Closed May 7, 1995)

Henry Ford ....John Cunningham   Thomas Alva Edison ....Robert Prosky
Warren G. Harding.................. Ken Howard   Col. Edmund Starling ....John Prosky

Standbys: Robert Prosky—Ben Hammer; Messrs. Cunningham, Howard, John Prosky—Evan Thompson.

Directed by Paul Lazarus; scenery, James Leonard Joy; costumes, Ann Hould-Ward; lighting, Phil Monat; sound, Otts Munderloh; special effects, Gregory Meeh; dance consultant, Leah Kreutzer; casting, Stephanie Klapper; production stage manager, Renee Lutz; press, Philip Rinaldi, Barbara Carroll, James Morrison.

Time: July 24, 1921. Place: The woods outside Licking Creek, Md. The play was presented in two parts.

An author's note in the program describes the play as "a fiction suggested by facts. That President Harding went camping with Henry Ford and Thomas Edison is fact; their evening 'escape' from the media-packed campsite is fictional. Conversations are fictional, but based on factual events." Previously produced at the Berkshire Theater Festival, Stockbridge, Mass.

A Best Play; see page 187.

*The Compleat Works of Wllm Shkspr (Abridged) (100). Revue by Adam Long, Daniel Singer and Jess Winfield. Produced by Jeffrey Richards, Richard Gross and Jamie deRoy at the Westside Theater Downstairs. Opened February 26, 1995.

Christopher Duva
Peter Jacobson
Jon Patrick Walker

Directed by Jess Winfield; scenery, Edward Gianfrancesco; costumes, Sa Winfield; sound, Jim van Bergen; casting, Johnson-Liff Associates, Andrew Zerman; production stage manager, Mark Cole; stage manager, Karen Evanouskas; press, Jeffrey Richards Associates, Irene Gandy, Kevin Rehac.

Shakespeare excerpted at top speed in a spoof of academic pretensions and other conceits, originally produced by the Reduced Shakespeare Company of San Francisco, which has previously presented portions of this show in limited New York engagements. The show was presented in two parts.

Circus Life (16). By Murray Schisgal. Produced by Martin R. Kaufman, Mike Burstyn and Keith Langsdale at the Kaufman Theater. Opened February 27, 1995. (Closed March 12, 1995)

Nick Schwab ....Mike Burstyn   Barbara "Bobbie"
Howard Corey ....Keith Langsdale   Bluestone ....Tresha Rodriguez

Directed by Larry Arrick; scenery, Edward Gianfrancesco; costumes, Mimi Maxmen; lighting, Robert Jared; sound, Darren Clark; casting, Pat McCorkle; production stage manager, Andrea Testani; press, David Rothenberg.

Act I: The present, the law firm of Corey and Schwab. Act II: five weeks later.

Two middle-aged law partners in love with the same seductive female.

*Death Defying Acts (98). Program of three one-act comedies: *An Interview* by David Mamet, *Hotline* by Elaine May and *Central Park West* by Woody Allen. Produced by Julian Schlossberg and Jean Doumanian at the Variety Arts Theater. Opened March 6, 1995.

An Interview	Dorothy .... Linda Lavin
The Attorney .... Paul Guilfoyle	Delivery Boy .... Aasif Mandvi
The Attendant .... Gerry Becker	*Central Park West*
Hotline	Phyllis .... Debra Monk
Ken .... Gerry Becker	Carol .... Linda Lavin
Dr. Russell .... Paul Guilfoyle	Howard .... Gerry Becker
Marty .... Paul O'Brien	Sam .... Paul Guilfoyle
	Juliet .... Tari T. Signor

Standbys: Misses Lavin, Monk—Lauren Klein; Mr. Guilfoyle—Chuck Stransky, Paul O'Brien; Mr. Becker—Dan Desmond; Miss Signor—Jennifer London; Messrs. O'Brien, Mandvi—Dan Desmond, Chuck Stransky.

Directed by Michael Blakemore; scenery, Robin Wagner; costumes, Jane Greenwood; lighting, Peter Kaczorowski; sound, Jan Nebozenko; associate producers, Letty Aronson, Meyer Ackerman; casting, Stuart Howard, Amy Schecter; production supervisor, Steven Zweigbaum; press, Boneau/Bryan-Brown, Jackie Green, Andy Shearer.

In *An Interview,* a lawyer tries to argue his way past a guardian of the pearly gates. In *Hotline,* a would-be suicide tries to capture the attention and concern of a support group. In *Central Park West,* a husband is the target of competition between three women, one of them his wife.

*Swingtime Canteen (91). Musical with book by Linda Thorsen Bond, William Repicci and Charles Busch; music from 1940s Hit Parade songs. Produced by William Repicci and Michael Minichiello in association with Ken Jillson, Robert Massimi and Patricia Greenwald at the Blue Angel. Opened March 14, 1995.

Marian Ames .... Alison Fraser	Jo Sterling; Drums .... Marcy McGuigan
Topeka Abotelli; Piano .... Debra Barsha	Lilly McBain; Saxophone;
Katie Gammersflugel .... Emily Loesser	Banjo .... Jackie Sanders

Side Musicians: Kim Bonsanti—WAC, trumpet, flugelhorn; Mary Ann McSweeney—WAC, bass violin, piano; Micki Ryan—WAC, clarinet, saxophone.

Directed by Kenneth Elliott; choreography, Barry McNabb; musical direction and supervision, Lawrence Yurman; scenery, B.T. Whitehill; costumes, Robert Mackintosh; lighting, Michael Lincoln; sound, Fox & Perla, Ltd.; arrangements and orchestrations, Bob McDowell; special material, Dick Gallagher; associate producers, Mel Borowka, James H. Ellis, Joyce M. Sarner, Michael Estwanik; casting, Stephanie Klapper; production stage manager, J. Andrew Burgreen; press, David Rothenberg Associates.

Time: 1944. Place: Onstage at a concert for the Eighth Air Force in London. The play was presented without intermission.

Group of women entertain the troops with songs by such as Frank Loesser, Johnny Mercer, Jimmy Van Heusen and Harry Warren. Previously produced at the Bay Street Theater Festival, Sag Harbor, N.Y.

*The Only Thing Worse You Could Have Told Me ... (67). Solo performance by Dan Butler; written by Dan Butler. Produced by Scott Allyn at Actor's Playhouse. Opened April 2, 1995.

Directed by Randy Brenner; scenery, James Noone; costumes, Parker Poole; lighting, Ken Billington; sound, Jim van Bergen; associate producer, Robert M. Browne; production stage manager, M.A. Howard; press, Cromarty & Company, Peter Cromarty, Hugh Hayes.

The Evening: Jimmy, Questions, Looking Good, Tommy Bastress, Conversations With My Mother, Act Up, Dancer, Joey, Critic I, Derek, Critic II, Precious, Critic III, The Only Thing Worse . . . , Leslie. The show was presented without intermission.

Panoramic view of contemporary gay culture, with Butler portraying a dozen characters in a series of vignettes. Previously produced in regional theater at Theater Geo, Los Angeles.

*__London Suite__ (60). Program of four one-act plays by Neil Simon: *Settling Accounts, Going Home, Diana & Sidney* and *The Man on the Floor.* Produced by Emanuel Azenberg and Leonard Soloway at the Union Square Theater. Opened April 9, 1995.

Settling Accounts

Brian	Jeffrey Jones
Billy	Paxton Whitehead

Going Home

Lauren	Kate Burton
Mrs. Semple	Carole Shelley

Diana & Sidney

Diana	Carole Shelley
Grace	Kate Burton
Sidney	Paxton Whitehead

The Man on the Floor

Mark	Jeffrey Jones
Annie	Kate Burton
Mrs. Sitgood	Carole Shelley
Bellman	Brooks Ashmanskas
Dr. McMerlin	Paxton Whitehead

Understudies: Miss Shelley—Patricia Kilgarriff; Mr. Whitehead—Paul Hecht; Miss Burton—Monique Fowler; Mr. Jones—Munson Hicks; Mr. Ashmanskas—Augie Mericola.

Directed by Daniel Sullivan; scenery, John Lee Beatty; costumes, Jane Greenwood; lighting, Ken Billington; sound, Tom Clark; associate producer, Ginger Montel; casting, Jay Binder; production stage manager, John Vivian; stage manager, Augie Mericola; press, Bill Evans & Associates, Jim Randolph, Terry M. Lilly, Tom D'Ambrosio.

Time: The present. Place: A hotel in London. The play was presented in two parts with the intermission following *Going Home.*

In "an old but very fashionable hotel in London, much like the Connaught," a Welsh writer is quarreling with his larcenous business manager in *Settling Accounts;* a mother and her daughter are at the end of a shopping trip, principally for shoes, in *Going Home;* and a bad back and missing Wimbledon tickets plague a New York couple in *The Man on the Floor.* in *Diana & Sidney,* a couple we have met before in the author's *California Suite*—an Oscar-nominated actress and her bisexual husband—are meeting for the first time in many years after their divorce. The program was previously presented in regional theater at Seattle Repertory Theater.

*__Travels With My Aunt__ (57). Adapted by Giles Havergal from the novel by Graham Greene. Produced by Bill Kenwright at the Minetta Lane Theater. Opened April 12, 1995.

CAST: Henry Pulling, Augusta Bertram—Jim Dale; Henry Pulling, Richard Pulling, A Vicar, Miss Keene, Tooley, Italian Girl, Frau General Schmidt, O'Toole, Yolanda—Brian Murray; Henry Pulling, Taxi Driver, Wordsworth, Det. Sgt. Sparrow, Hatty, Mr. Visconti, Col. Hakim, Miss Paterson, Spanish Gentleman—Martin Rayner; Henry Pulling, Girl in Jodhpurs, Wolf, Hotel Receptionist, Bodyguard—Tom Beckett.

Understudies: Mr. Dale—Tom Beckett; Messrs. Beckett, Murray, Rayner—Michael Lasswell.

Directed by Giles Havergal; scenery and costumes, Stewart Laing; lighting, Gerry Jenkinson; casting, Pat McCorkle; production stage manager, Jane Grey; press, Philip Rinaldi, James Morrison.

Henry Pulling (played by all four actors) meets his aunt at his mother's funeral and is taken by her on an eventful journey, as in the 1969 novel. A foreign play previously produced at Citizen's Theater, Glasgow; London (two 1993 Olivier Awards), and the Long Wharf Theater, New Haven, Conn.

The Cryptogram (62). By David Mamet. Produced by Frederick Zollo, Nicholas Paleologos, Gregory Mosher and Jujamcyn Theaters in association with Herb Alpert and Margo Lion in the American Repertory Theater production at the Westside Theater. Opened April 13, 1995. (Closed June 4, 1995)

John	Shelton Dane	Donny	Felicity Huffman
Del	Ed Begley Jr.		

Directed by David Mamet; scenery, John Lee Beatty; costumes, Harriet Voyt; lighting, Dennis Parichy; associate director, Scott Zigler; co-producers, Evangeline Morphos, Nancy Richards; associate producers, Joan Firestone, Richard Firestone; casting, Bernard Telsey Casting; production stage manager, Carol Dawes; stage manager, Rebecca C. Monroe; press, Bill Evans & Associates, Jim Randolph, Terry M. Lilly, Tom D'Ambrosio.

Time: 1959. Place: Donny's living room. Scene 1: One evening. Scene 2: The next night. Scene 3: One month later, evening. The play was presented without intermission.

A child is at the center of pressures exerted by his mother, her gay friend and his absent father, vaguely sensed but clearly felt. Previously produced at the Ambassadors Theater in London and the American Repertory Theater in Cambridge, Mass.

A Best Play; see page 247.

*Party (24). By David Dillon. Produced by Michael Leavitt, Fox Theatricals, Leonard Soloway, Peter Breger, Jerry Frankel, Dennis J. Grimaldi and Steven M. Levy at the Douglas Fairbanks Theater. Opened May 11, 1995.

Kevin	David Pevsner	Peter	Tom Stuart
Ray	Ted Bales	James	Jay Corcoran
Philip	Larry Alexander	Andy	Vince Gatton
Brian	Kellum Lewis		

Understudies: Messrs. Gatton, Stuart—Eric Bernat; Messrs. Lewis, Corcoran, Alexander—Brian Keith Lewis.

Directed by David Dillon; scenery, James Noone; costumes, Gail Cooper-Hecht; lighting, Ken Billington; sound, Tom Clark; associate producer, Libby Adler Mages; casting, Alan Filderman; production stage manager, Bruce Greenwood; press, Bill Evans & Associates, Jim Randolph, Terry M. Lilly, Tom D'Ambrosio.

Time: Tonight. Place: The living room of Kevin's apartment in New York City. The play was presented without intermission.

Comedy about seven gay men playing a truth-or-dare game in which they finally strip to the buff. Originally produced by Bailiwick Repertory, Chicago.

*Coming Through (14). Adapted by Wynn Handman from recorded interviews of the Ellis Island Oral History Project. Produced by American Place Theater, Wynn Handman artistic director, Susannah Halston executive director, at American Place Theater. Opened May 14, 1995.

CAST: David Kener, Shawn McNesby, Thomas Pennacchini, Mara Stephens, David Warren.

Directed by Wynn Handman; scenery, Vladimir Shpitalnik; costumes, Kim Wilcox; lighting, Rui Rita; assistant to the director, Dina Brody; production stage manager, Sue Jane Stoker; press, Jonathan Slaff.

Accounts of immigrants who came to America through Ellis Island, portraying their resilience and ingenuity. The play was presented without intermission.

The Acting Company. Repertory of two revivals in a limited engagement. **A Doll's House** (3). By Henrik Ibsen; translated by Gerry Bamman and Irene B. Berman. Opened May 15, 1995. **Othello** (6). by William Shakespeare. Opened May 15, 1995. Produced by the Acting Company, Margot Harley producing director, Pegge Logefeil managing director, at TriBeCa Performing Arts Center. (Repertory closed May 25, 1995)

PERFORMER	"A DOLL'S HOUSE"	"OTHELLO"
Gregory Lamont Allen		Solino
Kathleen Christal	Mrs. Kristine Linde	Bianca
Stevie Ray Dallimore	Henrik	Montano
Frank Deal		Duke of Venice
Kate Forbes	Nora Helmer	Desdemona
Allen Gilmore		Iago
Ezra Knight		Othello
Mark Lewis	Torvald Helmer	Lodovico

Derek Meader	Dr. Rank	Brabantio
Kevin Orton		Roderigo
Andy Paterson		Gratiano; Clown
Shona Tucker	Nurse Anne Marie	Emilia
Anthony Ward	Nils Krogstad	Cassio

A DOLL'S HOUSE: Helmer Children—Emily and Ted Kaplan or Ada and Gabriel Meyers.

Understudies: Miss Forbes—Kathleen Christal; Mr. Lewis—Stevie Ray Dallimore; Mr. Meader—Frank Deal; Mr. Ward—Kevin Orton; Miss Christal—Shona Tucker; Miss Tucker—Felicia Wilson.

Directed by Zelda Fichandler; scenery, Douglas Stein; costumes, Marjorie Slaiman; sound, Susan R. White; vocal consultant, Deborah Hecht.

Time: the end of the 19th century. Place: the home of Torvald and Nora Helmer, Christiana, Norway. Act I: the day before Christmas. Act II: Christmas Day. Act III: the following night.

This production of *A Doll's House* was presented last season at the Public Theater 5/20/94 for 3 performances, after its premiere 3/5/94 at the University of Texas at Austin.

OTHELLO: Cypriots—Frank Deal, Mark Lewis, Derek Meader.

Directed by Penny Mitropulos; scenery, Michael Vaughn Sims; costumes, James Scott; sound and music, Deena Kaye; fight choreographer and movement consultant, Felix Ivanov; voice and text consultant, Eva Wielgat Barnes.

Place: The city of Venice and the isle of Cyprus. The play was presented in two parts.

The premiere of this production of *Othello* took place at the Albert Bair Theater, Billings, Mont. on 2/1/95. The last major New York revival of the play was in the Public Theater's Shakespeare Marathon 6/21/91 for 21 performances.

BOTH PLAYS: Lighting, Dennis Parichy; casting, Barbara Hipkiss; production stage manager, Daniel L. Bello; press, Jeffrey Richards Associates, Kevin Rehac.

*__Loose Lips__ (16). Comedy revue conceived and written by Kurt Andersen, Lisa Birnbach and Jamie Malanowski. Produced by Channel Zero in association with Martin & McCall Productions at the Triad. Opened May 18, 1995.

James Biberi	Keith Primi
Scott Bryant	Ingrid Rockefeller
Sara Pratter	Luke Toma

Directed by Martin Charnin; scenery, Ken Foy; costumes, Joan Vass; lighting, Ken Billington; incidental music, Keith Levenson; production stage manager, Nancy Wernick; press, Cromarty & Company, Peter Cromarty, Philip Thurston.

Transcripts of records, quotations and other sources, reenacted in a comedy vein.

*__Fortune's Fools__ (9). By Frederick Stroppel. Produced by Stewart F. Lane at the Cherry Lane Theater. Opened May 24, 1995.

| Jay Morrison | Tuc Watkins | Gail Hildebrandt | Dorrie Joiner |
| Chuck Galluccio | Danton Stone | Bonnie Sparks | Marissa Chibas |

Directed by John Rando; scenery and projections, Loren Sherman; costumes, David Murin; lighting, Phil Monat; sound, Jim van Bergen; casting, Hughes Moss Casting; production stage manager, Christopher De Camillis; press, Keith Sherman & Associates, Jim Byk, Stuart Ginsberg.

Comedy, two Generation X couples cope with marriage. The play was presented in two parts.

CAST REPLACEMENTS AND TOURING COMPANIES

Compiled by Jeffrey A. Finn

The following is a list of the major cast replacements of record in productions which opened in previous years, but were still playing in New York during a substantial part of the 1994–95 season; or were on a first-class tour in 1994–95.

The name of each major role is listed in *italics* beneath the title of the play in the first column. In the second column directly opposite appears the name of the actor who created the role in the original New York production (whose opening date appears in *italics* at the top of the column). In shows of the past five years, indented immediately beneath the original actor's name are the names of subsequent New York replacements, together with the date of replacement when available. In shows that have run longer than five years, only this season's or the most recent cast replacements are listed under the names of the original cast members.

The third column gives information about first-class touring companies. When there is more than one roadshow company, #1, #2, etc., appear before the name of the performer who created the role in each company (and the city and date of each company's first performance appears in *italics* at the top of the column). Their subsequent replacements are also listed beneath their names in the same manner as the New York companies, with dates when available.

ALL IN THE TIMING

New York 2/17/94

Robert Stanton
  Jason Graae 9/94
  Ray Wills 1/95

Nancy Opel
  Jan Neuberger 2/95

Michael Countryman
  Philip Hoffman 9/94
  Stuart Zagnit 1/95

Wendy Lawless
  Kathy Morath 9/94

Ted Neustadt
  Danny Burstein 11/94

ANGELS IN AMERICA

	Part I, New York 5/4/93 *Part II, New York 11/23/93*	*Chicago 2/26/95*
Roy Cohn	Ron Leibman F. Murray Abraham 1/11/94	Jonathan Hadary

368

Prior Walter	Stephen Spinella	Robert Sella
Joe Pitt	David Marshall Grant	Philip Earl Johnson
Harper Pitt	Marcia Gay Harden Susan Bruce 1/94 Cynthia Nixon 4/94	Kate Goehring
Belize	Jeffrey Wright	Reg Flowers
Angel	Ellen McLaughlin	Carolyn Swift
Hannah Pitt	Ellen McLaughlin	Barbara Robertson

BEAUTY AND THE BEAST

	New York 4/18/94	*Los Angeles 4/12/95*
Beast	Terrence Mann Jeff McCarthy	Terrence Mann
Belle	Susan Egan Sarah Uriarte	Susan Egan
Lefou	Kenny Raskin	Jaime Torcelinni
Gaston	Burke Moses Marc Kudisch	Burke Moses
Maurice	Tom Bosley MacIntyre Dixon Tom Bosley Kurt Knudson	Tom Bosley
Cogsworth	Heath Lamberts	Fred Applegate
Lumiere	Gary Beach Lee Roy Reams	Gary Beach
Babette	Stacey Logan	Heather Lee
Mrs. Potts	Beth Fowler Cass Morgan	Beth Fowler

BLOOD BROTHERS

	New York 4/25/93	*Dallas 9/6/94*
Mrs. Johnson	Stephanie Lawrence Petula Clark Carole King Regina O'Malley Helen Reddy	Petula Clark
Narrator	Warwick Evans Richard Cox Adrian Zmed Richard Cox Domenick Allen 2/7/95	Mark McGrath
Mickey	Con O'Neill David Cassidy Philip Lehl	David Cassidy

Eddie	Mark Michael Hutchinson	Tif Luckinbill
	Shaun Cassidy	
	Ric Ryder	
Mrs. Lyons	Barbara Walsh	Priscilla Quinby
	Regina O'Malley	
Linda	Jan Graveson	Yvette Lawrence
	Shauna Hicks	

CAROUSEL

New York 3/24/44

Billy Bigelow	Michael Hayden
	James Barber 12/94
Julie Jordan	Sally Murphy

CATS

	New York 10/7/82	*#1 National tour 1993–94* *#2 National tour 1/94*
Alonzo	Hector Jaime Mercado Hans Kriefall	#1 William Patrick Dunne #2 William Patrick Dunne
Bustopher	Stephen Hanan Joel Briel Richard Poole	#1 Buddy Crutchfield #2 Richard Poole William R. Park
Bombalurina	Donna King Marlene Danielle	#1 Wendy Walter #2 Helen Frank
Cassandra	Rene Ceballos Amy N. Henning Sara Henry Ida Gilliams	#1 Laura Quinn #2 Laura Quinn Stephanie Lang
Coricopat	Rene Clemente David E. Liddell James Hadley	(not in tour)

Demeter	Wendy Edmead
	Mercedes Perez
		#1 N. Elaine Wiggins
		#2 N. Elaine Wiggins
		   J. Kathleen Lamb
		   Susan Lamontagne

Grizabella	Betty Buckley Liz Callaway	#1 Mary Gutzi #2 Mary Gutzi Jeri Sager
Jellylorum	Bonnie Simmons Nina Hennessey	#1 Linda Strassler #2 Patty Goble Jean Arbiter
Jennyanydots	Anna McNeely Carol Dilley	#1 Alice C. DeChant #2 Alice C. DeChant
Mistoffeles	Timothy Scott Lindsay Chambers	#1 Christopher Gattelli #2 Christopher Gattelli Joseph Favolora

Mungojerrie	Rene Clemente Roger Kachel	#1 Gavan Palmer #2 Gavan Palmer Ned Hannah Billy Johnstone
Munkustrup	Harry Groener Keith Bernardo	#1 Robert Amirante #2 Robert Amirante Randy Clements
Old Deuteronomy	Ken Page Ken Prymus	#1 Jimmy Lockett #2 John Treacy Egan Larry Small Doug Eskew
Plato/Macavity	Kenneth Ard Jim T. Ruttman Philip Michael Baskerville	#1 Taylor Wicker #2 Steve Bertles Taylor Wicker
Pouncival	Herman W. Sebek Jacob Brent	#1 Joey Gyondla #2 Joey Gyondla Randy Andre Davis
Rum Tum Tugger	Terrence Mann David Hibbard	#1 David Hibbard #2 Ron Seykell Ron DeVito J. Robert Spencer
Rumpleteazer	Christine Langner Jennifer Cody Jeanine Meyers Kristi Sperling	#1 Jennifer Cody #2 Jennifer Cody Maria Jo Ralabate
Sillabub	Whitney Kershaw Bethany Samuelson	#1 Bethany Samuelson #2 Lanene Charters
Skimbleshanks	Reed Jones Eric Scott Kincaid	#1 Carmen Yurich #2 Carmen Yurich Mickey Nugent Blair Bybee
Tantomile	Janet L. Hubert Jill Nicklaus	(not in tour)
Tumblebrutus	Robert Hoshour Levensky Smith	#1 Tim Hunter #2 Joseph Favalora Tim Hunter
Victoria	Cynthia Onrubia Nadine Isenegger	#1 Tricia Mitchell #2 Tricia Mitchell Kirstie Tice

Note: Only this season's or the most recent cast replacements are listed above under the names of the original cast members. For previous replacements, see previous volumes of *Best Plays*.

CRAZY FOR YOU

	New York 2/19/92	*Dallas 5/11/93*
Polly Baker	Jodi Benson Karen Ziemba	Karen Ziemba Crista Moore Beverly Ward
Bobby Child	Harry Groener James Brennan 1/2/95	James Brennan Kirby Ward

Lank Hawkins	John Hillner	Chris Coucill
		Daren Kelly
Tess	Beth Leavel	Cathy Susan Pyles
	Melinda Buckley	
Bela Zangler	Bruce Adler	Stuart Zagnit
	John Jellison	Paul Keith
	Bruce Adler	
Irene Roth	Michele Pawk	Kay McClelland
	Kay McClelland	Belle Callaway
	Sandy Edgerton	Riette Burdick
	Kay McClelland	
	Sandy Edgerton	
Mother	Jane Connell	Lanka Peterson
		Ann B. Davis
Everett Baker	Ronn Carroll	Carleton Carpenter
	Carleton Carpenter	Al Checco
	Roger Horchow	Raymond Thorne
	Carleton Carpenter	
	John Jellison	
	Al Checco	
	John Jellison	
Eugene	Stephen Temperley	Geoffrey Wade
		John Curless
Patricia	Amelia White	Jeanette Landis
	Colleen Smith Wallnau	(part dropped)
Patsy	Stacey Logan	Sally Boyet
	Jill Matson	Joan Leslie Simms

DAMN YANKEES

New York 3/3/94

Applegate	Victor Garber
	Jerry Lewis 3/12/95
Lola	Bebe Neuwirth
	Nancy Ticotin
	Charlotte D'Amboise 3/12/95
Joe Hardy	Jarrod Emick
	Jason Workman
	Jarrod Emick
	Eric Kunze
Joe Boyd	Dennis Kelly
Gloria Thorpe	Vicki Lewis
	Liz Larsen 3/12/95
Meg Boyd	Linda Stephens
Sister	Susan Mansur
Benny Van Buren	Dick Latessa

BEAUTY AND THE BEAST—Sarah Uriarte as Belle and Jeff McCarthy as Beast

THE FANTASTICKS

	New York 5/3/60
El Gallo	Jerry Orbach John Savarese
Luisa	Rita Gardner Natasha Harper Lisa Mayer Kristin Chenoweth
Matt	Kenneth Nelson Josh Miller

Note: Only this season's or the most recent cast replacements are listed above under the names of the original cast members. For previous replacements, see previous volumes of *Best Plays.*

GREASE

	New York 5/11/94	*Syracuse—9/19/94*
Vince Fontaine	Brian Bradley Micky Dolenz Brian Bradley	Davy Jones Micky Dolenz

Miss Lynch	Marcia Lewis Mimi Hines JoAnne Worley	Sally Struthers Dody Goodman
Betty Rizzo	Rosie O'Donnell Maureen McCormick Brooke Shields Joely Fisher Tia Riebling	Angela Pupello
Doody	Sam Harris Ray Walker	Scott Beck Ric Ryder
Kenickie	Jason Opsahl	Douglas Crawford
Roger	Hunter Foster	Nick Cavarra Erick Buckley
Sonny Latierri	Carlos Lopez Brad Kane Nick Cavarra	Danny Cistone
Frenchy	Jessica Stone Monica Lee Gradischek	Beth Lipari
Jan	Heather Stokes	Robin Irwin
Marty	Megan Mullally Sherie Rene Scott Leah Hocking	Deirdre O'Neil
Danny Zuko	Ricky Paull Goldin Adrian Zmed Ricky Paull Goldin Jon Secada	Rex Smith Adrian Zmed
Sandy Dumbrowski	Susan Wood Susan Moniz	Trisha M. Gorman
Patty Simcox	Michelle Blakely Christine Toy Carrie Ellen Austin	Melissa Papp
Eugene Florczyk	Paul Castree	Christopher Youngsman
Cha-Cha DiGregorio	Sandra Purpuro Jennifer Cody	Jennifer Cody Michelle Bombacie
Teen Angel	Billy Porter Mary Bond Davis Charles Gray Jennifer Holliday Charles Gray	Kevin-Anthony

GUYS AND DOLLS

	New York 4/14/92	*Hartford 9/15/92*
Sky Masterson	Peter Gallagher Tom Wopat 10/12/92 Burke Moses 4/12/93 Tom Wopat Martin Vidnovic	Richard Muenz

Nathan Detroit	Nathan Lane	Lewis J. Stadlen
	Jonathan Hadary 5/17/93	David Garrison
	Jamie Farr 3/15/94	Philip LeStrange
	Jeff Brooks	Steve Landesberg
Sarah Brown	Josie de Guzman	Patricia Ben Peterson
	Kim Crosby	
Miss Adelaide	Faith Prince	Lorna Luft
	Jennifer Allen	Beth McVey

HYSTERICAL BLINDNESS

New York 5/19/94

| *Storyteller* | Leslie Jordan |
| | Mark Baker 8/11/94 |

AN INSPECTOR CALLS

New York 4/27/94

Sybil Berling	Rosemary Harris
	Sian Phillips
Edna	Jan Owen
Arthur Berling	Philip Bosco
	Roy Cooper
Gerald Croft	Aden Gillett
	Maxwell Caulfield
Sheila Berling	Jane Adams
	Susannah Hoffmann
Eric Berling	Marcus D'Amico
	Harry Carnahan
Inspector Goole	Kenneth Cranham
	Nicholas Woodeson
Boy	Christopher Marquette
	Frank John Galasso

KISS OF THE SPIDER WOMAN

	New York 5/3/93	*Tampa 11/1/94*
Molina	Brent Carver	Juan Chioran
	Jeff Hyslop	Jeff Hyslop
	Howard McGillin 6/6/94	Juan Chioran
Warden	Herndon Lackey	Mark Zimmerman
Valentin	Anthony Crivello	John Dossett
	Brian Mitchell	Dorian Harewood
Spider Woman/Aurora	Chita Rivera	Chita Rivera
	Vanessa Williams 6/27/94	Carol Lawrence
	Maria Conchita Alonso 3/20/95	Chita Rivera

| *Molina's Mother* | Merle Louise
Mimi Turque | Rita Gardner |
| *Marta* | Kirsti Carnahan | Juliet Lambert |

LAUGHTER ON THE 23RD FLOOR

	New York 11/22/93	*Detroit 1/10/95*
Lucas	Stephen Mailer	Matthew Arkin
Milt	Lewis J. Stadlen	Lewis J. Stadlen
Carol	Randy Graff	Alison Martin
Max Prince	Nathan Lane	Howard Hesseman
Val	Mark Linn-Baker	Michael Countryman
Brian	J.K. Simmons	J.K. Simmons
Kenny	John Slattery	Anthony Cummings
Helen	Bitty Schram	Michelle Schumacher
Ira	Ron Orbach	Alan Blumenfeld

LES MISERABLES

	New York 3/12/87	*Tampa 11/18/88*
Jean Valjean	Colm Wilkinson Donn Cook	Gary Barker William Solo
Javert	Terrence Mann Merwin Foard	Peter Samuel Richard Kinsey
Fantine	Randy Graff Paige O'Hara	Hollis Resnik Jacqueline Piro
Enjolras	Michael Maguire Ron Bohmer	Greg Zerkle Robert Vernon
Marius	David Bryant Craig Rubano	Matthew Porretta Tom Donoghue
Cosette	Judy Kuhn Tamra Hayden	Jacqueline Piro Jodie Langel
Eponine	Frances Ruffelle Jessica Snow-Wilson	Michele Maika Caryn Lyn Manuel
Thenardier	Leo Burmester Drew Eshelman	Paul Ainsley J.P. Dougherty
Mme. Thenardier	Jennifer Butt Gina Ferrall	Linda Kerns Kelly Ebsary

Note: Only this season's or the most recent cast replacements are listed above under the names of the original cast members. For previous replacements, see previous volumes of *Best Plays*.

MISS SAIGON

	New York 4/11/91	#1 Chicago 10/12/93 #2 Seattle 3/16/95
The Engineer	Jonathan Pryce Francis Ruivivar 8/19/91 Jonathan Pryce 9/30/91 Francis Ruivivar 12/16/91 Herman Sebek Alan Muraoka Raul Aranas	#1 Raul Aranas Kevin Gray #2 Thom Sesma
Kim	Lea Salonga Lelia Florentino 3/16/92 Rona Figueroa Emy Baysic (alt.)	#1 Jennie Kwan Jennifer C. Paz (alt.) Jennifer C. Paz Hazel Raymundo (alt.) Melanie Mariko Tojio (alt.) #2 Deedee Lynn Magno Cristina Paras (alt.)
Chris	Willy Falk Sean McDermott 12/16/91 Chris Peccaro Jarrod Emick Eric Kunze	#1 Jarrod Emick Eric Kunze Peter Lockyer #2 Matt Bogart

THE PHANTOM OF THE OPERA

	New York 1/26/88	#1 Los Angeles 5/31/90 #2 Chicago 5/24/90 #3 Seattle 12/13/92
The Phantom	Michael Crawford Davis Gaines	#1 Michael Crawford Frank D'Ambrosio #2 Mark Jacoby Rick Hilsabeck #3 Frank D'Ambrosio Grant Norman
Christine Daae	Sarah Brightman Tracy Shayne Laurie Gayle Stephenson (alt.)	#1 Dale Kristien Lisa Vroman Cristin Mortenson #2 Karen Culliver Sarah Pfisterer Rita Harvey (alt.) #3 Tracy Shane Diane Frantantoni Susan Facer (alt.)
Raoul	Steve Barton Brad Little	#1 Reece Holland Aloysius Gigl #2 Keith Buterbaugh Nat Chandler #3 Ciaran Sheehan John Schroeder

Note: Alternates play the role of Christine Daae Monday and Wednesday evenings. Only this season's or the most recent cast replacements are listed above under the names of the original cast members. For previous replacements, see previous volumes of *Best Plays*.

THE SISTERS ROSENSWEIG

	New York 3/18/93	*Norfolk, Va. 1/7/94*
Sara Goode	Jane Alexander Michael Learned 8/16/93	Mariette Hartley Linda Thorson
Gorgeous Teitelbaum	Madeline Kahn Linda Lavin 8/16/93	Caroline Aaron Nancy Dussault
Pfeni Rosensweig	Christine Estabrook Joanne Camp	Joan McMurtrey Stephanie Dunham
Mervyn Kant	Robert Klein Hal Linden 8/16/93 Tony Roberts 1/18/94	Charles Cioffi Greg Mullavey

THREE TALL WOMEN

	New York 4/5/94
A	Myra Carter Lucille Patton Marian Seldes
B	Marian Seldes Joan Van Ark
C	Jordan Baker Christina Rouner
The Boy	Michael Rhodes

THE WHO'S TOMMY

	New York 4/22/93	*Dallas 10/12/93*
Tommy Walker	Michael Cerveris Peter Ermides	Steve Isaacs
Captain Walker	Jonathan Dokuchitz J. Mark McVey	Jason Workman Jordan Leeds
Mrs. Walker	Marcia Mitzman Laura Dean Jessica Molaskey Christy Tarr	Jessica Molaskey Christy Tarr
Uncle Ernie	Paul Kandel	William Youmans Stephen Lee Anderson
Cousin Kevin	Anthony Barrile	Roger Bart Michael Arnold
The Gypsy	Cheryl Freeman	Kennya Ramsey
Sally Simpson	Sherie Scott Lacey Hornkohl	Hilary Morse
Tommy, Age 10	Buddy Smith Travis Jordan Greisler Michael Zeidman	Robert Mann Keyser Brett Levenson

Tommy, Age 4	Carly Jane Steinborn	Kelly Mady (alt.)
	Crysta Macalush	Caitlin Newman (alt.)
	Emily Hart	Rachel Ben Levenson (alt.)
	Kimberly Hannon	
	Nicole Zeidman	

OTHER SHOWS
ON FIRST CLASS TOURS IN 1994–95

HELLO, DOLLY!

Denver 7/12/94

Mrs. Dolly Gallagher Levi	Carol Channing
Ernestina	Monica M. Wemitt
Ambrose Kemper	James Darrah
Horace Vandergelder	Jay Garner
Ermengarde	Christine DeVito
Cornelius Hackl	Michael DeVries
Barnaby Tucker	Cory English
Minnie Fay	Lori Ann Mahl
Irene Molloy	Florence Lacey
Mrs. Rose	Elizabeth Green
Rudolph	Steve Pudenz
Stanley	Julian Brightman
Judge	Bill Bateman

JELLY'S LAST JAM

Hartford 10/25/94

Jelly Roll Morton	Maurice Hines
Chimney Man	Mel Johnson Jr.
Anita	Nora Cole
Young Jelly	Savion Glover
Jack the Bear	Stanley Wayne Mathis
Miss Mamie	Cleo King
Gran Mimi	Freda Payne
Buddy Bolden	Ted L. Levy

JOSEPH AND THE AMAZING TECHNICOLOR DREAMCOAT

West Point, NY— 1/13/95

Joseph	Sam Harris
Narrator	Kristine Fraelich
Jacob/Potiphar/Guru	Russell Leib
Pharaoh	John Ganun
Butler	Glenn Sneed
Baker	Paul J. Gallagher
Mrs. Potiphar	Justine DiCostanzo
	Mindy Franzese

THE SOUND OF MUSIC

Baltimore—11/29/93

Maria Rainer	Marie Osmond
Capt. Georg Von Trapp	Laurence Guittard
	Neal Ben-Ari
Liesl	Vanessa Dorman
Friedrich	Erik McCormack
	James J. Kee
Louisa	Laura Bundy
	Mandy Henderson
Kurt	Stephen Blosil
Brigitta	Sara Zelle
Marta	Jacy DeFilippo
	Christy Romano
Gretl	Lisbeth Zelle
Rolf Gruber	Richard H. Blake
Elsa Schraeder	Jane Seaman
	Lauren Thompson
Max Detweiler	John Tillotson
	Terry Runnels
Mother Abbess	Claudia Cummings

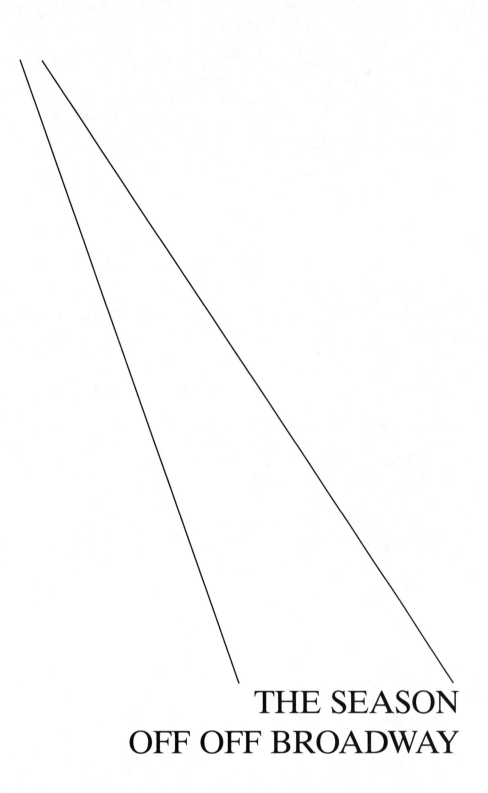

THE SEASON
OFF OFF BROADWAY

OFF OFF BROADWAY

○   *By Mel Gussow*

AFTER only four years of operation, the Signature Theater Company has become an integral part of off off Broadway and a significant force in the American theater. As artistic director, James Houghton had the idea of devoting an entire season to a single playwright. For the first season, the choice was Romulus Linney, and he was followed by Lee Blessing, Edward Albee and Horton Foote, four exceptional American dramatists, each represented by a selection of his strongest recent work. During his Signature year, Albee won the Pulitzer Prize for Drama, although not for one of the plays produced at that theater. In 1995, Foote won his Pulitzer for a play done at the Signature, *The Young Man From Atlanta,* named in this volume as one of the ten Best Plays.

The Young Man From Atlanta, one of four Footes new to New York this season, is a challenging work for the author, but not in my opinion the best of the four plays. That honor would go to *Talking Pictures,* which opened the Signature series and was apparently ineligible for a Pulitzer because it had already been produced in regional theater. Ostensibly, the prize was in recognition of the entire Foote festival, and, in a broader sense, for the playwright's rich body of work.

Moving and melancholic, *The Young Man From Atlanta* is characteristic of its author, while also acting as a change of pace in that it has a homosexual subtext. After the death of their adult son, a married couple tries to come to terms with inexplicable elements in his life as well as their own shared loneliness. The mother (Carlin Glynn), grasping for memories, allows herself to be taken advantage of by a mysterious and demanding friend of the son, as the father (Ralph Waite) tries to awaken her to her gullibility. On the sidelines is James Pritchett as Ms. Glynn's well-meaning but helpless stepfather. All three delivered beautifully modulated performances under the direction of Peter Masterson.

Talking Pictures was an even more resonant play, a lovely portrait of a stressful Texas family in the 1920s. At the center is an archetypal Foote character, a lonely single parent who plays the piano for silent movies and finds her career closing down and her personal life in limbo. Hallie Foote, the playwright's daughter, suffused the character with a transforming tenderness. This was a small canvas but one painted with the most precise painterly strokes. Sensitively directed by Carol Goodheart,

383

Talking Pictures is cited as an outstanding 1995 OOB production. A citation could have also gone to *Night Seasons,* a look at a mean and miserly family headed by a self-centered matriarch (Jean Stapleton). The character and the play are not so distant from Lillian Hellman's *The Little Foxes.* Goodness is represented by Sister Laura Lee (another splendid performance by Hallie Foote), a woman so beaten down that she has missed out on love and life. This is a quietly rambling domestic drama but one with a heartbeat of reality.

The Signature series ended with *Laura Dennis,* the least of the Foote quartet and the most plot-filled. There were two killings offstage, illicit affairs and an outbreak of illegitimacy (and confused parentage). Hallie Foote lapsed into histrionics as a sad town drunk, but Missy Yager (in a more typical Hallie Foote part) added poignancy to the play. After a triumphant season, Foote and company could easily be forgiven a *Laura Dennis.* Taken together, the plays offered additional proof that the playwright is an eloquent chronicler of small-town American life.

Houghton and his company are performing an invaluable service for theatergoers and playwrights, bringing attention to careers as well as to individual plays. Next season will be devoted to Adrienne Kennedy, another fine writer whose work has not been amply represented in New York in recent years. And there are numerous other playwrights who clearly qualify for the Signature treatment, beginning with a trio introduced at the Actors Theater of Louisville—Jane Martin, Beth Henley and Marsha Norman—and including Eric Overmyer, Steve Carter and Michael Weller. Unfortunately, Signature lost its temporary home in Greenwich Village and has had to look for a new space.

In a truly healthy theatrical climate, Signature would be prospering economically as well as artistically, but its financial difficulty is endemic of an underlying crisis off off Broadway (as in other areas of the American theater). With threatened cutbacks in funding, theaters are desperately seeking support. At the same time, enterprise continues to exist in this arena, with new companies springing up and more experienced ones like New York Theater Workshop and Primary Stages furthering their efforts. As always, OOB is defined by its diversity.

Just as there are many more Foote plays unseen in New York (enough for a second Signature season), there are also more neglected plays by Romulus Linney. One of his most compelling, *2* (now subtitled *Goering at Nuremberg*), finally opened in New York. Previously produced at the Actors Theater of Louisville and the Williamstown Theater Festival, *2* is not so much a play about the nature of evil as a play about the nature of Hermann Goering. The paradox under scrutiny is how a leader (and an esthete) so admired by his people could become a monster slavishly devoted to Hitler, even after the dictator's death. In its long delayed New York premiere, *2* is cited as an outstanding 1995 OOB production. Staged with stark simplicity by Thomas Bullard (at Primary Stages), the play starred Clarence Felder as Goering: arrogant, assured and erudite, a kind of porcine Richard III. Ezra Pound in prison was the subject of another political play, Tom Dulack's *Incommunicado.* First produced at Philadelphia's Wilma Theater, this provocative drama opened in New York with Tom Aldredge in the central role.

In addition to 2, Primary Stages presented *You Should Be So Lucky,* in which its author and star Charles Busch appeared in masculine garb rather than in his customary drag; *I Sent a Letter to My Love,* a chamber musical by Melissa Manchester and Jeffrey Sweet, a 1950s American version of Bernice Rubens's novel about the strangest of pen pals; and *Don Juan in Chicago,* an ambitious but unfulfilled modernization from David Ives. Last season Ives proved himself a master of one-act comedy in *All in the Timing.* The actresses almost rescued the new show, especially J. Smith-Cameron as Don Juan's enticing Donna Elvira.

The New York Theater Workshop highlighted its season with Tony Kushner's *Slavs,* a one-act postscript or pendant to his extravaganza, *Angels in America;* and *The Family Business,* a collaborative work by David Gordon and Ain Gordon (father and son), with Valda Setterfield (wife and mother) prominently in the cast. Coming after *What's So Funny?,* an earlier, self-indulgent family performance piece, *The Family Business* was a definite surprise. A funny and touching show about a death in a family, it is cited as an outstanding 1995 OOB production. When an aged aunt falls down and hurts herself, her relatives, especially her nephew, have to decide what to do with her. As played by David Gordon, the aunt was crotchety and colorful. Ain Gordon took the role of the son and nephew, a caretaker to his aunt's quirks and Miss Setterfield played all the other women on stage. The staging was minimal, the acting occasionally awkward, but the spirit was willing, and the play is an original.

As a performance artist, Ron Athey is literally on the cutting edge. *Four Scenes in a Harsh Life,* created by and starring Athey, called for him to make superficial slashes on another actor's body in the name of ritual. The play (at Performance Space 122) veered between masochism and mythology. At the risk of sounding over avant garded, one must say that the show added up to nothing new and was also oddly self-exploitative.

Far more interesting experimentation took place at the Soho Rep, where Mac Wellman offered *Swoop,* a coda to his *Dracula* of last season and itself a witty contemplation of vampire lore and language. In *I've Got the Shakes,* at the Ontological-Hysteric Theater, Richard Foreman continued his iconographic exploration of his mind and memory book. Education is on the line in this surrealistic schoolroom, tended by Jan Leslie Harding as a teacher who confesses that she does not know what she is teaching. The air is full of noises and portents, religious symbols as well as signs of death. Foreman faces questions of mortality with vaudeville humor as well as philosophical panache. He and Wellman continue to be sentinels on the advance line of theater.

In *Nothing So Powerful as Truth,* at the Dance Theater Workshop, Dan Hurlin created a kind of song and dance performance piece cousin to *Citizen Kane.* Inspired by the story of William Loeb, the reactionary publisher of the Manchester, N.H. *Union-Leader,* the show tripped lightly through the cultural history of the 20th century, but the text was not on a level with the concept and Hurlin's own staging. With *Luck, Pluck and Virtue* at the Atlantic Theater Company, James Lapine took off from Nathanael West's novel, *A Cool Million,* an idea previously investigated by

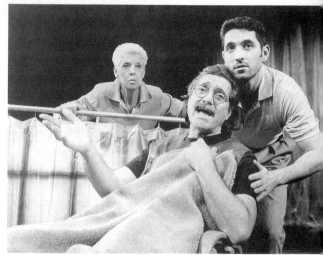

Left, Clarence Felder, Dion Graham, Craig Wroe and Kevin Cutts in Romulus Linney's *2* at Primary Stages ("About the nature of Hermann Goering ..... staged with stark simplicity")

Right, Valda Setterfield, David Gordon and Ain Gordon in *The Family Business* at N.Y. Theater Workshop ("A funny and touching show about a death in the family"); *below,* Jodi Lennon, Jackie Hoffman, Sarah Thyre and Amy Sedaris in *One Woman Shoe* by Amy and David Sedaris at LaMama ("A rambunctious and timely satirical revue")

Mel Gussow
Citations

Left, Hallie Foote and Eddie Kaye Thomas in *Talking Pictures* by Horton Foote at Signature Theater ("A lovely portrait of a stressful Texas family in the 1920s")

Hurlin. As adapter and director, Lapine sacrificed the Westian malice for something far less grotesque and randomly musical. The play was buoyed by Neil Patrick Harris's highly physicalized performance in the central role.

As in other areas of the theater, monologues proliferated. One of the most moving was *My Left Breast,* Susan Miller's intimate reflections on her own breast cancer and mastectomy. As performed by the author as part of a festival of monologues at the Watermark Theater, the play became a confessional. Treating the traumas of her life without self-pity, the author hauntingly personalized her experience: she ended her narrative by taking off her blouse and revealing her surgical wounds to the audience.

James Lecesne was represented by two simultaneous performance pieces, in which he played all the characters, both male and female: *Word of Mouth,* eight monologues of his authorship; and *Extraordinary Measures,* a musical drama by Eve Ensler and William Harper about the death of the actor-director Paul Walker. Lecesne is an artful quick-change actor. The most impressive scene in *Word of Mouth*—about Trevor, a gay man coming out and overcoming suicide—was previously made into an Oscar-winning short. The other sketches varied in quality, but the show was a better showcase for Lecesne's talents than *Extraordinary Measures,* an uneven tapestry of longing and futility. Singers behind a scrim added texture to this chamber musical, a production of Lyn Austin's Music Theater Group. It was presented at

Here, a comfortable new off-off-Broadway arts center. With its art gallery and coffee bar, Here is the New York equivalent of a London fringe theater.

Allen Havis's *Hospitality* at the Workhouse Theater, a play about detained aliens, lacked the swiftness and the urgency of the author's *Morocco,* on a related subject. *Raised in Captivity* at the Vineyard Theater was another hypertense Nicky Silver comedy about an impossibly dysfunctional family. Though there was little humor behind the hysteria, Peter Frechette's performance was engaging. In *Girl Gone,* Jacquelyn Reingold offered a fuzzy picture of the world of topless dancers. Kelly Bishop gave a sharply etched portrait of an Ava Gardner-like actress in *The Last Girl Singer* by Deborah Grace Winer but was unable to cosmetize the play's cliches.

Everett Quinton, as Charles Ludlam's successor, continued to put his own comic imprint on the Ridiculous Theatrical Company, this season branching into classics with *A Midsummer Night's Dream* and *Carmen.* Quinton was hilarious as Bottom in *A Midsummer Night's Dream,* and the Ridiculous fairies were large, bulky and hirsute. Coincidentally, there was a one-man treatment of the same material by Fred Curchack, as part of the International Festival of Puppet Theater at the Public Theater. Although Curchack's *What Fools These Mortals Be* was not as imaginative as his solo *Tempest,* it had its virtuosic moments. Outdoing Quinton, Curchack played all the characters, including Bottom and Titania at the same time.

New versions of classics proliferated. There were individual views of *Phaedra,* by Elizabeth Egloff at the Vineyard Theater and Matthew Maguire at Here; *Iphigenia and Other Daughters* by Ellen McLaughlin; and *Amphitryon* by Eric Overmyer, the last two at the CSC. McLaughlin's play was a modern feminist take on the House of Atreus. Despite the disparities from the original story, the play retained an instinctual intensity. Though somewhat lacking in the usual Overmyer linguistic cleverness, *Amphitryon* was an amusing variation on Heinrich von Kleist, focusing on women who are fooled and befuddled by godly pranks. Another version of the legend, Cole Porter's musical *Out of This World,* received a concert revival as part of the *Encores!* series of musicals at City Center: snappy songs and a sharply cut book. Irving Berlin's *Call Me Madam,* also in this series, was closer to a rediscovery; and *Pal Joey* reasserted itself as a vintage musical, with credit to Peter Gallagher, ideal as the caddish Joey.

The Brooklyn Academy of Music continued its mission of presenting the most farsighted theater directors, this season offering an international triple header: Peter Brook with *The Man Who,* Giorgio Strehler with Pirandello's unfinished play *The Mountain Giants* and Ingmar Bergman with *The Winter's Tale* and, in June, a return visit of Yukio Mishima's *Madame de Sade.* Earlier in the year, BAM had welcomed Lev Dodin and the Maly Theater of St. Petersburg with *Gaudeamus,* a play that used New Vaudeville techniques to deal with the dehumanization of soldiers in battle. It could be regarded as a service comedy with tragic undertones. All of these companies demanded to be seen.

Anne Bogart, who was the subject of a festival at the Actors Theater of Louisville, was briefly represented at Performance Space 122 with *Small Lives/Big Dreams,* a collage of dialogue extracted from the plays of Chekhov, sifted and transformed into a choreographic performance piece. At the center was Konstantin from *The Seagull* who seemed to have been released from a madhouse. Though deconstructive, the play unveiled the Beckett side of Chekhov, in contrast to the Wooster Group's deconstruction of *Three Sisters* that stopped far short of reconstruction. The play told us little about *Three Sisters* except that it is indestructible.

While the Jean Cocteau continued to provide a diet of classics, including *The Country Wife* and *The Cherry Orchard* (as well as *The Keepers,* a new play by Barbara Lebow), other newer companies reached further out in their choices. The tiny Mint Theater Company unearthed James M. Barrie's *Quality Street.* A creaky, old-fashioned romantic comedy about self-denial, it slowly came to life in the second act. This community-theater-style production was elevated by the performance of Lisa M. Bostnar in the central role as a woman making one final desperate stab at happiness.

In the spring, the Ensemble Studio Theater holds its annual Marathon of one-act plays, presenting plays by newcomers as well as experienced professionals. Of the 11 plays offered in three evenings (including works by Arthur Miller and Bill Bozzone), the most rewarding were by Thornton Wilder and David Mamet. Wilder's *Wreck on the Five-Twenty-Five,* never produced in New York before, is about the depressive decline of an all American family man. It is more venturesome than the plays by younger authors that surrounded it in the festival. Mamet's *No One Will Be Immune* was a nightmarish fantasy trip about air crashes and abduction by aliens, with David Rasche underscoring language with portent.

In terms of entertainment quotient, nothing could quite match *One Woman Shoe,* a rambunctious and timely satiric revue by Amy and David Sedaris (a brother and sister team that bills itself as the Talent Family). The premise: to retain welfare payments, people have to become performance artists. The result: a screwball send-up of public assistance, experimental theater, and let's-put-on-a-show movie musicals. The revue (at La Mama), with a clownish cast headed by Miss Sedaris, was brought back at the end of the season for an extended run and is cited as an outstanding OOB production.

PLAYS PRODUCED
OFF OFF BROADWAY

AND ADDITIONAL PRODUCTIONS

Compiled by Camille Croce Dee

Here is a comprehensive sampling of off-off-Broadway and other experimental or peripheral 1994–95 productions in New York. There is no definitive "off-off-Broadway" area or qualification. To try to define or regiment it would be untrue to its fluid, exploratory purpose. The listing below of hundreds of works produced by more than 100 OOB groups and others is as inclusive as reliable sources will allow, however, and takes in all leading Manhattan-based, new-play producing, English-language organizations.

The more active and established producing groups are identified in bold face type, in alphabetical order, with artistic policies and the names of the managing directors given whenever these are a matter of record. Each group's 1994–95 schedule, with emphasis on new plays and with revivals of classics usually omitted, is listed with play titles in CAPITAL LETTERS. Often these are works-in-progress with changing scripts, casts and directors, sometimes without an engagement of record (but an opening or early performance date is included when available).

Many of these off-off-Broadway groups have long since outgrown a merely experimental status and are offering programs which are the equal in professionalism and quality (and in some cases the superior) of anything in the New York theater, with special contractual arrangements like the showcase code, letters of agreement (allowing for longer runs and higher admission prices than usual) and, closer to the edge of the commercial theater, a so-called "mini-contract." In the list below, all available data on opening dates, performance numbers and major production and acting credits (almost all for Equity members) is included in the entries of these special-arrangement offerings.

A large selection of lesser-known groups and other shows that made appearances off off Broadway during the season appears under the "Miscellaneous" heading at the end of this listing.

American Place Theater. New American plays in their world premieres. Wynn Handman artistic director, Susannah Halston executive director.

BEAUTY'S DAUGHTER (one-woman show) (44). By and with Dael Orlandersmith. February 5, 1995. Director, Peter Askin; scenery, Joel Reynolds; lighting, Jane Reisman; costumes, Emma Cairns.

SPOONBREAD AND STRAWBERRY WINE (34). By Norma Jean Darden, based on the cookbook of the same title by Norma Jean and Carole Darden. February 8, 1995. Director, Josh Broder; scenery, Ken Rothchild; lighting, Christopher Boll. With Norma Jean Darden, Jou Jou Papailler.

COMING THROUGH (30). Adapted from immigrants' oral histories and directed by Wynn Handman. May 14, 1995; see its entry in the Plays Produced off Broadway section of this volume.

American Theater of Actors. Dedicated to providing a creative atmosphere for new American playwrights, actors and directors. James Jennings artistic director.

HENRY VI, PART 1. By William Shakespeare. June 1, 1994. Director, James Jennings. With Pat Connelly, Tom Bruce, Pam Everly, Jeff Sult.

THE COMEDY OF ERRORS. By William Shakespeare. July 6, 1994. Director, David LeBarron. With Jean Colvin, Cindy Gibson, Sherri Langsam.

LOCKIN' LOAD. By Daniel Kinch. July 20, 1994. Director, Ellen Bay. With Valentino Ferreira, Gary Lamadore.

MY SON, MY FATHER. Written and directed by James Jennings. August 3, 1994. With Tom Bruce, Jane Culley, Benjamin Quinto.

MARY. By Alex Menza. August 10, 1994. Director, Michael Gardner. With Flip Brown, Evalyn Taucher, Ken Coughlin.

PHILOCTETES. By Sophocles. August 10, 1994. Director, James Jennings. With Jon Panczyk, Ray Laudo, Gregory Pekar.

ES' O ES'. By Dave Ryan. August 17, 1994. Director, Luciana Polney. With John Borras, James Crawford, Connie Giordano.

SECRETS AND ORPHANS by Kevin Brofsky and SEA GLASS by Bill McMahon (one-act plays). September 7, 1994. Director, John Paine. With Louise Clay, Matt Collins, Douglas Houston, Mike Bancroft, Mary Kate Murphy, Greg Hirsh.

ETERNITY ROAD. By Peter Chelnik. September 14, 1994. Director, James Jennings. With Clark Reiner, Ken Coughlin, Pat Waggoner.

KOMICS, CLOWNS AND KRAZY KATS. By Judy Williams. October 12, 1994. Director, Michael Muzio. With Clayton Bartner, Shonnese Coleman, Ellie Dirraine.

WHEN THE SMITHS CAME TO DINNER. By Mara Dresner. October 26, 1994. Director, Tom Bruce. With Carollyne Ascher, Anne Correa, Ken Coughlin, Jocelyn Druyan.

NOVEMBER '63. By Frank Cossa. November 9, 1994. Director, David Platt. With Cheryl Adam, Jeff Lynn, Kelly Ann Moore, Richard Mowat, Chris Groenewold.

THE DANCE OF THE SEVEN-HEADED-MOUSE. By Carol Gaunt. November 16, 1994. Director, Luciana Polney. With Kerry Burns, Catherine Corcoran, Lauren Levy, Solveig Foster.

BAILEY. By Larry Manes. November 21, 1994. Director, James Jennings. With Tom Bruce, Susan Wise, Mat Sarter, Antoinette Gallo, Patti Sands, Larry Landau.

THE INTERVIEW. Written and directed by D.A.G. Burgos. December 7, 1994. With David Lipson, Sheik Mahmud-Bey, Aaron Nay, Ron LaVenture, Dean Negri.

A MOTHER'S DEATH WISH. By Jay Folb. December 14, 1994. Director, Michael Arzouane. With John Combs, Catherine Bush, Eddie Daniels, David Kachoui.

UGLY OLD BABIES. By Jerry Berk. December 19, 1994. Director, James Jennings. With Karron Haines, Jerry Berk.

SOLEMN PACT by Rob Santana, directed by Richard Quebral; COYOTE REBEL written and directed by James Jennings (one-act plays). January 11, 1995. With Robert Kelly, Rob Cividanes, Cinda Lawrence, Alex Jordan, Tom Bruce.

THE PURSUIT OF HAPPINESS. By Jerry Kaufman. February 15, 1995. Director, Ibrahim Quraishi. With Jonah Bay, Tom Bruce, Lulu D'Agostino, Adrian Lee.

MRS. HOLLISTER'S TROJAN HORSE. By Nancy Gardner. February 22, 1995. Director, Judith Caporale. With Stephen Kelly, Andrew Lerer, Jordan Torjussen, Elizabeth Vessels, Tom Fattoruso, John Koprowski.

TWENTY-NINE PINE. By Michael Moss. March 1, 1995. Director, Richard Quebral. With Catherine Corcoran, Antoinette Gallo, Dean Negri, Susan Wise, Lou Lagalante, Bill Garrity.

NARCISSIST IN EXILE by Greg Cummings, directed by Jeff Lynn; PRODIGY written and directed by Richard Quebral (one-act plays). April 5, 1995. With Cheryl Adam, Jonathan Webb, Bill Miller, Damien Langan, Thomas John Houfe.

THE SENTENCE. By Alex Menza. April 6, 1995. Director, Judith Caporale. With Ed Mahler, Antoinette Gallo, Tom Weyburn, Sue Bredenberg, Jerry Lewkowitz, Louis Rodgers.

THE OUTER-LOPER. Written and directed by James Jennings. April 12, 1995. With James Cronin, Stephanie Johnson, Tom Fattoruso.

THE SKY ABOVE THE BEST MEN. By Paul Rawlings. May 3, 1995. Director, Robert Engstrom. With Gary Lewis, Robert Engstrom.

EMPTY NESTERS. By Doug Williams. May 10, 1995. Director, David Kreuz. With John Borras, Faith Whitehill, Mike Columbo, Joe Iacona, David Sweeney.

LOVE TO HATE. By Norman Rhodes. May 17, 1995. Director, Marc Anthony Thomas. With Alixandree Antoine, Gordon Giddings, Scott Haskell, Rochelle Henderson, Miho Inoue, Susan Kaessinger, George Ratchford, Barrie Snider, Russell Stewart, Michele Lee Sung.

A SHORT VISIT. By Alex Menza. May 24, 1995. Director, Jason Russio. With Ed Mahler, Antoinette Gallo.

Atlantic Theater Company. Produces new plays or reinterpretations of classics that speak to audiences in a contemporary voice on issues reflecting today's society. Neil Pepe artistic director, Joshua Lehrer managing director.

TRAFFICKING IN BROKEN HEARTS (29). By Edwin Sanchez. December 13, 1994. Director, Anna D. Shapiro. Scenery and lighting, Kevin Rigdon; costumes, Laura Cunningham. With Giancarlo Esposito, Neil Pepe, Anthony Rapp.

MISSING PERSONS (34). By Craig Lucas. February 1, 1995. Director, Michael Mayer; scenery, David Gallo and Lauren Helpern; lighting, Howard Werner; costumes, Laura Cunningham; music, Jill Jaffe. With Mary Beth Peil, Todd Weeks, Cameron Boyd, Mary McCann, Camryn Manheim, Jordan Lage, John Cameron Mitchell.

LUCK, PLUCK & VIRTUE (26). Adapted from Nathanael West's novel *A Cool Million* and directed by James Lapine. April 4, 1995. Scenery, Derek McLane; lighting, Donald Holder; costumes, Laura Cunningham, Martin Pakledinaz; music, Allen Shawn. With Neil Patrick Harris, Elaina Davis, MacIntyre Dixon, Marge Redmond, Steven Goldstein, Adrianne Krstansky, Chris Bauer, Siobhan Fallon, Geoffrey Owens, Stephen Lee Anderson.

Circle Repertory Projects-in-Process. Program which is an essential part of the play development process. Tanya Berezin artistic director, Meredith Freeman managing director.

THE SUN AND THE MOON LIVE IN THE SKY (4). By Ellen Lewis. February 13, 1995. Director, Michael Warren Powell; lighting, Jennifer S. Lyons. With Sandra Daley, Laurine Towler, Brenda Denmark, Frank Mayers, Robert Jiminez, Angela Bullock, Rafeal Clements, Nashawn Kearse, Julius Hollingsworth.

Classic Stage Company. Reinventing and revitalizing the classics for contemporary audiences. David Esbjornson artistic director.

THE SCARLET LETTER (35). By Phyllis Nagy, adapted from Nathaniel Hawthorne's novel. October 19, 1994. Director, Lisa Peterson; scenery, Neil Patel; lighting, Kenneth Posner; costumes,

Michael Krass; music and sound, Mark Bennett. With Cynthia Nixon, Erin Cressida Wilson, Dan Daily, Bill Cwikowski, Sheila Tousey, Stephen Caffrey, Jon DeVries.

THE DREAM EXPRESS: THE ORIGINAL OUTLAW LOUNGE ACT (15). Written and directed by Len Jenkin. November 17, 1994. Musical direction, John Kilgore. With Steve Mellor, Deirdre O'Connell.

IPHIGENIA AND OTHER DAUGHTERS (35). By Ellen McLaughlin. February 8, 1995. Director, David Esbjornson; scenery, Narelle Sissons; lighting, Christopher Akerlind; costumes, Susan Hilferty; music and sound, Gina Leishman. With Susan Heimbinder, Kathleen Chalfant, Sheila Tousey, Deborah Hedwall, Seth Gilliam, Jasmine Curry, Carley Dubicki, Cari Kosins, Karen Sackman, Jill Vinci.

AMPHITRYON (35). By Eric Overmyer. April 26, 1995. Director, Brian Kulick; scenery and costumes, Mark Wendland; lighting, Kevin Adams. With Peter Francis James, Arthur Hanket, Gina Torres, Katherine Leask, David Edward Jones, Ken Cheeseman, Michael James Reed.

En Garde Arts. Dedicated to developing the concept of "site-specific theater" in the streets, parks and buildings of the city. Anne Hamburger founder and producer.

STONEWALL, NIGHT VARIATIONS (30). Written and directed by Tina Landau. June 23, 1994. Scenery, James Schuette; lighting, Brian Aldous; costumes, Elizabeth Fried; music, Ricky Ian Gordon; film segments, Jennie Livingston. With Joseph Mahan, Michael Malone, Jim Mahady, Tyrone Mitchell Henderson, Camilla Sanes, Sharon Scruggs, Steven Skybell, Barney O'Hanlon, Theresa McCarthy, Bruce Katzman, Will Warren, Andrea Darriau, Stefanie Zadravec, Rita Menu, Michael St. Clair.

Ensemble Studio Theater. Membership organization of playwrights, actors, directors and designers dedicated to supporting individual theater artists and developing new works for the stage. Over 250 projects each season, ranging from readings to fully-mounted productions. Curt Dempster artistic director, Jacqueline A. Siegel managing director.

SUDDEN DEVOTION (12). By Stuart Spencer. September 13, 1994. Director, Andrew Volkoff. With Christopher Berger, Kevin O'Keefe, Frank Raiter.

OCTOBERFEST. Festival of over 70 new plays by members. October 6–31, 1994.

MARATHON '95 (festival of one-act plays). THE RYAN INTERVIEW by Arthur Miller, directed by Curt Dempster; A DEAD MAN'S APARTMENT by Edward Allan Baker, directed by Ron Stetson; WRECK ON THE FIVE-TWENTY-FIVE by Thornton Wilder, directed by Richard Lichte; FLYBOY by Yvonne Adrian, directed by Maggie Mancinelli-Cahill; RAIN by Garry Williams, directed by Jamie Richards; CREDO by Craig Lucas, directed by Kirsten Sanderson; WATER AND WINE by Stuart Spencer, directed by Nicholas Martin; SONNY DEERE'S LIFE FLASHES BEFORE HIS EYES by Bill Bozzone, directed by Keith Reddin; NO ONE WILL BE IMMUNE by David Mamet, directed by Curt Dempster; FREUD'S HOUSE by Laurence Klavan, directed by Charles Karchmer; DEARBORN HEIGHTS by Cassandra Medley, directed by Irving Vincent. May 3–June 11, 1995.

INTAR. Mission is to identify, develop and present the talents of gifted Hispanic American theater artists and multicultural visual artists. Max Ferra artistic director.

27 performances each
HEART OF THE EARTH: A POPOL VUH STORY. By Cherrie Moraga, adapted from the Mayan sacred text. January 14, 1995. Director, Ralph Lee; music, Glen Velez. With Adrian Bethea, Caroline Stephanie Clay, Doris Difarnecio, William Ha'o, Wilson Jermaine Heredia, Joe Herrera, Stephanie Marshall, Dawnnie Mercado-Hernandez, Reggie Valdez.

A ROYAL AFFAIR. By Luis Santeiro. April 9, 1995. Director, Max Ferra; scenery, Loren Sherman; lighting, Phil Monat; costumes, Donna Zakowska. With Tobi Brydon, Sergio Cruz, Adriana Inchaustegui, Maritza Rivera, Gary Perez, Ed Trucco, Marta Vidal.

ENSEMBLE STUDIO THEATER—Melinda Hamilton, James Murtaugh and Deborah Hedwall in Thornton Wilder's *Wreck on the Five-Twenty-Five,* in its first New York production in Ensemble's 18th annual one-act play festival, Marathon '95

Irish Arts Center. Provides a range of contemporary Irish drama, classics and new works by Irish and Irish-American playwrights. Nye Heron artistic director.

SANCTIFYING GRACE (one-man show). By and with Colin Quinn. June 22, 1994. Director, Robert Moresco.

PUBLIC ENEMY (133). By Kenneth Branagh. November 3, 1994; see its entry in the Plays Produced off Broadway section of this volume.

THE DONAHUE SISTERS and BAR AND GER (48+). By Geraldine Aron. May 11, 1995. Director, Nye Heron; scenery, David Raphel; lighting, Mauricio Saavedra; costumes, Mimi Maxmen. With Carolyn McCormick, Alma Cuervo, Terry Donnelly, John Keating, Aedin Maloney.

La Mama (a.k.a LaMama) Experimental Theater Club (ETC). A busy workshop for experimental theater of all kinds. Ellen Stewart founder and artistic director.

Schedule included:

YARA'S FOREST SONG. Conceived and directed by Virlana Tkacz, based on Lesia Ukrainka's play. June 10, 1994. Music, Genji Ito. With Yara Arts Group.

MUGEN (ENDLESS). By Eiji Kusanaga. June 23, 1994. Directors, Sejishiro and Shirou Mihara. With Ken Togo and Company.

THE STORY OF DOU-E/SNOW IN JUNE. By Guan Han-Quing, adapted by Joanna Chan. September 29, 1994. Director, Lu Yu; music, Peter Gingerich. With Yangtze Repertory Theater of America.

IS THAT ALL THERE IS? By Amir Hosseinpour. October 13, 1994. Director, Kfir Yefet. With Liliane Montevecchi, Sarah Toner, Floyd Hendricks.

MOTHER. By Patricia Spears Jones. October 21, 1994. Co-presented by Mabou Mines; see its entry under Mabou Mines.

MARY STUART. By and with Denise Stoklos. October 27, 1994.

WINTERREISE. By Wilhelm Mueller. November 10, 1994. Director, Gabrielle Jakobi. With Michael Altman.

NOTES OF A MADMAN. Adapted from Nikolai Gogol's *Diary of a Madman* and performed by Ivan Franko State Drama Theater, translated by Kaksym Rylsky. November 25, 1994. Director, Vasyl Sechin.

EPPURE SI MUOVE (IT'S GOING AROUND). By Josef Mundi, translated by Avi Hoffman. November 30, 1994. Director, Geula Jeffet-Attar.

UNDER THE KNIFE II (multimedia work). Conceived, directed and designed by Theodora Skipitares. December 8, 1994.

THE BLUES STORIES: BLACK EROTICA ABOUT LETTING GO by Rhodessa Jones, directed by Idris Ackamoor; SHOEHORN by Idris Ackamoor and Mark Goodman, directed by Kerman Levern Jones. December 8, 1994.

PASS THE BLUTWURST, BITTE. Conceived, directed and choreographed by John Kelly. December 30, 1994. Lighting, Stan Pressner; costumes, Gary Lisz and Trine Walther; film, Anthony Chase. With Marleen Menard, Dina Emerson, John Kelly, Steven Craig, Jonathan Kinzel. Reopened March 15, 1995.

THE TIGHT FIT. Written, directed and designed by Susan Mosakowski. January 5, 1995. Scenery, Michael Casselli; lighting, Pat Dignan. With Tom Cayler, Louise Favier, Tina Preston, Jeff Sugarman.

CASCANDO and EH, JOE (one-act plays). By Samuel Beckett. January 19, 1995. Director, Erica Bilder; scenery, Peter Ungerleider; lighting, Howard Thies; costumes, Theodora Skipitares. With Mik-Michele, Stuart Pyle, Sarah Schilling, John Giorno.

WATERFALL/REFLECTIONS. Conceived and directed by Virlana Tkacz. January 27, 1995. Music, Genji Ito. With Yara Arts Group.

WINTER MAN. By Andy Tierstein and Lance Henson. February 2, 1995. Director, George Ferencz.

YOUNG GOODMAN BROWN. Libretto, Richard Foreman, based on Nathaniel Hawthorne's story; music, Phillip Johnston. February 16, 1995. Director, David Herskovits; scenery, Erika Belsey; lighting, Lenore Doxsee; costumes, David Zinn. With Jamie Callahan, David Eye, Michael Gans, Nicole Halmos, Julie Fain Lawrence, Randolph Curtis Rand, Suzanne Rose, Henry Steele, Andrei Clark, Gretchen Krich, Jennifer Westfeldt, Amy Wilson. Co-produced by Target Margin Theater.

SLIGHT RETURN. Written, directed and designed by John Jesurun. February 16, 1995.

DA CAPO. By and with Jun Maeda. March 2, 1995.

SPEAKEASY. By Joanna Scott. March 2, 1995. Director, Mervyn Willis; music, Obadiah Eaves.

HERE EVERYTHING STILL FLOATS. Written and directed by Michael Rush. March 30, 1995.

FRAGMENTS FROM THREE SISTERS. Adapted from Anton Chekhov's play and directed by Richard Schechner, translated by Michelle Minnick. April 12, 1995. Music, Ralph Denzer. With Drew Barr, Shaula Chambliss, Rebecca Ortese, Ulla Neuerberg.

MACBETH. Adapted from William Shakespeare's play by Luc van Meerbeke. April 20, 1995. With Stuffed Puppet Theater.

THE MANHATTAN BOOK OF THE DEAD. Libretto, music and lyrics by David First. April 27, 1995. Director, Ching Valdes-Aran; choreography, Gloria McLean. With Thomas Buckner.

THE RAINBOW FLEA: INSECTS AS ACTORS. Written and directed by Charles Allcroft. May 4, 1995. With Bill Rice, Jim Neu.

WILD ANCESTORS. Conceived and directed by Beth Skinner. May 18, 1995. Music, Edward Herbst. With Thunder Bay Ensemble.

BETTY SUFFER'S THEORY OF RELATIVITY. Written and composed by Ellen Maddow. May 18, 1995. Director, Brian Jucha. With the Talking Band (Ellen Maddow, Tina Shepard, Dale Soules, Paul Zimet).

The Club

RETURN OF THE SODOMITE WARRIORS by and with Kurt Fulton and Allan M. Tibbets; CRAZY HE CALLS ME by and with R.N. Schachter. June 16, 1994.

TAKE MY DOMESTIC PARTNER—PLEASE!. By and with Sara Cytron. June 23, 1994. Director, Harriet Malinowitz.

BUCK SIMPLE. By Craig Fols. September 22, 1994. Director, David Briggs. With Leah Hocking, Craig Fols.

WHY HANNAH'S SKIRTS WON'T STAY DOWN. By Tom Eyen. October 6, 1994. With Terry Vaughan, Tom Gilster.

HANDS IN WARTIME. By Edgar Oliver. October 27, 1994. Director, Jason Bauer. With Michael Laurence, Edgar Oliver.

A TATTLE TALE (one-woman show). By Judith Sloan and Warren Lehrer. November 10, 1994.

CHORES: THE BIG MAN IN THE ORANGE RUBBER RAIN SUIT. Written and directed by the Fabulous Giggin' Brothers (Will and Mike Gorman). November 25, 1994.

FOUR SHOTS OF ABSOLUTE. By Charles E. Drew Jr. and Felix Rodriguez; music, Janice Lowe; lyrics, Charles E. Drew Jr. November 28, 1994. With Absolute Theater Company.

EVAPROO'S BARBIE-O. By and with Evy Gildrie and Chris Andersson. December 19, 1994. Director, Ben Nadler.

CHANG IN A VOID MOON. Written, directed and designed by John Jesurun. January 9, 1995.

ENDANGERED SPECIES: THE BRENDA BERGMAN STORY. Written and directed by Kevin Maloney. January 16, 1995. Musical direction, Gabriel Rotello.

ONE WOMAN SHOE. By the Talent Family (David and Amy Sedaris). January 19, 1995. Director, Mick Napier; choreography, David Combs; scenery, Hugh Hamrick; lighting, Howard Thies. With Jackie Hoffman, Jodi Lennon, David Rakoff, Amy Sedaris, Sarah Thyre.

RED AND GREEN (one-act plays). Written and directed by Stuart Sherman. February 6, 1995. With Black-Eyed Susan, Bill Rice.

THE WOMAN WHO WOULDN'T COME OUT FROM UNDER THE BED (one-act play). By Louisa Benton, adapted with music and dance by Laraine Goodman. February 20, 1995.

THE STATE I'M IN (one-woman show). By and with Paula Killen. February 23, 1995.

THE FLOATONES. By Jim Neu; music, Harry Mann and Neal Kirkwood. March 9, 1995. Director, Rocky Bornstein. With Bill Rice, Mary Schultz, John Nesci, Jim Neu.

THE KNIVES AND FORKS OF LANA LYNX. By and with Ruth Fuglistaller. March 13, 1995. Director, Patricia Hoffbauer.

CHEMISE. By Elaine Patrice Simpleton. March 20, 1995. Director, Lithgow Osborne.

SWEET DREAMS. By Tony Ingrassia. March 23, 1995.

THE TEN COMMANDMENTS. By Gary Hill and Perry Arthur Kroeger. April 6, 1995. With Ralph Cole Jr., W. David Wilkins, Mary Ann Conk, Evelyn Tuths.

LOOKING FOR MR. AMERICA. By and with George Bermisia. April 10, 1995. Director, Joseph Leonardi.

NATASHA FEARLESS LIEDER (songs). By Natasha; music, David Cherins and Bill Ruyle. April 17, 1995.

ON THE BLOCK. By Donald Arrington and Camille Tibaldeo. April 24, 1995. Musical direction, Zecca.

JULIA DARES HERSELF . . . AGAIN (one-woman show). By and with Julia Dares. May 8, 1995.

LUST AND COMFORT. By Peggy Shaw, Lois Weaver and James Neale-Kennerly. May 11, 1995. Director, James Neale-Kennerly. With Peggy Shaw, Lois Weaver.

Lamb's Theater Company. Committed to developing and presenting new works in their most creative and delicate beginnings. Carolyn Rossi Copeland producing director.

JOHN & JEN (18+). Book, Tom Greenwald and Andrew Lippa; music, Andrew Lippa; lyrics, Tom Greenwald. May 16, 1995. Director, Gabriel Barre; scenery, Charles McCarry; costumes, D. Polly Kendrick; musical direction, Joel Fram. With Carolee Carmello, James Ludwig.

Mabou Mines. Theater collaborative whose work is a synthesis of motivational acting, narrative acting and mixed-media performance. Collective artistic leadership. Frederick Neumann, Terry O'Reilly, Ruth Maleczech, Lee Breuer artistic directors.

MOTHER (14). By Patricia Spears Jones. October 21, 1994. Director, John Edward McGrath; choreography, David Neumann; scenery and lighting, Paul Clay; music, Carter Burwell. With Oscar de la Fe Colon, Ruth Maleczech, David Neumann, Darryl Theirse, Ching Valdes-Aran. Co-presented by La Mama E.T.C.

Manhattan Class Company. Dedicated to the promotion of emerging writers, actors, directors and theatrical designers. Robert LuPone and Bernard Telsey executive directors.

GIRL GONE (25). By Jacquelyn Reingold. November 14, 1994. Director, Brian Mertes; choreography, Mark Dendy; scenery, Christine Jones; lighting, Scott Zielinski; costumes, Karen Perry; music, Delfeayo Marsalis. With Brenda Bakke, Sarita Choudhury, Seth Gilliam, Jack Gwaltney, Adina Porter, Dina Spybey, David Thornton, Kelly Wolf.

CLASS ONE-ACTS FESTIVAL (one-act plays): SWEET TALK by Peter Lefcourt, directed by Stephen Willems; HARD HATS by Rafael Lima, directed by Max Mayer; IT'S ALMOST LIKE A FAVOR THAT I DO by Patrick Breen, directed by Brian Mertes; THE ROCKS HAVE EARS (one-man show) by and with Tom Burnett. March 13–April 1, 1995. Scenery, Rob Odorisio; lighting, Darrel Maloney; costumes, Judy Jerald Sackheim. With Keith Reddin, Julie Boyd, James Colby, Dan Moran, Neal Huff, Cara Buono.

Music-Theater Group. Pioneering in the development of new music-theater. Lyn Austin producing director, Diane Wondisford general director.

AMERICA DREAMING (32). By Chiori Miyagawa; music, Tan Dun. December 8, 1994. Director, Michael Mayer; choreography, Doug Varone; scenery, Riccardo Hernandez; lighting, Michael Chybowski; costumes, Michael Krass; musical direction, Bruce Gremo. With Liana Pai, Billy Crudup, P.J. Brown, Shi-Zheng Chen, Joel de la Fuente, Beth Dixon, Ann Harada, Aleta Hayes, Michael Lewis, Virginia Wing, David Cossin, Elise Morris. Co-produced by Vineyard Theater.

EXTRAORDINARY MEASURES (26). Written and directed by Eve Ensler; music, William Harper. April 27, 1995. Scenery, Bradley Wester; lighting, Michael Chybowski; costumes, Donna Zakowska. With James Lecesne, Serafina Martino, Jeannine Otis, Christine Sperry.

New Dramatists. An organization devoted to playwrights; member writers may use the facilities for anything from private cold readings of their material to public script-in-hand readings. Elana Greenfield director of artistic programming, Jana Jevnikar director of finance, Paul A. Slee executive director.

Rehearsed Readings

LANDSCAPE OF DESIRE. By Barry Jay Kaplan. September 19, 1994. Director, Torben Brooks. With Jordan Baker, Glen Fitzgerald, Trish Hawkins, Kevin Kilner, Tom Ligon, Reese Madigan, Daniel Mastrogiorno, Henry Stram, Richard Topol.

A FOREST OF STONE. By Dmitri Lipkin. September 23, 1994. Director, Eduardo Machado. With Philip Courtney, Elzbieta Czyzewska, Kathryn Meisle, Irma St. Paule, David Strathairn.

JULY 7, 1994. Written and directed by Donald Margulies. October 13, 1994. With Kate Burton, Sharon Hope, Karen Evans Kandel, Bruce MacVittie, Jay O. Sanders, Teresa Yenque.

THREE VIEWINGS. By Jeffrey Hatcher. October 17, 1994. Director, Vivian Matalon. With Debra Drummond, Harry Groener, Frances Sternhagen.

VOIR DIRE. By Joe Sutton. October 18, 1994. Director, Doug Hughes. With Vanessa Aspillago, Robin Morse, Gus Rogerson, Brooke Smith, Mary Testa, Sharon Washington.

GERALD'S GOOD IDEA. By Y York. October 25, 1994. Director, Mark Lutwak. With Betsy Aidem, Alan Alda, Patrick Garner, Gail Grate, Tommy Hollis, Mary Beth Hurt, Marjorie Johnson, Chris McCann, Mark Smaltz, Lynne Thigpen.

THE SECRET WIFE. By Y York. October 25, 1994. Director, Mark Lutwak. With Ray Ford, Susan Greenhill, Lianne Kressin, Michael Mantell, Maryann Plunkett, Remak Ramsay, Jay O. Sanders.

LATINS IN LA-LA LAND. By Migdalia Cruz. October 26, 1994. Director, Lisa Peterson. With Raphael Baez, Lazaro Perez, Maritza Rivera, Anthony Michael Ruivivar, Cristina Sanjuan, Sandra Santiago, Jose Zuniga.

FUR. By Migdalia Cruz. October 26, 1994. Director, Dan Hurlin. With Sharon Hope, Melissa Smith, J. Ed Araiza.

NIGHT SKY. By Susan Yankowitz. October 27, 1994. Director, Joe Chaikin. With Steve Coats, Joan MacIntosh, Alate Mitchell, Polly Noonan, Austin Pendleton, Francis Ruivivar.

A KNIFE IN THE HEART. By Susan Yankowitz. October 27, 1994. Director, Jack Hofsiss. With Betsy Aidem, Larry Bryggman, Michael Conner, Tony Goldwyn, Elizabeth Lande, Nancy Marchand, Debra Monk, Paul Sparer.

MY NEBRASKA. Written and directed by Lenora Champagne. November 3, 1994. With Matthew Farrell, Mervyn Haines, Judith Hawking, Chris McCann, Margaret Ritchie.

INTO THE FIRE. By Deborah Baley. November 10, 1994. Director, Liz Diamond. With Jake Cooper, Brendan Corbalis, Philip De Bono, Mia Dillon, Patrick Garner, Fanni Green, Peggy Moran Rosado, Mark Smaltz, June Stein, Vince Trani.

BRAILLE GARDEN. By Darrah Cloud. November 17, 1994. Director, Dave Owens. With David Ethan, Stephanie Bell, Susan G. Bob, Trevor Hardwick, David Logan, Patricia A. Chilsen.

S. By Constance Congdon. November 21, 1994. Director, Mark Harrison. With June Ballinger, Kelly Bishop, Yusef Bulos, Richmond Hoxie, Mary Layne, Alison Sheehy, Susan Willis.

U GOT THE LOOK. By Silvia Gonzalez S. December 8, 1994. Director, Melanie White. With Vivienne Benesch, Aldo Cana, Al Espinoza, Jamison Shelby, Wendy Falcone, Katherine Freedman, Novella Nelson, Jorge Oliver, Clea Rivera.

HONOR SONG FOR CRAZY HORSE. By Darrah Cloud. December 11, 1994. Music, Kim Sherman. With Philip Anthony, Joseph Barbara, Catherine Dupuis, Elise Hernandez, Jack Kirk, Angela Lanza, Perry Silverbird, Jeff Stackhouse.

A FOREST OF STONE. By Dmitri Lipkin. January 13, 1995. Director, Eduardo Machado. With Lynn Cohen, Frances Conroy, Philip Courtney, Ellen McLaughlin, David Strathairn.

THE BIG BLUE NAIL. By Carlyle Brown. February 9, 1995. Director, Kirsten Sanderson. With Stephanie Cannon, Jed Diamond, Richard Ebihara, Ray Ford, Dwayne Gurley, Jasper McGruder, Jerome Davis, Disko Petkovich.

New Federal Theater. Dedicated to presenting new playwrights and plays dealing with the minority and Third World experiences. Woodie King Jr. producer.

THE SPIRIT MOVES (one-woman show) (16). By and with Trazana Beverley. June 23, 1994. Director, A. Dean Irby; scenery and lighting, Jeff Richardson.

BESSIE SPEAKS (one-woman show) (16). By China Clark. October 27, 1994. Director, Dwight R.B. Cook; choreography, Louis Johnson; scenery, Chris Cumberbatch; lighting, Ric Rogers; costumes, Judy Dearing; musical direction, Grenoldo G. Frazier. With Debbi Blackwell-Cook, Troy Blackwell-Cook.

THE MATADOR OF 1ST AND 1ST (one-man show) (12). By and with Oliver Lake. March 9, 1995. Director, Oz Scott.

New York Shakespeare Festival/Joseph Papp Public Theater. Schedule of special projects, in addition to its regular off-Broadway productions. George C. Wolfe producer, Rosemarie Tichler, Kevin Kline associate producers.

Schedule included:

INTERNATIONAL FESTIVAL OF PUPPET THEATER. Works included WOYZECK ON THE HIGHVELD by Handspring Puppet Company; see its entry in the Plays Produced off Broadway section of this volume. A PLAY CALLED NOT AND NOW by Hanne Tierney; THE ADVENTURES OF GINOCCHIO by Teatro Hugo and Ines; KIYOHIME MANDARA by Dondoro; THE GHOST SONATA by Marionetteatern; PETER BETWIXT AND BETWEEN by Teatro Gioco Vita; BOX OF NIGHT, ARNIE'S COW GOES TO NEW YORK and THE MYSTERY PLAY by Suzy Ferriss; SOLITUDE by Banialuka; HEART OF THE EARTH: A POPUL VUH STORY by Ralph Lee and INTAR; see also its entry under INTAR; ENVELOPPES ET DEBALLAGES by Velo Theater; IN XANADU ... INVISIBLE CITIES by Larry Reed; WHAT FOOLS THESE MORTALS BE by Fred Curchack; SAFE AS MILK by Jon Ludwig; PIPES: A COURTROOM DRAMA by Garland Farwell. September 6–18, 1994.

THEATRON '95/'96 (readings of new Israeli plays). DIFFICULT PEOPLE by Yosef Bar-Yosef; GAMES IN THE BACKYARD by Edna Mayza; HEFETZ by Hanoch Levin; EXILE IN JERUSALEM by Motti Lerner. February 13–March 6, 1995.

NEW WORK NOW (festival of staged readings). Schedule included HOUSE OF LEAR adapted from William Shakespeare's play and directed by Reginald T. Jackson; AN UNDIVIDED HEART by Brandon Toropov, directed by Christopher Fields; THE ESSENCE by Bunky Echo-Hawk Jr., directed by William S. Yellow Robe; INTER-TRIBAL by Terry Gomez, directed by Elizabeth Theobald; FISHES by Diana Son, directed by Carlos A. Murillo; LATINS IN LA-LA LAND by Migdalia Cruz, directed by Juliette Carrillo; MISS RUBY'S BLUES: THE STORY OF A MURDER IN FLORIDA by Thulani Davis, directed by Rae C. Wright; DIGGING ELEVEN by Kia Corthron, directed by Robert O'Hara; PRIVATE BATTLE by Lynn Manning; CHANG FRAGMENTS by Han Ong, directed by Marcus Stern; THE PEACOCK SCREAMS WHEN THE LIGHTS GO OUT by Kelly Stuart, directed by Jim Simpson; LAST OF THE SUNS by Alice Tuan; MUNDA NEGRA by Bonnie Greer, directed by Albee James; A GREATER GOOD by Keith Huff, directed by Randall Sommer; INSURRECTION PART ONE: HOLDING HISTORY by Robert O'Hara, directed by Timothy Douglas. April 30–May 21, 1995.

New York Theater Workshop. Produces new theater by American and international artists and encourages risk and stimulates experimentation in theatrical form. James C. Nicola artistic director, Nancy Kassak Diekmann managing director.

101 HUMILITATING STORIES (one-woman show) (30). By and with Lisa Kron. June 20, 1994. Director, John Robert Hoffman; scenery, Amy Shock; lighting, Dan Kotlowitz; costumes, Jose Gutierrez, Chip White.

OUT LATE (gay and lesbian solo performers): Performances by Michael Red Earth, Monica Palacios and Cowboy Girl; THE SCRUB by Chris Cinque; DIVA by Thomas Pasley; ONE MORMON SHOW by Emmett Foster. June 21–24, 1994. (101 HUMILIATING STORIES and OUT LATE ran in repertory as part of the O Solo Homo Festival.)

THE SECRETARIES (35). By and with the Five Lesbian Brothers (Maureen Angelos, Babs Davy, Dominique Dibbell, Peg Healey, Lisa Kron). September 19, 1994. Director, Kate Stafford; scenery, James Schuette; lighting, Nancy Schertler; costumes, Susan Young.

N.Y. THEATER WORKSHOP—John Christopher Jones
and Marisa Tomei in a scene from *Slavs* by Tony Kushner

SLAVS (64). By Tony Kushner. December 12, 1994. Director, Lisa Peterson; scenery, Neil Patel; lighting, Christopher Akerlind; costumes, Gabriel Berry. With Mischa Barton, David Chandler, Barbara Eda-Young, Ben Hammer, Gerald Hiken, John Christopher Jones, Mary Shultz, Marisa Tomei, Joseph Wiseman.

THE FAMILY BUSINESS (35). Written, directed and choreographed by Ain Gordon and David Gordon. April 3, 1995. Scenery and costumes, Anita Stewart; lighting, Stan Pressner. With Ain Gordon, David Gordon, Valda Setterfield.

PRISONER OF LOVE (35). By Jean Genet, translated by Barbara Bray, adapted by JoAnne Akalaitis, Ruth Maleczech and Chiori Miyagawa. May 22, 1995. Director, JoAnne Akalaitis; scenery and costumes, Amy Shock; lighting, Frances Aronson; music, Philip Glass. With Ruth Maleczech.

Studio Production

RENT (rock opera) (8). Book, music and lyrics, Jonathan Larson, based on Puccini's *La Boheme*. October 29, 1994. Director, Michael Greif. With Deirdre Boddie-Henderson, Pat Briggs, Gilles Chiasson, Sheila Kay Davis, Shelley Dickinson, Erin Hill, Tony Hoylen, Sarah Knowlton, John Lathan, Jesse Sinclair Lenat, Michael Potts, Anthony Rapp, Daphne Rubin-Vega, Mark Setlock.

The Open Eye Theater. Goal is to create a theater in which plays for multi-generational audiences are developed, produced and performed with skill, integrity and creative excellence. Amie Brockway producing artistic director, Jean Erdman founder.

A WOMAN CALLED TRUTH (7). By Sandra Fenichel Asher. February 17, 1995. Director, Ernest Johns. With Beresford Bennett, John DiLeo, Patricia Floyd, Ricky Genaro, Harlin Kearsley, Sheryl Greene Leverett, Stephanie Marshall, Jen Wolfe.

Pan Asian Repertory Theater. Strives to provide opportunities for Asian American artists to perform under the highest professional standards and to create and promote plays by and about Asians and Asian Americans. Tisa Chang artistic/producing director.

ARTHUR AND LEILA (21). By Cherylene Lee. October 7, 1994. Director, Ron Nakahara; scenery, Robert Klingelhoefer; lighting, William Simmons; costumes, Eiko Yamaguchi. With Tina Chen, Jon Lee.

YELLOW FEVER (20). By R.A. Shiomi. November 4, 1994. Director, Andrew Tsao; scenery, Robert Klingelhoefer; lighting, Richard Schaefer; costumes, Eiko Yamaguchi. With Ernest Abuba, Eleonora Kihlberg, Robert Baumgardner, David Beyda, Carol A. Honda, Glenn Kubota, Gay Reed, Michael Twaine.

RITA'S RESOURCES (21). By Jeannie Barroga. April 28, 1995. Director, Kati Kuroda; scenery, Dunsi Dai; costumes, Hugh Hanson. With Luna Borromeo, Marshall Factora, Lydia Gaston, Mirla Criste, Zar Acayan, Cortez Nance Jr.

Playwrights Horizons New Theater Wing. Full productions of new works, in addition to the regular off-Broadway productions. Don Scardino artistic director.

BABY ANGER (17). Written and directed by Peter Hedges. September 5, 1994. Lighting, Annie Padien; costumes, Therese Bruck; sound, Michael Clark. With Barbara Garrick, Patrick Breen, Paul Giamatti, Moira Driscoll, Judith Moreland, Damian Young, Shelton Dane, Travis DeLingua.

SOMEWHERE IN THE PACIFIC (15). By Neal Bell. May 17, 1995. Director, Mark Brokaw; lighting, Annie Padien; costumes, Therese Bruck; sound, Michael Clark. With Ross Bickell, Peter Rini, Leo Marx, Michael Gaston, Adam Trese, Charlie Schiff, Silas Weir Mitchell, Ross Salinger, Ari Fliakos.

Primary Stages Company. Dedicated to new American plays by new American playwrights. Casey Childs artistic director, Gina Gionfriddo general manager, Janet Reed associate artistic director, Seth Gordon associate producer.

YOU SHOULD BE SO LUCKY (41). By Charles Busch. October 19, 1994. Director, Kenneth Elliott; scenery, B.T. Whitehill; lighting, Michael Lincoln; costumes, Suzy Benzinger. With Charles Busch, Stephen Pearlman, Nell Campbell, Matthew Arkin, Julie Halston, Jennifer Kato.

I SENT A LETTER TO MY LOVE (34). Book, Jeffrey Sweet, based on Bernice Rubens's novel; music, Melissa Manchester; lyrics, Melissa Manchester and Jeffrey Sweet. January 18, 1995. Director, Pat Birch; scenery, James Noone; lighting, Kirk Bookman; costumes, Rodney Munoz; musical direction, Aaron Hagan. With Lynne Wintersteller, Robert Westenberg, John Hickok, Bethe B. Austin, Meagen Fay.

DON JUAN IN CHICAGO (38). By David Ives. March 3, 1995. Director, Robert Stanton; scenery, Bob Phillips; lighting, Deborah Constantine; costumes, Jennifer Von Mayrhauser; music and sound, David van Tieghem. With Simon Brooking, Larry Block, Peter Bartlett, J. Smith-Cameron, Nancy Opel, Mark Setlock, T. Scott Cunningham, Dina Spybey.

2: GOERING AT NUREMBERG (34). By Romulus Linney. May 10, 1995. Director, Thomas Bullard; scenery, E. David Cosier; lighting, Jeffrey S. Koger; costumes, Teresa Snider-Stein. With Alexandra Cohen-Spiegler, Kevin Cutts, Clarence Felder, Dion Graham, Laurie Kennedy, Matthew Lewis, Peter Ashton Wise, Craig Wroe.

Puerto Rican Traveling Theater. Professional company presenting bilingual productions primarily of Puerto Rican and Hispanic playwrights, emphasizing subjects of relevance today. Miriam Colon founder and producer.

THE FICKLE FINGER OF LADY DEATH. By Eduardo Rodriguez-Solis. July 29, 1994. Director, Jorge Huerta. With Tony Chiroldes, Sandra Rodriguez.

YEPETO (25). By Roberto Cossa. April 13, 1995. Director, Rafael Acevedo, translated by Jack Agueros; scenery, Eric Lowell Renschler; lighting, Peter Greenbaum. With Priscilla Garita, Bruno Irizarry, Nelson Landrieu.

SIMPSON STREET (42). By Eduardo Gallardo. May 24, 1995. Director, Alba Oms; scenery, Carl Baldasso; lighting, Peter Greenbaum. With Anamaria Correa, Martha De La Cruz, Selenis Leyva, Iraida Polanco, Carmen Rosario, Douglas Santiago.

The Ridiculous Theatrical Company. The late Charles Ludlam's comedic troupe devoted to productions of his original scripts and new adaptations of the classics. Everett Quinton artistic director, Adele Bove managing director.

A MIDSUMMER NIGHT'S DREAM. By William Shakespeare. September 29, 1994. Director, Everett Quinton; scenery, Tom Greenfield; lighting, Richard Currie; costumes, Ramona Ponce. With Everett Quinton, Wilfredo Medina, John Cassaras, Christine Weiss, Jimmy Szczepanek, Grant Neale, Beth Dodye Bass, Noelle Kalom, Lenys Sama, Eureka.

CARMEN. Adapted from Jacques Bizet's opera and directed by Everett Quinton. January 17, 1995. Choreography, Barbara Allen; scenery, Tom Greenfield; lighting, Richard Currie; costumes, Cory Lipiello, Ramona Ponce, Toni Nanette Thompson; music, Tony Stavick. With Everett Quinton, Julia Dares, Lenys Sama, Cheryl Reeves, Eureka, Beth Dodye Bass, Larry McLeon, Michael Van Meter, Jimmy Szczepanek.

Second Stage Theater. Committed to producing plays believed to deserve another look, as well as new works. Carole Rothman artistic director, Suzanne Schwartz Davidson producing director.

UNCOMMON WOMEN AND OTHERS (116). By Wendy Wasserstein. October 27, 1994. Director, Carole Rothman; scenery, Heidi Landesman; lighting, Richard Nelson; costumes, Jennifer Von Mayrhauser. With Stephanie Roth, Mary McCann, Jessica Lundy, Rosemary Murphy, Julie Dretzin, Haviland Morris, Robin Morse, Danielle Ferland, Joan Buddenhagen.

ZOOMAN AND THE SIGN (64). By Charles Fuller. November 22, 1994. Director, Seret Scott; scenery, Marjorie Bradley Kellogg; lighting, Michael Gilliam; costumes, Karen Perry. With Larry Gilliard Jr., Oni Faida Lampley, Tony Todd, Stephen M. Henderson, Alex Bess, Willie Stiggers Jr., Ed Wheeler, Saundra McClain, Kim Bey.

RUSH LIMBAUGH IN NIGHT SCHOOL (one-man show) (48). By and with Charlie Varon; developed with David Ford. February 22, 1995. Director, Martin Higgins; scenery, Sherri Adler; lighting, Donald Holder.

CRUMBS FROM THE TABLE OF JOY (64). By Lynn Nottage. May 9, 1995. Director, Joe Morton; scenery, Myung Hee Cho; lighting, Donald Holder; costumes, Karen Perry. With Daryl Edwards, Kisha Howard, Ella Joyce, Nicole Leach, Stephanie Roth.

Signature Theater Company. Dedicated to the exploration of a playwright's body of work. James Houghton artistic director, Thomas Proehl managing director.

24 performances each

TALKING PICTURES. By Horton Foote. September 23, 1994. Director, Carol Goodheart; scenery, Colin D. Young; lighting, Jeffrey S. Koger; costumes, Teresa Snider-Stein, Jonathan Green. With Hallie Foote, Seth Jones, Alice McLane, Isaiah G. Cazares, Samantha Reynolds, Sarah Paulson, Frank Girardeau, Eddie Kaye Thomas, Ed Hodson, Kenneth Cavett, Susan Wands.

NIGHT SEASONS. Written and directed by Horton Foote. November 4, 1994. Scenery, E. David Cosier; lighting, Jeffrey S. Koger; costumes, Barbara A. Bell, Teresa Snider-Stein. With Jean Stapleton, Hallie Foote, Devon Abner, George Bamford, Jo Ann Cunningham, Frank Girardeau, Michael Hadge, Howard Hensel, James Pritchett, Barbara Caren Sims, Elizabeth Stearns, Beatrice Winde, Ted Zurkowski.

THE YOUNG MAN FROM ATLANTA. By Horton Foote. January 27, 1995. A Best Play; see its entry in the Plays Produced off Broadway section of this volume.

LAURA DENNIS. By Horton Foote. March 10, 1995. Director, James Houghton; scenery, E. David Cosier; lighting, Jeffrey S. Koger; costumes, Jonathan Green. With Victoria Fischer, Missy Yager, Stacey Moseley, Pamela Lewis, Barbara Caren Sims, Horton Foote Jr., Peter Sarsgaard, Becky Ann Baker, Hallie Foote, Andrew Finney, Janet Ward, Eric Williams, Michael Hadge.

Soho Rep. Dedicated to new and avant garde American playwrights. Julian Webber artistic director, Chris Kelly managing director.

WARREN G. HARDING (one-man show) (3). By and with David Greenspan. June 16, 1994.

SWOOP (18). By Mac Wellman. November 3, 1994. Director, Julian Webber; scenery and lighting, Kyle Chepulis; costumes, James Sauli; music, David van Tieghem. With John Nesci, Zivia Flomen-haft, Jan Leslie Harding, Lauren Hamilton.

THE HOUSE OF YES (24). By Wendy MacLeod. January 12, 1995. Director, Julian Webber; scenery, Sarah Lambert; lighting, Joe Saint; costumes, James Sauli; music, David van Tieghem. With Christopher Eigeman, Neal Huff, Allison Janney, Jodie Markell, Kim Soden.

SKIN (23). By Naomi Iizuka. April 28, 1995. Director, John Edward McGrath; scenery and lighting, Paul Clay; costumes, Tracy Dorman. With Adam Stein, Karenjune Sanchez, Sarah Rose, Joey Dedio, Ronald Riley, Michael Wiener, Richard Scheinmel, Anthony Ruiz, Jacinto Riddick.

Theater for the New City. Developmental theater and new American experimental works. Crystal Field executive director.

Schedule included:

OUT OF THE BLUE (one-man show). By and with Richard Hoehler. June 9, 1994. Director, Catherine Coray; scenery and costumes, Richard Hoehler; lighting, Neil Galen.

BOB LOVES BONNIE. Written and directed by Bina Sharif. June 9, 1994.

WRATH OF KALI. By Leslie Mohn. June 16, 1994. Directors, Leslie Mohn and Lee Breuer. With Lucy Payjack, Rosemary Close.

LIVE! FROM THE BETTY FORD CLINIC. By and with Michael West. June 16, 1994. Director, Michael Leeds.

SQUEEGEE. Lyrics and direction, Crystal Field; music, Christopher Cherney. August 6, 1994. Scenery and lighting, Anthony Angel; costumes, Carol Tauser, Moira L. Shaughnessy. With Joe Davies, Cheryl Gadsen, Jerry Jaffe, Steven Long.

THE NEST. By Franz Xaver Kroetz, translated by Roger Downey. September 14, 1994. Director, Moises Kaufman. With David Bishins.

VOICES FROM THE RESPLENDENT ISLAND: STORIES FROM SRI LANKA (one-act plays). By Toby Armour. October 20, 1994. Director, Aileen Passloff; scenery, Kathy Joba; lighting, Ellen Bone. With Yolande Bevan, Angela Chale-Millington, Alka Khushalani, Hesh Malkar, Sally Stewart.

THE PERFECT MEATLOAF and LOVE IS A STRANGER IN A WINDOWLESS ROOM. Written and directed by Bina Sharif. November 10, 1994. With Cynthia Burbage, Kevin P. Martin, Ted Powers, Bina Sharif, Wonderly White.

MEISTER HEMMELIN. Written and directed by E. Macer-Story. November 10, 1994. With Eileen Aranas, Nicole Bernadette, Richard Craven, Bill Dobbins, Douglas Stone, James Sturtevant, Kimberly Weiant.

DROPPING IN ON THE EARTH. Book and lyrics, Tom Attea and Mark Marcante; music and musical direction, Arthur Abrams. November 25, 1994. Director, Mark Marcante; choreography, Craig Meade; scenery, Donald L. Brooks; lighting, Paul Ferri; costumes, Moira L. Shaughnessy. With Cheryl Gadsen, Donn Grebner, Mark Marcante, Craig Meade, Judy Nock, Michael Vazquez.

COME WEST. By Akeh Ugah Ufumaka III. December 1, 1994. Director, Rich Crooks; scenery, Evan Remnik, Rich Crooks. With Daniel Carlton, Daryl Dismond, Andrew R. Grant, Eboni Cooper.

THE LITTLE BOOK OF PROFESSOR ENIGMA. By Harry Kondoleon. December 15, 1994. Director, Tom Gladwell. With Andy Reynolds, Crystal Field, Stephen Sinclair, Bethany Smith, Donald Brooks, Laurie Wickens.

BREAD & PUPPET THEATER: NATIVITY. December 20, 1994.

SEXUAL PSYCHOBABBLE: POETIC INJUSTICE, LOW ACCOMMODATIONS, SEXLAX and A SPACE FOR SEDUCTION by Lissa Moira and Richard West; YOU ARE WHO YOU EAT by Ultra Violet. December 22, 1994. Director, Lissa Moira; scenery and costumes, Peter Janis; lighting and sound, George Kodar. With Lissa Moira, Robert Croft, Ray Capuana, Heathcliff Harris, Peter Hopkins, Rachel Isaacson, Aimee Jolson, Hal Smith Reynolds, Jo Lynn Sciarro, Ivy Levinson, Jiggers Turner, Kenya De Rosa.

POLKA. By Tony Greenleaf. December 29, 1994. Direction and scenery, Richard Hoehler; lighting, Rob Kaplowitz. With Cam Kornman, Keely Madden, Tony Greenleaf, Jonathan Teague Cook.

MR. BUDHOO'S LETTER OF RESIGNATION FROM THE I.M.F. By and with the Bread & Puppet Theater. February 8, 1995.

THE WORLD . . . IN SEVEN PLAYS (short sketches). By Walter Corwin. February 9, 1995. Director, Lee Gundersheimer; music, Arthur Abrams. With Elizabeth Baird, Mark Elliot, Lee Gundersheimer, Ruth Jaffe, Troy Rich.

TALKIN' TO THE DEVIL and SE JUDY'S BLANK VACATION. Written and directed by Karen Williams. February 9, 1995. Lighting, Paul Clay. With Marion Appel, Billy Clark, Ed Greer, Leo Marks, Susan Mumford, Roderick Murray, George Norfleet Jr., Heaven Phillips, Colleen Werthmann, Jeanne Wilcoxon.

HOW I GOT TO CLEVELAND (monologue). By and with Karen Williams. February 12, 1995. Director, Jo Bonney.

UNDERSTANDING DESIRE. By Anita Sieff, Anna Maria Cianciulli and Elizabeth Woodruff Thompson. February 16, 1995. Director, Anita Sieff. With Lisa M. Bobonis, Anna Maria Cianciulli, Michael Hladio.

UNORTHODOX BEHAVIOR. Written and directed by Barbara Kahn. March 9, 1995. Scenery, Donald L. Brooks; lighting, Paul Ferri; costumes, Linda Gui. With Jolie Dechev, Jackie S. Freeman, Gary Lamadore, Lenore Loveman.

ODD LIASONS: DELHI DUO and VULCANIC SURRENDER. By J. Lois Diamond. March 9, 1995. Directors, J. Lois Diamond, Anthony Patton. With Meryl Harris, Ken Valentino, Mair Immel, Katie Atcheson, Michael Mitchell.

CULTURE SHOCK. By Sebastian Liotta. March 16, 1995. Director, Rosalinda Zepeda; scenery, Shawn Ventura; lighting, David Scott. With John Cates, Tracy Costen, John DiGennaro, Christopher Kearns, Terry Lee King, Michael Martinez, Dennis Morton.

M: THE MANDELA SAGA. By Laurence Holder. March 16, 1995. Director, Randy Frazier; lighting, David Sheppard. With Marjorie Johnson, Todd Davis, Dominic Marcus.

THE CELEBRATION RECLAIMED. By Arthur Sainer. April 20, 1995. Director, Donald L. Brooks; costumes, Irene V. Nolan. With Mark Marcante, Pietro Gonzalez, Raquel Yossiffon, Jocelyn S. Druyan, Michael Keyloun, Reyn Williams, Katherine Adamenko, Anthony Craig, David Scott, Laurie Wickens.

COFFEE WITH KURT COBAIN. By Larry Myers. April 27, 1995. Director, Shellen Lubin. With Marilyn Duryea, Theo Polites, Paul Francis Scott, Angelica Torn.

THE CAUSE. By Yolanda Rodriguez. May 11, 1995. Director, Crystal Field; scenery, Mark Marcante; lighting, Donald L. Brooks. With Venus Velazquez, Joel Arandia, Donald L. Brooks, Isrial Cruz, Joseph C. Davies, Sol Echeverria, Pietro Gonzales, Bob Grimm, Jerry Jaffe.

THE HEART IS A LONELY HUNTER. Adapted from Carson McCullers's novel and directed by David Willinger. May 18, 1995. Scenery, Clark Fidelia; costumes, Tanya Serdiuk; lighting, Zdenek

Kriz. With Anthony Greenleaf, Aixa Kendrick, Shane Blodgett, Caesar Paul Del Trecco, Lea Antolini, Dennis R. Jones, Jonathan Teague Cook, Mari Prentice.

Ubu Repertory Theater. Committed to acquainting American audiences with new works by contemporary French-speaking playwrights from around the world. Francoise Kourilsky artistic director.

A MODEST PROPOSAL (18). By Tilly, translated by Richard Miller. October 4, 1994. Director, Saundra McClain; scenery, Watoku Ueno; lighting, Greg MacPherson; costumes, Carol Ann Pelletier. With Melissa Chalsma, Abdoulaye N'Gom, Fred Burrell, Elizabeth Hess, Elizabeth Perry.

THE TROPICAL BREEZE HOTEL (14). By Maryse Conde, translated by Barbara Brewster Lewis and Catherine Temerson. February 14, 1995. Director, Shauneille Perry; scenery, Watoku Ueno; lighting, Greg MacPherson; costumes, Carol Ann Pelletier. With Jane White, Patrick Rameau.

ANOTHER STORY (14). By Julius Amedee Laou, translated by Richard Miller. March 14, 1995. Director, Francoise Kourilsky; scenery, Watoku Ueno; lighting, Greg MacPherson; costumes, Carol Ann Pelletier. With La Tonya Borsay, Erika L. Heard, Robert Morgan, Andrea Smith.

Staged Readings

MARIE HASPARREN. By Jean-Marie Besset, translated by Richard Miller. October 17, 1994.
THE CHILD IN OBOCK. By Daniel Besnehard, translated by Stephen J. Vogel. October 24, 1994.
STILL LIFE FOR 3 DANCERS. By Philippe Faure, translated by Yan Senouf. October 31, 1994.

The Vineyard Theater. Multi-art chamber theater dedicated to the development of new plays and musicals, music-theater collaborations and innovative revivals. Douglas Aibel artistic director, Barbara Zinn Krieger executive director, Jon Nakagawa managing director.

AMERICA DREAMING. By Chiori Miyagwa. December 6, 1994. Co-produced by Music-Theater Group; see its entry under Music-Theater Group.

RAISED IN CAPTIVITY (42). By Nicky Silver. February 9, 1995. Director, David Warren; scenery, James Youmans; lighting, Donald Holder; costumes, Teresa Snider-Stein; music and sound, John Gromada. With Peter Frechette, Patricia Clarkson, Brian Kerwin, Leslie Ayvazian, Anthony Rapp.

PHAEDRA (32). By Elizabeth Egloff. April 21, 1995. Director, Evan Yionoulis; scenery, James Youmans; lighting, Donald Holder; costumes, Constance Hoffman. With Randy Danson, David Chandler, Mark Rosenthal, Sam Tsoutsouvas, Susan Blommaert, Mark Smaltz, Fanni Green, David Greenspan.

The Women's Project and Productions. Nurtures, develops and produces plays written and directed by women. Julia Miles founder and artistic director.

27 performances each

WHY WE HAVE A BODY. By Claire Chafee. November 8, 1994. Director, Evan Yionoulis; scenery, Peter B. Harrison; lighting, Donald Holder; costumes, Teresa Snider-Stein. With Jayne Atkinson, Trish Hawkins, Deborah Hedwall, Nancy Hower.

THE LAST GIRL SINGER. By Deborah Grace Winer. May 9, 1995. Director, Charles Maryan; scenery, Atkin Pace; lighting, John Gleason; costumes, Lana Fritz. With Kelly Bishop, Bill Tatum, Charlotte Maier.

WPA Theater. Produces new American plays and musicals in the realistic idiom. Kyle Renick artistic director, Lori Sherman managing director.

THE NAKED TRUTH (40). By Paul Rudnick. June 16, 1994. Director, Christopher Ashley; scenery, James Youmans; lighting, Donald Holder; costumes, David Woolard. With Peter Bartlett, J. Smith-

Cameron, John Cunningham, Cynthia Darlow, Debra Messing, Mary Beth Peil, Valarie Pettiford, Victor Slezak.

UNEXPECTED TENDERNESS (32). By Israel Horovitz. October 16, 1994. Director, Steve Zuckerman; scenery, Edward T. Gianfrancesco; lighting, Richard Winkler; costumes, Mimi Maxmen. With Steve Ryan, Jonathan Marc Sherman, Caitlin Clarke, Karen Goberman, Scotty Bloch, Sol Frieder, Paul O'Brien.

THE SUGAR BEAN SISTERS (26). By Nathan Sanders. January 19, 1995. Director, Evan Yionoulis; scenery, David Gallo; lighting, Jack Mehler; costumes, Mary Myers. With Annie Golden, Beth Dixon, Margo Martindale.

WATBANALAND (24). By Doug Wright. March 29, 1995. Director, Christopher Ashley; scenery, Rob Odorisio; lighting, Donald Holder; costumes, Anne C. Patterson; music and sound, Guy Sherman. With Lisa Emery, Emily Skinner, David Chandler, Ken Garito, Susan Greenhill, Dion Graham.

HUNDREDS OF HATS (40). Conceived and directed by Michael Mayer; music, Alan Menken, Jonathan Sheffer, Marvin Hamlisch and Barry Mann; lyrics, Howard Ashman. May 25, 1995. Choreography, John Ruocco; scenery, Mark Beard; lighting, Jack Mehler; costumes, Michael Krass; musical direction, Helen Gregory. With John Ellison Conlee, Bob Kirsh, Philip Lehl, Amanda Naughton, Nancy Opel.

York Theater Company. Specializing in producing new works as well as in reviving unusual, forgotten or avant-garde musicals. Janet Hayes Walker producing director.

DOWN BY THE OCEAN (30). Written and directed by P.J. Barry. September 24, 1994. Scenery, James Morgan; lighting, Stan Pressner; costumes, Elizabeth Besom. With Dennis Parlato, Sam Groom, Ross Bickell, Melina Kanakaredes, John Newton, Pamela Burrell.

A DOLL'S LIFE. Book and lyrics by Betty Comden and Adolph Green; music, Larry Grossman. December 21, 1994. Director, Robert Brink; scenery, James Morgan; lighting, Mary Jo Dondlinger; costumes, Patricia Adshead; musical direction, David Kirshenbaum. With Jill Geddes, Seth Jones, Jeff Herbst, Paul Schoeffler, Tom Galantich, Robin Skye.

LOVE! FOR BETTER AND VERSE (one-woman show) (13). Conceived and performed by Barbara Feldon. February 15, 1995. Director, Barry McNabb; scenery, James Morgan; lighting, Mary Jo Dondlinger.

CLOTHES FOR A SUMMER HOTEL. By Tennessee Williams. April 20, 1995. Director, Tony Giordano; lighting, Mary Jo Dondlinger; sound, Jim van Bergen; music, Michael Valenti. With Diane Kagan, Robert LuPone, Doug Stender, Robert Duncan, Terrence Markovich, Maeve McGuire, Conrad Osborn.

Musicals in Mufti. 4 performances each

ONWARD VICTORIA. Book and lyrics, Charlotte Anker and Irene Rosenberg; music, Keith Herrmann. May 6, 1995. Director, Adele Aronheim; musical direction, David Kirshenbaum.

MATA HARI. Book, Jerome Coopersmith; music, Edward Thomas; lyrics and direction by Martin Charnin. May 13, 1995. Musical direction, Keith Levinson.

GOLDEN BOY. Book by Leslie Lee, based on Clifford Odets's play; music, Charles Strouse; lyrics, Lee Adams and Charles Strouse. May 20, 1995. Director, Jeffrey B. Moss.

Miscellaneous

In the additional listing of 1994–95 off-off-Broadway productions below, the names of the producing groups or theaters appear in CAPITAL LETTERS and the titles of the works in *italics*. This list consists largely of new or reconstituted works. It includes a few productions staged by groups which rented space from the more established organizations listed previously.

ACTORS PLAYHOUSE. *The Truth About Ruth: The Musical Memoirs of a Bearded Lady* book and lyrics by Peter Morris; music by Brad Ellis. July 7, 1994. Directed by Phillip George; with Toni Dibuono, David Lowenstein. *Two Hearts Over Easy* book, music, lyrics and direction by Robert W. Cabell. August 24, 1994. With Melanie Demitri, Bill Ebbesmeyer, Randy Weiss, Maggie Wirth.

ACTOR'S INSTITUTE THEATER. *Not Responsible!* (one-man show) by and with Rich Stone. November 4, 1994. Directed by Quiche Lloyd-Kemble.

ALICE'S FOURTH FLOOR. *Thanatos* by Ron Simonian. March 12, 1995. Directed by Sidonie Garrett; with Richard Augustine, Phil Fiorni, R.D. Mangels, Tess Brubeck, Matthew Rapport.

AMERICAN JEWISH THEATER. *Hey, Buddy* by Bryan Goluboff. November 13, 1994. Directed by George Ferencz; with Mark Auerbach, Anthony Grasso. *Have You Spoken to Any Jews Lately?* by Bruce Jay Friedman. January 23, 1995. Directed by Michael Rudman; with Larry Pine, Richard M. Davidson, Stephen Singer, Penny Balfour, Christina Haag, Judith Granite, Gene Canfield, Brennan Brown. *Shabbatai* book, music and lyrics by Michael Schubert and Michael Edwin. May 10, 1995. Directed by Stanley Brechner; with Romain Fruge, Maggi-Meg Reed, Rex Hays, Ken Jennings.

AMERICAN THEATER ENSEMBLE. *Mother and Child* written and directed by Matthew Lombardo. September 22, 1994. With Helen Harrelson, Anthony Brown.

BANK STREET THEATER. *Blood Orgy of the Carnival Queens!* by Robin Carrigan and Jim Fall. June 23, 1994. Directed by Jim Fall; with Robin Carrigan, Kristine Zbornik, Eric Bernat, John Cantwell, Pall Gale, John O'Brien, Ronnie Ascher.

THE BARROW GROUP. *Ghost in the Machine* by David Gilman. September 18, 1994. Directed by Seth Barrish; with Lee Brock, Susan Floyd, Reade Kelly, Ken Leung, Herbert Rubens, Stephen Singer. *Trust* by Steven Dietz. March 13, 1995. Directed by Larry Green; with Elizabeth Rice, Ilene Kristen, Lee Brock, Amy Hargreaves, Holter Graham, Seth Barrish.

BROOKLYN ACADEMY OF MUSIC. *Next Wave Festival.* Works included *Gaudeamus* conceived and performed by the Maly Drama Theater and students of the Academy of Theater Arts, St. Petersburg, adapted and directed by Lev Dodin. November 2, 1994. With Igor Chernevich, Oleg Dmitriyev, Sergei Kargin, Yuri Kordonsky, Natalya Kromina, Igor Koniayev, Igor Nikolayev, Tatyana Olear, Irina Tychinina. *La Belle et La Bete* (opera) by Philip Glass, based on Jean Cocteau's film. December 7, 1994. Directed by Charles Otte; with Alexandra Montano, Hailie Neill, Gregory Purnhagen, Zheng Zhou.

CHAIN LIGHTNING THEATER. Fourth Annual Short Play Festival: *Shelter* by Sandford Stokes; *Live Witness* by Jim Neu; *Older People* by John Ford Noonan. December 4, 1994. With Leslie Colucci, Max Faugno, Kricker James, Cheryl Horne, Jerry Mettner, Sandi Skodnik, Sanford Morris, Mark Barkan, Frank O'Brien.

CREATIVE VOICES THEATER. *Tell Veronica* by Tony Jerris. November 13, 1994. Directed by Jeffrey J. Albright; with CaSandra Brooks, Lisa O'Brien, Wende O'Reilly, Jeff Paul, Joanie Schumacher, Lee Steinhardt.

CSC THEATER. *Box Office of the Damned!* book, music and lyrics by Michael James Ogborn. June 3, 1994. Directed by Barry McNabb; with Marcy McGuigan.

CUCHARACHA THEATER. *Apocrypha* by Travis Preston and Royston Coppenger; music by David van Tieghem. June 3, 1994. Directed by Travis Preston.

CURRICAN THEATER. *The Borderland* by Jim Grimsley. October 21, 1994. Directed by Dean Gray; with Elizabeth Lewis Corley, Laurence Lau, Sarah McCord, David Van Pelt. *Young Hitler* by and with Marshall Davis. April 24, 1995. Directed by Keith Fadelici.

DIXON PLACE. *My Tiny Life* by and with Hapi Phace (Mark F. Rizzo). November 4, 1994. *Jumping Off the Fridge* (one-woman show) by and with Ellen Hulkower. November 30, 1994.

DO GOODER PRODUCTIONS. *My Soul Is Mine: A Runaway's Story* by and with Mark Robert Gordon. February 8, 1995. Directed by Jon Michael Johnson.

DON'T TELL MAMA. *Honky-Tonk Highway* book by Richard Berg; music and lyrics by Robert Lindsey-Nassif. June 13, 1994. Directed by Gabriel Barre; with Rick Leon, Matthew Bennett, Sean McCourt, Kevin Fox, Erin Hill.

FOOLS COMPANY SPACE. *The Blindfold* by Jose Lopez Rubio, translated by Marion Peter Holt. September 28, 1994. Directed by Sara Louise Lazarus; with Richard Charles Hoh, Rica Martens, Steve Parris. *2266* by Alan Yeck. November 30, 1994.

45TH ST. THEATER. *The Castle* by Howard Barker. December 6, 1994. Directed by Michael E. Nassar.

FREE THEATER PROJECT. Reading by Marian Seldes. July 29, 1994.

THE GLINES. *Key West* by John Glines. October 5, 1994. Directed by Randy Buck. *Lady-Like* by Laura Shamas. May 18, 1995. Directed by Vivian Sorenson; with Angela McKinney, Laura Jane Salvato.

HAROLD CLURMAN THEATER. *Andrew My Dearest One* by Mary Mitchell. February 2, 1995. Directed by Tanya Kane-Parry; with Brenda Smiley, Jason Tyler White, Rafael Petlock.

HERE. *Killer in Love, The Group* and *1984* (one-act plays) by Sarah Schulman. June 1, 1994. Directed by Angela Robinson, Mark Owen and Rich Rubin; with Bina Sharif, Liz Stearns, Anna Padgett, Mark Ameen, Lisa Marie Bronson, Anna Grace. *Lizzie Borden* conceived and directed by Tim Maner; music and lyrics by Steven Cheslik-DeMeyer. September 9, 1994. With Loren Kidd, Alison White, Annette Houlihan Verdolino, Abigail Gampel. *Tip or Die* (one-woman show) by and with Linda Mancini. September 9, 1994. Directed by Pablo Vela. *Phaedra* written and directed by Matthew Maguire. April 12, 1995. With Socorro Santiago, George Bartenieff, Andy Paris, Ray Xifo, Nicole Alifante, Verna Hampton.

INTAR THEATER. *A Field in Heat* by Ricky Spears. September 25, 1994. Directed by Michael Piatkowski; with Christina Burz, Ray Pirkle, Jill Jackson, Melinda Eades, Steve Sherling, Justin Malone, Todd Lewis.

IRONDALE ENSEMBLE PROJECT. *You Can't Win* by Joshua Taylor and Jim Niesen, adapted from Jack Black's memoirs. November 6, 1994. Directed by Jim Niesen; with Georgina Corbo, Paul Ellis, Michael-David Gordon, Terry Greiss, Robin Kurtz, Ellen Orenstein, Joshua Taylor. *Ghost Sonata* by August Strindberg, translated by Harry G. Carlson. April 24, 1995. Directed by Johan Petri; with Terry Greiss, Joshua Taylor, Robin Kurtz, Georgina Corbo, Michael-David Gordon.

JEAN COCTEAU REPERTORY. *Marie Antoinette* by Conrad Bishop and Elizabeth Fuller. June 7, 1994. Directed by Conrad Bishop; with Elizabeth Fuller, Craig Smith, Elise Stone. Co-produced by Independent Eye. *The Keepers* by Barbara Lebow. August 28, 1994. Directed by Scott Shattuck; with Craig Smith, Elise Stone, Adrienne D. Williams. *The Country Wife* by William Wycherley. October 9, 1994. Directed by Tori Haring-Smith; with Mark Waterman, Harris Berlinsky, Elise Stone, Abner Genece, David Snider, Christopher Black, Adrienne Williams, Sandra Sciford, Jon Ecklund, Kennedy Brown, Craig Smith, Angela Vitale, Pat Edwards, Molly Pietz. *The Cherry Orchard* by Anton Chekhov. December 2, 1994. Directed by Eve Adamson; with Christopher Black, Angela Vitale. *Napoli Milionaria* by Eduardo De Filippo, translated by Tori Haring-Smith. January 22, 1995. Directed by Robert Hupp; with Craig Smith, Elise Stone, Christopher Black, Angela Vitale, Mark Waterman, Abner Genece, Jon Ecklund, David Snider, Kennedy Brown, Harris Berlinsky, Molly O'Donnell, Molly Pietz, Monique Vukovic. *Hamlet* by William Shakespeare. March 19, 1995. Directed by Eve Adamson; with Harris Berlinsky, Mark Waterman.

JEWISH REPERTORY THEATER. *That's Life!* (musical revue) conceived and directed by Helen Butleroff. June 20, 1994. With David Beach, Stephen Berger, Lisa Rochelle, Cheryl Stern, Steve Sterner. *The Gift Horse* by Michael Hardstark. November 6, 1994. Directed by Robert Kalfin; with Brian Rose, Ed Kershen, Jon Avner, Lex Monson, Bernie Passeltiner. *Living Proof* by Gordon Rayfield. January 15, 1995. Directed by Allen Coulter; with Rebecca Waxman, Amy Hargreaves, Michael D. Gallagher, Lee Brock, Lee Shepherd, Jeffrey Spolan. *Awake and Sing!* by Clifford Odets. March 19, 1995. Directed by Larry Arrick; with Tovah Feldshuh, Stephen Lang, Stephen Mailer, David Rosenbaum, Amanda Peet, Salem Ludwig, Tim Zay, Avery Schreiber, Jeff Casper. *Angel Levine* book (adapted from Bernard Malamud's story), music and lyrics by Phyllis K. Robinson. May 14, 1995. Directed by Peter Bennett; with Andre De Shields, Marilyn Sokol, Michael Ingram, Jordan Leeds, Pauline Frommer.

JOHN HOUSEMAN THEATER. *Spontaneous Broadway* by and with Freestyle Repertory Theater. March 8, 1995. *Brimstone and Treacle* by Dennis Potter. March 10, 1995. Directed by Edward Einhorn. *Ecstasy* by Mike Leigh. April 20, 1995. Directed by Scott Elliott; with John Wojda, Caroline Seymour, Marian Quinn, Zaniz Jakubowski, Jared Harris, Patrick Fitzgerald.

LARK THEATER COMPANY—Peter Daniel, Jeremy Shamos and Il-yana Kadushin in the revue *Commedia Tonite!* featuring original music by Frank Schiro

JUDITH ANDERSON THEATER. *Men: the Musical* (musical revue) music by C. Colby Sachs; lyrics by Kevin Hammonds. October 6, 1994. With Gary R. Ramsey, Mark Irish, Michael J. Isennock, Kevin Hammonds, J.B. McLendon. *Three by Beckett: Play, That Time* and *Not I* by Samuel Beckett. December 9, 1994. Directed by Mary Forcade, Joseph Chaikin, Luly Santangelo; with Ron Faber, Rosemary Quinn, Luly Santangelo, Henry Steele, Wendy vanden Heuvel. *Ferryboat* book by Sam Midwood; music and lyrics by Bart Midwood. December 23, 1994. *Niagara Falls and So Do I* by and with Gary Schiro. January 26, 1995. Directed by Robert Burns. *Incommunicado* by Tom Dulack. March 16, 1995. Directed by Richard Corley; with Tom Aldredge, Darryl Theirse, Scott Whitehurst, Brian Dykstra, Baxter Harris. *The Lysistrata Affair* book by Sally M. Gall; music and lyrics by Michael Cook and Eben W. Keyes II. April 21, 1995. Directed by Nancy Hancock.

JUDSON MEMORIAL CHURCH. *Heroes and Saints* by Cherrie Moraga. December 7, 1994. Directed by Albert Takazauckas; with Isaiah Cazares, Doris Difarnecio, Matt Edwards, Elsie Hilario, Adriana Inchaustegui, Mario Mendoza, Claudia Rocofort, Jualkyris Santiago, Marta Vidal.

THE KITCHEN. *Mathew in the School of Life* (opera) by John Moran. October 6, 1994. Directed by Bob McGrath.

LAMB'S THEATER. *St. Mark's Gospel* (one-man performance) by Alec McCowen of the Gospel According to St. Mark. March 29, 1995.

LARK THEATER COMPANY. *Commedia Tonite!* (musical revue) music by Frank Schiro. November 27, 1994. Directed by Erin B. Mee; with Peter Daniel, Jeremy Shamos, Ilyana Kadushin, Shaun M. Powell, Michael Cone, Stephen Gleason. *Playwrights Week '95* (staged readings): *Helmut Sees America* by George Malko, directed by John Stewart; *Question of Mercy* by Robert Trumbull, directed by Ray Gordon; *Swollen* by Ron Burch, directed by Martha Banta; *The Corridor* by Diane Kagan, directed by Gregory Abels; *Hothouse Burbs* by John Stewart, directed by William Woodman; *Dog and His Master* by Wang Luoyong and Michael Johnson, directed by John Morrison; *Old Man River* by Cynthia Gates

Fujikawa, directed by John Clinton Eisner; *The Goddess Cure* by Adam Kraar, directed by Paula Cole. May 11–14, 1995.

LINCOLN CENTER. *Serious Fun!* Schedule included *Schlemiel the First* by Robert Brustein, adapted from Isaac Bashevis Singer's play, music, Hankus Netsky, lyrics, Arnold Weinstein, directed by David Gordon, with Larry Block, Charles Levin, Rosalie Gerut, Remo Airaldi, Marilyn Sokol; *The Notebooks of Leonardo da Vinci* adapted and directed by Mary Zimmerman, with Mariann Mayberry, Tracy Walsh, Laura Eason, Krzysztof Pieczynski, Paul Oakley Stovall; *Chippy: Diary of a West Texas Hooker* by Jo Harvey Allen and Terry Allen, music by Jo Harvey Allen, Terry Allen, Butch Hancock, Joe Ely, Wayne Hancock and Jo Carol Pierce, directed by Evan Yionoulis; performance by Pomo Afro Homos. July 6–30, 1994.

MINT THEATER COMPANY. *Lady Windermere's Fan* by Oscar Wilde. October 7, 1994. Directed by James C. Nicola; with Barbara Reierson, Jennifer Rohn, Tercio Bretas, Barbara Becker, Peter Husovsky, Craig Dean Mason, James Conant, Julie Mer. *Uncle Bob* by Austin Pendleton. February 1, 1995. Directed by Kelly Morgan; with George Morfogen, Adam Sumner Stein. *Quality Street* by James M. Barrie. April 20, 1995. Directed by Jonathan Bank; with Lisa M. Bostnar, Tim Goldrick, Barbara Becker.

MIRANDA THEATER COMPANY. *Cinoman and Rebeck* (one act plays): *The Bull, The Sineater of Cork, Hysteria* and *Truth & Sex* by Susan Cinoman; *The Drinking Problem* and *Does This Woman Have A Name?* by Theresa Rebeck. June 1, 1994. With Geneva Carr, Wayne Adam Farness, Sally Frontman, Raymond Haigler, Ibi Janko, Jerry Mettner, Patricia Migliori, Matt Mutrie, Alexandra Napier, Paul O'Brien, Polly Segal, Diego Taborda. *Kidnapped* by Sean O'Connor. January 25, 1995. Directed by Jude Schanzer; with Sally Frontman, Raymond Haigler, Earle Hugens, Ibi Janko, Tim McCracken, Clark Middleton, Polly Segal, Andre Sogliuzzo. *Regrets Only* and *Knowing the Questions* (monologues) by and with Jamie Berger. February 15, 1995. Directed by Roberta D'Alois.

NADA. Faust Festival (over fifty productions of *Faust* at various sites by different groups). October 12, 1994–May 31, 1995.

NEGRO ENSEMBLE COMPANY. *Ballad for Bimshire* book by Irving Burgie and Loften Mitchell; music and lyrics by Irving Burgie. November 18, 1994. Directed by Susan Watson Turner; with Lisa Hunt, Amy-Monique Waddell.

NEW YORK GILBERT AND SULLIVAN PLAYERS. *The Yeoman of the Guard.* October 16, 1994. *Princess Ida.* December 29, 1994. *The Mikado.* January 5, 1995. Directed by Albert Bergeret; with Steve Allen, Marc Heller, Belinda Bronaugh, Cedric Cannon, Carrie Wilshusen, Kathleen Larson, Stephen O'Brien, Philip Reilly.

NEW YORK PUBLIC LIBRARY FOR THE PERFORMING ARTS READING ROOM READINGS. *Somewhere in the Pacific* by Neal Bell. October 17, 1994. Directed by Michael Greif; with John Cameron Mitchell, Adam Trese, John Benjamin Hickey, Gabriel Macht, Richmond Hoxie, Steve Zahn, David Warshofsky, Ross Salinger, Jonathan Fried. *Fear Itself* by Eugene Lee. November 14, 1994. Directed by Liz Diamond; with Jayne Haynes, Larry Pine, Lisa Benavides, Gabriel Macht, Bruce MacVittie. *Making Gingers* by Dan Kagan. December 12, 1994. Directed by John Ferraro; with Mary Testa, Paul Giamatti. *The Promise* by Jose Rivera. January 23, 1995. Directed by Susana Tubert; with Richard Petrocelli, Camilla Sanes, John Ortiz, Virginia Rambal, Joe Quintero, Jorge Rios. *Boca* by Christopher Kyle. February 27, 1995. Directed by Alice Jankell; with Meg Anderson, Sandra Bernhard, Ross Bickell, Mark W. Conklin, Jon Ecklund, Tibor Feldman, Stephanie Mnookin, Scott Sherman, Isa Thomas. *Going, Going, Gone* by and with Saratoga International Theater Institute. March 27, 1995. *Hard Work* by Ain Gordon. April 24, 1995. Directed by Michael Sexton; with Kirk Jackson, Chuck Coggins, Welker White, Jon Ecklund, Valda Setterfield, Michelle Hurst, Isa Thomas, Tibor Feldman, Oliver Wadsworth, Siobhan Fallon. *My Virginia* by and with Darci Picoult. May 22, 1995. Directed by Suzanne Shepherd.

NUYORICAN POETS CAFE. *The Preacher and the Rapper* by Ishmael Reed. November 10, 1994. Directed by Rome Neal; with William Williams, Ray Campbell, Robert N. Lin.

OHIO THEATER. *XXX Love Act* by Cintra Wilson. April 19, 1995. Directed by Troy Hollar; with Lynn Cohen, Jennifer Esposito, Adam Nelson, Courtney Rackley, Daniel Reinish, Nadine Stenovitch, Shea Whigham.

ONE DREAM THEATER. *Living in Pieces* by and with Julie Flanders. January 19, 1995. Directed by Stephen Jobes. *A Lie of the Mind* by Sam Shepard. March 19, 1995. Directed by April Shawhan; with

Paul Geiser, Irene Glezos, Kyle McMurry, Rosemary McNamara, David Phillips, Suzanne Shepherd, Sam Trammell, Jeannie Zusy. *Vertigo Park* by Mark O'Donnell. May 14, 1995. Directed by Matt Ames; with Margaret Howard, Josh Liveright, Christopher Marobella.

ONTOLOGICAL-HYSTERIC THEATER. *I've Got the Shakes* written, directed and designed by Richard Foreman. January 5, 1995. With Jan Leslie Harding, Mary McBride, Rebecca Moore, Michael Osano.

PEARL THEATER COMPANY. *King Lear* by William Shakespeare. September 18, 1994. Directed by Shepard Sobel; with Robert Hock, Chris O'Neill. *The Beaux' Stratagem* by George Farquhar. November 6, 1994. Directed by Mary Lou Rosato; with Michael Butler, Joanne Camp, Robin Leslie Brown, Robert Hock. *The Venetian Twins* by Carlo Goldoni, translated by Michael Feingold. December 24, 1994. Directed by John Rando; with Arnie Burton, Robin Leslie Brown, Clement Fowler, Kevin Black. *Oedipus at Colonus* by Sophocles. February 12, 1995. Directed by Shepard Sobel; with Robert Blackburn, Bernard K. Addison, Fred Burrell, Robert Hock. *Mrs. Warren's Profession* by George Bernard Shaw. April 2, 1995. Directed by Alex Dmitriev; with Margo Skinner, Chelsea Altman, Bradford Cover, John Braden, Woody Sempliner, Robert Hock.

PERFORMANCE SPACE 122. Queer Performance '94 Festival. Schedule included *The Dish* by Paul Hallam, directed by Bruno Santini, with Bette Bourne; *Virtually Yours* by and with Kate Bornstein, directed by Jayne Wenger; *Asian Boys* by and with Nicky Paraiso; *In Your Face* by and with Gay Sweatshop Theater Company. June 2–July 2, 1994. *Of Mice, Bugs and Women* by and with Deb Margolin. October 6, 1994. Directed by Kent Alexander. *Four Scenes in a Harsh Life* by and with Ron Athey. October 27, 1994. Directed by Ron Athey and Julie Tolentino Wood; with Ron Athey, Darryl Carlton, Mark Seitchik, Dug McDowell, Clint Colker, Laura Goodwin, Debbi Tay, Scott Ewalt, Patty Powers, Julie Tolentino Wood. *Naked Breath* by and with Tim Miller. December 1, 1994. *Small Lives/Big Dreams* conceived from Anton Chekhov's plays and directed by Anne Bogart. February 2, 1995. With Saratoga International Theater Institute (J. Ed Araiza, Will Bond, Kelly Maurer, Barney O'Hanlon, Karenjune Sanchez). *Wrapped Up, Tied Up and Tangled* by and with Peggy Pettitt. March 2, 1995. Directed by Remy Tissier. *The Mathematics of Change* by Josh Kornbluth and John Bellucci. May 12, 1995. Directed by John Bellucci; with Josh Kornbluth.

PERRY STREET THEATER. *Simply Cole Porter* (musical revue). By and with Deborah Ausemus and J. Kent Barnhart. June 9, 1994. *Dylan Thomas: Return Journey* (one-man show) by and with Bob Kingdom and *The Truman Capote Talk Show* (one man show) by and with Bob Kingdom; see their entries in the Plays Produced off Broadway section of this volume. *Morticians in Love* by Christi Stewart-Brown. April 15, 1995. Directed by Jennifer Mendenhall; with Bernadette Flagler, Warren Keith, Carol Monda, Eric Nolan, Gabriela May Ladd.

PLAYHOUSE 91. *The Fall Guy* by Tsuka Kohei, based on his play *Kamata Koshinkyoku,* translated by Gary Perlman. April 12, 1995. Directed by Mako; with Andrew Pang, Keone Young, Stephen Lee, Roger Ma.

PLAYHOUSE 125. *The Conquest of the South Pole* by Manfred Karge, translated by Ralf E. Remshardt, Caron Cadle and Calvin MacLean. April 20, 1995. Directed by Nigel Maister; with Dominic Comperatore, Sergio Cacciotti, Peggy Jo Brenneman, Christopher Mako, Edward Vassallo, William McCall, Linnea Pyne, Kevin Connell.

PLAYHOUSE ON VANDAM. *Grandma Sylvia's Funeral* by Gary Wein and Amy Lord Blumsack. October 1, 1994. Directed by Gary Wein.

PROMENADE THEATER. *James Lecesne's Word of Mouth* (one-man show) by and with James Lecesne. May 8, 1995. Directed by Eve Ensler.

PULSE ENSEMBLE THEATER. *Oh What a Lovely War* by Joan Littlewood. December 1, 1994. Directed by Alexa Kelly.

SAMUEL BECKETT THEATER. *Tower of Burden* by Onukaba A. Ojo. November 3, 1994. Directed by Adusah Boakye; with Arthur French, Ahmat Jallo, Richard Abrams, Tamika Lamison, William Francis Smith, Messeret Stroman. *Hooters* by Ted Tally. December 4, 1994. *The Rehearsal* by Jean Anouilh. January 8, 1995. Directed by John Daines; with George Millenbach, Fiona Hutchinson. *Fortinbras* by Lee Blessing. February 7, 1995.

AT THE PROMENADE—James Lecesne
in his solo performance *Word of Mouth*

SANFORD MEISNER THEATER. *Conversations With the Pool Boy* by Robert Coles. September 9, 1994. *Three Years From Thirty* by Mike O'Malley. November 8, 1994. Directed by John Znidarsic; with Jim Barry, Jack Carey, Victoria Labalme, Richard Munroe, Mike O'Malley, Jackie Phelan, Maria Sucharetza.

SYNCHRONICITY SPACE. *Jenny and Phineas* by Seth Hamilton. July 21, 1994. With Seth Hamilton, Jenifer Jordan.

THEATER BY THE BLIND. *The Flip Side* (musical revue) by and with Theater by the Blind. June 10, 1994. Directed by Ike Schambelan. *Blinks* (short plays): *Both and Neither* by Peter Seymour; *Clearing a Path* by Jaime Ituarte; *Honorary Member* by George Ashiotis; *Shoot* by Lynn Manning; *Double Vision* by Peter Mikochik. May 25, 1995. With Kristine Watt, George Ashiotis, Karen Lynn Gorney, Brian Evaret Chandler, Mark C. Tafoya, Peter Seymour.

THEATER EAST. *This Is Magic* by and with Doc Boston and Betty London. September 24, 1995.

THEATER OFF PARK. *Judy at the Stonewall Inn* by Thomas O'Neill. June 16, 1994. Directed by Kenneth Elliott; with Jackie Sanders, Bryce Jenson. *Banner* by Kathleen Clark. October 11, 1994. Directed by Alison Summers; with Lois Robbins, Michael Piontek, Kevin Geer, Schuyler Grant, Maduka Steady, James Doerr. *Most Men Are* book, music and lyrics by Stephen Dolginoff. February 6, 1995. Directed by Daniel Simmons; with Joel Carlton, James Heatherly, Mark Peters, Ed Walker. *The Secret Sits in the Middle* by Lisa-Maria Radano. April 24, 1995. Directed by Deena Levy; with Marnie Pomerantz, Andrea Maulella, Brian Vincent, John DiBenedetto, Kate Shein. *Dates and Nuts* by Gary Lennon. May 22, 1995. Directed by Donald Douglass; with Terumi Matthews, Dina Spybey, Mark Nassar, Thomas Michael Allen.

THEATER ROW THEATER. *The Manchurian Candidate* by John Lahr, adapted from Richard Condon's novel and film. July 16, 1994. Directed by Perry Liu; with Ann Guilford-Grey, Richard Bourg, Lawrence Comp, David Frank, Alicia Genetski. *The Green Turtle* by Patrick Gabridge. January 31, 1995. Directed by Michael McKenzie Wills; with Cheryl Ann Allen, Dean Bradshaw, Teddy Coluca, Dana Grant, Jill Leslie, Tim Miller, Alex Roe, Jayne Ross, JoAnn Wahl.

13TH STREET REPERTORY COMPANY. *Out of the Blue* (one-man show) by and with Richard Hoehler. October, 1994.

30TH STREET THEATER. *Shades of Grey* by Kirk Aanes. December 4, 1994. Directed by Nick Gregory; with Jan Leslie Harding, Stewart Clarke, Brian Tarantina.

TRIANGLE THEATER COMPANY. *Gunplay* by Frank Higgins. November 19, 1994. Directed by Charles R. Johnson; with Chris Hietikko, Charlotte Maier, Joanna Rhinehart, Scott Whitehurst. *The Arrangement* by Eric Eisenberg. February 16, 1995.

TRIBECA PERFORMING ARTS CENTER. *The Crossroads* by Juan Tovar, adapted from Juan Rulfo's stories. October 23, 1994. Directed by Susana Tubert; with Diego Taborda, George Bass.

28TH STREET THEATER. *Broken English* by Geraldine Sherman. September 25, 1994. Directed by Stephen Hollis; Maxine Taylor-Morris, Fleur Phillips, Ahvi Spindell, Mary Testa. *The Swamp Dwellers* by Wole Soyinka. April 14, 1995. Directed by Patricia Floyd; with Arthur French, Geany Masai, Daniel Whitner, Todd-Anthony Jackson, Christopher Kirk Allen, Rochelle Henderson, James Abe.

29TH STREET REPERTORY THEATER. *Killer Joe* by Tracy Letts. October 6, 1994. Directed by Wilson Milam; with Leo Farley, Linda June Larson, Danna Lyons, David Mogentale, Thomas Wehrle.

WATERMARK THEATER. *Waiting at the Water's Edge* by Lucinda Coxon. June 5, 1994. Directed by Nela Wagman; with Patricia Scanlon, Isabel Keating, Simon Brooking, Sharon Laughlin, Craig Ugoretz. *Blaming Mom* and *Soupy and Adena* (one-act plays) by David Edelstein. October 15, 1994. Directed by Nela Wagman; with Sean Runnette, Patricia Scanlon. *Wordfire Festival '95* (solo performances): *My Left Breast* by and with Susan Miller, directed by Nela Wagman; *Just Beneath My Skin* by and with Patricia Scanlon; *One Mormon Show* by and with Emmett Foster. February 2–19, 1995. *Acts of Desire* (one-act plays) by Neena Beber. May 4, 1995. Directed by Nela Wagman.

WEILL RECITAL HALL. *Very Warm for May* book and lyrics by Oscar Hammerstein II; music by Jerome Kern. October 19, 1994. Directed by John McGlinn; with Brent Barrett, Donna Lynne Champlin, Kari duHoffman, Elizabeth Futral, John Hancock, Gregory Jbara, Damon Kirschenmann, Jon Lovitz, James Ludwig, Dina Merrill, Robert Nichols, Marguerite Shannon.

WEST END THEATER. *Soul Survivors* by Nancy Crist. October, 1994. Directed by Robert Armin.

WESTBETH THEATER CENTER. *Body Shop* book, music and lyrics by Walter Marks. December 5, 1994. Directed by Sue Lawless; with Tiffany Cooper, Justine DiConstanzo, Donna Drake, Susan Flynn, Beth Glover, Christopher Scott, Jodi Stevens.

WILLIAM REDFIELD THEATER. *Life Anonymous* by N. Richard Nash. November 6, 1994. *Heavy Breathing* by and with Scott Carter. February 19, 1995. Directed by Jim Fyfe. *Two Boys in Bed on a Cold Winter's Night* by James Edwin Parker. March 12, 1995. Directed by Tom Caruso; with Michael Curry, Paul C. Rice.

WILLOW CABIN THEATER. *Anatomy of Sound, El Capitan and the Corporal, Daybreak, Undecided Molecule, Untitled* and *14 August* (radio plays) by Norman Corwin, conceived and directed by Edward Berkeley. November 14, 1994. With Fiona Davis, Linda Powell. *Goose and Tomtom* by David Rabe. April 10, 1995. Directed by Adam Oliensis; with Laurence Gleason, Joe Pacheco, Tasha Lawrence, Angela Nevard, John Billeci, Ken Forman, Joseph Adams, Bjarni Thorsson.

THE WOOSTER GROUP. *Fish Story (An Epilogue to Brace Up!)* by and with the Wooster Group, based on Anton Chekhov's *Three Sisters,* translated by Paul Schmidt. November 17, 1994. Directed by Elizabeth LeCompte.

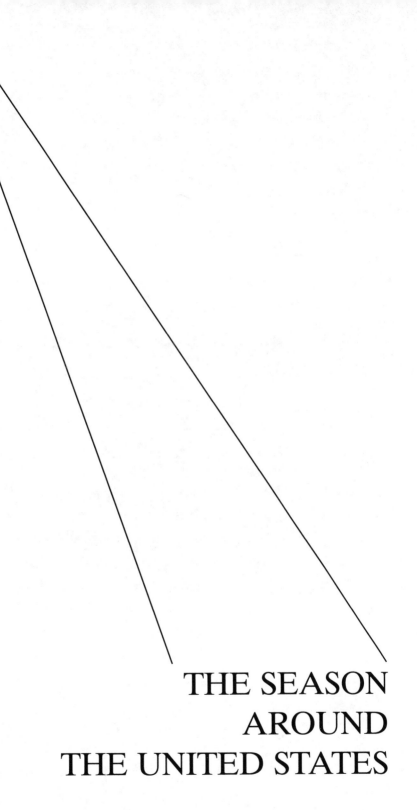

THE SEASON
AROUND
THE UNITED STATES

○
○
○

OUTSTANDING NEW PLAYS CITED BY AMERICAN THEATER CRITICS ASSOCIATION
and
A DIRECTORY OF NEW-PLAY PRODUCTIONS

○
○
○

THE American Theater Critics Association (ATCA) is the organization of over 250 leading drama critics in all media in all sections of the United States. One of this group's stated purposes is "To increase public awareness of the theater as a *national* resource" (italics ours). To this end, since 1974 ATCA has annually cited three outstanding new plays produced around the U.S., to be represented in our coverage by excerpts from each of their scripts demonstrating literary style and quality. And one of these—*The Nanjing Race* by Reggie Cheong-Leen—has been designated 1994's 10th annual ATCA New Play Award winner of $1,000.

A second 1994 ATCA citation went to *The Waiting Room* by Lisa Loomer. The second annual Elizabeth Osborn Award for an emerging playwright was voted to Charlie Varon for his one-actor, 24-character play *Rush Limbaugh in Night School,* in which he also performed all the roles. It has subsequently been produced off off Broadway.

The process of selection of these outstanding plays is as follows: any ATCA member critic may nominate a play which has been given a production in a professional house. It must be the first full professional production of a finished play (not a reading or an airing as a play-in-progress) during the calendar year. Nominated scripts were studied and discussed by an ATCA play-reading committee chaired by Michael Grossberg of the Columbus *Dispatch* and comprising Christine Dolen of the Miami *Herald,* Michael Sommers of the Newhouse Newspapers, Catherine Stadem of the Anchorage *Daily News,* Dennis Harvey of the San Francisco Bay *Guardian,* Misha Berson of the Seattle *Times,* Lawrence Bommer of the Chicago *Reader* and *Tribune* and alternates Michael Phillips of the San Diego *Union-Tribune* and Beatrice MacLeod of the Ithaca *Journal.* These committee members made their choices on the basis of script rather than production, thus placing very much the same emphasis as the editors of this volume in making the New York Best Play selections. If the timing of nominations and openings prevents some works from being considered in any given year, they will be eligible for consideration the following year if they haven't since moved to New York.

We offer our sincerest thanks and admiration to the ATCA members and their committee for the valuable insights into the 1994 theater season around the United States which their selections provide for this *Best Plays* record, in the form of excerpts from the outstanding scripts, with introductory reviews provided by Michael Sommers *(The Nanjing Race),* Misha Berson *(The Waiting Room)* and Michael Grossberg *(Rush Limbaugh in Night School)* .

ATCA Award

THE NANJING RACE

A Play in Two Acts

BY REGGIE CHEONG-LEEN

Cast and credits appear on page 476

REGGIE CHEONG-LEEN was born in Hong Kong and moved to the United States at age 15. He is a graduate of Notre Dame and since 1980 has lived in New York City, where two of his previous plays have been performed under the auspices of Asians & Friends: Cut Sleeves, *a musical, and* Squeeze, *a comedy. Prior to its world premiere at the McCarter Theater in Princeton, his prizewinning* The Nanjing Race *had received two staged readings as part of the Cleveland Public Theater's 11th Festival of New Plays.*

INTRODUCTION: Reggie Cheong-Leen's *The Nanjing Race* is a thoughtful drama about alienation. Its details relating to three characters are intimate and contemporary, but the canvas they are set against is a huge, historic and haunting one.

The play pivots about Philip, the New Jersey-born offspring of a Japanese mother and an American father. A 40-something businessman with scant awareness of his Asian heritage, Philip feels like an outsider in his own country. "One look and they'll label you minority," he says bitterly.

Philip has arrived in China for the first time to negotiate an important business deal. All too quickly, Philip discovers that he knows nothing about the Chinese way of doing business. He finds himself a stranger in the East, too.

In the venerable Nanjing hotel where much of the play occurs, Philip is rapidly pounced upon by Yu Ahn, a young hotel worker who is anxious to grow rich in America. Willing even to sell a kidney to bankroll the airfare out of a China that offers him only a bleak future, Yu Ahn will do almost anything for Philip's legal sponsorship. Philip, however, who is unabashedly gay, is soon taken with another hotel employee, Bao, a withdrawn fellow whose covert homosexuality has cost him dearly in China. Once Bao tried to escape to Hong Kong with his lover, who died in the attempt. Now, after spending a passionate night together, Philip wants to take Bao to live with him in America.

But history is against them. Nearly half a million Nanjing inhabitants were massacred by the Japanese during a few horrible weeks in 1937—the local water supply is said to be still faintly brown from the seepage of blood into the earth—and Bao is all too aware of Philip's Japanese background to link his future with the American visitor. "I do not have the strength to fight all that," Bao explains. "It is like to struggle against the state. It is too heavy and powerful. I cannot do it."

Despite Bao's refusal to go with Philip, a panicked Yu Ahn almost commits murder in his desperation to get out of China. In the end, the two Chinese men leave Philip to contemplate once more his uneasy place in the world.

The bitter ironies brewed up in Reggie Cheong-Leen's narrative are an effective contrast to the grace and subtle humor of his wordplay. The complex characters Cheong-Leen creates in his tenacious go-getter Yu-Ahn, the compassionate though wounded Bao, and the ever-alienated but still-so-American Philip make for a strong clash of different spirits as the play progresses.

The issue of homosexuality is practically incidental to this story, as the author concentrates far more upon the crushing weight of racial prejudice on the soul. For various reasons, each of these characters is rootless in his own society. The past history of prejudice and the current climate of misunderstanding that haunts these men in their present situations in life is a sad reminder that a genuine multicultural society in any part of the globe is still a long way off in the future.

The Nanjing Race is quite a good read as a play on the page, but it's one of those scripts that assumes extra urgency when it is performed. The McCarter Theater production was staged in an intimate arena setting by director Loretta Greco, which allowed the audience to register even the subtlest of facial expressions. Fluent lighting by Christopher Gorzelnik and Stephen Smith's sound design made for swift transitions in time and mood. The vibrant performances of Thom Sesma (Philip), B.D. Wong (Yu Ahn), and David Chung (Bao) further made *The Nanjing Race* a memorable theater experience.

Michael Sommers

Excerpts From *The Nanjing Race*

Bao is sitting on a bench. His hair is neatly combed, and his uniform is ironed and clean. From a large pile of dirty sheets, he takes each one and checks for holes before putting it into a bag. Yu Ahn enters. He pours himself some water to drink. His manner is full of strutting bravura. He hardly looks at Bao.

BAO: Where did your majesty disappear to for so long?

YU AHN: Hanging around, checking the rooms.

BAO: He's working! What god finally took mercy on us? I thought maybe you joined the ranks of the unemployed.

YU AHN: This shit is not employment. A grown man called a floor boy, standing with my hand out while they fish for a tip.

He goes downstage and opens the window. He breathes deeply, using his hands to slowly fan air towards his face.

BAO: What does it matter what they call you? Do your work. Get your salary. This is no different from any other profession.

YU AHN: Don't call this a profession. It's not even a trade. Slave labor, that's what this crap is.

BAO: I invite you to resign. You're enterprising. Scheme up some private business. You'd be a ten-thousander in no time, I'm sure.

YU AHN: Easy for you to say. I'm not pushing a cart to sell homemade soups for a few cents. Real business, you need backing. And luck. So much depends on luck.

BAO: Oh, I heard someone once whisper, "Hard work has something to do with it."

YU AHN: You're fucking right it has. You get no holidays, no sick pay, no insurance benefits. You know what they say, in your own business, your hands stop, your mouth stops.

BAO: So I guess my little job here isn't so bad after all.

YU AHN *(brings a rattan basket, takes out towels and folds them into a pile):* You don't mind the Japanese who overflow the tubs? Americans who leave tons of trash?

BAO: Water I mop. Trash I dump. I just wish they wouldn't chew gum. It sticks to everything. That's why they're fat, you know. They chew non-stop; their body thinks there's food coming, it creates more and more fat. They don't look like they have ever starved. Bunch of spoiled crybabies.

YU AHN: That's my old Bao.

Slaps Bao on the back.

Hate those foreigners, but love to work for them. You're all mixed up.

BAO: A job is a job. It doesn't mean I have to like them. Some of us know our history.

He goes and closes the window.

YU AHN: The hell with your history.

BAO: You are blessed. You have no conscience. So many in the past addicted to opium, it doesn't bother you.

YU AHN: It's called free trade. We were weak, people lost their desire to struggle, to go after their dreams. Sounds familiar?

He goes and opens the window.

BAO: I dream, like everyone else. We do it in our sleep. You're the only one who dreams while awake.

YU AHN: You pretend you are alive, but you're brain-dead. Know what I do? When I feel weak and frightened with doubt, I think of you. That gets my fighting spirit back, just like that.

He snaps his fingers in front of Bao's face. He goes back to his towels.

BAO: Think what you want. I don't have to broadcast my inner desires to feel secure.

YU AHN: You don't have to tell me your inner desires. I know what they are.

BAO: You're so smart, you know everything.

YU AHN: That's right. You forget how I got this job.

BAO: So you have a relative who has minor back-door connections.

YU AHN: Minor? My mother's cousin works for Public Security. She has the dirt on the assistant manager. That's not the only one she has the dirt on.

BAO: What are you telling me?

YU AHN: Forget it. Who has time for all that darkness in the past. My future is bright and happy. Far away from here.

BAO: Not that fantasy of yours again.

YU AHN: Not fantasy this time. It's going to happen.

BAO: That's what you said when you met Mr. Chicago.

YU AHN: How was I to know he was milking me for a story? Deadbeat journalist!

BAO: And Mrs. Florida? Mrs. Florida, I thought you loved him, but you got on that tourist bus, leaving the envelope with money, and such a sad note. Mrs. Florida, I wish you could have seen his face when he read your note.

YU AHN: You can't stand it, can you. Stuck here . . .

BAO *(goes to the window and closes it)*: You have your destiny, I have mine.

YU AHN: How can you breathe? Animals travel thousands of miles to the same spot each year. It's instinct. I must head west. I'll be a great success. Twenty-five inch color TV, giant refrigerator, a huge car. Girls are impressed with big things.

BAO: No one's impressed with you, the way you carry on. They come here to take pictures, buy souvenirs. The last thing they want is you as part of their luggage. It has to be a lot more subtle.

YU AHN: You brag so much, why don't I see you getting involved with any of them?

BAO: My Chinese nature and the white man's nature do not mix. They're all too aggressive. Not a bit of sensitivity or sublety. Think what China would be like un-corrupted by their Western influence.

YU AHN: I'd still be wearing a pigtail and get a hard-on when I see a woman's smelly bound feet.

BAO: You leave with one of these foreigners, the rest of your life will be indebted to them. That's not freedom. That's real slavery.

YU AHN: This time it's different. This one's part Asian, same blood as in my veins.

BAO: Don't fool yourself. You're nothing to them. They'll remember the hotel furniture before they remember you.

YU AHN: Day after day, life rushes by, while you sit in traffic with the other billion bicycles. One day you'll turn your head, there I'll be, next to you, driving a Mercedes-Benz. Everyone else will be driving cars, you'll still be on your bicycle, pedaling off to nowhere.

BAO: You'll never drive a Mercedes.

YU AHN: You want to bet? See who can get a sponsor first? I'll show you. Stay curled up in this tiny room, wait for old age. Then what? You retire to your one-room apartment; before you know it, you're buried in a box. It's not worth the effort of getting up in the morning, if that's all you have to look forward to. Try to live. Face upwind for a change. What have you got to lose?

BAO: Aren't you afraid I'll take the best sponsor away from you?

YU AHN: You can't take anything from me if you tried. Take my sponsor away. I could put the key that opens this cell in front of you, and you wouldn't have the guts to pick it up.

> *Yu Ahn leisurely puts some tea leaves into a cup, adds hot water from a thermos and puts a lid on it. He puts the cup on a tray.*

BAO: I ran away from home once, when I was nine, at the height of Cultural. All the neighborhood kids decided that was the thing to do. We didn't ask our mothers. With our red arm bands and little red book, no one dared refuse us a seat on the train. On the ninth morning, we get to Huang Shan. We climb all day, the mountain echoes with our reciting of Chairman Mao's teachings. By nightfall, we reach the monastery at the summit; all we see are clouds frozen in their turbulence. That night, I cannot sleep, so I go outside to pee. I suddenly get so homesick, I sit down by a tree and start to cry. A man comes and sits with me. It was so dark, I cannot see his face. He tells me he is a Buddhist monk, but because of his religion being looked down upon, he dresses in ordinary clothes and sits outside the monastery wall, just to feel close to the place he loves. In the darkness, he teaches me my first Tang poem.

> On the head of my bed
> Bright moon light
> How lucid the frost
> On barren ground of stone
> Raise my head I ponder
> The luminous moon
> Lower my head I crave
> For home lost and alone.

YU AHN: Spineless!

> *Yu ahn takes the tray with the cup and exits.*

BAO: He had such a bright, handsome voice, without seeing his face, I liked him.

> *Philip is sitting on the bed, wearing pajama pants. He dries his hair with a towel. Yu Ahn enters, once again assuming the obsequiousness of a servant.*

YU AHN: Water hot enough? Not too many guest in hotel. If many Japanese, no hot water in evening. If many Americans, no water pressure in morning. If European, no problem any time.

PHILIP: Do me a favor? Knock next time before you come in. I don't like people coming in uninvited.

YU AHN: Very sorry. I think you in bathroom, cannot hear me. Here is hot tea. This not best quality tea leaves, only domestic quality. Best quality save for export. They never keep good things. All export. Government say country need foreign exchange. We have five-year plan, ten-year plan, but what they promise never come. I want VCR, CD player now. Not wait five years. I meet rich businessman from Hong Kong, he has pocket telephone. He tells me he pays one thousand yuan a month for telephone bill. Very modern.

PHILIP: I hope you don't think that's what being modern is all about. I don't have a mobile phone. Very few Americans do. It's just a status symbol. Not everything has to have a dollar sign in front of it. We place more emphasis on things like integrity and friendship.

YU AHN: We have value for friend. I visit him, I bring him fruit or candy. Cost one yuan, or less. I visit supervisor for Chinese New Year, bring big chicken. Cost three yuan. Party boss of unit has daughter wedding, I give at least ten yuan present; that will smooth all future if I need favor. All this standard.

PHILIP: One billion Chinese doing exactly the same thing. Don't you feel the urge to break loose from the pack?

YU AHN: Chinese want no surprise. People think I lost common sense, my life has so many surprise.

PHILIP: We have so little, we must watch Freddy Krueger movies. Do they make Chinese horror movies?

YU AHN: Chinese movies very boring. We get enough shock from government policies.

PHILIP: You don't know what you're missing. Try putting it on slow motion, with the sound off, and play Richard Strauss's *Four Last Songs*. The melancholy of the music, the expression of the actors as they scream. That's what *Guernica* was supposed to convey when Picasso painted it.

YU AHN: Picasso? Who makes perfume.

PHILIP: Pablo Picasso was a painter. You heard of Debussy? Albert Camus?

YU AHN: Camus is brandy. I also know Rolex, Sony, Pe-yar Cardan.

PHILIP: Albert Camus was a philosopher. He won the Nobel prize writing about the benign indifference of the universe. He defined the raison d'etre for many of us.

YU AHN: What is raise on det?

PHILIP: That's French for your reason for being.

YU AHN: You speak French also? You so smart.

PHILIP: I lived in France for a year when I was in college.

YU AHN: America, there is chance to do everything. Here, I take one step forward, everyone pull me back two steps.

PHILIP: Not all Americans are emperors. Some of us have to do the grunt work.

McCARTER THEATER, PRINCETON, N.J.—B.D. Wong (Yu Ahn), David Chung (Bao) and Thom Sesma (Philip) in *The Nanjing Race*

YU AHN: You cannot be emperor, but you can be millionaire.

PHILIP: Where do you get your ideas of America from? I stretch too high, I hit that glass ceiling hard.

YU AHN: But you are rich man. You need buy anything? I get for you. I not collect commission, I swear you.

PHILIP: There is nothing I want.

YU AHN: Buy small gift, for someone special.

PHILIP: There is no one special. Unless I get some ginseng.

YU AHN: Do not know. What is jin sing?

PHILIP: A liquid that comes in little amber glass bottles. I think it's from a root.

YU AHN: Root? We have, called run shun. Very expensive.

PHILIP: No, ginseng. You drink it, like tea.

YU AHN: We have many teas.

PHILIP: Ginseng's much more potent. It cures cancer, lowers blood pressure, even makes sex better. So they say.

YU AHN: We have. You want deer horn. One cup, your thing stiff for two days.

PHILIP: I don't think that's what my mother needs. The ginseng's for her. She's recovering from a mastectomy. Big operation.

YU AHN: Then you should be with your mother.

PHILIP: This trip is important. It's a big step for my company. Our sales manager wanted his blond pet to come, but our president gave me the chance. He believes I have an edge, being part Asian, even though I'm an engineer. I'm going to prove he's right.

YU AHN: I know special Chinese medicine. Your mother drink, she will be healthy again in one week. I know best shop in Nanjing, they wrap in many small packet. One for each day. Very convenience. You want deer horn also?

PHILIP: No thanks.

YU AHN: But you will be so, strong. You married?

PHILIP: No. I'm not married. I'm tired.

YU AHN: You take deer horn, you will not be tired. Your girl friend not complain?

PHILIP: I don't have a girl friend.

YU AHN: Why? You handsome man. You walk in street, every female in Nanjing want you as husband. If I introduce you to beautiful girl, I will get big commission. But I am your friend; I will not collect commission. You need me introduce to you girl friend? She is very near. Can be here in five minutes.

PHILIP: No, thank you.

YU AHN: This is gentle girl, with good education. You will not be disappoint. Not expensive. Maybe she solve your problem without deer horn.

PHILIP: I am not interested.

YU AHN: I only offer. How old are you?

PHILIP: Thirty-nine, again.

YU AHN: That is almost same age as I am. You look young. Must be good life in America.

PHILIP: You know what my secret is? A good night's sleep.

YU AHN: I do not sleep well. I share room with my mother. She make noise when she sleep. Where you come from?

PHILIP: South Jersey.

YU AHN: Where is South Jersey?

PHILIP (sits up): Not where. It's a state of mind. Good night.

YU AHN: State of Mine? Where is state of Mine?

PHILIP: We've got to stop this yakking. I know you people are friendly, but this is ridiculous.

YU AHN: Excuse me. Please explain yakking.

He takes out his notebook and a pencil and writes.

PHILIP (goes to open the door): It doesn't matter. I haven't slept since I left New York over thirty-one hours ago. The fucking Air China connection was delayed six hours out of Shanghai, and the food was foul. I don't want to be here; I don't like my room and I'm not sure I can take any more of you. And tomorrow, I've got to negotiate the best prices my company has ever seen. So please, let's continue our wonderful relationship tomorrow.

YU AHN: You want me leave?

PHILIP: I want you to pirouette around, walk out that door and stay away till I ring that goddam bell on the wall. Comprendo?

YU AHN *(writes in his notebook):* Peer wet, com pren . . .

PHILIP *(shoves Yu Ahn towards the door):* Out!

YU AHN: You say you American? I am surprise. You no friendly.

PHILIP: No friendly? I'm only a guest here. I didn't realize I have to be nice.

YU AHN: You are like government official from small town, think you stay in hotel, you are big shot. White people not behave like this. You not white.

PHILIP: Not white? You tell me I have to be white? Back home, people can't understand why I don't speak Japanese, why I'm not soft-spoken and subservient. I tell them I'm born in Woodbury, New Jersey, they still refer to me as "You people." Now you accuse me of not being American enough? What am I supposed to do? Dye my hair blond?

YU AHN: I do not ask for special favor.

> *He takes his tray and turns to go.*

I just to make friend. I am sorry.

PHILIP: Wait. I . . .

> *He goes to his wallet, takes out some money and hands it to Yu Ahn.*

YU AHN: You tip already.

PHILIP: Take it. For your advice. I appreciate it. I didn't mean to push you. I'm . . . tired.

YU AHN *(takes the money):* We are friend?

PHILIP: Excuse me?

YU AHN *(extends his hand):* You are my friend?

PHILIP *(shakes Yu Ahn's hand):* Yes. I'm your friend.

YU AHN: So happy to meet you. My name is Wang Yu Ahn. It is an honor to be your friend, Mr . . .

PHILIP: Philip Hagen. Nice to meet you. I didn't mean to be rude. I'm sorry.

YU AHN: No worry. We are friend. You ring bell?

PHILIP: If I need anything. I will. I will.

YU AHN: Ring, I come. Jolly good. Good night, sir.

> *He exits.*

Bao recalls his failed attempt to flee to Hong Kong with his lover.

> *Spotlight on Bao.*

BAO: There was no moon, just as we had planned. The dark weighed heavily over the night, made all my senses go sharp. He was a better swimmer. I could barely see him up front, his head appearing and disappearing from the black ink water. I heard my own short breathing, which did not match the rhythm of my heart, pounding all the way up to my throat. The taste of salt numbed my lips, my gums, my tongue. The lights of Hong Kong started to glimmer in the distance. Suddenly, the sound of a motor. When he also started to swim faster, I knew he heard it too. He did not look back. Neither did I. All I could do was swim as fast as I could, trying not to splash the water. All of a sudden, he flung his left arm up, as if waving to someone. He sank out of sight. I thought he had reached a sandbar, or kicked a rock. Then his whole body came up sideways, turned back into the water and disappeared. The left side of his white shorts had a large rip. That's when I saw the sharks. I stopped breathing. A large wave came from behind; I turned; my eyes looked straight into the glare of searchlights, blinding me. Hands grabbed me and pulled me up. Later, the guards told me I had screamed. They said it sounded like someone's name. I have not said it out loud since. But tonight in room sixty-six, his name came to my lips.

The Nanjing Race *was first produced at the McCarter Theater, Princeton, N.J. in their Winter's Tales '94 series, January 12–23, 1994, under the direction of Loretta Greco.*

ATCA Citation

○○○
○○○
○○○
○○○
○○○
○○○ ## THE WAITING ROOM

A Play in Two Acts

BY LISA LOOMER

Cast and credits appear on pages 465–466

LISA LOOMER began her career onstage as an actress and comedienne but was deep into writing by 1985 when she was writer-in-residence at INTAR. Her plays have also been produced in New York at the Public Theater, American Place and Westside Arts; cross-country at the Mark Taper Forum (where this present work, The Waiting Room, *premiered), Kennedy Center, Williamstown and South Coast Repertory in Costa Mesa; and in Germany and Mexico. In addition to her* Birds, !Bocon!, Looking for Angels, Cuts, Chain of Life, A Crowd of Two, All by Herselves *and* Accelerando *for the theater, she has worked in films with Gabriel Garcia-Marquez and on many TV projects including* Hearts Afire *and* Women of the House. *She is a winner of the Jane Chambers Award, a runner-up for the Susan Blackburn Award, a recipient of NEA and NYFA grants and an alumna of New Dramatists.*

INTRODUCTION: Cancer is hardly a laughing matter. Nor are the negative complications of surgical breast implants, the gangrene that can result from foot-binding, or the hysteria and clinical depression endured by many upper-class Victorian women prime joke material.

In Lisa Loomer's *The Waiting Room,* however, all these conditions, their causes and aftereffects, and the social obsessions that contribute to them, are expertly mined for absurdist humor. And the laughter this dazzling comedy provokes is by no means frivolous. It's the stinging kind that clears the head the way a good cry or a healthy venting of rage can.

A seasoned writer for some of television's most topical, feminist-tinged situation comedies *(Hearts Afire, Women of the House),* Loomer clearly has a well-honed talent for pithy one-liners and quick-sketch caricature.

But one of the virtues of *The Waiting Room* is Loomer's refusal to confine her play to the snappy schmoozing and living room psychologizing of sitcom. To explore a great range of disturbing topics connected to the issues of women's health and self-image, Loomer exploits the elasticity of live theater. She conflates historical time zones, integrates the surreal and the mundane and presents a great deal of hard information—and protest—without overloading her satirical vessel with too much didactic cargo.

The variety of her central characters, and their screwball journeys of self-awareness, see to that. The play begins in a purgatorial waiting room, where three women patients await the same doctor. Each woman represents a cultural cliche—and later transcends it.

The character named Forgiveness From Heaven may be a victim of the draconian ancient Chinese beauty regimen of foot-binding. But she's a masterful player at the kind of marriage that, to women of her time (the 18th century) and place, meant survival.

Victoria, the corset-bound matron alternately petted and patronized by her smug husband, is also no straw woman. Coping with a horrific case of what used to be called "female troubles" induced in part by the stabbing bones of her undergarments, she studies the psychosexual theories of Drs. Freud and Reich on the sly and looks for a way out of the dutiful wife-and-mother trap.

The most surprising of the trio, though, is Wanda—the modern would-be-bimbo secretary. Yes, Wanda has bought into the hype that chin and cheekbone lifts, nose jobs, tummy tucks and three sets of toxic breast implants will make her attractive enough to overcome the allegedly dire odds of finding, at age 40, a husband.

But when all she gets for her massive expenditure on plastic surgery is an advanced case of double breast cancer, Wanda faces facts with a new sense of clarity and self-possession. Encouraged by a feisty Jamaican nurse, she takes control of her own illness instead of leaving all choice to the "experts" with little hope to offer her. "Dying would be a bitch," Wanda acknowledges. "But isn't it worse—not living while you're alive?"

Around the compelling dilemmas of these women, Loomer paints a cartoonish backdrop of greedy pharmaceutical executives, a clumsy male-dominated medical bureaucracy which seems largely indifferent to women's health concerns and a historical pattern of impossible feminine beauty standards.

The Waiting Room suggests a new way to see for several women whose mirrors have long betrayed them. And it manages to do so without indulging in wholesale male-bashing. The play also conjures empathy for Douglas, a doctor who learns a great deal about his patients (and his profession) through his own struggle against cancer. And in a slightly gratuitous shot, Loomer even mocks overzealous feminism by planting a strident man-hater in the play's antic bar scene. (Hygeia, goddess of health, also flits through that free-for-all passage.)

In the largely favorable reviews that greeted David Schweizer's premiere production of *The Waiting Room* at the Mark Taper Forum in Los Angeles, Loomer's vivacious mingling of comic styles, political jibes and historical references was likened to the oeuvre of British dramatist Caryl Churchill, and to the audacious American stage works of Tony Kushner.

But there's a kinship too, deliberate or not, with a more distant comedic relation: Molière. Just as Molière lampooned the deluded and incompetent and rapacious excesses of the French medical establishment of his own day, Loomer takes keen aim at our own. Her gifts for crafting the hip bon mot and capturing modern urban foibles may have been perfected in the Hollywood sitcom factory. But her willingness in *The Waiting Room* to leap beyond the topical into the fantastic, and beyond triviality into myth and mortality, link her to a tradition of satirical pathos that only the theater has kept alive.

—MISHA BERSON

Excerpts From *The Waiting Room*

The waiting room. Three chairs and a table with magazines. Boppy Muzak, preferably a Beatles tune. Victoria, dressed in 20 pounds of clothes and tightly corseted, and Forgiveness From Heaven, in ancient Chinese dress . . . wait. After several moments of waiting, Forgiveness picks up Vogue. She sniffs a perfume ad, delighted. Victoria picks up Cosmo, is horrified by the cover and quickly puts it down. Finally, she takes a book from under her skirt and begins to read.

FORGIVENESS: Pretty. Pretty, pretty . . .
Shows Victoria the magazine.
Pretty, huh?
VICTORIA (*politely*): Yes. (*She goes back to her book.*)
FORGIVENESS (*eager to chat*): Long wait, huh?
VICTORIA: He's thorough.
A bloodcurdling scream offstage. The women barely react.
FORGIVENESS: Good doctor.
VICTORIA: Oh, yes.
Forgiveness smiles. Victoria remembers her manners.
Ah—Victoria Smoot.
FORGIVENESS: Forgiveness From Heaven.
VICTORIA: How do you do. (*She goes back to her book.*)
FORGIVENESS: Oh, fine. (*Smiles.*) Little problem with little toe.
VICTORIA: Well, I'm sure the doctor will fix it.
FORGIVENESS: Fell off this morning.

VICTORIA: Well, I'm so sorry. And your family? Your husband is well?

FORGIVENESS *(smiles, covering pain)*: With other wives this week.

VICTORIA: Nice for you ... *(Sniffs.)* By the way, do you smell something—untoward?

FORGIVENESS *(proudly)*: My feet!

VICTORIA: I beg your pardon?

FORGIVENESS: My feet. Stink bad, huh?

VICTORIA: No, no, not—too awfully.

FORGIVENESS: I would wash them, but my husband, he's crazy for the smell. Likes to eat watermelon seeds from the toes. Almonds. *(Delighted.)* Dirt.

VICTORIA: *Well* ... *(Searches; what can she say?)* I like your shoes. *(She goes back to her book.)*

FORGIVENESS: Size three.

VICTORIA: Three *inches?*

FORGIVENESS *(competitive)*: What size your waist?

VICTORIA: Sixteen! I got my first corset quite young.

FORGIVENESS: How young?

VICTORIA: Fourteen!

FORGIVENESS *(tops her; shows feet)*: I was five. *(Almost hopeful.)* Corset hurts bad, huh?

VICTORIA: Oh, no. Only when I breathe.

FORGIVENESS: My feet, just first couple years.

VICTORIA: Really!

FORGIVENESS: My mother, you see—

VICTORIA *(reflexively polite)*: How is she?

FORGIVENESS: Oh, dead for long time now.

VICTORIA: Nice for her ...

FORGIVENESS: One day mother say to me, "Forgiveness From Heaven, today is lucky day by moon. Time to start binding ..."

VICTORIA: Ah.

FORGIVENESS *(like a recipe)*: Then mother takes bandage, place on inside of instep, and carry over small toes to force them in and towards the sole. Then bandage is wrapped around heel nice and forcefully, so heel and toes are drawn close, real close together.

VICTORIA: I see. *(Pause.)* Why?

FORGIVENESS: Make feet pretty for future husband! *(Laughs.)* That night, I tried to run away in the forest—my feet were on fire! But mother found me and forced me to walk. She was a good girl when her feet were bound and never cried.

Victoria and Forgiveness continue to speak matter-of-factly about the horrors of foot-binding. Then Forgiveness asks Victoria why she has come to the doctor.

VICTORIA: Me? Oh ... *(Yawns.)* Hysteria.

FORGIVENESS: Hys—teria? *(She gets up and examines the rubber plant.)*

VICTORIA: It's a disease of the ovaries.

FORGIVENESS: Hurts bad, huh?

VICTORIA (*condescending*): No, no, no. You see, the ovaries control the personality. I've done some reading on the matter. Though my husband says that reading makes me worse. Romantic novels especially. *(Proud.)* My husband is a doctor.

> Victoria has a tic. Whenever she says the word "husband," her arm flings out from the waist, as if to swat someone.

FORGIVENESS: Lucky. Has he treated you?

VICTORIA: Well, he did prescribe the rest cure.

FORGIVENESS: Nice and peaceful?

VICTORIA: Oh, very. Six weeks on one's back in a dimly lit room. No reading, no visitors, no ah . . . potty.

FORGIVENESS: Worked good?

VICTORIA: Well, I came out screaming, actually. But it was hardly my husband's fault. It seems—well, it seems I've had too much education and my uterus has atrophied commensurately.

FORGIVENESS: Glad I never went to school.

VICTORIA: Lucky.

FORGIVENESS: When I was a little girl, my husband liked my little feet so much, I never left the bedroom.

VICTORIA: Well, children need rest.

FORGIVENESS: Men crazy for the golden lotus. Feel much love and pity for your suffering . . . the tiny steps, the whispered walk. *(Demonstrates.)* And bound feet make buttocks larger, more attractive.

VICTORIA: Well, I assure you, it's a lot less fuss to wear a bustle.

FORGIVENESS: Bustle? Not natural! Also, foot-binding makes vagina tighter.

> Victoria has another tic. Sex makes her nose twitch.

When I walk, whole lower part of my body is in a state of tension, so vagina becomes like little fist!

VICTORIA (*after a beat*): Mrs. From Heaven, do you know erotic tendencies are one of the primary symptoms of ovarian disease—

FORGIVENESS (*worried*): Erotic tendencies are . . . ?

VICTORIA: Obviously you do not keep abreast of modern science.

FORGIVENESS: But what if husband *insists* on erotic tendencies?

VICTORIA: Well, that's not your "tendency," dear, that's your *duty. (Leans in.)* And need we mention the perils of the ah . . . well, the ah . . . vice?

FORGIVENESS: The vice?

VICTORIA: Leads to lesions, TB, dementia—I strap the children's hands down every night!

> A scream offstage.

And catch it early because clitorectomy and cauterization can be quite costly.

> Brenda enters with clipboard.

BRENDA: Which one of you ladies was here first?

VICTORIA and FORGIVENESS: She was.

BRENDA: The doctor will be right with you.
        She exits.
FORGIVENESS (*scared*): This—vice—can cause disease in grown women too?
VICTORIA: Mrs. From Heaven. There are even *some* women who become en-
thralled by the stimulation of gynecological instruments!— *(Twitching and insinu-
ating.)* begging every doctor to institute an examination of the, ah—the ah, sexual
ah—
FORGIVENESS: Wait just minute, Mrs. Smoot. *(Huffy.) I'm* only here to have toe
put back! Only here for that reason!
VICTORIA: Well! I'm just here to see about removing the ovaries!
        *Wanda enters in an outfit which pays homage to her enormous breasts.
        She carries a backbreaking pocketbook and a clipboard with her chart
        and takes the empty seat between them.*
WANDA: Excuse me, you reading that *Cosmo?*
VICTORIA: Take it!
FORGIVENESS: *Two* ovaries?
        As Victoria speaks, Wanda is distracted by Victoria's story.
VICTORIA (*with mounting hysteria*): Well, we've tried everything else! Injections
to the womb—water, milk, tea, a decoction of marshmallow. I've stopped reading
and writing, stopped stimulating my emotions with operas and French plays. Last
week the doctor placed leeches on my vulva—
        Wanda's mouth falls open. She gets out her cigarettes.
Some were quite adventurous, actually, and traveled all the way to the cervical
cavity! The pressure from the corset's forcing my uterus out through my vagina . . .
And according to my husband, my hysteria's only getting worse! My husband says
I've all the classic symptoms of ovarian disease: troublesomeness, eating like a
ploughman, painful menstruation—a desire to learn Greek! Attempted suicide, persecution mania and simple cussedness! Last night I sneezed continuously for twenty-
seven minutes and tried to *bite* my own husband! What can I do? I shan't be beaten
across the face and body with wet towels like an Irish woman—I JUST WANT THE
DAMN THINGS OUT!
WANDA (*after a beat*): Just the way I feel about my tits.

Douglas, the doctor all three women are waiting for, examines Wanda.

DOUGLAS: Have you noticed any change in your breasts, Ms. . . . *(Checks chart;
mispronounces.)* Koz . . . nicki? You haven't mentioned experiencing any pain.
WANDA: Only when I watch TV.
DOUGLAS: When you—
WANDA: You know, all those talk shows. "I Got Scleriowhatsis from My Implants," and Geraldo had on this transsexual typist who got rheumatoid arthritis and
couldn't type—I'm a secretary, doc; I gotta type. Hey, a gal in our office got a razor
and took hers out herself—
DOUGLAS: No, no, we can certainly do that for you. If that's what you decide.

MARK TAPER FORUM, LOS ANGELES—June Kyoko Lu as Forgiveness From Heaven, Jacalyn O'Shaugnessy as Wanda and Lela Ivey as Victoria in a scene from *The Waiting Room* by Lisa Loomer

WANDA (*flirtatious*): What do *you* think?

DOUGLAS: Well, the FDA believes that there is not enough evidence to justify having silicone implants removed if the woman is not having symptoms.

WANDA (*pats chest*): Good!

DOUGLAS: Unfortunately, there is no sure way to monitor for bleed, leakage, rupture—

WANDA: What would you advise your daughter?

DOUGLAS (*bewildered*): I don't have a daughter.

WANDA: But if you did.

DOUGLAS: And she had, uh . . .

WANDA: Yeah.

DOUGLAS: Well . . . (*Thinks.*) I'd have to speak with her doctor. (*Goes back to her chart.*) Any cancer in your family, Ms . . . (*Shakes head.*) Koz—niskaya?

WANDA: Uh . . . (*Pause.*) Sure. My grandmother on my father's side. My mother's sister . . . and brother. His wife—

DOUGLAS: Just blood relations, please.

WANDA: Oh. Okay. And my mother and father.

DOUGLAS: That's it?

WANDA: Well, I had an uncle who had it in the prostate. But he didn't die from it.

DOUGLAS (*writing*): That's good.

WANDA: He died in Atlantic City. Ever been there?

DOUGLAS: No, can't say I have.

WANDA: He died right on the boardwalk. (*Beat.*) With an ice pick in his head. He was lucky.

> She bursts out laughing. Douglas looks at her, confused. She lets it go.

DOUGLAS: Ever have a mammogram?

WANDA (*flirting*): I'm only thirty-five.

DOUGLAS: Well, I'm going to send you for one.

WANDA: I had one last year.

DOUGLAS: Oh, good. (*Rises.*) I'll have my nurse phone your previous physician and then we can compare.

WANDA: Nurses?

DOUGLAS: I'm sorry—?

> Wanda shakes her head, "never mind."

(*At the door; concerned*): By the way, did the doctor who gave you those implants ask you any questions?

WANDA: Yeah. "What size?"

> Douglas nods and leaves.

As the three women patients cope with their "conditions," Douglas discovers he (as well as Wanda) has cancer. He talks to his old friends and golf buddies: Larry, a pharmaceutical company executive and hospital board member, and Ken, a medical scientist, about a promising cancer drug not yet approved for the U.S. but administered by a Dr. Carson in a clinic in Jamaica. But they are more interested in INT-2, a drug Larry's company is developing.

DOUGLAS: What kind of side effects are you seeing with INT-2 and breast cancer?

LARRY: None at all so far.

KEN (*surprised*): You tested it on breast cancer?

LARRY: We haven't had the funding, Ken.

DOUGLAS: Studies I've been reading about prostate indicate that Carson's patients live twice as long as conventionally treated patients.

LARRY: Well, that's pretty darn impressive. Although often these *unpublished,* anecdotal studies reflect the bias toward longer survival in this type of patient— white, well-off patients who can afford to fly off to Jamaica for treatment.

DOUGLAS: I just thought it would be interesting for us to give Carson's serum a try, Larry. And I'd think you'd be interested too, as a member of the board of Smith Memorial . . . if not as a vice-president of Jones Pharmaceuticals.

KEN (*laughs*): Fellas—

LARRY: Well, I'm hurt that you see it that way. Are you implying a conflict of interest, my friend? Because all sorts of companies are represented on our little board, including the makers of petrochemicals and tobacco, which, I believe, are known to *cause* cancer. Me, I'm in the business of a *cure*. Hell, I'm interested in anything that'll cure cancer, Doug—apricot pits, vitamin C, snake oil, ozone, "eye of newt and toe of frog . . ."

DOUGLAS: This is not some quack cure. This Carson is not a nutritionist, or a chiropractor, or some . . . "healer." He's a scientist. We're talking about a serum made from human blood.

LARRY: I'm listening to you, Doug. I'm hearing you.

Brenda, Douglas's nurse, is angry because Dr. Carson's anti-cancer serum saved her mother's life but is not available to treat the breast cancer of Wanda and of so many other women. She suspects a conspiracy to suppress a cancer cure when she hears that the Jamaican clinic has been shut down by government authorities.

BRENDA: Maybe there's a cancer industry out there and it does not want to die. Big money in cancer! Hmmmn-hmmmn. 'Bout eighty billion a year, nuh? Now how a cure goin' be that profitable? Who goin' pay for such a profitable cure? The insurance company? Who goin' pay the insurance company? That chemical plant Ms. Kozynski work for, probably give her cancer in the first place?

DOUGLAS: Oh, fine. Now we are getting hysterical. (*She is.*)

BRENDA: Chu, don't listen to me, Douglas; I'm just a nurse. Ask your friend upstairs who closed that clinic. You went to school together, nuh? You play golf—

DOUGLAS: Brenda—

BRENDA: Lord have mercy, he's a breast man, isn't he?

DOUGLAS: I will ask you one more time—

BRENDA: You got a woman out there with breast cancer—you goin' cure Ms. Kozynski, doctor? Your friend upstairs goin' let you cure?

> Douglas takes a swipe at his desk or briefcase. Objects scatter on the floor. He is horrified.

DOUGLAS: I'm sorry. I'm sorry. You—you were getting hysterical—I—

BRENDA: I better bring in the next—

DOUGLAS (*shaken*): Brenda . . . There has always been cancer. There was cancer in the bones of dinosaurs, in Egyptian mummies—in Hippocrates' time. When it was deep-seated, he said to . . . just leave it alone. That the patient would live longer that way. And, yes, in two thousand years, when it gets bad, we don't have a lot more to offer. I wish to God we did. (*Fights tears.*) I'm a doctor! I want people to live. But I did not create cancer. And, God help me, I cannot cure it either.

> He picks up a picture of his wife which has fallen to the floor.

Still, I am bound by oath to try. *(Beat; adds quietly.)* And bound by the laws of this country which tell me how I may do so.

> *Brenda nods and starts to leave.*

Brenda—do you believe in Carson's *theory?*

BRENDA: What—?

DOUGLAS: Malignant cells will be destroyed by a healthy defense system, unless—unless that destruction is interfered with by something—

BRENDA: Something like greed?

DOUGLAS: If there is something in us—in our blood—in our genes that can overcome cancer—!

BRENDA: You think we goin' stop greed? Where we goin' catch it? I seen greed in a kiss, in a white man's billy club—I see doctors don't like their patients get too smart. Sure, I think Carson has a good theory. I think Mother Nature has a cure for most everything. *(Pause.)* 'Cept human nature.

All three women patients meet again in a hospital recovery room. Victoria has had her uterus removed and is beginning to take charge of her life. Forgiveness has had foot surgery. And Wanda has had a mastectomy, but the cancer has spread, and she is faced with a choice of chemotherapy, doses of experimental INT-2 or other unsure treatments.

VICTORIA: Are you going to try the new treatment or not?

WANDA: Don't know. It's an "unproven method."

VICTORIA: Then will you do as the doctor earlier prescribed?

WANDA *(shrugs)*: Don't know. All my life I've let men do pretty much what they wanted with my body . . .

> *Victoria goes back to her own bed.*

FORGIVENESS: Got to be First Wife! Not Fifth Wife! How you going to eat? Who going to take care of you?

WANDA: I really don't know. *(Beat.)* Hillary Clinton.

VICTORIA: Now just a minute, my dear. You have the vote, you can learn Greek, you have no obligations, you can read any book in the world—if you don't have a goddam answer, who does?

WANDA: Hey, I'm thinking, all right? Why do I always have to be the first one in the pool? Look. My grandmother— *(It's the first time she's said the word.)* had cancer. *(Touches her breast.)* My grandfather— *(Touches her stomach.)* My uncle— *(Touches her groin.)* My aunt— *(Touches her breast.)* My other uncle— *(Touches her brain.)* And my mother and father— *(She touches her lung, then motions "all over".)*

> *Brenda enters in street clothes, carrying a suitcase. She waits, not wanting to interrupt.*

. . . . . My father never got to see me . . . pretty. *(Forces a smile.)* Well, hey, I wouldn't want him to see me like this now, would I? And, you know, Vic, I got a girlfriend—they took a lump, they gave her chemo and she's just fine. She's fine! Well, her hair fell out, and she went through menopause at thirty-six, and her boyfriend left her for the radiologist . . . but she's fine. But I don't have a little lump of cancer. I'm a big girl. I got a lot of it. The hospital says my insurance won't kick in for *six* months now, at which point I may not be around to enjoy my benefits—which may all be beside the point anyway, because this morning I called my job and I'm fired.

BRENDA (*moves closer*): I hear they have a bed waiting for you upstairs, chile . . .

WANDA: Hey. Sit down. Have a Ding Dong; they took our cigars.

BRENDA (*sits on the bed*): Don't eat nuh sugar.

WANDA: You got a suitcase.

BRENDA (*smiles*): Me No Send, You No Come . . .

WANDA (*to Victoria*): You know, maybe I'll see Tijuana or Guadalajara—

FORGIVENESS: But doctor say—

WANDA (*explodes*): I KNOW! I know what the doctor said.

FORGIVENESS: No need to speak loudly.

WANDA: Forgive me. But this cancer . . . it's in *my* body. It's not in your body— or the good doctor's body—I know he's got his cancer, but this cancer is . . . mine. For better or worse, till death do us part, it's about the one thing I got left that's all—mine. And if I want to take it to Tijuana or Guadafuckinglajara—I've never been out of the tri-state area! (*Fights tears.*) If I want to die. If I want to call up my doctor and say, "No thank you very much," or "Please, God help me . . ." —for once in my lousy screwed-up life, it's MY BODY! MY BODY! MINE! (*Pause; laughs.*) And you know what I figured out this morning?

BRENDA (*gently*): What?

VICTORIA (*overlapping*): Frankly, you baffle me—

WANDA: I sat down with a pencil and figured out I've spent six thousand, seven hundred and fifty hours of my life . . . on my hair! Nine months washing off my waterproof mascara.

FORGIVENESS: Mascara?

WANDA: You don't wanna know. So, with all the time I'm going to save from now on, going around looking like shit . . . what if I take a *little* time—and make up my mind. Maybe I will do the chemo. Or, hey, maybe I'll find . . . something. I mean, this is America, right? Gal oughta be free to try, right?

Brenda smiles, picks up her suitcase.

For Chrissakes, I'm only forty—

VICTORIA (*shocked*): Forty!?

WANDA: And, you know, dying would be a bitch. But isn't it worse—not living while you're alive?

In the play's final scene, the women are still in the hospital, and telling each other bedtime stories. It is Wanda's turn.

WANDA: Okay. Once upon a time, there were three sisters. All of them stupid. One thought her feet were too big, one thought her waist was too big, and the really stupid one thought her tits weren't big *enough*. So they went to a Magician and said,

"Make us perfect." And he held up a magic mirror which made the sisters look like—

FORGIVENESS: Woman in Taurus commercial.

Hygeia enters, refills their water glasses and quietly leaves.

WANDA: Okay. And the Magician said, "You, too, can look just like this." And the sisters gave him a pile of gold and the Magician worked his magic . . . and built a new tennis court with their money. But, after a few years, the magic started to . . . go bad.

FORGIVENESS (*softly*): Sisters not lucky—

WANDA: No. And the sisters went back to the Magician and he said, "Hey, I said I'd make you perfect. I didn't say you'd be perfect *forever*. Check out the shingle. It says 'Magician' not 'God'." And the sisters were really pissed off. So what did they do?

FORGIVENESS: Wait for luck to change . . . *(She closes her eyes and nods every once in a while at the story.)*

WANDA: First they took all the mirrors in the kingdom and smashed 'em . . . and recycled the glass. Then they told all their girlfriends and daughters, "Next time you want to look in a mirror, don't go to the Magician, come to us." And when the women came to check out their thighs and their noses and all their other problems, they had to look in the sisters' eyes. And the sisters would say, "Oh, gimme a break, you look fine." At first, the women didn't believe them 'cause who believes you when you tell 'em they look good, right? But the sisters kept saying, "You're beautiful . . ."

FORGIVENESS: Beautiful . . .

Forgiveness smiles and lies perfectly still. Wanda continues, unaware.

WANDA: And eventually the women started to buy it. And the Magicians were doing such a lousy business they all had to move to . . . Europe. It was like magic. Everybody got kissed and the women who felt like it got married. And the ones who didn't got good jobs in the kingdom. *(Realizes.)* And some got both. And everybody lived a whole lot happier ever after.

She turns to Forgiveness.

Forgiveness? *(Waits.)* Forgiveness!? *(She understands.)* Good night, Forgiveness From Heaven. Sweet dreams.

Wanda turns out the light next to her bed. After a moment, a white spot comes up over Forgiveness. Slowly, she sits up into the light. Then she stands up on the bed and has a good stretch. Ancient Chinese music begins. Forgiveness jumps down and starts to unwrap her feet, as if unwrapping the bound years . . . first with the relief of the aging woman, then faster, with the joy of the bound five-year-old child. She begins to dance an ancient Chinese ribbon dance with her bindings. She dances and dances, spinning off the yoke of the centuries . . . And the light fades on her dancing.

The Waiting Room *was first produced at the Mark Taper Forum, Los Angeles, August 11, 1994 under the direction of David Schweizer.*

Elizabeth Osborn Award

○○○
○○○
○○○
○○○
○○○
○○○
RUSH LIMBAUGH IN NIGHT SCHOOL

A Play in Two Acts

BY CHARLIE VARON
DEVELOPED WITH DAVID FORD

Cast and credits appear on page 477

CHARLIE VARON is a New Yorker who gravitated to San Francisco in 1978 after a brief stint of theater study at Brown University. In the 1980s he toured the U.S., Britain and Canada as half of the political comedy team The Atomic Comics and collaborated on radio comedy with Jim Rosenau on Station KQED-FM's West Coast Weekend. *His first solo show,* Honest Prophets, *premiered at The Marsh in San Francisco in 1991 and was featured at the Solo Mio Festival the following year. He was commissioned to write and perform a Chanukah story,* The Grobinza, *for San Francisco's 1993 Klezmer Mania celebration. Varon's humor pieces have appeared in many newspapers and magazines, and he teaches a comedy performance workshop in association with The Marsh.*

David Ford, the director of Rush Limbaugh in Night School *as well as of Varon's* Honest Prophets, *is credited with collaboration in the development of both these programs. In addition to staging many others including those of Josh Kornbluth, a 1993 Best Play author, Ford is the author of two plays,* The Interrogation of Nathan Hale *and* Frankenthaler's Monster.

INTRODUCTION: Poor Rush Limbaugh. For the moment, he's everybody's favorite. To the Right, Limbaugh is a favorite champion in the conservative battle against liberalism and unchecked government power. To the Left, Limbaugh is a favorite whipping boy of unchecked conservative backlash. To actor-playwright Charlie Varon, Limbaugh is a fellow radio personality and a human being. Varon, a San Francisco radio humorist, refuses to idealize or demonize his target. Instead, he portrays the radio-television commentator as someone who can learn from new experiences, someone who can love and be affected by that love.

His 90-minute, one-man play, which Varon developed with David Ford, starts with an impish fish-out-of-water premise. Varon sets his near-future story in 1996 in New York City, where Limbaugh enrolls under another name in a Spanish class at the New School for Social Research in Greenwich Village. There, he falls in love with Nina, a radical feminist who herself assumed another name years ago after provoking J. Edgar Hoover as a member of the Weather Underground.

In Varon's PBS-style "mockumentary," Limbaugh becomes a sort of right wing Candide, a Newt-era innocent who blithely enters a wider world of New York feminists, New School progressives and New Age cultists. Complications and deceptions multiply and eventually collide with dizzyingly funny results on one summer night when Limbaugh accepts an invitation to play the black-faced title role in director Spalding Gray's summer revival of *Othello* opposite Garrison Keillor's Iago, Cokie Roberts's Desdemona and Jackie Mason's Roderigo at the Delacorte Theater.

Limbaugh embarks on his journey to broaden his talk show's multicultural appeal in response to the threat of a rival Hispanic radio host, but the farcically unexpected consequences of that journey end up broadening the character's personal and professional life in significant ways.

Rush Limbaugh can be enjoyed on several levels: as a thoroughly modern satire of the cultural-political zeitgeist, as a romantic comedy of mistaken (and shifting) identities, and as a picaresque New Age fantasy of transformation. Just thinking about the idea of a satire of Rush Limbaugh makes one laugh, but Varon doesn't go for the obvious punch lines.

One would expect a conventional satire of a conservative celebrity to take pot shots at his more extreme views while painting a largely unsympathetic portrait. Varon's approach is kinder, gentler and more whimsical. Although Varon writes from a liberal perspective, he does not reduce Limbaugh to caricature as Tony Kushner did to another right-wing celebrity (attorney Roy Cohn) in *Angels in America.*

Varon, a wild card of an emerging playwright, isn't interested in preaching to the converted Left or converting the preachy Right. Instead, he transforms Limbaugh into a playful symbol of change. Transformation, in fact, is the perfect word to sum up Varon's satirical but gently serious theme.

The sure-fire farcical structure generates laughs, but much of the play's charm derives from Varon's cheerful imagination and knowing wit. His background as a radio humorist obviously helped Varon portray the manic ins and outs of Limbaugh's workaday world. Varon, whose humor pieces have been published in *The*

Atlantic Monthly, Utne Reader and *The New Yorker,* is a regular personality on San Francisco's KQED-FM, where he is known for his send-ups of the BBC News.

The versatile solo performer, who has some of the chameleonic talents of a Robin Williams or a Rich Little, developed his play from a 15-minute comedy skit at The Marsh, a San Francisco theater that launched other off-Broadway monologuists like Josh Kornbluth *(Red Diaper Baby)* and Marga Gomez *(Memory Tricks).* Varon plays Limbaugh, Nina and 20 other roles in scenes that move so rapidly between characters that it's hard to imagine one actor delivering all the dialogue. Varon does so impressively, given the minimal staging: a chair, a table, an "On Air" sign and a few props. The one-man format gives *Rush Limbaugh* the added power of a personal tour-de-force. Varon can be compared to Gray or the early Eric Bogosian, but is more than an intriguing monologuist in the growing trend toward semiautobiographical one-man and one-woman shows.

Varon, who has faced the pressures of filling up the airwaves with talk, imagines Limbaugh unconsciously imbibing ideas and attitudes willy-nilly from his new cultural milieu and repeating them in hilariously garbled form for his daily gabfest. Here is a Limbaugh full of himself but empty of deep-rooted conviction. Is Varon's Limbaugh reality or parody? Varon's fantasy Limbaugh aptly symbolizes a talkshow culture run amok on its own inflated, self-reverential pomposities.

Varon's subject is a harder nut to crack than one might think, for how do you satirize a satirist? Limbaugh has referred to himself as "talent on loan from God," yet he also has an undeniable sense of humor that creeps into everything he talks about—including himself. Limbaugh might loosen up even more if he changed his mind about seeing *Rush Limbaugh in Night School.* A few weeks before Varon's play opened off Broadway in March at New York's Second Stage Theater, Limbaugh issued a dismissive one-line statement to the New York *Times:* "Call me if I ever reach the real Broadway."

Much satire brims with cynicism about the perennial follies of humanity. This satire is distinctive for its refreshingly hopeful, even upbeat vision. Varon's spacey bits about metaphoric pears and alternative cancer cures are not merely jokey asides about the excesses of the New Age. They are integral to his fantasy about the very real possibilities of personal and political transformation.

If even a hidebound conservative like Limbaugh can change, Varon seems to suggest, then is genuine transformation really so difficult for anyone else?

—MICHAEL GROSSBERG

Excerpts From
Rush Limbaugh in Night School

NARRATOR: The following morning Rush Limbaugh got up as usual at 4 A.M. and began his daily routine: scanning his faxes, E-mail messages and seven morning newspapers; shaving. In the shower, Limbaugh watches video highlights of the previous evening's *Nightline, Charlie Rose* and *Dan Quayle* programs.

6:22 A.M.: A stretch limousine pulls up outside One Rockefeller Center. Rush Limbaugh steps out, and is immediately surrounded by two dozen private security guards. Like many other celebrities, Limbaugh has beefed up his personal protection following the 1995 assassination attempt on Barbra Streisand. Beyond the ring of security agents, there is an outer circle of approximately eighty people wearing blue-and-orange armbands and pressing in with cameras and video recorders. These are fans of Mr. Limbaugh who for $250 have purchased day passes allowing them to be part of Mr. Limbaugh's entourage. Now, catching sight of the celebrity, they begin chanting in unison: "Limbaugh! Limbaugh! Limbaugh!" Smiling, waving, Mr. Limbaugh leaves the crowd behind and enters the building.

BARRY: Have a seat, Rush. You wanna cuppa coffee? Sit. Take a look at *these.* They're from Fred.

RUSH: What is this? My numbers, my audience curve plotted against that of Dick Cavett at the same GRC point in his career. "While Limbaugh's share has continued to increase, the pace of increase itself has slowed. When the numbers are fed into the Microsoft audience projection software, they produce *disturbingly Cavett-like results.* Rodriguez, by contrast, is showing the kind of meteoric gain that Limbaugh showed in 1990 and 1991."

BARRY: Fred thinks you've got six to eight weeks. Then? Cancellation.

RUSH: Barry! This doesn't make any sense. I'm at sixty million! Rodriguez is only—

BARRY: Rush, four years ago, my wife was having an affair. Nkay, and the investigators I hired to see what she and this Donald were doing—the videotapes they brought back showed that every time the two of them got together, they were doing something different. One time they made love with a lot of asparagus. Another time they got—not the Guarneri Quartet, but one of the major string quartets, to play Vivaldi while they made love on the living room rug. *(Stands.)* My point, Rush, is not the affair! My point is that they, like the American public, have an insatiable desire for novelty. *(Sits.)* And Rodriguez is—*new.*

RUSH: Six to eight weeks?? Barry, do something! Get me *out* of this! You're supposed to take care of this for me.

BARRY: Nkay, let's keep our heads about us. I've been through this before. What did we do with Henry Winkler? It didn't work. Like it or not, we are now in the ring with Rodriguez. *(Pause.)* Rush, have you ever thought about learning Spanish? Yeah, Spanish—beat Rodriguez at his own game. Rush, can you learn enough Spanish in four weeks to go on the air bilingual?

RUSH: Barry, Sp—Sp—

BARRY: This is not primarily an English-speaking hemisphere. And then, even if we do lose ground in North America, we've got still Central America, South America, open up a *new* market. Hell, we could go from sixty million to six hundred million!

NARRATOR: That day Barry Granatour enrolled Rush Limbaugh in an intensive Spanish class at the New School for Social Research, a politically progressive adult-education center in Greenwich Village. He chose the New School because he thought no one there would recognize Mr. Limbaugh. Still, as a precaution, Granatour enrolled him under the name "Russell Lindbergh." Three years later, the question remains: Why did Rush Limbaugh fail to question the computer projections that forecast his demise? Psychologist Ray Parnassus.

RAY PARNASSUS (*interview*): As I point out in my book, *The Half Life of a Celebrity,* the American celebrity lives in a state of perpetual terror, much like a chicken inching its way forward on the slaughter-house conveyor belt.

NARRATOR: May 29, 1996. Barry Granatour applies spirit gum to Rush Limbaugh's upper lip and chin, and pastes on a false mustache and goatee beard. Then he hands him a bag of clothes. Limbaugh puts on blue jeans, Birkenstock sandals and a T-shirt bearing the logo of Ben and Jerry's Ice Cream. Barry Granatour recalls what happened.

BARRY (*retrospect interview*): Rush showed absolutely no hesitation in putting on those clothes. He was like a seven-year-old with a new Halloween costume. He was happy.

NARRATOR: That evening, Spanish class at the New School.

ITCOTLELIAN: My name is Barbara Itcotlelian. I'm taking the class because I'm the new executive director of Shopping for Change; we're a non-profit, socially-responsible cable shopping channel.

HOROWITZ: My name is Daniel Horowitz. I was on one of the first Venceremos Brigades to Coova, back in the Sixties.

COLON: Okay. My name is Luis Colon. I'm with the Mayor's Advisory Task Force on Youth. I'm Puerto Rican, born and raised in the Bronx, but I never learned Spanish.

RUSH: *Me llamo* Russell Lindbergh, no relation to Charles, never been kidnapped. Taking the class purely for pleasure.

NARRATOR: The last of the ten students to introduce herself was a middle-aged woman. Rush Limbaugh immediately noticed that like him, she was wearing a Ben and Jerry's T-shirt. And then he saw her face: dangling from her ears, two gigantic ice-cream-cone earrings, and between them a mischievous smile framed by small dimples in the cheeks. Rush Limbaugh felt his heart pound in his chest.

NINA: I'm Nina Eggly. For the past twenty-one years, I lived in Santa Fe. And then last year my marriage ended—which incidentally, if you're thinking of leaving your spouse, was the best thing that's ever happened to me. Anyway, I made a commitment to myself to be fluent in Spanish by my fiftieth birthday. I'm forty-eight and a half now. I should also say that I do massage, and I'm still building up my practice here in the Village, so if you know anybody who's looking for massage, I'm available.

NARRATOR: What Nina Eggly did not say was that that was not her real name. Born Jean Brook, she had grown up the daughter of a wealthy New England industrialist. Then, in college, she joined the militant left-wing Weather Underground. Though she was not involved in any of the Weather Underground's violent acts, Jean Brook did manage to incur the wrath of the Federal Government. In 1969, in an act of puckish pranksterism, Jean Brook produced and distributed an FBI-style

WANTED poster showing FBI Chief J. Edgar Hoover wearing a pink chiffon gown. She unwittingly touched a nerve in the FBI director, who immediately placed her at the top of the FBI's Most Wanted List, where she remained even after Hoover's death. In 1971, Jean Brook left the Weather Underground and assumed the new identity of Nina Eggly.

After Spanish class, Rush Limbaugh lingered outside the classroom, thinking that when Nina Eggly emerged, he might ask her to join him for an ice cream cone and some Spanish conversation. But when she finally did come out, she was moving briskly. Rush Limbaugh tried to speak, but no words came out of his mouth.

RUSH: Ww—uh—

NARRATOR: Rush Limbaugh then followed Nina Eggly up two flights of stairs to a crowded lecture hall. The room was filled with more than a hundred students, most of them wearing Ben and Jerry's T-shirts. By the time he had found a seat, next to a tall man with a pencil moustache and dark glasses, Rush Limbaugh had lost sight of Nina Eggly. He resigned himself to staying through the class, whatever it turned out to be, in the hope of catching another glimpse of Nina Eggly.

KARL BRAUTERFELD: Good evening, welcome, first a word about the *title* of this seminar: "Millennial Musings: Reconstructing Meaning in the Age of Letterman and Limbaugh." Is there anyone here tonight who is *not* familiar with David Letterman? All right, we all know who *that* is. How about Rush Limbaugh? Anyone who has never heard or even heard *of* Rush Limbaugh? I see one hand.

NARRATOR: The one hand that went up was that of Nina Eggly. Rush Limbaugh's heart skipped a beat when he saw her.

KARL BRAUTERFELD: Well, I do not mean in any way to disparage the work of either Letterman or Limbaugh. They are both very intelligent, very skilled at what they do, and they work very hard at it. And they are part of a very important industry: The American Cleverness Industry—whose aim is to take from our culture, our society, our communal life such as it is, elements of our shared existence and turn them into nuggets of amusement which will take the place in our consciousness where meaning should be. Well. I'm going to shut up and turn it over to tonight's guest lecturer, Dr. Alvin Volt.

NARRATOR: During the lecture that followed, Rush Limbaugh's attention was divided between the speaker at the front of the room and Nina Eggly. He noticed that when Nina laughed, her ice cream cone earrings shook back and forth and small dimples formed once again in her cheeks.

Limbaugh consummates his blossoming romantic relationship with Nina Eggly while hiding his right-wing identity from her under an assumed name, just as she continues to hide her real name from him. Meanwhile, as Rush Limbaugh, he has accepted an invitation to perform onstage in an outdoor summer revival at the New York Shakespeare Festival—one more assumed role for Varon to juggle in a farce of multiple, shifting and mistaken identities.

NINA: . . . I'm too accepting of men. Of course, there *was* a time when I was ready to kill all men. I think that was during the Ford Administration.

THE MARSH, SAN FRANCISCO—Charlie Varon, author
of and solo performer in *Rush Limbaugh in Night School*

NARRATOR: As he listens to her speak, Rush Limbaugh looks around the room.
He sees a Guerrilla Girls poster, a signed first edition of *Our Bodies, Ourselves* and
a framed photograph of Bella Abzug. Suddenly, it dawns on him that he has just
gone to bed with a feminist. Rush Limbaugh feels dizzy and reaches for the table to
steady himself. A voice inside tells him to leave her apartment at once, but then he
sees the dimples in Nina's cheeks. He stays, telling himself that he needs Nina to
help him learn Spanish.

NINA: And then I met Walt. Walt Walt Walt. You know, the day Walt told me he was sleeping with Cherisse, was, I think, the angriest I've ever been in my life. Eighteen years! Two kids! And what does he say? It's biological. Men need to be allowed to fuck more than one woman. And then he backs it up with something from Joseph Campbell. And the thing that was so humiliating for me was, I thought I had put all the anger behind me. I had even stopped talking about patriarchy and the legitimate rage of all women. Everything was about healing and letting go— letting go!

> *Picks up phone.*

Hello? Oh, hi! Yeah, oh right! No, no, that's okay. We'll do it another time. 'Bye.

> *Hangs up. Pause.*

Huh. What a coincidence. Remember in Millennial Musings, that Rush Limbaugh guy who I'd never heard of?

RUSH: Yeah, the, uh, talk show personality.

NINA: Well, my friend Jenny does costumes for the New York Shakespeare Festival, where this Rush Limbaugh is evidently playing Othello. Anyway, there's this big rehearsal supposed to be happening now and Rush Limbaugh is not there and he didn't call, so they're holding everything up and Jenny's not gonna be able to come by later for coffee. Which is just as well because I'd forgotten that I'd invited her—*(Abruptly.)* Russell, why you getting dressed? Where you going?

NARRATOR: In hindsight, it appears that the lateness incident was the moment things began to unravel for Rush Limbaugh. Barry Granatour recalls what happened . . .

BARRY *(retrospect interview)*: They had phoned me at the office: Where's Rush?—and everything I tried: No answer! The phone, the beeper, the limo. Nada. So I personally go down to the rehearsal at the Delacorte, and the first thing I see is the guy who's playing Iago—Garrison Keillor.

KEILLOR: I have looked upon the world for four times seven years, and since I could distinguish between a benefit and an injury, I never found a man that knew how to love himself . . . Drown thyself! Drown cats and blind puppies!

BARRY *(retrospect interview)*: Now! There was a big crowd gathered around Jackie Mason. Jackie Mason who was in the production, cast as—now I'm trying to remember. Roderigo! Roderigo! Anyway, he's got some people, he's got some time to kill, so what's he doing?—he's working up some new material.

JACKIE MASON: You go to any bookstore, you look at all the books on all the shelves, why is it that ninety-nine percent of all the books are written by Jews? Mistuh, you know the answer to this? Because in a Jewish family, everybody's always talking at the same time. Don't eat that! I'm going to eat that! You can't eat that, it has cholesterol! But it's good cholesterol! No, it's bad chol—. And a certain percentage of Jews get tired of being interrupted and want to finish what they're saying; and so they write a book. Which is the complete opposite of White Anglo Saxon Gentiles. In a White Anglo Saxon Gentile family nobody talks. All year long they say maybe three woids. Then one time a year, at Christmas, they have a conversation. When should we open the presents? Most Gentile children do not talk before the age of eighteen. This is a fact. Which explains the phenomenon of our fellow acta, Mr. Rush Limbaugh. Why is Rush Limbaugh the only talk show host in the woild who never has a guest? Because for him talking is still a novelty and he can't get over it. Which is exactly the same situation as Garrison Keillor: you ever listen to his show on the radio? What he does on the radio: he could never get away with in a Jewish family. He starts talking, he says about six woids, then he comes up for air. Vell, it's been a quiet week. *(Inhales very deeply.)* In a Jewish family, inhaling like that is a big mistake because you'll never finish your sentence. NO, IT'S NOT A QUIET WEEK, it was a NOISY week, what are you talking about, it's been a very NOISY week, there's never a moment's peace around here, and that's the PROBlem.

NARRATOR: Later that night, Nina Eggly received another phone call from her friend Jenny Captanian.

NINA: This is *after* showing up two hours late? He won't let you take his measurements because he wants it done by someone who isn't a man-hater? *(Laughs.)* Well, this Limbaugh guy sure has your number, huh, Jen? *(Pause.)* No, I'm sorry I said that. It *was* insensitive. Look, Jen, you can't let him get to you. You have to find a way to do something with your anger, you've got to transform the energy.

NARRATOR: June 5, 1996. Millennial Musings. The lecture that night is given by the Israeli somatic feminist, Elea Avon.

ELEA: Before anything else I want you to get really comfortable. Feel your bottom on your seat. When you look around the island of Manhattan, what do you see? You see heads bobbing around; you don't see bodies. Am I correct, people? This is what you see. I'm not talking about quadriplegics and paraplegics; I'm not talking about Stephen Hawking. I'm talking about office workers and taxicab drivers and everybody else on the island of Manhattan who acts as if they only have a head and do not have—a body! Feel your bodies, people. Feel them! Feel your arms, feel your hands, feel your fingers as they come out of your hands. Do you know what your hands are for—evolutionarily speaking? They are not for sitting in front of a terminal and punching numbers into a computer. They're for making stone tools! Feel your bodies, people. Feel your legs. Evolutionarily—for running! Women, feel your breasts! Stick them out! Feel them! You know what your breasts are for— evolutionarily speaking? Do you realize what this society has done to breasts? This society has taken breasts . . . and has pasted them on billboards to sell Calvin Klein bluejeans. I have news for you: that is not what breasts are for! Form follows function, people. Really! There's a nipple at the end; that's where the milk comes out. Breasts are for suckling a baby. Feel your genitalia! We have become so completely confused because we live in a stupid century. The twentieth century is the stupidest century there has ever been. Really! Because in this century we have become so totally intelligent: we have super machines: supercolliders, supercomputers, super- conductors. We have forgotten all about our super *bodies!* Feel your genitalia! Is there anyone here tonight who can tell me what are the two purposes, evolutionarily speaking, for your genitalia?

NARRATOR: After class, at her apartment, Nina Eggly gives Rush Limbaugh a massage.

RUSH: Oh yes! Mmm. Hold on a sec, Nina. You hear that up there, your neighbor's radio? Nina, mind if I turn on your radio?

RODRIGUEZ: . . . treating cancer patients—and these are federally funded programs! And that is today's BIG QUESTION, The Big Porque of the Day on the J. Neil Hrodriguez Show is why—why why why why—why should you and I pay with *our* tax dollars—for so-called alternative cancer therapies: acupuncture, visualization, breathing exercises, massage! Tell me, who in their right mind would treat cancer with *massage?!*

NINA: Turn it off, Russell.

RUSH: No, no, I want to hear this.

RODRIGUEZ: Now let's go to our phone. The number to call . . .

NINA: What are you doing, Russell?

RODRIGUEZ: Talk to me, America! Agree, disagree, make me laugh, make me cry, *pero no me aburras:* don't bore me, America!

RUSH (*fingers over nose*): Yes, this is Roland in Manhattan, and I have a cancer experience I think is relevant. Yes, I'll hold. Watch what I do to this guy, Nina.

RODRIGUEZ: Roland in Manhattan, *you* are on the J. Neil Rodriguez Program.

RUSH/ROLAND: First, I'd like to say I listen to your program whenever I can: at home, in the car, in the operating room.

RODRIGUEZ: You are in the medical profession, sir?

RUSH/ROLAND: I'm an oncologist.

RODRIGUEZ: An oncologist! An oncologist! Ring the bell, Marylou!
    He rings the bell himself.
This is the first time to my knowledge that an oncologist has called in to the J. Neil Rodriguez Program. And do you have a comment, doctor, about these so-called alternative cancer therapies?

RUSH/ROLAND: I wouldn't be speaking to you today if it were not for massage. Four years ago I had pancreatic cancer . . .

RODRIGUEZ: Hold on, hold on, sir, you are a cancer doctor who yourself had cancer! Ring the bell, Marylou!
    He rings the bell himself.
A cancer doctor who himself had cancer!

RUSH/ROLAND: Upon diagnosis *my* oncologist told me I had six months to live. Then, against his advice, I began receiving intensive *massage* treatments, four to six hours every day. Can I prove that it cured me? No. Can you prove that it *didn't* cure me? No. I'm still alive. I think it did.

RODRIGUEZ: Sir, were you additionally taking chemotherapy or radiation?

RUSH/ROLAND: You know what your problem is, J. Neil Rodriguez? Your problem is that you live in a stupid century. See, in this century we've become so intelligent with all our supermachines, our EKGs and our MRIs and our Catscans, that we've forgotten about our super bodies and their ability to heal themselves.

RODRIGUEZ: But can you verify . . . ?

RUSH/ROLAND: In every stupid period in history, there are stupid talk show hosts who uphold outdated belief systems. Oh excuse me, I'm being paged. I have a bone marrow transplant on the ninth floor!

> *Hangs up.*

NINA (*laughing*): Do you call these shows a lot?

Limbaugh's attempts to juggle an increasingly complex schedule and contradictory roles have begun to change him in subtle and not-so-subtle ways—most obviously, through his feelings of love for Nina. He accompanies her on a midnight plane trip to Chicago to visit her daughter.

NARRATOR: Takeoff is delayed for over two hours because of unexpected local thunderstorms. Rush Limbaugh, unaccustomed to the narrow coach seats, shifts uncomfortably.

NINA: Hey, I forgot to tell you. I listened to your pal Rush Limbaugh today.

RUSH: Oh yeah?!! What'd you think?

NINA: Well, first of all, has anybody ever told you, he sounds a little like you? Anyway, it's true, his politics are really lousy. But—he did this thing about Homo Ludens, y'know, the gay performance with the NEA grant controversy: the guy who goes on stage and takes a picture of Jesse Helms and pees on it? Anyway, what Rush Limbaugh does is, he says, "I'm *so* offended by Homo Ludens." He said it about eight times. Then he says, "I'm so offended that Homo Ludens hasn't peed on *my* picture. I keep sending him glossy photographs of myself . . ." I'm not telling it really well . . . but the guy's a satirist. Kind of like Homo Ludens. Homo Ludens pees on Jesse Helms. Rush Limbaugh pees on Homo Ludens. I don't know, it's what boys do to each other.

> *Rush looks startled.*

NARRATOR: The plane finally leaves the ground at 2:26 a.m. New York time.

NINA: Sunset's a great kid but she got involved with one of her professors, a guy in the art department. And they took precautions, used one of those "automatic condoms," but it never inflated. Not that I didn't do some pretty dumb stuff when I was her age.

NARRATOR: Slowly, Nina Eggly begins telling Russell Lindbergh the story of her life, from her childhood as Jean Brook, through the three years she spent in the Weather Underground, and her subsequent life under an assumed name. Rush Limbaugh reaches overhead to open his air vent. But the flow of air does nothing to quiet the throbbing at the back of his skull. Should he turn her in to the authorities? Should he tell her that her parents are looking for her? Should he reveal to her *his own* true identity? But the question that comes out of his mouth is a different one entirely:

RUSH: Are you—going to eat those peanuts?

NINA: Russell, you know, you're the only person I've ever told about this. Don't turn me in, okay?

RUSH: Isn't it hard—living a double life?

NINA: For the first ten years it drove me completely crazy. Especially when Sunset was little—I thought, I'm denying her grandparents. Of course, then I remembered my dad would never have anything to do with grandkids who weren't white. And God!, underneath everything there was always this layer of paranoia that somebody might figure out who I was and turn me in. There came a point where I was so obsessed by the fear—I remember it was right around Sunset's third birthday, and I was still pregnant with Shiatsu. Finally, I went and saw a shaman, this Taos Indian guy, Crying Eagle. He took me up to the top of Taos Mountain and I had with me a picture of myself as Jean Brook, standing next to my sister and my mom and dad in front of the Christmas tree. And at sunset, Crying Eagle lit some cedar and sage. And I took the photograph and I held it over the burning cedar; and then I let it go. And I watched the smoke go up. And then Crying Eagle said—in Tiwa, he said: "We die many times, we have many griefs. We continue." And then he gave me a quartz crystal. The same one I wear now. And after that I was really okay with it. I *was* Nina Eggly.

NARRATOR: For a moment, Russell Lindbergh considers what would happen if he tried the same thing—a ceremony to let go of his old identity as Rush Limbaugh. He imagines himself holding a blue-and-orange armband over a fire of burning cedar. He imagines a new life, in a new country—perhaps Denmark—an ordinary life, in which he and Nina Eggly are letter carriers in a small town, delivering the mail by bicycle, getting into really good shape, staying up late together working on their Danish pronouns. Rush Limbaugh is drawn further and further into the dream of a new life. But then the captain puts on the FASTEN SEAT BELTS sign and announces the local weather and time.

NARRATOR: O'Hare Airport. While Nina Eggly uses the restroom, Rush Limbaugh calls his manager's voice mail.

RUSH: Barry, Rush. Working very hard on my Spanish; will not be in tomorrow. Put on a rerun. Oh—and call Spalding. Tell him if he ever wants to see me again— *no more stories!*

NARRATOR: Evanston, Illinois. Rush Limbaugh and Nina Eggly prepare to sleep on the floor of Sunset Eggly's college dorm room. Lying under the down comforter, Rush Limbaugh again sees the image of the burning blue-and-orange armband. He looks at the woman sleeping next to him, and a tear rolls down his cheek. Rush Limbaugh leans over and lightly kisses the sleeping Nina Eggly.

Monday, June 17, 1996. New York City. Rush Limbaugh is in a taxicab on his way from LaGuardia Airport to his studios in midtown. He looks at his watch and sees that he's late.

RUSH: What's going on; why is there so much traffic?

TAXI DRIVER: *Lo siento, no hablo ingles.*

RUSH: Okay, *espanol. (Falteringly.) Porque no podemos movernos en este—trafficojam?*

TAXI DRIVER: *Aah, los Limbaughistas! No ha oido? (Laughs.) Hay un gran tumulto.*

NARRATOR: As Rush Limbaugh tries to figure out the meaning of the word *"Limbaughistas,"* he sees a group of looters run by carrying computer terminals, telephones, Scotch tape dispensers. They are wearing the blue-and-orange armbands of the Rush Limbaugh Entourage. Limbaugh leaves the cab and runs up to his broadcast studio.

BARRY: Rush, where the hell have you been? When you didn't show on time, they went crazy. The whole Entourage! What they did to the offices of the New York *Times!* What— *(Points to ON AIR sign and mouths the words.)* Rush, you're on the air!

RUSH: This is the Rush Limbaugh Program, and let's go right to our phones. Cos Cob, Connecticut, you are on the Rush Limbaugh Program.

DELBERT BROOK *(very slowly)*: Mr. Limbaugh, my name is Delbert Brook. I am the father of Jean Brook, whom you refer to as a Leftover Lefty of the Sixties. I refer to her as my daughter. Sir, what you are doing to my family is cruel, and I ask you to stop it.

RUSH *(disoriented; in shock)*: Reasonable people may disagree. Commercial. *(Falls into chair.)*

BARRY: Rush, did I mention that Rodriguez is up to nineteen? Ever since this Roland guy has been calling in, his ratings have gone through the fucking roof!

NARRATOR: Wednesday, June 19, 1996. 12:51 P.M. Spalding Gray writes in his diary: "Tonight we open the definitive *Othello*."

2:37 P.M. Barry Granatour sells ABC-TV exclusive rights to a backstage, Barbara Walters interview of Rush Limbaugh as Othello.

3:09 P.M. Delbert and Harriet Brook, acting on a tip, begin driving from Cos Cob, Connecticut to New York City.

3:22 P.M. J. Neil Rodriguez begins secret talks with programming executives at ABC-TV.

3:27 P.M. Jenny Captanian distributes costumes and goes over plans with twenty-one fellow members of the women's direct action collective, Pants on Fire.

4:03 P.M. Opening night of *Othello* now less than four hours away. As he showers, Rush Limbaugh agonizes over whether to keep his 4:30 P.M. date with Nina Eggly. Soon, his mind drifts back to one of the Millennial Musings lectures: the lecture given by the Indian philosopher, Dr. Ginta Rosh.

GINTA ROSH: Transformation. People think transformation is very complicated. Not complicated. Simple. You want to understand transformation, look at a snake. Watch the snake shed its skin. That's all you need to know about transformation.

NARRATOR: In the shower, Rush Limbaugh's mind returns to the dream of a new life as a Danish letter carrier . . . meeting Nina for lunch in a clean, safe park, finding a secluded spot to make love. Then, suddenly, Limbaugh bolts naked out of the shower.

Rush Limbaugh in Night School *was first produced at The Marsh, San Francisco, October 6, 1994 under the direction of Martin Higgins. It has since been produced by the Second Stage Theater, New York City, March 28, 1995.*

A DIRECTORY OF NEW-PLAY PRODUCTIONS

Compiled by Sheridan Sellers

Professional 1994–95 productions of new plays by leading companies around the United States that supplied information on casts and credits at Sheridan Sellers's request, plus a few reported by other reliable sources, are listed below in alphabetical order of the locations of 56 producing organizations. Date given is opening date, included whenever a record was obtained from the producing management. All League of Resident Theaters (LORT) and other Equity groups were queried for this comprehensive Directory. Those not listed here either did not produce new or newly revised scripts in 1994–95 or had not responded by press time. Most of the productions listed—but not all—are American or world premieres. Some are new revisions, second looks or scripts produced previously but not previously reported in *Best Plays*.

Abingdon, Va.: Barter Theater

(Artistic director, Richard Rose)

THE LAST LEAF. By Peter Ekstrom. December 6, 1994. Director, John Hardy; musical direction, Winston Clark; scenery, James Gross; costumes, Amanda Aldridge; lighting, David Friedl; sound, Scott Koenig.

Doctor	Mark Delabarre
Sue	Stephanie Pope
Johnsy	Glory Crampton
Behrman	Peter Johl

Time and place: 1905, April and November. Adjoining garrets, Greenwich Village, New York City. One intermission.
Early Stages, 1994: Barter Stage II

PARTIAL OBJECTS. By Sherry Kramer. Director, Michael Champagne.
THE MOVING OF LILLA BARTON. By John MacNicholas. Director, Susanne Boulle.
DR. JEKYLL AND MISS HYDE. By David DeBoy. Director, Randall Rapstine.
THE LAST LEAF. By Peter Ekstrom. Director, John Hardy.
SWEET DELIVERANCE. By Eric Houston. Director, Bob Anglin.
THE CHERRY ORCHARD. Adapted by Michael Medeiros and Joseph Kline. Director, Michael Medeiros.

Ashland: Oregon Shakespeare Festival

(Artistic director, Henry Woronicz)

EMMA'S CHILD. By Kristine Thatcher. March 28, 1995. Director, Cynthia White; scenery, Curt Enderle; costumes, Alvin Perry; lighting, Robert Peterson; musical direction, Todd Barton.

Jean Farrell	Linda Emond
Henry Farrell	Dan Kremer
Tess; Dr. Arbaugh	Debra Lynne Wicks
Franny	Kirsten Giroux
Emma; Michelle	Christine Williams
Laurence	Ray Porter
Mary Joe	Cindy Basco
Vivien	Judith Sanford
Sam	Mark Murphey

Time and place: Between the fall of 1990 and the summer of 1991. The intensive care unit for newborns at Christ Hospital, Chicago, 1991.

THIS DAY AND AGE. By Nagle Jackson. April 19, 1995. Director, Pat Patton; scenery, William Bloodgood; costumes, Susan Mickey; lighting, Dawn Chiang; music, David deBerry.

Marjorie	Susan Corzatte

Ann .... Robin Goodrin Nordli
Brian .... James Newcomb
Joy .... Bonnie Akimoto
Tony .... Raymond L. Chapman

Man .... Clayton Corzatte
Time and place: The present. Connecticut:
One of New York City's more affluent suburbs.

Berkeley, Calif.: Berkeley Repertory Theater

(Artistic director, Sharon Ott; managing director, Susan Medak)

DON JUAN GIOVANNI. By Steven Epp, Felicity Jones, Dominique Serrand and Paul Walsh, based on the work of Molière and Mozart. September 7, 1994. Director, Dominique Serrand; scenery, Dominique Serrand; costumes, Sonya Berlovitz; lighting, Marcus Dilliard.

Sganarelle .... Steven Epp
Diva .... Mary Rempalski
Don Juan .... Dominique Serrand
Don Giovanni .... Gary Briggle
Leporello .... Bradley Greenwald
Zerlina .... Kathleen Humphrey
Charlotte .... Sarah Agnew
Peter .... Luverne Seifert
Elvire .... Felicity Jones
Donna Elvira .... Cynthia Lohman
Chorus .... Milissa Carey, Nadia Mahdi
    One intermission.

THE WOMAN WARRIOR. By Deborah Rogin. September 15, 1994. See its entry in the Huntington Theater Company, Boston, listing in this section of this volume.

LAST OF THE SUNS. By Alice Tuan. December 30, 1994. Director, Phyllis S.K. Look; scenery, Barbara Mesney; costumes, Lydia Tanji; lighting, Kurt Landisman; sound, J.A. Deane, choreography, Jamie H.J. Guan.

Yeh Yeh .... Sab Shimono
Twila .... Jacqueline Kim
Buddha; Ho Ping .... Alberto Isaac
1st Wife; Ni Lee .... Jeanne Sakata
May Lee .... Jacqueline Kim
Monkey King; Mao Cap #1;
    Lt. Gen. King .... Michael Ordona
Eight Pig; Mao Cap #2;
    Major Go .... Kelvin Han Yee
Sonny .... Sean San José Blackman
    One intermission.

GENI(US). By Geoff Hoyle and Tony Taccone. February 3, 1995. Director, Tony Taccone; scenery, Peggy Snider; costumes, Christine Dougherty; lighting, Kent Dorsey; sound, Matthew Spiro.
    With Geoff Hoyle, Sharon Lockwood. One intermission.

Boca Raton, Fla.: Caldwell Theater Company

(Artistic and managing director, Michael Hall)

COWGIRLS. Concept by Mary Murfitt; book by Betsy Howie; music and lyrics by Mary Murfitt. July 15, 1994. Director, Eleanor Reissa; musical direction, Mary Ehlinger; scenery, Tim Bennett; costumes, Patricia Bowes; lighting, Thomas Salzman; sound, Steve Shapiro.

Jo Carlson .... Audrey Lavine
Mickey .... Claudia Schneider
Mo .... Betsy Howie
Lee .... Brook Ann Hedick
Mary Lou .... Mary Murfitt
Rita .... Mary Ehlinger
    Time and place: The present. Hiram Hall, a

country Western music hall in Rexford, Kansas. Act I: Friday. Act II: Saturday. One intermission.

BUT NOT FOR ME. Musical by Christopher Cooper, Michael Hall, Dana P. Rowe and Avery Sommers. August 12, 1994. Director, Michael Hall; musical direction, Dana P. Rowe; scenery, Tim Bennett; costumes, Patricia Bowes; lighting, Thomas Salzman; sound, Steve Shapiro.

Avery .... Avery Sommers
Dana .... Dana P. Rowe
    Place: On and around various stages in the world of show business. One intermission.

Boston: Huntington Theater Company

(Producing director, Peter Altman; managing director, Michael Maso)

THE WOMAN WARRIOR. By Deborah Rogin; adapted from Hong Kingston's *The Woman Warrior* and *China Men*. September 14, 1994. Director,

Sharon Ott; scenery, Ming Cho Lee; costumes, Susan Hilferty; lighting, Peter Maradudin; original music, Jon Jang; additional musical compositions,

BERKELEY, CALIF. REPERTORY—Gary Briggle and Dominique Serrand in *Don Juan Giovanni*

Liu Qi-Chao; sound, Stephen LeGrand; produced in association with Martin Rosen and Nepenthe Productions, the Berkeley, Calif. Repertory Theater and the Center Theater Group, Los Angeles.

With Lydia Look, Lisa Lu, Soon-Teck Oh, Wang Luoyong, Emily Kuroda, Kim Miyori, Lisa Tejero, Jonathan Cho, Janis Chow, David Furumoto, Mel Duane Gionson, Charles Hu, David Johann, Michael Edo Keane, Dian Kobayashi, Brian Kwan, Miko Lee, Wood Moy, Donna Mae Wong, Man Wong.

Two intermissions.

Buffalo, N.Y.: Studio Arena Theater

(Artistic director, Gavin Cameron-Webb; producing director, Raymond Bonnard)

OVER THE TAVERN. By Tom Dudzick. December 6, 1994. Director, Terence Lamude; scenery, Russell Metheny; costumes, Maureen Carr; lighting, John McClain; sound, Rick Menke; choreography, Lynne Kurdziel-Formato.

Rudy .... Yvon Pasquarello
Sister Clarissa .... Jeanne Cairns
Ellen .... Susanne Marley
Georgie .... Chad Vahue
Eddie .... Jamie Bennett
Annie .... Fleur Phillips
Chet .... Tom Bloom
Rudy (alternate) .... Bob de la Plante

Time and place: 1950, Buffalo. One intermission.

Cambridge, Mass.: American Repertory Theater

(Artistic director, Robert Brustein; managing director, Robert J. Orchard; associate artistic director, Ron Daniels)

THE ORESTEIA. By Aeschylus; translated and adapted by Robert Auletta. November 30, 1994 (Part I, *Agamemnon*); December 4, 1994 (Part II, *The Libation Bearers* and *The Eumenides*). Director, Francois Rochaix; scenery, Robert Dahlstrom; costumes, Catherine Zuber; lighting, Mimi Jordan Sherin; music, Jan Garbarek; sound, Christopher Walker.

Clytemnestra .... Randy Danson
Orestes .... Thomas Derrah
Chorus Leader .... Alvin Epstein
Herald .... Benjamin Evett
Watchman .... Jeremy Geidt
Aegisthus .... Will LeBow
Agamemnon .... Charles Levin
Electra .... Kerry O'Malley

With Remo Airaldi, Starla Benford, Jessalyn Gilsig, Granville Hatcher, Teresa Y. Hegji, Tom Hughes, Sherri Lee, Karen Phillips, Natacha Roi, Chandler Vinton.

THE CRYPTOGRAM. By David Mamet. February 8, 1995. Director, David Mamet. See its entry in the Plays Produced Off Broadway section of this volume.

THE ACCIDENT. By Carol K. Mack. April 9, 1995. Director, Marcus Stern; scenery, Allison Koturbash; costumes, Gail Astrid Buckley; lighting, John Ambrosone; sound, Marcus Stern, Christopher Walker.

Bessie ....Natacha Roi
John ....Jack Willis
Ben .... Nat DeWolf
Doreen ....Caroline Hall
Dr. Greyson .... Jeremiah Kissel
No intermission.

Chelsea, Mich.: Purple Rose Theater Company

(Artistic director, T. Newell Kring; executive director, Jeff Daniels; managing director, Alan Ribant)

THY KINGDOM'S COMING. By Jeff Daniels. October 14, 1994. Director, T. Newell Kring; scenery, Bartley H. Bauer; costumes, Susan Holls Naum; lighting, Gary Decker; sound, Joe Jenkins.
Derek Johansen .... Wayne-David Parker

Crash Baker .... Guy Sanville
Gordon Wessler .... Phillip Locker
Gerald Marushkin ....Anthony Caselli
One intermission.

Chicago: Goodman Theater

(Artistic director, Robert Falls; executive director, Roche Schulfer)

SIN. By Wendy MacLeod. October 31, 1994. Director, David Petrarca; scenery, Scott Bradley; costumes, Allison Reeds; lighting, Robert Christen; sound and music, Rob Milburn.
Avery .... Amy Morton
Man (Lust) .... Tim Rhoze
Michael (Sloth) ....David Pasquesi
Date (Greed) .... Steve Carell
Helen (Gluttony) .... Karen Vaccaro
Fred (Envy) ....Kyle Colerider-Krugh
Jason (Wrath) ....Steve Pickering
Gerard, Avery's brother
    (Pride) ....Jeffrey Hutchinson
    Time and place: October, 1989, San Francisco.
One intermission.

SEVEN GUITARS. By August Wilson. January 23, 1995. Director, Walter Dallas; scenery, Scott Bradley; costumes, Constanza Romero; lighting, Christopher Akerlind; sound, Tom Clark; musical direction, Dwight Andrews.
Louise ....Michele Shay
Canewell ....Ruben Santiago-Hudson
Red Carter ....Tommy Hollis
Vera ....Viola Davis
Hedley ....Albert Hall
Floyd Barton ....Jerome Preston Bates
Ruby .... Rosalyn Coleman
    Time and place: The spring of 1948, Pittsburgh, Pa. Act I, Scene 1: Wednesday afternoon. Scene 2: Wednesday, one week earlier. Scene 3: Thursday morning. Scene 4: Thursday afternoon. Scene 5: Thursday evening. Act II, Scene 1: Friday morning. Scene 2: Friday afternoon. Scene 3: Late Friday night. Scene 4: Saturday evening. Scene 5: Sunday, Mother's Day. Scene 6: Later Sunday night. Scene 7: The following Wednesday afternoon. One intermission.

GERTRUDE STEIN: EACH ONE AS SHE MAY. Adapted and directed by Frank Galati. February 13, 1995. Music, Reginald Robinson, Miriam Sturm; scenery, Mary Griswold; costumes, Birgit Rattenborg Wise; lighting, Robert Christen; sound, Rob Milburn; musical arrangement and direction, Rob Milburn, Miram Sturm.
Narrators ...... Cheryl Lynn Bruce, Rick Worthy
Melanctha Herbert ....Jacqueline Williams
Dr. Jefferson Campbell .. Johnny Lee Davenport
Musicians ....Miriam Sturm, Reginald Robinson

JOURNEY TO THE WEST. Adapted and directed by Mary Zimmerman. May 8, 1995. Scenery, Scott Bradley; costumes, Allison Reeds; lighting, T.J. Gerckens; sound, Michael Bodeen; music, William Schwarz, Miriam Sturm, Michael Bodeen.
Buddha; and others ....Jane C. Cho
Jade Emperor; T'ang
    Emperor ....Christopher Donahue
Kuan Yin .... Jenny Bacon
The Monkey; Sun Wu-K'ung ..... Douglas Hara
Woodsman .... Marc Vann
Subodhi ....Lisa Tejero
Dragon King .... Tim Rhoze
Yama .... David Kersnar

Moksa .... Maulik Pancholy
Tripitaka T'ang; Scripture Pilgrim . Bruce Norris
Green Orchid .... Manao DeMuth
Pig; Chu Pa-Chieh .... Steve Pickering

Sha Monk .... Paul Oakley Stovall
Fisherman Chang .... Tracy Walsh
    Place: China to India and back. One intermission.

Chicago: Organic Theater Company

(Producing director, Jeff Neal; artistic director, Paul Frellick; managing director, Ladonna Freidheim)

WOLFBANE. By Jeff Carey. November 12, 1994. Director, Lisa L. Abbott; scenery, Chris Corwin; costumes, Patrick Clayberg; lighting, Robert G. Smith; sound, Glenn Swan.
Destiny .... Susan Frampton
Larry .... Martin Bedoian
    Place: Destiny's apartment.

POCKET CHANGE. By Scott Anderson. November 19, 1994. Director, Paul Frellick; scenery, Chris Corwin; costumes, Renee Starr Liepins; lighting, Robert G. Smith; sound, Glenn Swan.
Johnny .... David Warren
Frank; Smilin' Jack; Sid; Rich .... Steve Heller
Flip .... Tim Herbert
Man; Vince; Charlie .... Danny McCarthy

Woman; Rachel .... Danica Ivancevic
Phil .... Thomas Gebbia
Todd; Bobby .... Philip D. Lortie
Beth .... Heidi Ammon

YOUR WEB FOOTED FRIENDS. By David Rush. February 25, 1995. Director, Steve Scott; scenery and lighting, Robert G. Smith; costumes, Paula Line; sound, Alison Hill.
Carla Fremski .... Michelle Renee Thompson
Larry Kimball .... Steve Heller
Utah Williams .... Murray McKay
Kim Valenko .... Tonray Ho
    Time and place: July 3, from early morning to about 10 that night, throughout the city of Chicago. One intermission.

Chicago: Remains Theater

(Artistic director, Neel Keller)

MOON UNDER MIAMI. By John Guare. April 30, 1995. Director, Neel Keller; scenery, Red Grooms, assisted by Stephan Olson; costumes, Allison Reeds; lighting, Adam Silverman; sound, Joseph Cerqua, Stu Greenspan; musical direction and arrangements, Jeremy Kahn.
Agent Presby .... Will Clinger
Fran Farkas .... Valorie Hubbard
Congressman Kayak .... Rick Almada

Congressman Munoz .... Noe Cuellar
Agent Wilcox .... Larry McCauley
Agent Belden .... Kevin Hurley
Shelley Slutzky .... Matt DeCaro
Giselle St. Just .... Kate Walsh
Congressman Bentine ...... G. Knight Houghton
Sheik Akbahran .... Jihad Harik
    One intermission.

Chicago: Steppenwolf Theater Company

(Artistic director, Randall Arney)

TALKING HEADS. By Alan Bennett. July 17, 1994. Director, John Mahoney; scenery, Linda Buchanan; costumes, Nan Cibula-Jenkins; lighting, Kevin Rigdon; sound, Richard Woodbury.
Irene .... Estelle Parsons
Susan .... Martha Lavey
Graham .... Alan Wilder

A CLOCKWORK ORANGE. By Anthony Burgess. September 24, 1994. Director, Terry Kinney; scenery, Robert Brill; costumes, Laura Cunningham; lighting, Kevin Rigdon; sound, Michael Bo-

deen; musical concept and direction, Willy Schwarz.
Alex .... K. Todd Freeman
Mrs. F. Alexander; Alex's
    Mother .... Martha Lavey
F. Alexander .... Robert Breuler
Alex's Father .... Cedric Young
Head Warder .... Skip Sudduth
    With Paul Adelstein, Carolyn Baeumler, William R. Bartlett, Christopher Bauer, Jef Bek, Daniel J. Bryant, Dana Eskelson, Patrick Fitzgerald, Edgar Gabriel, Steve Gibons, Pat Healy, Rich

Hutchman, Bill Kronenberg, Adrianne Krstansky, Nick Offerman, Robert Radkoff-Ek, Margaret Rattenbury, Daniel Ruben, Willy Schwarz, Kim Leigh Smith, Jeff Still, Todd Tesen, Benjamin Werling, Sara Wollan.

PICASSO AT THE LAPIN AGILE. By Steve Martin. October 22, 1994. Director, Randall Arney; scenery, Scott Bradley; costumes, Allison Reeds; lighting, Kevin Rigdon; sound, Richard Woodbury; co-produced in Los Angeles (Westwood Playhouse) by Stephen Eich, Joan Stein, Levitt/Fox Theatricals/Mages and Bette Cerf Hill.

With Nathan Davis, Tim Hopper, Paula Korologos, Tracy Letts, Rondi Reed, Joe Sagal, Rick Snyder, Troy Eric West, Alan Wilder.

No intermission.

TIME OF MY LIFE. By Alan Ayckbourn. February 12, 1995. Director, Michael Maggio; scenery, Linda Buchanan; costumes, Nan Cibula-Jenkins; lighting, Kevin Rigdon; sound, Richard Woodbury.
Gerry ....Robert Breuler
Laura .... Molly Regan
Adam ....Ian Barford

Glyn ....Neil Flynn
Stephanie ....Martha Lavey
Maureen ....Mariann Mayberry
Calvinu; Tuto; Aggi; Dinka;
Bengie ....David Alan Novak
One intermission.

NOMATHEMBA. Book and lyrics by Ntozake Shange, Joseph Shabalala and Eric Simonson; based on a song by Joseph Shabalala; music by Joseph Shabalala. April 9, 1995. Direction, Eric Simonson; scenery, Loy Arcenas; costumes, Karin Kopischke; lighting, James F. Ingalls; sound, Rob Milburn; choreography, Joseph Shabalala; additional choreography, Kenny Ingram, Dumisani Diamini.
Ma Alina .... Cheryl Lynn Bruce
Sissy .... Bernadette L. Clark
Nsizwa; Keo .... Johnny Lee Davenport
Welcome .... Dumisani Diamini
Nomathemba .... Vanita Harbour
Bongani ....Natare Mwine
With Maqhinga Radebe, Tania Richard, Frank Russell, Linda Maurel Sithole, Sipho Nxumalo, Michael Williams, Ladysmith Black Mambazo.
No intermission.

Chicago: Victory Gardens Theater

(Artistic director, Dennis Zacek)

JEST A SECOND. By James Sherman. May 25, 1995. Director, Dennis Zacek; scenery, Stephen Packard; costumes, Claudia Boddy; lighting, Larry Shoeneman; sound, Galen G. Ramsey.
Miriam Goldman ....Roslyn Alexander
Dr. Rosen ....Ted Kamp

Abe Goldman .... Bernie Landis
Sarah Goldman ....Anna Markin
Joel Goldman ....Greg Vinkler
Bob Schroeder .... Larry Yando
One intermission.

Cincinnati: Cincinnati Playhouse in the Park

(Producing artistic director, Edward Stern; executive director, Buzz Ward)

THE BROTHERS KARAMAZOV (co-produced with Repertory Theater of St. Louis). By Anthony Clarvoe, based on the novel by Fyodor Dostoyevsky. January 6, 1995. Director, Brian Kulick; scenery and costumes, Mark Wendland; lighting, Max De Volder.
The Karamazovs:
Fyodor .... Robert Elliott
Dmitri ....Michael Chaban
Ivan ....Michael Ornstein
Alyosha .... Matthew Rauch
Smerdyakov .... Ed Shea
The Monastery:
Father Zosima ....Joneal Joplin
Rakitin ....Paul DeBoy
The Town:
Katya Verkhovtsev ....Susan Ericksen
Grushenka Svetlov .... Katherine Heasley

Fenya; Samsonov ....Brooks Almy
Plotkinov .... Ed Shea
The Inn at Mokroye:
Plastunov .... Paul DeBoy
Mussyalovich ....Joneal Joplin
Gypsies ....Susan Ericksen, Brooks Almy
Constables .... Michael Ornstein, Matthew Rauch
The Trial:
Judge; Devil .... Robert Elliott
District Attorney ....Joneal Joplin
Time and place: The 1860s in a small town in Russia. Two intermissions.

HOMETOWN HEROES. By Ed Graczyk. March 28, 1995. Director, Edward Stern; scenery, Paul R. Shortt; costumes, Hollis Jenkins-Evans; lighting,

On Chicago Stages

At the Goodman Theater, *above,* Viola Davis and Jerome Preston Bates in August Wilson's *Seven Guitars*; at the Organic Theater, *right,* Martin Bedoian and Susan Frampton in *Wolfbane* by Jeff Carey

Jackie Manassee; sound, David E. Smith.

Willie ....Ralph Waite
Joe .... M. Emmet Walsh
      Time and place: The back porches of its title characters in a medium-sized industrial city in Ohio during an October night in 1987. One intermission.

Cleveland: The Cleveland Play House

(Acting artistic director, Roger T. Danforth; managing director, Dean R. Gladden)

JUNGLE ROT. By Seth Greenland. January 10, 1995. Director, Roger T. Danforth; scenery, James Noone; costumes, David Toser; lighting, Richard Winkler; sound, Jordan Davis.

African Man #1; Burkino .... Danny Johnson
African Man #2; M'Bekan ......Joseph Edwards
African Man #3; Ndolo ....Tony Sias
John Stillman ....Richmond Hoxie

Walter Clark .... David Adkins
Patience Stillman .... Kay Walbye
Young Man .... Daryl Trammer
Patrice Lumumba ....Leon Addison Brown
Alice Bradshaw .... Lianne Kressin
Bud Bradshaw ....Dudley Swetland
Dr. Felix Bender .... Robert Machray

Miss Rendelbaker ....Karen Ogle
Bodyguards, Waiters, Airport Guards, Porter:
Joseph Edwards, Tony Sias, Daryl Trammer.
Time and place: The autumn of 1960 (Eisenhower is still in the White House) in and around Leopoldville, the capital of the Congo. One intermission.

Costa Mesa, Calif.: South Coast Repertory

(Artistic directors, David Emmes, Martin Benson; managing director, Paula Tomei)

GREEN ICEBERGS. By Cecilia Fannon. October 21, 1994. Director, David Emmes; scenery, Robert Brill; costumes, Ann Bruice; lighting, Tom Ruzika; music and sound, Michael Roth.
Waiter ....Hal Landon Jr.
Veronica .... Nike Doukas
Claude .... Robert Curtis-Brown
Beth ....Annie LaRussa
Justus .... Jeff Allin
Place: In and around an outdoor cafe in the Tuscan Hills of Italy. One intermission.

LA POSADA MAGICA. By Octavio Solis. December, 1994. Director, Jose Cruz Gonzalez; scenery, Cliff Faulkner; costumes, Shigeru Yaji; lighting, Lonnie Alcaraz; music and musical direction, Marcos Loya.
Horacio ....Ruben Sierra
Consuelo; Widow .... Edna Alvarez
Caridad; Widow ....Christine Avila
Mom; Mariluz ....Teresa Velarde
Rufugio; Buzzard .... Vic Trevino
Papi; Josecruz ....George Galvan
Eli; Lauro; Bones ...... Phillip Daniel Rodriguez

Gracie ....Ruth Livier
Musician; Ensemble ....Marcos Loya, Lorenzo Martinez
Time and place: The present, Christmas Eve. One intermission.

WIT. By Margaret Edson. January 27, 1995. Director, Martin Benson; scenery, Cliff Faulkner; costumes, Kay Peebles; lighting, Paulie Jenkins; music and sound, Michael Roth.
Vivian Bearing .... Megan Cole
Harvey Kelekian; Mr. Bearing ... Richard Doyle
Susie Monahan .... Mary Kay Wulf
E.M. Ashford; Housekeeper ......Patricia Fraser
Jason Posner .... Brian Drillinger
Lab Technicians; Clinical Fellows; Students;
Code Blue Team ....Christopher DuVal, Kyle Jones
Clinical Fellow; Student;
Code Blue Team .... Stacy L. Porter
Place: Most of the action, but not all, takes place in a room of the University Hospital Comprehensive Cancer Center.

Denver: Denver Center Theater Company

(Artistic director, Donovan Marley)

STAR FEVER. Conceived, designed and directed by Pavel M. Dobrusky. September 30, 1994. Music, Larry Delinger; choreography, Gary Abbott; sound, Jason Foote Roberts.
Dios ....Tim DeKay
His Honor .... Bernard K. Addison
Debby .... Kathleen M. Brady
C.K. .... Archie Smith
Dr. Spinn ....Luan Schooler
I.C. ....William M. Whitehead
Satyr Peppi .... Jamie Horton
Maria ....Gabriella Canino
Dancers: Christina Chiodo, Lisa Corbell, Tobi H. Johnson-Compton, Angela Patel, Colleen Noelani Young. Ensemble: Roy Arias, Tara Blau, Lauren Bone, Sadie Chrestman, Melissa King, Robert MacMullan, Scott Meikle, Matthew Nowosielski, Amy Prosser, Jim Rodriguez, Nick Stabile, Kerry VanderGriend.

COMING OF THE HURRICANE. By Keith Glover. January 6, 1995. Director, Israel Hicks; scenery, Vicki Smith; costumes, David Kay Mickelsen; lighting, Charles R. MacLeod; sound, Jason F. Roberts; fight direction, David S. Leong.
Meadows ....Willian Denis
Shadow Jack .... Ray Aranha
Kazarah .... Cynthia Ruffin
Crixus ....Charles Weldon
Bigelow ....Count Stovall
Stolkes ....Roderick Aird
Cayman ....Christopher Birt
Hurricane .... Bill Christ
Time and place: During the Reconstruction, late 1800s. Bailerton, Maryland.

THE QUICK-CHANGE ROOM. By Nagle Jackson; music by Robert Sprayberry. January 13, 1995. Director, Paul Weidner; scenery, Michael

Ganio; costumes, David Kay Mickelsen; lighting, Charles R. MacLeod; sound, Don Tindall.

Nina .... Erin J. O'Brien
Marya .... Peggy Pope
Sergey .... Tony Church
Lena .... Alice White
Nikolai .... John Hutton
Ludmilla .... Annie Murray
Sasha .... Stephen Turner
Boris .... Alex Wipf
Timofey .... Michael John McGann
Anna .... Jacqueline Antaramian
    Time and place: July, 1991 to May, 1992. The Kuzlov Theater, St. Petersburg, Russia. One intermission.

THE EDUCATION OF WALTER KAUF-

MANN. Written and performed by Kevin Kling. March 3, 1995. Direction and scenery, Michael Sommers; costumes, Andrew V. Yelusich; lighting, Charles R. MacLeod; sound, Don Tindall.

Walter Kaufmann .... Kevin Kling

IT AIN'T NOTHIN' BUT THE BLUES. By Charles Bevel, Lita Gaithers, Randal Myler, Ron Taylor and Dan Wheetman. March 17, 1995. Director, Randal Myler; musical direction, Dan Wheetman; scenery, Andrew V. Yelusich; costumes, Patricia A. Whitelock; lighting, Don Darnutzer; sound, David R. White.
    Ensemble: Charles Bevel, Lita Gaithers, Eloise Laws, Chic Street Man, Ron Taylor, Laura Theodore, Dan Wheetman.
    One intermission.

East Farmingdale, N.Y.: Arena Players Repertory Company of Long Island

(Producer/director, Frederic De Feis)

NO MAN'S LAND. By Barbara Snow. February 16, 1995. Director, Frederic De Feis; scenery, Fred Sprauer; costumes, Karen Ackley; lighting, Al Davis.

Lila .... Debbie Cascio
Nancy .... Vicki Baum
Diane .... Susan Leslie Blake
Anne .... Linda Bub
Sara .... Linda Rameizl
Janelle .... Sunny Taylor
Jenny .... Gia Brooks

Rebecca .... Christine LaCamera
Terrorist .... Geoff Grady
Officer Bob .... Cliff Lee
Officer Donovan .... Frank McGeeney
Patients .... Gia Brooks, Christine LaCamera, Deborah Payton
    Time and place: A family planning clinic somewhere in the U.S.A. in the year 1992. Act I: Afternoon. Act II, Scene 1: The action continues. Scene 2: Early evening. Scene 3: Later that night. One intermission.

East Haddam, Conn.: Goodspeed Opera House

(Executive director, Michael P. Price)

STARCROSSED: THE TRIAL OF GALILEO. Book and lyrics by Keith Levenson and Alexa Junge; music by Jeanine Tesori. November 3, 1994. Director, Martin Charnin; scenery, Kenneth Foy; costumes, Gail Brassard; lighting, Ken Billington; musical direction, Michael O'Flaherty; choreography, Daniel Pelzig.

Inquisitor; Astrologer .... Tom Treadwell
Galileo Galilei .... Ed Dixon
Antonio Ponti .... Neal Mayer
Maffeo Barberini .... Cordell Stahl
Mara .... Elizabeth Richmond
Doge of Venice .... Kevin Berdini
Simon Faber .... Phillip Officer
Venetian Princess .... Ellyn Arons
Agnus Dei Soloists .... Catherine Ruivivar, Jennifer Neuland
    Members of the Inquisition, Clergy, Students, Nuns, Venetian Citizens: Ellyn Arons, Kevin Ber-

dini, Tim Bohle, Jane Brockman, Neal Mayer, Jennifer Neuland, Barbara Pflaumer, David Alan Quart, Catherine Ruivivar, Tom Treadwell.
    Time and place: Renaissance Italy in the 17th Century. One intermission.

HONKY-TONK HIGHWAY. Book by Richard Berg; music, lyrics and additional dialogue by Robert Nassif-Lindsey. April 27, 1995. Director, Gabriel Barre; scenery, Charles E. McCarry; costumes, Robert Strong Miller; lighting, Phil Monat; musical direction, Steve Steiner.

Nat Dawson .... Kevin Fox
Jenine-Kate McWhorter .... Erin Hill
Paulie Latner .... Rick Leon
Darrell Waller .... David M. Lutken
Curtis Patterson .... Sean McCourt
    Time and place: Tucker's Roadhouse, Alton Falls, Tennessee in 1970. One intermission.

Gloucester, Mass.: Gloucester Stage Company

(Artistic director, Israel Horovitz)

UNEXPECTED TENDERNESS. By Israel Horovitz. August 19, 1994. Director, Grey Johnson; scenery, Charles F. Morgan; costumes, Jane Stein; lighting, John Ambrosone.

Roddy Stern; Archie Stern	Will LeBow
Molly Stern	Paula Plum
Sylvie Stern	Jessica Semeraro
Young Roddy Stern	Ben Webster, David Rich
Haddie Stern	Patricia Pellows
Jacob Stern	Barry Zaslove
Willie	Mick Verga

Hartford, Conn.: Hartford Stage Company

(Artistic director, Mark Lamos; managing director, Stephen J. Albert)

A DYBBUK, OR BETWEEN TWO WORLDS. By S. Ansky, adapted by Tony Kushner; translated from the Yiddish by Joachim Neugroschel. February 17, 1995. Director, Mark Lamos; scenery, John Conklin; costumes, Jess Goldstein; lighting, Pat Collins; choreography, Mark Dendy; sound, David Budries.

Khonen	Michael Hayden
Batlon 1	Daniel Zelman
Batlon 2; Menashe	Richard Topol
Batlon 3	Eddie Castrodad
Messenger	Michael Stuhlbarg
Mayer	David Little
Old Woman	Nancy Franklin
Henekh; Rabbi Mendl; Rabbi Moritz	Gordon MacDonald
Leah	Julie Dretzin
Fradde	Judith Roberts
Gitl	Elizabeth Sastre
Sender	Robert LuPone
Bessye	Alison Russo
Wedding Guest	Herman Petras
Nakhman; Rabbi Shimshin	Yusef Bulos
Scribe	Mark Feuerstein
Rabbi Azriel	Sam Gray
Mikhl	Herman Petras
Rabbi Gershom	H.A. Shemonsky

Two intermissions.

CLEAN. By Edwin Sanchez. March 25, 1995. Director, Graciela Daniele; scenery, Christopher Barreca; costumes, Eduardo Sicangco; lighting, David F. Segal; sound, David Budries; music, Robert C. Cotnoir.

Gustavito	Joe Quintero
Mercy	Paula Pizzi
Kiko	Mateo Gomez
Father	Neil Maffin
Junior	Nelson Vasquez
Norry	A. Benard Cummings

Time: During the course of eight years. One intermission.

Houston: Alley Theater

(Artistic director, Gregory Boyd; managing director, Paul R. Tetreault)

JEKYLL & HYDE. Book and lyrics by Leslie Bricusse; music by Frank Wildhorn; conceived for the stage by Steve Cuden and Frank Wildhorn, from *The Strange Case of Dr. Jekyll and Mr. Hyde* by Robert Louis Stevenson. January 20, 1995. Director, Gregory Boyd; choreography, Barry McNabb; scenery, Vincent Mountain; costumes, David C. Woolard; lighting, Howell Binkley; sound, Karl Richardson and Scott Stauffer; orchestrations, Kim Scharnberg; musical direction, Jeremy Roberts.

Condemned Prisoner	Sven Toorvald
Dr. Henry Jekyll; Edward Hyde	Robert Cuccioli
Sir Danvers Carew	Rod Loomis
Gabriel John Utterson	Philip Hoffman
Lady Beaconsfield	Sandy Rosenberg
Lord Savage; Poole; Bisset	Brad Oscar
Two Young Men About Town: Hugo Carruthers	Bob Wrenn
Theo Davenport	Rob Evan
Butler	James Hadley
Simon Stride	Bill Nolte
Orderly to the Board of Governors	William Thomas Evans
Sir Archibald Proops; Spider	Martin Van Treuren
General Sir George Glossop	Raymond McLeod
Bishop of Basingstoke	Dave Clemmons
Prostitutes: Nellie	Nita Moore
Lucy Harris	Linda Eder
Jenny	Allyson Tucker
Lizzie	Amy Spanger
Mary	Lauren Goler-Kosarin

HARTFORD, CONN. STAGE—Joe Quintero and
Neil Maffin in a scene from *Clean* by Edwin Sanchez

Nancy ....Mary Jo Mecca
Rosie ....Andie L. Mellom
Ivy .... Michelle Mallardi
Lottie ....Judy Glass
Newsboy .... Amy Spanger
Fenwick ....Lenny Daniel

HAMLET: A MONOLOGUE. Solo performance
by Robert Wilson; adapted from the William
Shakespeare play by Wolfgang Wiens and Robert
Wilson. May 24, 1995. Director and designer, Rob-
ert Wilson; co-director, Ann-Christin Rommen;
costumes, Frida Parmeggiani; lighting, Stephen
Strawbridge; original music and sound, Hans Peter
Kuhn.

Indianapolis: Indiana Repertory Theater

(Artistic director, Libby Appel; managing director, Brian Payne)

GOD'S PICTURES. By Daisy Foote. January 3,
1995. Director, Andrew Tsao; scenery, Linda
Buchanan; costumes, Jeanette DeJong; lighting,
Victor En Yu Tan; music, Irwin Appel.
Cindy Levesque ....Hallie Foote
Ray Stark .... Horton Foote Jr.
Vick Wallace ....Ray Fry

Bea Wallace ....Bella Jarrett
Sue Wallace ....Priscilla Lindsay
Caroline Wallace ....Liz Stauber
    Time and place: The kitchen of Sally's Bakery
in Tremont, New Hampshire during the present.
One intermission.

Kansas City, Mo.: Coterie Theater

(Producing artistic director, Jeff Church; executive director, Joette Pelster)

OZ. By Patrick Shanahan. June 14, 1994. Director, Jeff Church; scenery, Brad Shaw; costumes, Gayla Voss; lighting, Art Kent; music and sound, Greg Mackender.

L. Frank Baum .... William Harper
Dot .... Amani Starnes
Bridgey Sullivan .... Brenda Mason
One intermission.

Kansas City, Mo.: Missouri Repertory Theater

(Artistic director, George Keathley; executive director, James Costin)

PAUL ROBESON. By Phillip Hayes Dean (revision). March 19, 1995. Director, Mary Guaraldi; scenery, Ron Murphy; costumes, Vincent Scasselati; lighting, Jarrett Bertoncin; sound, Tom Mardikes.

Paul Robeson .... Don Marshall
Larry Brown
(accompanist) .... Everett Freeman Jr.
One intermission.

Kansas City, Mo.: Unicorn Theater

(Producing artistic director, Cynthia Levin)

BETRAYAL OF THE BLACK JESUS. By David Barr III. January 25, 1995. Director, Jacqueline L. Gafford; scenery, B. Michael Yeager; costumes, Mary Traylor; lighting, Ruth E. Cain; sound, Roger Stoddard.
Steven Schaffer Downs .... L. Roi Hopkins
Jonathan (Skibow) Morrison ... Darryl A. Stamp
Shabazz ....Walter Coppage

Cassandra Taylor Atkinson ...Lynn Anitra King
Bobby Wright .... Kurtis Armstrong
Arnie Stamotokos; Man in
Audience .... Ken Boehr
Woman in Audience ....Carolyn Cox
Young Woman in Audience ...... Tiffany Sipple
Television Newscaster ....Beverly Chapman
One intermission.

La Jolla, Calif: La Jolla Playhouse

(Artistic director, Michael Greif)

THE GOOD PERSON OF SETZUAN. By Bertolt Brecht; adapted by Tony Kushner from a translation by Wendy Arons. July 31, 1994. Director, Lisa Peterson; original music and lyric adaptation, David Hidalgo, Louie Perez; musical direction, Doug Weiselman; scenery, Robert Brill; costumes, Candice Donnelly; lighting, James F. In-

galls; sound, Michael Roth.
    With Chris De Oni, Matthew Henerson, Lou Diamond Phillips, Diane Rodriguez, Maria Striar, Alison Tatlock, Francine Torres, Ching Valdes-Aran, Gedde Watanabe, Isaiah Whitlock Jr., David Wiater, Charlayne Woodard.
One intermission.

Los Angeles: Mark Taper Forum

(Artistic director, Gordon Davidson; managing director, Charles Dillingham)

THE WAITING ROOM. By Lisa Loomer. August 11, 1994. Director, David Schweizer; scenery, Mark Wendland; costumes, Deborah Nadoolman; lighting, Anne Militello; sound, Jon Gottlieb and Mitchell Greenhill; music, Mitchell Greenhill.
Forgiveness From Heaven ......June Kyoko Lu
Victoria .... Lela Ivey

Brenda; Bridget; Jade Ornament; Cerise; Nurse
    Bruce; Jamaican Waitress ......Leah Maddrie
Wanda .... Jacalyn O'Shaughnessy
Douglas ....Robert Picardo
Oliver ....Simon Templeman
Ken ....Tony Simotes
Larry .... Kurt Fuller
Blessing From Heaven .... Jim Ishida

Orderlies: Brian Brophy, Ken Narasaki, Jason Reed.

Time and place: The past, and the present, and often both at once. New York City, England and China. One intermission. An ATCA citation; see introduction to this section.

FLOATING ISLANDS (Part I, *The Family Business;* Part II, *After the Revolution*). By Eduardo Machado. October 23, 1994. Director, Oskar Eustis; scenery, Eugene Lee; costumes, Marianna Elliott; lighting, Paulie Jenkins; sound, Jon Gottlieb; choreography, Naomi Goldberg; music supervisor, Nathan Birnbaum; musical direction, Jeff Rizzo; fight director, Randy Kovitz.

Part I: The Modern Ladies of Guanabacoa

Maria Josefa .... Miriam Colon
Arturo .... Victor Argo
Manuela .... Marissa Chibas
Mario .... Shawn Elliott
Ernesto .... Jaime Sanchez
Miguel .... Tim Perez
Dolores .... Josie de Guzman
Adelita .... Wanda De Jesus
Oscar Hernandez .... Joe Urla

Time and place: Act I, Scene 1: A spring day in Guanabacoa, Cuba, 1928. The Ripoll home. Scene 2: Evening, the same day. Scene 3: April, 1931. After dinner. Scene 4: The field where the buses are kept, that night. Scene 5: Later that same night, the Ripoll home.

Part I: In the Eye of the Hurricane

Manuela .... Alma Cuervo
Maria Josefa .... Miriam Colon
Mario .... Shawn Elliott
Miguel .... Tim Perez
Ernesto .... Jaime Sanchez
Oscar .... Victor Argo
Sonia .... Josie de Guzman
Hugo .... Yul Vazquez
Rosa .... Marissa Chibas
Antonio .... William Marquez
Osvaldo; Miliciano .... Joe Urla
Miliciana .... Wanda De Jesus

Time and place: Act I, Scene 1: October, 1960. The dining room. Scene 2: Lunch in the dining room. Scene 3: The bus yard, dusk, the next day. Scene 4: Late at night in the dining room.

Part II: Fabiola

Pedro .... Yul Vazquez
Sonia .... Josie de Guzman
Cusa .... Rosana De Soto
Osvaldo .... Joe Urla
Alfredo .... Jaime Sanchez
Miriam .... Wanda De Jesus
Fernando .... Tim Perez
Clara .... Marissa Chibas
Oscar .... Victor Argo
Manuela .... Alma Cuervo

Mario .... Shawn Elliott
Sara .... Gloria Mann

Time and place: Act II, Scene 1: Castro's Cuba. A ballroom in a mansion in Guanabacoa, midnight. 1960. Scene 2: March 1961, late afternoon in the ballroom. Scene 3: Early morning, April 19, 1961. The rose garden. Scene 4: Six days later, late at night. The ballroom.

Part II: Broken Eggs

Sonia .... Alma Cuervo
Oscar .... Joe Urla
Lizette .... Kamala Dawson
Mimi .... Marissa Chibas
Manuela .... Miriam Colon
Osvaldo .... Shawn Elliott
Miriam .... Wanda De Jesus
Alfredo .... Victor Argo
Adam Rifkin .... Yul Vazquez

Time and place: Act II, Scene 1: A hot January morning, 1980. A country club in Woodland Hills, California. Scene 2: Afternoon the same day. One intermission.

Taper Lab 1994–95: New Work Festival

THE DREAM EXPRESS. By Len Jenkin. November 2, 1994. Director, Len Jenkin; musical direction, John Kilgore.

With Deirdre O'Connell, Steve Mellor.

Workshops:

PRIVATE BATTLE. By Lynn Manning. November 5, 1994. Director, L. Kenneth Richardson; scenery, Tom Brown; costumes, Kitty Murphy; lighting, D. Martyn Bookwalter; sound, Karl Fredrik Lundeberg.

Private Battle .... Monte Russell
Colonel; Ensemble .... Ron Canada
Andre Andrews .... Troy Winbush
Marie .... Natalie Belcon
Tayna; Ensemble .... Ellen Idelson
Nancy; Ensemble .... Lynsey McLeod
Thelonius .... Alfred Borders
Dolores .... O-Lan Jones
Nanmaw; Ensemble .... Pamela Gordon
Doctor; Ensemble .... John Towey
Female Barker;
  Ensemble .... Cheryl Francis Harrington
Gay Soldier; Ensemble .... Gregory Millar
Gay Man; Ensemble .... Jack Dwyer
Bernard .... Cress Williams
Brotherman .... Gregory Lemarr McQueary
Male Barker; Bartender;
  Proprietor .... Charles H. Hyman

Time and place: The present, U.S. Army Base at Fort Campbell, Kentucky and nearby city of Oak Grove. One intermission.

MIMI'S GUIDE. By Doris Baizley. November 9, 1994. Director, Robert Egan; scenery, Rachel

Houk; costumes, Stephanie Kerley; lighting, Mike Nevitt; sound, Karl Fredrik Lundeberg.

Mimi .... Jane Kaczmarek
Waterman .... David Dukes
Robert .... Ping Wu

Time and place: The present, the second week of August, writer's residence at a university in Louisiana.

THE INNOCENCE OF GHOSTS. By Rosanna Staffa. November 12, 1994. Director, Peter C. Brosius; scenery, Marsha Ginsburg; costumes, Durinda Wood; lighting, Geoff Korf; sound, Karl Fredrik Lundeberg.

Sophie .... Anna Gunn
Dr. Gao ....Jacqueline Kim
Man ....Tzi Ma

Time and place: Now, Hangzhou, People's Republic of China.

THE POSSUM PLAY. By Benjie Aerenson. November 19, 1994. Director, Stanley Soble; scenery, Victoria Petrovich; costumes, Kenton; lighting, Geoff Korf; sound, Mitchell Greenhill.

Adele .... Hope Alexander-Willis
Olson .... Spike Alexander
Cop; Mechanic; Bank
  Officer .... Michael Bofshever
Clark .... Gabriel Dell Jr.
Jordan .... Drew Ebersole
Sally .... Mariette Hartley
Irma .... Annette Helde
Evelyn .... Monica Parker
Sylvia ....Jana Robbins
Turner ....Nick Sadler
Stevens .... Barrett Sherwood
Mike ....Rudolph Willrich

Place: Outskirts of Miami. One intermission.

BIRD'S NEST SOUP. By Lucy Wang. December 7, 1994. Director, Tim Dan; scenery, Victoria Petrovich; costumes, Durinda Wood; lighting, Ves Weaver; sound, Michael K. Hooker.

Julie ....Jennifer Fujii
Mark .... Radmar Agana Jao
Daisy .... Emily Kuroda
Henry .... Richard Narita
Alice ....Joanne Takahashi

Time and place: Acorn, Ohio and Berry, Australia, 1973–75. Act I: Great Leap Forward; Act II: Cultural Revolution. One intermission.

BUFFALO HUNTERS. By Shem Bitterman. December 10, 1994. Director, Robert Egan; scenery, Clare Scarpulla; costumes, Candice Cain; lighting, Dan Ionazzi; sound, Karl Fredrik Lundeberg.

Martin ....David Birney
Sheila .... Christine Estabrook
Chris .... Adam Scott

Place: A suburban home in Orange County, California.

Performance Art:

SASSY GIRL: MEMOIRS OF A POSTER CHILD GONE AWRY. Written and performed by Cheryl Marie Wade. December 14, 1994. Director, Jace Alexander; scenery, Rachel Hauck; costumes, Stephanie Kerley; lighting, Kevin Adams; sound, Seth Mellman.

One intermission.

THE FIRST EFF. By Donna DiNovelli. December 14, 1994. Directors, Donna DiNovelli and Naomi Goldberg; scenery, Rachel Hauck; costumes, Stephanie Kerley; lighting, Kevin Adams; sound, Seth Mellman.

Cardigan Sweater Girls: Peggy Blow, Page Leong, Anne O'Sullivan, Kate Stern, Maura Vincent, Nancy Allison Wolfe.

A LINE AROUND THE BLOCK. Written and performed by Marga Gomez. December 17, 1994. Director, Corey Madden; scenery, Ramsey Avery; costumes, Kenton; lighting, Teresa Enroth; sound, Bryan Bowen.

Readings:

BEYOND THE RISING SUN. By Edward Sakamoto. February 7, 1995. Director, Mako.

THE LOST VEGAS SERIES. By Julie Jensen. February 9, 1995. Director, Jan Lewis.

THE SUMMER PEOPLE. By Maxim Gorky; translated by Nicholas Saunders and Frank Dwyer. February 10, 1995. Director, Frank Dwyer.

OFF THE MAP. By Joan Ackermann. February 11, 1995. Director, Deborah LaVine.

INSURRECTION. By Robert O'Hara. February 11, 1995. Director, Timothy Douglas.

PRICKLY PEARS. By Sharon Beatty. February 12, 1995. Director, Tiffany McLinn.

BONES. By Lillian Garrett-Groag. February 12, 1995. Director, Anne McNaughton.

Louisville: Actors Theater of Louisville

(Producing director, Jon Jory; literary manager, Michael Bigelow Dixon)

19th Annual Humana Festival of New American Plays, March 1-April 8, 1995

BETWEEN THE LINES. By Regina Taylor. Director, Shirley Jo Finney; scenery, Paul Owen; costumes, Myrna Colley-Lee; lighting, T.J. Gerckens; sound, Martin R. Desjardins.

Nina .... Ellen Bethea
Becca .... Dee Pelletier
Mother; Angela Davis .... Lizan Mitchell
Jonathan; George
    Jackson .... Jacinto Taras Riddick
Rufus .... Gordon Joseph Weiss
Mercedes .... Ashley Savage
Pam; Nancy; Nadine .... Denise Gientke
Supervisor; Marcus .... Andrew Pyle
Ensemble .... Jamison Newlander, Leah Price
    Time and place: From the late 1970s to the
present, between an American metropolis, memory and a dream.

CLOUD TECTONICS. By Jose Rivera. Director, Tina Landau; scenery, Paul Owen; costumes, Laura Patterson; lighting, T.J. Gerckens; sound, Martin R. Desjardins.
Celestina del Sol .... Camilia Sanes
Anibal de la Luna .... Robert Montano
Nelson de la Luna .... Javi Mulero
    Time and place: The present, Los Angeles.

MIDDLE-AGED WHITE GUYS. By Jane Martin. Director, Jon Jory; scenery, Paul Owen; costumes, Marcia Dixcy; lighting, Mimi Jordan Sherin; sound, Martin R. Desjardins.
R.V. .... Karenjune Sanchez
Roy .... John Griesemer
Clem .... Bob Burrus
Mona .... Karen Grassle
Moon .... Leo Burmester
King .... Larry Larson
Mrs. Mannering .... Anne Pitoniak
    Time and place: The play is current, in a dump.

BEAST ON THE MOON. By Richard Kalinoski. Director, Laszlo Marton; scenery, Paul Owen; costumes, Marcia Dixcy; lighting, T.J. Gerckens; sound, Martin R. Desjardins.
Gentleman .... Ray Fry
Aram Tomasian .... Faran Tahir
Seta Tomasian .... Vilma Silva
Vincent .... Dustin Longstreth
    Time and place: 1921–1933, Milwaukee, Wisconsin. One intermission.

BELOW THE BELT. By Richard Dresser. Director, Gloria Muzio; scenery, Paul Owen; costumes, Marcia Dixcy; lighting, T.J. Gerckens; sound, Martin R. Desjardins.
Hanrahan .... William McNulty
Dobbitt .... V Craig Heidenreich
Merkin .... Fred Major
    Place: An industrial compound in a distant land. One intermission.

TRUDY BLUE. By Marsha Norman. Director, George de la Pena; scenery, Paul Owen; costumes, Laura Patterson; lighting, Mimi Jordan Sherin; sound, Martin R. Desjardins.
Ginger .... Joanne Camp

Don .... Leo Burmester
Maria; Admirer .... Karenjune Sanchez
Sue .... Karen Grassle
Connie; Sales Person; Waitress .... Ann Bean
Annie .... Anne Pitoniak
Voice of Swami; Sales Person;
    Publisher .... Larry Larson
James .... Tony Coleman
Beth .... Jennifer Carpenter
Charlie .... Larry Barnett
Waiter .... James McDaniel

TOUGH CHOICES FOR THE NEW CENTURY: A SEMINAR FOR RESPONSIBLE LIVING. By Jane Anderson. Director, Lisa Peterson; scenery, Paul Owen; costumes, Laura Patterson; lighting, T.J. Gerckens; sound, Martin R. Desjardins.
Bob Dooley .... Kenneth L. Marks
Helen Dooley; Arden Shingles ..... Susan Knight
    Time and place: The present, a seminar room. One intermission.

JULY 7, 1994. By Donald Margulies. Director, Lisa Peterson; scenery, Paul Owen; costumes, Laura Patterson; lighting, T.J. Gerckens; sound, Martin R. Desjardins.
Kate .... Susan Knight
Mark .... Kenneth L. Marks
Senora Soto .... Miriam Cruz
Ms. Pike .... Myra Taylor
Mr. Caridi .... Edward Hyland
Paula .... Sandra Daley
    Time: A single day, July 7, 1994.

HELEN AT RISK. By Dana Yeaton. Director, Frazier W. Marsh; scenery, Paul Owen; costumes, Laura Patterson; lighting, Brian Scott; sound, Martin R. Desjardins.
Helen .... Adale O'Brien
Ronnie Guyette .... V Craig Heidenreich
Guard .... William McNulty
    Time and place: The present, a prison recroom.

YOUR OBITUARY IS A DANCE. By Benard Cummings. Director, Lorna Littleway; scenery, Paul Owen; costumes, Laura Patterson; lighting, Brian Scott; sound, Martin R. Desjardins.
Tommy .... Jacinto Taras Riddick
Nella .... Marcella Lowery
    Time and place: The present, the kitchen of a small home in East Texas.

HEAD ON. By Elizabeth Dewberry. Director, Shirley Jo Finney; scenery, Paul Owen; costumes, Laura Patterson; lighting, Brian Scott; sound, Martin R. Desjardins.
Anne .... Adale O'Brien
Anne's Therapist .... Dee Pelletier
    Time and place: The present, the Greenroom of the Oprah Winfrey Show.

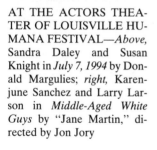

AT THE ACTORS THEA-
TER OF LOUISVILLE HU-
MANA FESTIVAL—*Above*,
Sandra Daley and Susan
Knight in *July 7, 1994* by Don-
ald Margulies; *right*, Karen-
june Sanchez and Larry Lar-
son in *Middle-Aged White
Guys* by "Jane Martin," di-
rected by Jon Jory

Lowell, Mass.: Merrimack Repertory Theater

(Artistic director, David G. Kent)

OPEN WINDOW. By Brad Korbesmeyer. October 31, 1994. Director, David G. Kent; scenery,
Crystal Tiala; costumes, Laura Crow; lighting,
Kendall Smith; produced in association with Connecticut Repertory Theater (Gary English artistic
director).

Leah Wilson	Cecilia de Wolf
Judy Wilson	Angela Parks
Betty Kaelin	Victoria Boothby
John Wilson	Mick Regan
Universal Father	Keith Randolph Smith
Brian Wilson	Brian Coughlin
Universal Mother	Mairzy Yost

One intermission.

Milford, N.H.: American Stage Festival

(Producing director, Matthew Parent; general manager, David Henderson)

AS SEEN FROM THE MOON. By Larry Grusin. August 17, 1994. Director, Kenneth Elliott; scenery, Rob Odorisio; costumes, George Bacon; lighting, Kendall Smith; sound, Marlow Seyffert.

Micki .... Holly Baron
Rueben .... Seth Altschull
Jack .... David Little
Janine .... Stephanie Pope
    One intermission.

Early Stages: Staged Readings
THIRST FOR FREEDOM. By Walt Wilson. June 25, 1994.
WUTHERING HEIGHTS. By Emily Bronte, dramatized by Michael Napier Brown. July 30, 1994.
GOLF WITH ALAN SHEPARD. By Carter W. Lewis. August 13, 1994.
LIFE IN THE FOOD CHAIN. By Jason Milligan. August 27, 1994.

Millburn, N.J.: Paper Mill Playhouse

(Artistic director, Robert Johanson; executive producer, Angelo Del Rossi)

THE PRISONER OF ZENDA. By Peter Manes; based on the novel by Anthony Hope. February 15, 1995. Director, Robert Johanson; scenery, Michael Anania; costumes, Gregg Barnes; lighting, Ken Billington; sound, David R. Paterson.

Robert, Lord of Burlesdon; Michael,
    Duke of Zenda .... Michael James Reed
Rose, Lady Burlesdon; Princess
    Flavia .... Nancy Bell
Rudolph Rassendyll; Crown
    Prince Rudolph .... Jonathan Wade

Burton; Johann .... Steve Boles
Olive; Frieda .... Therese M. McLaughlin
Col. Sapt .... John Wylie
Rupert of Hentzau .... Tito Enriquez
Detchard .... Teel James Glenn
Bersonin .... J. David Brimmer
    Guards; Soldiers: Sean Dougherty, Dan Olk, Al Espinoza, Corinna May, Andrew Palmer, J. David Brimmer.
    One intermission.

Milwaukee: Milwaukee Repertory Theater

(Artistic director, Joseph Hanreddy; managing director, Sara O'Connor)

THE GAMBLER. By Fyodor Dostoyevsky, dramatic adaptation by Lev Stoukalov; translation by Paul Schmidt. September 11, 1994. Director, Lev Stoukalov; scenery, Alexander Orlov; costumes, Irina Tcherednikova; lighting, Chris Parry; composer, Edward Gleizer.

General Zagoryansky .... Richard Halverson
Paulina .... Kellie Waymire
Alexei Ivanovich .... Torrey Hanson
Grandmother .... Ruby Holbrook
Mademoiselle Blanche ... Catherine Lynn Davis
Madame de Cominges .... Laura Gordon
Marquis des Grieux .... Richard Elmore
Mister Astley .... Andrew May
Baron Wurmerhelm; Soldier;
    Office Assistant .... Jerry Miller
Baroness Wurmerhelm .... Lynette DeWitt
Prince Nilsky .... Dwight Powell
Marfa .... Rose Pickering
Potapich .... James Pickering
Mr. Zero .... Stephen Hemming
Nadya .... Victoria Watson

Misha .....Nicholas Costantini, Benjamin Vance
Chambermaids ...Kari Boldon, Katheryn Phillips
    Beggars: Kari Boldon, Lynette DeWitt, Dominic Fumusa, Carolyne Haycraft, Dwight Powell. Lackeys: Dominic Fumusa, Jeremy Hawkinson, Ron Rittinger. Gamblers: Jeremy Hawkinson, Megan Oberle, Katheryn Phillips, Ron Rittinger, Monica Wyche.
    Time and place: 1864–1865. Roulettenburg, Germany. Two intermissions.

TWO SUITCASES. Written and directed by Barbara Damashek. October, 1994. Scenery, Linda Buchanan; costumes, Frances Maggio; lighting, Linda Essig; musical direction, Barbara Damashek.

Raisa .... Frances Chaney
Yakov .... Irwin Charone
Lyuba .... Tamara Daniel
Nick .... Dominic Fumusa
Viktor .... Jeff Gardner
Major; Party Official .... Jeremy Hawkinson

Yulya .... Angela Iannone
Andrei .... Andrew May
    Ensemble: Kari Boldon, Lynette DeWitt, Carolyne Haycraft, Megan Oberle.

WAR STORIES FROM THE 20TH CENTURY. By W. Frank. April, 1995. Director, Joseph Hanreddy; scenery, Kent Goetz; costumes, Mary Waldhart; lighting, Thomas C. Hase.
Narrator .... James Pickering
Johnny .... Ron Rittinger
Harry Blumenfeld .... Jim Mohr
Uncle Mike .... J.D. Nelson
Aunt Lily .... Kathleen Tague
Irish .... Norman Ross
1st Customer .... Scott Craig
2d Customer .... Jerry Miller
3d Customer .... Richard Blair
    Time and place: The present and 1957. Merrill Park, Milwaukee, Wisconsin.

DON JUAN ON TRIAL. By Eric-Emmanuel Schmitt, translated by Jeremy Sams. April 6, 1995. Director, Norma Saldivar; scenery, Kate Edmunds; costumes, Sam Fleming; lighting, Derek Duarte; sound, Michael Bodeen.
Marion .... Carolyne Haycraft
Comtesse de la Roche Piquet ... Angela Iannone
Hortense de la Hauteclaire .... Miriam A. Laube
Mademoiselle de la Frotte .... Laura Gordon
Madame Cassin .... Rose Pickering
Duchess de Vaubricourt ...... Carole Monferdini
Don Juan .... Marco Barricelli
Sganarelle .... Lee E. Ernst
Angelique .... Julia Klein
Chevalier de Chiffreville .... Rex Young
    Time and place: Mid-18th century. The salon of a provincial chateau. One intermission.

Montgomery: Alabama Shakespeare Festival

(Artistic director, Kent Thompson; managing director, Kevin K. Maifeld)

Southern Writers' Project

LIZARD. By Dennis Covington. November 8, 1994. Directors, Kent Thompson, Susan Willis; scenery, Michael C. Smith; costumes, Elizabeth Novak; lighting, William H. Grant III; sound, Kristen R. Kuipers.
Lucius Sims .... Norbert Butz
Miss Cooley; Ronnie; Woman at
   the Courthouse .... Mandy Peek
Bus Driver; Actor; Fire Chief ..... Kurt Kingsley
Mike; Roger; Actor .... Joey Collins

Walrus; Homer; Technician .... Danny Gilroy
Ricardo; Sammy; Actor .... Cedric Harris
Sallie; Albino Boy .... Raye Lankford
Nurse Barmore; Miranda .... Cheryl Turner
Mr. Tinker; Waldo Stakes .... Roger Forbes
Callahan .... Greg Thornton
Preacher; Willie J. Tyson; Boy ... Kevin N. Davis
Rain; Boy; Actor .... Stacy Highsmith
    Time and place: 1976. Various locations in Louisiana and Alabama.

Mountain View, Calif.: TheaterWorks

(Artistic director, Robert Kelley)

NAGASAKI DUST. By W. Colin McKay; story idea by W. Colin McKay and Jim Ishida. September 25, 1994. Director, Jules Aaron; scenery, Joe Bagey; costumes, Fumiko Bielefeldt; lighting, John Rathman; sound, Aodh Og O Tuama; fights, Bob Borwick.
John Okui .... Michael Ordona

Lt. Chuck Randolph .... Paul Mackley
    With Darren Bridgett, Darrow Carson, Conrad Cimarra, Joseph Dones, Kinji Hayshai, Craig C. Lewis, Randall Nakano, Mark Phillips, Lawrence Tho, Diana C. Weng.
    One intermission.

New Brunswick, N.J.: Crossroads Theater Company

(Artistic director, Ricardo Khan; managing director, Steve Warnick)

TAMER OF HORSES (revised version). By William Mastrosimone. October 11, 1994. Director, Sheldon Epps; scenery, Daniel Proett; costumes, Nancy Konrardy; lighting, Susan A. White; sound, Efrem Jenkins-Ahmad.

Hector St. Vincent .... Neko Parham
Ty Fletcher .... Terry Alexander
Georgiane Fletcher .... Gail Grate
    Time and place: Now. The barn and farmhouse kitchen of the Fletcher home in rural New Jersey.

HARRIET'S RETURN. By Karen Jones Meadows. March 7, 1995. Director, Ricardo Khan; scenery, John Ezell; costumes, Judy Dearing; lighting, Jackie Manassee; sound, Efrem Jenkins-Ahmad.

Harriet Tubman .... Trazana Beverley
    Time and place: The world of the late 20th century.

TWO HAH HAHS AND A HOMEBOY, OR, "HOW COME WE ALL AIN'T CRAZY." Compiled by Ruby Dee; music by Guy Davis. April 18, 1995. Director, Micki Grant; scenery and costumes, Felix E. Cochren; lighting, Shirley Prendergast.
    With Ruby Dee, Ossie Davis, Guy Davis.
    One intermission.

6th Annual Genesis Festival: A Celebration of New Voices in African American Theater: May 24-June 4, 1995

THE DARKER FACE OF THE EARTH. By Rita Dove. Director, Ricardo Khan. May 24, 1995.

2 POETS IN PERFORMANCE (one-acts): *Doors Open to One Love,* by Ozzie Jones, May 25, 1995; and *Chronicles of a Comic Mulatta: An Oreo/Choreo Poem,* by Josslyn Luckett, May 25, 1995. Director, Monica Johnson.

THE SCREENED-IN PORCH. By Marian X. Director, Judyie Al-Bilali. May 26, 1995.

THE QUADROON BALL. By Damon Wright. May 31, 1995.

PORTRAIT OF THE ARTIST AS A SOUL-DEAD MAN. By Jake-ann Jones. Director, Lou Bellamy. June 1, 1995.

ORIGINAL RAGS: A MUSICAL ABOUT SCOTT JOPLIN. By Michael Dinwiddie. June 2, 1995.

SERVANT TO THE PEOPLE, THE RISE AND FALL OF HUEY P. NEWTON AND THE BLACK PANTHER PARTY. By Robert Alexander. June 3, 1995.

BLUES TRAIN (play with music). By Ronald Wyche. June 4, 1995.

New Brunswick, N.J.: George Street Playhouse

(Producing artistic director, Gregory S. Hurst; managing director, Diane Glaussen)

RELATIVITY. By Mark Stein. October 29, 1994. Director, Gregory S. Hurst; scenery, Deborah Jasien; costumes, Barbara Forbes; lighting, Donald Holder; sound, Jeff Willens.

Neil .... Michael Rupert
Audrey .... Kit Flanagan
Vera .... Doris Belack
Susan .... Laura Sametz
Kirby ....David S. Howard
    One intermission.

OPAL. Book, music and lyrics by Robert Nassif Lindsey. February 18, 1995. Director and choreographer, Lynne Taylor-Corbett; musical direction, James Stenborg; scenery, Michael C. Smith; costumes, Ann Hould-Ward; lighting, Tom Sturge; orchestrations, Douglas Besterman; produced in association with Elliot Martin.

Girl That Has No Seeing .... Mana Allen
Opal ....Jackie Angelescu
Man Who Wears Gray
    Neckties ....Christopher Chew
Thought Girl With the Faraway Look
    in Her Eyes ....Erin Hill
Mamma ....Julie Johnson

Sadie McKibben .... Marni Nixon
    Narrators: Hal Davis, Deb G. Girdler, Judy Malloy, Ed Sala.
    No intermission.

OFF-KEY. Book by Bill C. Davis; music by Richard Adler; lyrics by Bill C. Davis and Richard Adler. April 1, 1995. Director and choreographer, Marcia Milgrom Dodge; musical direction, Darren R. Cohen; scenery, Narelle Sissons; costumes, Gail Brassard; lighting Chris Akerlind; sound, Jeff Willens.

Austin Quinn ....Christopher Sieber
Donna .... Lannyl Stephens
Ronald ....Paul Binotto
Ruth .... Mana Allen
Lauren ....Amanda Naughton
Charles .... Michael Greenwood
Diane .... Christy Baron
Lionel .... Derek Gentry
Mr. Lester ....Reathel Bean
Alex .... Robert Vargas
Mrs. Liebowitz ....Marcell Rosenblatt
Mr. Garfinkle .... Frank Raiter
Officer Pitts .... M. Eliot Beisner

New Haven, Conn.: Long Wharf Theater

(Artistic director, Arvin Brown; managing director, M. Edgar Rosenblum)

PADDYWACK. By Daniel Magee. September 27, 1994. Director, John Tillinger; scenery, James

Youmans; costumes, Candice Donnelly; lighting, Ken Billington.

Colin .... Alessandro Nivola
Brian .... Denis O'Hare
Michael .... Michael O'Hagan
Mrs. Somers .... Patricia Kilgarriff
Damien .... James Nesbitt
Annette ....Sarah Long
Time and place: The present, London.

TRAVELS WITH MY AUNT. By Graham
Greene, adapted and directed by Giles Havergal.
October 14, 1994. See its entry in the Plays Pro-
duced Off Broadway section of this volume.

SATURDAY, SUNDAY, MONDAY. By Ed-
uardo de Filippo; new translation by Thomas
Simpson. November 8, 1994. Director, Arvin
Brown; scenery, Marjorie Bradley Kellogg; cos-
tumes, David Murin; lighting, Dennis Parichy.
Priore Family:
    Rosa ....Lauren Klein
    Peppino .... Richard Venture
    Roberto ....Donald Berman
    Rocco .... James Andreassi
    Giulianella ....Marin Hinkle
Extended Family:
    Antonio Piscopo .... Dominic Chianese
    Aunt Meme .... Jan Miner
    Attilio .... Geoffrey P. Cantor
    Raffaele ....Frank Savino
    Maria Carolina ....Michelle Kronin
Near Family:
    Federico .... Peter Rini
    Virginia .... Stephanie Silverman
    Michele ....Saul Stein
Neighbors:
    Luigi Ianiello .... George Sperdakos
    Elena Ianiello ....Janis Dardaris

Friends:
    Doctor Cefercola; Catiello ....Richard Merrell
    Time and place: The Priore houshould. Na-
ples, Italy. Spring, early 1960s. Act I: Saturday,
late afternoon. Act II: Sunday, early afternoon.
Act III: Monday morning. One intermission.

Workshop Series:

IN THE HEART OF AMERICA. By Naomi
Wallace. November 29, 1994. Director, Tony
Kushner; scenery, David Fletcher; costumes, Pa-
tricia M. Risser; lighting, Kirk Matson; sound,
Brenton Evans.
Craver Perry ....David Van Pelt
Fairouz Saboura .... Irene Glezos
Lue Ming ....Wai Ching Ho
Remzi Saboura .... Firdous Bamji
Boxler ....Lanny Flaherty
    Time and place: Before, during and several
months after the Gulf War. A motel room, a mil-
itary camp in Saudi Arabia, another room, the
Iraqi desert.

RULER OF MY DESTINY. By Jocelyn Mein-
hardt. March 21, 1995. Director, Pamela Berlin;
scenery, David Fletcher; costumes, Patricia M.
Risser; lighting, Kirk Matson; sound, Brenton Ev-
ans.
Joan .... Priscilla Shanks
Jane .... Angela Marie Bettis
Audrey .... Carrie Luft
Lydia .... Jenny Maguire
Hart ....Charlie Hofheimer
Bruno .... Malachy Cleary
Gretchen .... Diana Henry
    Time and place: The present, New York City.
One intermission.

New Haven, Conn.: Yale Repertory Theater

(Artistic director, Stan Wojewodski Jr.; managing director, Victoria Nolan)

THE MARRIAGE OF FIGARO/FIGARO
GETS A DIVORCE. By Pierre Caron de-
Beaumarchais and Odon von Horvath; adapted
by Eric Overmyer. December 1, 1994. Director,
Stan Wojewodski Jr.; scenery, Derek McLane;
costumes, Jess Goldstein; lighting, Stephen Straw-
bridge; sound, Christopher Cronin.
Figaro ....Reg Rogers
Susanna .... Susan Cremin
Cherubino ....Lynn Hawley
Count Almaviva ....Byron Jennings
Countess .... Carolyn McCormick
Antonio ....Herbert Rubens
Pedrillo .... Max Chalawsky
Fanchette ....Amy Malloy
1st Guard; Constable .............D.B. Woodside
2d Guard; Commissioner ....David Grillo

3d Guard; Schoolmaster ....Michael Eaddy
4th Guard; Cafe Guest ..... Michael Goodfriend
Officer; Captain .... Michael Strickland
Assistant Forester .... Christopher McHale
Midwife ....Lynn Cohen
Josepha ....Jennie Israel
    Palace Staff, New Year's Eve Guests, Soldiers,
Cafe Guests: Michael Eaddy, Michael Good-
friend, David Grillo, Jennie Israel, Amy Malloy,
Michael Strickland, D.B. Woodside.
    Orphans: Matthew F. Dolan, Michael Dubrov-
sky, Nicole L. Fleming, Charlette Renee Ham-
mett, Jason Inman, Maureen M. Keefer, Julia W.
Miller, Lenee Shanette Myers, Leididiana Ortega,
Edwin Polanco Jr., Rachel Stone, Zachary Stone,
Risheda C. Turner.
    Time and place: Part I, Scene 1: Six years be-

fore the Revolution, morning. An Antechamber in the palace of Count Almaviva. Scene 2: The Countess's bedroom, late morning. Scene 3: Outside the palace, early afternoon. Scene 4: A gallery in the palace, afternoon. Scene 5: The palace garden, night. Part II, Scene 1: Immediately following the Revolution, night. A deep forest near the border. (Intermission.) Scene 2: Later that night. A guardhouse just across the border. Scene 3: Three months later, a hotel high in the mountains. Scene 4: One year later. A hair salon in Grosshadersdorf. Scene 5: A cheaply furnished room in a large foreign city. Scene 6: New Year's Eve. The Postal Tavern, Grosshadersdorf. Scene 7: Six months later. An orphanage in the land of the Revolution, formerly the palace of Count Almaviva. Scene 8: One year later. A cafe in a large foreign city. Scene 9: A deep forest near the border. Scene 10: The garden of the orphanage.

Philadelphia: American Music Festival

(Artistic director, Ben Levit; managing director, Donna Vidas Owell; producing director, Marjorie Samoff)

THE BONES OF LOVE and OLD AUNT DINAH'S SURE GUIDE TO DREAMS AND LUCKY NUMBERS. Program of two one-act musicals by Edward Barnes. April 9, 1995. Director and choreographer, Kim Okada; musical direction, Edward Barnes; scenery, Neil Patel; costumes, Maria Jurglanis; lighting, Michael Gilliam; sound, Darron L. West.

Vocalist—Katherine Peterson; Dancers—Sharon Marie Desmarais, Meredith Magoon; Lead Keyboard—Edward Barnes; Second Keyboard—Andrea Clearfield; Percussion—John Fitzgerald.

Philadelphia: Philadelphia Theater Company

(Producing artistic director, Sara Garonzik)

MASTER CLASS. By Terrence McNally. February 24, 1995. Director, Leonard Foglia; scenery, Michael McGarty; costumes, Jane Greenwood; lighting, Brian MacDevitt; sound, John Gromada; musical supervision, David Loud.
Manny .... David Loud

Maria Callas .... Zoe Caldwell
Sophie .... Karen Kay Cody
Stagehand .... Michael Friel
Sharon .... Audra McDonald
Tony .... Jay Hunter Morris
  One intermission.

Philadelphia: Walnut Street Theater

(Executive director, Bernard Havard)

ITALIAN FUNERALS AND OTHER FESTIVE OCCASIONS. By John Miranda. January 18, 1995. Director, Scott Reiniger; scenery, John Iacovelli; costumes, Gail Cooper-Hecht; lighting, F. Mitchell Dana; sound, Lewis Mead.
John .... Tom Teti
Little Johnny .... Emmanuel Carrera
Young Mama; Rosalie .... Christine Vanacore
Brigida ....Carla Belver
Mama .... Mildred Clinton
Grandmother; Big Man's
  Housekeeper .... Irma St. Paule
Dad .... Patrick DeSantis
Uncle Dom .... Fil Formicola
Aunt Mary .... Emelise Aleandri
Andrea ....Maura Russo
Fatty Townsend ....Tom McCarthy
Big Man .... Carl Don
  Time and place: Between the present (1984–

The Masiellos' mobile home in a trailer park, Port St. Lucie, Florida) and the past (1930s Greenport, Long Island and 1970s Little Italy, New York). One intermission.

THE OLD, WICKED SONGS. By Jon Marans. April 25, 1995. Director, Frank Ferrante; scenery, Thom Bumblauskas; costumes, Lani Apperson; lighting, Troy Martin-O'Shia; sound, Phil Cassidy.
Professor Josef Mashkan .... Hal Robinson
Stephen Hoffmann .... Roy Abramsohn
  Time and place: Professor Mashkan's rehearsal studio in Vienna, Austria. The play begins in spring of 1986 and continues through to Summer. Act I, Scene 1: Spring afternoon, 1986. Scene 2: Tuesday morning, the next week. Scene 3: Late Wednesday night, two weeks later. Scene 4: Friday afternoon, two days later. Act II, Scene 1: Tuesday morning, two weeks later. Scene 2: Friday after-

PHILADELPHIA THEATER COMPANY—David Loud, Audra
McDonald and Zoe Caldwell in *Master Class* by Terrence McNally

noon, three days later. Scene 3: Hours later, night;
Scene 4: Tuesday, June 10, 1986. One intermission.

LUST. Book, music and lyrics by The Heather
Brothers; freely adapted from William Wycher-
ley's *The Country Wife.* May 3, 1995. Director,
Bob Carlton; musical direction, John Johnson;
scenery, Rodney Ford; lighting, F. Mitchell Dana;
sound, Scott Smith; musical staging, Barry Finkel.
Horner .... Denis Lawson
Quack .... Robert McCormick
Pinchwife .... David Barron

Margery Pinchwife .... Jennifer Lee Andrews
Sir Jasper Fidget .... Lee Golden
Lady Fidget .... Judith Moore
Mistress Dainty .... Janet Aldrich
Misstress Squeamish .... Suzanne Ishee
Alithea Pinchwife; Wench .... Jennifer Piech
Harcourt .... A.J. Vincent
Dorilant .... Dan Schiff
Sparkish .... Barry Finkel
Servants; Townspeople .... Adam Giordano,
Kirk Brown, Larry Weiss
Time and place: 1661. London.

Portland, Me.: Portland Stage Company

(Artistic director, Greg Leaming; managing director, William Chance)

CHURCH OF THE SOLE SURVIVOR. By
Keith Curran. February 12, 1995. Director, Greg
Leaming; scenery, Rob Odorisio; costumes, Mar-
cia Whitney; lighting, Mark McCullough; sound,
Thomas Ciufo.
Man .... Jamison Selby
Cassie Doob .... Deirdre Lovejoy
Alba Doob .... Lucy Martin
Katie Doob .... Anne Swift

Sinjin Walker .... Michael Lipton
Patrick Delaware .... Michael Connor
Place: The play takes place at a beachfront
Cape Cod cottage. One intermission.

*6th Annual Little Festival of the Unexpected
March 10–13, 1995—Staged Readings*

THE LOVER. By Elizabeth Egloff. Director, Michael Wilson.

Elena Andreyevna .... Alyssa Bresnahan	Hem .... Richard Poe
Dmitri Insarov .... Philip Goodwin	Joris .... Rainn Wilson
Stahov .... Richard Poe	Dos .... Philip Goodwin
Anna .... Pamela Nyberg	Marty .... Alyssa Bresnahan
Shubin .... Rainn Wilson	One intermission.
Bersyenev; Rendic .... Jeffrey Hayenga	A TURN OF THE SCREW. By Jeffrey Hatcher.
Tanya; Landlady .... Kym Dakin	Director, Greg Leaming.
One intermission.	Man .... Jeffrey Hayenga
SHOOTING IN MADRID. By Tug Yourgrau.	Woman .... Pamela Nyberg
Director, Tom Prewitt.	

Princeton, N.J.: McCarter Theater

(Artistic director, Emily Mann; managing director, Jeffrey Woodward)

THE NANJING RACE. By Reggie Cheong-Leen. January 12, 1995. Director, Loretta Greco; scenery, Philip Creech; costumes, Catherine Homa-Rocchio; lighting, Christopher Gorzelnik; sound, Stephen Smith.

Philip .... Thom Sesma
Yu Ahn .... B.D. Wong
Bao .... David Chung

Time: The present. Place: A hotel in Nanjing. One intermission. ATCA Award; see introduction to this section.

HAVING OUR SAY: DELANY SISTERS' FIRST 100 YEARS. By Emily Mann; adapted from the book by Sarah L. Delany and A. Elizabeth Delany, with Amy Hill Hearth. February 7, 1995. Director, Emily Mann. See its entry in the Plays Produced on Broadway section of this volume.

MIRANDOLINA (The Mistress of the Inn). By Carlo Goldoni; adapted and based upon a translation by Stephen Wadsworth. March 14, 1995. Director, Stephen Wadsworth; scenery, Thomas Lynch; costumes, Martin Pakledinaz; lighting, Christopher J. Akerlind.

Marchese of Forlipopoli .... Robin Chadwick
Count of Albafiorita .... Sebastian Roche
Fabrizio .... Derek Smith
Cavaliere of Ripafratta .... John Michael Higgins
Mirandolina .... Mary Lou Rosato
Cavaliere's Servant .... Laurence O'Dwyer
Ortensia .... Elizabeth Van Dyke
Desianza .... Wendy Kaplan
Count's Servant; Guest .... Sewell Whitney
Flavio; Jeweler .... Reid Armbruster
Serpetta .... Maggie Lacey
Vecchia .... Rhonda King

Time and place: Mirandolina's Inn, Florence, September, 1753. Two intermissions.

Providence, R.I.: Trinity Repertory Company

(Artistic director, Oskar Eustis; managing director, Patricia Egan)

GOD'S HEART. By Craig Lucas. May 9, 1995. Director, Norman Rene; scenery, Eugene Lee; costumes, Walker Hicklin; lighting, Debra J. Kletter; sound, David E. Smith.

Carlin .... Ray Ford
Janet; Carol .... Phyllis Kay
David; Customer; Reese .... Ed Shea
Eleanor .... Harriet Harris

Barbara .... Janice Duclos
Angela; Whitney .... Brienin Bryant
Ana; Volunteer; Night Nurse .... Avaan Patel
Dr. Farkas; Cashmere;	
Valerie .... Rosalyn Coleman
Patty .... Barbara Olson
Two intermissions.	

St. Louis: Repertory Theater of St. Louis

(Artistic director, Steven Woolf; managing director, Mark D. Bernstein)

THE BROTHERS KARAMAZOV. By Anthony Clarvoe; based on the novel by Fyodor Dostoyevsky. January 6, 1995. See its entry in the Cincinnati Playhouse in the Park listing in this section of this volume.

OFF THE ICE. By Barbara Field. January 20, 1995. Director, Susan Gregg; scenery and lighting, Dale F. Jordan; costumes, John Carver Sullivan.

Beth .... Kim Sebastian
Jo .... Alison Stair Neet

Meg .... Carol Schultz
Amy .... Sherry Skinker
Eliza .... Sybyl Walker
Time: 1866–67. Place: Suburban Boston. One intermission.

ESMERALDA. Book by Kathryn Placzek and David Schechter; music and lyrics by Steven Lutvak; based on the play *The Hunchback of Notre Dame* by Andrew Dallmeyer and the novel *Notre Dame de Paris* by Victor Hugo. March 24, 1995. Director, David Schechter; musical direction, Michael Horsley; scenery, John Ezell; costumes, James Scott; lighting, Peter E. Sargent.
Pierre .... Price Waldman
Esmeralda .... Kimberly JaJuan

Phoebus .... Steve Blanchard
Frollo .... George Merritt
Clothilde .... Suzanne Costallos
Fleur .... Marian Murphy
Innkeeper .... Jennifer Jonassen
Time and place: 1485 and a few years before. In and around the Cathedral of Notre Dame, Paris. One intermission.

The Lab Project:

IT'S A RATTY OLD WORLD, AIN'T IT. By Michael Ornstein. April 7, 1995. Director, Susan Gregg.
MISSISSIPPI SUGAR. By Randy Redd. April 7, 1995. Director, Tom Martin.

San Francisco: American Conservatory Theater

(Artistic director, Carey Perloff)

HECUBA. By Euripides, translated and adapted by Timberlake Wertenbaker. April 27, 1995. Director, Carey Perloff; scenery, Kate Edmunds; costumes, Donna Zakowska; lighting, Peter Maradudin; music, David Lang; sound, Stephen LeGrand.
Voice of Polydorus .... Darren Bridgett
Hecuba, Queen of Troy .... Olympia Dukakis
Chorus Leader .... Viola Davis
Polyxena .... Shirley Roecca
Odysseus .... Ken Ruta
Talthibios .... Gerald Hiken

Serving Woman .... Remy Barclay Bosseau
Agamemnon .... James Carpenter
Polymestor .... Stephen Markle
Polymestor's Sons: Dylan Hackett, Eli Marienthal, James Milber, Ari Rosenman. Chorus: Bob Brown, Catherine Rose Crowther, Deborah Dietrich, Irina Mikhailova, Janet Kutulas, Julie Graffagna, Michele Simon, Shira Cion, Tatiana Sarbinsky.
Time and place: The coast of Thrace, in a Greek slave camp immediately after the Trojan War.

San Francisco: Magic Theater

(Artistic director, Mame Hunt)

NIGHT TRAIN TO BOLINA. By Nilo Cruz. November 15, 1994. Director, Mary Coleman; scenery, Jeff Rowlings; costumes, Derek Sullivan; lighting, Jose Lopez; sound, J.A. Deane.
Mateo .... Sean San Jose Blackman
Clara .... Greta Sanchez Ramirez
Talita .... Minerva Garcia
Sister Nora .... Tessa Koning-Martinez
Dr. Martin .... Luis Saguar
One intermission.

SAY GRACE. By Gary Leon Hill. January 24, 1995. Director, David Dower; scenery and lighting, Jeff Rowlings; costumes, Cassandra Carpenter; sound, Scott Koue.
Ida; Dottie .... Abigail Van Alyn
Swain/Sky .... John Balma
Bruno .... Ronnie Dee Blair
Opal; Emma .... Jeri Lynn Cohen
Llewellyn .... Howard Swain
One intermission.

San Francisco: The Marsh

(Artistic director, Stephanie Weisman)

RUSH LIMBAUGH IN NIGHT SCHOOL. Solo performance by Charlie Varon; written by Charlie Varon; developed with David Ford, in association with The Marsh. Opened October 6, 1994. Director, Martin Higgins.

Time: May and June of 1996. Place: New York City. One intermission. Elizabeth Osborn Award; see introduction to this section.

Sarasota: Florida Studio Theater

(Artistic director, Richard Hopkins)

VERONICA'S POSITION. By Rich Orloff. March 2, 1995. Director, Richard Hopkins; scenery, Jeffrey W. Dean; costumes, Susan Douglas; lighting, Joseph P. Oshry.

Veronica Fairchild	Kim Crow
Harvey Johnson	Douglas Jones
Philip Wilder	Robert D. Mowry
Alan Croft	Russell Goldberg
Mallory	Debra Whitfield
Ezekiel Barrows North	Blake Walton

One intermission.

Seattle: A Contemporary Theater

(Founding director, Gregory A. Falls; artistic director, Jeff Steitzer; producing director, Phil Schermer)

VOICES IN THE DARK. By John Pielmeier. October 20, 1994. Director, John Pielmeier; scenery, Kent Dorsey; costumes, Christine Dougherty; lighting, Rick Paulsen; sound, Steven M. Klein; original music, Albert Ahronheim.

Caller #1	Karen Kay Cody
Lil	Jacqueline Knapp
Owen	James Marsters
Hack	Mark Chamberlin
Red	Lenny Blackburn
Bill	Alec Dennis
Blue	Eddie Levi Lee
Egan	Michael MacRae

One intermission.

Seattle: Intiman Theater Company

(Artistic director, Warner Shook; managing director, Laura Penn)

New Voices at Intiman—New Play Reading Series:
HANDLER. By Robert Schenkkan. July 22, 1994. Director, Warner Shook.
NINE ARMENIANS. By Leslie Ayvazian. August 29, 1994. Director, Victor Pappas.

THE LAST SURVIVOR. By Eleanor Reissa. October 17, 1994. Director, Victor Pappas.
MIMI'S GUIDE. By Doris Baizley. November 14, 1994. Director, Daniel Renner.

Seattle: Seattle Repertory Theater

(Artistic director, Daniel Sullivan; managing director, Benjamin Moore)

LONDON SUITE. Program of four one-act plays by Neil Simon: *Going Home, Settling Accounts, Diana and Sidney* and *The Man on the Floor.* October 12, 1994. See its entry in the Plays Produced Off Broadway section of this volume.
JOLSON SINGS AGAIN. By Arthur Laurents. February 8, 1995. Director, Daniel Sullivan; scenery, David Mitchell, Thomas Gregg Meyer; costumes, Theoni V. Aldredge; lighting, Pat Collins; music, Ken Benshoof; sound, Steven M. Klein.

Julian	Evan Handler
Robbie	Laura Esterman
Sydney	Daniel Oreskes
Andreas	Dennis Boutsikaris

SCAPIN. By Molière; adapted by Bill Irwin and Mark O'Donnell. March 15, 1995. Director, Bill Irwin; scenery, Doug Stein; costumes, Victoria Petrovich; lighting, Greg Sullivan; music, Bruce Hurlbut; sound, Steven M. Klein.

Octave	R. Hamilton Wright
Silvestre	Christopher Evan Welch
Scapin	Bill Irwin
Chief Gendarme; Porter	Jeff Gordon
Gendarme; Porter	David-Paul Wichert
Hyacinth	Peggy Poage
Argante	William Biff McGuire
Geronte	John Aylward
Leandre	Kevin Carroll
Zerbinette	Katie Forgette
Nerine	Mary Bond Davis

Keyboards: Bruce Hurlbut. One intermission.

Stockbridge, Mass.: Berkshire Theater Festival

(Artistic director, Julianne Boyd; managing director, Cynthia Wassell)

BRIMSTONE. Musical with book and lyrics by Mary Bracken Phillips; music by Patrick Meegan. June 29, 1994. Director, Julianne Boyd; choreography, Daniel Levans; musical direction, Christine Caderette; scenery, Ken Foy; costumes, David Murin; lighting, Victor En Yu Tan; sound, Abe Jacob; arrangements, Keith Levenson; orchestrations, Aaron Hagan.

Captain	Mark Honan
Corporal	John Leone
Protestant Boy	Scott Wichmann
Catholic Boy	Jeff Gurner
Eamon Dunne	Jeff McCarthy
R.U.C. Policeman	James Judy
Seamus	Nick Wyman
Paddy	Richard Pelzman
Bridget	Mary Beth Griffith
Roisin Dunne	Brooks Almy
Katherine	Michele Sheehy
Miraid	Colleen Quinn
Caithal	Ed Sala

One intermission.

Troy: New York State Theater Institute

(Producing artistic director, Patricia Di Benedetto Snyder)

A TALE OF CINDERELLA. Book by W.A. Frankonis; music by Will Severin and George David Weiss; lyrics by George David Weiss. Director, Patricia Di Benedetto Snyder; choreographic director, Adrienne Posner; scenery, Richard Finkelstein; costumes, Brent Griffin; lighting, John McLain; sound, Dan Toma; orchestrations, Larry Moore; musical supervision and dance arrangements, Dennis Buck; musical direction, Mark Brockley.

Principals:

Rafael the Gondolier	John T. McGuire
Prince Nicolo di Cuore	Sean Frank Sullivan
Angelina	Catherine Wronowski
Paolo	Joel Aroeste
Giametta; Cinderella	Christianne Tisdale
Pulchitruda	Erika Newell
Moltovoce	Michele Golden
Seppia	Margaret Robinson
La Stella	Lorraine Serabian
Il Compari	John Romeo
Peliculo	David Bunce

Citizens of Venice:

Floira; Waltzer	Laura Roth
Roberto	David Bunce
Riccardo; Waltzer	John R. McEnerney
Sorella Philomena	Sara Biggs
Cardinale Francesco	Michael Steese
Pietro; Waltzer	A.J. Michaels
Lucia; Floreale	Vanessa Thorpe
Guillermo; Waltzer	Christopher Bessette
Giorgio; Pasticceri	Shawn Michael Cahill
Michelena; Waltzer	Patti Edelmann
Nistina; Waltzer	Shira Ginsburg
Vincenzo; Acolyte	Peter Kutchukian
Montano; Juggler	Matthew Ostroff
Isabella	Arwen Spargo
Araldo	Kevin C. West

Children of Venice:

Gabriella	Kerry Conte
Marielena	Dulcinea Vega Cuprill
Rosa	Brittany Engel-Adams
Christina	Sarah Koblenz
Rita	Alyson Lange
Santoro	Sean Mack
Pippinella	Dana Mainella

Time and place: The city of Venice, in the time of fairy tales.

Concert Reading Series:

FINAL EDITION. By Donald Drake. November 5, 1994. Director, Helen Binder Bress.

A WRINKLE IN TIME. By Madeleine L'Engel; adapted by Marjorie Bradley Kellogg. November 6, 1994. Director, Freda Scott Giles.

Washington, D.C.: Arena Stage

(Artistic director, Douglas C. Wager; executive director, Stephen Richard)

THE ODYSSEY. By Derek Walcott; music for songs composed and arranged by Galt MacDermot. September 30, 1994. Director, Douglas C. Wager; scenery, Thomas Lynch; costumes, Paul Tazewell; lighting, Allen Lee Hughes; musical direction, incidental music, sound, Carol La Chapelle; movement and fight director, David S. Leong.

NEW YORK STATE THEATER INSTITUTE, TROY—The Prince (Sean Frank Sullivan, *right*) finds that the shoe fits Cinderella (Christianne Tisdale), as other characters (John Romeo, Joel Aroeste, Erika Newell, Michele Golden and Margaret Robinson) look on in the musical *A Tale of Cinderella* by W.A. Frankonis, Will Severin and George David Weiss

"Blind" Billy Blue .... Wendell Wright
Odysseus .... Casey Biggs
Athena ....Pamela Nyberg
Penelope .... Cordelia Gonzalez
Telemachus .... Teagle F. Bougere
Eurycleia .... Marilyn Coleman
Antinous .... Gary Sloan
Eumaeus .... Ralph Cosham
Menelaus .... Henry Strozier
Eurylochus .... TJ Edwards
Nausicaa .... Kristina Nielsen
Anemone .... Yvonne Racz
Chloe ....Crystal Simone Wright
Cyclops .... Richard Bauer
Circe .... Stephanie Pope

Anticlea ....Helen Carey
Achilles .... M.E. Hart
Thersites .... Michael W. Howell
Wrestler .... Ernest Robert Mercer
Leodes ....Cornell Womack
Boy ....Dominic Dickerson, Kieron Anthony Pickett Lee

A MONTH IN THE COUNTRY. By Brian Friel; adapted from Turgenev. April 28, 1995. Director, Kyle Donnelly; scenery, Linda Buchanan; costumes, Lindsay W. Davis; lighting, Rita Pietraszek; sound, Rob Milburn.
Herr Schaaf .... Richard Bauer
Lizaveta Bogdonovna .... Tana Hicken

Anna Semyonovna Islayeva ....Halo Wines
Natalya Petrovna ....Mary Beth Peil
Katya .... Melissa Flaim
Michel Aleksandrovich Rakitin ...... Gary Sloan
Aleksey Nikolayevich Belyayev ... Joseph Fuqua
Matvey .... Ralph Cosham
Ignaty Ilyich Shpigelsky .... Henry Strozier
Vera Aleksandrovna ....Kristine Nielson
Arkady Sergeyevich Islayev ..... Wendell Wright
Afanasy Ivanovich
    Bolshintsov .... Jeffrey V. Thompson
    Time and place: On the Islayev estate at the beginning of the 1840s. One intermission.

PlayQuest Workshop

LIFE GO BOOM! By Alonzo D. Lamont Jr. December 2, 1994. Director, Laurence Maslon; scenery, Dawn Robyn Petrlik; costumes, Kendra Johnson; lighting, R. Lap-Chi Chu; sound, Daniel L. Schrader.
Jasper Imhotep .... Teagle F. Bougere
Dr. Ashanti Barnes ....Charlotte Gibson
Ray-Ray DuRoy .... Christopher Bauer
Cameraman ....Steven Box
    Time and place: The present. The Jasper Imhotep Show.

Waterbury, Conn.: Seven Angels Theater

(Artistic director, Semina De Laurentis)

EXPATRIATE. By Bill C. Davis. April 29, 1995. Director, Andre Ernotte; scenery, Rorie Fitzsimons; lighting, Paul Miller.
Kemper .... Patrick Boll
Lynne ....Joan Buddenhagen
Mr. Nolan .... David Logan
Roscoe ....Larkin Malloy
Gram .... Rosemary Prinz
    One intermission.

FACTS AND
FIGURES

LONG RUNS ON BROADWAY

The following shows have run 500 or more continuous performances in a single production, usually the first, not including previews or extra non-profit performances, allowing for vacation layoffs and special one-booking engagements, but not including return engagements after a show has gone on tour. In all cases, the numbers were obtained directly from the show's production offices. Where there are title similarities, the production is identified as follows: (p) straight play version, (m) musical version, (r) revival, (tr) transfer.

THROUGH MAY 31, 1995

(PLAYS MARKED WITH ASTERISK WERE STILL PLAYING JUNE 1, 1995)

Plays	Number Performances	Plays	Number Performances
A Chorus Line	6,137	Dreamgirls	1,522
Oh! Calcutta! (r)	5,959	Mame (m)	1,508
*Cats	5,281	Same Time, Next Year	1,453
42nd Street	3,486	Arsenic and Old Lace	1,444
Grease	3,388	The Sound of Music	1,443
*Les Misérables	3,368	Me and My Girl	1,420
Fiddler on the Roof	3,242	How to Succeed in Business Without	
Life With Father	3,224	Really Trying	1,417
Tobacco Road	3,182	Hellzapoppin	1,404
*The Phantom of the Opera	3,074	The Music Man	1,375
Hello, Dolly!	2,844	*Crazy for You	1,370
My Fair Lady	2,717	Funny Girl	1,348
Annie	2,377	Mummenschanz	1,326
Man of La Mancha	2,328	Angel Street	1,295
Abie's Irish Rose	2,327	Lightnin'	1,291
Oklahoma!	2,212	Promises, Promises	1,281
Pippin	1,944	The King and I	1,246
South Pacific	1,925	Cactus Flower	1,234
The Magic Show	1,920	Sleuth	1,222
Deathtrap	1,793	Torch Song Trilogy	1,222
Gemini	1,788	1776	1,217
Harvey	1,775	Equus	1,209
Dancin'	1,774	Sugar Babies	1,208
La Cage aux Folles	1,761	Guys and Dolls	1,200
Hair	1,750	Amadeus	1,181
*Miss Saigon	1,725	Cabaret	1,165
The Wiz	1,672	Mister Roberts	1,157
Born Yesterday	1,642	Annie Get Your Gun	1,147
The Best Little Whorehouse in		Guys and Dolls (r)	1,144
Texas	1,639	The Seven Year Itch	1,141
Ain't Misbehavin'	1,604	Butterflies Are Free	1,128
Mary, Mary	1,572	Pins and Needles	1,108
Evita	1,567	Plaza Suite	1,097
The Voice of the Turtle	1,557	They're Playing Our Song	1,082
Barefoot in the Park	1,530	Grand Hotel (m)	1,077
Brighton Beach Memoirs	1,530	Kiss Me, Kate	1,070
		Don't Bother Me, I Can't Cope	1,065

Plays	*Number Performances*	Plays	*Number Performances*
The Pajama Game	1,063	Anything Goes (r)	804
Shenandoah	1,050	No Time for Sergeants	796
The Teahouse of the August		Fiorello!	795
Moon	1,027	Where's Charley?	792
Damn Yankees	1,019	The Ladder	789
Never Too Late	1,007	Forty Carats	780
Big River	1,005	Lost in Yonkers	780
The Will Rogers Follies	983	The Prisoner of Second Avenue	780
Any Wednesday	982	M. Butterfly	777
A Funny Thing Happened on the Way		Oliver!	774
to the Forum	964	The Pirates of Penzance (1980 r)	772
The Odd Couple	964	Woman of the Year	770
Anna Lucasta	957	My One and Only	767
Kiss and Tell	956	Sophisticated Ladies	767
*The Who's Tommy	928	Bubbling Brown Sugar	766
Dracula (r)	925	Into the Woods	765
Bells Are Ringing	924	State of the Union	765
The Moon Is Blue	924	Starlight Express	761
Beatlemania	920	The First Year	760
The Elephant Man	916	Broadway Bound	756
Luv	901	You Know I Can't Hear You When	
Chicago (m)	898	the Water's Running	755
Applause	896	Two for the Seesaw	750
Can-Can	892	Joseph and the Amazing Technicolor	
Carousel	890	Dreamcoat (r)	747
I'm Not Rappaport	890	Death of a Salesman	742
Hats Off to Ice	889	For Colored Girls, etc.	742
Fanny	888	Sons o' Fun	742
Children of a Lesser God	887	Candide (m, r)	740
Follow the Girls	882	Gentlemen Prefer Blondes	740
City of Angels	878	The Man Who Came to Dinner	739
Camelot	873	Nine	739
I Love My Wife	872	Call Me Mister	734
*Kiss of the Spider Woman	868	West Side Story	732
The Bat	867	High Button Shoes	727
My Sister Eileen	864	Finian's Rainbow	725
No, No, Nanette (r)	861	Claudia	722
Song of Norway	860	The Gold Diggers	720
Chapter Two	857	Jesus Christ Superstar	720
A Streetcar Named Desire	855	Carnival	719
Barnum	854	The Diary of Anne Frank	717
Comedy in Music	849	I Remember Mama	714
Raisin	847	Tea and Sympathy	712
Blood Brothers	839	Junior Miss	710
You Can't Take It With You	837	Last of the Red Hot Lovers	706
La Plume de Ma Tante	835	The Secret Garden	706
Three Men on a Horse	835	Company	705
The Subject Was Roses	832	Seventh Heaven	704
Black and Blue	824	Gypsy (m)	702
Inherit the Wind	806	The Miracle Worker	700

Plays	Number Performances	Plays	Number Performances
That Championship Season	700	Irene (r)	604
Da	697	Sunday in the Park With George	604
The King and I (r)	696	Adonis	603
Cat on a Hot Tin Roof	694	Broadway	603
Li'l Abner	693	Peg o' My Heart	603
The Children's Hour	691	Street Scene (p)	601
Purlie	688	Flower Drum Song	600
Dead End	687	Kiki	600
The Lion and the Mouse	686	A Little Night Music	600
White Cargo	686	Agnes of God	599
Dear Ruth	683	Don't Drink the Water	598
East Is West	680	Wish You Were Here	598
Come Blow Your Horn	677	Sarafina!	597
The Most Happy Fella	676	A Society Circus	596
The Doughgirls	671	Absurd Person Singular	592
The Impossible Years	670	A Day in Hollywood/A Night in the	
Irene	670	Ukraine	588
Boy Meets Girl	669	The Me Nobody Knows	586
The Tap Dance Kid	669	The Two Mrs. Carrolls	585
Beyond the Fringe	667	Kismet (m)	583
Who's Afraid of Virginia Woolf?	664	Gypsy (m, r)	582
Blithe Spirit	657	Brigadoon	581
A Trip to Chinatown	657	Detective Story	581
The Women	657	No Strings	580
Bloomer Girl	654	Brother Rat	577
The Fifth Season	654	Blossom Time	576
Rain	648	Pump Boys and Dinettes	573
Witness for the Prosecution	645	Show Boat	572
Call Me Madam	644	The Show-Off	571
Janie	642	Sally	570
The Green Pastures	640	Jelly's Last Jam	569
Auntie Mame (p)	639	Golden Boy (m)	568
A Man for All Seasons	637	One Touch of Venus	567
Jerome Robbins' Broadway	634	The Real Thing	566
The Fourposter	632	Happy Birthday	564
The Music Master	627	Look Homeward, Angel	564
Two Gentlemen of Verona (m)	627	Morning's at Seven (r)	564
The Tenth Man	623	The Glass Menagerie	561
The Heidi Chronicles	621	I Do! I Do!	560
Is Zat So?	618	Wonderful Town	559
Anniversary Waltz	615	Rose Marie	557
The Happy Time (p)	614	Strictly Dishonorable	557
Separate Rooms	613	Sweeney Todd, the Demon Barber of	
Affairs of State	610	Fleet Street	557
Oh! Calcutta! (tr)	610	The Great White Hope	556
Star and Garter	609	A Majority of One	556
The Mystery of Edwin Drood	608	The Sisters Rosensweig	556
The Student Prince	608	Sunrise at Campobello	556
Sweet Charity	608	Toys in the Attic	556
Bye Bye Birdie	607	Jamaica	555

Plays	Number Performances	Plays	Number Performances
Stop the World—I Want to Get Off	555	Rosalinda	521
Florodora	553	The Best Man	520
Noises Off	553	Chauve-Souris	520
Ziegfeld Follies (1943)	553	Blackbirds of 1928	518
Dial "M" for Murder	552	The Gin Game	517
Good News	551	Sunny	517
Peter Pan (r)	551	Victoria Regina	517
Let's Face It	547	Fifth of July	511
Milk and Honey	543	Half a Sixpence	511
Within the Law	541	The Vagabond King	511
Pal Joey (r)	540	The New Moon	509
What Makes Sammy Run?	540	The World of Suzie Wong	508
The Sunshine Boys	538	The Rothschilds	507
What a Life	538	On Your Toes (r)	505
Crimes of the Heart	535	Sugar	505
The Unsinkable Molly Brown	532	Shuffle Along	504
The Red Mill (r)	531	Up in Central Park	504
Rumors	531	Carmen Jones	503
A Raisin in the Sun	530	The Member of the Wedding	501
Godspell (tr)	527	Panama Hattie	501
Fences	526	Personal Appearance	501
The Solid Gold Cadillac	526	Bird in Hand	500
Biloxi Blues	524	Room Service	500
Irma La Douce	524	Sailor, Beware!	500
The Boomerang	522	Tomorrow the World	500
Follies	521		

LONG RUNS OFF BROADWAY

Plays	Number Performances	Plays	Number Performances
*The Fantasticks	14,518	One Mo' Time	1,372
Nunsense	3,672	Let My People Come	1,327
*Perfect Crime	3,334	Driving Miss Daisy	1,195
The Threepenny Opera	2,611	The Hot l Baltimore	1,166
*Tony 'n' Tina's Wedding	2,461	I'm Getting My Act Together and	
Forbidden Broadway 1982–87	2,332	Taking It on the Road	1,165
Little Shop of Horrors	2,209	Little Mary Sunshine	1,143
Godspell	2,124	Steel Magnolias	1,126
Vampire Lesbians of Sodom	2,024	El Grande de Coca-Cola	1,114
Jacques Brel	1,847	The Proposition	1,109
Forever Plaid	1,811	Beau Jest	1,069
Vanities	1,785	Tamara	1,036
You're a Good Man Charlie		One Flew Over the Cuckoo's	
Brown	1,597	Nest (r)	1,025
*Tubes	1,574	The Boys in the Band	1,000
The Blacks	1,408	Fool for Love	1,000

Plays	Number Performances	Plays	Number Performances
Other People's Money	990	America Hurrah	634
Cloud 9	971	Oil City Symphony	626
Sister Mary Ignatius Explains It All for You & The Actor's		Hogan's Goat	607
		Beehive	600
Nightmare	947	The Trojan Women	600
Your Own Thing	933	The Dining Room	583
Curley McDimple	931	Krapp's Last Tape & The Zoo Story	582
Leave It to Jane (r)	928	The Dumbwaiter & The Collection	578
The Mad Show	871	Forbidden Broadway 1990	576
Scrambled Feet	831	Dames at Sea	575
The Effect of Gamma Rays on Man-		The Crucible (r)	571
in-the-Moon Marigolds	819	The Iceman Cometh (r)	565
A View From the Bridge (r)	780	The Hostage (r)	545
The Boy Friend (r)	763	What's a Nice Country Like You	
True West	762	Doing in a State Like This?	543
Isn't It Romantic	733	Forbidden Broadway 1988	534
Dime a Dozen	728	Frankie and Johnny in the Clair de	
The Pocket Watch	725	Lune	533
The Connection	722	Six Characters in Search of an	
The Passion of Dracula	714	Author (r)	529
Adaptation & Next	707	All in the Timing	526
Oh! Calcutta!	704	*Stomp	523
Scuba Duba	692	Oleanna	513
The Foreigner	686	The Dirtiest Show in Town	509
The Knack	685	Happy Ending & Day of Absence	504
The Club	674	Greater Tuna	501
The Balcony	672	A Shayna Maidel	501
Penn & Teller	666	The Boys From Syracuse (r)	500

NEW YORK DRAMA CRITICS CIRCLE AWARDS, 1935–36 TO 1994–95

Listed below are the New York Drama Critics Circle Awards from 1935–36 through 1994–95 classified as follows: (1) Best American Play, (2) Best Foreign Play, (3) Best Musical, (4) Best, regardless of category (this category was established by new voting rules in 1962–63 and did not exist prior to that year.)

1935–36—(1) Winterset
1936–37—(1) High Tor
1937–38—(1) Of Mice and Men, (2) Shadow and Substance
1938–39—(1) No award, (2) The White Steed
1939–40—(1) The Time of Your Life
1940–41—(1) Watch on the Rhine, (2) The Corn Is Green
1941–42—(1) No award, (2) Blithe Spirit
1942–43—(1) The Patriots
1943–44—(2) Jacobowsky and the Colonel
1944–45—(1) The Glass Menagerie
1945–46—(3) Carousel
1946–47—(1) All My Sons, (2) No Exit, (3) Brigadoon
1947–48—(1) A Streetcar Named Desire, (2) The Winslow Boy
1948–49—(1) Death of a Salesman, (2) The Madwoman of Chaillot, (3) South Pacific
1949–50—(1) The Member of the Wedding, (2) The Cocktail Party, (3) The Consul
1950–51—(1) Darkness at Noon, (2) The Lady's Not for Burning, (3) Guys and Dolls
1951–52—(1) I Am a Camera, (2) Venus Observed, (3) Pal Joey (Special citation to Don Juan in Hell)
1952–53—(1) Picnic, (2) The Love of Four Colonels, (3) Wonderful Town
1953–54—(1) The Teahouse of the August Moon, (2) Ondine, (3) The Golden Apple
1954–55—(1) Cat on a Hot Tin Roof, (2) Witness for the Prosecution, (3) The Saint of Bleecker Street
1955–56—(1) The Diary of Anne Frank, (2) Tiger at the Gates, (3) My Fair Lady
1956–57—(1) Long Day's Journey Into Night, (2) The Waltz of the Toreadors, (3) The Most Happy Fella
1957–58—(1) Look Homeward, Angel, (2) Look Back in Anger, (3) The Music Man
1958–59—(1) A Raisin in the Sun, (2) The Visit, (3) La Plume de Ma Tante
1959–60—(1) Toys in the Attic, (2) Five Finger Exercise, (3) Fiorello!

1960–61—(1) All the Way Home, (2) A Taste of Honey, (3) Carnival
1961–62—(1) The Night of the Iguana, (2) A Man for All Seasons, (3) How to Succeed in Business Without Really Trying
1962–63—(4) Who's Afraid of Virginia Woolf? (Special citation to Beyond the Fringe)
1963–64—(4) Luther, (3) Hello, Dolly! (Special citation to The Trojan Women)
1964–65—(4) The Subject Was Roses, (3) Fiddler on the Roof
1965–66—(4) The Persecution and Assassination of Marat as Performed by the Inmates of the Asylum of Charenton Under the Direction of the Marquis de Sade, (3) Man of La Mancha
1966–67—(4) The Homecoming, (3) Cabaret
1967–68—(4) Rosencrantz and Guildenstern Are Dead, (3) Your Own Thing
1968–69—(4) The Great White Hope, (3) 1776
1969–70—(4) Borstal Boy, (1) The Effect of Gamma Rays on Man-in-the-Moon Marigolds, (3) Company
1970–71—(4) Home, (1) The House of Blue Leaves, (3) Follies
1971–72—(4) That Championship Season, (2) The Screens (3) Two Gentlemen of Verona (Special citations to Sticks and Bones and Old Times)
1972–73—(4) The Changing Room, (1) The Hot l Baltimore, (3) A Little Night Music
1973–74—(4) The Contractor, (1) Short Eyes, (3) Candide
1974–75—(4) Equus (1) The Taking of Miss Janie, (3) A Chorus Line
1975–76—(4) Travesties, (1) Streamers, (3) Pacific Overtures
1976–77—(4) Otherwise Engaged, (1) American Buffalo, (3) Annie
1977–78—(4) Da, (3) Ain't Misbehavin'
1978–79—(4) The Elephant Man, (3) Sweeney Todd, the Demon Barber of Fleet Street
1979–80—(4) Talley's Folly, (2) Betrayal, (3) Evita (Special citation to Peter Brook's Le

Centre International de Créations Théâtrales for its repertory)

1980–81—(4) A Lesson From Aloes, (1) Crimes of the Heart (Special citations to Lena Horne: The Lady and Her Music and the New York Shakespeare Festival production of The Pirates of Penzance)

1981–82—(4) The Life & Adventures of Nicholas Nickleby, (1) A Soldier's Play

1982–83—(4) Brighton Beach Memoirs, (2) Plenty, (3) Little Shop of Horrors (Special citation to Young Playwrights Festival)

1983–84—(4) The Real Thing, (1) Glengarry Glen Ross, (3) Sunday in the Park With George (Special citation to Samuel Beckett for the body of his work)

1984–85—(4) Ma Rainey's Black Bottom

1985–86—(4) A Lie of the Mind, (2) Benefactors (Special citation to The Search for Signs of Intelligent Life in the Universe)

1986–87—(4) Fences, (2) Les Liaisons Dangereuses , (3) Les Misérables

1987–88—(4) Joe Turner's Come and Gone, (2) The Road to Mecca, (3) Into the Woods

1988–89—(4) The Heidi Chronicles, (2) Aristocrats (Special citation to Bill Irwin for Largely New York)

1989–90—(4) The Piano Lesson, (2) Privates on Parade, (3) City of Angels

1990–91—(4) Six Degrees of Separation, (2) Our Country's Good, (3) The Will Rogers Follies (Special citation to Eileen Atkins for her portrayal of Virginia Woolf in A Room of One's Own)

1991–92—(4) Dancing at Lughnasa, (1) Two Trains Running

1992–93—(4) Angels in America: Millennium Approaches, (2) Someone Who'll Watch Over Me, (3) Kiss of the Spider Woman

1993–94—(4) Three Tall Women (Special citation to Anna Deavere Smith for her unique contribution to theatrical form)

1994–95—(4) Arcadia, (1) Love! Valour! Compassion! (Special citation to Signature Theater Company for outstanding artistic achievement)

NEW YORK DRAMA CRITICS CIRCLE VOTING 1994–95

The New York Drama Critics Circle named Tom Stoppard's *Arcadia* the best play of the season, regardless of category, by a majority of 10 votes on the first ballot of first choices only. The runner-up was Terrence McNally's *Love! Valour! Compassion!* with 4 votes, with 1 vote each for David Mamet's *The Cryptogram,* Nicky Silver's *Raised in Captivity* and Giles Havergal's *Travels With My Aunt.*

Having named a foreign play best of bests, the critics proceeded to first-ballot voting on best American play. The majority went to *Love! Valour! Compassion!* with 10 votes to 2 votes each for *The Cryptogram* and *Raised in Captivity* and 1 vote each for Tony Kushner's *Slavs,* Horton Foote's *Talking Pictures* and Jeffrey Hatcher's *Three Viewings.*

The critics voted a special 1994–95 citation for outstanding achievement to Signature Theater Company (producer of this year's Pulitzer Prize winner, Horton Foote's *The Young Man From Atlanta* and other Foote plays) but voted not to give an award for best musical this season.

The 17 members of the Circle present and voting cast their 1994–95 ballots as follows.

Critic	*Best Play*	*Best American Play*
Clive Barnes *Post*	Arcadia	Talking Pictures
Mary Campbell AP	Love! Valour! Compassion!	Love! Valour! Compassion!

Greg Evans *Variety*	Arcadia	Love! Valour! Compassion!
Michael Feingold *Village Voice*	The Cryptogram	The Cryptogram
Jeremy Gerard *Variety*	Arcadia	The Cryptogram
John Heilpern *Observer*	Arcadia	Raised in Captivity
Howard Kissel *Daily News*	Love! Valour! Compassion!	Love! Valour! Compassion!
Jack Kroll *Newsweek*	Arcadia	Slavs
Michael Kuchwara AP	Arcadia	Love! Valour! Compassion!
Jacques le Sourd Gannett Newspapers	Arcadia	Love! Valour! Compassion!
Donald Lyons *Wall St. Journal*	Arcadia	Love! Valour! Compassion!
Frank Scheck *Monitor*	Love! Valour! Compassion!	Love! Valour! Compassion!
John Simon *New York*	Travels With My Aunt	Three Viewings
Michael Sommers Newhouse Newspapers	Love! Valour! Compassion!	Love! Valour! Compassion!
David Patrick Stearns *USA Today*	Raised in Captivity	Raised in Captivity
Jan Stuart *Newsday*	Arcadia	Love! Valour! Compassion!
Linda Winer *Newsday*	Arcadia	Love! Valour! Compassion!

CHOICES OF SOME OTHER CRITICS

Critic	*Best Play*	*Best Musical*
Casper Citron WOR	Having Our Say	Sunset Boulevard
Sylviane Gold *New York Newsday*	Arcadia	Sunset Boulevard
Ralph Howard WINS Radio	Arcadia	Sunset Boulevard
Stewart Klein WNYW-TV	Central Park West	Smokey Joe's Cafe
Pia Lindstrom WNBC, NBC	The Heiress	Show Boat
James McLaughlin CBS Sunday Morning	Hapgood	Sunset Boulevard
Liz Smith *Tribune-News* Syndicate	Arcadia	Show Boat
David Sheward *Backstage*	Love! Valour! Compassion!	Abstain

PULITZER PRIZE WINNERS 1916–17 to 1994–95

1916–17—No award

1917–18—Why Marry?, by Jesse Lynch Williams

1918–19—No award

1919–20—Beyond the Horizon, by Eugene O'Neill

1920–21—Miss Lulu Bett, by Zona Gale

1921–22—Anna Christie, by Eugene O'Neill

1922–23—Icebound, by Owen Davis

1923–24—Hell-Bent fer Heaven, by Hatcher Hughes

1924–25—They Knew What They Wanted, by Sidney Howard

1925–26—Craig's Wife, by George Kelly

1926–27—In Abraham's Bosom, by Paul Green

1927–28—Strange Interlude, by Eugene O'Neill

1928–29—Street Scene, by Elmer Rice

1929–30—The Green Pastures, by Marc Connelly

1930–31—Alison's House, by Susan Glaspell

1931–32—Of Thee I Sing, by George S. Kaufman, Morrie Ryskind, Ira and George Gershwin

1932–33—Both Your Houses, by Maxwell Anderson

1933–34—Men in White, by Sidney Kingsley

1934–35—The Old Maid, by Zoe Akins

1935–36—Idiot's Delight, by Robert E. Sherwood

1936–37—You Can't Take It With You, by Moss Hart and George S. Kaufman

1937–38—Our Town, by Thornton Wilder

1938–39—Abe Lincoln in Illinois, by Robert E. Sherwood

1939–40—The Time of Your Life, by William Saroyan

1940–41—There Shall Be No Night, by Robert E. Sherwood

1941–42—No award

1942–43—The Skin of Our Teeth, by Thornton Wilder

1943–44—No award

1944–45—Harvey, by Mary Chase

1945–46—State of the Union, by Howard Lindsay and Russel Crouse

1946–47—No award

1947–48—A Streetcar Named Desire, by Tennessee Williams

1948–49—Death of a Salesman, by Arthur Miller

1949–50—South Pacific, by Richard Rodgers, Oscar Hammerstein II and Joshua Logan

1950–51—No award

1951–52—The Shrike, by Joseph Kramm

1952–53—Picnic, by William Inge

1953–54—The Teahouse of the August Moon, by John Patrick

1954–55—Cat on a Hot Tin Roof, by Tennessee Williams

1955–56—The Diary of Anne Frank, by Frances Goodrich and Albert Hackett

1956–57—Long Day's Journey Into Night, by Eugene O'Neill

1957–58—Look Homeward, Angel, by Ketti Frings

1958–59—J.B., by Archibald MacLeish

1959–60—Fiorello!, by Jerome Weidman, George Abbott, Sheldon Harnick and Jerry Bock

1960–61—All the Way Home, by Tad Mosel

1961–62—How to Succeed in Business Without Really Trying, by Abe Burrows, Willie Gilbert, Jack Weinstock and Frank Loesser

1962–63—No award

1963–64—No award

1964–65—The Subject Was Roses, by Frank D. Gilroy

1965–66—No award

1966–67—A Delicate Balance, by Edward Albee

1967–68—No award

1968–69—The Great White Hope, by Howard Sackler

1969–70—No Place To Be Somebody, by Charles Gordone

1970–71—The Effect of Gamma Rays on Man-in-the-Moon Marigolds, by Paul Zindel

1971–72—No award

1972–73—That Championship Season, by Jason Miller

1973–74—No award

1974–75—Seascape, by Edward Albee

1975–76—A Chorus Line, by Michael Bennett, James Kirkwood, Nicholas Dante, Marvin Hamlisch and Edward Kleban

1976–77—The Shadow Box, by Michael Cristofer

1977–78—The Gin Game, by D.L. Coburn

1978–79—Buried Child, by Sam Shepard

1979–80—Talley's Folly, by Lanford Wilson

1980–81—Crimes of the Heart, by Beth Henley

1981–82—A Soldier's Play, by Charles Fuller

1982–83—'night, Mother, by Marsha Norman

1983–84—Glengarry Glen Ross, by David Mamet

1984–85—Sunday in the Park With George, by James Lapine and Stephen Sondheim

1985–86—No award

1986–87—Fences, by August Wilson

1987–88—Driving Miss Daisy, by Alfred Uhry

1988–89—The Heidi Chronicles, by Wendy Wasserstein

1989–90—The Piano Lesson, by August Wilson

1990–91—Lost in Yonkers, by Neil Simon

THE TONY AWARDS, 1994–95

The American Theater Wing's Antoinette Perry (Tony) Awards are presented annually in recognition of distinguished artistic achievement in the Broadway theater. The League of American Theaters and Producers and the American Theater Wing present the Tony Awards, founded by the Wing in 1947. Legitimate theater productions opening in eligible Broadway theaters during the eligibility season of the current year—May 12, 1994 to May 3, 1995—were considered for Tony nominations.

The Tony Awards Administration Committee appoints the Tony Awards Nominating Committee which makes the actual nominations. The 1994–95 Nominating Committee consisted of Donald Brooks, costume designer; Marge Champion, choreographer; Betty Comden, writer and performer; Betty L. Corwin, theater archivist; Gretchen Cryer, composer; Thomas Dillon, administrator; Brendan Gill, historian and writer; Jay Harnick, artistic director; Charles Hollerith, producer; Earle Hyman, actor; Robert Kamlot, general manager; Ming Cho Lee, set designer; Robert Lewis, director and educator; Robert McDonald, union administrator; Sister Francesca Thompson, theater educator; Douglas Watt, critic; and George White, administrator.

For the second time, because of the large number of revivals that opened on Broadway, the category of best revival was split in two (for play and musical). Since there was only one eligible nominee in the best book of a musical and best original score (music & lyrics) written for the theater categories, the Nominating Committee granted Tony Awards in these two categories.

The Tony Awards are voted from the list of nominees by the members of the governing boards of the five theater artists' organizations: Actors' Equity Association, the Dramatists Guild, the Society of Stage Directors and Choreographers, the United Scenic Artists and the Casting Society of America, plus the members of the designated first night theater press, the board of directors of the American Theater Wing and the membership of the League of American Theaters and Producers. Because of the fluctuation within these boards, the size of the Tony electorate varies from year to year. In the 1994–95 season, there were 714 qualified Tony voters.

The list of 1994–95 nominees follows, with winners in each category listed in **bold face type.**

BEST PLAY (award goes to both author and producer). *Arcadia* by Tom Stoppard, produced by Lincoln Center Theater, Andre Bishop, Bernard Gersten; *Having Our Say* by Emily Mann, produced by Camille O. Cosby, Judith Rutherford James; *Indiscretions* by Jean Cocteau, produced by The Shubert Organization, Roger Berlind, Capital Cities/ ABC, Scott Rudin; ***Love! Valour! Compassion!*** by **Terrence McNally,** produced by

Manhattan Theater Club, Lynne Meadow, Barry Grove, Jujamcyn Theaters.

BEST MUSICAL (award goes to the producer; only two nominees in this category). *Smokey Joe's Cafe* produced by Richard Frankel, Thomas Viertel, Steven Baruch, Jujamcyn Theaters/Jack Viertel, Rick Steiner, Frederic H. Mayerson, Center Theater Group/Ahmanson Theater/Gordon Davidson; *Sunset Boulevard* produced by **The Really Useful Company**.

BEST BOOK OF A MUSICAL. *Sunset Boulevard* by **Don Black** and **Christopher Hampton**.

BEST ORIGINAL SCORE (music & lyrics) WRITTEN FOR THE THEATER. *Sunset Boulevard,* music by **Andrew Lloyd Webber,** lyrics by **Don Black** and **Christopher Hampton**.

BEST LEADING ACTOR IN A PLAY. Brian Bedford in *The Molière Comedies,* **Ralph Fiennes** in *Hamlet,* Roger Rees in *Indiscretions,* Joe Sears in *A Tuna Christmas.*

BEST LEADING ACTRESS IN A PLAY. Mary Alice in *Having Our Say,* Eileen Atkins in *Indiscretions,* **Cherry Jones** in *The Heiress,* Helen Mirren in *A Month in the Country.*

BEST LEADING ACTOR IN A MUSICAL. **Matthew Broderick** in *How to Succeed in Business Without Really Trying,* Alan Campbell in *Sunset Boulevard,* Mark Jacoby in *Show Boat,* John McMartin in *Show Boat.*

BEST LEADING ACTRESS IN A MUSICAL. (Only two nominees in this category). **Glenn Close** in *Sunset Boulevard,* Rebecca Luker in *Show Boat.*

BEST FEATURED ACTOR IN A PLAY. Stephen Bogardus in *Love! Valour! Compassion!,* **John Glover** in *Love! Valour! Compassion!,* Anthony Heald in *Love! Valour! Compassion!,* Jude Law in *Indiscretions.*

BEST FEATURED ACTRESS IN A PLAY. Suzanne Bertish in *The Molière Comedies,* Cynthia Nixon in *Indiscretions,* Mercedes Ruehl in *The Shadow Box,* **Frances Sternhagen** in *The Heiress.*

BEST FEATURED ACTOR IN A MUSICAL. Michel Bell in *Show Boat,* Joel Blum in *Show Boat,* Victor Trent Cook in *Smokey Joe's Cafe,* **George Hearn** in *Sunset Boulevard.*

BEST FEATURED ACTRESS IN A MUSICAL. **Gretha Boston** in *Show Boat,* Brenda Braxton in *Smokey Joe's Cafe,* B.J. Crosby in *Smokey Joe's Cafe,* DeLee Lively in *Smokey Joe's Cafe.*

BEST DIRECTION OF A PLAY. **Gerald Gutierrez** for *The Heiress,* Emily Mann for *Having Our Say,* Joe Mantello for *Love! Valour! Compassion!,* Sean Mathias for *Indiscretions.*

BEST DIRECTION OF A MUSICAL. Des McAnuff for *How to Succeed in Business Without Really Trying,* Trevor Nunn for *Sunset Boulevard,* **Harold Prince** for *Show Boat,* Jerry Zaks for *Smokey Joe's Cafe.*

BEST SCENIC DESIGN. John Lee Beatty for *The Heiress,* Stephen Brimson Lewis for *Indiscretions,* **John Napier** for *Sunset Boulevard,* Mark Thompson for *Arcadia.*

BEST COSTUME DESIGN. Jane Greenwood for *The Heiress,* **Florence Klotz** for *Show Boat,* Stephen Brimson Lewis for *Indiscretions,* Anthony Powell for *Sunset Boulevard.*

BEST LIGHTING DESIGN. **Andrew Bridge** for *Sunset Boulevard,* Beverly Emmons for *The Heiress,* Mark Henderson for *Indiscretions,* Paul Pyant for *Arcadia.*

BEST CHOREOGRAPHY. Bob Avian for *Sunset Boulevard,* Wayne Cilento for *How to Succeed in Business Without Really Trying,* Joey McKneely for *Smokey Joe's Cafe,* **Susan Stroman** for *Show Boat.*

BEST REVIVAL OF A PLAY (award goes to the producer). *Hamlet* produced by Dodger Productions, Roger Berlind, Endemol Theater Productions, Inc., Jujamcyn Theaters, Kardana Productions, Inc., Scott Rudin, The Almeida Theater Company; *The Heiress* produced by **Lincoln Center Theater, Andre Bishop, Bernard Gersten;** *The Molière Comedies* produced by Roundabout Theater Company, Todd Haimes; *The Rose Tattoo*

HAMLET—Ralph Fiennes in his Tony Award-winning performance in the title role of Shakespeare's play

produced by Circle in the Square Theater, Theodore Mann, Josephine R. Abady, Robert Bennett.

BEST REVIVAL OF A MUSICAL (award goes to the producer; only two nominees in this category). *How to Succeed in Business Without Really Trying* produced by Dodger Productions & Kardana Productions, Inc., The John F. Kennedy Center for the Performing Arts, The Nederlander Organiza-tion; *Show Boat* produced by **Livent (U.S.) Inc.**

SPECIAL TONY AWARDS. Lifetime Achievement Awards to **Carol Channing** and **Harvey Sabinson.** Regional Theater Award to **Goodspeed Opera House,** East Haddam, Conn.

TONY HONOR. **National Endowment for the Arts.**

TONY AWARD WINNERS, 1947–95

Listed below are the Antoinette Perry (Tony) Award winners in the categories of Best Play and Best Musical from the time these awards were established until the present.

1947—No play or musical award
1948—Mister Roberts; no musical award
1949—Death of a Salesman; Kiss Me, Kate
1950—The Cocktail Party; South Pacific
1951—The Rose Tattoo; Guys and Dolls
1952—The Fourposter; The King and I
1953—The Crucible; Wonderful Town
1954—The Teahouse of the August Moon; Kismet
1955—The Desperate Hours; The Pajama Game

1956—The Diary of Anne Frank; Damn Yankees
1957—Long Day's Journey Into Night; My Fair Lady
1958—Sunrise at Campobello; The Music Man
1959—J.B.; Redhead
1960—The Miracle Worker; Fiorello! and The Sound of Music (tie)
1961—Becket; Bye Bye Birdie

1962—A Man for All Seasons; How to Succeed in Business Without Really Trying

1963—Who's Afraid of Virginia Woolf?, A Funny Thing Happened on the Way to the Forum

1964—Luther; Hello, Dolly!

1965—The Subject Was Roses; Fiddler on the Roof

1966—The Persecution and Assassination of Marat as Performed by the Inmates of the Asylum of Charenton Under the Direction of the Marquis de Sade; Man of La Mancha

1967—The Homecoming; Cabaret

1968—Rosencrantz and Guildenstern Are Dead; Hallelujah, Baby!

1969—The Great White Hope; 1776

1970—Borstal Boy; Applause

1971—Sleuth; Company

1972—Sticks and Bones; Two Gentlemen of Verona

1973—That Championship Season; A Little Night Music

1974—The River Niger; Raisin

1975—Equus; The Wiz

1976—Travesties; A Chorus Line

1977—The Shadow Box; Annie

1978—Da; Ain't Misbehavin'

1979—The Elephant Man; Sweeney Todd, the Demon Barber of Fleet Street

1980—Children of a Lesser God; Evita

1981—Amadeus; 42nd Street

1982—The Life & Adventures of Nicholas Nickleby; Nine

1983—Torch Song Trilogy; Cats

1984—The Real Thing; La Cage aux Folles

1985—Biloxi Blues; Big River

1986—I'm Not Rappaport; The Mystery of Edwin Drood

1987—Fences; Les Misérables

1988—M. Butterfly; The Phantom of the Opera

1989—The Heidi Chronicles; Jerome Robbins' Broadway

1990—The Grapes of Wrath; City of Angels

1991—Lost in Yonkers; The Will Rogers Follies

1992—Dancing at Lughnasa; Crazy for You

1993—Angels in America, Part I: Millennium Approaches; Kiss of the Spider Woman

1994—Angels in America, Part II: Perestroika; Passion

1995—Love! Valour! Compassion!; Sunset Boulevard

THE LUCILLE LORTEL AWARDS

The Lucille Lortel Awards were established in 1985 by a resolution of the League of Off-Broadway Theaters and Producers, which administers them and has presented them annually since 1986 for outstanding off-Broadway achievement. Eligible for the 9th annual awards in 1995 were all off-Broadway productions which opened between March 1, 1994 and March 31, 1995 except any which had moved from an off-Broadway to a Broadway theater. The 1995 selection committee was composed of Clive Barnes, Jeremy Gerard, Brendan Gill, Howard Kissel, Alvin Klein, Jack Kroll, Michael Kuchwara, Edith Oliver, Edwin Wilson and Miss Lortel.

PLAY. *Camping With Henry and Tom* by Mark St. Germain.

MUSICAL. *Jelly Roll!* by Vernel Bagneris.

REVIVAL. York Theater Company's *Merrily We Roll Along* by Stephen Sondheim and George Furth.

DIRECTION. **Jack O'Brien** for *Hapgood*

PERFORMANCE. Actor, **Ed Harris** in *Simpatico;* actress, **Eileen Atkins** in *Vita & Virginia* and **Linda Lavin** in *Death Defying Acts* (tie).

DESIGN: Scenery, **James Leonard Joy** for *Camping With Henry and Tom;* costumes, **Judy Dolan** for *The Petrified Prince;* lighting, **Phil Monat** for *Camping With Henry and Tom.*

BODY OF WORK. Individual, **Horton Foote;** company, **Signature Theater Company.**

LIFETIME ACHIEVEMENT. **Uta Hagen.**

SPECIAL AWARD. City Center's *Encores! Great American Musicals in Concert.*

LORTEL AWARD WINNERS, 1986–95

Listed below are the Lucille Lortel Award winners in the categories of Outstanding Play and Outstanding Musical from the time these awards were established until the present.

1986—Woza Africa!; no musical award
1987—The Common Pursuit; no musical award
1988—No play or musical award
1989—The Cocktail Hour; no musical award
1990—No play or musical award
1991—Aristocrats; Falsettoland

1992—Lips Together, Teeth Apart; And the World Goes 'Round
1993—The Destiny of Me; Forbidden Broadway
1994—Three Tall Women; Wings
1995—Camping With Henry & Tom; Jelly Roll!

ADDITIONAL PRIZES AND AWARDS, 1994–95

The following is a list of major prizes and awards for achievement in the theater this season. In all cases the names and/or titles of the winners appear in **bold face type.**

14th ANNUAL WILLIAM INGE FESTIVAL AWARD. For distinguished achievement in the American Theater. **Arthur Miller.**

10th ANNUAL ATCA AWARDS. For outstanding new plays in cross-country theater, voted by a committee of the American Theater Critics Association. New Play Award: **The Nanjing Race** by Reggie Cheong-Leen. Citation: **The Waiting Room** by Lisa Loomer. Elizabeth Osborn Award: **Rush Limbaugh in Night School** by Charlie Varon.

1994 ELIZABETH HULL-KATE WARRINER AWARD. To the playwright whose work dealt with controversial subjects involving the fields of political, religious or social mores of the time, selected by the Dramatists Guild Council. **Edward Albee** for **Three Tall Women.**

14th ANNUAL TDF ASTAIRE AWARDS. For excellence in dance on Broadway, voted by a nominating committee administered by the Theater Development Fund. **Susan Stroman** for *Show Boat;* **Charlotte D'Amboise** for *Damn Yankees.*

1994 MR. ABBOTT AWARD. Presented by the Stage Directors and Choreographers

Foundation for lifetime achievement. **Jerry Zaks.**

3d ANNUAL ROBERT WHITEHEAD AWARD. For distinguished producing. **Kevin McCollum.**

11th ANNUAL GEORGE AND ELISABETH MARTON AWARD. To an American playwright, selected by a committee of Young Playwrights Inc. **David Ives** for *All in the Timing.*

1994 KESSELRING PRIZE. For best new American play, selected by a committee of the National Arts Club comprising Anne Cattaneo, John Guare and John Lahr. *Pterodactyls* by Nicky Silver.

17th ANNUAL KENNEDY CENTER HONORS. For distinguished achievement by individuals who have made significant contributions to American culture through the arts. **Kirk Douglas, Aretha Franklin, Morton Gould, Harold Prince, Pete Seeger.**

1994 MUSICAL THEATER HALL OF FAME AWARDS. In recognition of musical theater greats whose lives and work have contributed to sustaining the art form. **George Abbott, Betty Comden, Adolph Green.**

61st ANNUAL DRAMA LEAGUE AWARDS. For distinguished achievement in musical theater, **Andrew Lloyd Webber.** For distinguished performance, **Cherry Jones** in *The Heiress.* For unique contribution to the theater, **Manhattan Theater Club.**

11th ANNUAL JUJAMCYN THEATERS AWARD. Honoring outstanding contributions to the development of creative talent for the theater. **Market Theater,** South Africa.

1994 THEATER HALL OF FAME FOUNDERS AWARD. **Kitty Carlisle Hart.**

1995 AMERICAN THEATER WING DESIGN AWARDS. For design originating in the U.S., voted by a committee comprising Tish Dace (chair), Alexis Greene, Henry Hewes and Joan Ungaro. Scenic design, **John Lee Beatty** for *The Heiress.* Costume design, **Jane Greenwood** for *The Heiress* and other shows. Lighting design, **Beverly Emmons** for *The Heiress* and *Hapgood.* Noteworthy unusual effects, **Ralph Lee** for *Heart of the Earth: A Popul Vuh Story.*

6th ANNUAL OSCAR HAMMERSTEIN AWARD. For achievement in musical theater, presented by the York Theater Company. **Arthur Laurents.** (Past recipients were **Stephen Sondheim, Harold Prince, Betty Comden & Adolph Green, Cy Coleman** and **Charles Strouse.**)

51st ANNUAL *THEATER WORLD* AWARDS. For outstanding new talent during the 1994–95 Broadway and off-Broadway seasons, selected by a committee comprising Clive Barnes, Frank Scheck, Michael Sommers, Douglas Watt and John Willis. **Gretha Boston** in *Show Boat,* **Billy Crudup** in *Arcadia,* **Beverly D'Angelo** in *Simpatico,* **Ralph Fiennes** in *Hamlet,* **Calista Flockhart** and **Kevin Kilner** in *The Glass Menagerie,* **Julie Johnson** in *Das Barbecü,* **Anthony LaPaglia** in *The Rose Tattoo,* **Jude Law** in *Indiscretions,* **Helen Mirren** in *A Month in the Country,* **Rufus Sewell** in *Translations,* **Vanessa Williams** in *Kiss of the Spider Woman.* Special awards: **Jerry Lewis** in *Damn Yankees;* **Brooke Shields** in *Grease.*

50th ANNUAL CLARENCE DERWENT AWARDS. For the most promising male and female actors on the metropolitan scene. **Calista Flockhart** in *The Glass Menagerie;* **Billy Crudup** in *Arcadia.*

JOE A. CALLAWAY AWARD. To the author of a first New York production, presented by Young Playwrights. **Kia Corthron** for *Come Down Burning.*

40th ANNUAL DRAMA DESK AWARDS. For outstanding achievement in the 1994–95 season, voted by an association of New York drama reporters, editors and critics. New play: *Love! Valour! Compassion!* by Terrence McNally. Musical production: *Show Boat.* Actor in a play: **Ralph Fiennes** in *Hamlet.* Actress in a play: **Cherry Jones** in *The Heiress.* Actor in a musical: **Matthew Broderick** in *How to Succeed in Business Without Really Trying.* Actress in a musical: **Glenn Close** in *Sunset Boulevard.* Featured actor in a play: **Nathan Lane** in *Love! Valour! Compassion!* Featured actress in a play, **Tara FitzGerald** in *Hamlet* and **Hallie Foote** in the Horton Foote plays at Signature Theater. Director of a play, **Gerald Gutierrez** for *The Heiress.* Director of a musical, **Harold Prince** for *Show Boat.* One-person show: **James Lecesne** for *Word of Mouth.* Revival/reinterpretation: *The Heiress.* Design: **Eugene Lee** (scenery), **Florence Klotz** (costumes), **Richard Pilbrow** (lighting) for *Show Boat.*

Off-off-Broadway Achievement Award: **The Barrow Group,** Seth Barrish founder. Honorary Awards: **Sam Norkin** for his distinguished body of work and contributions to the Drama Desk; **The Non-Traditional Casting Project** for its persuasive advocacy of equal employment opportunities in the arts and crafts of theater; **Otis L. Guernsey Jr.** for the *Best Plays* annual's 75th anniversary and for becoming its longest-running editor.

40th ANNUAL *VILLAGE VOICE* OBIE AWARDS. For outstanding achievement in off- and off-off-Broadway theater, chosen by a panel of judges chaired by Ross Wetzsteon and comprising Michael Feingold, Lisa Kennedy, Michael Sommers, JoAnne Akalaitis and Lynne Thigpen. Best play: *The Cryptogram* by David Mamet. Sustained achievement: **Ming Cho Lee.** Playwriting: **David Hancock** for *The Convention of Cartography,*

Tony Kushner for *Slavs,* Terrence McNally for *Love! Valour! Compassion!,* Susan Miller for *My Left Breast.* Performances: Joanna Adler in *The Boys in the Basement;* Eileen Atkins and Vanessa Redgrave in *Vita & Virginia;* Paul Calderon in *Blade to the Heat;* Malcolm Gets in *Merrily We Roll Along* and *The Two Gentlemen of Verona;* Felicity Huffman in *The Cryptogram;* Linda Lavin in *Death Defying Acts;* Ron Leibman in *The Merchant of Venice;* Camryn Manheim in *Missing Persons;* Kristine Nielsen in *Dog Opera;* Mary Beth Peil in *The Naked Truth, Missing Persons* and *A Cheever Evening;* Barbara Eda Young in *Slavs.* Ensemble performance: The cast of *Love! Valour! Compassion!* and its director, Joe Mantello. Direction: Robert Falls for *SubUrbia,* Don Scardino for *A Cheever Evening,* Susan Shulman for *Merrily We Roll Along.* Design: Wendall K. Harrington for sustained excellence of projection; Jennifer Von Mayrhauser for sustained excellence of costume design.

Special citations: Vernel Bagneris and Morten Gunnar Larsen for *Jelly Roll!,* The Five Lesbian Brothers for *The Secretaries,* The New Group for *Ecstasy,* Dael Orlandersmith for *Beauty's Daughter,* Amy and David Sedaris for *One Woman Shoe.* Grants: Archives at LaMama; Blueprint Series at Ontological-Hysteric Theater; Nada.

45th ANNUAL OUTER CRITICS CIRCLE AWARDS. For outstanding achievement in the 1994–95 New York season, voted by an organization of critics on out-of-town periodicals and media. Broadway play: *Love! Valour! Compassion!.* Performance in a play: actor, Nathan Lane in *Love! Valour! Compassion!;* actress, Cherry Jones in *The Heiress.* Broadway musical: *Sunset Boulevard.* Performance in a musical: actor, Matthew Broderick in *How to Succeed Without Really Trying;* actress, Glenn Close in *Sunset Boulevard.* Off-Broadway play: *Camping With Henry & Tom.* Off-Broadway musical: *Jelly Roll!.* Design: production, Eugene Lee; costumes, Florence Klotz; lighting, Richard Pilbrow, all for *Show Boat.* Direction: play, Joe Mantello for *Love! Valour! Compassion!* musical, Harold Prince for *Show Boat.* Choreography: Susan Stroman for *A Christmas Carol* and *Show Boat.* Revival: play, *The*

Heiress; musical, *Show Boat.* Solo Performance: James Lecesne in *James Lecesne's Word of Mouth.* Debut: actor, Billy Crudup in *Arcadia;* actress, Helen Mirren in *A Month in the Country.* John Gassner Playwriting Award: Anne Meara for *After-Play.*

Special achievement: Jerry Lewis for dazzling the Great White Way in *Damn Yankees;* the Horton Foote plays (*Night Seasons, Talking Pictures, The Young Man From Atlanta,* Laura Dennis) presented at the Signature Theater Company; *Encores! Great American Musicals in Concert* at City Center; the cast of *Travels With My Aunt* for an outstanding ensemble performance.

2d ANNUAL BOSTON THEATER AWARDS (formerly Elliot Norton Awards). For outstanding contribution to the theater in Boston, voted by a committee comprising Carolyn Clay, Iris Fanger, Arthur Friedman, Joyce Kulhawik, Jon Lehman, Bill Marx and Caldwell Titcomb. Guest of honor, Irene Worth "whose artistry in classical and contemporary theater has graced and illuminated the stage." (1994 guest of honor was Stockard Channing.) Elliot Norton Price for sustained excellence, Cherry Jones. Outstanding productions: by a large visiting company, *Angels in America;* by a small visiting company Mump & Smoot's *Caged* and *Ferno;* by a large resident company, *The Woman Warrior* at Huntington Theater Company; by a small resident company, *Krazy Kat* at Beau Jest Moving Theater. Director, Robert Scanlon for *An Evening of Beckett.* Designer, Howard Crabtree for the *Howard Crabtree's Whoop-Dee-Doo* costumes. Script in a local premiere, *The America Play* by Suzan-Lori Parks. Actress, Paula Plum for Molly in *Unexpected Tenderness* and Bella in *Lost in Yonkers.* Actor, Jack Willis for Clyde in *Hot 'n' Throbbing,* Mitch in *A Streetcar Named Desire* and Ken in *Three Hotels.*

Special citations: Trinity Repertory Company "for the ongoing excellence of its acting ensemble." Trinidad Theater Workshop for its production of Derek Walcott's *Dream on Monkey Mountain..*

11th ANNUAL HELEN HAYES AWARDS. In recognition of excellence in Washington, D.C. Theater, presented by the

Washington Theater Awards Society. Resident productions—Play: *Dream of a Common Language* by Heather MacDonald, produced by Theater of the First Amendment. Musical: *Into the Woods* by James Lapine and Stephen Sondheim, produced by Signature Theater. Charles MacArthur Award for outstanding new play: *Rhythms* by Chris White, produced by Horizons Theater. Director: *Michael Kahn* for *Henry IV, Parts 1 & 2.* Lead actor, play: **Robert Prosky** in *The Price.* Lead actress, play: **Ellen Karas** in *The Revengers' Comedies.* Lead actor, musical: **Ross Lehman** in *The Hot Mikado.* Lead actress, musical: **Dana Kreuger** in *Wings.*

KMPG Peat Marwick Award for distinguished service to the Washington theater community: **Fanny Mae Corporation.** Washington *Post* Award for distinguished community service: **Wolly Mammoth Theater Company.** American Express Tribune recognizing artists and their essential, unique contribution to our lives: **Julie Harris.**

26th ANNUAL JOSEPH JEFFERSON AWARDS. For achievement in Chicago theater during the 1993–94 season. Production—Play: *The Triumph of Love* produced by **Court Theater;** musical: *A Little Night Music* produced by **Goodman Theater;** revue (tie): *Blues in the Night* produced by **Northlight Theater,** *Michael, Margaret, Pat & Kate* produced by **Victory Gardens Theater.** Director—Play: **Mary Zimmerman** for *The Notebooks of Leonardo da Vinci;* musical: **Michael Maggio** for *A Little Night Music;* revue: **Jim Corti** for *Blues in the Night.* Actress in a principal role—Play: **Cherry Jones** in *The Night of the Iguana;* musical: **Jennifer Rosin** in *West Side Story.* Actor in a principal role—Play: **B.J. Jones** in *Someone Who'll Watch Over Me;* musical: **Mark Zimmerman** in *A Little Night Music.* Actress in a supporting role—Play: **Kate Buddeke** in *Dancing at Lughnasa;* musical: **Hollis Resnik** in *A Little Night Music.* Actor in a supporting role—Play (tie): **Lawrence McCauley** in *It Runs in the Family,* **Darryl Alan Reed** in *The Ties That Bind;* musical: **Guy Adkins** in *Oklahoma!* Actress in a revue: **Nia Vardalos** in *Whitewater for Chocolate.* Actor in a revue: **Michael Smith** in *Michael, Margaret, Pat & Kate.* Ensemble: *Phil Hill.* Design—Scenery: **Loy Arcenas** for *The*

Night of the Iguana; costumes: **Virgil Johnson** for *A Little Night Music;* lighting: **John Culbert** for *The Triumph of Love;* sound: **The Dogs** for *Dogtown.* New work/adaptation (multiple choices permitted): **Michael Smith** and **Peter Glazer** for *Michael, Margaret, Pat & Kate,* **Mary Zimmerman** for *The Notebooks of Leonardo da Vinci.* Original music: **Michael Smith** for *Michael, Margaret, Pat & Kate.* Choreography: **Kenny Ingram** for *Forty-Second Street.* Musical direction: **Bradley Vieth** for *A Little Night Music.*

Touring productions—Production: *Crazy for You* produced by **Roger Horchow** and **Elizabeth Williams.** Actress in a principal role (tie): **Lynn Redgrave** in *Shakespeare for My Father,* **Karen Ziemba** in *Crazy for You.* Actor in a principal role: **James Brennan** in *Crazy for You.* Actress in a supporting role: **Brenda Braxton** in *Baby That's Rock 'n' Roll.* Actor in a supporting role: **Kevin Ligon** in *Guys and Dolls.*

19th ANNUAL CARBONELL AWARDS. For achievement in South Florida theater during the 1993–94 season. New work: *Chaplin* produced by **Shores Performing Arts Theater.** Production—Play: *Papa* produced by **Caldwell Theater Company;** musical: *The Most Happy Fella* produced by **Jupiter Theater.** Director—Play: **Rafael de Acha** for *A Perfect Ganesh;* musical: **Norb Joerder** for *The Most Happy Fella.* Actor—Play: **Len Cariou** in *Papa;* musical: **David Holliday** in *The Most Happy Fella.* Actress—Play: **Brenda Foley** in *Keely and Du;* musical: **Avery Sommers** in *But Not for Me.* Supporting actor—Play: **John Rodaz** in *The Homecoming;* musical: **Michael Martino** in *West Side Story.* Supporting actress—Play: **Kimberly Daniel** in *To Gillian on Her 37th Birthday;* musical: **Connie Saloutous** in *West Side Story.* Choreographer: **Andrew Glant-Linden** for *West Side Story.* Musical direction: **Douglass Lutz** for *West Side Story.* Design—Scenery: **Gary Douglas** for *To Gillian on Her 37th Birthday;* costumes: **Vickie Bast** for *The Most Happy Fella;* lighting: **F. Mitchell Dana** for *Papa.* George Abbott Award for outstanding achievement in the arts: **Bill Cosford.**

Spanish-language theater awards—Production: *Mirando al Tendido* produced by **Teatro Avante.** Director: **Rolando Moreno** for *Jesus.* Actor: **Gerardo Riveron** for *Fresa y Chocolate.* Actress: **Griselda Noguera** for *Sarah.*

26th ANNUAL LOS ANGELES DRAMA CRITICS CIRCLE AWARDS. For distinguished achievement in Los Angeles Theater during 1994 (as they do not designate "bests," there can be multiple recipients, or none, in any category). Production: *Counsellor-at-Law* at Interact Theater; *The Seagull* at Matrix Theater; *The Visit* at Pacific Resident Theater Ensemble. Direction: **Alan Johnson** for *The 1940s Radio Hour;* **Milton Katselas** for *The Seagull;* **John Rubinstein** and **Anita Khanzadian** for *Counsellor-at-Law;* **Stephanie Shroyer** for *The Visit.* Writing: **Scott McPherson** for *Marvin's Room.* Lead performance: **Nancy Linehan Charles** in *The Visit;* **Pat Destro** and **Dave Higgins** in *Dylan;* **Marilyn Fox** in *Awake and Sing!;* **John Rubinstein** in *Counsellor-at-Law.* Featured performance: **Mary Carver, Jane Lanier** and **Marilyn McIntyre** in *Counsellor-at-Law.* Creation performance: **Colin Martin** in *Virgins &*

Other Myths. Scenic design: **John Arnone** for *The Who's Tommy;* **Matthew C. Jacobs** for *The Visit;* **Bradley Kaye** for *Counsellor-at-Law.* Costume design: **Jonathan Bixby** for *Sayonara;* **Cara Varnett** for *The Visit.* Lighting design; **Deena Lynn Mullen** for *The Visit;* **Chris Parry** for *The Who's Tommy.* Sound design: **Alan Faulkner** for *The 1940s Radio Hour.* Musical direction: **Brian Miller** for *The 1940s Radio Hour;* **Louis St. Louis** for *Smokey Joe's Cafe.* Choreography: **Wayne Cilento** for *The Who's Tommy.* Music and lyrics: **Stephen Sondheim** for *Assassins.* Original music: **Tom Gerou** for *The Visit.*

Ted Schmitt Award (for an outstanding world premiere presented in Los Angeles or Orange County): **Justin Tanner** for *Pot Mom.* Margaret Harford Award (for continuous achievement in the smaller theater arena): **Theater 40.** Angstrom Lighting Award: **Ken Booth.** Lifetime achievement: **Betty Garrett.**

Special awards: **The Cast Theater** and **Justin Tanner** for *The Collected Plays of Justin Tanner;* **Tim Miller** and **Highways**.

THE THEATER HALL OF FAME

The Theater Hall of Fame was created to honor those who have made outstanding contributions to the American theater in a career spanning at least 25 years. Members are elected annually by the nation's drama critics and editors (names of those so elected in 1994 and inducted January 23, 1995 appear in ***bold face italics***).

GEORGE ABBOTT	EDWIN BOOTH	***OSSIE DAVIS***
MAUDE ADAMS	JUNIUS BRUTUS BOOTH	RUBY DEE
VIOLA ADAMS	SHIRLEY BOOTH	ALFRED DE LIAGRE JR.
STELLA ADLER	ALICE BRADY	AGNES DEMILLE
EDWARD ALBEE	FANNIE BRICE	COLLEEN DEWHURST
THEONI V. ALDREDGE	PETER BROOK	HOWARD DIETZ
IRA ALDRIDGE	JOHN MASON BROWN	DUDLEY DIGGES
JANE ALEXANDER	BILLIE BURKE	MELVYN DOUGLAS
WINTHROP AMES	ABE BURROWS	ALFRED DRAKE
JUDITH ANDERSON	RICHARD BURTON	MARIE DRESSLER
MAXWELL ANDERSON	MRS. PATRICK CAMPBELL	JOHN DREW
ROBERT ANDERSON	ZOE CALDWELL	MRS. JOHN DREW
MARGARET ANGLIN	EDDIE CANTOR	WILLIAM DUNLAP
HAROLD ARLEN	MORRIS CARNOVSKY	MILDRED DUNNOCK
GEORGE ARLISS	MRS. LESLIE CARTER	ELEANORA DUSE
BORIS ARONSON	GOWER CHAMPION	JEANNE EAGELS
ADELE ASTAIRE	FRANK CHANFRAU	FRED EBB
FRED ASTAIRE	CAROL CHANNING	FLORENCE ELDRIDGE
BROOKS ATKINSON	RUTH CHATTERTON	LEHMAN ENGEL
PEARL BAILEY	PADDY CHAYEFSKY	MAURICE EVANS
GEORGE BALANCHINE	INA CLAIRE	JOSE FERRER
WILLIAM BALL	BOBBY CLARK	***CY FEUER***
ANNE BANCROFT	HAROLD CLURMAN	DOROTHY FIELDS
TALLULAH BANKHEAD	LEE J. COBB	HERBERT FIELDS
RICHARD BARR	GEORGE M. COHAN	LEWIS FIELDS
PHILIP BARRY	JACK COLE	W.C. FIELDS
ETHEL BARRYMORE	CY COLEMAN	***JULES FISHER***
JOHN BARRYMORE	CONSTANCE COLLIER	MINNIE MADDERN FISKE
LIONEL BARRYMORE	BETTY COMDEN	CLYDE FITCH
NORA BAYES	MARC CONNELLY	GERALDINE FITZGERALD
S.N. BEHRMAN	BARBARA COOK	HENRY FONDA
NORMAN BEL GEDDES	KATHARINE CORNELL	LYNN FONTANNE
DAVID BELASCO	NOEL COWARD	EDWIN FORREST
MICHAEL BENNETT	JANE COWL	BOB FOSSE
RICHARD BENNETT	LOTTA CRABTREE	RUDOLF FRIML
IRVING BERLIN	CHERYL CRAWFORD	CHARLES FROHMAN
SARAH BERNHARDT	HUME CRONYN	GRACE GEORGE
LEONARD BERNSTEIN	RUSSEL CROUSE	GEORGE GERSHWIN
EARL BLACKWELL	CHARLOTTE CUSHMAN	IRA GERSHWIN
KERMIT BLOOMGARDEN	JEAN DALRYMPLE	JOHN GIELGUD
JERRY BOCK	AUGUSTIN DALY	JACK GILFORD
RAY BOLGER	E.L. DAVENPORT	WILLIAM GILLETTE

GEORGE C. SCOTT	DOROTHY STICKNEY	JOSEPH WEBER
SAM SHEPARD	FRED STONE	MARGARET WEBSTER
ROBERT E. SHERWOOD	LEE STRASBERG	KURT WEILL
J.J. SHUBERT	JULE STYNE	ORSON WELLES
LEE SHUBERT	MARGARET SULLAVAN	MAE WEST
HERMAN SHUMLIN	JESSICA TANDY	ROBERT WHITEHEAD
NEIL SIMON	LAURETTE TAYLOR	THORNTON WILDER
LEE SIMONSON	ELLEN TERRY	BERT WILLIAMS
EDMUND SIMPSON	TOMMY TUNE	TENNESSEE WILLIAMS
OTIS SKINNER	GWEN VERDON	LANFORD WILSON
MAGGIE SMITH	ELI WALLACH	P.G. WODEHOUSE
OLIVER SMITH	JAMES WALLACK	PEGGY WOOD
STEPHEN SONDHEIM	LESTER WALLACK	IRENE WORTH
E.H. SOTHERN	TONY WALTON	ED WYNN
KIM STANLEY	DAVID WARFIELD	VINCENT YOUMANS
MAUREEN STAPLETON	ETHEL WATERS	STARK YOUNG
ROGER L. STEVENS	CLIFTON WEBB	FLORENZ ZIEGFELD
ELLEN STEWART		

MUSICAL THEATER HALL OF FAME

This organization was established at New York University on November 10, 1993. Names of those elected in 1994 appear in *bold face italics.*

IRVING BERLIN	*E.Y. HARBURG*	*COLE PORTER*
GEORGE GERSHWIN	JEROME KERN	ETHEL MERMAN
IRA GERSHWIN	ALAN JAY LERNER	RICHARD RODGERS
OSCAR HAMMERSTEIN II	FREDERICK LOEWE	

MARGO JONES
CITIZEN OF THE THEATER
MEDAL

Presented annually to a citizen of the theater who has made a lifetime commitment to the encouragement of the living theater in the United States and has demonstrated an understanding and affirmation of the craft of playwriting.

1961 LUCILLE LORTEL	EDWARD ALBEE &	1966 JON JORY
1962 MICHAEL ELLIS	CLINTON WILDER	ARTHUR BALLET
1963 JUDITH RUTHERFORD	RICHARD A. DUPREY	(University Award)
MARECHAL	(University Award)	1967 PAUL BAKER
GEORGE SAVAGE	1965 WYNN HANDMAN	GEORGE C. WHITE
(University Award)	MARSTON BALCH	(Workshop Award)
1964 RICHARD BARR,	(University Award)	1968 DAVEY MARLIN-JONES

ELLEN STEWART
(Workshop Award)
1969 ADRIAN HALL
EDWARD PARONE &
GORDON DAVIDSON
(Workshop Award)
1970 JOSEPH PAPP
1971 ZELDA FICHANDLER
1972 JULES IRVING
1973 DOUGLAS TURNER
WARD

1974 PAUL WEIDNER
1975 ROBERT KALFIN
1976 GORDON DAVIDSON
1977 MARSHALL W. MASON
1978 JON JORY
1979 ELLEN STEWART
1980 JOHN CLARK DONAHUE
1981 LYNNE MEADOW
1982 ANDRE BISHOP
1983 BILL BUSHNELL
1984 GREGORY MOSHER

1985 JOHN LION
1986 LLOYD RICHARDS
1987 GERALD CHAPMAN
1988 NO AWARD
1989 MARGARET GOHEEN
1990 RICHARD COE
1991 OTIS L. GUERNSEY JR.
1992 ABBOTT VAN
NOSTRAND
1993 HENRY HEWES
1994 JANE ALEXANDER

1994–95 PUBLICATION OF
RECENTLY-PRODUCED NEW PLAYS
AND NEW TRANSLATIONS/ADAPTATIONS

Absolute Turkey. Georges Feydeau, adapted by Nicki Frei and Peter Hall from *Le Dindon.* Absolute
    Press (paperback).
Amphitryon. Molière, newly translated by Richard Wilbur. Harcourt Brace (also paperback).
Aven'U Boys. Frank Pugliese. Broadway Play (paperback).
Bright Room Called Day, A. Tony Kushner. TCG (paperback).
Broken Glass. Arthur Miller. Penguin (paperback).
Cryptogram, The. David Mamet. Random House (paperback).
Eating Chicken Feet. Kitty Chen. Dramatic Publishing (acting edition).
Hapgood: Broadway Edition. Tom Stoppard. Faber & Faber (paperback).
I Am a Man. OyamO. Applause (paperback).
Jake's Women. Neil Simon. Random House.
Laughter on the 23rd Floor. Neil Simon. Random House.
Les Parents Terribles. Jean Cocteau. Nick Hern (paperback).
Passion: A Musical. Stephen Sondheim and James Lapine. TCG (paperback).
Pounding Nails in the Floor With My Forehead. Eric Bogosian. TCG (paperback).
Pretty Fire. Charlayne Woodard. N.A.L. (paperback).
Shriker, The. Caryl Churchill. TCG (paperback).
SubUrbia. Eric Bogosian. TCG (paperback).
Three Sisters. Anton Chekhov, newly translated by Lanford Wilson. Smith & Kraus (paperback).
Three Tall Women. Edward Albee. Dutton.
Thyestes. Seneca, newly translated by Caryl Churchill. Nick Hern (paperback).
Two Plays: A Murder of Crows/The Hyacinth Macaw. Mac Wellman. Sun and Moon Press.
Wildest Dreams. Alan Ayckbourn. Faber & Faber.

A SELECTED LIST OF OTHER PLAYS
PUBLISHED IN 1994–95

All in the Timing: Fourteen Plays. David Ives. Vintage/Random House (paperback).
Alternate Roots: Plays From the Southern Theater. Kathie deNobriga and Valetta Anderson, editors.
    Heinemann (paperback).
American Play and Other Works, The. Suzan-Lori Parks. TCG (paperback).
Approaching Zanzibar and Other Plays. Tina Howe. TCG (paperback).
Best American Short Plays 1993–1994, The. Howard Stein and Glenn Young, editors (paperback).
Best of Off-Broadway: Eight Contemporary Obie-Winning Plays, The. Ross Wetzsteon, editor. New
    American Library (paperback).
Buried Child & Seduced & Suicide in B. Sam Shepard. Talonbooks (paperback).
Collected Works of Paddy Chayefsky: The Screenplays—Volume I, The. Applause (paperback).
Collected Works of Paddy Chayefsky: The Screenplays—Volume II, The. Applause (paperback).
Collected Works of Paddy Chayefsky: The Stage Plays, The. Applause (paperback).
Collected Works of Paddy Chayefsky: The Television Plays, The. Applause (paperback).
Chekhov: The Major Plays. Anton Chekhov, English version by Jean-Claude Van Itallie. Applause
    (paperback).
Cyrano de Bergerac. Edmond Rostand, English version by Charles Marowitz. Smith and Kraus (paper-
    back).

Essential Bogosian, The. Eric Bogosian. TCG (paperback).

Fifteen Short Plays. Terrence McNally. Smith and Kraus.

Humana Festival '94: the Complete Plays. Marisa Smith, editor. Smith and Kraus (paperback).

Israel Horovitz: 16 Short Plays. Smith and Kraus. (paperback).

Look Back in Anger and Other Plays: Collected Plays—Volume I. John Osborne. Faber and Faber (paperback).

Meridian Anthology of Restoration and Eighteenth-Century Plays by Women, The. Katharine M. Rogers, editor. New American Library (paperback).

New French-Language Plays. C. Rosette Lamont. UBU/TCG (paperback).

Patient A and Other Plays: Five Plays by Lee Blessing. Heinemann (paperback).

Perfectionist and Other Plays, The. Joyce Carol Oates. Ecco Press.

Plays by Early American Women, 1775–1850. Amelia Howe Kritzer, editor. University of Michigan (paperback).

Plays Four: Arthur Miller. Methuen (paperback).

Plays Two: David Storey. Methuen (paperback).

Real Inspector Hound and Other Entertainments, The. Tom Stoppard. Faber and Faber.

South Africa Plays; New Drama from Southern Africa. Stephen Gray, selector. Nick Hern (paperback).

Tales of the Lost Formicans and Other Plays. Constance Congdon. TCG (paperback).

Ten "Lost" Plays. Eugene O'Neill. Dover (paperback).

Three Hotels: Plays and Monologues. Jon Robin Baitz. TCG (paperback).

Voicings: Ten Plays From the Documentary Theater. Attilio Favorini, editor. Ecco Press.

NECROLOGY

MAY 1994—MAY 1995

Adrian, Iris (81)—September 17, 1994
Albin, Andy (86)—December 27, 1994
Aldridge, Kay (77)—January 12, 1995
Allen, Randy (38)—May 11, 1995
Anderson, Evelyn (87)—October 29, 1994
Anderson, Herbert (77)—June 11, 1994
Andersen-Gimbel, Elga (55)—December 7, 1994
Arden, Donn (78)—November 2, 1994
Aviles, Rick (41)—March 17, 1995
Azito, Tony (46)—May 26, 1995
Beery, Noah Jr. (81)—November 1, 1994
Benson, Courtenay E. (80)—February 5, 1995
Bird, Bonnie (80)—April 9, 1995
Bishop, David (66)—August 19, 1994
Bissainthe, Toto (60)—June 4, 1994
Blair, Frank (79)—March 14, 1995
Boatwright, McHenry (74)—November 5, 1994
Bondarchuk, Sergei (74)—October 20, 1994
Boylan, John (82)—November 16, 1994
Bramson, Berenice (65)—March 23, 1995
Brancato, Rosemarie (83)—June 18, 1994
Brazzi, Rossano (78)—December 24, 1994
Brock, Alan (85)—March 19, 1995
Brockett, Don (65)—May 2, 1995
Brown, Roderick Ewing (38)—November 8, 1994
Burton, Philip (90)—February 4, 1995
Bulgakova, Maya (62)—October 11, 1994
Cameron, Donna (71)—February 25, 1995
Campbell, Miff (89)—April 2, 1995
Carson, Doris (83)—February 20, 1995
Carter, Janis (80)—July 30, 1994
Cass, Lee (70)—April 30, 1995
Chaney, Lon (68)—January 31, 1995
Collins, Christopher (44)—June 11, 1994
Collins, Dorothy (67)—July 21, 1994
Colon, Alex (53)—January 6, 1995
Cook, Peter (57)—January 9, 1995
Cossart, Valerie (87)—December 31, 1994
Cushing, Peter (81)—August 11, 1994
Dale, Virginia (77)—October 3, 1994
Darden, Severn (65)—May 26, 1995
Dash, Michael (36)—March 11, 1995
Dengel, Jack (61)—November 14, 1994
Dodson, Jack (63)—September 16, 1994
Dolberg, Nola L. (99)—October 10, 1994
Donaldson, Norma (68)—November 22, 1994

Dönch, Karl (80)—September 16, 1994
Doucette, John (73)—August 16, 1994
Downs, Johnny (81)—June 6, 1994
Drake, Charles (76)—September 10, 1994
Duff-Griffin, William (54)—November 13, 1994
Dulo, Jane (75)—May 22, 1994
Dunfee, Nora (76)—December 23, 1994
Emhardt, Robert (80)—December 26, 1994
Ergas, Joseph (72)—February 3, 1995
Ewell, Tom (85)—September 12, 1994
Flanders, Ed (60)—February 22, 1995
Fowler, Wally (77)—June 3, 1994
Franklin, Melvin (52)—February 23, 1995
Freed, Bert (74)—August 2, 1994
Fuller, Frederick (86)—February 3, 1995
Gentry, Eve (84)—June 17, 1994
George, Zelma (90)—July 3, 1994
Gibberson, William (74)—September 25, 1994
Gilmore, Phillip (38)—August 29, 1994
Gitlin, Murray (67)—June 22, 1994
Gladstone, Henry (83)—January 22, 1995
Godunov, Alexander (45)—May 15, 1995
Goff-Doerfler, Eleanor (71)—February 4, 1995
Graff, Uta (80)—February 17, 1995
Granger, Dorothy (83)—January 4, 1995
Gray, Nadia (70)—June 13, 1994
Haas, Dolly (84)—September 16, 1994
Harris, Robert (95)—May 18, 1995
Harrison, Wilbert (65)—October 26, 1994
Harrold, Jack (74)—July 22, 1994
Hawkins, Corwin (29)—August 5, 1994
Hawkins, Yvette (54)—April 10, 1995
Haydon, Julie (84)—December 24, 1994
Hayman, Lillian (72)—October 25, 1994
Hayward, Thomas (77)—February 2, 1995
Holland, Joseph (84)—December 29, 1995
Hordern, Michael (83)—May 2, 1995
Howard, John (82)—February 19, 1995
Humann, Helena E. (52)—December 13, 1994
Hurst, Margaret (75)—November 11, 1994
Hutton, Robert (73)—August 7, 1994
Ives, Burl (85)—April 14, 1995
Julia, Raul (54)—October 24, 1994
Keats, Stephen (49)—May 8, 1994
Kelly, Nancy (73)—January 2, 1995
Kermoyan, Michael (73)—September 21, 1994
Knapp, Sally A. (68)—November 1, 1994
Knox, Alexander (88)—April 25, 1995
Koscina, Sylva (61)—December 26, 1994
Kronstam, Henning (60)—May 28, 1995
Lancaster, Burt (80)—October, 1994

509

Lane, Priscilla (76)—April 4, 1995
Lansing, Robert (66)—October 23, 1994
Lindroth, Lloyd (63)—June 9, 1994
Livingston, Valerie Cossart (87)—December 31, 1994
Lukas, Karl (75)—January 16, 1995
Luxford, Nola (97)—October 10, 1994
Manuell, Barbara (58)—February 12, 1995
Martin, Richard (75)—September 4, 1994
McClure, Doug (59)—February 5, 1995
McCoy, Dan (37)—February 7, 1995
McDaniel, Keith (38)—January 2, 1995
McNally, Stephen (82)—June 4, 1994
McRae, Carmen (74)—November 10, 1994
Meisner, Gunter (66)—December 5, 1994
Mensinger, Jon (37)—September 13, 1994
Mitchell, Cameron (75)—July 6, 1994
Mitty, Nomi (54)—August 24, 1994
Moffet, Sally (63)—May 9, 1995
Moncion, Francisco (76)—April 1, 1995
Monks, James (81)—October 9, 1994
Montgomery, Elizabeth (57)—May 18, 1995
Morrill, Priscilla (67)—November 9, 1994
Namoura, Litia (83)—April 13, 1995
Natwick, Mildred (89)—October 25, 1994
Nelli, Herva (85)—May 30, 1994
Nelson, Harriet (85)—October 2, 1994
Nobles, Gerald (58)—August 23, 1994
O'Connor, Hugh (33)—March 28, 1995
O'Hare, Stephen (43)—October 1, 1994
Oliver, Gordon (84)—January 26, 1995
O'Neal, Patrick (66)—September 9, 1994
O'Shea, Tessie (82)—April 21, 1995
Ott, Dennis C. (36)—November 3, 1994
Palmer, Thomas M. (59)—June 11, 1994
Pennell, Nicholas (56)—February 22, 1995
Peterkoch, Lydia (29)—October 30, 1994
Pleasence, Donald (75)—February 2, 1995
Porter, Eric (67)—May 15, 1995
Quinn, Katherine DeMille (83)—April 27, 1995
Raines, Walter (54)—August 28, 1994
Rathgeb, Joanne (64)—November 19, 1994
Raye, Martha (78)—October 19, 1994
Renaud, Madeleine (94)—September 23, 1994
Richards, Jess (51)—November 6, 1994
Richardson, Ron (43)—April 5, 1995
Robin, Dany (68)—May 25, 1995
Rocca, Daniela (57)—May 28, 1995
Roebling, Paul (60)—July 27, 1994
Rogers, Ginger (83)—May 2, 1995
Rubinstein, Sarah (94)—July 1994
Sargent, Dick (64)—July 8, 1994
Scanlan, John (73)—June 26, 1994
Scott, Terry (67)—July 26, 1994
Silber, David (41)—December 29, 1994
Simek, Vasek (66)—May 16, 1994
Skala, Lilia (90s)—December 19, 1994
Smith, John (68)—January 25, 1995
Smith, Martin (37)—November 12, 1994

Somes, Michael (77)—November 18, 1994
Squire, Katherine (92)—March 19, 1995
Stander, Lionel (86)—November 30, 1994
Stevens, K.T. (74)—June 13, 1994
Strode, Woody (80)—December 31, 1994
Sulka, Elaine (61)—December 24, 1994
Sullivan, Barry (81)—June 6, 1994
Swift, Paul (60)—October 7, 1994
Tagliavini, Ferruccio (81)—January 29, 1995
Tandy, Jessica (85)—September 11, 1994
Tate, Robin (40)—August 19, 1994
Taylor, Dub (87)—October 3, 1994
Teas, William Ellis (80)—November 25, 1994
Teng, Teresa (40)—May 8, 1995
Thomas, Rachel (90)—February 9, 1995
Thurston, Ted (77)—July 23, 1994
Tikanova, Nina (84)—January 4, 1995
Valenti, Dino (57)—November 16, 1994
Vance, Danitra (35)—August 21, 1994
Velis, Andrea (67)—October 4, 1994
Villard, Tom (40)—November 14, 1994
Wadlington, Jeff (29)—September 24, 1994
Walker, Sydney (73)—September 30, 1994
Walters, Jeannette (52)—June 1, 1994
Washington, Fredi (90)—June 28, 1994
Waterman, Willard (80)—February 2, 1995
Wayne, David (81)—February 9, 1995
Welsh, Patricia (79)—January 26, 1995
Williams, Frances E. (89)—January 2, 1995
Williams, Marion (66)—July 2, 1994
Wolfberg, Dennis (48)—October 3, 1994
Woolf, Charles (67)—June 18, 1994
Workman, Nimrod (99)—November 26, 1994
Wright, Eric (31)—March 26, 1995
Youskevitch, Igor (82)—June 13, 1994
Zamora, Pedro (22)—November 22, 1994
Zane, Bartine (96)—May 20, 1994

MUSICIANS

Balsam, Artur (88)—September 1, 1994
Bollig, Richard Charles (51)—October 6, 1994
Bogue, Merwyn (86)—June 5, 1994
Buckner, Teddy (85)—September 26, 1994
Cherico, Gene (62)—August 13, 1994
Dillard, William (83)—January 16, 1995
Ehrhart, Raymond A. (86)—June 20, 1994
Firkusney, Rudolf (82)—July 19, 1994
Fischer, Annie (81)—April 20, 1995
Garvey, David (72)—February 14, 1995
Gatton, Danny (49)—October 4, 1994
Gingold, Josef (85)—January 11, 1995
Goldschmidt, Bernhard (69)—October 29, 1994
Hamilton, Jimmy (77)—September 20, 1994
Haywood, Henry (81)—September 15, 1994
Herman, Samuel Herbert (91)—April 23, 1995

Humphrey, Willie (93)—June 7, 1994
Jackson, Oliver (61)—May 29, 1994
James, George Richard Sr. (88)—January 30, 1995
Jefferson, Carl (75)—March 29, 1995
Kaminsky, Max (85)—September 6, 1994
Kay, Connie (67)—November 30, 1994
Krasner, Louis (91)—May 4, 1995
Lawson, Yank (84)—February 18, 1995
Levitt, Al (62)—November 28, 1994
Lipman, Samuel (60)—December 17, 1994
Marcus, Adele (89)—May 3, 1995
McDougal, E. Parker (69)—July 18, 1994
Menard, Pierre (53)—August 3, 1994
Mitchell, Jeanne (70)—June 6, 1994
Noss, Luther N. (87)—February 9, 1995
Parsons, Geoffrey (65)—January 26, 1995
Pointer, Noel (39)—December 19, 1994
Pullen, Dan (53)—April 22, 1995
Rogers, Milton (70)—November 7, 1994
Rothfuss, Levering (42)—November 21, 1994
Sharrock, Sonny (53)—May 26, 1994
Shure, Leonard (84)—February 28, 1995
Simon, Louis (79)—January 17, 1995
Smith, Fred (44)—November 4, 1994
Solomonoff, Henry (87)—March 4, 1995
Stacy, Jess (90)—January 1, 1995
Stinson, Bob (35)—February 19, 1995
Sunnyland Slim (87)—March 17, 1995
Taylor, Art (65)—February 6, 1995
van de Kamp, Peter (93)—May 19, 1995
Villa, Joseph (48)—April 13, 1995
Warren, Earle (79)—June 4, 1994
Willie, Vic (72)—January 15, 1995
Worth, Stanley (82)—July 31, 1994
Zimmerman, Jerry (52)—February 4, 1995

CONDUCTORS, BAND LEADERS

Allers, Franz (89)—January 19, 1995
Bastar, Francisco (58)—July 31, 1994
Calloway, Cab (86)—November 18, 1994
Colman, John (82)—March 5, 1995
Echols, Paul C. (50)—September 25, 1994
Kostal, Irwin (83)—November 30, 1994
Lewis, Sabby (79)—July 9, 1994
McKinley, Ray (84)—May 7, 1995
Rachlin, Ezra (79)—January 21, 1995
Rodney, Red (66)—May 27, 1994
Rudolf, Max (92)—March 1, 1995
Seuffert, George Jr. (82)—May 6, 1995
Shirley, Charles (74)—December 23, 1994
Simmons, Harwood (92)—November 14, 1994
Simon, Eric (87)—October 6, 1994
Strasser, Conrad (44)—January 5, 1995

PLAYWRIGHTS

Abbott, George (107)—January 31, 1995
Alexander, Ronald (78)—April 24, 1995
Avidan, David (61)—May 11, 1995
Block, Robert (77)—September 23, 1994
Blum, Edwin (89)—May 2, 1995
Bolt, Robert (70)—February 20, 1995
Bosakowski, Philip (47)—September 11, 1994
Brooks, Jeremy (67)—June 27, 1994
Childress, Alice (77)—August 14, 1994
Davies, Jack (80)—June 22, 1994
Drayton, Mary (89)—June 24, 1994
Dugan, John T. (74)—December 24, 1994
Gazzo, Michael V. (71)—February 14, 1995
Gilliat, Sidney—May 31, 1994
Hackett, Albert (95)—March 16, 1995
Harrison, Joan (83)—August 14, 1994
Horne, Charles (48)—September 2, 1994
Irizarry, Richard B. (38)—September 19, 1994
Kingsley, Sidney (88)—March 20, 1995
Kroll, Abraham (91)—May 25, 1994
Lee, Robert E. (75)—July 8, 1994
Leighton, Isabel (95)—April 22, 1995
Lieberson, William (79)—December 7, 1994
Osborne, John (65)—December 24, 1994
Potter, Dennis (59)—June 7, 1994
Povod, Reinaldo (34)—July 30, 1994
Randall, Bob (57)—February 11, 1995
Resnik, Muriel (78)—March 8, 1995
Rosten, Norman (81)—March 7, 1995
Shulman, Irving (82)—March 23, 1995
Smith, Mark Stow (45)—August 28, 1994
Willingham, Calder (72)—February 19, 1995

COMPOSERS, LYRICISTS

Apolinar, Danny (61)—March 23, 1995
Ashwander, Donald (65)—October 26, 1994
Bernat, Robert (63)—December 1, 1994
Boyce, Tommy (55)—November 23, 1994
Buchholz, Robert (40)—June 27, 1994
Carlebach, Shlomo (69)—October 20, 1994
Elton, John M. (73)—May 19, 1995
Feather, Leonard (80)—September 22, 1994
Fusco, Nelly (85)—July 29, 1994
Gaste, Louis (88)—January 8, 1995
Hadjidakis, Manos (68)—June 15, 1994
Hawkins, Ted (58)—December 29, 1994
Hayes, Kendall L. (59)—February 10, 1995
Hemphill, Julius (57)—April 2, 1995
Jobin, Antonio Carlos (67)—December 8, 1994
Kay, Ulysses (78)—May 20, 1995
Linn, Michael—March 23, 1995
Lopez, Francis (79)—January 12, 1995

Mancini, Henry (70)—June 14, 1994
Roussakis, Nicolas (60)—October 23, 1994
Salter, Hans J. (98)—July 23, 1994
Siegel, Arthur (70)—September 13, 1994
Stravinsky, Soulima (84)—November 28, 1994
Styne, Jule (88)—September 20, 1994
Tobias, Harry (99)—December 15, 1994
Vassy, Kin (50)—June 23, 1994
Zabrack, Harold (66)—February 2, 1995

DESIGNERS

Allio, Rene (71)—March 27, 1995
Barcelo, Randy (48)—December 6, 1994
Bardyguine, George (74)—September 11, 1994
Fuchs, Theodore (90)—January 25, 1995
Gould, Peter D. (50)—October 17, 1994
Harrison, Llewellyn (47)—November 14, 1994
Horner, Harry (84)—December 5, 1994
Johnston, Romain (65)—March 17, 1995
Miller, Craig (43)—June 7, 1994
Morrow, Milo (73)—March 14, 1995
Shovestull, Thomas B. (45)—June 25, 1994
Skelton, Thomas R. (66)—August 9, 1994
Zuberano, Maurice—July 2, 1994

PRODUCERS, DIRECTORS, CHOREOGRAPHERS

Anderson, Lindsay (71)—August 30, 1994
Beatty, Talley (76)—April 29, 1995
Bedsow, Len (76)—May 14, 1994
Blasi, Silverio (73)—April 27, 1995
Borsos, Philip (41)—February 9, 1995
Campbell, Dick (91)—December 20, 1994
Caro, Warren (87)—January 1, 1995
Chadman, Christopher (47)—April 30, 1995
Clayton, Jack (73)—February 25, 1995
Djordjadze, Timor (49)—August 11, 1994
Fearnley, John (80)—November 29, 1994
Fedicheva, Kaleria (58)—September 13, 1994
Finch, Nigel (45)—February 14, 1995
Fisher, Nelle (79)—October 19, 1994
Francis, Ron (57)—March 11, 1995
Hawkins, Erick (85)—November 23, 1994
Hazen, Joseph (96)—November 13, 1994
Hill, James (75)—October 9, 1994
Houlton, Loyce (70)—March 14, 1995
Hudson, Louise Y. (52)—October 11, 1994
Kasdan, Michael (66)—October 22, 1994
Lubin, Arthur (96)—May 11, 1995
March, Donald (53)—May 3, 1995
Martin, Ernest (75)—May 7, 1995
Minskoff, Jerome (78)—August 13, 1994

Moore, Sonia (92)—May 19, 1995
Moses, Gilbert (52)—April 14, 1995
Peck, Thomas (56)—June 8, 1994
Peters, Michael (46)—August 19, 1994
Primus, Pearl (74)—October 29, 1994
Rawson, Ron (76)—July 19, 1994
Rea, Oliver (71)—March 31, 1995
Reinhardt, Gottfried (80)—July 18, 1994
Rice, Marion Burbank Stevens (90)—April 12, 1995
Roberson, Will (36)—December 12, 1994
Ross, William (78)—August 23, 1994
Rowland, Toby (77)—August 9, 1994
Rushton, Matthew (43)—March 26, 1995
Saltzman, Harry (78)—September 28, 1994
Scevers, Robert (54)—December 15, 1994
Simonov, Yevgeny (69)—August 4, 1994
Sloan, Larry (34)—January 18, 1995
Talin, Nikita (75)—March 16, 1995
Tornberg, Jeff (43)—December 21, 1994
Totten, Robert (57)—January 27, 1995
Warner, Jack M. (79)—April 1, 1995
Wilson, Billy (59)—August 14, 1994
Young, Terence (79)—September 7, 1994

CRITICS

Fox, David (29)—Winter 1995
Gardner, R.H. (76)—March 4, 1995
Hatch, Robert (83)—May 31, 1994
Henry, William A. III (44)—June 28, 1994
Kahn, Nathan (80)—March 26, 1995
Kelly, Kevin (64)—November 28, 1994
Kubasik, Ben A. (65)—October 19, 1994
Lerman, Leo (80)—August 22, 1994
Stuart, Otis (43)—February 28, 1995
Wiley, Mason (39)—October 7, 1994

OTHERS

Abdoh, Reza (32)—May 11, 1995
    Artist
Aubrey, James T. (75)—September 3, 1994
    Producer MGM, CBS
Barison, David (30)—January 1, 1995
    Agent
Barr, Geoffrey (70)—January 4, 1995
    Personal manager
Barrett, Kay Brown (93)—January 18, 1995
    Agent
Baumgarten, David (77)—April 25, 1995
    Agency for the Performing Arts
Becker, Ralph E. (87)—August 24, 1994
    The Wolf Trap Foundation

Belfrage, Julian (60)—December 29, 1994
  Agent
Blackwell, Earl (85)—March 1, 1995
  Celebrity Service
Bindle, Thomas (63)—April 28, 1995
  Scholar
Bufano, Anthony (53)—July 6, 1994
  Organ curator
Cagney, Frances (95)—October 10, 1994
  Widow of James Cagney
Cliburn, Rildia Bee (97)—August 3, 1994
  Piano teacher
Cohen, Martin (69)—February 17, 1995
  Company manager
Crawford, Oliver H. (83)—January 4, 1995
  TV Guide
Davis, Keith (85)—September 9, 1994
  Singing teacher
DiTolla, Al (68)—December 20, 1994
  IATSE president
Espy, Hilda Cole (83)—January 20, 1995
  Publicist
Ferrari, Irene Elaine (42)—December 13, 1994
  Wardrobe supervisor
Foladare, Maury (86)—August 20, 1994
  Publicist
Frame, Paul (80)—November 8, 1994
  Illustrator
Glaser, Elizabeth—December 3, 1994
  AIDS activist
Goldfarb, Herman (85)—August 8, 1994
  Lawyer
Highsmith, Patricia (74)—February 4, 1995
  Mystery writer
Hooten, Bruce (66)—May 17, 1995
  Living Theater
Huntly, David V. (47)—July 1, 1994
  Music executive
Inglis, Frances (83)—October 22, 1994
  Writers Guild of America, West
Joslyn, Donald (50)—January 1, 1995
  Company manager
Kaufman, Brian (40)—August 22, 1994
  Stage manager
Krim, Arthur (84)—September 21, 1994
  Lawyer
Ladd, David—October 12, 1994
  Registrar of Copyrights

Lees, Beatrice (84)—May 1, 1995
  Dance teacher
Lefko, Morris (87)—January 26, 1995
  Sales manager
Leonard, William (78)—October 23, 1994
  Journalist
Markson, Edith (81)—September 10, 1994
  Promoter, regional theater
McHugh, James F. (79)—October 25, 1994
  Talent agent
McNaspy, Clement J. (79)—February 3, 1995
  Musicologist, historian
Mead, Edward Shepherd (80)—August 15, 1994
  Novelist
Meighan, Howard S. (88)—March 8, 1995
  CBS
Merrill, James (68)—February 6, 1995
  Poet
Nathan, Fred (38)—June 28, 1994
  Publicist
O'Casey, Eileen (95)—April 9, 1995
  Widow of Sean O'Casey
Pagliotti, Douglas A. (36)—September 27, 1994
  Stage manager
Ratliff, Neil M. (58)—September 17, 1994
  Music librarian
Roberts, Janet (68)—January 31, 1995
  Agent
Rogers, Henry (82)—April 28, 1995
  Publicist
Rosenthal, Barry E. (53)—May 11, 1994
  Lawyer
Scott-Fox, Judy (56)—August 18, 1994
  Agent
Scouten, Arthur (85)—April 30, 1995
  Scholar
Shouse, Catherine Filene (98)—December 14,
  1994
  Philanthropist
Spolin, Viola (88)—November 22, 1994
  Improvisational theater
Taper, S. Mark (92)—December 15, 1994
  Philanthropist
Valando, Tommy (72)—February 14, 1995
  Music publisher
Zahn, Anita (91)—November 3, 1994
  Dance teacher

THE BEST PLAYS, 1894–1994

Listed in alphabetical order below are all those works selected as Best Plays in previous volumes of the *Best Plays* series. Opposite each title is given the volume in which the play appears, its opening date and its total number of performances. Two separate opening-date and performance-number entries signify two separate engagements off Broadway and on Broadway when the original production was transferred from one area to the other, usually in an off-to-on direction. Those plays marked with an asterisk (*) were still playing on June 1, 1995 and their number of performances was figured through May 31, 1995. Adaptors and translators are indicated by (ad) and (tr), the symbols (b), (m) and (l) stand for the author of the book, music and lyrics in the case of musicals and (c) signifies the credit for the show's conception, (i) for its inspiration.

PLAY	VOLUME	OPENED	PERFS
ABE LINCOLN IN ILLINOIS—Robert E. Sherwood	38–39	Oct. 15, 1938	472
ABRAHAM LINCOLN—John Drinkwater	19–20	Dec. 15, 1919	193
ACCENT ON YOUTH—Samson Raphaelson	34–35	Dec. 25, 1934	229
ADAM AND EVA—Guy Bolton, George Middleton	19–20	Sept. 13, 1919	312
ADAPTATION—Elaine May; and NEXT—Terrence McNally	68–69	Feb. 10, 1969	707
AFFAIRS OF STATE—Louis Verneuil	50–51	Sept. 25, 1950	610
AFTER THE FALL—Arthur Miller	63–64	Jan. 23, 1964	208
AFTER THE RAIN—John Bowen	67–68	Oct. 9, 1967	64
AGNES OF GOD—John Pielmeier	81–82	Mar. 30, 1982	599
AH, WILDERNESS!—Eugene O'Neill	33–34	Oct. 2, 1933	289
AIN'T SUPPOSED TO DIE A NATURAL DEATH—(b, m, l) Melvin Van Peebles	71–72	Oct. 20, 1971	325
ALIEN CORN—Sidney Howard	32–33	Feb. 20, 1933	98
ALISON'S HOUSE—Susan Glaspell	30–31	Dec. 1, 1930	41
ALL MY SONS—Arthur Miller	46–47	Jan. 29, 1947	328
ALL IN THE TIMING—David Ives	93–94	Feb. 17, 1994	526
ALL OVER TOWN—Murray Schisgal	74–75	Dec. 29, 1974	233
ALL THE WAY HOME—Tad Mosel, based on James Agee's novel *A Death in the Family*	60–61	Nov. 30, 1960	333
ALLEGRO—(b, l) Oscar Hammerstein II, (m) Richard Rodgers	47–48	Oct. 10, 1947	315
AMADEUS—Peter Shaffer	80–81	Dec. 17,1980	1,181
AMBUSH—Arthur Richman	21–22	Oct. 10, 1921	98
AMERICA HURRAH—Jean-Claude van Itallie	66–67	Nov. 6, 1966	634
AMERICAN BUFFALO—David Mamet	76–77	Feb. 16, 1977	135
AMERICAN ENTERPRISE—Jeffrey Sweet (special citation)	93–94	Apr. 13, 1994	15
AMERICAN PLAN, THE—Richard Greenberg	90–91	Dec. 16, 1990	37
AMERICAN WAY, THE—George S. Kaufman, Moss Hart	38–39	Jan. 21, 1939	164
AMPHITRYON 38—Jean Giraudoux, (ad) S.N. Behrman	37–38	Nov. 1, 1937	153
AND A NIGHTINGALE SANG . . .—C.P. Taylor	83–84	Nov. 27, 1983	177
ANDERSONVILLE TRIAL, THE—Saul Levitt	59–60	Dec. 29, 1959	179
ANDORRA—Max Frisch, (ad) George Tabori	62–63	Feb. 9, 1963	9
ANGEL STREET—Patrick Hamilton	41–42	Dec. 5, 1941	1,295

PLAY	VOLUME	OPENED	PERFS
HAPPY TIME, THE—Samuel Taylor, based on Robert Fontaine's book	49–50	Jan. 24, 1950	614
HARRIET—Florence Ryerson, Colin Clements	42–43	Mar. 3, 1943	377
HARVEY—Mary Chase	44–45	Nov. 1, 1944	1,775
HASTY HEART, THE—John Patrick	44–45	Jan. 3, 1945	207
HE WHO GETS SLAPPED—Leonid Andreyev, (ad) Gregory Zilboorg	21–22	Jan. 9, 1922	308
HEART OF MARYLAND, THE—David Belasco	94–99	Oct. 22, 1895	240
HEIDI CHRONICLES, THE—Wendy Wasserstein	88–89	Dec. 11, 1988	81
	88–89	Mar. 9, 1989	621
HEIRESS, THE—Ruth and Augustus Goetz, suggested by Henry James's novel *Washington Square*	47–48	Sept. 29, 1947	410
HELL-BENT FER HEAVEN—Hatcher Hughes	23–24	Jan. 4, 1924	122
HELLO, DOLLY!—(b) Michael Stewart, (m, l) Jerry Herman, based on Thornton Wilder's *The Matchmaker*	63–64	Jan. 16, 1964	2,844
HER MASTER'S VOICE—Clare Kummer	33–34	Oct. 23, 1933	224
HERE COME THE CLOWNS—Philip Barry	38–39	Dec. 7, 1938	88
HERO, THE—Gilbert Emery	21–22	Sept. 5, 1921	80
HIGH TOR—Maxwell Anderson	36–37	Jan. 9, 1937	171
HOGAN'S GOAT—William Alfred	65–66	Nov. 11, 1965	607
HOLIDAY—Philip Barry	28–29	Nov. 26, 1928	229
HOME—David Storey	70–71	Nov. 17, 1970	110
HOME—Samm-Art Williams	79–80	Dec. 14, 1979	82
	79–80	May 7, 1980	279
HOMECOMING, THE—Harold Pinter	66–67	Jan. 5, 1967	324
HOME OF THE BRAVE—Arthur Laurents	45–46	Dec. 27, 1945	69
HOPE FOR A HARVEST—Sophie Treadwell	41–42	Nov. 26, 1941	38
HOSTAGE, THE—Brendan Behan	60–61	Sept. 20, 1960	127
HOT L BALTIMORE, THE—Lanford Wilson	72–73	Mar. 22, 1973	1,166
HOUSE OF BLUE LEAVES, THE—John Guare	70–71	Feb. 10, 1971	337
HOUSE OF CONNELLY, THE—Paul Green	31–32	Sept. 28, 1931	91
HOW TO SUCCEED IN BUSINESS WITHOUT REALLY TRYING—(b) Abe Burrows, Jack Weinstock, Willie Gilbert, based on Shepherd Mead's novel, (m, l) Frank Loesser	61–62	Oct. 14, 1961	1,417
HURLYBURLY—David Rabe	84–85	June 21, 1984	45
	84–85	Aug. 7, 1984	343
I AM A CAMERA—John van Druten, based on Christopher Isherwood's Berlin stories	51–52	Nov. 28, 1951	214
I KNOW MY LOVE—S.N. Behrman, based on Marcel Achard's *Auprès de Ma Blonde*	49–50	Nov. 2, 1949	246
I NEVER SANG FOR MY FATHER—Robert Anderson	67–68	Jan. 25, 1968	124
I OUGHT TO BE IN PICTURES—Neil Simon	79–80	Apr. 3, 1980	324
I REMEMBER MAMA—John van Druten, based on Kathryn Forbes's book *Mama's Bank Account*	44–45	Oct. 19, 1944	714
ICEBOUND—Owen Davis	22–23	Feb. 10, 1923	171
ICEMAN COMETH, THE—Eugene O'Neill	46–47	Oct. 9, 1946	136
IDIOT'S DELIGHT—Robert E. Sherwood	35–36	Mar. 24, 1936	300
IF I WERE KING—Justin Huntly McCarthy	99–09	Oct. 14, 1901	56
I'M NOT RAPPAPORT—Herb Gardner	85–86	June 6, 1985	181
	85–86	Nov. 18, 1985	890

PLAY	VOLUME	OPENED	PERFS
REMAINS TO BE SEEN—Howard Lindsay, Russel Crouse	51–52 ..	Oct. 3, 1951 ..	199
REQUIEM FOR A NUN—Ruth Ford, William Faulkner, adapted from William Faulkner's novel	58–59 ..	Jan. 30, 1959 ..	43
REUNION IN VIENNA—Robert E. Sherwood.....................	31–32 ..	Nov. 16, 1931 ..	264
RHINOCEROS—Eugene Ionesco, (tr) Derek Prouse.............	60–61 ..	Jan. 9, 1961 ..	240
RITZ, THE—Terrence McNally	74–75 ..	Jan. 20, 1975 ..	400
RIVER NIGER, THE—Joseph A. Walker.........................	72–73 ..	Dec. 5, 1972 ..	120
	72–73 ..	Mar. 27, 1973 ..	280
ROAD—Jim Cartwright...	88–89 ..	July 28, 1988 ..	62
ROAD TO MECCA, THE—Athol Fugard	87–88 ..	Apr. 12, 1988 ..	172
ROAD TO ROME, THE—Robert E. Sherwood	26–27 ..	Jan. 31, 1927 ..	392
ROCKABY—(see *Enough, Footfalls* and *Rockaby*)			
ROCKET TO THE MOON—Clifford Odets.........................	38–39 ..	Nov. 24, 1938 ..	131
ROMANCE—Edward Sheldon......................................	09–19 ..	Feb. 10, 1913 ..	160
ROPE DANCERS, THE—Morton Wishengrad....................	57–58 ..	Nov. 20, 1957 ..	189
ROSE TATTOO, THE—Tennessee Williams.......................	50–51 ..	Feb. 3, 1951 ..	306
ROSENCRANTZ AND GUILDENSTERN ARE DEAD—Tom Stoppard...	67–68 ..	Oct. 16, 1967 ..	420
ROUND AND ROUND THE GARDEN—Alan Ayckbourn	75–76 ..	Dec. 7, 1975 ..	76
ROYAL FAMILY, THE—George S. Kaufman, Edna Ferber......	27–28 ..	Dec. 28, 1927 ..	345
ROYAL HUNT OF THE SUN—Peter Shaffer.......................	65–66 ..	Oct. 26, 1965 ..	261
RUGGED PATH, THE—Robert E. Sherwood.....................	45–46 ..	Nov. 10, 1945 ..	81
RUNNER STUMBLES, THE—Milan Stitt	75–76 ..	May 18, 1976 ..	191
ST. HELENA—R.C. Sheriff, Jeanne de Casalis	36–37 ..	Oct. 6, 1936 ..	63
SAME TIME, NEXT YEAR—Bernard Slade	74–75 ..	Mar. 13, 1975 ..	1,453
SATURDAY'S CHILDREN—Maxwell Anderson....................	26–27 ..	Jan. 26, 1927 ..	310
SCREENS, THE—Jean Genet, (tr) Minos Volanakis	71–72 ..	Nov. 30, 1971 ..	28
SCUBA DUBA—Bruce Jay Friedman...............................	67–68 ..	Oct. 10, 1967 ..	692
SEA HORSE, THE—Edward J. Moore (James Irwin).............	73–74 ..	Apr. 15, 1974 ..	128
SEARCHING WIND, THE—Lillian Hellman	43–44 ..	Apr. 12, 1944 ..	318
SEASCAPE—Edward Albee	74–75 ..	Jan. 26, 1975 ..	65
SEASON IN THE SUN—Wolcott Gibbs.............................	50–51 ..	Sept. 28, 1950 ..	367
SEASON'S GREETINGS—Alan Ayckbourn	85–86 ..	July 11, 1985 ..	20
SECOND THRESHOLD—Philip Barry, revisions by Robert E. Sherwood...	50–51 ..	Jan. 2, 1951 ..	126
SECRET SERVICE—William Gillette................................	94–99 ..	Oct. 5, 1896 ..	176
SEPARATE TABLES—Terence Rattigan............................	56–57 ..	Oct. 25, 1956 ..	332
SERENADING LOUIE—Lanford Wilson	75–76 ..	May 2, 1976 ..	33
SERPENT: A CEREMONY, THE—Jean-Claude van Itallie	69–70 ..	May 29, 1973 ..	3
SEVEN KEYS TO BALDPATE—(ad) George M. Cohan, from the novel by Earl Derr Biggers....................................	09–19 ..	Sept. 22, 1913 ..	320
1776—(b) Peter Stone, (m, l) Sherman Edwards, based on a conception by Sherman Edwards	68–69 ..	Mar. 16, 1969 ..	1,217
SEX, DRUGS, ROCK & ROLL—Eric Bogosian	89–90 ..	Feb. 8, 1990 ..	103
SHADOW AND SUBSTANCE—Paul Vincent Carroll	37–38 ..	Jan. 26, 1938 ..	274
SHADOW BOX, THE—Michael Cristofer..........................	76–77 ..	Mar. 31, 1977 ..	315
SHADOW OF HEROES—(see *Stone and Star*)			
SHADOWLANDS—William Nicholson	90–91 ..	Nov. 11, 1990 ..	169
SHE LOVES ME—(b) Joe Masteroff, based on Miklos Laszlo's play *Parfumerie,* (l) Sheldon Harnick, (m) Jerry Bock	62–63 ..	Apr. 23, 1963 ..	301

PLAY	VOLUME	OPENED	PERFS
SUGAR BABIES—(ad) Ralph G. Allen from traditional material (special citation)	79–80	Oct. 8, 1979	1,208
SUM OF US, THE—David Stevens	90–91	Oct. 16, 1990	335
SUMMER OF THE 17TH DOLL—Ray Lawler	57–58	Jan. 22, 1958	29
SUNDAY IN THE PARK WITH GEORGE—(b) James Lapine, (m, l) Stephen Sondheim	83–84	May 2, 1984	604
SUNRISE AT CAMPOBELLO—Dore Schary	57–58	Jan. 30, 1958	556
SUNSHINE BOYS, THE—Neil Simon	72–73	Dec. 20, 1972	538
SUN-UP—Lula Vollmer	22–23	May 25, 1923	356
SUSAN AND GOD—Rachel Crothers	37–38	Oct. 7, 1937	288
SWAN, THE—Ferenc Molnar, (tr) Melville Baker	23–24	Oct. 23, 1923	255
SWEENEY TODD, THE DEMON BARBER OF FLEET STREET— (b) Hugh Wheeler, (m, l) Stephen Sondheim, based on a version of *Sweeney Todd* by Christopher Bond	78–79	Mar. 1, 1979	557
SWEET BIRD OF YOUTH—Tennessee Williams	58–59	Mar. 10, 1959	375
TABLE MANNERS—Alan Ayckbourn	75–76	Dec. 7, 1975	76
TABLE SETTINGS—James Lapine	79–80	Jan. 14, 1980	264
TAKE A GIANT STEP—Louis Peterson	53–54	Sept. 24, 1953	76
TAKING OF MISS JANIE, THE—Ed Bullins	74–75	May 4, 1975	42
TALLEY'S FOLLEY—Lanford Wilson	78–79	May 1, 1979	44
	79–80	Feb. 20, 1980	277
TARNISH—Gilbert Emery	23–24	Oct. 1, 1923	248
TASTE OF HONEY, A—Shelagh Delaney	60–61	Oct. 4, 1960	376
TCHIN-TCHIN—Sidney Michaels, based on François Billetdoux's play	62–63	Oct. 25, 1962	222
TEA AND SYMPATHY—Robert Anderson	53–54	Sept. 30, 1953	712
TEAHOUSE OF THE AUGUST MOON, THE—John Patrick, based on Vern Sneider's novel	53–54	Oct. 15, 1953	1,027
TENTH MAN, THE—Paddy Chayefsky	59–60	Nov. 5, 1959	623
THAT CHAMPIONSHIP SEASON—Jason Miller	71–72	May 2, 1972	144
	72–73	Sept. 14, 1972	700
THERE SHALL BE NO NIGHT—Robert E. Sherwood	39–40	Apr. 29, 1940	181
THEY KNEW WHAT THEY WANTED—Sidney Howard	24–25	Nov. 24, 1924	414
THEY SHALL NOT DIE—John Wexley	33–34	Feb. 21, 1934	62
THOUSAND CLOWNS, A—Herb Gardner	61–62	Apr. 5, 1962	428
THREE POSTCARDS—(b) Craig Lucas, (m, l) Craig Carnelia	86–87	May 14, 1987	22
*THREE TALL WOMEN—Edward Albee	93–94	Apr. 5, 1994	478
THREEPENNY OPERA—(b, l) Bertolt Brecht, (m) Kurt Weill, (tr) Ralph Manheim, John Willett	75–76	Mar. 1, 1976	307
THURBER CARNIVAL, A—James Thurber	59–60	Feb. 26, 1960	127
TIGER AT THE GATES—Jean Giraudoux's *La Guerre de Troie n'Aura Pas Lieu,* (tr) Christopher Fry	55–56	Oct. 3, 1955	217
TIME OF THE CUCKOO, THE—Arthur Laurents	52–53	Oct. 15, 1952	263
TIME OF YOUR LIFE, THE—William Saroyan	39–40	Oct. 25, 1939	185
TIME REMEMBERED—Jean Anouilh's *Léocadia,* (ad) Patricia Moyes	57–58	Nov. 12, 1957	248
TINY ALICE—Edward Albee	64–65	Dec. 29, 1964	167
TOILET, THE—LeRoi Jones (a.k.a. Amiri Baraka)	64–65	Dec. 16, 1964	151
TOMORROW AND TOMORROW—Philip Barry	30–31	Jan. 13, 1931	206
TOMORROW THE WORLD—James Gow, Arnaud d'Usseau	42–43	Apr. 14, 1943	500

INDEX

INDEX

Play titles appear in **bold face**. *Bold face italic* page numbers refer to those pages where complete cast and credit listings for New York productions may be found